A *New York Times Book Review* Notable Book

Named a Best Book of the Year by *The Economist,*
New York Magazine, Amazon.com, and
Barnesandnoble.com

Winner—Book Sense Nonfiction Book of the Year
Winner—Quill Award for Business Book of the Year
Finalist—*Financial Times*/Goldman Sachs
Business Book of the Year

"Levitt and Dubner's clever juxtapositions, the way they consistently mine illuminating truths by contrasting seemingly unrelated topics, is what makes *Freakonomics* a romp of a read. . . . *Freakonomics* is a splendid book, full of unlikely but arresting historical details that distinguish the authors from the run of pop social scientists."

—*The New York Times*

"If Indiana Jones were an economist, he'd be Steven Levitt. . . . A maverick treasure hunter who relies for success on his wit, pluck and disregard for conventional wisdom. . . . *Freakonomics* reads like a detective novel. . . . Economists, ever wary of devaluing their currency, tend to be stinting in their praise. I therefore tried hard to find something in this book that I could complain about. But I give up. Criticizing *Freakonomics* would be like criticizing a hot fudge sundae. . . . The cherry on top of the sundae is Mr. Levitt's co-author, Stephen Dubner, a journalist who clearly understands what he is writing about and explains it in prose that has you chuckling one minute and gasping in amazement the next. Mr. Dubner is a treasure of the rarest sort; we are fortunate that Mr. Levitt managed to find him."

—*The Wall Street Journal*

"A delight. . . . It shows, in fact, what plain old-fashioned economics can do in the hands of a boundlessly curious and superbly skilled practitioner. . . . The material is quite fascinating. . . . Always it finds questions that are mischievously intriguing in themselves but that also shed light on broader matters as well— and then it finds ingenious ways of answering them."

—*The Economist*

"An engaging and always interesting work, rich in insights, full of surprises. . . . *Freakonomics* is packed with fascinating ideas."

—*Washington Post Book World*

"We think we know how the world operates, but we really don't. . . . *Freakonomics* uses the science of economics and concrete data to challenge our assumptions about everything. . . . You'll walk away with not only a few good party tidbits, but also a more critical eye to many things presented as fact."

—*Harvard Business Review*

"Instructive and entertaining . . . the trivia alone is worth the cover price. . . . It might appear presumptuous of Steven Levitt to see himself as an all-purpose intellectual detective, fit to take on whatever puzzle of human behavior grabs his fancy. But on the evidence of *Freakonomics,* the presumption is earned."

—*The New York Times Book Review*

"Imagine a whip-smart economist with a sprawling imagination. Now imagine he's 9 years old and wants to know everything. That is the basic profile of Steven Levitt. . . . Each chapter is an enlightening field trip, like the investigations into human nature in Malcolm Gladwell's books, *The Tipping Point* and *Blink*."

—*Time*

"Steven Levitt has the most interesting mind in America, and reading *Freakonomics* is like going for a leisurely walk with him on a sunny summer day, as he waves his fingers in the air and turns everything you once thought to be true inside out. Prepare to be dazzled."

—Malcolm Gladwell

"Levitt employs statistical tools that are simple yet elegant. He cuts to the heart of a question and picks topics that are fascinating. All social scientists should ask themselves if the problems they are working on are as interesting or important as those in this superb work."

—*Los Angeles Times Book Review*

"The funkiest study of statistical mechanics ever by a world-renowned economist . . . Levitt (along with coauthor Dubner) searches for logic in the messy mathematics of human behavior. His conclusions are often eye-opening and sometimes eye-popping (his theory that high abortion rates help reduce crime probably won't get him invited to the White House anytime soon). . . . fun to read."

—*Entertainment Weekly*

"While legions of his fellow economists toil to decipher the intricacies of, say, monetary policy, Steven D. Levitt has become something of a sensation by using its models to tease out the answers to livelier questions."

—*San Francisco Chronicle*

"Maverick economist Steven Levitt explains why a lot of the things you thought you knew about money are wrong. . . . A fresh look at everyday topics through an economic lens."

—*Money*

"Principles of economics are used to examine daily life in this fun read."

—*People* (Great Reads)

"*Freakonomics* unfolds much less like a typical arcane economic treatise and more like the type of detective story that has you reading late into the night. . . . compelL[ing]."

—*Chicago Tribune*

"*Freakonomics* presents Levitt's findings in accessible, nonacademic terms. It is an engaging and always interesting work, rich in insights, full of surprises. . . . *Freakonomics* is packed with fascinating ideas."

—*Houston Chronicle*

"Imagine the best of Levitt put into readable form by an excellent journalist. When it comes to the popular exposition of contemporary economic research, this book is a milestone."

—Tyler Cowen, MarginalRevolution.com

"It's not often an economist writes a book that people untutored in the complicated science might actually want to read. But University of Chicago economist Steven Levitt seems to have pulled it off."

—*Chicago Sun-Times*

"An econ tome for both freaks and geeks. . . . Armed with the attitude of a puzzle solver and the tools of statistical economics, Levitt finds different ways to get answers. . . . In his hands, economics, far from being a dismal science, is a tool for the curious."

—*Fortune*

"Fun yet substantial . . . a mind-bending variety of questions in fascinating ways."

—*Detroit Free Press*

"In recent memory, there has not been an economics text that has gripped the popular consciousness like this intriguing and strikingly original collaborative offering. . . . One of the singular accomplishments of this book is its ability to bring together analyses of seemingly unrelated situations, and explain all of them through imparting a simple truth; namely, that people respond, more or less rationally, to economic incentives."

—*Washington Times*

"There's plenty in these pages to warrant a long-form treatment of Levitt's peculiar points of view. . . . Levitt never fails to emerge left-of-center from a mountain of data, with ideas that make us do a double take on wisdom we've long taken for granted. . . . Levitt extrapolates his material with an apparent lack of agenda.

Neither politically correct nor pushing a political viewpoint, he displays rare common sense-and uncommon sense as well."

—*Time Out New York*

"*Freakonomics,* shows Levitt at his best, asking questions that nobody else thought of and sometimes finding answers that nobody else imagined."

—*Atlanta Journal-Constitution*

"Forget your image of an economist as a crusty professor worried about fluctuating interest rates: Levitt focuses his attention on more intimate real-world issues. . . . Underlying all [Levitt's] research subjects is a belief that complex phenomena can be understood if we find the right perspective. Levitt has a knack for making that principle relevant to our daily lives, which could make this book a hit."

—*Publishers Weekly* (starred review)

"In an age of too much wishful, faith-based conventional wisdom on the right and left, and too much intellectual endeavor squeezed into pre-fab ideological containers, *Freakonomics* is politically incorrect in the best, most essential way. Levitt and Dubner suss out all kinds of surprising truths—sometimes important ones, sometimes merely fascinating ones—by means of a smart, deep, rigorous, open-minded consideration of facts, with a fearless disregard for whom they might be upsetting. This is bracing fun of the highest order."

—Kurt Andersen

"A showcase for Levitt's intriguing explorations into a number of disparate topics. . . . Plenty of fun."

—Salon.com

"*Freakonomics* [is] an addictive, irresistible crash course in the populist application of economics. . . . Levitt has a remarkable gift for gazing into a dry pile of statistics and coming away with a novel, exciting theory about how the world works, and in *Freakonomics,* it's well matched by Dubner's gift for conveying Levitt's ideas and theories in vivid, fun, conversational language."

—*The Onion*

"Riveting, funny, and surprising. I can't think of a single adult I know who wouldn't enjoy reading it."

—*San Francisco Weekly*

"[An] innovative and brilliant way of looking at the world. . . . In spite of the controversy that *Freakonomics* is almost certain to cause, Levitt has produced a work full of stunning insights that can rightfully be called genius. . . . In spite of the dense and complex nature of its many arguments, it is from start to finish a good read. . . . Levitt has described aspects of that 'actual world' with stunning originality and breathtaking audacity. How our society responds to these realities is of course an open question, but Levitt and Dubner have done their job. They have written one of the decade's most intelligent and provocative books."

—*The Daily Standard* (UK)

"*Freakonomics* is full of stunning data analysis, the kind that shatters conventional wisdom and leads you to yell across the room to your spouse, 'Hey, listen to this . . . '"

—*Toronto Star*

"*Freakonomics* just might be the first data-analysis book that also qualifies as a beach read. . . . [It] is a series of provocative but persuasive, clearly articulated conclusions about hot-button social issues—crime, abortion, cheating on tests, class consciousness, parenting—leavened by anecdotes and dryly humorous asides."

—*Minneapolis Star Tribune*

"In non-stick prose *Freakonomics* explains how the world really works, popularizing a science or scientific insight while forever hitting the reader on the head with how damnably clever the author is. . . . Entertaining."

—*New York Observer*

"The lasting reason Levitt and Dubner's book will be remembered for decades to come is that it is a tour de force of analysis and logical rigor. *Freakonomics* can legitimately be called dazzling. . . . *Freakonomics'* intellectual fearlessness isn't just welcome. It's something to treasure.

—*Orange County Register*

"Levitt is a brilliant mind applying itself to the mysteries of everyday life, like an economic Sherlock Holmes . . . *Freakonomics* offers nonstop counterintuitive fun."

—*The Evening Standard* (UK)

"*Freakonomics* is about unconventional wisdom, using the raw data of economics in imaginative ways to ask clever and diverting questions . . . Levitt has a genius for wacky inquiry . . . Hallucinatory and mesmerizing . . . Brilliant."

—*The Observer* (UK)

"Vivid, readily understandable and consistently convincing. . . . Levitt tries to serve as a guide for us in opening up a different perspective on the world and its works. . . . He is a compellingly clever economist."

—*Canberra Times* (Australia)

"A thoughtful and provocative analysis."

—*Legal Times*

"Asking provocative and profound questions about human motivation and contemporary living, and reaching some astonishing conclusions, *Freakonomics* shows you a familiar world through a totally new lens. . . . Levitt puts forward a theory that keeps you wondering for a long time after finishing the last page."

—*Business Day* (South Africa)

"Anybody who is interested in the answers to [an] eclectic set of questions should read *Freakonomics,* one of the smartest, politically incorrect and definitely the most entertaining book you will ever read about economics. . . . So skillful is Dubner that even a two-page definition of regression analysis passes by not just painlessly, but pleasurably."

—*The Jakarta Post* (Indonesia)

"*Freakonomics* is Economics 101 meets Sherlock Holmes meets *Ripley's Believe It or Not.*"

—*Times Colonist* (Victoria, British Columbia)

"This book is a brilliant, provocative investigation into motives: what they are, how they can be changed, and how they affect what people do. It is also a deceptively easy read: its style is so light, its tone so sunny and humorous, that it is hard to realise the extent to which the arguments in *Freakonomics* attack some of our most basic assumptions about the way people, and society, work. . . . I can't recommend this book highly enough. Wherever you read it—on the beach, at home, on a train or in an office—you will be stimulated, provoked and entertained."

—*Sunday Telegraph* (UK)

"A thoughtful and provocative analysis"

—*The Legal Intelligencer*

"*Freakonomics* is filled with fascinating revelations.

—*Tulsa World*

"Levitt's curiosity is contagious. He has never lost that toddler's desire to know why, and with that he encourages us to keep questioning, to keep looking for answers and perhaps to look somewhere we hadn't thought of before. . . . An entertaining work highlighting economic theory. Something previously thought impossible."

—*Buffalo News*

"I can't imagine anyone reading this book and not stopping every once in a while and saying, 'Whoa, that goes against everything I've believed for a long time.' . . . Fascinating. I highly recommend it"

—*Green Bay Press Gazette*

"A fun and fascinating book that applies economics to interesting questions of our times . . . *Freakonomics* is a quick and enjoyable read that's thought-provoking at the same time. Levitt's use of statistical analysis to answer quirky questions may help corporate executives find new ways of looking at their problems."

—*Texas Lawyer*

"Levitt's interests are immediately attractive to non-specialists, and he and Dubner tackle them in a lively, conversational style. . . . For readers unfamiliar with the way economists think, *Freakonomics* is likely to be enlightening as well as entertaining."

—*New Statesman* (UK)

"*Freakonomics* is an incredibly stunning book, full of insights that will leave you gasping in amazement. . . . Stephen Levitt is one of the most original thinkers around."

—*Business World*

"An eye-opening, and most interesting, approach to the world."

—*Kirkus Reviews*

FREAKONOMICS

FREAKONOMICS

A Rogue Economist Explores the
Hidden Side of Everything

STEVEN D. LEVITT &
STEPHEN J. DUBNER

HARPER PERENNIAL

NEW YORK • LONDON • TORONTO • SYDNEY • NEW DELHI • AUCKLAND

Freakonomics
Copyright © 2005, 2006 by Steven D. Levitt and Stephen J. Dubner.
All rights reserved.

Published by Harper Perennial, an imprint of HarperCollins Publishers Ltd.

First Canadian trade paperback edition: 2009

HARPER ● PERENNIAL®
is a registered trademark of HarperCollins Publishers

HarperCollins books may be purchased for educational, business,
or sales promotional use through our Special Markets Department.

HarperCollins Publishers Ltd
2 Bloor Street East, 20th Floor
Toronto, Ontario, Canada
M4W 1A8

www.harpercollins.ca

Library and Archives Canada
Cataloguing in Publication information is available

ISBN: 978-1-55468-636-0

Designed by Number 17, NYC

Printed and bound in the United States
RRD 9 8 7 6 5 4 3 2 1

CONTENTS

In which the origins of this book are clarified.

In which the book's central idea is set forth: namely, if morality represents how people would like the world to work, then economics shows how it actually does work.

Why the conventional wisdom is so often wrong... How "experts"—from criminologists to real-estate agents to political scientists—bend the facts... Why knowing what to measure, and how to measure it, is the key to understanding modern life... What is "freakonomics," anyway?

CONTENTS

Chapter 1

WHAT DO SCHOOLTEACHERS AND SUMO WRESTLERS HAVE IN COMMON?

In which we explore the beauty of incentives, as well as their dark side—cheating.

Who cheats? Just about everyone . . . How cheaters cheat, and how to catch them . . . Stories from an Israeli day-care center . . . The sudden disappearance of seven million American children . . . Cheating schoolteachers in Chicago . . . Why cheating to lose is worse than cheating to win . . . Could sumo wrestling, the national sport of Japan, be corrupt? . . . What the Bagel Man saw: mankind may be more honest than we think.

Chapter 2

HOW IS THE KU KLUX KLAN LIKE A GROUP OF REAL-ESTATE AGENTS?

In which it is argued that nothing is more powerful than information, especially when its power is abused.

Spilling the Ku Klux Klan's secrets . . . Why experts of every kind are in the perfect position to exploit you . . . The antidote to information abuse: the Internet . . . Why a new car is suddenly worth so much less the moment it leaves the lot . . . Breaking the real-estate agent code: what "well maintained" really means . . . Is Trent Lott more racist than the average Weakest Link contestant? . . . What do online daters lie about?

Chapter 3

In which the conventional wisdom is often found to be a web of fabrication, self-interest, and convenience.

Why experts routinely make up statistics; the invention of chronic halitosis . . . How to ask a good question . . . Sudhir Venkatesh's long, strange trip into the crack den . . . Why prostitutes earn more than architects . . . What a drug dealer, a high-school quarterback, and an editorial assistant have in common . . . How the invention of crack cocaine mirrored the invention of nylon stocking . . . Was crack the worst thing to hit black Americans since Jim Crow?

Chapter 4

In which the facts of crime are sorted out from the fictions.

What Nicolae Ceauşescu learned—the hard way— about abortion . . . Why the 1960s was a great time to be a criminal . . . Think the roaring 1990s economy put a crimp on crime? Think again . . . Why capital punishment doesn't deter criminals . . . Do police actually lower crime rates? . . . Prisons, prisons everywhere . . . Seeing through the New York City police "miracle" . . . What is a gun, really? . . . Why early crack dealers were like Microsoft millionaires and later crack dealers were like Pets.com . . . The superpredator versus the senior citizen . . . Jane Roe, crime stopper: how the legalization of abortion changed everything.

In the summer of 2003, *The New York Times Magazine* sent Stephen J. Dubner, an author and journalist, to write a profile of Steven D. Levitt, a heralded young economist at the University of Chicago.

Dubner, who was researching a book about the psychology of money, had lately been interviewing many economists and found that they often spoke English as if it were a fourth or fifth language. Levitt, who had just won the John Bates Clark Medal (a sort of junior Nobel Prize for young economists), had lately been interviewed by many journalists and found that their thinking wasn't very . . . robust, as an economist might say.

But Levitt decided that Dubner wasn't a complete idiot. And Dubner found that Levitt wasn't a human slide rule. The writer was dazzled by the inventiveness of the economist's work and his knack for explaining it. Despite Levitt's elite credentials (Harvard undergrad, a PhD from MIT, a stack of awards), he approached economics in a notably unorthodox way. He seemed to look at the world not so much as an academic but as a very smart and curious explorer—a documentary filmmaker, perhaps, or a forensic investigator or a bookie whose markets ranged from sports to crime to pop culture. He professed little interest in the sort of monetary issues that come to mind when most people think about economics; he practically blustered with self-effacement. "I just don't know very much about the field of economics," he told Dubner at one point, swiping the hair from his eyes. "I'm not good at math, I don't know a lot of econometrics, and I also don't know how to do theory. If you ask me about whether the stock market's going to go up or down, if you ask me whether the economy's going to grow or shrink, if you ask me whether deflation's good or bad, if you ask me about taxes—I mean, it would be total fakery if I said I knew anything about any of those things."

What interested Levitt were the riddles of everyday life. His investigations were a feast for anyone wanting to know how the world really works. His singular attitude was evoked in Dubner's resulting article:

> As Levitt sees it, economics is a science with excellent tools for gaining answers but a serious shortage of interesting questions. His particular gift is the ability to ask such questions. For instance: If drug dealers make so much money, why do they still live with their mothers? Which is more dangerous, a gun or a swimming pool? What really caused crime rates to plunge during the past decade? Do real-estate agents have their clients' best interests at heart? Why do black parents give their children names that may hurt their career prospects?

Do schoolteachers cheat to meet high-stakes testing standards? Is sumo wrestling corrupt?

Many people—including a fair number of his peers—might not recognize Levitt's work as economics at all. But he has merely distilled the so-called dismal science to its most primal aim: explaining how people get what they want. Unlike most academics, he is unafraid of using personal observations and curiosities; he is also unafraid of anecdote and storytelling (although he is afraid of calculus). He is an intuitionist. He sifts through a pile of data to find a story that no one else has found. He figures a way to measure an effect that veteran economists had declared unmeasurable. His abiding interests— though he says he has never trafficked in them himself—are cheating, corruption, and crime.

Levitt's blazing curiosity also proved attractive to thousands of *New York Times* readers. He was beset by questions and queries, riddles and requests—from General Motors and the New York Yankees and U.S. senators but also from prisoners and parents and a man who for twenty years had kept precise data on his sales of bagels. A former Tour de France champion called Levitt to ask his help in proving that the current Tour is rife with doping; the Central Intelligence Agency wanted to know how Levitt might use data to catch money launderers and terrorists.

What they were all responding to was the force of Levitt's underlying belief: that the modern world, despite a surfeit of obfuscation, complication, and downright deceit, is *not* impenetrable, is *not* unknowable, and—if the right questions are asked—is even more intriguing than we think. All it takes is a new way of looking.

In New York City, the publishers were telling Levitt he should write a book.

"Write a book?" he said. "I don't want to write a book." He already had a million more riddles to solve than time to solve them. Nor did he think himself much of a writer. So he said that no, he wasn't interested—"unless," he proposed, "maybe Dubner and I could do it together."

Collaboration isn't for everyone. But the two of them—henceforth known as the two of *us*—decided to talk things over to see if such a book might work. We decided it could. We hope you agree.

FREAKONOMICS

INTRODUCTION:
THE HIDDEN SIDE OF EVERYTHING

Anyone living in the United States in the early 1990s and paying even a whisper of attention to the nightly news or a daily paper could be forgiven for having been scared out of his skin.

The culprit was crime. It had been rising relentlessly—a graph plotting the crime rate in any American city over recent decades looked like a ski slope in profile—and it seemed now to herald the end of the world as we knew it. Death by gunfire, intentional and otherwise, had become commonplace. So too had carjacking and crack dealing, robbery and rape. Violent crime was a gruesome, constant companion. And things were about to get even worse. Much worse. All the experts were saying so.

The cause was the so-called superpredator. For a time, he was everywhere. Glowering from the cover of newsweeklies. Swaggering his way through foot-thick government reports. He was a scrawny, big-city teenager with a cheap gun in his hand and nothing in his heart but ruthlessness. There were thousands out there just like him, we were told, a generation of killers about to hurl the country into deepest chaos.

In 1995 the criminologist James Alan Fox wrote a report for the U.S. attorney general that grimly detailed the coming spike in murders by teenagers. Fox proposed optimistic and pessimistic scenarios. In the optimistic scenario, he believed, the rate of teen homicides would rise another 15 percent over the next decade; in the pessimistic scenario, it would more than double. "The next crime wave will get so bad," he said, "that it will make 1995 look like the good old days."

Other criminologists, political scientists, and similarly learned forecasters laid out the same horrible future, as did President Clinton. "We know we've got about six years to turn this juvenile crime thing around," Clinton said, "or our country is going to be living with chaos. And my successors will not be giving speeches about the wonderful opportunities of the global economy; they'll be trying to keep body and soul together for people on the streets of these cities." The smart money was plainly on the criminals.

And then, instead of going up and up and up, crime began to fall. And fall and fall and fall some more. The crime drop was startling in several respects. It was ubiquitous, with every category of crime falling in every part of the country. It was persistent, with incremental decreases year after year. And it was entirely unanticipated—especially by the very experts who had been predicting the opposite.

The magnitude of the reversal was astounding. The teenage murder rate, instead of rising 100 percent or even 15 percent as James Alan Fox had warned, fell more than 50 percent within five years. By 2000 the overall murder rate in the United States had dropped to its lowest level in thirty-five years. So had the rate of just about every other sort of crime, from assault to car theft.

Even though the experts had failed to anticipate the crime drop—which was in fact well under way even as they made their horrifying predictions—they now hurried to explain it. Most of their theories sounded perfectly logical. It was the roaring 1990s economy, they said, that helped turn back crime. It was the proliferation of gun control laws, they said. It was the sort of innovative policing strategies put into place in New York City, where murders would fall from 2,262 in 1990 to 540 in 2005.

These theories were not only logical; they were also *encouraging*, for they attributed the crime drop to specific and recent human initiatives. If it was gun control and clever police strategies and better-paying jobs that quelled crime—well then, the power to stop criminals had been within our reach all along. As it would be the next time, God forbid, that crime got so bad.

These theories made their way, seemingly without friction, from the experts' mouths to journalists' ears to the public's mind. In short course, they became conventional wisdom.

There was only one problem: they weren't true.

There was another factor, meanwhile, that *had* greatly contributed to the massive crime drop of the 1990s. It had taken shape more than twenty years earlier and concerned a young woman in Dallas named Norma McCorvey.

Like the proverbial butterfly that flaps its wings on one continent and eventually causes a hurricane on another, Norma McCorvey dramatically altered the course of events without intending to. All she had wanted was an abortion. She was a poor, uneducated, unskilled, alcoholic, drug-using twenty-one-year-old woman who had already given up two children for adoption and now, in 1970, found herself pregnant again. But in Texas, as in all but a few states at that time, abortion was illegal. McCorvey's cause came to be adopted by people far more powerful than she. They made her the lead plaintiff in a class-action lawsuit seeking to legalize abortion. The defendant was Henry Wade, the Dallas County district attorney. The case ultimately made it to the U.S. Supreme Court, by which time McCorvey's name had been disguised as Jane Roe. On January 22, 1973, the court ruled in favor of Ms. Roe, allowing legalized abortion throughout the United States. By this time, of course, it was far too late for Ms. McCorvey/Roe to have her abortion. She had given birth and put the child up for adoption. (Years later she would renounce her allegiance to legalized abortion and become a pro-life activist.)

So how did *Roe v. Wade* help trigger, a generation later, the greatest crime drop in recorded history?

As far as crime is concerned, it turns out that not all children are born equal. Not even close. Decades of studies have shown that a child born into an adverse family environment is far more likely than other children to become a criminal. And the millions of women most likely to have an abortion in the wake of *Roe v. Wade*—poor, unmarried, and teenage mothers for whom illegal abortions had been too expensive or too hard to get—were often models of adversity. They were the very women whose children, if born, would have been much more likely than average to become criminals. But because of *Roe v. Wade*, these children *weren't* being born. This powerful cause would have a drastic, distant effect: years later, just as these unborn children would have entered their criminal primes, the rate of crime began to plummet.

It wasn't gun control or a strong economy or new police strategies that finally blunted the American crime wave. It was, among other factors, the reality that the pool of potential criminals had dramatically shrunk.

Now, as the crime-drop experts (the former crime doomsayers) spun their theories to the media, how many times did they cite legalized abortion as a cause?

Zero.

It is the quintessential blend of commerce and camaraderie: you hire a real-estate agent to sell your home.

She sizes up its charms, snaps some pictures, sets the price, writes a seductive ad, shows the house aggressively, negotiates the offers, and sees the deal through to its end. Sure, it's a lot of work, but she's getting a nice cut. On the sale of a $300,000 house, a typical 6 percent agent fee yields $18,000. Eighteen thousand dollars, you say to yourself: that's a lot of money. But you also tell yourself that you never could have sold the house for $300,000 on your own. The agent knew how to—what's that phrase she used?—"maximize the house's value." She got you top dollar, right?

Right?

A real-estate agent is a different breed of expert than a criminologist, but she is every bit the expert. That is, she knows her field far better than the layman on whose behalf she is acting. She is better informed about the house's value, the state of the housing market, even the buyer's frame of mind. You depend on her for this information. That, in fact, is why you hired an expert.

As the world has grown more specialized, countless such experts have made themselves similarly indispensable. Doctors, lawyers, contractors, stockbrokers, auto mechanics, mortgage brokers, financial planners: they all enjoy a gigantic informational advantage. And they use that advantage to help you, the person who hired them, get exactly what you want for the best price.

Right?

It would be lovely to think so. But experts are human, and humans respond to incentives. How any given expert treats you, therefore, will depend on how that expert's incentives are set up. Sometimes his incentives may work in your favor. For instance: a study of California auto mechanics found they often passed up a small repair bill by letting failing cars pass emissions inspections—the reason being that lenient mechanics are rewarded with repeat business. But in a different case, an expert's incentives may work against you. In a medical study, it turned out that obstetricians in areas with declining birth rates are much more likely to perform cesarean-section deliveries than obstetricians in growing areas—suggesting that, when business is tough, doctors try to ring up more expensive procedures.

It is one thing to muse about experts' abusing their position and another to prove it. The best way to do so would be to measure how an expert treats you versus how he performs the same service for himself. Unfortunately a surgeon doesn't operate on himself. Nor is his medical file a matter of public record; neither is an auto mechanic's repair log for his own car.

Real-estate sales, however, *are* a matter of public record. And real-estate agents often do sell their own homes. A recent set of data covering the sale of nearly 100,000 houses in suburban Chicago shows that more than 3,000 of those houses were owned by the agents themselves.

Before plunging into the data, it helps to ask a question: what is the real-estate agent's incentive when she is selling her own home? Simple: to make the best deal possible. Presumably this is also your incentive when you are selling your home. And so your incentive and the real-estate agent's incentive would seem to be nicely aligned. Her commission, after all, is based on the sale price.

But as incentives go, commissions are tricky. First of all, a 6 percent real-estate commission is typically split between the seller's agent and the buyer's. Each agent then kicks back roughly half of her take to the agency. Which means that only 1.5 percent of the purchase price goes directly into your agent's pocket.

So on the sale of your $300,000 house, her personal take of the $18,000 commission is $4,500. Still not bad, you say. But what if the house was actually worth more than $300,000? What if, with a little more effort and patience and a few more newspaper ads, she could have sold it for $310,000? After the commission, that puts an additional $9,400 in your pocket. But the agent's additional share—her personal 1.5 percent of the extra $10,000—is a mere $150. If you earn $9,400 while she earns only $150, maybe your incentives aren't aligned after all. (Especially when she's the one paying for the ads and doing all the work.) Is the agent willing to put out all that extra time, money, and energy for just $150?

There's one way to find out: measure the difference between the sales data for houses that belong to real-estate agents themselves and the houses they sold on behalf of clients. Using the data from the sales of those 100,000 Chicago homes, and controlling for any number of variables—location, age and quality of the house, aesthetics, whether or not the property was an investment, and so on—it turns out that a real-estate agent keeps her own home on the market an average of ten days longer and sells it for an extra 3-plus percent, or $10,000 on a $300,000 house. When she sells her own house, an agent holds out for the best offer; when she sells yours, she encourages you to take the first decent offer that comes along. Like a stockbroker churning commissions, she wants to make deals and make them fast. Why not? Her share of a better offer—$150—is too puny an incentive to encourage her to do otherwise.

Of all the truisms about politics, one is held to be truer than the rest: money buys elections. Arnold Schwarzenegger, Michael Bloomberg, Jon Corzine—these are but a few recent, dramatic examples of the truism at work. (Disregard for a moment the contrary examples of Steve Forbes, Michael Huffington, and especially Thomas Golisano, who over the course of three gubernatorial elections in New York spent $93 million of his own money and won 4 percent, 8 percent, and 14 percent, respectively, of the vote.) Most people would agree that money has an undue influence on elections and that far too much money is spent on political campaigns.

Indeed, election data show it is true that the candidate who spends more money in a campaign usually wins. But is money the *cause* of the victory?

It might seem logical to think so, much as it might have seemed logical that a booming 1990s economy helped reduce crime. But just because two things are correlated does not mean that one causes the other. A correlation simply means that a relationship exists between two factors—let's call them X and Y—but it tells you nothing about the direction of that relationship. It's possible that X causes Y; it's also possible that Y causes X; and it may be that X and Y are both being caused by some other factor, Z.

Think about this correlation: cities with a lot of murders also tend to have a lot of police officers. Consider now the police/murder correlation in a pair of real cities. Denver and Washington, D.C., have about the same population—but Washington has nearly three times as many police as Denver, and it also has eight times the number of murders. Unless you have more information, however, it's hard to say what's causing what. Someone who didn't know better might contemplate these figures and conclude that it is all those extra police in Washington who are causing the extra murders. Such wayward thinking, which has a long history, generally provokes a wayward response. Consider the folktale of the czar who learned that the most disease-ridden province in his empire was also the province with the most doctors. His solution? He promptly ordered all the doctors shot dead.

Now, returning to the issue of campaign spending: in order to figure out the relationship between money and elections, it helps to consider the incentives at play in campaign finance. Let's say you are the kind of person who might contribute $1,000 to a candidate. Chances are you'll give the money in one of two situations: a close race, in which you think the money will influence the outcome; or a campaign in which one candidate is a sure winner and you would like to bask in reflected glory or receive some future in-kind consideration. The one candidate you *won't* contribute to is a sure loser. (Just ask any presidential hopeful who bombs in Iowa and New Hampshire.) So front-runners and incumbents raise a lot more money than long shots. And what about spending that money? Incumbents and front-runners obviously have more cash, but they only spend a lot of it when they stand a legitimate chance of losing; otherwise, why dip into a war chest that might be more useful later on, when a more formidable opponent appears?

Now picture two candidates, one intrinsically appealing and the other not so. The appealing candidate raises much more money and wins easily. But was it the money that won him the votes, or was it his appeal that won the votes *and* the money?

That's a crucial question but a very hard one to answer. Voter appeal, after all, isn't easy to quantify. How can it be measured?

It can't, really—except in one special case. The key is to measure a candidate against . . . himself. That is, Candidate A today is likely to be similar to Candidate A two or four years hence. The same could be said for Candidate B. If only Candidate A ran against Candidate B in two consecutive elections but in each case spent different amounts of money. Then, with the candidates' appeal more or less constant, we could measure the money's impact.

As it turns out, the same two candidates run against each other in consecutive elections all the time—indeed, in nearly a thousand U.S. congressional races since 1972. What do the numbers have to say about such cases?

Here's the surprise: the amount of money spent by the candidates *hardly matters at all.* A winning candidate can cut his spending in half and lose only 1 percent of the vote. Meanwhile, a losing candidate who doubles his spending can expect to shift the vote in his favor by only that same 1 percent. What really matters for a political candidate is *not* how much you spend; what matters is who you are. (The same could be said—and will be said, in chapter 5—about parents.) Some politicians are inherently attractive to voters and others simply aren't, and no amount of money can do much about it. (Messrs. Forbes, Huffington, and Golisano already know this, of course.)

And what about the other half of the election truism—that the amount of money spent on campaign finance is obscenely huge? In a typical election period that includes campaigns for the presidency, the Senate, and the House of Representatives, about $1 billion is spent per year—which sounds like a lot of money, unless you care to measure it against something seemingly less important than democratic elections.

It is the same amount, for instance, that Americans spend every year on chewing gum.

This isn't a book about the cost of chewing gum versus campaign spending per se, or about disingenuous real-estate agents, or the impact of legalized abortion on crime. It will certainly address these scenarios and dozens more, from the art of parenting to the mechanics of cheating, from the inner workings of a crack-selling gang to racial discrimination on *The Weakest Link*. What this book *is* about is stripping a layer or two from the surface of modern life and seeing what is happening underneath. We will ask a lot of questions, some frivolous and some about life-and-death issues. The answers may often seem odd but, after the fact, also rather obvious. We will seek out these answers in the data—whether those data come in the form of schoolchildren's test scores or New York City's crime statistics or a crack dealer's financial records. Often we will take advantage of patterns in the data that were incidentally left behind, like an airplane's sharp contrail in a high sky. It is well and good to opine or theorize about a subject, as humankind is wont to do, but when moral posturing is replaced by an honest assessment of the data, the result is often a new, surprising insight.

Morality, it could be argued, represents the way that people would like the world to work—whereas economics represents how it actually *does* work. Economics is above all a science of measurement. It comprises an extraordinarily powerful and flexible set of tools that can reliably assess a thicket of information to determine the effect of any one factor, or even the whole effect. That's what "the economy" is, after all: a thicket of information about jobs and real estate and banking and investment. But the tools of economics can be just as easily applied to subjects that are more—well, more *interesting*.

This book, then, has been written from a very specific worldview, based on a few fundamental ideas:

Incentives are the cornerstone of modern life. And understanding them—or, often, ferreting them out—is the key to solving just about any riddle, from violent crime to sports cheating to online dating.

The conventional wisdom is often wrong. Crime didn't keep soaring in the 1990s, money alone doesn't win elections, and—surprise—drinking eight glasses of water a day has never actually been shown to do a thing for your health. Conventional wisdom is often shoddily formed and devilishly difficult to see through, but it can be done.

Dramatic effects often have distant, even subtle, causes. The answer to a given riddle is not always right in front of you. Norma McCorvey had a far greater impact on crime than did the combined forces of gun control, a strong economy, and innovative police strategies. So did, as we shall see, a man named Oscar Danilo Blandon, aka the Johnny Appleseed of Crack.

"Experts"—from criminologists to real-estate agents—use their informational advantage to serve their own agenda. However, they can be beat at their own game. And in the face of the Internet, their informational advantage is shrinking every day—as evidenced by,

among other things, the falling price of coffins and life-insurance premiums.

Knowing what to measure and how to measure it makes a complicated world much less so. If you learn to look at data in the right way, you can explain riddles that otherwise might have seemed impossible. Because there is nothing like the sheer power of numbers to scrub away layers of confusion and contradiction.

So the aim of this book is to explore the hidden side of . . . everything. This may occasionally be a frustrating exercise. It may sometimes feel as if we are peering at the world through a straw or even staring into a funhouse mirror; but the idea is to look at many different scenarios and examine them in a way they have rarely been examined. In some regards, this is a strange concept for a book. Most books put forth a single theme, crisply expressed in a sentence or two, and then tell the entire story of that theme: the history of salt; the fragility of democracy; the use and misuse of punctuation. This book has no such unifying theme. We did consider, for about six minutes, writing a book that would revolve around a single theme—the theory and practice of applied microeconomics, anyone?—but opted instead for a sort of treasure-hunt approach. Yes, this approach employs the best analytical tools that economics can offer, but it also allows us to follow whatever freakish curiosities may occur to us. Thus our invented field of study: Freakonomics. The sort of stories told in this book are not often covered in Econ 101, but that may change. Since the science of economics is primarily a set of tools, as opposed to a subject matter, then no subject, however offbeat, need be beyond its reach.

It is worth remembering that Adam Smith, the founder of classical economics, was first and foremost a philosopher. He strove to be a moralist and, in doing so, became an economist. When he published *The Theory of Moral Sentiments* in 1759, modern capitalism was just getting under way. Smith was entranced by the sweeping changes wrought by this new force, but it wasn't just the numbers that interested him. It was the human effect, the fact that economic forces were vastly changing the way a person thought and behaved in a given situation. What might lead one person to cheat or steal while another didn't? How would one person's seemingly innocuous choice, good or bad, affect a great number of people down the line? In Smith's era, cause and effect had begun to wildly accelerate; incentives were magnified tenfold. The gravity and shock of these changes were as overwhelming to the citizens of his time as the gravity and shock of modern life may seem to us today.

Smith's true subject was the friction between individual desire and societal norms. The economic historian Robert Heilbroner, writing in *The Worldly Philosophers*, wondered how Smith was able to separate the doings of man, a creature of self-interest, from the greater moral plane in which man operated. "Smith held that the answer lay in our ability to put ourselves in the position of a third person, an impartial observer," Heilbroner wrote, "and in this way to form a notion of the objective . . . merits of a case."

Consider yourself, then, in the company of a third person—or, if you will, a pair of third people—eager to explore the objective merits of interesting cases. These explorations generally begin with the asking of a simple unasked question. Such as: what do schoolteachers and sumo wrestlers have in common?

Chapter 1

WHAT DO SCHOOLTEACHERS AND SUMO WRESTLERS HAVE IN COMMON?

Imagine for a moment that you are the manager of a day-care center. You have a clearly stated policy that children are supposed to be picked up by 4 p.m. But very often parents are late. The result: at day's end, you have some anxious children and at least one teacher who must wait around for the parents to arrive. What to do?

A pair of economists who heard of this dilemma—it turned out to be a rather common one—offered a solution: fine the tardy parents. Why, after all, should the day-care center take care of these kids for free?

The economists decided to test their solution by conducting a study of ten day-care centers in Haifa, Israel. The study lasted twenty weeks, but the fine was not introduced immediately. For the first four weeks, the economists simply kept track of the number of parents who came late; there were, on average, eight late pickups per week per day-care center. In the fifth week, the fine was enacted. It was announced that any parent arriving more than ten minutes late would pay $3 per child for each incident. The fee would be added to the parents' monthly bill, which was roughly $380.

After the fine was enacted, the number of late pickups promptly went . . . up. Before long there were twenty late pickups per week, more than double the original average. The incentive had plainly backfired.

Economics is, at root, the study of incentives: how people get what they want, or need, especially when other people want or need the same thing. Economists love incentives. They love to dream them up and enact them, study them and tinker with them. The typical economist believes the world has not yet invented a problem that he cannot fix if given a free hand to design the proper incentive scheme. His solution may not always be pretty—it may involve coercion or exorbitant penalties or the violation of civil liberties—but the original problem, rest assured, will be fixed. An incentive is a bullet, a lever, a key: an often tiny object with astonishing power to change a situation.

We all learn to respond to incentives, negative and positive, from the outset of life. If you toddle over to the hot stove and touch it, you burn a finger. But if you bring home straight A's from school, you get a new bike. If you are spotted picking your nose in class, you get ridiculed. But if you make the basketball team, you move up the social ladder. If you break curfew, you get grounded. But if you ace your SATs, you get to go to a good college. If you flunk out of law school, you have to go to work at your father's insurance company. But if you perform so well that a rival company comes calling, you become a vice president and no longer have to work for your father. If you become so excited about your new vice president job that you drive home at eighty mph, you get pulled over by the police and fined $100. But if you hit your sales projections and collect a year-end bonus, you not only aren't worried about the $100 ticket but can also afford to buy that Viking range you've always wanted—and on which your toddler can now burn her own finger.

An incentive is simply a means of urging people to do more of a good thing and less of a bad thing. But most incentives don't come about organically. Someone—an economist or a politician or a parent—has to invent them. Your three-year-old eats all her vegetables for a week? She wins a trip to the toy store. A big steelmaker belches too much smoke into the air? The company is fined for each metric ton of pollutants over the legal limit. Too many Americans aren't paying their share of income tax? It was the economist Milton Friedman who helped come up with a solution to this one: automatic tax withholding from employees' paychecks.

There are three basic flavors of incentive: economic, social, and moral. Very often a single incentive scheme will include all three varieties. Think about the anti-smoking campaign of recent years. The addition of a $3-per-pack "sin tax" is a strong economic incentive against buying cigarettes. The banning of cigarettes in restaurants and bars is a powerful social incentive. And when the U.S. government asserts that terrorists raise money by selling black-market cigarettes, that acts as a rather jarring moral incentive.

Some of the most compelling incentives yet invented have been put in place to deter crime. Considering this fact, it might be worthwhile to take a familiar question—why is there so much crime in modern society?—and stand it on its head: why isn't there a lot *more* crime?

After all, every one of us regularly passes up opportunities to maim, steal, and defraud. The chance of going to jail—thereby losing your job, your house, and your freedom, all of which are essentially economic penalties—is certainly a strong incentive. But when it comes to crime, people also respond to moral incentives (they don't want to do something they consider wrong) and social incentives (they don't want to be seen by others as doing something wrong). For certain types of misbehavior, social incentives are terribly powerful. In an echo of Hester Prynne's scarlet letter, many American cities now fight prostitution with a "shaming" offensive, posting pictures of convicted johns (and prostitutes) on websites or on local-access television. Which is a more horrifying deterrent: a $500 fine for soliciting a prostitute or the thought of your friends and family ogling you on www.HookersAndJohns.com?

So through a complicated, haphazard, and constantly readjusted web of economic, social, and moral incentives, modern society does its best to militate against crime. Some people would argue that we don't do a very good job. But taking the long view, that is clearly not true. Consider the historical trend in homicide (not including wars), which is both the most reliably measured crime and the best barometer of a society's overall crime rate. These statistics, compiled by the criminologist Manuel Eisner, track the historical homicide levels in five European regions.

HOMICIDES

(PER 100,000 PEOPLE)

	ENGLAND	NETHERLANDS & BELGIUM	SCANDINAVIA	GERMANY & SWITZERLAND	ITALY
13TH&14TH C.	23.0	47.0	N.A.	37.0	56.0
15TH C.	N.A.	45.0	46.0	16.0	73.0
16TH C.	7.0	25.0	21.0	11.0	47.0
17TH C.	5.0	7.5	18.0	7.0	32.0
18TH C.	1.5	5.5	1.9	7.5	10.5
19TH C.	1.7	1.6	1.1	2.8	12.6
1900–1949	0.8	1.5	0.7	1.7	3.2
1950–1994	0.9	0.9	0.9	1.0	1.5

The steep decline of these numbers over the centuries suggests that, for one of the gravest human concerns—getting murdered—the incentives that we collectively cook up are working better and better.

So what was wrong with the incentive at the Israeli day-care centers?

You have probably already guessed that the $3 fine was simply too small. For that price, a parent with one child could afford to be late every day and only pay an extra $60 each month—just one-sixth of the base fee. As babysitting goes, that's pretty cheap. What if the fine had been set at $100 instead of $3? That would have likely put an end to the late pickups, though it would have also engendered plenty of ill will. (Any incentive is inherently a trade-off; the trick is to balance the extremes.)

But there was another problem with the day-care center fine. It substituted an economic incentive (the $3 penalty) for a moral incentive (the guilt that parents were supposed to feel when they came late). For just a few dollars each day, parents could buy off their guilt. Furthermore, the small size of the fine sent a signal to the parents that late pickups weren't such a big problem. If the day-care center suffers only $3 worth of pain for each late pickup, why bother to cut short your tennis game? Indeed, when the economists eliminated the $3 fine in the seventeenth week of their study, the number of late-arriving parents didn't change. Now they could arrive late, pay no fine, *and* feel no guilt.

Such is the strange and powerful nature of incentives. A slight tweak can produce drastic and often unforeseen results. Thomas Jefferson noted this while reflecting on the tiny incentive that led to the Boston Tea Party and, in turn, the American Revolution: "So inscrutable is the arrangement of causes and consequences in this world that a two-penny duty on tea, unjustly imposed in a sequestered part of it, changes the condition of all its inhabitants."

In the 1970s, researchers conducted a study that, like the Israeli day-care study, pitted a moral incentive against an economic incentive. In this case, they wanted to learn about the motivation behind blood donations. Their discovery: when people are given a small stipend for donating blood rather than simply being praised for their altruism, they tend to donate *less* blood. The stipend turned a noble act of charity into a painful way to make a few dollars, and it wasn't worth it.

What if the blood donors had been offered an incentive of $50, or $500, or $5,000? Surely the number of donors would have changed dramatically.

But something else would have changed dramatically as well, for every incentive has its dark side. If a pint of blood were suddenly worth $5,000, you can be sure that plenty of people would take note. They might literally steal blood at knifepoint. They might pass off pig blood as their own. They might circumvent donation limits by using fake IDs. Whatever the incentive, whatever the situation, dishonest people will try to gain an advantage by whatever means necessary.

Or, as W. C. Fields once said: a thing worth having is a thing worth cheating for.

Who cheats?

Well, just about anyone, if the stakes are right. You might say to yourself, *I* don't cheat, regardless of the stakes. And then you might remember the time you cheated on, say, a board game. Last week. Or the golf ball you nudged out of its bad lie. Or the time you really wanted a bagel in the office break room but couldn't come up with the dollar you were supposed to drop in the coffee can. And then took the bagel anyway. And told yourself you'd pay double the next time. And didn't.

For every clever person who goes to the trouble of creating an incentive scheme, there is an army of people, clever and otherwise, who will inevitably spend even more time trying to beat it. Cheating may or may not be human nature, but it is certainly a prominent feature in just about every human endeavor. Cheating is a primordial economic act: getting more for less. So it isn't just the boldface names—inside-trading CEOs and pill-popping ballplayers and perk-abusing politicians—who cheat. It is the waitress who pockets her tips instead of pooling them. It is the Wal-Mart payroll manager who goes into the computer and shaves his employees' hours to make his own performance look better. It is the third grader who, worried about not making it to the fourth grade, copies test answers from the kid sitting next to him.

Some cheating leaves barely a shadow of evidence. In other cases, the evidence is massive. Consider what happened one spring evening at midnight in 1987: seven million American children suddenly disappeared. The worst kidnapping wave in history? Hardly. It was the night of April 15, and the Internal Revenue Service had just changed a rule. Instead of merely listing the name of each dependent child, tax filers were now required to provide a Social Security number. Suddenly, seven million children—children who had existed only as phantom exemptions on the previous year's 1040 forms—vanished, representing about one in ten of all dependent children in the United States.

The incentive for those cheating taxpayers was quite clear. The same for the waitress, the payroll manager, and the third grader. But what about that third grader's *teacher*? Might she have an incentive to cheat? And if so, how would she do it?

Imagine now that instead of running a day-care center in Haifa, you are running the Chicago Public Schools, a system that educates 400,000 students each year.

The most volatile current debate among American school administrators, teachers, parents, and students concerns "high-stakes" testing. The stakes are considered high because instead of simply testing students to measure their progress, schools are increasingly held accountable for the results.

The federal government mandated high-stakes testing as part of the No Child Left Behind law, signed by President Bush in 2002. But even before that law, most states gave annual standardized tests to students in elementary and secondary school. Twenty states rewarded individual schools for good test scores or dramatic improvement; thirty-two states sanctioned the schools that didn't do well.

The Chicago Public School system embraced high-stakes testing in 1996. Under the new policy, a school with low reading scores would be placed on probation and face the threat of being shut down, its staff to be dismissed or reassigned. The CPS also did away with what is known as social promotion. In the past, only a dramatically inept or difficult student was held back a grade. Now, in order to be promoted, every student in third, sixth, and eighth grade had to manage a minimum score on the standardized, multiple-choice exam known as the Iowa Test of Basic Skills.

Advocates of high-stakes testing argue that it raises the standards of learning and gives students more incentive to study. Also, if the test prevents poor students from advancing without merit, they won't clog up the higher grades and slow down good students. Opponents, meanwhile, worry that certain students will be unfairly penalized if they don't happen to test well, and that teachers may concentrate on the test topics at the exclusion of more important lessons.

Schoolchildren, of course, have had incentive to cheat for as long as there have been tests. But high-stakes testing has so radically changed the incentives for teachers that they too now have added reason to cheat. With high-stakes testing, a teacher whose students test poorly can be censured or passed over for a raise or promotion. If the entire school does poorly, federal funding can be withheld; if the school is put on probation, the teacher stands to be fired. High-stakes testing also presents teachers with some positive incentives. If her students do well enough, she might find herself praised, promoted, and even richer: the state of California at one point introduced bonuses of $25,000 for teachers who produced big test-score gains.

And if a teacher were to survey this newly incentivized landscape and consider somehow inflating her students' scores, she just might be persuaded by one final incentive: teacher cheating is rarely looked for, hardly ever detected, and just about never punished.

How might a teacher go about cheating? There are any number of possibilities, from brazen to subtle. A fifth-grade student in Oakland recently came home from school and gaily told her mother that her super-nice teacher had written the answers to the state exam right there on the chalkboard. Such instances are certainly rare, for placing your fate in the hands of thirty prepubescent witnesses doesn't seem like a risk that even the worst teacher would take. (The Oakland teacher was duly fired.) There are more nuanced ways to inflate students' scores. A teacher can simply give students extra time to complete the test. If she obtains a copy of the exam early—that is, illegitimately—she can prepare them for specific questions. More broadly, she can "teach to the test," basing her lesson plans on questions from past years' exams, which isn't considered cheating but may well violate the spirit of the test. Since these tests all have multiple-choice answers, with no penalty for wrong guesses, a teacher might instruct her students to randomly fill in every blank as the clock is winding down, perhaps inserting a long string of Bs or an alternating pattern of Bs and Cs. She might even fill in the blanks for them after they've left the room.

But if a teacher *really* wanted to cheat—and make it worth her while—she might collect her students' answer sheets and, in the hour or so before turning them in to be read by an electronic scanner, erase the wrong answers and fill in correct ones. (And you always thought that no. 2 pencil was for the *children* to change their answers.) If this kind of teacher cheating is truly going on, how might it be detected?

To catch a cheater, it helps to think like one. If you were willing to erase your students' wrong answers and fill in correct ones, you probably wouldn't want to change too many wrong answers. That would clearly be a tip-off. You probably wouldn't even want to change answers on every student's test—another tip-off. Nor, in all likelihood, would you have enough time, because the answer sheets have to be turned in soon after the test is over. So what you might do is select a string of eight or ten consecutive questions and fill in the correct answers for, say, one-half or two-thirds of your students. You could easily memorize a short pattern of correct answers, and it would be a lot faster to erase and change that pattern than to go through each student's answer sheet individually. You might even think to focus your activity toward the end of the test, where the questions tend to be harder than the earlier questions. In that way, you'd be most likely to substitute correct answers for wrong ones.

If economics is a science primarily concerned with incentives, it is also—fortunately—a science with statistical tools to measure how people respond to those incentives. All you need are some data.

In this case, the Chicago Public School system obliged. It made available a database of the test answers for every CPS student from third grade through seventh grade from 1993 to 2000. This amounts to roughly 30,000 students per grade per year, more than 700,000 sets of test answers, and nearly 100 million individual answers. The data, organized by classroom, included each student's question-by-question answer strings for reading and math tests. (The actual paper answer sheets were not included; they were habitually shredded soon after a test.) The data also included some information about each teacher and demographic information for every student, as well as his or her past and future test scores—which would prove a key element in detecting the teacher cheating.

Now it was time to construct an algorithm that could tease some conclusions from this mass of data. What might a cheating teacher's classroom look like?

The first thing to search for would be unusual answer patterns in a given classroom: blocks of identical answers, for instance, especially among the harder questions. If ten very bright students (as indicated by past and future test scores) gave correct answers to the exam's first five questions (typically the easiest ones), such an identical block shouldn't be considered suspicious. But if ten poor students gave correct answers to the *last* five questions on the exam (the hardest ones), that's worth looking into. Another red flag would be a strange pattern within any one student's exam— such as getting the hard questions right while missing the easy ones—especially when measured against the thousands of students in other classrooms who scored similarly on the same test. Furthermore, the algorithm would seek out a classroom full of students who performed far better than their past scores would have predicted and who then went on to score significantly lower the following year. A dramatic one-year spike in test scores might initially be attributed to a *good* teacher; but with a dramatic fall to follow, there's a strong likelihood that the spike was brought about by artificial means.

Consider now the answer strings from the students in two sixth-grade Chicago classrooms who took the identical math test. Each horizontal row represents one student's answers. The letter a, b, c, or d indicates a correct answer; a number indicates a wrong answer, with 1 corresponding to a, 2 corresponding to b, and so on. A zero represents an answer that was left blank. One of these classrooms almost certainly had a cheating teacher and the other did not. Try to tell the difference—although be forewarned that it's not easy with the naked eye.

CLASSROOM A

```
112a4a342cb214d0001acd24a3a12dadbcb4a0000000
d4a2341cacbddad3142a2344a2ac23421c00adb4b3cb
1b2a34d4ac42d23b141acd24a3a12dadbcb4a2134141
dbaab3dcacb1dadbc42ac2cc31012dadbcb4adb40000
d12443d43232d32323c213c22d2c23234c332db4b300
db2abad1acbdda212b1acd24a3a12dadbcb400000000
d4aab2124cbddadbcb1a42cca3412dadbcb423134bc1
1b33b4d4a2b1dadbc3ca22c00000000000000000000
d43a3a24acb1d32b412acd24a3a12dadbcb422143bc0
313a3ad1ac3d2a23431223c000012dadbcb400000000
db2a33dcacbd32d313c21142323cc300000000000000
d43ab4d1ac3dd43421240d24a3a12dadbcb400000000
db223a24acb11a3b24cacd12a241cdadbcb4adb4b300
db4abadcacb1dad3141ac212a3a1c3a144ba2db41b43
1142340c2cbddadb4b1acd24a3a12dadbcb43d133bc4
214ab4dc4cbdd31b1b2213c4ad412dadbcb4adb00000
1423b4d4a23d24131413234123a243a2413a21441343
3b3ab4d14c3d2ad4cbcac1c003a12dadbcb4adb40000
```

dba2ba21ac3d2ad3c4c4cd40a3a12dadbcb400000000
d122ba2cacbd1a13211a2d02a2412d0dbcb4adb4b3c0
144a3adc4cbddadbcbc2c2cc43a12dadbcb4211ab343
d43aba3cacbddadbcbca42c2a3212dadbcb42344b3cb

CLASSROOM B

db3a431422bd131b4413cd422a1acda332342d3ab4c4
d1aa1a11acb2d3dbc1ca22c23242c3a142b3adb243c1
d42a12d2a4b1d32b21ca2312a3411d00000000000000
3b2a34344c32d21b1123cdc000000000000000000000
34aabad12cbdd3d4c1ca112cad2ccd00000000000000
d33a3431a2b2d2d44b2acd2cad2c2223b40000000000
23aa32d2a1bd2431141342c13d212d233c34a3b3b000
d32234d4a1bdd23b242a22c2a1a1cda2b1baa33a0000
d3aab23c4cbddadb23c322c2a222223232b443b24bc3
d13a14313c31d42b14c421c42332cd2242b3433a3343
d13a3ad122b1da2b11242dc1a3a12100000000000000
d12a3ad1a13d23d3cb2a21ccada24d2131b440000000
314a133c4cbd142141ca424cad34c122413223ba4b40
d42a3adcacbddadbc42ac2c2ada2cda341baa3b24321
db1134dc2cb2dadb24c412c1ada2c3a341ba20000000
d1341431acbddad3c4c213412da22d3d1132a1344b1b
1ba41a21a1b2dadb24ca22c1ada2cd32413200000000
dbaa33d2a2bddadbcbca11c2a2accda1b2ba20000000

If you guessed that classroom A was the cheating classroom, congratulations. Here again are the answer strings from classroom A, now reordered by a computer that has been asked to apply the cheating algorithm and seek out suspicious patterns.

CLASSROOM A	(WITH CHEATING ALGORITHM APPLIED)

1 112a4a342cb214d0001**acd24a3a12dadbcb4**a0000000
2 1b2a34d4ac42d23b141**acd24a3a12dadbcb4**a2134141
3 db2abad1acbdda212b1**acd24a3a12dadbcb4**00000000
4 d43a3a24acb1d32b412**acd24a3a12dadbcb4**22143bc0
5 1142340c2cbddadb4b1**acd24a3a12dadbcb4**3d133bc4
6 d43ab4d1ac3dd43421240d24**a3a12dadbcb4**00000000
7 dba2ba21ac3d2ad3c4c4cd40**a3a12dadbcb4**00000000
8 144a3adc4cbddadbcbc2c2cc4**3a12dadbcb4**211ab343
9 3b3ab4d14c3d2ad4cbcac1c003**a12dadbcb4**adb40000
10 d43aba3cacbddadbcbca42c2a32**12dadbcb4**2344b3cb
11 214ab4dc4cbdd31b1b2213c4ad4**12dadbcb4**adb00000
12 313a3ad1ac3d2a23431223c0000**12dadbcb4**00000000
13 d4aab2124cbddadbcb1a42cca34**12dadbcb4**23134bc1
14 dbaab3dcacb1dadbc42ac2cc3101**2dadbcb4**adb40000
15 db223a24acb11a3b24cacd12a241c**dadbcb4**adb4b300
16 d122ba2cacbd1a13211a2d02a2412d0dbcb4adb4b3c0
17 1423b4d4a23d24131413234123a243a2413a21441343
18 db4abadcacb1dad3141ac212a3a1c3a144ba2db41b43
19 db2a33dcacbd32d313c21142323cc300000000000000
20 1b33b4d4a2b1dadbc3ca22c00000000000000000000
21 d12443d43232d32323c213c22d2c23234c332db4b300
22 d4a2341cacbddad3142a2344a2ac23421c00adb4b3cb

Take a look at the answers in bold. Did fifteen out of twenty-two students somehow manage to reel off the same six consecutive correct answers (the d-a-d-b-c-b string) all by themselves? There are at least four reasons this is unlikely. One: those questions, coming near the end of the test, were harder than the earlier questions. Two: these were mainly subpar students to begin with, few of whom got six consecutive right answers elsewhere on the test, making it all the more unlikely they would get right the same six hard questions. Three: up to this point in the test, the fifteen students' answers were virtually uncorrelated. Four: three of the students (numbers 1, 9, and 12) left more than one answer blank *before* the suspicious string and then ended the test with another string of blanks. This suggests that a long, unbroken string of blank answers was broken not by the student but by the teacher.

There is another oddity about the suspicious answer string. On nine of the fifteen tests, the six correct answers are preceded by another identical string, 3-a-1-2, which includes three of four *incorrect* answers. And on all fifteen tests, the six correct answers are followed by the same incorrect answer, a 4. Why on earth would a cheating teacher go to the trouble of erasing a student's test sheet and then fill in the *wrong* answer?

Perhaps she is merely being strategic. In case she is caught and hauled into the principal's office, she could point to the wrong answers as proof that she didn't cheat. Or perhaps—and this is a less charitable but just as likely answer—she doesn't know the right answers herself. (With standardized tests, the teacher is typically not given an answer key.) If this is the case, then we have a pretty good clue as to why her students are in need of inflated grades in the first place: they have a bad teacher.

Another indication of teacher cheating in classroom A is the class's overall performance. As sixth graders who were taking the test in the eighth month of the academic year, these students needed to achieve an average score of 6.8 to be considered up to national standards. (Fifth graders taking the test in the eighth month of the year needed to score 5.8, seventh graders 7.8, and so on.) The students in classroom A averaged 5.8 on their sixth-grade tests, which is a full grade level below where they should be. So plainly these are poor students. A year earlier, however, these students did even worse, averaging just 4.1 on their fifth-grade tests. Instead of improving by one full point between fifth and sixth grade, as would be expected, they improved by 1.7 points, nearly two grades' worth. But this miraculous improvement was short-lived. When these sixth-grade students reached seventh grade, they averaged 5.5—more than two grade levels below standard and even *worse* than they did in sixth grade. Consider the erratic year-to-year scores of three particular students from classroom A:

	5TH GRADE SCORE	6TH GRADE SCORE	7TH GRADE SCORE
STUDENT 3	3.0	6.5	5.1
STUDENT 5	3.6	6.3	4.9
STUDENT 14	3.8	7.1	5.6

The three-year scores from classroom B, meanwhile, are also poor but at least indicate an honest effort: 4.2, 5.1, and 6.0. So an entire roomful of children in classroom A suddenly got very smart one year and very dim the next, or more likely, their sixth-grade teacher worked some magic with her pencil.

There are two noteworthy points to be made about the children in classroom A, tangential to the cheating itself. The first is that they are obviously in poor academic shape, which makes them the very children whom high-stakes testing is promoted as helping the most. The second point is that these students (and their parents) would be in for a terrible shock once they reached the seventh grade. All they knew was that they had been successfully promoted due to their test scores. (No child left behind, indeed.) *They* weren't the ones who artificially jacked up their scores; they probably expected to do great in the seventh grade—and then they failed miserably. This may be the cruelest twist yet in high-stakes testing. A cheating teacher may tell herself that she is helping her students, but the fact is that she would appear far more concerned with helping herself.

An analysis of the entire Chicago data reveals evidence of teacher cheating in more than two hundred classrooms per year, roughly 5 percent of the total. This is a conservative estimate, since the algorithm was able to identify only the most egregious form of cheating—in which teachers systematically changed students' answers—and not the many subtler ways a teacher might cheat. In a recent study among North Carolina schoolteachers, some 35 percent of the respondents said they had witnessed their colleagues cheating in some fashion, whether by giving students extra time, suggesting answers, or manually changing students' answers.

What are the characteristics of a cheating teacher? The Chicago data shows that male and female teachers are equally prone to cheating. A cheating teacher tends to be younger and less qualified than average. She is also more likely to cheat after her incentives change. Because the Chicago data ran from 1993 to 2000, it bracketed the introduction of high-stakes testing in 1996. Sure enough, there was a pronounced spike in cheating in 1996. Nor was the cheating random. It was the teachers in the lowest-scoring classrooms who were most likely to cheat. It should also be noted that the $25,000 bonus for California teachers was eventually revoked, in part because of suspicions that too much of the money was going to cheaters.

Not every result of the Chicago cheating analysis was so dour. In addition to detecting cheaters, the algorithm could also identify the best teachers in the school system. A good teacher's impact was nearly as distinctive as a cheater's. Instead of getting random answers correct, her students would show real improvement on the easier types of questions they had previously missed, an indication of actual learning. And a good teacher's students carried over all their gains into the next grade.

Most academic analyses of this sort tend to languish, unread, on a dusty library shelf. But in early 2002, the new CEO of the Chicago Public Schools, Arne Duncan, contacted the study's authors. He didn't want to protest or hush up their findings. Rather, he wanted to make sure that the teachers identified by the algorithm as cheaters were truly cheating—and then do something about it.

Duncan was an unlikely candidate to hold such a powerful job. He was only thirty-six when appointed, a onetime academic all-American at Harvard who later played pro basketball in Australia. He had spent just three years with the CPS—and never in a job important enough to have his own secretary—before becoming its CEO. It didn't hurt that Duncan had grown up in Chicago. His father taught psychology at the University of Chicago; his mother ran an afterschool program for forty years, without pay, in a poor neighborhood. When Duncan was a boy, his afterschool playmates were the underprivileged kids his mother cared for. So when he took over the public schools, his allegiance lay more with schoolchildren and their families than with teachers and their union.

The best way to get rid of cheating teachers, Duncan had decided, was to readminister the standardized exam. He only had the resources to retest 120 classrooms, however, so he asked the creators of the cheating algorithm to help choose which classrooms to test.

How could those 120 retests be used most effectively? It might have seemed sensible to retest only the classrooms that likely had a cheating teacher. But even if their retest scores were lower, the teachers could argue that the students did worse merely because they were told that the scores wouldn't count in their official record—which, in fact, all retested students would be told. To make the retest results convincing, some non-cheaters were needed as a control group. The best control group? The classrooms shown by the algorithm to have the best teachers, in which big gains were thought to have been legitimately attained. If those classrooms held their gains while the classrooms with a suspected cheater lost ground, the cheating teachers could hardly argue that their students did worse only because the scores wouldn't count.

So a blend was settled upon. More than half of the 120 retested classrooms were those suspected of having a cheating teacher. The remainder were divided between the supposedly excellent teachers (high scores but no suspicious answer patterns) and, as a further control, classrooms with mediocre scores and no suspicious answers.

The retest was given a few weeks after the original exam. The children were not told the reason for the retest. Neither were the teachers. But they may have gotten the idea when it was announced that CPS officials, not the teachers, would administer the test. The teachers were asked to stay in the classroom with their students, but they would not be allowed to even touch the answer sheets.

The results were as compelling as the cheating algorithm had predicted. In the classrooms chosen as controls, where no cheating was suspected, scores stayed about the same or even rose. In contrast, the students with the teachers identified as cheaters scored far worse, by an average of more than a full grade level.

As a result, the Chicago Public School system began to fire its cheating teachers. The evidence was only strong enough to get rid of a dozen of them, but the many other cheaters had been duly warned. The final outcome of the Chicago study is further testament to the power of incentives: the following year, cheating by teachers fell more than 30 percent.

You might think that the sophistication of teachers who cheat would increase along with the level of schooling. But an exam given at the University of Georgia in the fall of 2001 disputes that idea. The course was called Coaching Principles and Strategies of Basketball, and the final grade was based on a single exam that had twenty questions. Among the questions:

How many halves are in a college basketball game?

a. 1   b. 2   c. 3   d. 4

How many points does a 3-pt. field goal account for in a basketball game?

a. 1   b. 2   c. 3   d. 4

What is the name of the exam which all high school seniors in the state of Georgia must pass?

a. Eye Exam
b. How Do the Grits Taste Exam
c. Bug Control Exam
d. Georgia Exit Exam

In your opinion, who is the best Division I assistant coach in the country?

a. Ron Jirsa
b. John Pelphrey
c. Jim Harrick Jr.
d. Steve Wojciechowski

If you are stumped by the final question, it might help to know that Coaching Principles was taught by Jim Harrick Jr., an assistant coach with the university's basketball team. It might also help to know that his father, Jim Harrick Sr., was the head basketball coach. Not surprisingly, Coaching Principles was a favorite course among players on the Harricks' team. Every student in the class received an A. Not long afterward, both Harricks were relieved of their coaching duties.

If it strikes you as disgraceful that Chicago schoolteachers and University of Georgia professors will cheat—a teacher, after all, is meant to instill values along with the facts—then the thought of cheating among sumo wrestlers may also be deeply disturbing. In Japan, sumo is not only the national sport but also a repository of the country's religious, military, and historical emotion. With its purification rituals and its imperial roots, sumo is sacrosanct in a way that American sports will never be. Indeed, sumo is said to be less about competition than about honor itself.

It is true that sports and cheating go hand in hand. That's because cheating is more common in the face of a bright-line incentive (the line between winning and losing, for instance) than with a murky incentive. Olympic sprinters and weightlifters, cyclists in the Tour de France, football linemen and baseball sluggers: they have all been shown to swallow whatever pill or powder may give them an edge. It is not only the participants who cheat. Cagey baseball managers try to steal an opponent's signs. In the 2002 Winter Olympic figure-skating competition, a French judge and a Russian judge were caught trying to swap votes to make sure their skaters medaled. (The man accused of orchestrating the vote swap, a reputed Russian mob boss named Alimzhan Tokhtakhounov, was also suspected of rigging beauty pageants in Moscow.)

An athlete who gets caught cheating is generally condemned, but most fans at least appreciate his motive: he wanted so badly to win that he bent the rules. (As the baseball player Mark Grace once said, "If you're not cheating, you're not trying.") An athlete who cheats to *lose*, meanwhile, is consigned to a deep circle of sporting hell. The 1919 Chicago White Sox, who conspired with gamblers to throw the World Series (and are therefore known forever as the Black Sox), retain a stench of iniquity among even casual baseball fans. The City College of New York's championship basketball team, once beloved for its smart and scrappy play, was instantly reviled when it was discovered in 1951 that several players had taken mob money to shave points—intentionally missing baskets to help gamblers beat the point spread. Remember Terry

Malloy, the tormented former boxer played by Marlon Brando in *On the Waterfront*? As Malloy saw it, all his troubles stemmed from the one fight in which he took a dive. Otherwise, he could have had class; he could have been a contender.

If cheating to lose is sport's premier sin, and if sumo wrestling is the premier sport of a great nation, cheating to lose couldn't possibly exist in sumo. Could it?

Once again, the data can tell the story. As with the Chicago school tests, the data set under consideration here is surpassingly large: the results from nearly every official match among the top rank of Japanese sumo wrestlers between January 1989 and January 2000, a total of 32,000 bouts fought by 281 different wrestlers.

The incentive scheme that rules sumo is intricate and extraordinarily powerful. Each wrestler maintains a ranking that affects every slice of his life: how much money he makes, how large an entourage he carries, how much he gets to eat, sleep, and otherwise take advantage of his success. The sixty-six highest-ranked wrestlers in Japan, comprising the *makuuchi* and *juryo* divisions, make up the sumo elite. A wrestler near the top of this elite pyramid may earn millions and is treated like royalty. Any wrestler in the top forty earns at least $170,000 a year. The seventieth-ranked wrestler in Japan, meanwhile, earns only $15,000 a year. Life isn't very sweet outside the elite. Low-ranked wrestlers must tend to their superiors, preparing their meals, cleaning their quarters, and even soaping up their hardest-to-reach body parts. So ranking is everything.

A wrestler's ranking is based on his performance in the elite tournaments that are held six times a year. Each wrestler has fifteen bouts per tournament, one per day over fifteen consecutive days. If he finishes the tournament with a winning record (eight victories or better), his ranking will rise. If he has a losing record, his ranking falls. If it falls far enough, he is booted from the elite rank entirely. The eighth victory in any tournament is therefore critical, the difference between promotion and demotion; it is roughly four times as valuable in the rankings as the typical victory.

So a wrestler entering the final day of a tournament on the bubble, with a 7–7 record, has far more to gain from a victory than an opponent with a record of 8–6 has to lose.

Is it possible, then, that an 8–6 wrestler might allow a 7–7 wrestler to beat him? A sumo bout is a concentrated flurry of force and speed and leverage, often lasting only a few seconds. It wouldn't be very hard to let yourself be tossed. Let's imagine for a moment that sumo wrestling *is* rigged. How might we measure the data to prove it?

The first step would be to isolate the bouts in question: those fought on a tournament's final day between a wrestler on the bubble and a wrestler who has already secured his eighth win. (Because more than half of all wrestlers end a tournament with either seven, eight, or nine victories, hundreds of bouts fit these criteria.) A final-day match between two 7–7 wrestlers isn't likely to be fixed, since both fighters badly need the victory. A wrestler with ten or more victories probably wouldn't throw a match either, since he has his own strong incentive to win: the $100,000 prize for overall tournament champion and a series of $20,000 prizes for the "outstanding technique" award, "fighting spirit" award, and others.

Let's now consider the following statistic, which represents the hundreds of matches in which a 7–7 wrestler faced an 8–6 wrestler on a tournament's final day. The left column tallies the probability, based on all past meetings between the two wrestlers fighting that day, that the 7–7 wrestler will win. The right column shows how often the 7–7 wrestler actually did win.

7–7 WRESTLER'S PREDICTED WIN PERCENTAGE AGAINST 8–6 OPPONENT	7–7 WRESTLER'S ACTUAL WIN PERCENTAGE AGAINST 8–6 OPPONENT
48.7	79.6

So the 7–7 wrestler, based on past outcomes, was expected to win just less than half the time. This makes sense; their records in this tournament indicate that the 8–6 wrestler is slightly better. But in actuality, the wrestler on the bubble won *almost eight out of ten* matches against his 8–6 opponent. Wrestlers on the bubble also do astonishingly well against 9–5 opponents:

7–7 WRESTLER'S PREDICTED WIN PERCENTAGE AGAINST 9–5 OPPONENT	7–7 WRESTLER'S ACTUAL WIN PERCENTAGE AGAINST 9–5 OPPONENT
47.2	73.4

As suspicious as this looks, a high winning percentage alone isn't enough to prove that a match is rigged. Since so much depends on a wrestler's eighth win, he should be expected to fight harder in a crucial bout. But perhaps there are further clues in the data that prove collusion.

It's worth thinking about the incentive a wrestler might have to throw a match. Maybe he accepts a bribe (which would obviously not be recorded in the data). Or perhaps some other arrangement is made between the two wrestlers. Keep in mind that the pool of elite sumo wrestlers is extraordinarily tight-knit. Each of the sixty-six elite wrestlers fights fifteen of the others in a tournament every two months. Furthermore, each wrestler belongs to a stable that is typically managed by a former sumo champion, so even the rival stables have close ties. (Wrestlers from the same stable do not wrestle one another.)

Now let's look at the win-loss percentage between the 7–7 wrestlers and the 8–6 wrestlers the *next* time they meet, when neither one is on the bubble. In this case, there is no great pressure on the individual match. So you might expect the wrestlers who won their 7–7 matches in the previous tournament to do about as well as they had in earlier matches against these same opponents— that is, winning roughly 50 percent of the time. You certainly wouldn't expect them to uphold their 80 percent clip.

As it turns out, the data show that the 7–7 wrestlers win only 40 percent of the rematches. Eighty percent in one match and 40 percent in the next? How do you make sense of that?

The most logical explanation is that the wrestlers made a quid pro quo agreement: you let me win today, when I really need the victory, and I'll let you win the next time. (Such an arrangement wouldn't preclude a cash bribe.) It's especially interesting to note that by the two wrestlers' *second* subsequent meeting, the win percentages revert to the expected level of about 50 percent, suggesting that the collusion spans only two matches.

And it isn't only the individual wrestlers whose records are suspect. The collective records of the various sumo stables are similarly aberrational. When one stable's wrestlers fare well on the bubble against wrestlers from a second stable, they tend to do especially *poorly* when the second stable's wrestlers are on the bubble. This indicates that some match rigging may be choreographed at the highest level of the sport—much like the Olympic skating judges' vote swapping.

No formal disciplinary action has ever been taken against a Japanese sumo wrestler for match rigging. Officials from the Japanese Sumo Association typically dismiss any such charges as fabrications by disgruntled former wrestlers. In fact, the mere utterance of the words "sumo" and "rigged" in the same sentence can cause a national furor. People tend to get defensive when the integrity of their national sport is impugned.

Still, allegations of match rigging do occasionally find their way into the Japanese media. These occasional media storms offer one more chance to measure possible corruption in sumo. Media scrutiny, after all, creates a powerful incentive: if two sumo wrestlers or their stables *have* been rigging matches, they might be leery to continue when a swarm of journalists and TV cameras descend upon them.

So what happens in such cases? The data show that in the sumo tournaments held immediately after allegations of match rigging, 7–7 wrestlers win only 50 percent of their final-day matches against 8–6 opponents instead of the typical 80 percent. No matter how the data are sliced, they inevitably suggest one thing: it is hard to argue that sumo wrestling isn't rigged.

Several years ago, two former sumo wrestlers came forward with extensive allegations of match rigging—and more. Aside from the crooked matches, they said, sumo was rife with drug use and sexcapades, bribes and tax evasion, and close ties to the *yakuza*, the Japanese mafia. The two men began to receive threatening phone calls; one of them told friends he was afraid he would be killed by the *yakuza*. Still, they went forward with plans to hold a press conference at the Foreign Correspondents' Club in Tokyo. But shortly beforehand, the two men died—hours apart, in the same hospital, of a similar respiratory ailment. The police declared there had been no foul play but did not conduct an investigation. "It seems very strange for these two people to die on the same day at the same hospital," said Mitsuru Miyake, the editor of a sumo magazine. "But no one has seen them poisoned, so you can't prove the skepticism."

Whether or not their deaths were intentional, these two men had done what no other sumo insider had previously done: named names. Of the 281 wrestlers covered in the data cited above, they identified 29 crooked wrestlers and 11 who were said to be incorruptible.

What happens when the whistle-blowers' corroborating evidence is factored into the analysis of the match data? In matches between two supposedly corrupt wrestlers, the wrestler who was on the bubble won about 80 percent of the time. In bubble matches against a supposedly clean opponent, meanwhile, the bubble wrestler was no more likely to win than his record would predict. Furthermore, when a supposedly corrupt wrestler faced an opponent whom the whistle-blowers did not name as either corrupt or clean, the results were nearly as skewed as when two corrupt wrestlers met—suggesting that most wrestlers who *weren't* specifically named were also corrupt.

So if sumo wrestlers, schoolteachers, and day-care parents all cheat, are we to assume that mankind is innately and universally corrupt? And if so, how corrupt?

The answer may lie in . . . bagels. Consider this story about a man named Paul Feldman.

Once upon a time, Feldman dreamed big dreams. With early training in agricultural economics, he wanted to tackle world hunger. Instead, he took a job in Washington, analyzing weapons expenditures for the U.S. Navy. This was in 1962. For the next twenty-odd years, he did further analytic work in Washington. He held senior-level jobs and earned good money, but he wasn't always recognized for his best work. At the office Christmas party, colleagues would introduce him to their wives not as "the head of the public research group" (which he was) but as "the guy who brings in the bagels."

The bagels had begun as a casual gesture: a boss treating his employees whenever they won a research contract. Then he made it a habit. Every Friday, he would bring in some bagels, a serrated knife, and cream cheese. When employees from neighboring floors heard about the bagels, they wanted some too. Eventually he was bringing in fifteen dozen bagels a week. In order to recoup his costs, he set out a cash basket and a sign with the suggested price. His collection rate was about 95 percent; he attributed the underpayment to oversight, not fraud.

In 1984, when his research institute fell under new management, Feldman took a look at his future and grimaced. He decided to quit his job and sell bagels. His economist friends thought he had lost his mind, but his wife supported him. The last of their three children was finishing college, and they had retired their mortgage.

Driving around the office parks that encircle Washington, he solicited customers with a simple pitch: early in the morning, he would deliver some bagels and a cash basket to a company's snack room; he would return before lunch to pick up the money and the leftovers. It was an honor-system commerce scheme, and it worked. Within a few years, Feldman was delivering 8,400 bagels a week to 140 companies and earning as much as he had ever made as a research analyst. He had thrown off the shackles of cubicle life and made himself happy.

He had also—quite without meaning to—designed a beautiful economic experiment. From the beginning, Feldman kept rigorous data on his bagel business. So by measuring the money collected against the bagels taken, he found it possible to tell, down to the penny, just how honest his customers were. Did they steal from him? If so, what were the characteristics of a company that stole versus a company that did not? Under what circumstances did people tend to steal more, or less?

As it happens, Feldman's accidental study provides a window onto a form of cheating that has long stymied academics: white-collar crime. (Yes, shorting the bagel man is white-collar crime, writ however small.) It might seem ludicrous to address as large and intractable a problem as white-collar crime through the life of a bagel man. But often a small and simple question can help chisel away at the biggest problems.

Despite all the attention paid to rogue companies like Enron, academics know very little about the practicalities of white-collar crime. The reason? There are no good data. A key fact of white-collar crime is that we hear about only the very slim fraction of people who are *caught* cheating. Most embezzlers lead quiet and theoretically happy lives; employees who steal company property are rarely detected.

With street crime, meanwhile, that is not the case. A mugging or a burglary or a murder is usually tallied whether or not the criminal is caught. A street crime has a victim, who typically reports the crime to the police, who generate data, which in turn generate thousands of academic papers by criminologists, sociologists, and economists. But white-collar crime presents no obvious victim. From whom, exactly, did the masters of Enron steal? And how can you measure something if you don't know to whom it happened, or with what frequency, or in what magnitude?

Paul Feldman's bagel business was different. It did present a victim. The victim was Paul Feldman.

When he started his business, he expected a 95 percent payment rate, based on the experience at his own office. But just as crime tends to be low on a street where a police car is parked, the 95 percent rate was artificially high: Feldman's presence had deterred theft. Not only that, but those bagel eaters knew the provider and had feelings (presumably good ones) about him. A broad swath of psychological and economic research has shown that people will pay different amounts for the same item depending on who is providing it. The economist Richard Thaler, in his 1985 "Beer on the Beach" study, showed that a thirsty sunbather would pay $2.65 for a beer delivered from a resort hotel but only $1.50 for the same beer if it came from a shabby grocery store.

In the real world, Feldman learned to settle for less than 95 percent. He came to consider a company "honest" if its payment rate was above 90 percent. He considered a rate between 80 and 90 percent "annoying but tolerable." If a company habitually paid below 80 percent, Feldman might post a hectoring note, like this one:

The cost of bagels has gone up dramatically since the beginning of the year. Unfortunately, the number of bagels that disappear without being paid for has also gone up. Don't let that continue. I don't imagine that you would teach your children to cheat, so why do it yourselves?

In the beginning, Feldman left behind an open basket for the cash, but too often the money vanished. Then he tried a coffee can with a money slot in its plastic lid, which also proved too tempting. In the end, he resorted to making small plywood boxes with a slot cut into the top. The wooden box has worked well. Each year he drops off about seven thousand boxes and loses, on average, just one to theft. This is an intriguing statistic: the same people who routinely steal more than 10 percent of his bagels almost never stoop to stealing his money box—a tribute to the nuanced social calculus of theft. From Feldman's perspective, an office worker who eats a bagel without paying is committing a crime; the office worker probably doesn't think so. This distinction probably has less to do with the admittedly small amount of money involved (Feldman's bagels cost one dollar each, cream cheese included) than with the context of the "crime." The same office worker who fails to pay for his bagel might also help himself to a long slurp of soda while filling a glass in a self-serve restaurant, but he is very unlikely to leave the restaurant without paying.

So what do the bagel data have to say? In recent years, there have been two noteworthy trends in the overall payment rate. The first was a long, slow decline that began in 1992. By the summer of 2001, the overall rate had slipped to about 87 percent. But immediately after September 11 of that year, the rate spiked a full 2 percent and hasn't slipped much since. (If a 2 percent gain in payment doesn't sound like much, think of it this way: the nonpayment rate fell from 13 to 11 percent, which amounts to a 15 percent decline in theft.) Because many of Feldman's customers are affiliated with national security, there may have been a patriotic element to this 9/11 Effect. Or it may have represented a more general surge in empathy.

The data also show that smaller offices are more honest than big ones. An office with a few dozen employees generally outpays by 3 to 5 percent an office with a few hundred employees. This may seem counterintuitive. In a bigger office, a bigger crowd is bound to convene around the bagel table, providing more witnesses to make sure you drop your money in the box. But in the big-office/small-office comparison, bagel crime seems to mirror street crime. There is far less street crime per capita in rural areas than in cities, in large part because a rural criminal is more likely to be known (and therefore caught). Also, a smaller community tends to exert greater social incentives against crime, the main one being shame.

The bagel data also reflect how much personal mood seems to affect honesty. Weather, for instance, is a major factor. Unseasonably pleasant weather inspires people to pay at a higher rate. Unseasonably cold weather, meanwhile, makes people cheat prolifically; so do heavy rain and wind. Worst are the holidays. The week of Christmas produces a 2 percent drop in payment rates—again, a 15 percent increase in theft, an effect on the same magnitude, in reverse, as that of 9/11. Thanksgiving is nearly as bad; the week of Valentine's Day is also lousy, as is the week straddling April 15. There are, however, several good holidays: the weeks that include the Fourth of July, Labor Day, and Columbus Day. The difference in the two sets of holidays? The low-cheating holidays represent little more than an extra day off from work. The high-cheating holidays are fraught with miscellaneous anxieties and the high expectations of loved ones.

Feldman has also reached some of his own conclusions about honesty, based more on his experience than the data. He has come to believe that morale is a big factor—that an office is more honest when the employees like their boss and their work. He also believes that employees further up the corporate ladder cheat more than those down below. He got this idea after delivering for years to one company spread out over three floors—an executive floor on top and two lower floors with sales, service, and administrative employees. (Feldman wondered if perhaps the executives cheated out of an overdeveloped sense of entitlement. What he didn't consider is that perhaps cheating was how they got to *be* executives.)

If morality represents the way we would like the world to work and economics represents how it actually does work, then the story of Feldman's bagel business lies at the very intersection of morality and economics. Yes, a lot of people steal from him, but the vast majority, even though no one is watching over them, do not. This outcome may surprise some people—including Feldman's economist friends, who counseled him twenty years ago that his honor-system scheme would never work. But it would not have surprised Adam Smith. In fact, the theme of Smith's first book, *The Theory of Moral Sentiments*, was the innate honesty of mankind. "How selfish soever man may be supposed," Smith wrote, "there are evidently some principles in his nature, which interest him in the fortune of others, and render their happiness necessary to him, though he derives nothing from it, except the pleasure of seeing it."

There is a tale, "The Ring of Gyges," that Feldman sometimes tells his economist friends. It comes from Plato's *Republic*. A student named Glaucon offered the story in response to a lesson by Socrates—who, like Adam Smith, argued that people are generally good even without enforcement. Glaucon, like Feldman's economist friends, disagreed. He told of a shepherd named Gyges who stumbled upon a secret cavern with a corpse inside that wore a ring. When Gyges put on the ring, he found that it made him invisible. With no one able to monitor his behavior, Gyges proceeded to do woeful things—seduce the queen, murder the king, and so on. Glaucon's story posed a moral question: could any man resist the temptation of evil if he knew his acts could not be witnessed? Glaucon seemed to think the answer was no. But Paul Feldman sides with Socrates and Adam Smith—for he knows that the answer, at least 87 percent of the time, is yes.

Chapter 2

HOW IS THE KU KLUX KLAN LIKE A GROUP OF REAL-ESTATE AGENTS?

As institutions go, the Ku Klux Klan has had a markedly up-and-down history. It was founded in the immediate aftermath of the Civil War by six former Confederate soldiers in Pulaski, Tennessee. The six young men, four of whom were budding lawyers, saw themselves as merely a circle of like-minded friends. Thus the name they chose, "kuklux," a slight mangling of *kuklos*, the Greek word for "circle." In the beginning, their activities were said to be harmless midnight pranks—for instance, riding horses through the countryside while draped in white sheets and pillowcase hoods. But soon the Klan evolved into a multistate terrorist organization designed to frighten and kill emancipated slaves. Among its regional leaders were five former Confederate generals; its staunchest supporters were the plantation owners for whom Reconstruction posed an economic and political nightmare. In 1872, President Ulysses S. Grant spelled out for the House of

Representatives the true aims of the Ku Klux Klan: "By force and terror, to prevent all political action not in accord with the views of the members, to deprive colored citizens of the right to bear arms and of the right of a free ballot, to suppress the schools in which colored children were taught, and to reduce the colored people to a condition closely allied to that of slavery."

The early Klan did its work through pamphleteering, lynching, shooting, burning, castrating, pistol-whipping, and a thousand forms of intimidation. They targeted former slaves and any whites who supported the blacks' rights to vote, acquire land, or gain an education. But within barely a decade, the Klan had been extinguished, largely by legal and military interventions out of Washington, D.C.

If the Klan itself was defeated, however, its aims had largely been achieved through the establishment of Jim Crow laws. Congress, which during Reconstruction had been quick to enact measures of legal, social, and economic freedom for blacks, just as quickly began to roll them back. The federal government agreed to withdraw its occupation troops from the South, allowing the restoration of white rule. In *Plessy v. Ferguson*, the U.S. Supreme Court gave the go-ahead to full-scale racial segregation.

The Ku Klux Klan lay largely dormant until 1915, when D. W. Griffith's film *The Birth of a Nation* (originally titled *The Clansman*) helped spark its rebirth. Griffith presented the Klan as crusaders for white civilization itself, and as one of the noblest forces in American history. The film quoted a line from *A History of the American People*, written by a renowned historian: "At last there had sprung into existence a great Ku Klux Klan, a veritable empire of the South, to protect the Southern country." The historian in question was U.S. president Woodrow Wilson, one-time scholar and president of Princeton University.

By the 1920s, a revived Klan claimed eight million members. This time around, the Klan was not confined to the South but ranged throughout the country; this time, it concerned itself not only with blacks but also with Catholics, Jews, communists, unionists, immigrants, agitators, and other disrupters of the status quo. In 1933, with Hitler ascendant in Germany, Will Rogers was the first to draw a line between the new Klan and the new threat in Europe: "Papers all state Hitler is trying to copy Mussolini," he wrote. "Looks to me like it's the Ku Klux that he is copying."

The onset of World War II and a number of internal scandals once again laid the Klan low. Public sentiment turned against the Klan as the unity of a country at war trumped its message of separatism.

But within a few years, there were already signs of a massive revival. As wartime anxiety gave way to postwar uncertainty, Klan membership flourished. Barely two months after V-J Day, the Klan in Atlanta burned a 300-foot cross on the face of Stone Mountain, site of a storied rock carving of Robert E. Lee. The extravagant cross burning, one Klansman later said, was intended "just to let the niggers know the war is over and that the Klan is back on the market."

Atlanta had by now become Klan headquarters. The Klan was thought to hold great sway with key Georgia politicians, and its Georgia chapters were said to include many policemen and sheriff's deputies. Yes, the Klan was a secret society, reveling in passwords and cloak-and-dagger ploys, but its real power lay in

the very public fear that it fostered, exemplified by the open secret that the Ku Klux Klan and the law-enforcement establishment were brothers in arms.

Atlanta—the Imperial City of the KKK's Invisible Empire,
in Klan jargon—was also home to Stetson Kennedy, a thirty-
year-old man with the bloodlines of a Klansman but a tempera-
ment that ran opposite. He came from a good southern family
which claimed ancestors including two signers of the Declaration
of Independence, an officer in the Confederate Army, and John
B. Stetson, founder of the famed hat company and the man for
whom Stetson University was named.

Stetson Kennedy grew up in a fourteen-room house in Jackson-
ville, Florida, the youngest of five children. His uncle Brady was a
Klansman. But Kennedy would go on to become a self-described
"dissident at large," writing numberless articles and several books
that railed against bigotry. He first worked as a folklorist, traveling around Florida to collect old native tales and songs. Years
later, when he served as a rare white correspondent for the *Pittsburgh Courier*, the country's largest black newspaper, he wrote under the pseudonym Daddy Mention—after a black folk hero who,
as myth told it, could outrun the blast of a sheriff's shotgun.

What drove Kennedy was a hatred of small-mindedness, ignorance, obstructionism, and intimidation—which, in his view,
were displayed by no organization more proudly than the Ku
Klux Klan. Kennedy saw the Klan as the terrorist arm of the
white establishment itself. This struck him as an intractable
problem, for a variety of reasons. The Klan was in cahoots with
political, business, and law-enforcement leaders. The public was
frightened and felt powerless to act against the Klan. And the
few anti-hate groups that existed at the time had little leverage or

even information about the Klan. "Almost all of the things written on the subject were editorials, not exposés," Kennedy would later explain. "The writers were *against* the Klan, all right, but they had precious few inside facts *about* it."

So Kennedy set out to gather those facts. He would spend years interviewing Klan leaders and sympathizers, sometimes taking advantage of his own background and lineage to pretend that he was on their side of the issues. He also attended public Klan events and, as he would later write, he even set about to infiltrate the Klan in Atlanta.

The Klan Unmasked, Kennedy's memoir of his exploits "inside" the Klan, is in fact more of a novelization than a straight nonfiction account. Kennedy, a folklorist at heart, apparently wanted to put across the most dramatic story possible, and therefore included not only his own anti-Klan activities but those of another man, code-named John Brown. Brown was a union worker and a former Klan official who had changed his ways and offered to infiltrate the Klan. It was John Brown who apparently performed many of the most dramatic and dangerous episodes portrayed in *The Klan Unmasked*—physically attending Klan meetings and other functions in Atlanta—but since Stetson Kennedy was the man who later wrote the book, he rendered Brown's actions as his own.

Regardless, there was a great deal of information to be gleaned from this Brown/Kennedy collaboration. Brown divulged what he was learning at the weekly Klan meetings: the identities of the Klan's local and regional leaders; their upcoming plans; the Klan's current rituals, passwords, and language. It was Klan custom, for instance, to append a *Kl* to many words. (Thus would two Klansmen hold a Klonversation in the local Klavern.) The secret Klan handshake was a left-handed, limp-wristed fish wiggle. When a traveling Klansman wanted to locate brethren in a strange town, he would ask for a "Mr. Ayak"—"Ayak" being code for "Are You a Klansman?" He would hope to hear this response: "Yes, and I also know a Mr. Akai"—code for "A Klansman Am I."

Before long, John Brown was invited to join the Klavaliers, the Klan's secret police and "flog squad." For an infiltrator, this posed a particularly sticky problem: What would happen if he were called upon to inflict violence?

But as it happened, a central tenet of life in the Klan—and of terrorism in general—is that most of the threatened violence never goes beyond the threat stage.

Consider lynching, the Klan's hallmark sign of violence. Here, compiled by the Tuskegee Institute, are the decade-by-decade statistics on the lynching of blacks in the United States:

YEARS	LYNCHINGS OF BLACKS
1890–1899	1,111
1900–1909	791
1910–1919	569
1920–1929	281
1930–1939	119
1940–1949	31
1950–1959	6
1960–1969	3

Bear in mind that these figures represent not only lynchings attributed to the Ku Klux Klan but the total number of reported lynchings. The statistics reveal at least three noteworthy facts. The first is the obvious decrease in lynchings over time. The second is the absence of a correlation between lynchings and Klan membership: there were actually *more* lynchings of blacks between 1900 and 1909, when the Klan was dormant, than during the 1920s, when the Klan had millions of members—which suggests that the Ku Klux Klan carried out far fewer lynchings than is generally thought.

Third, relative to the size of the black population, lynchings were exceedingly rare. To be sure, one lynching is one too many. But by the turn of the century, lynchings were hardly the everyday occurrence that they are often considered in the public recollection. Compare the 281 victims of lynchings in the 1920s to the number of black infants who were dying at that time as a result of malnutrition, pneumonia, diarrhea, and the like. As of 1920, about 13 out of every 100 black children died in infancy, or roughly 20,000 children each year—compared to 28 people who were lynched in a year. As late as 1940, about 10,000 black infants died each year.

What larger truths do these lynching figures suggest? What does it mean that lynchings were relatively rare and that they fell precipitously over time, even in the face of a boom in Klan membership?

The most compelling explanation is that all those early lynchings *worked*. White racists—whether or not they belonged to the Ku Klux Klan—had through their actions and their rhetoric developed a strong incentive scheme that was terribly clear and terribly frightening. If a black person violated the accepted code of behavior, whether by talking back to a bus driver or daring to try to vote, he knew he might well be punished, perhaps by death.

So it may be that by the mid-1940s, when Stetson Kennedy was trying to bust up the Klan, it didn't really *need* to use as much violence. Many blacks, having long been told to behave like second-class citizens—or else—simply obliged. One or two lynchings went a long way toward inducing docility among even a large group of people, for people respond strongly to strong incentives. And there are few incentives more powerful than the fear of random violence—which, in essence, is why terrorism is so effective.

But if the Ku Klux Klan of the 1940s wasn't uniformly violent, what was it? The Klan that Stetson Kennedy wrote about was in fact a sorry fraternity of men, most of them poorly educated and with poor prospects, who needed a place to vent—and an excuse for occasionally staying out all night. That their fraternity engaged in quasi-religious chanting and oath taking and hosanna hailing, all of it top secret, made it that much more appealing.

Kennedy also found the Klan to be a slick money-making operation, at least for those near the top of the organization. Klan leaders had any number of revenue sources: thousands of dues-paying rank-and-file members; business owners who hired the Klan to scare off the unions or who paid the Klan protection money; Klan rallies that generated huge cash donations; even the occasional gunrunning or moonshine operation. Then there were rackets like the Klan's Death Benefit Association, which sold insurance policies to Klan members and accepted only cash or personal checks made out to the Grand Dragon himself.

And, even though the Klan may not have been as deadly as generally thought, it was plenty violent and, perhaps worse, had ever greater designs on political influence. Kennedy was therefore eager to damage the Klan in any way he could. When he heard about Klan plans for a union-busting rally, he fed the information to a union friend. He passed along Klan information to the assistant attorney general of Georgia, an established Klan buster. After researching the Klan's corporate charter, Kennedy wrote to the governor of Georgia suggesting the grounds upon which the charter should be revoked: the Klan had been designated a non-profit, non-political organization, but Kennedy had proof that it was clearly devoted to both profits and politics.

The problem was that most of Kennedy's efforts weren't producing the desired effect. The Klan was so entrenched and broad-based that Kennedy felt as if he were tossing pebbles at a giant. And even if he could somehow damage the Klan in Atlanta, the hundreds of other chapters around the country would go untouched.

Kennedy was supremely frustrated, and out of this frustration was born a new strategy. He had noticed one day a group of young boys playing some kind of spy game in which they exchanged silly secret passwords. It reminded him of the Klan. Wouldn't it be nice, he thought, to get the Klan's passwords and the rest of its secrets into the hands of kids all across the country—and their parents too? What better way to defang a secret society than to make public its most secret information? Instead of futilely attacking the Klan from the outside, what if he could somehow unleash all the secret inside information that John Brown was gathering from the Klan's weekly meetings? Between Brown's inside dope and everything that Kennedy had learned via his own investigations, he probably knew more Klan secrets than the average Klansman.

Kennedy turned to the most powerful mass medium of his day: radio. He began feeding Klan reports to the journalist Drew

Pearson, whose *Washington Merry-Go-Round* program was heard by millions of adults every day, and to the producers of the *Adventures of Superman* show, which reached millions of children each night. He told them about Mr. Ayak and Mr. Akai, and he passed along overheated passages from the Klan's bible, which was called the Kloran. (Kennedy never did learn why a white Christian supremacist group would give its bible essentially the same name as the most holy book of Islam.) He explained the role of Klan officers in any local Klavern: the Klaliff (vice president), Klokard (lecturer), Kludd (chaplain), Kligrapp (secretary), Klabee (treasurer), Kladd (conductor), Klarogo (inner guard), Klexter (outer guard), the Klokann (a five-man investigative committee), and the Klavaliers (whose leader was called Chief Ass Tearer). He spelled out the Klan hierarchy as it proceeded from the local to the national level: an Exalted Cyclops and his twelve Terrors; a Great Titan and his twelve Furies; a Grand Dragon and his nine Hydras; and the Imperial Wizard and his fifteen Genii. And Kennedy passed along all the information and gossip that John Brown gleaned by infiltrating the main Klan chapter, Nathan Bedford Forrest Klavern No. 1, Atlanta, Realm of Georgia.

During the war, the *Adventures of Superman* program had portrayed its hero fighting Hitler and Mussolini and Hirohito. But now he was in need of fresh villains. The Klan was a perfect target, and Superman turned his powers against them. Drew Pearson, an avowed Klan hater, now began giving regular Klan updates on his radio show, and then gave further updates, based on John Brown's inside reports, to show how the original updates were infuriating Klan officials. Pearson's work created an echo chamber that seemed to be driving Grand Dragon Samuel Green crazy. Here is Pearson's radio report from November 17, 1948:

Speaking at Klavern No. 1, Atlanta, Ga., the week after elections, the Grand Dragon wrung his hands and once again cautioned Klansmen to be careful about leaks.

"I have to talk frankly at these meetings," he said, "but I might as well call Drew Pearson before I come to the meeting and give him the information, for {the} next day he gives it out to everybody from coast to coast. The A.P. and U.P. are both calling me about it next morning while I am eating breakfast." . . .

The Grand Dragon spoke about plans for a big cross-burning to be held in Macon, Ga., on Dec. 10. It would be the biggest in Klan history, he said, and he expected 10,000 Klansmen to be there—in their robes. . . .

He added that the Klavalier Klub—the Klan's whipping and flogging department—was now on the job and had plenty of friends on the Atlanta police force.

As the Pearson and *Superman* radio shows played on, and as Stetson Kennedy continued to relay the Klan secrets obtained by John Brown to other broadcast and print outlets, a funny thing happened: attendance at Klan meetings began to fall, as did applications for new membership. Of all the ideas that Kennedy had thought up to fight bigotry, this campaign was easily the cleverest. He turned the Klan's secrecy against itself by making its private information public; he converted heretofore precious knowledge into ammunition for mockery.

Americans who might have been philosophically inclined to oppose the Klan had now been given enough specific information to oppose them more actively, and public sentiment began to shift. Americans who might have been philosophically inclined to *embrace* the Klan had now been given all sorts of caution against doing so. Although the Klan would never quite die, especially down south—David Duke, a smooth-talking Klan leader from Louisiana, mounted substantive bids for the U.S. Senate and other offices—it was certainly handicapped, at least in the short term, by Kennedy's brazen dissemination of inside information. While it is impossible to tease out the exact impact that his work had on the Klan, many people have given him a great deal of credit for damaging an institution that was in grave need of being damaged.

This did not come about because Stetson Kennedy was courageous or resolute or unflappable, even though he was all of these. It happened because he understood the raw power of information. The Ku Klux Klan—much like politicians or real-estate agents or stockbrokers—was a group whose power was derived in large part from the fact that it hoarded information. Once that information falls into the wrong hands (or, depending on your point of view, the *right* hands), much of the group's advantage disappears.

In the late 1990s, the price of term life insurance fell dramatically. This posed something of a mystery, for the decline had no obvious cause. Other types of insurance, including health and automobile and homeowners' coverage, were certainly not falling in price. Nor had there been any radical changes among insurance companies, insurance brokers, or the people who buy term life insurance. So what happened?

The Internet happened. In the spring of 1996, Quotesmith.com became the first of several websites that enabled a customer to compare, within seconds, the price of term life insurance sold by dozens of different companies. For such websites, term life insurance was a perfect product. Unlike other forms of insurance—

especially whole life insurance, which is a far more complicated financial instrument—term life policies are fairly homogeneous: any given thirty-year, guaranteed policy for $1 million is essentially identical to the next. So what really matters is the price. Shopping around for the cheapest policy, a process that had been convoluted and time-consuming, was suddenly made simple. With customers able to instantaneously find the cheapest policy, the more expensive companies had no choice but to lower their prices. Suddenly customers were paying $1 billion less a year for term life insurance.

It is worth noting that these websites only listed prices; they didn't even sell the policies. So it wasn't really insurance they were peddling. Like Stetson Kennedy, they were dealing in information. (Had the Internet been around when Kennedy was attacking the Klan, he probably would have been blogging his brains out.) To be sure, there are differences between exposing the Ku Klux Klan and exposing insurance companies' high premiums. The Klan trafficked in secret information whose secrecy engendered fear, while insurance prices were less a secret than a set of facts dispensed in a way that made comparisons difficult. But in both instances, the dissemination of the information diluted its power. As Supreme Court Justice Louis D. Brandeis once wrote, "Sunlight is said to be the best of disinfectants."

Information is a beacon, a cudgel, an olive branch, a deterrent—all depending on who wields it and how. Information is so powerful that the *assumption* of information, even if the information does not actually exist, can have a sobering effect. Consider the case of a one-day-old car.

The day that a car is driven off the lot is the worst day in its life, for it instantly loses as much as a quarter of its value. This might seem absurd, but we know it to be true. A new car that was bought for $20,000 cannot be resold for more than perhaps $15,000. Why? Because the only person who might logically want to resell a brand-new car is someone who found the car to be a lemon. So even if the car isn't a lemon, a potential buyer assumes that it is. He assumes that the seller has some information about the car that he, the buyer, does not have—and the seller is punished for this assumed information.

And if the car *is* a lemon? The seller would do well to wait a year to sell it. By then, the suspicion of lemonness will have faded; by then, some people will be selling their perfectly good year-old cars, and the lemon can blend in with them, likely selling for more than it is truly worth.

It is common for one party to a transaction to have better information than another party. In the parlance of economists, such a case is known as an information asymmetry. We accept as a verity of capitalism that someone (usually an expert) knows more than someone else (usually a consumer). But information asymmetries everywhere have in fact been gravely wounded by the Internet.

Information is the currency of the Internet. As a medium, the Internet is brilliantly efficient at shifting information from the hands of those who have it into the hands of those who do not. Often, as in the case of term life insurance prices, the information existed but in a woefully scattered way. (In such instances, the Internet acts like a gigantic horseshoe magnet waved over an endless sea of haystacks, plucking the needle out of each one.) The Internet has accomplished what even the most fervent consumer advocates usually cannot: it has vastly shrunk the gap between the experts and the public.

The Internet has proven particularly fruitful for situations in which a face-to-face encounter with an expert might actually *exacerbate* the problem of asymmetrical information—situations in which an expert uses his informational advantage to make us feel stupid or rushed or cheap or ignoble. Consider a scenario in which your loved one has just died and now the funeral director (who knows that you know next to nothing about his business and are under emotional duress to boot) steers you to the $8,000 mahogany casket. Or consider the automobile dealership: a salesman does his best to obscure the car's base price under a mountain of add-ons and incentives. Later, however, in the cool-headed calm of your home, you can use the Internet to find out exactly how much the dealer paid the manufacturer for that car. Or you might just log on to www.TributeDirect.com and buy that mahogany casket yourself for only $3,595, delivered overnight. Unless you decide to spend $2,300 for "The Last Hole" (a casket with golf scenes) or "Memories of the Hunt" (featuring big-racked bucks and other prey) or one of the much cheaper models that the funeral director somehow failed even to mention.

The Internet, powerful as it is, has hardly slain the beast that is information asymmetry. Consider the corporate scandals of the early 2000s. The crimes committed by Enron included hidden partnerships, disguised debt, and the manipulation of energy markets. Henry Blodget of Merrill Lynch and Jack Grubman of Salomon Smith Barney wrote glowing research reports of companies they knew to be junk. Sam Waksal dumped his ImClone stock when he got early word of a damaging report from the Food and Drug Administration; his friend Martha Stewart also dumped her shares, then lied about the reason. WorldCom and Global Crossing fabricated billions of dollars in revenues to pump up their stock prices. One group of mutual fund companies let preferred customers trade at preferred prices, and another group was charged with hiding management fees.

Though extraordinarily diverse, these crimes all have a common trait: they were sins of information. Most of them involved an expert, or a gang of experts, promoting false information or hiding true information; in each case the experts were trying to keep the information asymmetry as asymmetrical as possible.

The practitioners of such acts, especially in the realm of high finance, inevitably offer this defense: "Everybody else was doing it." Which may be largely true. One characteristic of information crimes is that very few of them are detected. Unlike street crimes, they do not leave behind a corpse or a broken window. Unlike a bagel criminal—that is, someone who eats one of Paul Feldman's bagels but doesn't pay—an information criminal typically doesn't have someone like Feldman tallying every nickel. For an information crime to reach the surface, something drastic must happen. When it does, the results tend to be pretty revealing. The perpetrators, after all, weren't thinking about their private actions being made public. Consider the "Enron tapes," the secretly recorded conversations of Enron employees that surfaced after the company imploded. During a phone conversation on August 5, 2000, two traders chatted about how a wildfire in California would allow Enron to jack up its electricity prices. "The magical word of the day," one trader said, "is 'Burn, Baby, Burn.' " A few months later, a pair of Enron traders named Kevin and Bob talked about how California officials wanted to make Enron refund the profits of its price gouging.

KEVIN: *They're fucking taking all the money back from you guys? All the money you guys stole from those poor grandmas in California?*

BOB: *Yeah, Grandma Millie, man.*

KEVIN: *Yeah, now she wants her fucking money back for all the power you jammed right up her ass for fucking $250 a megawatt hour.*

If you were to assume that many experts use their information to your detriment, you'd be right. Experts depend on the fact that you don't have the information they do. Or that you are so befuddled by the complexity of their operation that you wouldn't know what to do with the information if you had it. Or that you are so in awe of their expertise that you wouldn't dare challenge them. If your doctor suggests that you have angioplasty—even though some current research suggests that angioplasty often does little to prevent heart attacks—you aren't likely to think that the doctor is using his informational advantage to make a few thousand dollars for himself or his buddy. But as David Hillis, an interventional cardiologist at the University of Texas Southwestern Medical Center in Dallas, explained to *The New York Times*, a doctor may have the same economic incentives as a car salesman or a funeral director or a mutual fund manager: "If you're an invasive cardiologist and Joe Smith, the local internist, is sending you patients, and if you tell them they don't need the procedure, pretty soon Joe Smith doesn't send patients anymore."

Armed with information, experts can exert a gigantic, if unspoken, leverage: fear. Fear that your children will find you dead on the bathroom floor of a heart attack if you do not have angioplasty surgery. Fear that a cheap casket will expose your grandmother to a terrible underground fate. Fear that a $25,000 car will crumple like a toy in an accident, whereas a $50,000 car will wrap your loved ones in a cocoon of impregnable steel. The fear created by commercial experts may not quite rival the fear created by terrorists like the Ku Klux Klan, but the principle is the same.

Consider a transaction that wouldn't seem, on the surface, to create much fear: selling your house. What's so scary about that? Aside from the fact that selling a house is typically the largest financial transaction in your life, and that you probably have scant experience in real estate, and that you may have an enormous emotional attachment to your house, there are at least two pressing fears: that you will sell the house for far less than it is worth and that you will not be able to sell it at all.

In the first case, you fear setting the price too low; in the second, you fear setting it too high. It is the job of your real-estate agent, of course, to find the golden mean. She is the one with all the information: the inventory of similar houses, the recent sales trends, the tremors of the mortgage market, perhaps even a lead on an interested buyer. You feel fortunate to have such a knowledgeable expert as an ally in this most confounding enterprise.

Too bad she sees things differently. A real-estate agent may see you not so much as an ally but as a mark. Think back to the study cited at the beginning of this book, which measured the difference between the sale prices of homes that belonged to real-estate agents themselves and the houses they sold for their clients. The study found that an agent keeps her own house on the market an average ten extra days, waiting for a better offer, and sells it for over 3 percent more than your house—or $10,000 on the sale of a $300,000 house. That's $10,000 going into her pocket that does not go into yours, a nifty profit produced by the abuse of information and a keen understanding of incentives. The problem is that the agent only stands to personally gain an additional $150 by selling your house for $10,000 more, which isn't much reward for a lot of extra work. So her job is to convince you that a $300,000 offer is in fact a very good offer, even a generous one, and that only a fool would refuse it.

This can be tricky. The agent does not want to come right out and call you a fool. So she merely implies it—perhaps by telling you about the much bigger, nicer, newer house down the block that has sat unsold for six months. Here is the agent's main weapon: the conversion of information into fear. Consider this true story, related by John Donohue, a law professor who in 2001 was teaching at Stanford University: "I was just about to buy a house on the Stanford campus," he recalls, "and the seller's agent kept telling me what a good deal I was getting because the market was about to zoom. As soon as I signed the purchase contract, he asked me if I would need an agent to sell my previous Stanford house. I told him that I would probably try to sell without an agent, and he replied, 'John, that might work under normal conditions, but with the market tanking now, you really need the help of a broker.' "

Within five minutes, a zooming market had tanked. Such are the marvels that can be conjured by an agent in search of the next deal.

Consider now another true story of a real-estate agent's information abuse. The tale involves K., a close friend of one of this book's authors. K. wanted to buy a house that was listed at $469,000. He was prepared to offer $450,000 but he first called the seller's agent and asked her to name the lowest price that she thought the homeowner might accept. The agent promptly scolded K. "You ought to be ashamed of yourself," she said. "That is clearly a violation of real-estate ethics."

K. apologized. The conversation turned to other, more mundane issues. After ten minutes, as the conversation was ending, the agent told K., "Let me say one last thing. My client is willing to sell this house for a lot less than you might think."

Based on this conversation, K. then offered $425,000 for the house instead of the $450,000 he had planned to offer. In the end, the seller accepted $430,000. Thanks to *his own agent's* intervention, the seller lost at least $20,000. The agent, meanwhile, only lost $300—a small price to pay to ensure that she would quickly and easily lock up the sale, which netted her a commission of $6,450.

So a big part of a real-estate agent's job, it would seem, is to persuade the homeowner to sell for less than he would like while at the same time letting potential buyers know that a house can be bought for less than its listing price. To be sure, there are more subtle means of doing so than coming right out and telling the buyer to bid low. The study of real-estate agents cited above also includes data that reveals how agents convey information through the for-sale ads they write. A phrase like "well maintained," for instance, is as full of meaning to an agent as "Mr. Ayak" was to a Klansman; it means that a house is old but not quite falling down. A savvy buyer will know this (or find out for himself once he sees the house), but to the sixty-five-year-old retiree who is selling his house, "well maintained" might sound like a compliment, which is just what the agent intends.

An analysis of the language used in real-estate ads shows that certain words are powerfully correlated with the final sale price of a house. This doesn't necessarily mean that labeling a house "well maintained" *causes* it to sell for less than an equivalent house. It does, however, indicate that when a real-estate agent labels a house "well maintained," she may be subtly encouraging a buyer to bid low.

Listed below are ten terms commonly used in real-estate ads. Five of them have a strong positive correlation to the ultimate sale price, and five have a strong negative correlation. Guess which are which.

TEN COMMON REAL-ESTATE AD TERMS

Fantastic

Granite

Spacious

State-of-the-Art

!

Corian

Charming

Maple

Great Neighborhood

Gourmet

A "fantastic" house is surely fantastic enough to warrant a high price, isn't it? What about a "charming" and "spacious" house in a "great neighborhood!"? No, no, no, and no. Here's the breakdown:

FIVE TERMS CORRELATED TO A HIGHER SALE PRICE

Granite

State-of-the-Art

Corian

Maple

Gourmet

FIVE TERMS CORRELATED TO A LOWER SALE PRICE

Fantastic

Spacious

!

Charming

Great Neighborhood

Three of the five terms correlated with a higher sale price are physical descriptions of the house itself: granite, Corian, and maple. As information goes, such terms are specific and straightforward—and therefore pretty useful. If you like granite, you might like the house; but even if you don't, "granite" certainly doesn't connote a fixer-upper. Nor does "gourmet" or "state-of-the-art," both of which seem to tell a buyer that a house is, on some level, truly fantastic.

"Fantastic," meanwhile, is a dangerously ambiguous adjective, as is "charming." Both these words seem to be real-estate agent code for a house that doesn't have many specific attributes worth describing. "Spacious" homes, meanwhile, are often decrepit or impractical. "Great neighborhood" signals a buyer that, well, *this* house isn't very nice but others nearby may be. And an exclamation point in a real-estate ad is bad news for sure, a bid to paper over real shortcomings with false enthusiasm.

If you study the words in ads for a real-estate agent's *own* home, meanwhile, you see that she indeed emphasizes descriptive terms (especially "new," "granite," "maple," and "move-in condition") and avoids empty adjectives (including "wonderful," "immaculate," and the telltale "!"). Then she patiently waits for the best buyer to come along. She might tell this buyer about a house nearby that just sold for $25,000 *above* the asking price, or another house that is currently the subject of a bidding war. She is careful to exercise every advantage of the information asymmetry she enjoys.

Does this make her a bad person? That's hard to say, at least hard for *us* to say. The point here is not that real-estate agents are bad people, but that they simply *are* people—and people inevitably respond to incentives. The incentives of the real-estate business, as currently configured, plainly encourage some agents to act against the best interests of their customers.

But like the funeral director and the car salesman and the life-insurance company, the real-estate agent has also seen her advantage eroded by the Internet. After all, anyone selling a home can now get online and gather her own information about sales trends and housing inventory and mortgage rates. The information has been set loose. And recent sales data show the results. Real-estate agents still get a higher price for their own homes than comparable homes owned by their clients, but since the proliferation of real-estate websites, the gap between the two prices has shrunk by a third.

It would be naïve to suppose that people abuse information only when they are acting as experts or as agents of commerce. After all, agents and experts are people too—which suggests that we are likely to abuse information in our personal lives as well, whether by withholding true information or editing the information we choose to put forth. A real-estate agent may wink and nod when she lists a "well-maintained" house, but we each have our equivalent hedges.

Think about how you describe yourself during a job interview versus how you might describe yourself on a first date. (For even more fun, compare that first-date conversation to a conversation with the same person during your tenth year of marriage.) Or think about how you might present yourself if you were going on national television for the first time. What sort of image would you want to project? Perhaps you want to seem clever or kind or good-looking; presumably you *don't* want to come off as cruel or bigoted. During the heyday of the Ku Klux Klan, its members took pride in publicly disparaging anybody who wasn't a conservative white Christian. But public bigotry has since been vastly curtailed. Even subtle displays of bigotry, if they become public, are now costly. Trent Lott, the majority leader of the U.S. Senate, learned this in 2002 after making a toast at a one hundredth birthday party for Strom Thurmond, his fellow senator and fellow southerner. Lott made a reference in his toast to Thurmond's 1948 campaign for president, which was built on a platform of segregation; Mississippi—Lott's home state—was one of just four states that Thurmond carried. "We're proud of it," Lott told the partygoers. "And if the rest of the country had followed our lead, we wouldn't have had all these problems over all these years either." The implication that Lott was a fan of segregation raised enough of a fury that he was forced to quit his Senate leadership post.

Even if you are a private citizen, you surely wouldn't want to seem bigoted while appearing in public. Might there be a way to test for discrimination in a public setting?

Unlikely as it may seem, the television game show *The Weakest*

Link provides a unique laboratory to study discrimination. An import from the United Kingdom, *The Weakest Link* for a short time became wildly popular in the United States. The game includes eight contestants (or, in a later daytime version, six) who each answer trivia questions and compete for a single cash jackpot. But the player who answers the most questions correctly isn't necessarily the player who advances. After each round, every contestant votes to eliminate one other contestant. A player's trivia-answering ability is presumably the only worthwhile factor to consider; race, gender, and age wouldn't seem to matter. But do they? By measuring a contestant's actual votes against the votes that would truly best serve his self-interest, it's possible to tell if discrimination is at play.

The voting strategy changes as the game progresses. In the first several rounds, it makes sense to eliminate bad players since the jackpot grows only when correct answers are given. In later rounds, the strategic incentives are flipped. The value of building the jackpot is now outweighed by each contestant's desire to win the jackpot. It's easier to do that if you eliminate the other good players. So, roughly speaking, the typical contestant will vote to eliminate the worse players in the early rounds and the better players in the later rounds.

The key to measuring the *Weakest Link* voting data is to tease out a contestant's playing ability from his race, gender, and age. If a young black man answers a lot of questions correctly but is voted off early, discrimination would seem to be a factor. Meanwhile, if an elderly white woman doesn't answer a single question correctly and is still not voted off, some sort of discriminatory favoritism would seem to be at play.

Again, keep in mind that all of this is happening on camera. A contestant knows that his friends, family, and co-workers—along with a few million strangers—are watching. So who, if anyone, is discriminated against on *The Weakest Link*?

Not, as it turns out, blacks. An analysis of more than 160 episodes reveals that black contestants, in both the early and late rounds of the game, are eliminated at a rate commensurate with their trivia-answering abilities. The same is true for female contestants. In a way, neither of these findings is so surprising. Two of the most potent social campaigns of the past half-century were the civil rights movement and the feminist movement, which demonized discrimination against blacks and women, respectively.

So perhaps, you say hopefully, discrimination was practically eradicated during the twentieth century, like polio.

Or more likely, it has become so unfashionable to discriminate against certain groups that all but the most insensitive people take pains to at least *appear* fair-minded, at least in public. This hardly means that discrimination itself has ended—only that people are embarrassed to show it. How might you determine whether the lack of discrimination against blacks and women represents a true absence or just a charade? The answer can be found by looking at other groups that society doesn't protect as well. Indeed, the *Weakest Link* voting data do indicate two kinds of contestants who *are* consistently discriminated against: the elderly and Latinos.

Among economists, there are two leading theories of discrimination. Interestingly, elderly *Weakest Link* contestants seem to suffer from one type, while Latinos suffer the other. The first type is called taste-based discrimination, which means that one person discriminates simply because he prefers to not interact with a particular type of other person. In the second type, known as information-based discrimination, one person believes that another type of person has poor skills, and acts accordingly.

On *The Weakest Link*, Latinos suffer information-based discrimination. Other contestants seem to view the Latinos as poor players, even when they are not. This perception translates into Latinos' being eliminated in the early rounds even if they are doing well and *not* being eliminated in the later rounds, when other contestants want to keep the Latinos around to weaken the field.

Elderly players, meanwhile, are victims of taste-based discrimination: in the early rounds *and* late rounds, they are eliminated far out of proportion to their skills. It seems as if the other contestants—this is a show on which the average age is thirty-four—simply don't want the older players around.

It's quite possible that a typical *Weakest Link* contestant isn't even cognizant of his discrimination toward Latinos and the elderly (or, in the case of blacks and women, his *lack* of discrimination). He is bound to be nervous, after all, and excited, playing a fast-moving game under the glare of television lights. Which naturally suggests another question: how might that same person express his preferences—and reveal information about himself—in the privacy of his home?

In a given year, some forty million Americans swap intimate truths about themselves with complete strangers. It all happens on Internet dating sites. Some of them, like Match.com, eHarmony .com, and Yahoo! Personals, appeal to a broad audience. Others cater to more specific tastes: ChristianSingles.com, JDate.com, Latin Matcher.com, BlackSinglesConnection.com, CountryWestern Singles.com, USMilitarySingles.com, OverweightDate.com, and

Gay.com. Dating websites are the most successful subscription-based business on the Internet.

Each site operates a bit differently, but the gist is this: You compose a personal ad about yourself that typically includes a photo, vital statistics, your income range, level of education, likes and dislikes, and so on. If the ad catches someone's fancy, that someone will e-mail you and perhaps arrange a date. On many sites, you also specify your dating aims: "long-term relationship," "a casual lover," or "just looking."

So there are two massive layers of data to be mined here: the information that people include in their ads and the level of response gleaned by any particular ad. Each layer of the data can be asked its own question. In the case of the ads, how forthright (and honest) are people when it comes to sharing their personal information? And in the case of the responses, what kind of information in personal ads is considered the most (and least) desirable?

Two economists and a psychologist recently banded together to address these questions. Günter J. Hitsch, Ali Hortaçsu, and Dan Ariely analyzed the data from one of the mainstream dating sites, focusing on more than 20,000 active users, half in Boston and half in San Diego. Fifty-six percent of the users were men, and the median age range for all users was twenty-one to thirty-five. Although they represented an adequate racial mix to reach some conclusions about race, they were predominantly white.

They were also a lot richer, taller, skinnier, and better-looking than average. That, at least, is what they wrote about themselves. More than 4 percent of the online daters claimed to earn more than $200,000 a year, whereas fewer than 1 percent of typical Internet users actually earn that much, suggesting that three of the four big earners were exaggerating. Male and female users typically reported that they are about an inch taller than the national average. As for weight, the men were in line with the national average, but the women typically said they weighed about twenty pounds less than the national average.

Most impressively, fully 72 percent of the women claimed "above average" looks, including 24 percent claiming "very good looks." The online men too were gorgeous: 68 percent called themselves "above average," including 19 percent with "very good looks." This leaves only about 30 percent of the users with "average" looks, including a paltry 1 percent with "less than average" looks—which suggests that the typical online dater is either a fabulist, a narcissist, or simply resistant to the meaning of "average." (Or perhaps they are all just pragmatists: as any real-estate agent knows, the typical house isn't "charming" or "fantastic," but unless you say it is, no one will even bother to take a look.) Twenty-eight percent of the women on the site said they were blond, a number far beyond the national average, which indicates a lot of dyeing, or lying, or both.

Some users, meanwhile, were bracingly honest. Seven percent of the men conceded that they were married, with a significant minority of these men reporting that they were "happily married." But the fact that they were honest doesn't mean they were rash. Of the 243 "happily married" men in the sample, only 12 chose to post a picture of themselves. The reward of gaining a mistress was evidently outweighed by the risk of having your wife discover your personal ad. ("And what were *you* doing on that website?" the husband might bluster, undoubtedly to little avail.)

Of the many ways to fail on a dating website, not posting a photo of yourself is perhaps the most certain. (Not that the photo necessarily *is* a photo of yourself; it may well be some better-looking stranger, but such deception would obviously backfire in time.) A man who does not include his photo gets only 60 percent of the volume of e-mail response of a man who does; a woman who doesn't include her photo gets only 24 percent as much. A low-income, poorly educated, unhappily employed, not very attractive, slightly overweight, and balding man who posts his photo stands a better chance of gleaning some e-mails than a man who says he makes $200,000 and is deadly handsome but doesn't post a photo. There are plenty of reasons someone might not post a photo—he's technically challenged or is ashamed of being spotted by friends or is just plain unattractive—but as in the case of a brand-new car with a For Sale sign, prospective customers will assume he's got something seriously wrong under the hood.

Getting a date is hard enough as it is. Fifty-six percent of the men who post ads don't receive even one e-mail; 21 percent of the women don't get a single response. The traits that do draw a big response, meanwhile, will not be a big surprise to anyone with even a passing knowledge of the sexes. In fact, the preferences expressed by online daters fit snugly with the most common stereotypes about men and women.

For instance, men who say they want a long-term relationship do much better than men looking for an occasional lover. But women looking for an occasional lover do great. For men, a woman's looks are of paramount importance. For women, a man's income is terribly important. The richer a man is, the more e-mails he receives. But a woman's income appeal is a bell-shaped curve: men do not want to date *low*-earning women, but once a woman starts earning too much, they seem to be scared off. Women are eager to date military men, policemen, and firemen (possibly the result of a 9/11 Effect, like the higher payments to Paul Feldman's bagel business), along with lawyers and doctors; they generally avoid men with manufacturing jobs. For men, being short is a big disadvantage (which is probably why so many lie about it), but weight doesn't much matter. For women, being overweight is deadly (which is probably why *they* lie). For a man, having red hair or curly hair is a downer, as is "bald with a fringe"—but a shaved head is okay. For a woman, salt-and-pepper hair is bad, while blond hair is, not surprisingly, very good.

In addition to all the information about income, education, and looks, men and women on the dating site listed their race. They were also asked to indicate a preference regarding the race of their potential dates. The two preferences were "the same as mine" or "it doesn't matter." Like the *Weakest Link* contestants, the website users were now publicly declaring how they felt about people who didn't look like them. They would reveal their *actual* preferences later, in confidential e-mails to the people they wanted to date.

Roughly half of the white women on the site and 80 percent of the white men declared that race didn't matter to them. But the response data tell a different story. The white men who said that race didn't matter sent 90 percent of their e-mail queries to white women. The white women who said race didn't matter sent about 97 percent of their e-mail queries to white men. This means that an Asian man who is good-looking, rich, and well educated will receive fewer than 25 percent as many e-mails from white women as a white man with the same qualifications would receive; similarly, black and Latino men receive about half as many e-mails from white women as they would if they were white.

Is it possible that race really didn't matter for these white women and men and that they simply never happened to browse a non-white date that interested them? Or, more likely, did they say that race didn't matter because they wanted to come across—especially to potential mates of their own race—as open-minded?

The gulf between the information we publicly proclaim and the information we know to be true is often vast. (Or, put a more familiar way: we say one thing and do another.) This can be seen in personal relationships, in commercial transactions, and of course in politics.

By now we are fully accustomed to the false public proclamations of politicians themselves. But voters lie too. Consider an election between a black candidate and a white candidate. Might white voters lie to pollsters, claiming they will vote for the black candidate in order to appear more color-blind than they actually are? Apparently so. In New York City's 1989 mayoral race between David Dinkins (a black candidate) and Rudolph Giuliani (who is white), Dinkins won by only a few points. Although Dinkins became the city's first black mayor, his slender margin of victory came as a surprise, for pre-election polls showed Dinkins winning by nearly 15 points. When the white supremacist David Duke ran for the U.S. Senate in 1990, he garnered nearly 20 percent more of the vote than pre-election polls had projected, an indication that thousands of Louisiana voters did not want to admit their preference for a candidate with racist views.

Duke, though he never won the high political office he often sought, proved himself a master of information abuse. As Grand Wizard of the Knights of the Ku Klux Klan, he was able to compile a mailing list of thousands of rank-and-file Klansmen and other supporters who would eventually become his political base. Not content to use the list only for himself, he sold it for $150,000 to the governor of Louisiana. Years later, Duke would once again use the list himself, letting his supporters know that he'd fallen on hard times and needed their donations. In this way Duke was able to raise hundreds of thousands of dollars for his continuing work in the field of white supremacy. He had explained to his supporters in a letter that he was so broke that the bank was trying to repossess his house.

In truth, Duke had already sold his house for a solid profit. (It isn't known whether he used a real-estate agent.) And most of the money he raised from his supporters was being used not to promote any white supremacist cause but rather to satisfy Duke's gambling habit. It was a sweet little scam he was running—until he was arrested and sent to federal prison in Big Spring, Texas.

Chapter 3

WHY DO DRUG DEALERS STILL LIVE WITH THEIR MOMS?

The two previous chapters were built around a pair of admittedly freakish questions: *What do schoolteachers and sumo wrestlers have in common?* and *How is the Ku Klux Klan like a group of real-estate agents?* But if you ask enough questions, strange as they seem at the time, you may eventually learn something worthwhile.

The first trick of asking questions is to determine if your question is a good one. Just because a question has never been asked does not make it good. Smart people have been asking questions for quite a few centuries now, so many of the questions that *haven't* been asked are bound to yield uninteresting answers.

But if you can question something that people really care about and find an answer that may surprise them—that is, if you can overturn the conventional wisdom—then you may have some luck.

It was John Kenneth Galbraith, the hyperliterate economic

sage, who coined the phrase "conventional wisdom." He did not consider it a compliment. "We associate truth with convenience," he wrote, "with what most closely accords with self-interest and personal well-being or promises best to avoid awkward effort or unwelcome dislocation of life. We also find highly acceptable what contributes most to self-esteem." Economic and social behaviors, Galbraith continued, "are complex, and to comprehend their character is mentally tiring. Therefore we adhere, as though to a raft, to those ideas which represent our understanding."

So the conventional wisdom in Galbraith's view must be simple, convenient, comfortable, and comforting—though not necessarily true. It would be silly to argue that the conventional wisdom is *never* true. But noticing where the conventional wisdom may be false—noticing, perhaps, the contrails of sloppy or self-interested thinking—is a nice place to start asking questions.

Consider the recent history of homelessness in the United States. In the early 1980s, an advocate for the homeless named Mitch Snyder took to saying that there were about 3 million homeless Americans. The public duly sat up and took notice. More than 1 of every 100 people were homeless? That sure seemed high, but . . . well, the expert said it. A heretofore quiescent problem was suddenly catapulted into the national consciousness. Snyder even testified before Congress about the magnitude of the problem. He also reportedly told a college audience that 45 homeless people die each second—which would mean a whopping 1.4 billion dead homeless every year. (The U.S. population at the time was about 225 million.) Assuming that Snyder misspoke or was misquoted and meant to say that *one* homeless person died *every forty-five seconds*, that's still 701,000 dead homeless people every year—roughly one-third of all deaths in the United States. Hmm.

Ultimately, when Snyder was pressed on his figure of 3 million homeless, he admitted that it was a fabrication. Journalists had been hounding him for a specific number, he said, and he hadn't wanted them to walk away empty-handed.

It may be sad but not surprising to learn that experts like Snyder can be self-interested to the point of deceit. But they cannot deceive on their own. Journalists need experts as badly as experts need journalists. Every day there are newspaper pages and television newscasts to be filled, and an expert who can deliver a jarring piece of wisdom is always welcome. Working together, journalists and experts are the architects of much conventional wisdom.

Advertising too is a brilliant tool for creating conventional wisdom. Listerine, for instance, was invented in the nineteenth century as a powerful surgical antiseptic. It was later sold, in distilled form, as a floor cleaner and a cure for gonorrhea. But it wasn't a runaway success until the 1920s, when it was pitched as a solution for "chronic halitosis"—a then obscure medical term for bad breath. Listerine's new ads featured forlorn young women and men, eager for marriage but turned off by their mate's rotten breath. "Can I be happy with him in spite of *that?*" one maiden asked herself. Until that time, bad breath was not conventionally considered such a catastrophe. But Listerine changed that. As the advertising scholar James B. Twitchell writes, "Listerine did not make mouthwash as much as it made halitosis." In just seven years, the company's revenues rose from $115,000 to more than $8 million.

However created, the conventional wisdom can be hard to budge. The economist Paul Krugman, a *New York Times* columnist and devout critic of George W. Bush, bemoaned this fact as the President's reelection campaign got under way in early 2004:

"The approved story line about Mr. Bush is that he's a bluff, honest, plainspoken guy, and anecdotes that fit that story get reported. But if the conventional wisdom were instead that he's a phony, a silver-spoon baby who pretends to be a cowboy, journalists would have plenty of material to work with."

In the months leading up to the U.S. invasion of Iraq in 2003, dueling experts floated diametrically opposite forecasts about Iraq's weapons of mass destruction. But more often, as with Mitch Snyder's homeless "statistics," one side wins the war of conventional wisdom. Women's rights advocates, for instance, have hyped the incidence of sexual assault, claiming that one in three American women will in her lifetime be a victim of rape or attempted rape. (The actual figure is more like one in eight—but the advocates know it would take a callous person to publicly dispute their claims.) Advocates working for the cures of various tragic diseases regularly do the same. Why not? A little creative lying can draw attention, indignation, and—perhaps most important—the money and political capital to address the actual problem.

Of course an expert, whether a women's health advocate or a political advisor or an advertising executive, tends to have different incentives than the rest of us. And an expert's incentives may shift 180 degrees, depending on the situation.

Consider the police. A recent audit discovered that the police in Atlanta were radically underreporting crime since the early 1990s. The practice apparently began when Atlanta was working to land the 1996 Olympics. The city needed to shed its violent image, and fast. So each year thousands of crime reports were either downgraded from violent to nonviolent or simply thrown away. (Despite these continuing efforts—there were more than

22,000 missing police reports in 2002 alone—Atlanta regularly ranks among the most violent American cities.)

Police in other cities, meanwhile, were spinning a different story during the 1990s. The sudden, violent appearance of crack cocaine had police departments across the country scrapping for resources. They made it known that it wasn't a fair fight: the drug dealers were armed with state-of-the-art weapons and a bottomless supply of cash. This emphasis on illicit cash proved to be a winning effort, for nothing infuriated the law-abiding populace more than the image of the millionaire crack dealer. The media eagerly glommed on to this story, portraying crack dealing as one of the most profitable jobs in America.

But if you were to have spent a little time around the housing projects where crack was so often sold, you might have noticed something strange: not only did most of the crack dealers still live in the projects, but most of them still lived at home with their moms. And then you may have scratched your head and said, "Why is that?"

The answer lies in finding the right data, and the secret to finding the right data usually means finding the right person—which is more easily said than done. Drug dealers are rarely trained in economics, and economists rarely hang out with crack dealers. So the answer to this question begins with finding someone who *did* live among the drug dealers and managed to walk away with the secrets of their trade.

Sudhir Venkatesh—his boyhood friends called him Sid, but he has since reverted to Sudhir—was born in India, raised in the suburbs of upstate New York and southern California, and graduated from the University of California at San Diego with a degree in mathematics. In 1989 he began to pursue his PhD in sociology at the University of Chicago. He was interested in understanding how young people form their identities; to that end, he had just spent three months following the Grateful Dead around the country. What he was not interested in was the grueling fieldwork that typifies sociology.

But his graduate advisor, the eminent poverty scholar William Julius Wilson, promptly sent Venkatesh into the field. His assignment: to visit Chicago's poorest black neighborhoods with a clipboard and a seventy-question, multiple-choice survey. This was the first question on the survey:

How do you feel about being black and poor?

a. Very bad
b. Bad
c. Neither bad nor good
d. Somewhat good
e. Very good

One day Venkatesh walked twenty blocks from the university to a housing project on the shore of Lake Michigan to administer his survey. The project comprised three sixteen-story buildings made of yellow-gray brick. Venkatesh soon discovered that the names and addresses he had been given were badly outdated. These buildings were condemned, practically abandoned. Some families lived on the lower floors, pirating water and electricity, but the elevators didn't work. Neither did the lights in the stairwell. It was late afternoon in early winter, nearly dark outside.

Venkatesh, who is a thoughtful, handsome, and well-built but not aberrationally brave person, had made his way up to the sixth floor, trying to find someone willing to take his survey. Suddenly, on the stairwell landing, he startled a group of teenagers shooting dice. They turned out to be a gang of junior-level crack dealers who operated out of the building, and they were not happy to see him.

"I'm a student at the University of Chicago," Venkatesh sputtered, sticking to his survey script, "and I am administering—"

"Fuck you, nigger, what are you doing in our stairwell?"

There was an ongoing gang war in Chicago. Things had been violent lately, with shootings nearly every day. This gang, a branch of the Black Gangster Disciple Nation, was plainly on edge. They didn't know what to make of Venkatesh. He didn't *seem* to be a member of a rival gang. But maybe he was some kind of spy? He certainly wasn't a cop. He wasn't black, wasn't white. He wasn't exactly threatening—he was armed only with his clipboard—but he didn't seem quite harmless either. Thanks to his three months trailing the Grateful Dead, he still looked, as he would later put it, "like a genuine freak, with hair down to my ass."

The gang members started arguing over what should be done with Venkatesh. Let him go? But if he *did* tell the rival gang about this stairwell hangout, they'd be susceptible to a surprise attack. One jittery kid kept wagging something back and forth in his hands—in the dimming light, Venkatesh eventually realized it was a gun—and muttering, "Let me have him, let me have him." Venkatesh was very, very scared.

The crowd grew bigger and louder. Then an older gang member appeared. He snatched the clipboard from Venkatesh's hands and, when he saw that it was a written questionnaire, looked puzzled.

"I can't read any of this shit," he said.

"That's because you can't *read*," said one of the teenagers, and everyone laughed at the older gangster.

He told Venkatesh to go ahead and ask him a question from the survey. Venkatesh led with the how-does-it-feel-to-be-black-and-poor question. It was met with a round of guffaws, some angrier than others. As Venkatesh would later tell his university colleagues, he realized that the multiple-choice answers A through E were insufficient. In reality, he now knew, the answers should have looked like this:

a. Very bad
b. Bad
c. Neither bad nor good
d. Somewhat good
e. Very good
f. Fuck you

Just as things were looking their bleakest for Venkatesh, another man appeared. This was J. T., the gang's leader. J. T. wanted to know what was going on. Then he told Venkatesh to read him the survey question. He listened but then said he couldn't answer the question because he wasn't black.

"Well then," Venkatesh said, "how does it feel to be *African American* and poor?"

"I ain't no African American either, you idiot. I'm a *nigger*." J. T. then administered a lively though not unfriendly taxonomical lesson in "nigger" versus "African American" versus "black." When he was through, there was an awkward silence. Still nobody seemed to know what to do with Venkatesh. J. T., who was in his late twenties, had cooled down his subordinates, but he didn't seem to want to interfere directly with their catch. Darkness fell and J. T. left. "People don't come out of here alive," the jittery teenager with the gun told Venkatesh. "You know that, don't you?"

As night deepened, his captors eased up. They gave Venkatesh one of their beers, and then another and another. When he had to pee, he went where they went—on the stairwell landing one floor up. J. T. stopped by a few times during the night but didn't have much to say. Daybreak came and then noon. Venkatesh would occasionally try to discuss his survey, but the young crack dealers just laughed and told him how stupid his questions were. Finally, nearly twenty-four hours after Venkatesh stumbled upon them, they set him free.

He went home and took a shower. He was relieved but he was also curious. It struck Venkatesh that most people, including himself, had never given much thought to the daily life of ghetto criminals. He was now eager to learn how the Black Disciples worked, from top to bottom.

After a few hours, he decided to walk back to the housing project. By now he had thought of some better questions to ask.

Having seen firsthand that the conventional method of data gathering was in this case absurd, Venkatesh vowed to scrap his questionnaire and embed himself with the gang. He tracked down J. T. and sketched out his proposal. J. T. thought Venkatesh was crazy, literally—a university student wanting to cozy up to a crack gang? But he also admired what Venkatesh was after. As it happened, J. T. was a college graduate himself, a business major. After college, he had taken a job in the Loop, working in the marketing department of a company that sold office equipment. But he felt so out of place there—like a white man working at Afro Sheen headquarters, he liked to say—that he quit. Still, he never forgot what he learned. He knew the importance of collecting data and finding new markets; he was always on the lookout for better management strategies. It was no coincidence, in other words, that J. T. was the leader of this crack gang. He was bred to be a boss.

After some wrangling, J. T. promised Venkatesh unfettered access to the gang's operations as long as J. T. retained veto power over any information that, if published, might prove harmful.

When the yellow-gray buildings on the lakefront were demolished, shortly after Venkatesh's first visit, the gang relocated to another housing project even deeper in Chicago's south side. For the next six years, Venkatesh practically lived there. Under J. T.'s protection he watched the gang members up close, at work and at home. He asked endless questions. Sometimes the gangsters were annoyed by his curiosity; more often they took advantage of his willingness to listen. "It's a war out here, man," one dealer told him. "I mean, every day people struggling to survive, so you know, we just do what we can. We ain't got no choice, and if that means getting killed, well, shit, it's what niggers do around here to feed their family."

Venkatesh would move from one family to the next, washing their dinner dishes and sleeping on the floor. He bought toys for their children; he once watched a woman use her baby's bib to sop up the blood of a teenaged drug dealer who was shot to death in front of Venkatesh. William Julius Wilson, back at the U. of C., was having regular nightmares on Venkatesh's behalf.

Over the years the gang endured bloody turf wars and, eventually, a federal indictment. A member named Booty, who was one rank beneath J. T., came to Venkatesh with a story. Booty was being blamed by the rest of the gang for bringing about the indictment, he told Venkatesh, and therefore suspected that he would soon be killed. (He was right.) But first Booty wanted to do a little atoning. For all the gang's talk about how crack dealing didn't do any harm—they even liked to brag that it kept black money in the black community—Booty was feeling guilty. He wanted to leave behind something that might somehow benefit the next generation. He handed Venkatesh a stack of well-worn spiral notebooks—blue and black, the gang's colors. They represented a complete record of four years' worth of the gang's financial transactions. At J. T.'s direction, the ledgers had been rigorously compiled: sales, wages, dues, even the death benefits paid out to the families of murdered members.

At first Venkatesh didn't even want the notebooks. What if the Feds found out he had them—perhaps he'd be indicted too? Besides, what was he supposed to do with the data? Despite his math background, he had long ago stopped thinking in numbers.

Upon completing his graduate work at the University of Chicago, Venkatesh was awarded a three-year stay at Harvard's Society of Fellows. Its environment of sharp thinking and bonhomie—the walnut paneling, the sherry cart once owned by Oliver Wendell Holmes—delighted Venkatesh. He went so far as to become the society's wine steward. And yet he regularly left Cambridge, returning again and again to the crack gang in Chicago. This street-level research made Venkatesh something of an anomaly. Most of the other young Fellows were dyed-in-the-tweed intellectuals who liked to pun in Greek.

One of the society's aims was to bring together scholars from various fields who might not otherwise have occasion to meet. Venkatesh soon encountered another anomalous young Fellow, one who also failed the society stereotype. This one happened to be an economist who, instead of thinking grand macro thoughts, favored his own list of offbeat micro curiosities. At the very top of his list was crime. And so, within ten minutes of their meeting, Sudhir Venkatesh told Steven Levitt about the spiral notebooks from Chicago and they decided to collaborate on a paper. It would be the first time that such priceless financial data had fallen into an economist's hands, affording an analysis of a heretofore uncharted criminal enterprise.

So how *did* the gang work? An awful lot like most American businesses, actually, though perhaps none more so than McDonald's. In fact, if you were to hold a McDonald's organizational chart and a Black Disciples org chart side by side, you could hardly tell the difference.

The gang that Venkatesh had fallen in with was one of about a hundred branches—franchises, really—of a larger Black Disciples organization. J. T., the college-educated leader of his franchise, reported to a central leadership of about twenty men that was called, without irony, the board of directors. (At the same time that white suburbanites were studiously mimicking black rappers' ghetto culture, black ghetto criminals were studiously mimicking the suburbanites' dads' corp-think.) J. T. paid the board of directors nearly 20 percent of his revenues for the right to sell crack in a designated twelve-square-block area. The rest of the money was his to distribute as he saw fit.

Three officers reported directly to J. T.: an enforcer (who ensured the gang members' safety), a treasurer (who watched over the gang's liquid assets), and a runner (who transported large quantities of drugs and money to and from the supplier). Beneath the officers were the street-level salesmen known as foot soldiers. The goal of a foot soldier was to someday become an officer. J. T. had anywhere from twenty-five to seventy-five foot soldiers on his payroll at any given time, depending on the time of year (autumn was the best crack-selling season; summer and Christmastime were slow) and the size of the gang's territory (which doubled at one point when the Black Disciples engineered a hostile takeover of a rival gang's turf). At the very bottom of J. T.'s organization were as many as two hundred members known as the rank and file. They were not employees at all. They did, however, pay dues to the gang—some for protection from rival gangs, others for the chance to eventually earn a job as a foot soldier.

The four years recorded in the gang's notebooks coincided with the peak years of the crack boom, and business was excellent. J. T.'s franchise quadrupled its revenues during this period. In the first year, it took in an average of $18,500 each month; by the final year, it was collecting $68,400 a month. Here's a look at the monthly revenues in the third year:

DRUG SALES	$ 24,800
DUES	$ 5,100
EXTORTIONARY TAXES	$ 2,100
TOTAL MONTHLY REVENUES	$ 32,000

"Drug sales" represents only the money from dealing crack cocaine. The gang did allow some rank-and-file members to sell heroin on its turf but accepted a fixed licensing fee in lieu of a share of profits. (This was off-the-books money and went straight into J. T.'s pocket; he probably skimmed from other sources as well.) The $5,100 in dues came from rank-and-file members only, since full gang members didn't pay dues. The extortionary taxes were paid by other businesses that operated on the gang's turf, including grocery stores, gypsy cabs, pimps, and people selling stolen goods or repairing cars on the street.

Now, here's what it cost J. T., excluding wages, to bring in that $32,000 per month:

WHOLESALE COST OF DRUGS	$ 5,000
BOARD OF DIRECTORS FEE	$ 5,000
MERCENARY FIGHTERS	$ 1,300
WEAPONS	$ 300
MISCELLANEOUS	$ 2,400
TOTAL MONTHLY NONWAGE COSTS	**$14,000**

Mercenary fighters were nonmembers hired on short-term contracts to help the gang fight turf wars. The cost of weapons is small here because the Black Disciples had a side deal with local gunrunners, helping them navigate the neighborhood in exchange for free or steeply discounted guns. The miscellaneous expenses include legal fees, parties, bribes, and gang-sponsored "community events." (The Black Disciples worked hard to be seen as a pillar rather than a scourge of the housing-project community.) The miscellaneous expenses also include the costs associated with a gang member's murder. The gang not only paid for the funeral but often gave a stipend of up to three years' wages to the victim's family. Venkatesh had once asked why the gang was so generous in this regard. "That's a fucking stupid question," he was told, " 'cause as long as you been with us, you still don't understand that their families is our families. We can't just leave 'em out. We been knowing these folks our whole lives, man, so we grieve when they grieve. You got to respect the family." There was another reason for the death benefits: the gang feared community backlash (its enterprise was plainly a destructive one) and figured it could buy some goodwill for a few hundred dollars here and there.

The rest of the money the gang took in went to its members, starting with J. T. Here is the single line item in the gang's budget that made J. T. the happiest:

NET MONTHLY PROFIT ACCRUING TO LEADER.... $8,500

At $8,500 per month, J. T.'s annual salary was about $100,000—tax-free, of course, and not including the various off-the-books money he pocketed. This was a lot more than he earned at his short-lived office job in the Loop. And J. T. was just one of roughly 100 leaders at this level within the Black Disciples network. So there were indeed some drug dealers who could afford to live large—or, in the case of the gang's board of directors, *extremely* large. Each of those top 20 bosses stood to earn about $500,000 a year. (A third of them, however, were typically imprisoned at any time, a significant downside of an up position in an illicit industry.)

So the top 120 men on the Black Disciples' pyramid were paid very well. But the pyramid they sat atop was gigantic. Using J. T.'s franchise as a yardstick—3 officers and roughly 50 foot soldiers—there were some 5,300 other men working for those 120 bosses. Then there were another 20,000 unpaid rank-and-file members, many of whom wanted nothing more than an opportunity to become a foot soldier. They were even willing to pay gang dues to have their chance.

And how well did that dream job pay? Here are the monthly totals for the wages that J. T. paid his gang members:

COMBINED WAGES PAID TO ALL THREE OFFICERS	**$2,100**
COMBINED WAGES PAID TO ALL FOOT SOLDIERS	**$7,400**
TOTAL MONTHLY GANG WAGES (EXCLUDING LEADER)	**$9,500**

So J. T. paid his employees $9,500, a *combined* monthly salary that was only $1,000 more than his own official salary. J. T.'s hourly wage was $66. His three officers, meanwhile, each took home $700 a month, which works out to about $7 an hour. And the foot soldiers earned just $3.30 an hour, less than the minimum wage. So the answer to the original question—if drug dealers make so much money, why are they still living with their mothers?—is that, except for the top cats, they *don't* make much money. They had no choice but to live with their mothers. For every big earner, there were hundreds more just scraping along. The top 120 men in the Black Disciples gang represented just 2.2 percent of the full-fledged gang membership but took home well more than half the money.

In other words, a crack gang works pretty much like the standard capitalist enterprise: you have to be near the top of the pyramid to make a big wage. Notwithstanding the leadership's rhetoric about the family nature of the business, the gang's wages are about as skewed as wages in corporate America. A foot soldier had plenty in common with a McDonald's burger flipper or a Wal-Mart shelf stocker. In fact, most of J. T.'s foot soldiers also held minimum-wage jobs in the legitimate sector to supplement their skimpy illicit earnings. The leader of another crack gang once told Venkatesh that he could easily afford to pay his foot soldiers more, but it wouldn't be prudent. "You got all these niggers below you who want your job, you dig?" he said. "So, you know, you try to take care of them, but you know, you also have to show them you the boss. You always have to get yours first, or else you really ain't no leader. If you start taking losses, they see you as weak and shit."

Along with the bad pay, the foot soldiers faced terrible job conditions. For starters, they had to stand on a street corner all day and do business with crackheads. (The gang members were strongly advised against using the product themselves, advice that was enforced by beatings if necessary.) Foot soldiers also risked arrest and, more worrisome, violence. Using the gang's financial documents and the rest of Venkatesh's research, it is possible to construct an adverse-events index of J. T.'s gang during the four years in question. The results are astonishingly bleak. If you were a member of J. T.'s gang for all four years, here is the typical fate you would have faced during that period:

NUMBER OF TIMES ARRESTED	**5.9**
NUMBER OF NONFATAL WOUNDS OR INJURIES (NOT INCLUDING INJURIES METED OUT BY THE GANG ITSELF FOR RULES VIOLATIONS)	**2.4**
CHANCE OF BEING KILLED	**1 IN 4**

A 1-in-4 chance of being killed! Compare these odds with those for a timber cutter, which the Bureau of Labor Statistics calls the most dangerous job in the United States. Over four years' time, a timber cutter would stand only a 1-in-200 chance of being killed. Or compare the crack dealer's odds to those of a death-row inmate in Texas, which executes more prisoners than any other state. In 2003, Texas put to death twenty-four inmates—or just 5 percent of the nearly 500 inmates on its death row during that time. Which means that you stand a greater chance of dying while dealing crack in a Chicago housing project than you do while sitting on death row in Texas.

So if crack dealing is the most dangerous job in America, and if the salary was only $3.30 an hour, why on earth would anyone take such a job?

Well, for the same reason that a pretty Wisconsin farm girl moves to Hollywood. For the same reason that a high-school quarterback wakes up at 5 a.m. to lift weights. They all want to succeed in an extremely competitive field in which, if you reach the top, you are paid a fortune (to say nothing of the attendant glory and power).

To the kids growing up in a housing project on Chicago's south side, crack dealing seemed like a glamour profession. For many of them, the job of gang boss—highly visible and highly lucrative—was easily the best job they thought they had access to. Had they grown up under different circumstances, they might have thought about becoming economists or writers. But in the neighborhood where J. T.'s gang operated, the path to a decent legitimate job was practically invisible. Fifty-six percent of the neighborhood's children lived below the poverty line (compared to a national average of 18 percent). Seventy-eight percent came from single-parent homes. Fewer than 5 percent of the neighborhood's adults had a college degree; barely one in three adult men worked at all. The neighborhood's median income was about $15,000 a year, well less than half the U.S. average. During the years that Venkatesh lived with J. T.'s gang, foot soldiers often asked his help in landing what they called "a good job": working as a janitor at the University of Chicago.

The problem with crack dealing is the same as in every other glamour profession: a lot of people are competing for a very few prizes. Earning big money in the crack gang wasn't much more likely than the Wisconsin farm girl becoming a movie star or the high-school quarterback playing in the NFL. But criminals, like everyone else, respond to incentives. So if the prize is big enough, they will form a line down the block just hoping for a chance. On the south side of Chicago, people wanting to sell crack vastly outnumbered the available street corners.

These budding drug lords bumped up against an immutable law of labor: when there are a lot of people willing and able to do a job, that job generally doesn't pay well. This is one of four meaningful factors that determine a wage. The others are the specialized skills a job requires, the unpleasantness of a job, and the demand for services that the job fulfills.

The delicate balance between these factors helps explain why, for instance, the typical prostitute earns more than the typical architect. It may not seem as though she should. The architect would appear to be more skilled (as the word is usually defined) and better educated (again, as usually defined). But little girls don't grow up dreaming of becoming prostitutes, so the supply of potential prostitutes is relatively small. Their skills, while not necessarily "specialized," are practiced in a very specialized context. The job is unpleasant and forbidding in at least two significant ways: the likelihood of violence and the lost opportunity of having a stable family life. As for demand? Let's just say that an architect is more likely to hire a prostitute than vice versa.

In the glamour professions—movies, sports, music, fashion—there is a different dynamic at play. Even in second-tier glamour industries like publishing, advertising, and media, swarms of bright young people throw themselves at grunt jobs that pay poorly and demand unstinting devotion. An editorial assistant earning $22,000 at a Manhattan publishing house, an unpaid high-school quarterback, and a teenage crack dealer earning $3.30 an hour are all playing the same game, a game that is best viewed as a tournament.

The rules of a tournament are straightforward. You must start at the bottom to have a shot at the top. (Just as a Major League shortstop probably played Little League and just as a Grand Dragon of the Ku Klux Klan probably started out as a lowly spear-carrier, a drug lord typically began by selling drugs on a street corner.) You must be willing to work long and hard at substandard wages. In order to advance in the tournament, you must prove yourself not merely above average but spectacular. (The way to distinguish yourself differs from profession to profession, of course; while J. T. certainly monitored his foot soldiers' sales performance, it was their force of personality that really counted—more than it would for, say, a shortstop.) And finally, once you come to the sad realization that you will never make it to the top, you will quit the tournament. (Some people hang on longer than others—witness the graying "actors" who wait tables in New York—but people generally get the message quite early.)

Most of J. T.'s foot soldiers were unwilling to stay foot soldiers for long after they realized they weren't advancing. Especially once the shooting started. After several relatively peaceful years, J. T.'s gang got involved in a turf war with a neighboring gang. Drive-by shootings became a daily event. For a foot soldier—the gang's man on the street—this development was particularly dangerous. The nature of the business demanded that customers be able to find him easily and quickly; if he hid from the other gang, he couldn't sell his crack.

Until the gang war, J. T.'s foot soldiers had been willing to balance the risky, low-paying job with the reward of advancement. But as one foot soldier told Venkatesh, he now wanted to be compensated for the added risk: "Would you stand around here when all this shit is going on? No, right? So if I gonna be asked to put my life on the line, then front me the cash, man. Pay me more 'cause it ain't worth my time to be here when they're warring."

J. T. hadn't wanted this war. For one thing, he was forced to pay his foot soldiers higher wages because of the added risk. Far worse, gang warfare was bad for business. If Burger King and McDonald's launch a price war to gain market share, they partly make up in volume what they lose in price. (Nor is anyone getting shot.) But with a gang war, sales plummet because customers are so scared of the violence that they won't come out in the open to buy their crack. In every way, war was expensive for J. T.

So why did he start the war? As a matter of fact, he didn't. It was his foot soldiers who started it. It turns out that a crack boss didn't have as much control over his subordinates as he would have liked. That's because they had different incentives.

For J. T., violence was a distraction from the business at hand; he would have preferred that his members never fired a single gunshot. For a foot soldier, however, violence served a purpose. One of the few ways that a foot soldier could distinguish himself—and advance in the tournament—was by proving his mettle for violence. A killer was respected, feared, talked about. A foot soldier's incentive was to make a name for himself; J. T.'s incentive was, in effect, to keep the foot soldiers from doing so. "We try to tell these shorties that they belong to a serious organization," he once told Venkatesh. "It ain't all about killing. They see these movies and shit, they think it's all about running around tearing shit up. But it's not. You've got to learn to be part of an organization; you can't be fighting all the time. It's bad for business."

In the end, J. T. prevailed. He oversaw the gang's expansion and ushered in a new era of prosperity and relative peace. J. T. was a winner. He was paid well because so few people could do what he did. He was a tall, good-looking, smart, tough man who knew how to motivate people. He was shrewd too, never tempting arrest by carrying guns or cash. While the rest of his gang lived in poverty with their mothers, J. T. had several homes, several women, several cars. He also had his business education, of course. He constantly worked to extend this advantage. That was why he ordered the corporate-style bookkeeping that eventually found its way into Sudhir Venkatesh's hands. No other franchise leader had ever done such a thing. J. T. once showed his ledgers to the board of directors to prove, as if proof were needed, the extent of his business acumen.

And it worked. After six years running his local gang, J. T. was promoted to the board of directors. He was now thirty-four years old. He had won the tournament. But this tournament had a catch that publishing and pro sports and even Hollywood don't have. Selling drugs, after all, is illegal. Not long after he made the board of directors, the Black Disciples were essentially shut down by a federal indictment—the same indictment that led the gangster named Booty to turn over his notebooks to Venkatesh—and J. T. was sent to prison.

• • •

Now for another unlikely question: what did crack cocaine have in common with nylon stockings?

In 1939, when DuPont introduced nylons, countless American women felt as if a miracle had been performed in their honor. Until then, stockings were made of silk, and silk was delicate, expensive, and in ever shorter supply. By 1941, some sixty-four million pairs of nylon stockings had been sold—more stockings than there were adult women in the United States. They were easily affordable, immensely appealing, practically addictive.

DuPont had pulled off the feat that every marketer dreams of: it brought class to the masses. In this regard, the invention of nylon stockings was markedly similar to the invention of crack cocaine.

In the 1970s, if you were the sort of person who did drugs, there was no classier drug than cocaine. Beloved by rock stars and movie stars, ballplayers and even the occasional politician, cocaine was a drug of power and panache. It was clean, it was white, it was pretty. Heroin was droopy and pot was foggy but cocaine provided a beautiful high.

Alas, it was also very expensive. Nor did the high last long. This led cocaine users to try jacking up the drug's potency. They did this primarily by freebasing—adding ammonia and ethyl ether to cocaine hydrochloride, or powdered cocaine, and burning it to free up the "base" cocaine. But this could be dangerous. As more than a few flame-scarred drug users could attest, chemistry is best left to chemists.

Meanwhile, cocaine dealers and aficionados across the country, and perhaps also in the Caribbean and South America, were working on a safer version of distilled cocaine. They found that mixing powdered cocaine in a saucepan with baking soda and water, and then cooking off the liquid, produced tiny rocks of smokeable cocaine. It came to be called crack for the crackling sound the baking soda made when it was burned. More affectionate nicknames would soon follow: Rock, Kryptonite, Kibbles 'n Bits, Scrabble, and Love. By the early 1980s, the class drug was ready for the masses. Now only two things were needed to turn crack into a phenomenon: an abundant supply of raw cocaine and a way to get the new product to a mass market.

The cocaine was easy to come by, for the invention of crack coincided with a Colombian cocaine glut. During the late 1970s, the wholesale price of cocaine in the United States fell dramatically, even as its purity was rising. One man, a Nicaraguan émigré named Oscar Danilo Blandon, was suspected of importing far more Colombian cocaine than anyone else. Blandon did so much business with the budding crack dealers of South Central Los Angeles that he came to be known as the Johnny Appleseed of Crack. Blandon would later claim that he was selling the cocaine to raise money for the CIA-sponsored Contras back home in Nicaragua. He liked to say that the CIA was in turn watching his back in the United States, allowing him to sell cocaine with impunity. This claim would spark a belief that still seethes to this day, especially among urban blacks, that the CIA itself was the chief sponsor of the American crack trade.

Verifying that claim is beyond the purview of this book. What *is* demonstrably true is that Oscar Danilo Blandon helped establish a link—between Colombian cocaine cartels and inner-city crack merchants—that would alter American history. By putting massive amounts of cocaine into the hands of street gangs, Blandon and others like him gave rise to a devastating crack boom. And gangs like the Black Gangster Disciple Nation were given new reason to exist.

As long as there have been cities, there have been gangs of one sort or another. In the United States, gangs have traditionally been a sort of halfway house for recent immigrants. In the 1920s, Chicago alone had more than 1,300 street gangs, catering to every ethnic, political, and criminal leaning imaginable. As a rule, gangs would prove much better at making mayhem than money. Some fancied themselves commercial enterprises, and a few—the Mafia, most notably—actually did make money (at least for the higher-ups). But most gangsters were, as the cliché assures us, two-bit gangsters.

Black street gangs in particular flourished in Chicago, with membership in the tens of thousands by the 1970s. They constituted the sort of criminals, petty and otherwise, who sucked the life out of urban areas. Part of the problem was that these criminals never seemed to get locked up. The 1960s and 1970s were, in retrospect, a great time to be a street criminal in most American cities. The likelihood of punishment was so low—this was the heyday of a liberal justice system and the criminals' rights movement—that it simply didn't cost very much to commit a crime.

By the 1980s, however, the courts had begun to radically reverse that trend. Criminals' rights were curtailed and stricter sentencing guidelines put in place. More and more of Chicago's black gangsters were getting sent to federal prisons. By happy coincidence, some of their fellow inmates were Mexican gang members with close ties to Colombian drug dealers. In the past, the black gangsters had bought their drugs from a middleman, the

Mafia—which, as it happened, was then being pummeled by the federal government's new anti-racketeering laws. But by the time crack came to Chicago, the black gangsters had made the connections to buy their cocaine directly from Colombian dealers.

Cocaine had never been a big seller in the ghetto: it was too expensive. But that was before the invention of crack. This new product was ideal for a low-income, street-level customer. Because it required such a tiny amount of pure cocaine, one hit of crack cost only a few dollars. Its powerful high reached the brain in just a few seconds—and then faded fast, sending the user back for more. From the outset, crack was bound to be a huge success.

And who better to sell it than the thousands of junior members of all those street gangs like the Black Gangster Disciple Nation? The gangs already owned the territory—real estate was, in essence, their core business—and they were suitably menacing to keep customers from even thinking about ripping them off. Suddenly the urban street gang evolved from a club for wayward teenagers into a true commercial enterprise.

The gang also presented an opportunity for longtime employment. Before crack, it was just about impossible to earn a living in a street gang. When it was time for a gangster to start supporting a family, he would have to quit. There was no such thing as a thirty-year-old gangster: he was either working a legitimate job, dead, or in prison. But with crack, there was real money to be made. Instead of moving on and making way for the younger gangsters to ascend, the veterans stayed put. This was happening just as the old-fashioned sort of lifetime jobs—factory jobs especially—were disappearing. In the past, a semi-skilled black man in Chicago could earn a decent wage working in a factory. With that option narrowing, crack dealing looked even better.

How hard could it be? The stuff was so addictive that a fool could sell it.

Who cared if the crack game was a tournament that only a few of them could possibly win? Who cared if it was so dangerous—standing out there on a corner, selling it as fast and anonymously as McDonald's sells hamburgers, not knowing any of your customers, wondering who might be coming to arrest or rob or kill you? Who cared if your product got twelve-year-olds and grandmothers and preachers so addicted that they stopped thinking about anything except their next hit? Who cared if crack killed the neighborhood?

For black Americans, the four decades between World War II and the crack boom had been marked by steady and often dramatic improvement. Particularly since the civil rights legislation of the mid-1960s, the telltale signs of societal progress had finally taken root among black Americans. The black-white income gap was shrinking. So was the gap between black children's test scores and those of white children. Perhaps the most heartening gain had been in infant mortality. As late as 1964, a black infant was twice as likely to die as a white infant, often of a cause as basic as diarrhea or pneumonia. With segregated hospitals, many black patients received what amounted to Third World care. But that changed when the federal government ordered the hospitals to be desegregated: within just seven years, the black infant mortality rate had been cut in half. By the 1980s, virtually every facet of life was improving for black Americans, and the progress showed no sign of stopping.

Then came crack cocaine.

While crack use was hardly a black-only phenomenon, it hit black neighborhoods much harder than most. The evidence can be seen by measuring the same indicators of societal progress cited above. After decades of decline, black infant mortality began to soar in the 1980s, as did the rate of low-birthweight babies and parent abandonment. The gap between black and white school-children widened. The number of blacks sent to prison tripled. Crack was so dramatically destructive that if its effect is averaged for all black Americans, not just crack users and their families, you will see that the group's postwar progress was not only stopped cold but was often knocked as much as ten years backward. Black Americans were hurt more by crack cocaine than by any other single cause since Jim Crow.

And then there was the crime. Within a five-year period, the homicide rate among young urban blacks *quadrupled*. Suddenly it was just as dangerous to live in parts of Chicago or St. Louis or Los Angeles as it was to live in Bogotá.

The violence associated with the crack boom was various and relentless. It coincided with an even broader American crime wave that had been building for two decades. Although the rise of this crime wave long predated crack, the trend was so exacerbated by crack that criminologists got downright apocalyptic in their predictions. James Alan Fox, perhaps the most widely quoted crime expert in the popular press, warned of a coming "bloodbath" of youth violence.

But Fox and the other purveyors of conventional wisdom turned out to be wrong. The bloodbath did not materialize. The crime rate in fact began to fall—so unexpectedly and dramatically and thoroughly that now, from the distance of several years, it is almost hard to recall the crushing grip of that crime wave.

Why did it fall?

For a few reasons, but one of them more surprising than the

rest. Oscar Danilo Blandon, the so-called Johnny Appleseed of Crack, may have been the instigator of one ripple effect, in which by his actions a single person inadvertently causes an ocean of despair. But unbeknownst to just about everybody, another remarkably powerful ripple effect—this one moving in the opposite direction—had just come into play.

Chapter 4

WHERE HAVE ALL THE CRIMINALS GONE?

In 1966, one year after Nicolae Ceauşescu became the Communist dictator of Romania, he made abortion illegal. "The fetus is the property of the entire society," he proclaimed. "Anyone who avoids having children is a deserter who abandons the laws of national continuity."

Such grandiose declarations were commonplace during Ceauşescu's reign, for his master plan—to create a nation worthy of the New Socialist Man—was an exercise in grandiosity. He built palaces for himself while alternately brutalizing and neglecting his citizens. Abandoning agriculture in favor of manufacturing, he forced many of the nation's rural dwellers into unheated apartment buildings. He gave government positions to forty family members including his wife, Elena, who required forty homes and a commensurate supply of fur and jewels. Madame Ceauşescu, known officially as the Best Mother Romania Could

Have, was not particularly maternal. "The worms never get satisfied, regardless of how much food you give them," she said when Romanians complained about the food shortages brought on by her husband's mismanagement. She had her own children bugged to ensure their loyalty.

Ceaușescu's ban on abortion was designed to achieve one of his major aims: to rapidly strengthen Romania by boosting its population. Until 1966, Romania had had one of the most liberal abortion policies in the world. Abortion was in fact the main form of birth control, with four abortions for every live birth. Now, virtually overnight, abortion was forbidden. The only exemptions were mothers who already had four children or women with significant standing in the Communist Party. At the same time, all contraception and sex education were banned. Government agents sardonically known as the Menstrual Police regularly rounded up women in their workplaces to administer pregnancy tests. If a woman repeatedly failed to conceive, she was forced to pay a steep "celibacy tax."

Ceaușescu's incentives produced the desired effect. Within one year of the abortion ban, the Romanian birth rate had doubled. These babies were born into a country where, unless you belonged to the Ceaușescu clan or the Communist elite, life was miserable. But these children would turn out to have particularly miserable lives. Compared to Romanian children born just a year earlier, the cohort of children born after the abortion ban would do worse in every measurable way: they would test lower in school, they would have less success in the labor market, and they would also prove much more likely to become criminals.

The abortion ban stayed in effect until Ceaușescu finally lost his grip on Romania. On December 16, 1989, thousands of people took to the streets of Timisoara to protest his corrosive regime. Many of the protestors were teenagers and college students. The police killed dozens of them. One of the opposition leaders, a forty-one-year-old professor, later said it was his thirteen-year-old daughter who insisted he attend the protest, despite his fear. "What is most interesting is that we learned not to be afraid from our children," he said. "Most were aged thirteen to twenty." A few days after the massacre in Timisoara, Ceauşescu gave a speech in Bucharest before one hundred thousand people. Again the young people were out in force. They shouted down Ceauşescu with cries of "Timisoara!" and "Down with the murderers!" His time had come. He and Elena tried to escape the country with $1 billion, but they were captured, given a crude trial, and, on Christmas Day, executed by firing squad.

Of all the Communist leaders deposed in the years bracketing the collapse of the Soviet Union, only Nicolae Ceauşescu met a violent death. It should not be overlooked that his demise was precipitated in large measure by the youth of Romania—a great number of whom, were it not for his abortion ban, would never have been born at all.

The story of abortion in Romania might seem an odd way to begin telling the story of American crime in the 1990s. But it's not. In one important way, the Romanian abortion story is a reverse image of the American crime story. The point of overlap was on that Christmas Day of 1989, when Nicolae Ceauşescu learned the hard way—with a bullet to the head—that his abortion ban had much deeper implications than he knew.

On that day, crime was just about at its peak in the United States. In the previous fifteen years, violent crime had risen

80 percent. It was crime that led the nightly news and the national conversation.

When the crime rate began falling in the early 1990s, it did so with such speed and suddenness that it surprised everyone. It took some experts many years to even recognize that crime was falling, so confident had they been of its continuing rise. Long after crime had peaked, in fact, some of them continued to predict ever darker scenarios. But the evidence was irrefutable: the long and brutal spike in crime was moving in the opposite direction, and it wouldn't stop until the crime rate had fallen back to the levels of forty years earlier.

Now the experts hustled to explain their faulty forecasting. The criminologist James Alan Fox explained that his warning of a "bloodbath" was in fact an intentional overstatement. "I never said there would be blood flowing in the streets," he said, "but I used strong terms like 'bloodbath' to get people's attention. And it did. I don't apologize for using alarmist terms." (If Fox seems to be offering a distinction without a difference—"bloodbath" versus "blood flowing in the streets"—we should remember that even in retreat mode, experts can be self-serving.)

After the relief had settled in, after people remembered how to go about their lives without the pressing fear of crime, there arose a natural question: just where did all those criminals go?

At one level, the answer seemed puzzling. After all, if none of the criminologists, police officials, economists, politicians, or others who traffic in such matters had foreseen the crime decline, how could they suddenly identify its causes?

But this diverse army of experts now marched out a phalanx of hypotheses to explain the drop in crime. A great many newspaper articles would be written on the subject. Their conclusions often hinged on which expert had most recently spoken to which reporter. Here, ranked by frequency of mention, are the crime-drop explanations cited in articles published from 1991 to 2001 in the ten largest-circulation papers in the LexisNexis database:

CRIME-DROP EXPLANATION	NUMBER OF CITATIONS
1. INNOVATIVE POLICING STRATEGIES	52
2. INCREASED RELIANCE ON PRISONS	47
3. CHANGES IN CRACK AND OTHER DRUG MARKETS	33
4. AGING OF THE POPULATION	32
5. TOUGHER GUN-CONTROL LAWS	32
6. STRONG ECONOMY	28
7. INCREASED NUMBER OF POLICE	26
8. ALL OTHER EXPLANATIONS (INCREASED USE OF CAPITAL PUNISHMENT, CONCEALED-WEAPONS LAWS, GUN BUYBACKS, AND OTHERS)	34

If you are the sort of person who likes guessing games, you may wish to spend the next few moments pondering which of the preceding explanations seem to have merit and which don't. Hint: of the seven major explanations on the list, only three can be shown to have contributed to the drop in crime. The others are, for the most part, figments of someone's imagination, self-interest, or wishful thinking. Further hint: one of the greatest measurable causes of the crime drop does not appear on the list at all, for it didn't receive a single newspaper mention.

Let's begin with a fairly uncontroversial one: *the strong economy.* The decline in crime that began in the early 1990s was accompanied by a blistering national economy and a significant drop in unemployment. It might seem to follow that the economy was a hammer that helped beat down crime. But a closer look at the data destroys this theory. It is true that a stronger job market may make certain crimes relatively less attractive. But that is only the case for crimes with a direct financial motivation—burglary, robbery, and auto theft—as opposed to violent crimes like homicide, assault, and rape. Moreover, studies have shown that an unemployment decline of 1 percentage point accounts for a 1 percent drop in nonviolent crime. During the 1990s, the unemployment rate fell by 2 percentage points; nonviolent crime, meanwhile, fell by roughly 40 percent. But an even bigger flaw in the strong-economy theory concerns violent crime. Homicide fell at a greater rate during the 1990s than any other sort of crime, and a number of reliable studies have shown virtually *no* link between the economy and violent crime. This weak link is made even weaker by glancing back to a recent decade, the 1960s, when the economy went on a wild growth spurt—as did violent crime. So while a strong 1990s economy might have seemed, on the surface, a likely explanation for the drop in crime, it almost certainly didn't affect criminal behavior in any significant way.

Unless, that is, "the economy" is construed in a broader sense—as a means to build and maintain hundreds of prisons. Let's now consider another crime-drop explanation: *increased reliance on prisons*. It might help to start by flipping the crime question around. Instead of wondering what made crime fall, think about this: why had it risen so dramatically in the first place?

During the first half of the twentieth century, the incidence of violent crime in the United States was, for the most part, fairly steady. But in the early 1960s, it began to climb. In retrospect, it is clear that one of the major factors pushing this trend was a more lenient justice system. Conviction rates declined during the 1960s, and criminals who were convicted served shorter sentences. This trend was driven in part by an expansion in the rights of people accused of crimes—a long overdue expansion, some would argue. (Others would argue that the expansion went too far.) At the same time, politicians were growing increasingly softer on crime—"for fear of sounding racist," as the economist Gary Becker has written, "since African-Americans and Hispanics commit a disproportionate share of felonies." So if you were the kind of person who might want to commit a crime, the incentives were lining up in your favor: a slimmer likelihood of being convicted and, if convicted, a shorter prison term. Because criminals respond to incentives as readily as anyone, the result was a surge in crime.

It took some time, and a great deal of political turmoil, but these incentives were eventually curtailed. Criminals who would have previously been set free—for drug-related offenses and parole revocation in particular—were instead locked up. Between 1980 and 2000, there was a fifteenfold increase in the number of people sent to prison on drug charges. Many other sentences, especially for violent crime, were lengthened. The total effect was dramatic. By 2000, more than two million people were in prison, roughly four times the number as of 1972. Fully half of that increase took place during the 1990s.

The evidence linking increased punishment with lower crime rates is very strong. Harsh prison terms have been shown to act as both deterrent (for the would-be criminal on the street) and prophylactic (for the would-be criminal who is already locked up). Logical as this may sound, some criminologists have fought the logic. A 1977 academic study called "On Behalf of a Moratorium on Prison Construction" noted that crime rates tend to be high when imprisonment rates are high, and concluded that crime would fall if imprisonment rates could only be lowered. (Fortunately, jailers did not suddenly turn loose their wards and sit back waiting for crime to fall. As the political scientist John J. DiIulio Jr. later commented, "Apparently, it takes a Ph.D. in criminology to doubt that keeping dangerous criminals incarcerated cuts crime.")

The "Moratorium" argument rests on a fundamental confusion of correlation and causality. Consider a parallel argument. The mayor of a city sees that his citizens celebrate wildly when their team wins the World Series. He is intrigued by this correlation but, like the "Moratorium" author, fails to see the direction in which the correlation runs. So the following year, the mayor decrees that his citizens start celebrating the World Series *before the first pitch is thrown*—an act that, in his confused mind, will ensure a victory.

There are certainly plenty of reasons to dislike the huge surge in the prison population. Not everyone is pleased that such a significant fraction of Americans, especially black Americans, live behind bars. Nor does prison even begin to address the root causes of crime, which are diverse and complex. Lastly, prison is hardly a cheap solution: it costs about $25,000 a year to keep someone incarcerated. But if the goal here is to explain the drop in crime in the 1990s, imprisonment is certainly one of the key answers. It accounts for roughly one-third of the drop in crime.

Another crime-drop explanation is often cited in tandem with imprisonment: *the increased use of capital punishment.* The number of executions in the United States quadrupled between the 1980s and the 1990s, leading many people to conclude—in the context of a debate that has been going on for decades—that capital punishment helped drive down crime. Lost in the debate, however, are two important facts.

First, given the rarity with which executions are carried out in this country and the long delays in doing so, no reasonable criminal should be deterred by the threat of execution. Even though capital punishment quadrupled within a decade, there were still only 478 executions in the entire United States during the 1990s. Any parent who has ever said to a recalcitrant child, "Okay, I'm going to count to ten and this time I'm *really* going to punish you," knows the difference between deterrent and empty threat. New York State, for instance, has not as of this writing executed a single criminal since reinstituting its death penalty in 1995. Even among prisoners on death row, the annual execution rate is only 2 percent—compared with the 7 percent annual chance of dying faced by a member of the Black Gangster Disciple Nation crack gang. If life on death row is safer than life on the streets, it's hard to believe that the fear of execution is a driving force in a criminal's calculus. Like the $3 fine for late-arriving parents at the Israeli day-care centers, the negative incentive of capital punishment simply isn't serious enough for a criminal to change his behavior.

The second flaw in the capital punishment argument is even more obvious. Assume for a moment that the death penalty *is* a deterrent. How much crime does it actually deter? The economist Isaac Ehrlich, in an oft-cited 1975 paper, put forth an estimate that is generally considered optimistic: executing 1 criminal translates into 7 fewer homicides that the criminal might have committed. Now do the math. In 1991, there were 14 executions in the United States; in 2001, there were 66. According to Ehrlich's calculation, those 52 additional executions would have accounted for 364 fewer homicides in 2001—not a small drop, to be sure, but less than 4 percent of the actual decrease in homicides that year. So even in a death penalty advocate's best-case scenario, capital punishment could explain only one twenty-fifth of the drop in homicides in the 1990s. And because the death penalty is rarely given for crimes other than homicide, its deterrent effect cannot account for a speck of decline in other violent crimes.

It is extremely unlikely, therefore, that the death penalty, as currently practiced in the United States, exerts any real influence on crime rates. Even many of its onetime supporters have come to this conclusion. "I feel morally and intellectually obligated simply to concede that the death penalty experiment has failed," said U.S. Supreme Court Justice Harry A. Blackmun in 1994, nearly twenty years after he had voted for its reinstatement. "I no longer shall tinker with the machinery of death."

So it wasn't capital punishment that drove crime down, nor was it the booming economy. But higher rates of imprisonment did have a lot to do with it. All those criminals didn't march into jail by themselves, of course. Someone had to investigate the crime, catch the bad guy, and put together the case that would get him convicted. Which naturally leads to a related pair of crime-drop explanations:

Innovative policing strategies
Increased number of police

Let's address the second one first. The number of police officers per capita in the United States rose about 14 percent during the

1990s. Does merely increasing the number of police, however, reduce crime? The answer would seem obvious—yes—but proving that answer isn't so easy. That's because when crime is rising, people clamor for protection, and invariably more money is found for cops. So if you just look at raw correlations between police and crime, you will find that when there are more police, there tends to be more crime. That doesn't mean, of course, that the police are causing the crime, just as it doesn't mean, as some criminologists have argued, that crime will fall if criminals are released from prison.

To show causality, we need a scenario in which more police are hired for reasons completely unrelated to rising crime. If, for instance, police were randomly sprinkled in some cities and not in others, we could look to see whether crime declines in the cities where the police happen to land.

As it turns out, that exact scenario is often created by vote-hungry politicians. In the months leading up to Election Day, incumbent mayors routinely try to lock up the law-and-order vote by hiring more police—even when the crime rate is standing still. So by comparing the crime rate in one set of cities that have recently had an election (and which therefore hired extra police) with another set of cities that had no election (and therefore no extra police), it's possible to tease out the effect of the extra police on crime. The answer: yes indeed, additional police substantially lower the crime rate.

Again, it may help to look backward and see why crime had risen so much in the first place. From 1960 to 1985, the number of police officers *fell* more than 50 percent relative to the number of crimes. In some cases, hiring additional police was considered a violation of the era's liberal aesthetic; in others, it was simply deemed too expensive. This 50 percent decline in police translated into a roughly equal decline in the probability that a given criminal would be caught. Coupled with the above-cited leniency in the other half of the criminal justice system, the courtrooms, this decrease in policing created a strong positive incentive for criminals.

By the 1990s, philosophies—and necessities—had changed. The policing trend was put in reverse, with wide-scale hiring in cities across the country. Not only did all those police act as a deterrent, but they also provided the manpower to imprison criminals who might have otherwise gone uncaught. The hiring of additional police accounted for roughly 10 percent of the 1990s crime drop.

But it wasn't only the number of police that changed in the 1990s; consider the most commonly cited crime-drop explanation of all: *innovative policing strategies.*

There was perhaps no more attractive theory than the belief that smart policing stops crime. It offered a set of bona fide heroes rather than simply a dearth of villains. This theory rapidly became an article of faith because it appealed to the factors that, according to John Kenneth Galbraith, most contribute to the formation of conventional wisdom: the ease with which an idea may be understood and the degree to which it affects our personal well-being.

The story played out most dramatically in New York City, where newly elected mayor Rudolph Giuliani and his hand-picked police commissioner, William Bratton, vowed to fix the city's desperate crime situation. Bratton took a novel approach to policing. He ushered the NYPD into what one senior police official later called "our Athenian period," in which new ideas were given weight over calcified practices. Instead of coddling his precinct commanders, Bratton demanded accountability. Instead of relying solely on old-fashioned cop know-how, he introduced technological solutions like CompStat, a computerized method of addressing crime hot spots.

The most compelling new idea that Bratton brought to life stemmed from the broken window theory, which was conceived by the criminologists James Q. Wilson and George Kelling. The broken window theory argues that minor nuisances, if left unchecked, turn into major nuisances: that is, if someone breaks a window and sees it isn't fixed immediately, he gets the signal that it's all right to break the rest of the windows and maybe set the building afire too.

So with murder raging all around, Bill Bratton's cops began to police the sort of deeds that used to go unpoliced: jumping a subway turnstile, panhandling too aggressively, urinating in the streets, swabbing a filthy squeegee across a car's windshield unless the driver made an appropriate "donation."

Most New Yorkers loved this crackdown on its own merit. But they particularly loved the idea, as stoutly preached by Bratton and Giuliani, that choking off these small crimes was like choking off the criminal element's oxygen supply. Today's turnstile jumper might easily be wanted for yesterday's murder. That junkie peeing in an alley might have been on his way to a robbery.

As violent crime began to fall dramatically, New Yorkers were more than happy to heap laurels on their operatic, Brooklyn-bred mayor and his hatchet-faced police chief with the big Boston accent. But the two strong-willed men weren't very good at sharing the glory. Soon after the city's crime turnaround landed Bratton— and not Giuliani—on the cover of *Time*, Bratton was pushed to resign. He had been police commissioner for just twenty-seven months.

New York City was a clear innovator in police strategies during the 1990s crime drop, and it also enjoyed the greatest decline in crime of any large American city. Homicide rates fell from 30.7 per 100,000 people in 1990 to 8.4 per 100,000 people in 2000, a change of 73.6 percent. But a careful analysis of the facts shows that the innovative policing strategies probably had little effect on this huge decline.

First, the drop in crime in New York began in 1990. By the end of 1993, the rate of property crime and violent crime, including homicides, had already fallen nearly 20 percent. Rudolph Giuliani, however, did not become mayor—and install Bratton—until early 1994. Crime was well on its way down before either man arrived. And it would continue to fall long after Bratton was bumped from office.

Second, the new police strategies were accompanied by a much more significant change within the police force: a hiring binge. Between 1991 and 2001, the NYPD grew by 45 percent, more than three times the national average. As argued above, an increase in the number of police, regardless of new strategies, *has* been proven to reduce crime. By a conservative calculation, this huge expansion of New York's police force would be expected to reduce crime in New York by 18 percent relative to the national average. If you subtract that 18 percent from New York's homicide reduction, thereby discounting the effect of the police-hiring surge, New York no longer leads the nation with its 73.6 percent drop; it goes straight to the middle of the pack. Many of those new police were in fact hired by David Dinkins, the mayor whom

Giuliani defeated. Dinkins had been desperate to secure the law-and-order vote, having known all along that his opponent would be Giuliani, a former federal prosecutor. (The two men had run against each other four years earlier as well.) So those who wish to credit Giuliani with the crime drop may still do so, for it was his own law-and-order reputation that made Dinkins hire all those police. In the end, of course, the police increase helped everyone—but it helped Giuliani a lot more than Dinkins.

Most damaging to the claim that New York's police innovations radically lowered crime is one simple and often overlooked fact: crime went down *everywhere* during the 1990s, not only in New York. Few other cities tried the kind of strategies that New York did, and certainly none with the same zeal. But even in Los Angeles, a city notorious for bad policing, crime fell at about the same rate as it did in New York once the growth in New York's police force is accounted for.

It would be churlish to argue that smart policing isn't a good thing. Bill Bratton certainly deserves credit for invigorating New York's police force. But there is frighteningly little evidence that his strategy was the crime panacea that he and the media deemed it. The next step will be to continue measuring the impact of police innovations—in Los Angeles, for instance, where Bratton himself became police chief in late 2002. While he duly instituted some of the innovations that were his hallmark in New York, Bratton announced that his highest priority was a more basic one: finding the money to hire thousands of new police officers.

Now to explore another pair of common crime-drop explanations:

Tougher gun laws
Changes in crack and other drug markets

First, the guns. Debates on this subject are rarely coolheaded. Gun advocates believe that gun laws are too strict; opponents believe exactly the opposite. How can intelligent people view the world so differently? Because a gun raises a complex set of issues that change according to one factor: whose hand happens to be holding the gun.

It might be worthwhile to take a step back and ask a rudimentary question: what *is* a gun? It's a tool that can be used to kill someone, of course, but more significantly, a gun is a great disrupter of the natural order.

A gun scrambles the outcome of any dispute. Let's say that a tough guy and a not-so-tough guy exchange words in a bar, which leads to a fight. It's pretty obvious to the not-so-tough guy that he'll be beaten, so why bother fighting? The pecking order remains intact. But if the not-so-tough guy happens to have a gun, he stands a good chance of winning. In this scenario, the introduction of a gun may well lead to more violence.

Now instead of the tough guy and the not-so-tough guy, picture a high-school girl out for a nighttime stroll when she is suddenly set upon by a mugger. What if only the mugger is armed? What if only the girl is armed? What if *both* are armed? A gun opponent might argue that the gun has to be kept out of the mugger's hands in the first place. A gun advocate might argue that the high-school girl needs to have a gun to disrupt what has become the natural order: it's the bad guys that have the guns. (If the girl scares off the mugger, then the introduction of a gun in this case may lead to *less* violence.) Any mugger with even a little initiative is bound to be armed, for in a country like the United States, with a thriving black market in guns, anyone can get hold of one.

There are enough guns in the United States that if you gave one to every adult, you would run out of adults before you ran out of guns. Nearly two-thirds of U.S. homicides involve a gun, a far greater fraction than in other industrialized countries. Our homicide rate is also much higher than in those countries. It would therefore seem likely that our homicide rate is so high in part because guns are so easily available. Research indeed shows this to be true.

But guns are not the whole story. In Switzerland, every adult male is issued an assault rifle for militia duty and is allowed to keep the gun at home. On a per capita basis, Switzerland has more firearms than just about any other country, and yet it is one of the safest places in the world. In other words, guns do not cause crime. That said, the established U.S. methods of keeping guns away from the people who *do* cause crime are, at best, feeble. And since a gun—unlike a bag of cocaine or a car or a pair of pants— lasts pretty much forever, even turning off the spigot of new guns still leaves an ocean of available ones.

So bearing all this in mind, let's consider a variety of recent gun initiatives to see the impact they may have had on crime in the 1990s.

The most famous gun-control law is the Brady Act, passed in 1993, which requires a criminal check and a waiting period before a person can purchase a handgun. This solution may have seemed appealing to politicians, but to an economist it doesn't make much sense. Why? Because regulation of a legal market is bound to fail when a healthy black market exists for the same product. With guns so cheap and so easy to get, the standard criminal has no incentive to fill out a firearms application at his local gun shop and then wait a week. The Brady Act, accordingly, has proven to be practically impotent in lowering crime. (A study of imprisoned felons showed that even before the Brady Act, only about one-fifth of the criminals had bought their guns through a licensed dealer.) Various local gun-control laws have also failed. Washington, D.C., and Chicago both instituted handgun bans well before crime began to fall across the country in the 1990s, and yet those two cities were laggards, not leaders, in the national reduction in crime. One deterrent that *has* proven moderately effective is a stiff increase in prison time for anyone caught in possession of an illegal gun. But there is plenty of room for improvement. Not that this is likely, but if the death penalty were assessed to anyone carrying an illegal gun, and if the penalty were actually enforced, gun crimes would surely plunge.

Another staple of 1990s crime fighting—and of the evening news—was the gun buyback. You remember the image: a menacing, glistening heap of firearms surrounded by the mayor, the police chief, the neighborhood activists. It made for a nice photo op, but that's about as meaningful as a gun buyback gets. The guns that are turned in tend to be heirlooms or junk. The payoff to the gun seller—usually $50 or $100, but in one California buyback, three free hours of psychotherapy—isn't an adequate incentive for anyone who actually plans to use his gun. And the number of surrendered guns is no match for even the number of new guns simultaneously coming to market. Given the number of handguns in the United States and the number of homicides each year, the likelihood that a particular gun was used to kill someone that year is 1 in 10,000. The typical gun buyback program yields fewer than 1,000 guns—which translates into an expectation of less than one-tenth of one homicide per buyback. Not enough, that is, to make even a sliver of impact on the fall of crime.

Then there is an opposite argument—that we need *more* guns on the street, but in the hands of the right people (like the high-school girl above, instead of her mugger). The economist John R. Lott Jr. is the main champion of this idea. His calling card is the book *More Guns, Less Crime*, in which he argues that violent crime has decreased in areas where law-abiding citizens are allowed to carry concealed weapons. His theory might be surprising, but it is sensible. If a criminal thinks his potential victim may be armed, he may be deterred from committing the crime. Handgun opponents call Lott a pro-gun ideologue, and Lott let himself become a lightning rod for gun controversy. He exacerbated his trouble by creating a pseudonym, "Mary Rosh," to defend his theory in online debates. Rosh, identifying herself as a former student of Lott's, praised her teacher's intellect, his evenhandedness, his charisma. "I have to say that he was the best professor that I ever had," s/he wrote. "You wouldn't know that he was a 'right-wing' ideologue from the class. . . . There were a group of us students who would try to take any class that he taught. Lott finally had to tell us that it was best for us to try and take classes from other professors more to be exposed to other ways of teaching graduate material." Then there was the troubling allegation that Lott actually invented some of the survey data that support his more-guns/less-crime theory. Regardless of whether the data were faked, Lott's admittedly intriguing hypothesis doesn't seem to be true. When other scholars have tried to replicate his results, they found that right-to-carry laws simply don't bring down crime.

• • •

Consider the next crime-drop explanation: *the bursting of the crack bubble.* Crack cocaine was such a potent, addictive drug that a hugely profitable market had been created practically overnight. True, it was only the leaders of the crack gangs who were getting rich. But that only made the street-level dealers all the more desperate to advance. Many of them were willing to kill their rivals to do so, whether the rival belonged to the same gang or a different one. There were also gun battles over valuable drug-selling corners. The typical crack murder involved one crack dealer shooting another (or two of them, or three) and not, contrary to conventional wisdom, some bug-eyed crackhead shooting a shopkeeper over a few dollars. The result was a huge increase in violent crime. One study found that more than 25 percent of the homicides in New York City in 1988 were crack-related.

The violence associated with crack began to ebb in about 1991. This has led many people to think that crack itself went away. It didn't. Smoking crack remains much more popular today than most people realize. Nearly 5 percent of all arrests in the United States are still related to cocaine (as against 6 percent at crack's peak); nor have emergency room visits for crack users diminished all that much.

What *did* go away were the huge profits for selling crack. The price of cocaine had been falling for years, and it got only cheaper as crack grew more popular. Dealers began to underprice one another; profits vanished. The crack bubble burst as dramatically as the Nasdaq bubble would eventually burst. (Think of the first generation of crack dealers as the Microsoft millionaires; think of the second generation as Pets.com.) As veteran crack dealers were killed or sent to prison, younger dealers decided that the smaller profits didn't justify the risk. The tournament had lost its allure.

It was no longer worth killing someone to steal their crack turf, and certainly not worth being killed.

So the violence abated. From 1991 to 2001, the homicide rate among young black men—who were disproportionately represented among crack dealers—fell 48 percent, compared to 30 percent for older black men and older white men. (Another minor contributor to the falling homicide rate is the fact that some crack dealers took to shooting their enemies in the buttocks rather than murdering them; this method of violent insult was considered more degrading—and was obviously less severely punished—than murder.) All told, the crash of the crack market accounted for roughly 15 percent of the crime drop of the 1990s—a substantial factor, to be sure, though it should be noted that crack was responsible for far more than 15 percent of the crime *increase* of the 1980s. In other words, the net effect of crack is still being felt in the form of violent crime, to say nothing of the miseries the drug itself continues to cause.

The final pair of crime-drop explanations concern two demographic trends. The first one received many media citations: *aging of the population*.

Until crime fell so drastically, no one talked about this theory at all. In fact, the "bloodbath" school of criminology was touting exactly the opposite theory—that an increase in the teenage share of the population would produce a crop of superpredators who would lay the nation low. "Just beyond the horizon, there lurks a cloud that the winds will soon bring over us," James Q. Wilson wrote in 1995. "The population will start getting younger again. . . . Get ready."

But overall, the teenage share of the population *wasn't* getting much bigger. Criminologists like Wilson and James Alan Fox had badly misread the demographic data. The real population growth in the 1990s was in fact among the elderly. While this may have been scary news in terms of Medicare and Social Security, the average American had little to fear from the growing horde of oldsters. It shouldn't be surprising to learn that elderly people are not very criminally intent; the average sixty-five-year-old is about one-fiftieth as likely to be arrested as the average teenager. That is what makes this aging-of-the-population theory of crime reduction so appealingly tidy: since people mellow out as they get older, more older people must lead to less crime. But a thorough look at the data reveals that the graying of America did nothing to bring down crime in the 1990s. Demographic change is too slow and subtle a process—you don't graduate from teenage hoodlum to senior citizen in just a few years—to even begin to explain the suddenness of the crime decline.

There was another demographic change, however, unforeseen and long-gestating, that did drastically reduce crime in the 1990s.

Think back for a moment to Romania in 1966. Suddenly and without warning, Nicolae Ceauşescu declared abortion illegal. The children born in the wake of the abortion ban were much more likely to become criminals than children born earlier. Why was that? Studies in other parts of Eastern Europe and in Scandinavia from the 1930s through the 1960s reveal a similar trend. In most of these cases, abortion was not forbidden outright, but a woman had to receive permission from a judge in order to obtain one. Researchers found that in the instances where the woman was denied an abortion, she often resented her baby and failed to provide it with a good home. Even when controlling for the income, age, education, and health of the mother, the researchers found that these children too were more likely to become criminals.

The United States, meanwhile, has had a different abortion history than Europe. In the early days of the nation, it was permissible to have an abortion prior to "quickening"—that is, when the first movements of the fetus could be felt, usually around the sixteenth to eighteenth week of pregnancy. In 1828, New York became the first state to restrict abortion; by 1900 it had been made illegal throughout the country. Abortion in the twentieth century was often dangerous and usually expensive. Fewer poor women, therefore, had abortions. They also had less access to birth control. What they did have, accordingly, was a lot more babies.

In the late 1960s, several states began to allow abortion under extreme circumstances: rape, incest, or danger to the mother. By 1970 five states had made abortion entirely legal and broadly available: New York, California, Washington, Alaska, and Hawaii. On January 22, 1973, legalized abortion was suddenly extended to the entire country with the U.S. Supreme Court's ruling in *Roe v. Wade*. The majority opinion, written by Justice Harry Blackmun, spoke specifically to the would-be mother's predicament:

> *The detriment that the State would impose upon the pregnant woman by denying this choice altogether is apparent. . . . Maternity, or additional offspring, may force upon the woman a distressful life and future. Psychological harm may be imminent. Mental and physical health may be taxed by child care. There is also the distress, for all concerned, associated with the unwanted child, and there is the problem of bringing a child into a family already unable, psychologically and otherwise, to care for it.*

The Supreme Court gave voice to what the mothers in Romania and Scandinavia—and elsewhere—had long known: when a woman does not want to have a child, she usually has good reason. She may be unmarried or in a bad marriage. She may consider herself too poor to raise a child. She may think her life is too unstable or unhappy, or she may think that her drinking or drug use will damage the baby's health. She may believe that she is too young or hasn't yet received enough education. She may want a child badly but in a few years, not now. For any of a hundred reasons, she may feel that she cannot provide a home environment that is conducive to raising a healthy and productive child.

In the first year after *Roe v. Wade*, some 750,000 women had abortions in the United States (representing one abortion for every 4 live births). By 1980 the number of abortions reached 1.6 million (one for every 2.25 live births), where it leveled off. In a country of 225 million people, 1.6 million abortions per year—one for every 140 Americans—may not have seemed so dramatic. In the first year after Nicolae Ceauşescu's death, when abortion was reinstated in Romania, there was one abortion for every *twenty-two* Romanians. But still: 1.6 million American women a year who got pregnant were suddenly not having those babies.

Before *Roe v. Wade*, it was predominantly the daughters of middle- or upper-class families who could arrange and afford a safe illegal abortion. Now, instead of an illegal procedure that might cost $500, any woman could easily obtain an abortion, often for less than $100.

What sort of woman was most likely to take advantage of *Roe v. Wade*? Very often she was unmarried or in her teens or poor, and sometimes all three. What sort of future might her child have had? One study has shown that the typical child who went unborn in the earliest years of legalized abortion would have been 50 percent more likely than average to live in poverty; he would have also been 60 percent more likely to grow up with just one parent. These two factors—childhood poverty and a single-parent household—are among the strongest predictors that a child will have a criminal future. Growing up in a single-parent home roughly doubles a child's propensity to commit crime. So does having a teenage mother. Another study has shown that low maternal education is the single most powerful factor leading to criminality.

In other words, the very factors that drove millions of American women to have an abortion also seemed to predict that their children, had they been born, would have led unhappy and possibly criminal lives.

To be sure, the legalization of abortion in the United States had myriad consequences. Infanticide fell dramatically. So did shotgun marriages, as well as the number of babies put up for adoption (which has led to the boom in the adoption of foreign babies). Conceptions rose by nearly 30 percent, but births actually *fell* by 6 percent, indicating that many women were using abortion as a method of birth control, a crude and drastic sort of insurance policy.

Perhaps the most dramatic effect of legalized abortion, however, and one that would take years to reveal itself, was its impact on crime. In the early 1990s, just as the first cohort of children born after *Roe v. Wade* was hitting its late teen years—the years during which young men enter their criminal prime—the rate of crime began to fall. What this cohort was missing, of course, were the children who stood the greatest chance of becoming criminals. And the crime rate continued to fall as an entire generation came of age minus the children whose mothers had not wanted to bring a child into the world. Legalized abortion led to less unwantedness; unwantedness leads to high crime; legalized abortion, therefore, led to less crime.

This theory is bound to provoke a variety of reactions, ranging from disbelief to revulsion, and a variety of objections, ranging from the quotidian to the moral. The likeliest first objection is the most straightforward one: is the theory true? Perhaps abortion and crime are merely correlated and not causal.

It may be more comforting to believe what the newspapers say, that the drop in crime was due to brilliant policing and clever gun control and a surging economy. We have evolved with a tendency to link causality to things we can touch or feel, not to some distant or difficult phenomenon. We believe especially in near-term causes: a snake bites your friend, he screams with pain, and he dies. The snakebite, you conclude, must have killed him. Most of the time, such a reckoning is correct. But when it comes to cause and effect, there is often a trap in such open-and-shut thinking. We smirk now when we think of ancient cultures that embraced faulty causes—the warriors who believed, for instance, that it was their raping of a virgin that brought them victory on the battle-field. But we too embrace faulty causes, usually at the urging of an expert proclaiming a truth in which he has a vested interest.

How, then, can we tell if the abortion-crime link is a case of causality rather than simply correlation?

One way to test the effect of abortion on crime would be to measure crime data in the five states where abortion was made legal before the Supreme Court extended abortion rights to the rest of the country. In New York, California, Washington, Alaska, and Hawaii, a woman had been able to obtain a legal abortion for at least two years before *Roe v. Wade*. And indeed, those early-legalizing states saw crime begin to fall earlier than the other forty-five states and the District of Columbia. Between 1988 and 1994, violent crime in the early-legalizing states fell 13 percent compared to the other states; between 1994 and 1997, their murder rates fell 23 percent more than those of the other states.

But what if those early legalizers simply got lucky? What else might we look for in the data to establish an abortion-crime link?

One factor to look for would be a correlation between each state's abortion rate and its crime rate. Sure enough, the states with the highest abortion rates in the 1970s experienced the greatest crime drops in the 1990s, while states with low abortion rates experienced smaller crime drops. (This correlation exists even when controlling for a variety of factors that influence crime: a state's level of incarceration, number of police, and its economic situation.) Since 1985, states with high abortion rates have experienced a roughly 30 percent drop in crime relative to low-abortion states. (New York City had high abortion rates *and* lay within an early-legalizing state, a pair of facts that further dampen the claim that innovative policing caused the crime drop.) Moreover, there was no link between a given state's abortion rate and its crime rate *before* the late 1980s—when the first cohort affected by legalized abortion was reaching its criminal prime—which is yet another indication that *Roe v. Wade* was indeed the event that tipped the crime scale.

There are even more correlations, positive and negative, that shore up the abortion-crime link. In states with high abortion rates, the entire decline in crime was among the post-*Roe* cohort as opposed to older criminals. Also, studies of Australia and Canada have since established a similar link between legalized abortion and crime. And the post-*Roe* cohort was not only missing thousands of young male criminals but also thousands of single, teenage mothers—for many of the aborted baby girls would have been the children most likely to replicate their *own* mothers' tendencies.

To discover that abortion was one of the greatest crime-lowering factors in American history is, needless to say, jarring. It feels less Darwinian than Swiftian; it calls to mind a long-ago dart attributed to G. K. Chesterton: when there aren't enough hats to go around, the problem isn't solved by lopping off some heads. The crime drop was, in the language of economists, an "unintended benefit" of legalized abortion. But one need not oppose abortion on moral or religious grounds to feel shaken by the notion of a private sadness being converted into a public good.

Indeed, there are plenty of people who consider abortion itself to be a violent crime. One legal scholar called legalized abortion worse than either slavery (since it routinely involves death) or the Holocaust (since the number of post-*Roe* abortions in the United States, roughly thirty-seven million as of 2004, outnumber the six million Jews killed in Europe). Whether or not one feels so strongly about abortion, it remains a singularly charged issue. Anthony V. Bouza, a former top police official in both the Bronx and Minneapolis, discovered this when he ran for Minnesota governor in 1994. A few years earlier, Bouza had written a book in which he called abortion "arguably the only effective crime-prevention device adopted in this nation since the late 1960s." When Bouza's opinion was publicized just before the election, he fell sharply in the polls. And then he lost.

However a person feels about abortion, a question is likely to come to mind: what are we to make of the trade-off of more abortion for less crime? Is it even possible to put a number on such a complicated transaction?

As it happens, economists have a curious habit of affixing numbers to complicated transactions. Consider the effort to save the northern spotted owl from extinction. One economic study found that in order to protect roughly five thousand owls, the opportunity costs—that is, the income surrendered by the logging industry and others—would be $46 billion, or just over $9 million per owl. After the *Exxon Valdez* oil spill in 1989, another study estimated the amount that the typical American household would be willing to pay to avoid another such disaster: $31. An economist can affix a value even to a particular body part. Consider the schedule that the state of Connecticut uses to compensate for work-related injuries.

LOST OR DAMAGED BODY PART	COMPENSATED WEEKS OF PAY
FINGER (FIRST)	36
FINGER (SECOND)	29
FINGER (THIRD)	21
FINGER (FOURTH)	17
THUMB (MASTER HAND)	63
THUMB (OTHER HAND)	54
HAND (MASTER)	168
HAND (OTHER)	155
ARM (MASTER)	208
ARM (OTHER)	194
TOE (GREAT)	28
TOE (ANY OTHER)	9
FOOT	125

LOST OR DAMAGED BODY PART	COMPENSATED WEEKS OF PAY
NOSE	35
EYE	157
KIDNEY	117
LIVER	347
PANCREAS	416
HEART	520
MAMMARY	35
OVARY	35
TESTIS	35
PENIS	35–104
VAGINA	35–104

Now, for the sake of argument, let's ask an outrageous question: what is the relative value of a fetus and a newborn? If faced with the Solomonic task of sacrificing the life of one newborn for an indeterminate number of fetuses, what number might you choose? This is nothing but a thought exercise—obviously there is no right answer—but it may help clarify the impact of abortion on crime.

For a person who is either resolutely pro-life or resolutely pro-choice, this is a simple calculation. The first, believing that life begins at conception, would likely consider the value of a fetus versus the value of a newborn to be 1:1. The second person, believing that a woman's right to an abortion trumps any other factor, would likely argue that no number of fetuses can equal even one newborn.

But let's consider a third person. (If you identify strongly with either person number one or person number two, the following exercise might strike you as offensive, and you may want to skip this paragraph and the next.) This third person does not believe that a fetus is the 1:1 equivalent of a newborn, yet neither does he believe that a fetus has no relative value. Let's say that he is forced, for the sake of argument, to affix a relative value, and he decides that 1 newborn is worth 100 fetuses.

There are roughly 1.5 million abortions in the United States every year. For a person who believes that 1 newborn is worth 100 fetuses, those 1.5 million abortions would translate—dividing 1.5 million by 100—into the equivalent of a loss of 15,000 human lives. Fifteen thousand lives: that happens to be about the same number of people who die in homicides in the United States every year. And it is far more than the number of homicides eliminated each year due to legalized abortion. So even for someone who considers a fetus to be worth only one one-hundredth of a human being, the trade-off between higher abortion and lower crime is, by an economist's reckoning, terribly inefficient.

What the link between abortion and crime does say is this: when the government gives a woman the opportunity to make her own decision about abortion, she generally does a good job of figuring out if she is in a position to raise the baby well. If she decides she can't, she often chooses the abortion.

But once a woman decides she *will* have her baby, a pressing question arises: what are parents supposed to do once a child is born?

Chapter 5

WHAT MAKES A PERFECT PARENT?

Has there ever been another art so devoutly converted into a science as the art of parenting?

Over the recent decades, a vast and diverse flock of parenting experts has arisen. Anyone who tries even casually to follow their advice may be stymied, for the conventional wisdom on parenting seems to shift by the hour. Sometimes it is a case of one expert differing from another. At other times the most vocal experts suddenly agree en masse that the old wisdom was wrong and that the new wisdom is, for a little while at least, irrefutably right. Breast feeding, for example, is the only way to guarantee a healthy and intellectually advanced child—unless bottle feeding is the answer. A baby should always be put to sleep on her back—until it is decreed that she should only be put to sleep on her stomach. Eating liver is either a) toxic or b) imperative for brain development. Spare the rod and spoil the child; spank the child and go to jail.

In her book *Raising America: Experts, Parents, and a Century of Advice About Children*, Ann Hulbert documented how parenting experts contradict one another and even themselves. Their banter might be hilarious were it not so confounding and, often, scary. Gary Ezzo, who in the *Babywise* book series endorses an "infant-management strategy" for moms and dads trying to "achieve excellence in parenting," stresses how important it is to train a baby, early on, to sleep alone through the night. Otherwise, Ezzo warns, sleep deprivation might "negatively impact an infant's developing central nervous system" and lead to learning disabilities. Advocates of "co-sleeping," meanwhile, warn that sleeping alone is harmful to a baby's psyche and that he should be brought into the "family bed." What about stimulation? In 1983 T. Berry Brazelton wrote that a baby arrives in the world "beautifully prepared for the role of learning about him- or herself and the world all around." Brazelton favored early, ardent stimulation—an "interactive" child. One hundred years earlier, however, L. Emmett Holt cautioned that a baby is not a "plaything." There should be "no forcing, no pressure, no undue stimulation" during the first two years of a child's life, Holt believed; the brain is growing so much during that time that overstimulation might cause "a great deal of harm." He also believed that a crying baby should never be picked up unless it is in pain. As Holt explained, a baby should be left to cry for fifteen to thirty minutes a day: "It is the baby's exercise."

The typical parenting expert, like experts in other fields, is prone to sound exceedingly sure of himself. An expert doesn't so much argue the various sides of an issue as plant his flag firmly on one side. That's because an expert whose argument reeks of restraint or nuance often doesn't get much attention. An expert must be bold if he hopes to alchemize his homespun theory into conventional wisdom. His best chance of doing so is to engage the public's emotions, for emotion is the enemy of rational argument. And as emotions go, one of them—fear—is more potent than the rest. The superpredator, Iraqi weapons of mass destruction, mad-cow disease, crib death: how can we fail to heed the expert's advice on these horrors when, like that mean uncle telling too-scary stories to too-young children, he has reduced us to quivers?

No one is more susceptible to an expert's fearmongering than a parent. Fear is in fact a major component of the act of parenting. A parent, after all, is the steward of another creature's life, a creature who in the beginning is more helpless than the newborn of nearly any other species. This leads a lot of parents to spend a lot of their parenting energy simply being scared.

The problem is that they are often scared of the wrong things. It's not their fault, really. Separating facts from rumors is always hard work, especially for a busy parent. And the white noise generated by the experts—to say nothing of the pressure exerted by fellow parents—is so overwhelming that they can barely think for themselves. The facts they do manage to glean have usually been varnished or exaggerated or otherwise taken out of context to serve an agenda that isn't their own.

Consider the parents of an eight-year-old girl named, say, Molly. Her two best friends, Amy and Imani, each live nearby. Molly's parents know that Amy's parents keep a gun in their house, so they have forbidden Molly to play there. Instead, Molly spends a lot of time at Imani's house, which has a swimming pool in the backyard. Molly's parents feel good about having made such a smart choice to protect their daughter.

But according to the data, their choice isn't smart at all. In a given year, there is one drowning of a child for every 11,000 residential pools in the United States. (In a country with 6 million pools, this means that roughly 550 children under the age of ten drown each year.) Meanwhile, there is 1 child killed by a gun for every 1 million-plus guns. (In a country with an estimated 200 million guns, this means that roughly 175 children under ten die each year from guns.) The likelihood of death by pool (1 in 11,000) versus death by gun (1 in 1 million-plus) isn't even close: Molly is far more likely to die in a swimming accident at Imani's house than in gunplay at Amy's.

But most of us are, like Molly's parents, terrible risk assessors. Peter Sandman, a self-described "risk communications consultant" in Princeton, New Jersey, made this point in early 2004 after a single case of mad-cow disease in the United States prompted an antibeef frenzy. "The basic reality," Sandman told *The New York Times*, "is that the risks that scare people and the risks that kill people are very different."

Sandman offered a comparison between mad-cow disease (a superscary but exceedingly rare threat) and the spread of food-borne pathogens in the average home kitchen (exceedingly common but somehow not very scary). "Risks that you control are much less a source of outrage than risks that are out of your control," Sandman said. "In the case of mad-cow, it feels like it's beyond my control. I can't tell if my meat has prions in it or not. I can't see it, I can't smell it. Whereas dirt in my own kitchen is very much in my own control. I can clean my sponges. I can clean the floor."

Sandman's "control" principle might also explain why most people are more scared of flying in an airplane than driving a car. Their thinking goes like this: since I control the car, I am the one keeping myself safe; since I have no control of the airplane, I am at the mercy of myriad external factors.

So which should we actually fear more, flying or driving?

It might first help to ask a more basic question: what, exactly, are we afraid of? Death, presumably. But the fear of death needs to be narrowed down. Of course we all know that we are bound to die, and we might worry about it casually. But if you are told that you have a 10 percent chance of dying within the next year, you might worry a lot more, perhaps even choosing to live your life differently. And if you are told that you have 10 percent chance of dying within the next minute, you'll probably panic. So it's the *imminent* possibility of death that drives the fear—which means that the most sensible way to calculate fear of death would be to think about it on a per-hour basis.

If you are taking a trip and have the choice of driving or flying, you might wish to consider the per-hour death rate of driving versus flying. It is true that many more people die in the United States each year in motor vehicle accidents (roughly forty thousand) than in airplane crashes (fewer than one thousand). But it's also true that most people spend a lot more time in cars than in airplanes. (More people die even in boating accidents each year than in airplane crashes; as we saw with swimming pools versus guns, water is a lot more dangerous than most people think.) The per-*hour* death rate of driving versus flying, however, is about equal. The two contraptions are equally likely (or, in truth, unlikely) to lead to death.

But fear best thrives in the present tense. That is why experts rely on it; in a world that is increasingly impatient with long-term processes, fear is a potent short-term play. Imagine that you are a government official charged with procuring the funds to fight one of two proven killers: terrorist attacks and heart disease. Which cause do you think the members of Congress will open up the coffers for? The likelihood of any given person being killed in a terrorist attack is far smaller than the likelihood that the same person will clog up his arteries with fatty food and die of heart disease. But a terrorist attack happens *now;* death by heart disease is some distant, quiet catastrophe. Terrorist acts lie beyond our control; french fries do not. Just as important as the control factor is what Peter Sandman calls the dread factor. Death by terrorist attack (or mad-cow disease) is considered wholly dreadful; death by heart disease is, for some reason, not.

Sandman is an expert who works both sides of the aisle. One day he might help a group of environmentalists expose a public health hazard. His client the next day could be a fast-food CEO trying to deal with an *E. coli* outbreak. Sandman has reduced his expertise to a tidy equation: Risk = hazard + outrage. For the CEO with the bad hamburger meat, Sandman engages in "outrage reduction"; for the environmentalists, it's "outrage increase."

Note that Sandman addresses the outrage but not the hazard itself. He concedes that outrage and hazard do not carry equal weight in his risk equation. "When hazard is high and outrage is low, people underreact," he says. "And when hazard is low and outrage is high, they overreact."

So why is a swimming pool less frightening than a gun? The thought of a child being shot through the chest with a neighbor's gun is gruesome, dramatic, horrifying—in a word, outrageous. Swimming pools do not inspire outrage. This is due in part to the familiarity factor. Just as most people spend more time in cars than in airplanes, most of us have a lot more experience swimming in pools than shooting guns. But it takes only about thirty seconds for a child to drown, and it often happens noiselessly. An infant can drown in water as shallow as a few inches. The steps to prevent drowning, meanwhile, are pretty straightforward: a watchful adult, a fence around the pool, a locked back door so a toddler doesn't slip outside unnoticed.

If every parent followed these precautions, the lives of perhaps four hundred young children could be saved each year. That would outnumber the lives saved by two of the most widely promoted inventions in recent memory: safer cribs and child car seats. The data show that car seats are, at best, nominally helpful. It is certainly safer to keep a child in the rear seat than sitting on a lap in the front seat, where in the event of an accident he essentially becomes a projectile. But the safety to be gained here is from preventing the kids from riding shotgun, not from strapping them into a $200 car seat. Nevertheless, many parents so magnify the benefit of a car seat that they trek to the local police station or firehouse to have it installed just right. Theirs is a gesture of love, surely, but also a gesture of what might be called obsessive parenting. (Obsessive parents know who they are and are generally proud of the fact; non-obsessive parents also know who the obsessives are and tend to snicker at them.)

Most innovations in the field of child safety are affiliated with—shock of shocks—a new product to be marketed. (Nearly five million car seats are sold each year.) These products are often a response to some growing scare in which, as Peter Sandman might put it, the outrage outweighs the hazard. Compare the four hundred lives that a few swimming pool precautions might save to the number of lives saved by far noisier crusades: child-resistant packaging (an estimated fifty lives a year), flame-retardant pajamas (ten lives), keeping children away from airbags in cars (fewer than five young children a year have been killed by airbags since their introduction), and safety drawstrings on children's clothing (two lives).

Hold on a minute, you say. What does it matter if parents are manipulated by experts and marketers? Shouldn't we applaud any effort, regardless of how minor or manipulative, that makes even one child safer? Don't parents already have enough to worry about? After all, parents are responsible for one of the most awesomely important feats we know: the very shaping of a child's character. Aren't they?

The most radical shift of late in the conventional wisdom on parenting has been provoked by one simple question: how much do parents really matter?

Clearly, *bad* parenting matters a great deal. As the link between abortion and crime makes clear, unwanted children—who are disproportionately subject to neglect and abuse—have worse outcomes than children who were eagerly welcomed by their parents. But how much can those eager parents actually accomplish for their children's sake?

This question represents a crescendo of decades' worth of research. A long line of studies, including research into twins who were separated at birth, had already concluded that genes alone are responsible for perhaps 50 percent of a child's personality and abilities.

So if nature accounts for half of a child's destiny, what accounts for the other half? Surely it must be the nurturing—the Baby Mozart tapes, the church sermons, the museum trips, the French lessons, the bargaining and hugging and quarreling and punishing that, in toto, constitute the act of parenting. But how then to explain another famous study, the Colorado Adoption Project, which followed the lives of 245 babies put up for adoption and found virtually *no* correlation between the child's personality traits and those of his adopted parents? Or the other studies showing that a child's character wasn't much affected whether or not he was sent to day care, whether he had one parent or two, whether his mother worked or didn't, whether he had two mommies or two daddies or one of each?

These nature-nurture discrepancies were addressed in a 1998 book by a little-known textbook author named Judith Rich Harris. *The Nurture Assumption* was in effect an attack on obsessive parenting, a book so provocative that it required two subtitles: *Why Children Turn Out the Way They Do* and *Parents Matter Less than You Think and Peers Matter More.* Harris argued, albeit gently, that parents are wrong to think they contribute so mightily to their child's personality. This belief, she wrote, was a "cultural myth." Harris argued that the top-down influence of parents is overwhelmed by the grassroots effect of peer pressure, the blunt force applied each day by friends and schoolmates.

The unlikeliness of Harris's bombshell—she was a grandmother, no less, without PhD or academic affiliation—prompted both wonder and chagrin. "The public may be forgiven for saying, 'Here we go again,'" wrote one reviewer. "One year we're told bonding is the key, the next that it's birth order. Wait, what really matters is stimulation. The first five years of life are the most important; no, the first three years; no, it's all over by the first year. Forget that: It's all genetics!"

But Harris's theory was duly endorsed by a slate of heavyweights. Among them was Steven Pinker, the cognitive psychologist and bestselling author, who in his own book *Blank Slate* called Harris's views "mind-boggling" (in a good way). "Patients in traditional forms of psychotherapy while away their fifty minutes reliving childhood conflicts and learning to blame their unhappiness on how their parents treated them," Pinker wrote. "Many biographies scavenge through the subject's childhood for the roots of the grown-up's tragedies and triumphs. 'Parenting experts' make women feel like ogres if they slip out of the house to work or skip a reading of *Goodnight Moon*. All these deeply held beliefs will have to be rethought."

Or will they? Parents *must* matter, you tell yourself. Besides, even if peers exert so much influence on a child, isn't it the parents who essentially choose a child's peers? Isn't that why parents agonize over the right neighborhood, the right school, the right circle of friends?

Still, the question of how much parents matter is a good one. It is also terribly complicated. In determining a parent's influence, which dimension of the child are we measuring: his personality? his school grades? his moral behavior? his creative abilities? his salary as an adult? And what weight should we assign each of the many inputs that affect a child's outcome: genes, family environment, socioeconomic level, schooling, discrimination, luck, illness, and so on?

For the sake of argument, let's consider the story of two boys, one white and one black.

The white boy is raised in a Chicago suburb by parents who read widely and involve themselves in school reform. His father, who has a decent manufacturing job, often takes the boy on nature hikes. His mother is a housewife who will eventually go back to college and earn a bachelor's degree in education. The boy is happy and performs very well in school. His teachers think he may be a bona fide math genius. His parents encourage him and are terribly proud when he skips a grade. He has an adoring younger brother who is also very bright. The family even holds literary salons in their home.

The black boy is born in Daytona Beach, Florida, and his mother abandons him at the age of two. His father has a good job in sales but is a heavy drinker. He often beats the little boy with the metal end of a garden hose. One night when the boy is eleven, he is decorating a tabletop Christmas tree—the first one he has ever had—when his father starts beating up a lady friend in the kitchen. He hits her so hard that some teeth fly out of her mouth and land at the base of the boy's Christmas tree, but the boy knows better than to speak up. At school he makes no effort whatsoever. Before long he is selling drugs, mugging suburbanites, carrying a gun. He makes sure to be asleep by the time his father comes home from drinking, and to be out of the house before his father awakes. The father eventually goes to jail for sexual assault. By the age of twelve, the boy is essentially fending for himself.

You don't have to believe in obsessive parenting to think that the second boy doesn't stand a chance and that the first boy has it made. What are the odds that the second boy, with the added handicap of racial discrimination, will turn out to lead a productive life? What are the odds that the first boy, so deftly primed for success, will somehow fail? And how much of his fate should each boy attribute to his parents?

One could theorize forever about what makes the perfect parent. For two reasons, the authors of this book will not do so. The first is that neither of us professes to be a parenting expert (although between us we do have six children under the age of five). The second is that we are less persuaded by parenting theory than by what the data have to say.

Certain facets of a child's outcome—personality, for instance, or creativity—are not easily measured by data. But school performance is. And since most parents would agree that education lies at the core of a child's formation, it would make sense to begin by examining a telling set of school data.

These data concern school choice, an issue that most people feel strongly about in one direction or another. True believers of school choice argue that their tax dollars buy them the right to send their children to the best school possible. Critics worry that school choice will leave behind the worst students in the worst schools. Still, just about every parent seems to believe that her child will thrive if only he can attend the *right* school, the one with an appropriate blend of academics, extracurriculars, friendliness, and safety.

School choice came early to the Chicago Public School system. That's because the CPS, like most urban school districts, had a disproportionate number of minority students. Despite the U.S. Supreme Court's 1954 ruling in *Brown v. Board of Education of Topeka*, which dictated that schools be desegregated, many black CPS students continued to attend schools that were nearly all-black. So in 1980 the U.S. Department of Justice and the Chicago Board of Education teamed up to try to better integrate the city's schools. It was decreed that incoming freshmen could apply to virtually any high school in the district.

Aside from its longevity, there are several reasons the CPS school-choice program is a good one to study. It offers a huge data set—Chicago has the third-largest school system in the country, after New York and Los Angeles—as well as an enormous amount of choice (more than sixty high schools) and flexibility. Its take-up rates are accordingly very high, with roughly half of the CPS students opting out of their neighborhood school. But the most serendipitous aspect of the CPS program—for the sake of a study, at least—is how the school-choice game was played.

As might be expected, throwing open the doors of any school to every freshman in Chicago threatened to create bedlam. The schools with good test scores and high graduation rates would be rabidly oversubscribed, making it impossible to satisfy every student's request.

In the interest of fairness, the CPS resorted to a lottery. For a researcher, this is a remarkable boon. A behavioral scientist could hardly design a better experiment in his laboratory. Just as the scientist might randomly assign one mouse to a treatment group and another to a control group, the Chicago school board effec-tively did the same. Imagine two students, statistically identi-cal, each of whom wants to attend a new, better school. Thanks to how the ball bounces in the hopper, one student goes to the new school and the other stays behind. Now imagine multiplying those students by the thousands. The result is a natural experi-ment on a grand scale. This was hardly the goal in the mind of the Chicago school officials who conceived the lottery. But when viewed in this way, the lottery offers a wonderful means of mea-suring just how much school choice—or, really, a better school—truly matters.

So what do the data reveal?

The answer will not be heartening to obsessive parents: in this case, school choice barely mattered at all. It is true that the Chi-cago students who *entered* the school-choice lottery were more likely to graduate than the students who didn't—which seems to suggest that school choice does make a difference. But that's an illusion. The proof is in this comparison: the students who won the lottery and went to a "better" school did no better than equivalent students who lost the lottery and were left behind. That is, a student who opted out of his neighborhood school was more likely to graduate whether or not he actually won the opportunity to go to a new school. What appears to be an advantage gained by going to a new school isn't connected to the new school at all. What this means is that the students—and parents—who choose to opt out tend to be smarter and more academically motivated to begin with. But statistically, they gained no academic benefit by changing schools.

And is it true that the students left behind in neighborhood schools suffered? No: they continued to test at about the same levels as before the supposed brain drain.

There was, however, one group of students in Chicago who did see a dramatic change: those who entered a technical school or career academy. These students performed substantially better than they did in their old academic settings and graduated at a much higher rate than their past performance would have predicted. So the CPS school-choice program did help prepare a small segment of otherwise struggling students for solid careers by giving them practical skills. But it doesn't appear that it made anyone much smarter.

Could it really be that school choice doesn't much matter? No self-respecting parent, obsessive or otherwise, is ready to believe that. But wait: maybe it's because the CPS study measures high-school students; maybe by then the die has already been cast. "There are too many students who arrive at high school not prepared to do high school work," Richard P. Mills, the education commissioner of New York State, noted recently, "too many students who arrive at high school reading, writing, and doing math at the elementary level. We have to correct the problem in the earlier grades."

Indeed, academic studies have substantiated Mills's anxiety. In examining the income gap between black and white adults—it is well established that blacks earn significantly less—scholars have found that the gap is virtually eradicated if the blacks' lower eighth-grade test scores are taken into account. In other words, the black-white income gap is largely a product of a black-white education gap that could have been observed many years earlier. "Reducing the black-white test score gap," wrote the authors of one study, "would do more to promote racial equality than any other strategy that commands broad political support."

So where does that black-white test gap come from? Many theories have been put forth over the years: poverty, genetic makeup, the "summer setback" phenomenon (blacks are thought to lose more ground than whites when school is out of session), racial bias in testing or in teachers' perceptions, and a black backlash against "acting white."

In a paper called "The Economics of 'Acting White,' " the young black Harvard economist Roland G. Fryer Jr. argues that some black students "have tremendous disincentives to invest in particular behaviors (i.e., education, ballet, etc.) due to the fact that they may be deemed a person who is trying to act like a white person (a.k.a. 'selling-out'). Such a label, in some neighborhoods, can carry penalties that range from being deemed a social outcast, to being beaten or killed." Fryer cites the recollections of a young Kareem Abdul-Jabbar, known then as Lew Alcindor, who had just entered the fourth grade in a new school and discovered that he was a better reader than even the seventh graders: "When the kids found this out, I became a target. . . . It was my first time away from home, my first experience in an all-black situation, and I found myself being punished for everything I'd ever been taught was right. I got all A's and was hated for it; I spoke correctly and was called a punk. I had to learn a new language simply to be able to deal with the threats. I had good manners and was a good little boy and paid for it with my hide."

Fryer is also one of the authors of "Understanding the Black-White Test Score Gap in the First Two Years of School." This paper takes advantage of a new trove of government data that helps reliably address the black-white gap. Perhaps more interestingly, the data do a nice job of answering the question that every parent—black, white, and otherwise—wants to ask: what are the factors that do and do not affect a child's performance in the early school years?

In the late 1990s, the U.S. Department of Education undertook a monumental project called the Early Childhood Longitudinal Study. The ECLS sought to measure the academic progress of more than twenty thousand children from kindergarten through the fifth grade. The subjects were chosen from across the country to represent an accurate cross section of American schoolchildren.

The ECLS measured the students' academic performance and gathered typical survey information about each child: his or her race, gender, family structure, socioeconomic status, the level of his or her parents' education, and so on. But the study went well beyond these basics. It also included interviews with the students' parents (and teachers and school administrators), posing a long list of questions more intimate than those in the typical government interview: whether the parents spanked their children, and how often; whether they took them to libraries or museums; how much television the children watched.

The result is an incredibly rich set of data—which, if the right questions are asked of it, tells some surprising stories.

How can this type of data be made to tell a reliable story? By subjecting it to the economist's favorite trick: regression analysis. No, regression analysis is not some forgotten form of psychiatric treatment. It is a powerful—if limited—tool that uses statistical techniques to identify otherwise elusive correlations.

Correlation is nothing more than a statistical term that indicates whether two variables move together. It tends to be cold outside when it snows; those two factors are positively correlated. Sunshine and rain, meanwhile, are negatively correlated. Easy enough—as long as there are only a couple of variables. But with a couple of *hundred* variables, things get harder. Regression analysis is the tool that enables an economist to sort out these huge piles of data. It does so by artificially holding constant every variable except the two he wishes to focus on, and then showing how those two co-vary.

In a perfect world, an economist could run a controlled experiment just as a physicist or a biologist does: setting up two samples, randomly manipulating one of them, and measuring the effect. But an economist rarely has the luxury of such pure experimentation. (That's why the school-choice lottery in Chicago was such a happy accident.) What an economist typically has is a data set with a great many variables, none of them randomly generated, some related and others not. From this jumble, he must determine which factors are correlated and which are not.

In the case of the ECLS data, it might help to think of regression analysis as performing the following task: converting each of those twenty thousand schoolchildren into a sort of circuit board with an identical number of switches. Each switch represents a single category of the child's data: his first-grade math score, his third-grade math score, his first-grade reading score, his third-grade reading score, his mother's education level, his father's income, the number of books in his home, the relative affluence of his neighborhood, and so on.

Now a researcher is able to tease some insights from this very complicated set of data. He can line up all the children who share many characteristics—all the circuit boards that have their switches flipped the same direction—and then pinpoint the single characteristic they *don't* share. This is how he isolates the true impact of that single switch on the sprawling circuit board. This is how the effect of that switch—and, eventually, of every switch—becomes manifest.

Let's say that we want to ask the ECLS data a fundamental question about parenting and education: does having a lot of books in your home lead your child to do well in school? Regression analysis can't quite answer that question, but it can answer a subtly different one: does a child with a lot of books in his home tend to do better than a child with no books? The difference between the first and second questions is the difference between causality (question 1) and correlation (question 2). A regression analysis can demonstrate correlation, but it doesn't prove cause. After all, there are several ways in which two variables can be correlated. X can cause Y; Y can cause X; or it may be that some other factor is causing both X and Y. A regression alone can't tell you whether it snows because it's cold, whether it's cold because it snows, or if the two just happen to go together.

The ECLS data do show, for instance, that a child with a lot of books in his home tends to test higher than a child with no books. So those factors are correlated, and that's nice to know. But higher test scores are correlated with many other factors as well. If you simply measure children with a lot of books against children with no books, the answer may not be very meaningful. Perhaps the number of books in a child's home merely indicates how much money his parents make. What we really want to do is measure two children who are alike in every way except one—in this case, the number of books in their homes—and see if that one factor makes a difference in their school performance.

It should be said that regression analysis is more art than science. (In this regard, it has a great deal in common with parenting itself.) But a skilled practitioner can use it to tell how meaningful a correlation is—and maybe even tell whether that correlation does indicate a causal relationship.

So what does an analysis of the ECLS data tell us about school-children's performance? A number of things. The first one concerns the black-white test score gap.

It has long been observed that black children, even before they set foot in a classroom, underperform their white counterparts. Moreover, black children didn't measure up even when controlling for a wide array of variables. (To control for a variable is essentially to eliminate its influence, much as one golfer uses a handicap against another. In the case of an academic study such as the ECLS, a researcher might control for any number of disadvantages that one student might carry when measured against the average student.) But this new data set tells a different story. After controlling for just a few variables—including the income and education level of the child's parents and the mother's age at the birth of her first child—the gap between black and white children is virtually eliminated at the time the children enter school.

This is an encouraging finding on two fronts. It means that young black children have continued to make gains relative to their white counterparts. It also means that whatever gap remains can be linked to a handful of readily identifiable factors. The data reveal that black children who perform poorly in school do so not because they are black but because a black child is more likely to come from a low-income, low-education household. A typical black child and white child from the same socioeconomic background, however, have the same abilities in math and reading upon entering kindergarten.

Great news, right? Well, not so fast. First of all, because the average black child *is* more likely to come from a low-income, low-education household, the gap is very real: on average, black children still *are* scoring worse. Worse yet, even when the parents' income and education are controlled for, the black-white gap re-appears within just two years of a child's entering school. By the end of first grade, a black child is underperforming a statistically equivalent white child. And the gap steadily grows over the second and third grades.

Why does this happen? That's a hard, complicated question. But one answer may lie in the fact that the school attended by the typical black child is not the same school attended by the typical white child, and the typical black child goes to a school that is simply . . . bad. Even fifty years after *Brown v. Board,* many

American schools are virtually segregated. The ECLS project surveyed roughly one thousand schools, taking samples of twenty children from each. In 35 percent of those schools, not a single black child was included in the sample. The typical white child in the ECLS study attends a school that is only 6 percent black; the typical black child, meanwhile, attends a school that is about 60 percent black.

Just how are the black schools bad? Not, interestingly, in the ways that schools are traditionally measured. In terms of class size, teachers' education, and computer-to-student ratio, the schools attended by blacks and whites are similar. But the typical black student's school has a far higher rate of troublesome indicators, such as gang problems, nonstudents loitering in front of the school, and lack of PTA funding. These schools offer an environment that is simply not conducive to learning.

Black students are hardly the only ones who suffer in bad schools. White children in these schools also perform poorly. In fact, there is essentially no black-white test score gap *within* a bad school in the early years once you control for students' backgrounds. But all students in a bad school, black and white, *do* lose ground to students in good schools. Perhaps educators and researchers are wrong to be so hung up on the black-white test score gap; the bad-school/good-school gap may be the more salient issue. Consider this fact: the ECLS data reveal that black students in good schools *don't* lose ground to their white counterparts, and black students in good schools outperform whites in poor schools.

So according to these data, a child's school does seem to have a clear impact on his academic progress, at least in the early years. Can the same be said for parenting? Did all those Baby Mozart tapes pay off? What about those marathon readings of *Goodnight*

Moon? Was the move to the suburbs worthwhile? Do the kids with PTA parents do better than the kids whose parents have never heard of the PTA?

The wide-ranging ECLS data offer a number of compelling correlations between a child's personal circumstances and his school performance. For instance, once all other factors are controlled for, it is clear that students from rural areas tend to do worse than average. Suburban children, meanwhile, are in the middle of the curve, while urban children tend to score higher than average. (It may be that cities attract a more educated workforce and, therefore, parents with smarter children.) On average, girls test higher than boys, and Asians test higher than whites—although blacks, as we have already established, test similarly to whites from comparable backgrounds and in comparable schools.

Knowing what you now know about regression analysis, conventional wisdom, and the art of parenting, consider the following list of sixteen factors. According to the ECLS data, eight of the factors show a strong correlation—positive or negative—with test scores. The other eight don't seem to matter. Feel free to guess which are which. Keep in mind that these results reflect only a child's early test scores, a useful but fairly narrow measurement; poor testing in early childhood isn't necessarily a great harbinger of future earnings, creativity, or happiness.

The child has highly educated parents.
The child's family is intact.
The child's parents have high socioeconomic status.
The child's parents recently moved into a better neighborhood.
The child's mother was thirty or older at the time of her first child's birth.

The child's mother didn't work between birth and kindergarten.
The child had low birthweight.
The child attended Head Start.
The child's parents speak English in the home.
The child's parents regularly take him to museums.
The child is adopted.
The child is regularly spanked.
The child's parents are involved in the PTA.
The child frequently watches television.
The child has many books in his home.
The child's parents read to him nearly every day.

Here now are the eight factors that *are* strongly correlated with test scores:

The child has highly educated parents.
The child's parents have high socioeconomic status.
The child's mother was thirty or older at the time of her first child's birth.
The child had low birthweight.
The child's parents speak English in the home.
The child is adopted.
The child's parents are involved in the PTA.
The child has many books in his home.

And the eight that aren't:

The child's family is intact.
The child's parents recently moved into a better neighborhood.
The child's mother didn't work between birth and kindergarten.

The child attended Head Start.
The child's parents regularly take him to museums.
The child is regularly spanked.
The child frequently watches television.
The child's parents read to him nearly every day.

Now, two by two:

MATTERS: *The child has highly educated parents.*
DOESN'T: *The child's family is intact.*

A child whose parents are highly educated typically does well in school; not much surprise there. A family with a lot of schooling tends to value schooling. Perhaps more important, parents with higher IQs tend to get more education, and IQ is strongly hereditary. But whether a child's family is intact doesn't seem to matter. Just as the earlier-cited studies show that family structure has little impact on a child's personality, it does not seem to affect his academic abilities either, at least in the early years. This is not to say that families ought to go around splitting up willy-nilly. It should, however, offer encouragement to the roughly twenty million American schoolchildren being raised by a single parent.

MATTERS: *The child's parents have high socioeconomic status.*

DOESN'T: *The child's parents recently moved into a better neighborhood.*

A high socioeconomic status is strongly correlated to higher test scores, which seems sensible. Socioeconomic status is a strong indicator of success in general—it suggests a higher IQ and more education—and successful parents are more likely to have successful children. But moving to a better neighborhood doesn't improve a child's chances in school. It may be that moving itself is a disruptive force; more likely, it's because a nicer house doesn't improve math or reading scores any more than nicer sneakers make you jump higher.

MATTERS: *The child's mother was thirty or older at the time of her first child's birth.*

DOESN'T: *The child's mother didn't work between birth and kindergarten.*

A woman who doesn't have her first child until she is at least thirty is likely to see that child do well in school. This mother tends to be a woman who wanted to get some advanced education or develop traction in her career. She is also likely to *want* a child more than a teenage mother wants a child. This doesn't mean that an older first-time mother is necessarily a better mother, but she has put herself—and her children—in a more advantageous position. (It is worth noting that this advantage is nonexistent for a teenage mother who waits until she is thirty to have her *second* child. The ECLS data show that her second child will perform no better than her first.) At the same time, a mother who stays home from work until her child goes to kindergarten does not seem to provide any advantage. Obsessive parents might find this lack of correlation bothersome—what was the point of all those Mommy and Me classes?—but that is what the data tell us.

MATTERS: *The child had low birthweight.*

DOESN'T: *The child attended Head Start.*

A child who had a low birthweight tends to do poorly in school. It may be that being born prematurely is simply hurtful to a child's overall well-being. It may also be that low birthweight is a strong forecaster of poor parenting, since a mother who smokes or drinks or otherwise mistreats her baby in utero isn't likely to turn things around just because the baby is born. A low-birthweight child, in turn, is more likely to be a poor child—and, therefore, more likely to attend Head Start, the federal preschool program. But according to the ECLS data, Head Start does nothing for a child's future test scores. Despite a deep reservoir of appreciation for Head Start (one of this book's authors was a charter student), we must acknowledge that it has repeatedly been proven ineffectual in the long term. Here's a likely reason: instead of spending the day with his own undereducated, overworked mother, the typical Head Start child spends the day with someone else's undereducated, overworked mother. (And a whole roomful of similarly needy children.) As it happens, fewer than 30 percent of Head Start teachers have even a bachelor's degree. And the job pays so poorly—about $21,000 for a Head Start teacher versus $40,000 for the average public-school kindergarten teacher—that it is unlikely to attract better teachers any time soon.

MATTERS: *The child's parents speak English in the home.*

DOESN'T: *The child's parents regularly take him to museums.*

A child with English-speaking parents does better in school than one whose parents don't speak English. Again, not much of a surprise. This correlation is further supported by the performance of Hispanic students in the ECLS study. As a group, Hispanic students test poorly; they are also disproportionately likely to have non-English-speaking parents. (They do, however, tend to catch up with their peers in later grades.) So how about the opposite case: what if a mother and father are not only proficient in English but spend their weekends broadening their child's cultural horizons by taking him to museums? Sorry. Culture cramming may be a foundational belief of obsessive parenting, but the ECLS data show no correlation between museum visits and test scores.

MATTERS: *The child is adopted.*

DOESN'T: *The child is regularly spanked.*

There is a strong correlation—a negative one—between adoption and school test scores. Why? Studies have shown that a child's academic abilities are far more influenced by the IQs of his biological parents than the IQs of his adoptive parents, and mothers who offer up their children for adoption tend to have significantly lower IQs than the people who are doing the adopting. There is another explanation for low-achieving adoptees which, though it may seem distasteful, jibes with the basic economic theory of self-interest: a woman who knows she will offer her baby for adoption may not take the same prenatal care as a woman who is keeping her baby. (Consider—at the risk of furthering the distasteful thinking—how you treat a car you own versus a car you are renting for the weekend.)

But if an adopted child is prone to lower test scores, a spanked child is not. This may seem surprising—not because spanking itself is necessarily detrimental but because, conventionally xpeaking, spanking is considered an unenlightened practice. We might therefore assume that parents who spank are unenlightened in other ways. Perhaps that isn't the case at all. Or perhaps there is a different spanking story to be told. Remember, the ECLS survey included direct interviews with the children's parents. So a parent would have to sit knee to knee with a government researcher and admit to spanking his child. This would suggest that a parent who does so is either unenlightened or—more interestingly—congenitally honest. It may be that honesty is more important to good parenting than spanking is to bad parenting.

MATTERS: *The child's parents are involved in the PTA.*

DOESN'T: *The child frequently watches television.*

A child whose parents are involved in the PTA tends to do well in school—which probably indicates that parents with a strong relationship to education get involved in the PTA, not that their PTA involvement somehow makes their children smarter. The ECLS data show no correlation, meanwhile, between a child's test scores and the amount of television he watches. Despite the conventional wisdom, watching television apparently does not turn a child's brain to mush. (In Finland, whose education system has been ranked the world's best, most children do not begin school until age seven but have often learned to read on their own by watching American television with Finnish subtitles.) Nor, however, does using a computer at home turn a child into Einstein: the ECLS data show no correlation between computer use and school test scores.

Now for the final pair of factors:

MATTERS: *The child has many books in his home.*

DOESN'T: *The child's parents read to him nearly every day.*

As noted earlier, a child with many books in his home has indeed been found to do well on school tests. But regularly reading to a child *doesn't* affect early childhood test scores.

This would seem to present a riddle. It bounces us back to our original question: just how much, and in what ways, do parents really matter?

Let's start with the positive correlation: books in the home equal higher test scores. Most people would look at this correlation and infer an obvious cause-and-effect relationship. To wit: a little boy named Isaiah has a lot of books at home; Isaiah does beautifully on his reading test at school; this must be because his mother or father regularly reads to him. But Isaiah's friend Emily, who also has a lot of books in her home, practically never touches them. She would rather dress up her Bratz or watch cartoons. And Emily tests just as well as Isaiah. Meanwhile, Isaiah and Emily's friend Ricky doesn't have *any* books at home. But Ricky goes to the library every day with his mother. And yet he does *worse* on his school tests than either Emily or Isaiah.

What are we to make of this? If reading books doesn't have an impact on early childhood test scores, could it be that the books' mere physical presence in the house makes the children smarter? Do books perform some kind of magical osmosis on a child's brain? If so, one might be tempted to simply deliver a truckload of books to every home that contains a preschooler. That, in fact, is what the governor of Illinois tried to do. In early 2004, Governor Rod Blagojevich announced a plan to mail one book a month to every child in Illinois from the time they were born until they entered kindergarten. The plan would cost $26 million a year. But, Blagojevich argued, this was a vital intervention in a state where 40 percent of third graders read below their grade level. "When you own [books] and they're yours," he said, "and they just come as part of your life, all of that will contribute to a sense . . . that books should be part of your life."

So all children born in Illinois would end up with a sixty-volume library by the time they entered school. Does this mean they would all perform better on their reading tests?

Probably not. (Although we may never know for sure: in the end, the Illinois legislature rejected the book plan.) After all, the ECLS data don't say that books in the house *cause* high test scores; it says only that the two are correlated.

How should this correlation be interpreted? Here's a likely theory: most parents who buy a lot of children's books tend to be smart and well educated to begin with. (And they pass on their smarts and work ethic to their kids.) Or perhaps they care a great deal about education, and about their children in general. (Which means they create an environment that encourages and rewards learning.) Such parents may believe—as fervently as the governor of Illinois believed—that every children's book is a talisman that leads to unfettered intelligence. But they are probably wrong. A book is in fact less a cause of intelligence than an *indicator*.

So what does all this have to say about the importance of parents in general? Consider again the eight ECLS factors that are correlated with school test scores:

The child has highly educated parents.
The child's parents have high socioeconomic status.
The child's mother was thirty or older at the time of her first child's birth.
The child had low birthweight.
The child's parents speak English in the home.
The child is adopted.
The child's parents are involved in the PTA.
The child has many books in his home.

And the eight factors that are not:

The child's family is intact.
The child's parents recently moved into a better neighborhood.
The child's mother didn't work between birth and kindergarten.
The child attended Head Start.
The child's parents regularly take him to museums.
The child is regularly spanked.
The child frequently watches television.
The child's parents read to him nearly every day.

To overgeneralize a bit, the first list describes things that parents *are;* the second list describes things that parents *do.* Parents who are well educated, successful, and healthy tend to have children who test well in school; but it doesn't seem to much matter whether a child is trotted off to museums or spanked or sent to Head Start or frequently read to or plopped in front of the television.

For parents—and parenting experts—who are obsessed with

child-rearing technique, this may be sobering news. The reality is that technique looks to be highly overrated.

But this is not to say that parents don't matter. Plainly they matter a great deal. Here is the conundrum: by the time most people pick up a parenting book, it is far too late. Most of the things that matter were decided long ago—who you are, whom you married, what kind of life you lead. If you are smart, hardworking, well educated, well paid, and married to someone equally fortunate, then your children are more likely to succeed. (Nor does it hurt, in all likelihood, to be honest, thoughtful, loving, and curious about the world.) But it isn't so much a matter of what you *do* as a parent; it's who you are. In this regard, an overbearing parent is a lot like a political candidate who believes that money wins elections—whereas in truth, all the money in the world can't get a candidate elected if the voters don't like him to start with.

In a paper titled "The Nature and Nurture of Economic Outcomes," the economist Bruce Sacerdote addressed the nature-nurture debate by taking a long-term quantitative look at the effects of parenting. He used three adoption studies, two American and one British, each of them containing in-depth data about the adopted children, their adoptive parents, and their biological parents. Sacerdote found that parents who adopt children are typically smarter, better educated, and more highly paid than the baby's biological parents. But the adoptive parents' advantages had little bearing on the child's school performance. As also seen in the ECLS data, adopted children test relatively poorly in school; any influence the adoptive parents might exert is seemingly outweighed by the force of genetics. But, Sacerdote found, the parents were not powerless forever. By the time the adopted children became adults, they had veered sharply from the destiny that IQ alone might have predicted. Compared to similar children who were *not* put up for adoption, the adoptees were far more likely to attend college, to have a well-paid job, and to wait until they were out of their teens before getting married. It was the influence of the adoptive parents, Sacerdote concluded, that made the difference.

Chapter 6

**PERFECT PARENTING, PART II;
OR: WOULD A ROSHANDA BY ANY
OTHER NAME SMELL AS SWEET?**

Obsessive or not, any parent *wants* to believe that she is making a big difference in the kind of person her child turns out to be. Otherwise, why bother?

The belief in parental power is manifest in the first official act a parent commits: giving the baby a name. As any modern parent knows, the baby-naming industry is booming, as evidenced by a proliferation of books, websites, and baby-name consultants. Many parents seem to believe that a child cannot prosper unless it is hitched to the right name; names are seen to carry great aesthetic or even predictive powers.

This might explain why, in 1958, a New York City man named Robert Lane decided to call his baby son Winner. The Lanes, who lived in a housing project in Harlem, already had several children, each with a fairly typical name. But this boy—well, Robert Lane apparently had a special feeling about this one. Winner Lane: how could he fail with a name like that?

Three years later, the Lanes had another baby boy, their seventh and last child. For reasons that no one can quite pin down today, Robert decided to name this boy Loser. It doesn't appear that Robert was unhappy about the new baby; he just seemed to get a kick out of the name's bookend effect. First a Winner, now a Loser. But if Winner Lane could hardly be expected to fail, could Loser Lane possibly succeed?

Loser Lane did in fact succeed. He went to prep school on a scholarship, graduated from Lafayette College in Pennsylvania, and joined the New York Police Department (this was his mother's longtime wish), where he made detective and, eventually, sergeant. Although he never hid his name, many people were uncomfortable using it. "So I have a bunch of names," he says today, "from Jimmy to James to whatever they want to call you. Timmy. But they rarely call you Loser." Once in a while, he said, "they throw a French twist on it: 'Losier.' " To his police colleagues, he is known as Lou.

And what of his brother with the can't-miss name? The most noteworthy achievement of Winner Lane, now in his midforties, is the sheer length of his criminal record: nearly three dozen arrests for burglary, domestic violence, trespassing, resisting arrest, and other mayhem.

These days, Loser and Winner barely speak. The father who named them is no longer alive. Clearly he had the right idea—that naming is destiny—but he must have gotten the boys mixed up.

Then there is the recent case of Temptress, a fifteen-year-old girl whose misdeeds landed her in Albany County Family Court in New York. The judge, W. Dennis Duggan, had long taken note of the strange names borne by some offenders. One teenage boy, Amcher, had been named for the first thing his parents saw upon reaching the hospital: the sign for Albany Medical Center Hospital Emergency Room. But Duggan considered Temptress the most outrageous name he had come across.

"I sent her out of the courtroom so I could talk to her mother about why she named her daughter Temptress," the judge later recalled. "She said she was watching *The Cosby Show* and liked the young actress. I told her the actress's name was actually *Tempestt* Bledsoe. She said she found that out later, that they had misspelled the name. I asked her if she knew what 'temptress' meant, and she said she also found that out at some later point. Her daughter was charged with ungovernable behavior, which included bringing men into the home while the mother was at work. I asked the mother if she had ever thought the daughter was living out her name. Most all of this went completely over her head."

Was Temptress actually "living out her name," as Judge Duggan saw it? Or would she have wound up in trouble even if her mother had called her Chastity? *

It isn't much of a stretch to assume that Temptress didn't have ideal parents. Not only was her mother willing to name her Temptress in the first place, but she wasn't smart enough to know what that word even meant. Nor is it so surprising, on some level, that a boy named Amcher would end up in family court. People who can't be bothered to come up with a name for their child aren't likely to be the best parents either.

So does the name you give your child affect his life? Or is it *your* life reflected in his name? In either case, what kind of signal does a child's name send to the world—and most important, does it really matter?

* See footnote, p. 290.

• • •

As it happens, Loser and Winner, Temptress and Amcher were all black. Is this fact merely a curiosity or does it have something larger to say about names and culture?

Every generation seems to produce a few marquee academics who advance the thinking on black culture. Roland G. Fryer Jr., the young black economist who analyzed the "acting white" phenomenon and the black-white test score gap, may be among the next. His ascension has been unlikely. An indifferent high-school student from an unstable family, he went to the University of Texas at Arlington on an athletic scholarship. Two things happened to him during college: he quickly realized he would never make the NFL or the NBA; and, taking his studies seriously for the first time in his life, he found he liked them. After graduate work at Penn State and the University of Chicago, he was hired as a Harvard professor at age twenty-five. His reputation for candid thinking on race was already well established.

Fryer's mission is the study of black underachievement. "One could rattle off all the statistics about blacks not doing so well," he says. "You can look at the black-white differential in out-of-wedlock births or infant mortality or life expectancy. Blacks are the worst-performing ethnic group on SATs. Blacks earn less than whites. They are still just not doing well, period. I basically want to figure out where blacks went wrong, and I want to devote my life to this."

In addition to economic and social disparity between blacks and whites, Fryer had become intrigued by the virtual segregation of culture. Blacks and whites watch different television shows. (*Monday Night Football* is the only show that typically appears on each group's top ten list; *Seinfeld,* one of the most popular sitcoms in history, never ranked in the top fifty among blacks.) They smoke different cigarettes. (Newports enjoy a 75 percent market share among black teenagers versus 12 percent among whites; the white teenagers are mainly smoking Marlboros.) And black parents give their children names that are starkly different from white children's.

Fryer came to wonder: is distinctive black culture a *cause* of the economic disparity between blacks and whites or merely a reflection of it?

As with the ECLS study, Fryer went looking for the answer in a mountain of data: birth-certificate information for every child born in California since 1961. The data, covering more than sixteen million births, included standard items such as name, gender, race, birthweight, and the parents' marital status, as well as more telling factors about the parents: their zip code (which indicates socioeconomic status and a neighborhood's racial composition), their means of paying the hospital bill (again, an economic indicator), and their level of education.

The California data prove just how dissimilarly black and white parents name their children. White and Asian-American parents, meanwhile, give their children remarkably similar names; there is some disparity between white and Hispanic-American parents, but it is slim compared to the black-white naming gap.

The data also show the black-white gap to be a recent phenomenon. Until the early 1970s, there was a great overlap between black and white names. The typical baby girl born in a black neighborhood in 1970 was given a name that was twice as common among blacks as whites. By 1980 she received a name that was *twenty* times more common among blacks. (Boys' names moved in the same direction but less aggressively—probably because parents of all races are less adventurous with boys' names than with girls'.) Given the location and timing of this change—dense urban areas where Afro-American activism was gathering strength—the most likely cause of the explosion in distinctively black names was the Black Power movement, which sought to accentuate African culture and fight claims of black inferiority. If this naming revolution was indeed inspired by Black Power, it would be one of the movement's most enduring remnants. Afros today are rare, dashikis even rarer; Black Panther founder Bobby Seale is best known today for peddling a line of barbecue products.

A great many black names today are unique to blacks. More than 40 percent of the black girls born in California in a given year receive a name that not *one* of the roughly 100,000 baby white girls received that year. Even more remarkably, nearly 30 percent of the black girls are given a name that is unique among the names of every baby, white and black, born that year in California. (There were also 228 babies named Unique during the 1990s alone, and 1 each of Uneek, Uneque, and Uneqqee.) Even among very popular black names, there is little overlap with whites. Of the 626 baby girls named Deja in the 1990s, 591 were black. Of the 454 girls named Precious, 431 were black. Of the 318 Shanices, 310 were black.

What kind of parent is most likely to give a child such a distinctively black name? The data offer a clear answer: an unmarried, low-income, undereducated teenage mother from a black neighborhood who has a distinctively black name herself. In

Fryer's view, giving a child a superblack name is a black parent's signal of solidarity with the community. "If I start naming my kid Madison," he says, "you might think, 'Oh, you want to go live across the railroad tracks, don't you?' " If black kids who study calculus and ballet are thought to be "acting white," Fryer says, then mothers who call their babies Shanice are simply "acting black."

The California study shows that many white parents send as strong a signal in the opposite direction. More than 40 percent of the white babies are given names that are at least four times more common among whites. Consider Connor and Cody, Emily and Abigail. In one recent ten-year stretch, each of these names was given to at least two thousand babies in California—fewer than 2 percent of them black.

So what are the "whitest" names and the "blackest" names?

THE TWENTY "WHITEST" GIRL NAMES			
1. Molly	6. Madeline	11. Jenna	16. Holly
2. Amy	7. Katelyn	12. Heather	17. Allison
3. Claire	8. Emma	13. Katherine	18. Kaitlyn
4. Emily	9. Abigail	14. Caitlin	19. Hannah
5. Katie	10. Carly	15. Kaitlin	20. Kathryn

THE TWENTY "BLACKEST" GIRL NAMES

1. Imani	6. Nia	11. Jada	16. Jasmin
2. Ebony	7. Deja	12. Tierra	17. Jazmin
3. Shanice	8. Diamond	13. Tiara	18. Jasmine
4. Aaliyah	9. Asia	14. Kiara	19. Alexus
5. Precious	10. Aliyah	15. Jazmine	20. Raven

THE TWENTY "WHITEST" BOY NAMES

1. Jake	6. Dustin	11. Cole	16. Dylan
2. Connor	7. Luke	12. Lucas	17. Maxwell
3. Tanner	8. Jack	13. Bradley	18. Hunter
4. Wyatt	9. Scott	14. Jacob	19. Brett
5. Cody	10. Logan	15. Garrett	20. Colin

THE TWENTY "BLACKEST" BOY NAMES

1. DeShawn	6. Malik	11. Demetrius	16. Darius
2. DeAndre	7. Trevon	12. Reginald	17. Xavier
3. Marquis	8. Tyrone	13. Jamal	18. Terrance
4. Darnell	9. Willie	14. Maurice	19. Andre
5. Terrell	10. Dominique	15. Jalen	20. Darryl

So how does it matter if you have a very white name or a very black name? Over the years, a series of "audit studies" have tried to measure how people perceive different names. In a typical audit study, a researcher would send two identical (and fake) résumés, one with a traditionally white name and the other with an immigrant or minority-sounding name, to potential employers. The "white" résumés have always gleaned more job interviews.

According to such a study, if DeShawn Williams and Jake Williams sent identical résumés to the same employer, Jake Williams would be more likely to get a callback. The implication is that black-sounding names carry an economic penalty. Such studies are tantalizing but severely limited, for they can't explain *why* DeShawn didn't get the call. Was he rejected because the employer is a racist and is convinced that DeShawn Williams is black? Or did he reject him because "DeShawn" sounds like someone from a low-income, low-education family? A résumé is a fairly undependable set of clues—a recent study showed that more than 50 percent of them contain lies—so "DeShawn" may simply signal a disadvantaged background to an employer who believes that workers from such backgrounds are undependable.

Nor do the black-white audit studies predict what might have happened in a job interview. What if the employer *is* racist, and if he unwittingly agreed to interview a black person who happened to have a white-sounding name—would he be any more likely to hire the black applicant after meeting face-to-face? Or is the interview a painful and discouraging waste of time for the black applicant—that is, an economic penalty for having a *white*-sounding name? Along those same lines, perhaps a black person with a white name pays an economic penalty in the *black* community; and what of the potential *advantage* to be gained in the black community by having a distinctively black name? But because the audit studies can't measure the actual life outcomes of the fictitious DeShawn Williams versus Jake Williams, they can't assess the broader impact of a distinctively black name.

Maybe DeShawn should just change his name.

People do this all the time, of course. The clerks in New York City's civil court recently reported that name changes are at an all-time high. Some of the changes are purely, if bizarrely, aesthetic. A young couple named Natalie Jeremijenko and Dalton Conley recently renamed their four-year-old son Yo Xing Heyno Augustus Eisner Alexander Weiser Knuckles Jeremijenko-Conley. Some people change names for economic purposes: after a New York livery-cab driver named Michael Goldberg was shot in early 2004, it was reported that Mr. Goldberg was in fact an Indian-born Sikh who thought it advantageous to take a Jewish name upon immigrating to New York. Goldberg's decision might have puzzled some people in show business circles, where it is a time-honored tradition to change Jewish names. Thus did Issur Danielovitch become Kirk Douglas; thus did the William Morris Agency rise to prominence under its namesake, the former Zelman Moses.

The question is, would Zelman Moses have done as well had he not become William Morris? And would DeShawn Williams do any better if he called himself Jake Williams or Connor Williams? It is tempting to think so—just as it is tempting to think that a truckload of children's books will make a child smarter.

Though the audit studies can't be used to truly measure how much a name matters, the California names data can.

How? The California data included not only each baby's vital statistics but information about the mother's level of education, income, and, most significantly, her own date of birth. This last fact made it possible to identify the hundreds of thousands of California mothers who had themselves been born in California and then to link them to their *own* birth records. Now a new and extremely potent story emerged from the data: it was possible to track the life outcome of any individual woman. This is the sort of data chain that researchers dream about, making it possible to identify a set of children who were born under similar circumstances, then locate them again twenty or thirty years later to see how they turned out. Among the hundreds of thousands of such women in the California data, many bore distinctively black names and many others did not. Using regression analysis to control for other factors that might influence life trajectories, it was then possible to measure the impact of a single factor—in this case, a woman's first name—on her educational, income, and health outcomes.

So does a name matter?

The data show that, on average, a person with a distinctively black name—whether it is a woman named Imani or a man named DeShawn—*does* have a worse life outcome than a woman named Molly or a man named Jake. But it isn't the fault of their names. If two black boys, Jake Williams and DeShawn Williams, are born in the same neighborhood and into the same familial and economic circumstances, they would likely have similar life outcomes. But the kind of parents who name their son Jake *don't* tend to live in the same neighborhoods or share economic circumstances with the kind of parents who name their son DeShawn. And that's why, on average, a boy named Jake will tend to earn more money and get more education than a boy named DeShawn. A DeShawn is more likely to have been handicapped by a low-income, low-education, single-parent background. His name is an indicator—not a cause—of his outcome. Just as a child with no books in his home isn't likely to test well in school, a boy named DeShawn isn't likely to do as well in life.

And what if DeShawn *had* changed his name to Jake or Connor: would his situation improve? Here's a guess: anybody who bothers to change his name in the name of economic success is—like the high-school freshmen in Chicago who entered the school-choice lottery—at least highly motivated, and motivation is probably a stronger indicator of success than, well, a name.

Just as the ECLS data answered questions about parenting that went well beyond the black-white test gap, the California names data tell a lot of stories in addition to the one about distinctively black names. Broadly speaking, the data tell us how parents see themselves—and, more significantly, what kind of expectations they have for their children.

Here's a question to begin with: where does a name come from, anyway? Not, that is, the actual source of the name—that much is usually obvious: there's the Bible, there's the huge cluster of traditional English and Germanic and Italian and French names, there are princess names and hippie names, nostalgic names and place names. Increasingly, there are brand names (Lexus, Armani, Bacardi, Timberland) and what might be called aspirational names. The California data show eight Harvards born during the 1990s (all of them black), fifteen Yales (all white), and eighteen Princetons (all black). There were no Doctors but three Lawyers (all black), nine Judges (eight of them white), three Senators (all white), and two Presidents (both black). Then there are the invented names. Roland G. Fryer Jr., while discussing his names research on a radio show, took a call from a black woman who was upset with the name just given to her baby niece. It was pronounced *shuh-TEED* but was in fact spelled "Shithead." *

Shithead has yet to catch on among the masses, but other names do. How does a name migrate through the population, and why? Is it purely a matter of zeitgeist, or is there some sensible explanation? We all know that names rise and fall and rise—witness the return of Sophie and Max from near extinction—but is there a discernible pattern to these movements?

The answer lies in the California data, and the answer is yes.

Among the most interesting revelations in the data is the correlation between a baby's name and the parents' socioeconomic status. Consider the most common female names found in middle-income white households versus low-income white households. (These and other lists to follow include data from the 1990s alone, to ensure a large sample that is also current.)

MOST COMMON MIDDLE-INCOME WHITE GIRL NAMES

1. Sarah	6. Amanda	11. Nicole	16. Jennifer
2. Emily	7. Megan	12. Taylor	17. Alexandra
3. Jessica	8. Samantha	13. Elizabeth	18. Brittany
4. Lauren	9. Hannah	14. Katherine	19. Danielle
5. Ashley	10. Rachel	15. Madison	20. Rebecca

* See note, p. 289.

MOST COMMON LOW-INCOME WHITE GIRL NAMES

1. Ashley	6. Sarah	11. Emily	16. Stephanie
2. Jessica	7. Kayla	12. Nicole	17. Jennifer
3. Amanda	8. Amber	13. Elizabeth	18. Hannah
4. Samantha	9. Megan	14. Heather	19. Courtney
5. Brittany	10. Taylor	15. Alyssa	20. Rebecca

There is considerable overlap, to be sure. But keep in mind that these are the most common names of all, and consider the size of the data set. The difference between consecutive positions on these lists may represent several hundred or even several thousand children. So if Brittany is number five on the low-income list and number eighteen on the middle-income list, you can be assured that Brittany is a decidedly low-end name. Other examples are even more pronounced. Five names in each category don't appear at all in the other category's top twenty. Here are the top five names among high-end and low-end families, in order of their relative disparity with the other category:

MOST COMMON HIGH-END WHITE GIRL NAMES

1. Alexandra	4. Madison
2. Lauren	5. Rachel
3. Katherine	

MOST COMMON LOW-END WHITE GIRL NAMES

1. Amber
2. Heather
3. Kayla
4. Stephanie
5. Alyssa

And for the boys:

MOST COMMON HIGH-END WHITE BOY NAMES

1. Benjamin
2. Samuel
3. Jonathan
4. Alexander
5. Andrew

MOST COMMON LOW-END WHITE BOY NAMES

1. Cody
2. Brandon
3. Anthony
4. Justin
5. Robert

Considering the relationship between income and names, and given the fact that income and *education* are strongly correlated, it is not surprising to find a similarly strong link between the parents' level of education and the name they give their baby. Once again drawing from the pool of most common names among white children, here are the top picks of highly educated parents versus those with the least education:

MOST COMMON WHITE GIRL NAMES
AMONG HIGH-EDUCATION PARENTS

1. Katherine
2. Emma
3. Alexandra
4. Julia
5. Rachel

MOST COMMON WHITE GIRL NAMES
AMONG LOW-EDUCATION PARENTS

1. Kayla
2. Amber
3. Heather
4. Brittany
5. Brianna

MOST COMMON WHITE BOY NAMES
AMONG HIGH-EDUCATION PARENTS

1. Benjamin
2. Samuel
3. Alexander
4. John
5. William

MOST COMMON WHITE BOY NAMES
AMONG LOW-EDUCATION PARENTS

1. Cody
2. Travis
3. Brandon
4. Justin
5. Tyler

The effect is even more pronounced when the sample is widened beyond the most common names. Drawing from the entire California database, here are the names that signify the most poorly educated white parents.

THE TWENTY WHITE GIRL NAMES THAT BEST SIGNIFY LOW-EDUCATION PARENTS *

(AVERAGE NUMBER OF YEARS OF MOTHER'S EDUCATION IN PARENTHESES)

1.	Angel	(11.38)	11.	Jazmine	(11.94)
2.	Heaven	(11.46)	12.	Shyanne	(11.96)
3.	Misty	(11.61)	13.	Britany	(12.05)
4.	Destiny	(11.66)	14.	Mercedes	(12.06)
5.	Brenda	(11.71)	15.	Tiffanie	(12.08)
6.	Tabatha	(11.81)	16.	Ashly	(12.11)
7.	Bobbie	(11.87)	17.	Tonya	(12.13)
8.	Brandy	(11.89)	18.	Crystal	(12.15)
9.	Destinee	(11.91)	19.	Brandie	(12.16)
10.	Cindy	(11.92)	20.	Brandi	(12.17)

* WITH A MINIMUM OF 100 OCCURRENCES.

If you or someone you love is named Cindy or Brenda and is over, say, forty, and feels that those names did not formerly connote a low-education family, you are right. These names, like many others, have shifted hard and fast of late. Some of the other low-education names are obviously misspellings, whether intentional or not, of more standard names. In most cases the standard spellings of the names—Tabitha, Cheyenne, Tiffany, Brittany, and Jasmine—also signify low education. But the various spellings of even one name can reveal a strong disparity:

TEN "JASMINES" IN ASCENDING ORDER OF MATERNAL EDUCATION

(YEARS OF MOTHER'S EDUCATION IN PARENTHESES)

1.	Jazmine	(11.94)	6. Jasmina	(12.50)
2.	Jazmyne	(12.08)	7. Jazmyn	(12.77)
3.	Jazzmin	(12.14)	8. Jasmine	(12.88)
4.	Jazzmine	(12.16)	9. Jasmin	(13.12)
5.	Jasmyne	(12.18)	10. Jasmyn	(13.23)

Here is the list of low-education white boy names. It includes the occasional misspelling (Micheal and Tylor), but more common is the nickname-as-proper-name trend.

THE TWENTY WHITE BOY NAMES THAT BEST SIGNIFY LOW-EDUCATION PARENTS *

(YEARS OF MOTHER'S EDUCATION IN PARENTHESES)

1.	Ricky	(11.55)	11. Tommy	(11.89)
2.	Joey	(11.65)	12. Tony	(11.96)
3.	Jessie	(11.66)	13. Micheal	(11.98)
4.	Jimmy	(11.66)	14. Ronnie	(12.03)
5.	Billy	(11.69)	15. Randy	(12.07)
6.	Bobby	(11.74)	16. Jerry	(12.08)
7.	Johnny	(11.75)	17. Tylor	(12.14)
8.	Larry	(11.80)	18. Terry	(12.15)
9.	Edgar	(11.81)	19. Danny	(12.17)
10.	Steve	(11.84)	20. Harley	(12.22)

* WITH A MINIMUM OF 100 OCCURRENCES

Now for the names that signify the *highest* level of parental education. These names don't have much in common, phonetically or aesthetically, with the low-education names. The girls' names are in most regards diverse, though with a fair share of literary and otherwise artful touches. A caution to prospective parents who are shopping for a "smart" name: remember that such a name won't *make* your child smart; it will, however, give her the same name as other smart kids—at least for a while. (For a much longer and more varied list of girls' and boys' names, see pp. 290–293.)

THE TWENTY WHITE GIRL NAMES
THAT BEST SIGNIFY HIGH-EDUCATION PARENTS *

(YEARS OF MOTHER'S EDUCATION IN PARENTHESES)

1.	Lucienne	(16.60)	11. Rotem	(16.08)
2.	Marie-Claire	(16.50)	12. Oona	(16.00)
3.	Glynnis	(16.40)	13. Atara	(16.00)
4.	Adair	(16.36)	14. Linden	(15.94)
5.	Meira	(16.27)	15. Waverly	(15.93)
6.	Beatrix	(16.26)	16. Zofia	(15.88)
7.	Clementine	(16.23)	17. Pascale	(15.82)
8.	Philippa	(16.21)	18. Eleanora	(15.80)
9.	Aviva	(16.18)	19. Elika	(15.80)
10.	Flannery	(16.10)	20. Neeka	(15.77)

* WITH A MINIMUM OF 10 OCCURRENCES

Now for the boys' names that are turning up these days in high-education households. This list is particularly heavy on the Hebrew, with a noticeable trend toward Irish traditionalism.

**THE TWENTY WHITE BOY NAMES
THAT BEST SIGNIFY HIGH-EDUCATION PARENTS***

(YEARS OF MOTHER'S EDUCATION IN PARENTHESES)

1.	Dov	(16.50)	11.	Finnegan	(16.13)
2.	Akiva	(16.42)	12.	MacGregor	(16.10)
3.	Sander	(16.29)	13.	Florian	(15.94)
4.	Yannick	(16.20)	14.	Zev	(15.92)
5.	Sacha	(16.18)	15.	Beckett	(15.91)
6.	Guillaume	(16.17)	16.	Kia	(15.90)
7.	Elon	(16.16)	17.	Ashkon	(15.84)
8.	Ansel	(16.14)	18.	Harper	(15.83)
9.	Yonah	(16.14)	19.	Sumner	(15.77)
10.	Tor	(16.13)	20.	Calder	(15.75)

* WITH A MINIMUM OF 10 OCCURRENCES

If many names on the above lists were unfamiliar to you, don't feel bad. Even boys' names—which have always been scarcer than girls'—have been proliferating wildly. This means that even the most popular names today are less popular than they used to be. Consider the ten most popular names given to black baby boys in California in 1990 and then in 2000. The top ten in 1990 includes 3,375 babies (18.7 percent of those born that year), while the top ten in 2000 includes only 2,115 (14.6 percent of those born that year).

MOST POPULAR BLACK BOY NAMES

(NUMBER OF OCCURRENCES IN PARENTHESES)

	1990			2000	
1.	Michael	(532)	1.	Isaiah	(308)
2.	Christopher	(531)	2.	Jordan	(267)
3.	Anthony	(395)	3.	Elijah	(262)
4.	Brandon	(323)	4.	Michael	(235)
5.	James	(303)	5.	Joshua	(218)
6.	Joshua	(301)	6.	Anthony	(208)
7.	Robert	(276)	7.	Christopher	(169)
8.	David	(243)	8.	Jalen	(159)
9.	Kevin	(240)	9.	Brandon	(148)
10.	Justin	(231)	10.	Justin	(141)

In the space of ten years, even the most popular name among black baby boys (532 occurrences for Michael) became far less popular (308 occurrences for Isaiah). So parents are plainly getting more diverse with names. But there's another noteworthy shift in these lists: a very quick rate of turnover. Note that four of the 1990 names (James, Robert, David, and Kevin) fell out of the top ten by 2000. Granted, they made up the bottom half of the 1990 list. But the names that replaced them in 2000 *weren't* bottom dwellers. Three of the new names—Isaiah, Jordan, and Elijah—were in fact numbers one, two, and three in 2000. For an even more drastic example of how quickly and thoroughly a name can cycle in and out of use, consider the ten most popular names given to white girls in California in 1960 and then in 2000.

MOST POPULAR WHITE GIRL NAMES

1960	2000
1. Susan	1. Emily
2. Lisa	2. Hannah
3. Karen	3. Madison
4. Mary	4. Sarah
5. Cynthia	5. Samantha
6. Deborah	6. Lauren
7. Linda	7. Ashley
8. Patricia	8. Emma
9. Debra	9. Taylor
10. Sandra	10. Megan

Not a single name from 1960 remains in the top ten. But, you say, it's hard to stay popular for forty years. So how about comparing today's most popular names with the top ten from only twenty years earlier?

MOST POPULAR WHITE GIRL NAMES

1980	2000
1. Jennifer	1. Emily
2. Sarah	2. Hannah
3. Melissa	3. Madison
4. Jessica	4. Sarah
5. Christina	5. Samantha
6. Amanda	6. Lauren

7.	Nicole	7.	Ashley
8.	Michelle	8.	Emma
9.	Heather	9.	Taylor
10.	Amber	10.	Megan

A single holdover: Sarah. So where do these Emilys and Emmas and Laurens all come from? Where on earth did *Madison* come from?* It's easy enough to see that new names become very popular very fast—but why?

Let's take another look at a pair of earlier lists. Here are the most popular names given to baby girls in the 1990s among low-income families and among families of middle income or higher.

MOST COMMON "HIGH-END" WHITE GIRL NAMES IN THE 1990S

1.	Alexandra	4.	Madison
2.	Lauren	5.	Rachel
3.	Katherine		

MOST COMMON "LOW-END" WHITE GIRL NAMES IN THE 1990S

1.	Amber	4.	Stephanie
2.	Heather	5.	Alyssa
3.	Kayla		

---

* Madison almost certainly came from the 1984 movie *Splash*, starring Darryl Hannah as a mermaid who comes ashore in New York City and takes her name from the street sign for Madison Avenue. For humans, the name soon progressed from exceedingly rare to a perennial top five choice.

Notice anything? You might want to compare these names with the "Most Popular White Girl Names" list on page 202 that includes the top ten overall names from 1980 and 2000. Lauren and Madison, two of the most popular "high-end" names from the 1990s, made the 2000 top ten list. Amber and Heather, meanwhile, two of the overall most popular names from 1980, are now among the "low-end" names.

There is a clear pattern at play: once a name catches on among high-income, highly educated parents, it starts working its way down the socioeconomic ladder. Amber and Heather started out as high-end names, as did Stephanie and Brittany. For every high-end baby named Stephanie or Brittany, another five lower-income girls received those names within ten years.

So where do lower-end families go name-shopping? Many people assume that naming trends are driven by celebrities. But celebrities actually have a weak effect on baby names. As of 2000, the pop star Madonna had sold 130 million records worldwide but hadn't generated even the ten copycat namings—in California, no less—required to make the master index of four thousand names from which the sprawling list of girls' names on page 290 was drawn. Or considering all the Brittanys, Britneys, Brittanis, Brittanies, Brittneys, and Brittnis you encounter these days, you might think of Britney Spears. But she is in fact a symptom, not a cause, of the Brittany/Britney/Brittani/Brittanie/Brittney/Brittni explosion. With the most common spelling of the name, Brittany, at number eighteen among high-end families and number five among low-end families, it is surely approaching its pull date. Decades earlier, Shirley Temple was similarly a symptom of the Shirley boom, though she is often now remembered as its cause. (It should also be noted that many girls' names, including Shirley,

Carol, Leslie, Hilary, Renee, Stacy, and Tracy began life as boys' names, but girls' names almost never cross over to boys.)

So it isn't famous people who drive the name game. It is the family just a few blocks over, the one with the bigger house and newer car. The kind of families that were the first to call their daughters Amber or Heather and are now calling them Lauren or Madison. The kind of families that used to name their sons Justin or Brandon and are now calling them Alexander or Benjamin. Parents are reluctant to poach a name from someone *too* near— family members or close friends—but many parents, whether they realize it or not, like the sound of names that sound "successful."

But as a high-end name is adopted en masse, high-end parents begin to abandon it. Eventually, it is considered so common that even lower-end parents may not want it, whereby it falls out of the rotation entirely. The lower-end parents, meanwhile, go looking for the next name that the upper-end parents have broken in.

So the implication is clear: the parents of all those Alexandras, Laurens, Katherines, Madisons, and Rachels should not expect the cachet to last much longer. Those names are already on their way to overexposure. Where, then, will the new high-end names come from?

It wouldn't be surprising to find them among the "smartest" girls' and boys' names in California, listed on pages 199–200, that are still fairly obscure. Granted, some of them—Oona and Glynnis, Florian and Kia—are bound to remain obscure. The same could be surmised of most of the Hebrew names (Rotem and Zofia, Akiva and Zev), even though many of today's most mainstream names (David, Jonathan, Samuel, Benjamin, Rachel, Hannah, Sarah, Rebecca) are of course Hebrew biblical names.

Aviva may be the one modern Hebrew name that is ready to break out: it's easy to pronounce, pretty, peppy, and suitably flexible.

Drawn from a pair of "smart" databases, here is a sampling of today's high-end names. Some of them, as unlikely as it seems, are bound to become tomorrow's mainstream names. Before you scoff, ask yourself this: do any of them seem more ridiculous than "Madison" might have seemed ten years ago?

MOST POPULAR GIRLS' NAMES OF 2015?

Annika	Eleanora	Isabel	Maya
Ansley	Ella	Kate	Philippa
Ava	Emma	Lara	Phoebe
Avery	Fiona	Linden	Quinn
Aviva	Flannery	Maeve	Sophie
Clementine	Grace	Marie-Claire	Waverly

MOST POPULAR BOYS' NAMES OF 2015?

Aidan	Bennett	Johan	Reagan
Aldo	Carter	Keyon	Sander
Anderson	Cooper	Liam	Sumner
Ansel	Finnegan	Maximilian	Will
Asher	Harper	McGregor	
Beckett	Jackson	Oliver	

Obviously, a variety of motives are at work when parents consider a name for their child. They may want something traditional or something bohemian, something unique or something perfectly trendy. It would be an overstatement to suggest that all parents are looking—whether consciously or not—for a "smart" name or a "high-end" name. But they are all trying to signal *something* with a name, whether the name is Winner or Loser, Madison or Amber, Shithead or Sander, DeShawn or Jake. What the California names data suggest is that an overwhelming number of parents use a name to signal *their own expectations* of how successful their children will be. The name isn't likely to make a shard of difference. But the parents can at least feel better knowing that, from the very outset, they tried their best.

EPILOGUE:
TWO PATHS TO HARVARD

And now, with all these pages behind us, an early promise has been confirmed: this book indeed has no "unifying theme."

But if there is no unifying theme to *Freakonomics*, there is at least a common thread running through the everyday application of Freakonomics. It has to do with thinking sensibly about how people behave in the real world. All it requires is a novel way of looking, of discerning, of measuring. This isn't necessarily a difficult task, nor does it require supersophisticated thinking. We have essentially tried to figure out what the typical gang member or sumo wrestler figured out on his own (although we had to do so in reverse).

Will the ability to think such thoughts improve your life materially? Probably not. Perhaps you'll put up a sturdy gate around your swimming pool or push your real-estate agent to work a little harder. But the net effect is likely to be more subtle than that.

You might become more skeptical of the conventional wisdom; you may begin looking for hints as to how things aren't quite what they seem; perhaps you will seek out some trove of data and sift through it, balancing your intelligence and your intuition to arrive at a glimmering new idea. Some of these ideas might make you uncomfortable, even unpopular. To claim that legalized abortion resulted in a massive drop in crime will inevitably lead to explosive moral reactions. But the fact of the matter is that *Freakonomics*-style thinking simply doesn't traffic in morality. As we suggested near the beginning of this book, if morality represents an ideal world, then economics represents the actual world.

The most likely result of having read this book is a simple one: you may find yourself asking a lot of questions. Many of them will lead to nothing. But some will produce answers that are interesting, even surprising. Consider the question posed at the beginning of this book's penultimate chapter: how much do parents really matter?

The data have by now made it clear that parents matter a great deal in some regards (most of which have been long determined by the time a child is born) and not at all in others (the ones we obsess about). You can't blame parents for trying to do something—anything—to help their child succeed, even if it's something as irrelevant as giving him a high-end first name.

But there is also a huge random effect that rains down on even the best parenting efforts. If you are in any way typical, you have known some intelligent and devoted parents whose child went badly off the rails. You may have also known of the opposite instance, where a child succeeds despite his parents' worst intentions and habits.

Recall for a moment the two boys, one white and one black,

who were described in chapter 5. The white boy who grew up outside Chicago had smart, solid, encouraging, loving parents who stressed education and family. The black boy from Daytona Beach was abandoned by his mother, was beaten by his father, and had become a full-fledged gangster by his teens. So what became of the two boys?

The second child, now twenty-eight years old, is Roland G. Fryer Jr., the Harvard economist studying black underachievement.

The white child also made it to Harvard. But soon after, things went badly for him. His name is Ted Kaczynski.

BONUS MATTER

THE PROBABILITY THAT A REAL-ESTATE AGENT IS CHEATING YOU (AND OTHER RIDDLES OF MODERN LIFE)

Inside the curious mind of the heralded young economist Steven Levitt

BY STEPHEN J. DUBNER

THE NEW YORK TIMES MAGAZINE

The most brilliant young economist in America—the one so deemed, at least, by a jury of his elders—brakes to a stop at a traffic light on Chicago's south side. It is a sunny day in mid-June. He drives an aging green Chevy Cavalier with a dusty dashboard and a window that doesn't quite shut, producing a dull roar at highway speeds.

But the car is quiet for now, as are the noontime streets: gas stations, boundless concrete, brick buildings with plywood windows.

An elderly homeless man approaches. It says he is homeless right on his sign, which also asks for money. He wears a torn jacket, too heavy for the warm day, and a grimy red baseball cap.

The economist doesn't lock his doors or inch the car forward. Nor does he go scrounging for spare change. He just watches, as if through one-way glass. After a while, the homeless man moves along.

"He had nice headphones," says the economist, still watching in the rearview mirror. "Well, nicer than the ones I have. Otherwise, it doesn't look like he has many assets."

Steven Levitt tends to see things differently than the average person. Differently, too, than the average economist. This is either a wonderful trait or a troubling one, depending on how you feel about economists. The average economist is known to wax oracularly about any and all monetary issues. But if you were to ask Levitt his opinion of some standard economic matter, he would probably swipe the hair from his eyes and plead ignorance. "I gave up a long time ago pretending that I knew stuff I didn't know," he says. "I mean, I just—I just don't know very much about the field of economics. I'm not good at math, I don't know a lot of econometrics, and I also don't know how to do theory. If you ask me about whether the stock market's going to go up or down, if you ask me whether the economy's going to grow or shrink, if you ask me whether deflation's good or bad, if you ask me about taxes— I mean, it would be total fakery if I said I knew anything about any of those things."

In Levitt's view, economics is a science with excellent tools for gaining answers but a serious shortage of interesting questions. His particular gift is the ability to ask such questions. For instance: If drug dealers make so much money, why do they still live with their mothers? Which is more dangerous, a gun or a swimming pool? What really caused crime rates to plunge during the past decade? Do real-estate agents have their clients' best interests at heart? Why do black parents give their children names that may hurt their career prospects? Do schoolteachers cheat to meet high-stakes testing standards? Is sumo wrestling corrupt?

And how does a homeless man afford $50 headphones?

Many people—including a fair number of his peers—might not recognize Levitt's work as economics at all. But he has merely distilled the so-called dismal science down to its most primal aim: explaining how people get what they want, or need. Unlike most academics, he is unafraid of using personal observations and curiosities (though he does fear calculus). He is an intuitionist. He sifts through a pile of data to find a story that no one else had found. He devises a way to measure an effect that veteran economists had declared unmeasurable. His abiding interests—though he says he has never trafficked in them himself—are cheating, corruption and crime.

His interest in the homeless man's headphones, meanwhile, didn't last long. "Maybe," he said later, "it was just testimony to the fact I'm too disorganized to buy a set of headphones that I myself covet."

Levitt is the first to say that some of his topics border on the trivial. But he has proved to be such an ingenious researcher and clear-eyed thinker that instead of being consigned to the fringe of his field, the opposite has happened: he has shown other economists just how well their tools can make sense of the real world.

"Levitt is considered a demigod, one of the most creative people in economics and maybe in all social science," says Colin Camerer, an economist at the California Institute of Technology. "He represents something that everyone thinks they will be when they go to grad school in econ, but usually they have the creative spark bored out of them by endless math—namely, a kind of intellectual detective trying to figure stuff out."

Levitt is a populist in a field that is undergoing a bout of popularization. Undergraduates are swarming the economics departments of elite universities. Economics is seen as the ideal blend of intellectual prestige (it does offer a Nobel, after all) and practical training for a high-flying finance career (unless, like Levitt, you choose to stay in academia). At the same time, economics is ever more visible in the real world, thanks to the continuing fetishization of the stock market and the continuing fixation with Alan Greenspan.

The greatest change, however, is within the scholarly ranks. Microeconomists are gaining on the macro crowd, empiricists gaining on the theorists. Behavioral economists have called into doubt the very notion of "homo economicus," the supposedly rational decision-maker in each of us. Young economists of every stripe are more inclined to work on real-world subjects and dip into bordering disciplines—psychology, criminology, sociology, even neurology—with the intent of rescuing their science from its slavish dependence upon mathematical models.

Levitt fits everywhere and nowhere. He is a noetic butterfly that no one has pinned down—he was once offered a job on the Clinton economic team, and the Bush campaign approached him about being a crime adviser—but who is widely appreciated.

"Steve isn't really a behavioral economist, but they'd be happy to have him," says Austan Goolsbee, who teaches economics at the University of Chicago's Graduate School of Business. "He's not really an old price-theory guy, but these Chicago guys are happy to claim him. He's not really a Cambridge guy"—although Levitt went to Harvard and then M.I.T.—"but they'd love him to come back."

He has critics, to be sure. Daniel Hamermesh, a prominent labor economist at the University of Texas, has taught Levitt's paper "The Impact of Legalized Abortion on Crime" to his undergraduates. "I've gone over this paper in draft, in its printed version, at great length, and for the life of me I can't see anything wrong with it," Hamermesh says. "On the other hand, I don't believe a word of it. And his stuff on sumo wrestlers—well, this is not exactly fundamental, unless you're Japanese and weigh 500 pounds."

But at 36, Levitt is a full professor in the University of Chicago's economics department, the most legendary program in the country. (He received tenure after only two years.) He is an editor of *The Journal of Political Economy,* a leading journal in the field. And the American Economic Association recently awarded him its John Bates Clark Medal, given biennially to the country's best economist under 40.

He is a prolific and diverse writer. But his paper linking a rise in abortion to a drop in crime has made more noise than the rest combined. Levitt and his co-author, John Donohue of Stanford Law School, argued that as much as 50 percent of the huge drop in crime since the early 1990's can be traced to *Roe v. Wade.* Their thinking goes like this: the women most likely to seek an abortion—poor, single, black or teenage mothers—were the very women whose children, if born, have been shown most likely to become criminals. But since those children *weren't* born, crime began to decrease during the years they would have entered their criminal prime. In conversation, Levitt reduces the theory to a tidy syllogism: "Unwantedness leads to high crime; abortion leads to less unwantedness; abortion leads to less crime."

Levitt had already published widely about crime and punishment. One paper he wrote as a graduate student is still regularly cited. His question was disarmingly simple: Do more police translate into less crime? The answer would seem obvious—yes—but had never been proved: since the number of police officers tends to rise along with the number of crimes, the effectiveness of the police was tricky to measure.

Levitt needed a mechanism that would unlink the crime rate from police hiring. He found it within politics. He noticed that mayors and governors running for re-election often hire more police officers. By measuring *those* police increases against crime rates, he was able to determine that additional officers do indeed bring down violent crime.

That paper was later disputed—another graduate student found a serious mathematical mistake in it—but Levitt's ingenuity was obvious. He began to be acknowledged as a master of the simple, clever solution. He was the guy who, in the slapstick scene, sees all the engineers futzing with a broken machine—and then realizes that no one has thought to plug it in.

Arguing that the police help deter crime didn't make Levitt any enemies. Arguing that abortion deterred crime was another matter.

In the abortion paper, published in 2001, he and Donohue warned that their findings should not be seen "as either an endorsement of abortion or a call for intervention by the state in the fertility decisions of women." They suggested that crime might just as easily be curbed by "providing better environments for those children at greatest risk for future crime."

Still, the very topic managed to offend nearly everyone. Conservatives were enraged that abortion could be construed as a crime-fighting tool. Liberals were aghast that poor and black women were singled out. Economists grumbled that Levitt's methodology was not sound. A syllogism, after all, can be a magic trick: All cats die; Socrates died; therefore Socrates was a cat.

"I think he's enormously clever in so many areas, focusing very much on the issue of reverse causality," says Ted Joyce, an economist at Baruch College who has written a critical response to the abortion paper. "But in this case I think he ignored it, or didn't tend to it well enough."

As the news media gorged on the abortion-crime story, Levitt came under direct assault. He was called an ideologue (by conservatives and liberals alike), a eugenicist, a racist and downright evil.

In reality, he seems to be very much none of those. He has little taste for politics and less for moralizing. He is genial, low-key and unflappable, confident but not cocky. He is a respected teacher and colleague; he is a sought-after collaborator who, because of the breadth of his curiosities, often works with scholars outside his field—another rarity for an economist.

"I hesitate to use these words, but Steve is a con man, in the best sense," says Sudhir Venkatesh, a sociologist at Columbia University. "He's the Shakespearean jester. He'll make you believe his ideas were yours." Venkatesh was Levitt's co-author on "An Economic Analysis of a Drug-Selling Gang's Finances," which found that the average street dealer lives with his mother because the take-home pay is, frankly, terrible. The paper analyzed one crack gang's financial activities as if it were any corporation. (It was Venkatesh who procured the data, from a former gang member.) Such a thing had never been tried. "This lack of focus," Levitt deadpanned in one version of the paper, "is perhaps partly attributable to the fact that few economists have been involved in the study of gangs."

Levitt speaks with a boyish lisp. His appearance is High Nerd: a plaid button-down shirt, nondescript khakis and a braided belt, sensible shoes. His pocket calendar is branded with the National Bureau of Economic Research logo. "I wish he would get more than three haircuts a year," his wife, Jeannette, says, "and that he wasn't still wearing the same glasses he got 15 years ago, which weren't even in fashion then." He was a good golfer in high school but has so physically atrophied that he calls himself "the weakest human being alive" and asks Jeannette to open jars around the house.

There is nothing in his appearance or manner, in other words, that suggests a flamethrower. He will tell you that all he does is sit at his desk, day and night, wrestling with some strange mountain of data. He will tell you that he would do it free (his salary is reportedly more than $200,000), and you tend to believe him. He may be an accidental provocateur, but he is a provocateur nonetheless.

He takes particular delight in catching wrongdoers. In one paper, he devised a set of algorithms that could identify teachers in the Chicago public-school system who were cheating. "Cheating classrooms will systematically differ from other classrooms along a number of dimensions," he and his co-author, Brian Jacob of the Kennedy School of Government, wrote in "Catching Cheating Teachers." "For instance, students in cheating classrooms are likely to experience unusually large test-score gains in the year of the cheating, followed by unusually small gains or even declines in the following year when the boost attributable to cheating disappears."

Levitt used test-score data from the Chicago schools that had long been available to other researchers. There were a number of ways, he realized, that a teacher could cheat. If she were particularly brazen (and stupid), she might give students the correct answers. Or, after the test, she might actually erase students' wrong answers and fill in correct ones. A sophisticated cheater would be careful to avoid conspicuous blocks of identical answers. But Levitt was more sophisticated. "The first step in analyzing suspicious strings is to estimate the probability each child would give a particular answer on each question," he wrote. "This estimation is done using a multinomial logit framework with past test scores, demographics and socioeconomic characteristics as explanatory variables."

So by measuring any number of factors—the difficulty of a particular question, the frequency with which students got hard questions right and easy ones wrong, the degree to which certain answers were highly correlated in one classroom—Levitt identified which teachers he thought were cheating. (Perhaps just as valuable, he was also able to identify the good teachers.) The Chicago school system, rather than disputing Levitt's findings, invited him into the schools for retesting. As a result, the cheaters were fired.

Then there is his coming "Understanding Why Crime Fell in the 1990's: Four Factors That Explain the Decline and Seven That Do Not." The entire drop in crime, Levitt says, was due to more police officers, more prisoners, the waning crack epidemic and *Roe v. Wade.*

One factor that probably *didn't* make a difference, he argues, was the innovative policing strategy trumpeted in New York by Rudolph Giuliani and William Bratton.

"I think," Levitt says, "I'm pretty much alone in saying that."

He comes from a Minneapolis family of high, if unusual, achievers. His father, a medical researcher, is considered a leading authority on intestinal gas. (He bills himself as "The Man Who Gave Status to Flatus and Class to Gas.") One of Levitt's great uncles, Robert May, wrote *Rudolph the Red-Nosed Reindeer*— the book, that is; another great uncle, Johnny Marks, later wrote the song.

At Harvard, Levitt wrote his senior thesis on thoroughbred breeding and graduated summa cum laude. (He is still obsessed with horse racing. He says he believes it is corrupt and has designed a betting system—the details of which he will not share— to take advantage of the corruption.) He worked for two years as a management consultant before enrolling at M.I.T. for a doctorate in economics. The M.I.T. program was famous for its mathematical intensity. Levitt had taken exactly one math course as an undergraduate and had forgotten even that. During his first graduate class, he asked the student next to him about a formula on the board: Is there any difference between the derivative sign that's straight up-and-down and the curly one? "You are in so much trouble," he was told.

"People wrote him off," recalls Austan Goolsbee, the Chicago economist who was then a classmate. "They'd say, 'That guy has no future.'"

Levitt set his own course. Other grad students stayed up all night working on problem sets, trying to make good grades. He stayed up researching and writing. "My view was that the way you succeed in this profession is you write great papers," he says. "So I just started."

Sometimes he would begin with a question. Sometimes it was a set of data that caught his eye. He spent one entire summer typing into his computer the results of years' worth of Congressional elections. (Today, with so much information so easily available on the Internet, Levitt complains that he can't get his students to input data at all.) All he had was a vague curiosity about why incumbents were so often re-elected.

Then he happened upon a political-science book whose authors claimed that money wins elections, period. "They were trying to explain election outcomes as a function of campaign expenditures," he recalls, "completely ignoring the fact that contributors will only give money to challengers when they have a realistic chance of winning, and incumbents only spend a lot when they have a chance of losing. They convinced themselves this was the causal story even though it's so obvious in retrospect that it's a spurious effect."

Obvious, at least, to Levitt. Within five minutes, he had a vision of the paper he would write. "It came to me," he says, "in full bloom."

The problem was that his data couldn't tell him who was a good candidate and who wasn't. It was therefore impossible to tease out the effect of the money. As with the police/crime rate puzzle, he had to trick the data.

Because he himself had typed in the data, he had noticed something: often, the same two candidates faced each other multiple times. By analyzing the data from only those elections, Levitt was able to find a true result. His conclusion: campaign money has about one-tenth the impact as was commonly accepted.

An unknown graduate student, he sent his paper to *The Journal of Political Economy*—one professor told him he was crazy for even trying—where it was published. He completed his Ph.D. in three years, but because of his priorities, he says, he was "invisible" to the faculty, "a real zero." Then he stumbled upon what he now calls the turning point in his career.

He had an interview for the Society of Fellows, the venerable intellectual Harvard clubhouse that pays young scholars to do their own work, for three years, with no commitments. Levitt felt he didn't stand a chance. For starters, he didn't consider himself an intellectual. He would be interviewed over dinner by the senior fellows, a collection of world-renowned philosophers, scientists and historians. He worried he wouldn't have enough conversation for even the first course.

Instead, he was on fire. Whatever subject came up—the brain, ants, philosophy—he just happened to remember something pithy he'd read. His wit crackled as it had never crackled before. When he told them about the two summers he spent betting the horses back in Minnesota, *they ate it up!*

Finally—disquietingly—one of them said: "I'm having a hard time seeing the unifying theme of your work. Could you explain it?"

Levitt was stymied. He had no idea what his unifying theme was, or if he even had one.

Amartya Sen, the future Nobel-winning economist, jumped in and neatly summarized what he saw as Levitt's theme.

Yes, Levitt said eagerly, that's my theme.

Another fellow then offered another theme.

You're right, Levitt said, *that's* my theme.

And so it went, like dogs tugging at a bone, until the philosopher Robert Nozick interrupted. If Levitt could have been said to have an intellectual hero, it would be Nozick.

"How old are you, Steve?" he asked.

"Twenty-six."

Nozick turned to the other fellows: "He's 26 years old. Why does he need to have a unifying theme? Maybe he's going to be one of those people who's so talented he doesn't need one. He'll take a question and he'll just answer it, and it'll be fine."

The University of Chicago's economics department had a famous unifying theme—the Gospel of Free Markets, with a conservative twist—and would therefore not have seemed the most likely fit for Levitt. As he sees it, Chicago is about theory, deep thinking and big ideas, while he is about empiricism, clever thinking and "cute but ultimately insubstantial ideas."

But Chicago also had Gary Becker. To Levitt, Becker is the most influential economist of the past 50 years. Long before it was fashionable, Becker brought microeconomic theory to offbeat topics, the family and crime in particular. For years, Becker was demonized—a single phrase like "the price of children" would set off untold alarms. "I took a lot of heat over my career from people who thought my work was silly or irrelevant or not economics," Becker says. But Chicago supported him; he persevered, winning the Nobel Prize in 1992; and he became Steven Levitt's role model.

Becker told Levitt that Chicago would be a great environment for him. "Not everybody agrees with all your results," he said, "but we agree what you're doing is very interesting work, and we'll support you in that."

Levitt soon found that the support at Chicago went beyond the scholarly. The year after he was hired, his wife gave birth to their first child, Andrew. One day, just after Andrew turned a year old, he came down with a slight fever. The doctor diagnosed an ear infection. When he started vomiting the next morning, his parents took him to the hospital. A few days later he was dead of pneumococcal meningitis.

Amid the shock and grief, Levitt had an undergraduate class that needed teaching. It was Gary Becker—a Nobel laureate nearing his 70th birthday—who sat in for him. Another colleague, D. Gale Johnson, sent a condolence card that Levitt still quotes from memory.

Levitt and Johnson, an agricultural economist in his 80's, began speaking regularly. Levitt learned that Johnson's daughter was one of the first Americans to adopt a daughter from China. Soon the Levitts adopted a daughter of their own, whom they named Amanda. In addition to Amanda, they have since had a daughter, now almost 3, and a son. But Andrew's death has played on, in various ways. They have become close friends with the family of the little girl to whom they donated Andrew's liver. (They also donated his heart, but that baby died.) And not surprisingly for a scholar who pursues real-life subjects, the death also informed Levitt's work.

He and Jeannette joined a support group for grieving parents. Levitt was struck by how many children had drowned in swimming pools. They were the kinds of deaths that don't make the newspaper—unlike, for instance, a child who dies while playing with a gun.

Levitt was curious and went looking for numbers that would tell the story. He wrote up the results as an op-ed article for *The Chicago Sun-Times*. It featured the sort of plangent counterintuition for which he has become famous: "If you own a gun and have a swimming pool in the yard, the swimming pool is almost 100 times more likely to kill a child than the gun is."

Trying to get his mind off death, Levitt took up a hobby: rehabbing and selling old houses in Oak Park, where he lives. This experience has led to yet another paper, about the real-estate market. It is his most Chicago-style paper yet, a romp in price theory, a sign that the university's influence on him is perhaps as strong as his influence on it. But Levitt being Levitt, it also deals with corruption.

While negotiating to buy old houses, he found that the seller's agent often encouraged him, albeit cagily, to underbid. This seemed odd: didn't the agent represent the seller's best interest? Then he thought more about the agent's role. Like many other "experts" (auto mechanics and stockbrokers come to mind), a real-estate agent is thought to know his field far better than a lay person. A homeowner is encouraged to trust the agent's information. So if the agent brings in a low offer and says it might just be the best the homeowner can expect, the homeowner tends to believe him. But the key, Levitt determined, lay in the fact that agents "receive only a small share of the incremental profit when a house sells for a higher value." Like a stockbroker churning commissions or a bookie grabbing his vig, an agent was simply looking to make a deal, any deal. So he would push homeowners to sell too fast and too cheap.

Now if Levitt could only measure this effect. Once again, he found a clever mechanism. Using data from more than 50,000 home sales in Cook County, Ill., he compared the figures for homes *owned* by real-estate agents with those for homes for which they acted only as agents. The agents' homes stayed on the market about 10 days longer and sold for 2 percent more.

Late on a summer afternoon, Levitt is in his office, deep inside one of the university's Gothic behemoths. The ceiling is stained, the plaster around the window crumbling. He is just back from sabbatical at Stanford, and his desk is a holy mess: stacks of books and journals, a green sippy cup and a little orange squeeze hippo.

This is his afternoon to meet with students. Levitt drinks a Mountain Dew and talks softly. Some students come for research assignments, some for advice. One has just written her undergraduate thesis: "The Labor Market Consequence of Graduating College in a Bad Economy." For a thesis, Levitt tells her, it's very good. But now she wants to have it published.

"You write like a college student, and that's a problem," he says. "The thing is, you're telling a story. There's foreshadowing going on, all those tricks. You want the reader going down a particular path so when they get the results, they understand them and believe them. But you also want to be honest about your weaknesses. People are much less harsh on weaknesses that are clear than weaknesses that are hidden—as they should be."

Be honest about your weaknesses. Has there ever been a prize-winning scholar as honest about his weaknesses as Steven Levitt? He doesn't understand economics, he claims, or math. He's a little thinker in a world of big thinkers. He can't even open a jar of spaghetti sauce at home, poor guy.

Friends say that Levitt's self-deprecation is as calculated as it is genuine. Within academia, economists take pride in being the most cutthroat of a cutthroat breed. Anyone who writes papers on *Weakest Link* (contestants discriminate against Latino and elderly peers, Levitt concluded, but not blacks or women) and sumo (to best manage their tournament rankings, wrestlers often conspire to throw matches) had better not also be arrogant.

Or maybe it is not self-deprecation at all. Maybe it is self-flagellation. Maybe what Steven Levitt really wants is to graduate from his "silly" and "trivial" and "shallow" topics.

He thinks he's onto something with a new paper about black names. He wanted to know if someone with a distinctly black name suffers an economic penalty. His answer—contrary to other recent research—is no. But now he has a bigger question: Is black culture a cause of racial inequality or is it a consequence? For an economist, even for Levitt, this is new turf—"quantifying culture," he calls it. As a task, he finds it thorny, messy, perhaps impossible and deeply tantalizing.

Driving home to Oak Park that evening, his Cavalier glumly thrumming along the Eisenhower Expressway, he dutifully addresses his future. Leaving academia for a hedge fund or a government job does not interest him (though he might, on the side, start a company to catch cheating teachers). He is said to be at the top of every economics department's poaching list. But the tree he and Jeannette planted when Andrew died is getting too big to move. You get the feeling he may stay at Chicago awhile.

There are important problems, he says, that he feels ready to address.

For instance? "Tax evasion. Money-laundering. I'd like to put together a set of tools that lets us catch terrorists. I mean, that's the goal. I don't necessarily know yet how I'd go about it. But given the right data, I have little doubt that I could figure out the answer."

It might seem absurd for an economist to dream of catching terrorists. Just as it must have seemed absurd if you were a Chicago schoolteacher, called into an office and told that, ahem, the algorithms designed by that skinny man with thick glasses had determined that you are a cheater. And that you are being fired. Steven Levitt may not fully believe in himself, but he does believe in this: teachers and criminals and real-estate agents may lie, and politicians, and even C.I.A. analysts. But numbers don't.

HOODWINKED?
January 8, 2006

Our book *Freakonomics* includes a chapter titled "How Is the Ku Klux Klan Like a Group of Real-Estate Agents?" This chapter was our effort to bring to life the economic concept known as information asymmetry, a state wherein one party to a transaction has better information than another party. It is probably obvious that real-estate agents typically have better information than their clients. The Klan story was perhaps less obvious. We argued that the Klan's secrecy—its rituals, made-up language, passwords and so on—formed an information asymmetry that furthered its aim of terrorizing blacks and others.

But the Klan was not the hero of our story. The hero was a man named Stetson Kennedy, a white Floridian from an old-line family who from an early age sought to assail racial and social injustices. Out of all of his crusades—for unionism, voting rights and numberless other causes—Kennedy is best known for taking on the Klan in the 1940's. In his book *The Klan Unmasked* (originally published in 1954 as *I Rode With the Ku Klux Klan*), Kennedy describes how he adopted a false identity to infiltrate the Klan's main chapter in Atlanta, was chosen to serve as a "klavalier" (a Klan strong-arm man) and repeatedly found himself at the center of astonishing events, all the while courting great personal risk.

What did Kennedy do with all the secret Klan information he gathered? He disseminated it like mad: to state prosecutors, to human rights groups and even to broadcasters like Drew Pearson and the producers of the *Superman* radio show, who publicly aired the Klan's heretofore hidden workings. Kennedy took an information asymmetry and dumped it on its head. And in doing so, we wrote, he played a significant role in quashing the renaissance of the Klan in postwar America.

Kennedy has been duly celebrated for his activism: his friend Woody Guthrie once wrote a song about him, and a Stetson Kennedy Day was recently declared in St. John's County, Fla., where Kennedy, 89, still lives. That is where we interviewed him nearly two years ago; our account of his amazing true story was based on those interviews, *The Klan Unmasked* and a small mountain of history books and newspaper articles.

But is Kennedy's story as true as it is amazing?

That was the disturbing question that began to haunt another Florida author, Ben Green, who in 1992 began writing a book about Harry T. Moore, a black civil rights advocate who was murdered in 1951. For a time, Stetson Kennedy was a collaborator on the book. Although Green was only tangentially interested in Kennedy's Klan infiltration—it wasn't central to the Moore story—he eventually checked out Kennedy's voluminous archives, held in libraries in New York and Atlanta.

These papers charted the extraordinarily colorful life of a man who had been, among other things, a poet, a folklorist, a muckraking journalist and a union activist. But Green was dismayed to find that the story told in Kennedy's own papers seemed to be quite different from what Kennedy wrote in *The Klan Unmasked.*

In *The Klan Unmasked,* Kennedy posed as an encyclopedia salesman named John S. Perkins who, in one of his first undercover maneuvers, visits the former governor of Georgia—a reputed Klan sympathizer—and ingratiates himself by offering to distribute some hate literature. A document in Kennedy's archives, however, suggests that Kennedy had indeed met the ex-governor, but not in any undercover capacity. Rather, he had interviewed him for a book he was writing—nor did this document mention any hate literature.

A close examination of Kennedy's archives seems to reveal a recurrent theme: legitimate interviews that he conducted with Klan leaders and sympathizers would reappear in *The Klan Unmasked* in different contexts and with different facts. In a similar vein, the archives offer evidence that Kennedy covered public Klan events as a reporter but then recast them in his book as undercover exploits. Kennedy had also amassed a great deal of literature about the Klan and other hate groups that he joined, but his own archives suggest that he joined most of these groups by mail.

So did Kennedy personally infiltrate the Klan in Atlanta, as portrayed in *The Klan Unmasked*?

In his archives are a series of memos that were submitted to the Anti-Defamation League, one of several civil rights groups to which Kennedy reported. Some of the memos were written by him; others were written by a man identified as John Brown, a union worker and former Klan official who had changed his ways and offered to infiltrate the Klan. "This worker is joining the

Klan for me," Kennedy wrote in one memo in early 1946. "I am certain that he can be relied on."

In Kennedy's subsequent memos—indeed, in hundreds of pages of Kennedy's various correspondence from the era—he matter-of-factly attributed some of his most powerful Klan information to John Brown: one of the memos he declared "a report from my informant inside the Klan on the meeting of Atlanta Klan No. 1 on August 12 and Atlanta Klan No. 297 on August 15." As John Brown fed inside information to Kennedy, Kennedy would then relay it to groups like the A.D.L., as well as to prosecutors and journalists. It wasn't until he wrote *The Klan Unmasked,* several years later, that Kennedy placed himself, Zelig-like, at the center of all the action.

Ben Green, despite months spent immersed in Kennedy's archives, could not identify the man once known as John Brown. Green did manage to interview Dan Duke, a former state prosecutor who, as rendered in *The Klan Unmasked,* worked closely with Kennedy. Duke agreed that Kennedy "got inside of some [Klan] meetings" but openly disputed Kennedy's dramatized account of their relationship. "None of that happened," he told Green. In 1999, when Green finally published his Harry T. Moore book, "Before His Time," it contained a footnote labeling *The Klan Unmasked* "a novelization."

Green is not the only person to have concluded that Kennedy has bent the truth. Jim Clark, who teaches history at the University of Central Florida, says that Kennedy "built a national reputation on many things that didn't happen." Meredith Babb, director of the University Press of Florida, which has published four of Kennedy's books, now calls Kennedy "an entrepreneurial folklorist." But except for Green's footnote, they all kept quiet until the retelling of Kennedy's exploits in *Freakonomics* produced a new round of attention. Why? "It would be like killing Santa Claus," Green says. "To me, the saddest part of this story is that what he actually did wasn't enough for him, and he has felt compelled to make up, embellish or take credit for things he didn't do."

When presented with documents from his own archives and asked outright, several weeks ago over lunch near his Florida home, if *The Klan Unmasked* was "somewhat conflated or fictionalized," Kennedy said no. "There may have been a bit of dialogue that was not as I remembered it," he answered. "But beyond that, no." When pressed, Kennedy did concede that "in some cases I took the reports and actions of this other guy and incorporated them into one narrative." As it turns out, Kennedy has made such an admission at least once before. Peggy Bulger, director of the American Folklife Center in the Library of Congress, wrote a 1992 dissertation called "Stetson Kennedy: Applied Folklore and Cultural Advocacy," based in part on extensive interviews with her subject. In an endnote, Bulger writes that "Kennedy combined his personal experiences undercover with the narratives provided by John Brown in writing *I Rode With the Ku Klux Klan* in 1954."

We weren't very happy, of course, to learn that a story we included in *Freakonomics* was built on such shaky foundations—especially since the book is devoted to upending conventional wisdoms rather than reinforcing them, and concerning Stetson Kennedy, the most conventional wisdom of all is his reputation as a Klan infiltrator.

There is also the fact that in our work we make a point of depending less on anecdote in favor of data, the idea being that numbers tend to lie less baldly than people do. But the story of Stetson Kennedy was one long series of anecdotes—which, no matter how many times they were cited over the decades, were nearly all generated by the same self-interested source.

Perhaps Kennedy's long life of fighting the good fight are all that matter. Perhaps, to borrow Peggy Bulger's phraseology, a goal of "cultural advocacy" calls for the use of "applied folklore" rather than the sort of forthrightness that should be more typical of history or journalism. One thing that does remain true is that Kennedy was certainly a master of information asymmetry. Until, that is, the data caught up with him.

WHY VOTE?
November 6, 2005

Within the economics departments at certain universities, there is a famous but probably apocryphal story about two world-class economists who run into each other at the voting booth.

"What are you doing here?" one asks.

"My wife made me come," the other says.

The first economist gives a confirming nod. "The same."

After a mutually sheepish moment, one of them hatches a plan: "If you promise never to tell anyone you saw me here, I'll never tell anyone I saw you." They shake hands, finish their polling business and scurry off.

Why would an economist be embarrassed to be seen at the voting booth? Because voting exacts a cost—in time, effort, lost productivity—with no discernible payoff except perhaps some vague sense of having done your "civic duty." As the economist Patricia Funk wrote in a recent paper, "A rational individual should abstain from voting."

The odds that your vote will actually affect the outcome of a given election are very, very, very slim. This was documented by the economists Casey Mulligan and Charles Hunter, who analyzed more than 56,000 Congressional and state-legislative elections since 1898. For all the attention paid in the media to close elections, it turns out that they are exceedingly rare. The median margin of victory in the Congressional elections was 22 percent; in the state-legislature elections, it was 25 percent. Even in the closest elections, it is almost never the case that a single vote is pivotal. Of the more than 40,000 elections for state legislator that Mulligan and Hunter analyzed, comprising nearly 1 billion votes, only 7 elections were decided by a single vote, with 2 others tied. Of the more than 16,000 Congressional elections, in which many more people vote, only one election in the past 100 years—a 1910 race in Buffalo—was decided by a single vote.

But there is a more important point: the closer an election is, the more likely that its outcome will be taken out of the voters' hands—most vividly exemplified, of course, by the 2000 presidential race. It is true that the outcome of that election came down to a handful of voters; but their names were Kennedy, O'Connor, Rehnquist, Scalia and Thomas. And it was only the votes they cast while wearing their robes that mattered, not the ones they may have cast in their home precincts.

Still, people do continue to vote, in the millions. Why? Here are three possibilities:

1. Perhaps we are just not very bright and therefore wrongly believe that our votes will affect the outcome.
2. Perhaps we vote in the same spirit in which we buy lottery tickets. After all, your chances of winning a lottery and of

affecting an election are pretty similar. From a financial perspective, playing the lottery is a bad investment. But it's fun
and relatively cheap: for the price of a ticket, you buy the
right to fantasize how you'd spend the winnings—much as
you get to fantasize that your vote will have some impact on
policy.

3. Perhaps we have been socialized into the voting-as-civic-duty
idea, believing that it's a good thing for society if people vote,
even if it's not particularly good for the individual. And thus
we feel guilty for not voting.

But wait a minute, you say. If everyone thought about voting
the way economists do, we might have no elections at all. No
voter goes to the polls actually believing that her single vote will
affect the outcome, does she? And isn't it cruel to even suggest
that her vote is not worth casting?

This is indeed a slippery slope—the seemingly meaningless behavior of an individual, which, in aggregate, becomes quite meaningful. Here's a similar example in reverse. Imagine that you and
your 8-year-old daughter are taking a walk through a botanical
garden when she suddenly pulls a bright blossom off a tree.

"You shouldn't do that," you find yourself saying.

"Why not?" she asks.

"Well," you reason, "because if everyone picked one, there
wouldn't be any flowers left at all."

"Yeah, but everybody *isn't* picking them," she says with a look.
"Only me."

In the old days, there were more pragmatic incentives to vote.
Political parties regularly paid voters $5 or $10 to cast the proper
ballot; sometimes payment came in the form of a keg of whiskey,

a barrel of flour or, in the case of an 1890 New Hampshire Congressional race, a live pig.

Now as then, many people worry about low voter turnout—only slightly more than half of eligible voters participated in the last presidential election—but it might be more worthwhile to stand this problem on its head and instead ask a different question: considering that an individual's vote almost never matters, why do so many people bother to vote at all?

The answer may lie in Switzerland. That's where Patricia Funk discovered a wonderful natural experiment that allowed her to take an acute measure of voter behavior.

The Swiss love to vote—on parliamentary elections, on plebiscites, on whatever may arise. But voter participation had begun to slip over the years (maybe they stopped handing out live pigs there too), so a new option was introduced: the mail-in ballot. Whereas each voter in the U.S. must register, that isn't the case in Switzerland. Every eligible Swiss citizen began to automatically receive a ballot in the mail, which could then be completed and returned by mail.

From a social scientist's perspective, there was beauty in the setup of this postal voting scheme: because it was introduced in different cantons (the 26 statelike districts that make up Switzerland) in different years, it allowed for a sophisticated measurement of its effects over time.

Never again would any Swiss voter have to tromp to the polls during a rainstorm; the cost of casting a ballot had been lowered significantly. An economic model would therefore predict voter turnout to increase substantially. Is that what happened?

Not at all. In fact, voter turnout often *decreased*, especially in smaller cantons and in the smaller communities within cantons.

This finding may have serious implications for advocates of Internet voting—which, it has long been argued, would make voting easier and therefore increase turnout. But the Swiss model indicates that the exact opposite might hold true.

But why is this the case? Why on earth would *fewer* people vote when the cost of doing so is lowered?

It goes back to the incentives behind voting. If a given citizen doesn't stand a chance of having her vote affect the outcome, why does she bother? In Switzerland, as in the U.S., "there exists a fairly strong social norm that a good citizen should go to the polls," Funk writes. "As long as poll-voting was the only option, there was an incentive (or pressure) to go to the polls only to be *seen* handing in the vote. The motivation could be hope for social esteem, benefits from being perceived as a cooperator or just the avoidance of informal sanctions. Since in small communities, people know each other better and gossip about who fulfills civic duties and who doesn't, the benefits of norm adherence were particularly high in this type of community."

In other words, we *do* vote out of self-interest—a conclusion that will satisfy economists—but not necessarily the same self-interest as indicated by our actual ballot choice. For all the talk of how people "vote their pocketbooks," the Swiss study suggests that we may be driven to vote less by a financial incentive than a social one. It may be that the most valuable payoff of voting is simply being seen at the polling place by your friends or co-workers.

Unless, of course, you happen to be an economist.

HOW MANY LIVES DID DALE EARNHARDT SAVE?
February 19, 2006

Five years ago this weekend, Dale Earnhardt crashed into a wall during the final lap of the Daytona 500 and was instantly killed. One of the most successful, beloved and intimidating drivers in Nascar history, Earnhardt is still actively mourned. (If you watch today's Daytona 500, the first and most prominent race of the Nascar season, you will surely see his No. 3 everywhere.) Earnhardt's death was to Nascar as 9/11 was to the federal government: a wake-up call leading to a radical overhaul of safety measures. "There were three or four bad accidents in a row there over two or three years," says Matt Kenseth, an elite Nascar driver. "Nascar was always working hard on safety, but that"—Earnhardt's death—"really sped things up."

Driving a race car is an obviously hazardous pursuit. When Earnhardt died, he was the seventh driver within Nascar's three major divisions—the Craftsman Truck Series, the Busch Series and the premier circuit now known as the Nextel Cup Series—to die within a period of seven years.

And how many drivers have been killed since his death in 2001?

Zero. In more than six million miles of racing—and many, many miles in practice and qualifying laps, which are plenty dangerous—not a single driver in Nascar's three top divisions has died.

On U.S. roads, meanwhile, roughly 185,000 drivers, passengers and motorcyclists have been killed during this same time frame. Those 185,000 deaths, though, came over the course of nearly 15 trillion miles driven. This translates into one fatality for every 81 million miles driven. Although traffic accidents are the leading cause of death for Americans from ages 3 to 33, this would seem to be a pretty low death rate (especially since it includes motorcycles, which are far more dangerous than cars or trucks). How long might it take one person to drive 81 million miles? Let's say that for a solid year you did nothing but drive, 24 hours a day, at 60 miles per hour. In one year, you'd cover 525,600 miles; to reach 81 million miles, you'd have to drive around the clock for 154 years. In other words, a lot of people die on U.S. roads each year not because driving is so dangerous, but because an awful lot of people are driving an awful lot of miles.

So Nascar's record of zero deaths in five years over six million miles is perhaps not as remarkable as it first sounded. Still, driving a race car would seem to be substantially more dangerous than taking a trip to the supermarket. What has Nascar done to produce its zero-fatality record?

It's a long list. Well before Earnhardt was killed, each driver was already wearing a helmet, fireproof suit and shoes and a five-point safety harness. Months after Earnhardt's death, Nascar began requiring the use of a head-and-neck restraint that is tethered to a driver's helmet and prevents his head from flying forward or sideways in a crash. (Like many race-car drivers who are killed, Earnhardt suffered a fracture to the base of the skull.) It erected safer walls on its race tracks. And it began to zealously collect crash data. This Incident Database (which Nascar politely declined to let us examine) is gleaned from two main sources: a black box now mounted on every vehicle and the work of a new Field Investigation unit. These field investigators meticulously take key measurements on every car before every race, and then if a car is involved in a crash, they retake those measurements.

"In the past, a car would be in an accident, the driver would have no injuries and the team would load up the car and go home," says Gary Nelson, who runs Nascar's research and development center. "But now they measure every car in certain areas, and we make a log of that. Like the width of the seat—it seems simple, the width of the headrest from left to right. But in an accident, those things can bend, and the amount they bend can help us understand the energy involved. When we began, we thought our seats were adequately strong, but we found these things to be bending more than we thought. So we've come back since and rewritten the regulations."

Although it is wildly reductive to put it this way, a Nascar driver has two main goals: to win a race and to not be killed. Nascar's recent safety measures seem to have considerably reduced the likelihood of being killed. So could it be that drivers are now willing to be more reckless? When crashing is made less costly, an economist would fully expect drivers to be crashing like crazy; could it be that Nascar's safety measures have led to fewer deaths but more crashes?

A quick look at the data seems to suggest so. In last year's Nextel Cup races, there were 345 cars involved in crashes, an all-time high. But, as Matt Kenseth points out, the two cup races held during 2005 at Lowe's Motor Speedway near Charlotte, N.C., were unusually brutal—the track had a new surface that caused numerous flat tires—and may have aberrationally affected the crash count. "In Charlotte, pretty much everybody wrecked in both races," he says. "It was the fault of the track and the tires—but if you take those races out of it, crashes are probably about even." And there were actually fewer crashes in 2004 than there were in 2003. While the number of overall crashes are up a bit since Earnhardt's death (Nascar will not release annual crash counts, but one official did confirm this trend), they haven't increased nearly as much as an economist might have predicted based on how Nascar's safety measures would seem to have shifted a driver's incentives.

Maybe that's because there are other, perhaps stronger, incentives at play. The first is that Nascar has increased its penalties for reckless driving, not only fining drivers but also subtracting points in their race for the cup championship. The other lies in how the cup championship itself has been restructured. Two years ago, Nascar gave its 36-race season a playoff format. In order to qualify for the playoffs—and have a chance at winning the $6 million-plus cup championship—a driver must be among the points leaders after the first 26 races of the season. While a couple of 20th-place finishes during those first 26 races won't necessary ruin your championship hopes (each race fields a slate of 43 cars), a few bad crashes might.

So Nascar has reduced a danger incentive but imposed a financial incentive, thus maintaining the delicate and masterful balance it has cultivated: it has enough crashes to satisfy its fans but not too many to destroy the sport—or its drivers. (Nascar fans love crashes the way hockey fans love fights; when you watch the Speed Channel's edited replays of Nascar races, the plot is always the same: green flag, crash, crash, crash, crash, crash, checkered flag.)

And here lies the most startling statistic concerning Nascar and driver safety. In the past five years, more than 3,000 vehicles have crashed in Nascar's three top divisions, with zero fatalities. How does this compare with crashes on American highways? For interstate travel, there are 5.2 driver deaths per 1,000 crashes. At this rate, it would seem likely that those 3,000 Nascar crashes would have produced at least 15 deaths—and yet there have been none. To be sure, there are significant differences between Interstate driving and Nascar driving. A driver on the Interstate has to contend with poor weather, drunken drivers and cars coming at him in the opposite direction. On the other hand, a driver in the Daytona 500 is often traveling at 180 miles per hour in bumper-to-bumper traffic.

With more than 37,000 Americans dying in traffic accidents each year, it might be tempting to impose some of Nascar's safety regulations on the average driver. But considering how relatively safe it is to drive in this country, the added costs, measured in both dollars and comfort, would be steep. You might be willing to wear a five-point safety harness instead of the typical three-point lap-and-shoulder belt, and you would almost certainly be safer if you did. But are you ready to put on a helmet and fireproof suit every time you drive to the supermarket?

THE GIFT-CARD ECONOMY
January 7, 2007

What do a gym membership, a bottle of prescription pills and a holiday gift card have in common? Each of them is a thing that is bought and then often goes unused.

In their recent paper "Paying Not to Go to the Gym," the economists Stefano DellaVigna and Ulrike Malmendier showed that people who buy an annual membership to a health club overestimate by more than 70 percent how much they'll actually use it. Many people, therefore, would be better off buying monthly or daily passes.

The Cochrane Collaboration, an evidence-based health-care research group, recently issued a report about patients who fail to take their medicine. "People who are prescribed self-administered medications," it began, "typically take less than half the prescribed doses." While this may be more troubling as a medical issue than a financial one, it is nevertheless true that the medicine cabinets of America are stuffed with billions of dollars of unused prescriptions.

As for gift cards—well, let's just say there is good reason that they are known within the retail industry as a stored-value product: they store their value very well, and often permanently. The financial-services research firm TowerGroup estimates that of the $80 billion spent on gift cards in 2006, roughly $8 billion will never be redeemed—"a bigger impact on consumers," Tower notes, "than the combined total of both debit- and credit-card fraud." A survey by Marketing Workshop Inc. found that only 30 percent of recipients use a gift card within a month of receiving it, while *Consumer Reports* estimates that 19 percent of the people who received a gift card in 2005 never used it.

Considering that two-thirds of all holiday shoppers in 2006 planned to give someone else a gift card, you most likely received one yourself in recent weeks. Perhaps you are among the exceptional minority, and you have already spent it, or soon will. But the odds say that it has instead wound up in your sock drawer.

Does this mean that a gift card is a bad gift? The answer depends on whom you ask, and it also requires the asking of a separate question: What is gift-giving meant to accomplish in the first place?

An economist might describe a gift as a signaling mechanism that allows one person to tell another person that she: a) is thinking about him; b) cares about him; and c) wants to give him something that he'll value.

Of course there are many different types of recipients and relationships. It's quite easy to give gifts to people who don't have the money or the wherewithal to get things for themselves—children, for instance. Since a child can't drive himself to Toys 'R' Us and probably doesn't have much money of his own, by giving him a toy you are substantially expanding the set of things he has access to. Which makes nearly any gift meaningful.

With adults, it's a bit trickier. An adult is free to buy whatever he wants, and presumably he knows what he likes. So ideally, you'd want to give him something he might like but doesn't know about, or some kind of guilty pleasure that he wouldn't buy for himself. In either case, you are creating value for the recipient by giving him something that is actually worth more to him than the money you spent on it.

But realistically, most of our gifts fall well short of that high standard. This creates a lot of inefficiency. In 1993, the economist Joel Waldfogel addressed this subject in a paper whose continuing fame in economics circles is due in part to its wonderfully Scrooge-ish title: "The Deadweight Loss of Christmas." Since gifts "may be mismatched with the recipients' preferences," Waldfogel argued, it is likely that "the gift will leave the recipient worse off than if she had made her own consumption choice with an equal amount of cash." He concluded that "holiday gift-giving destroys between 10 percent and a third of the value of gifts."

If gift-giving destroys so much value, why not take the most efficient route and simply give cash? Obviously, some people do. In the small survey of Yale undergraduates on which Waldfogel based his paper, grandparents gave cash 42 percent of the time, and parents gave cash 10 percent of the time. But not once did a student receive cash from his or her significant other. Plainly, there are a few relationships for which a cash gift is appropriate, but in most cases, the social taboo crushes the economist's dream of such a beautifully efficient exchange.

So if cash is inappropriate, and buying gifts is inefficient, wouldn't a gift card—not quite as fungible as cash but also not nearly as coldhearted—be a perfect solution?

You could certainly make that case. And for the merchant, at least, the gift card is a godsend. Just think of it: In the weeks leading up to Christmas, millions of people visit your store or Web site and hand you billions of dollars in exchange for nothing more than a plastic I.O.U. that may never even be redeemed. Best Buy, for instance, earned $16 million last year in gift-card "breakage," which is the industry's term for card value that was bought but never redeemed. Then there's what retailers call "upspending": most customers who do use their gift cards spend some of their own money to buy merchandise that is more expensive than the value of the card.

For the giver, meanwhile, a gift card could hardly be easier. But most economists would argue that if a gift card is so transparently good for the giver, it is necessarily bad for the recipient: the fact that it can be bought so easily signals to the recipient that the giver didn't put much effort into the gift.

In the end, the value of any gift is overwhelmingly dependent on the nature of the relationship between giver and recipient. The economist Alex Tabarrok, writing recently on the Marginal Revolution blog, put an even finer point on this fact, noting that each of us has many "selves," including a "wild self," and that "we want the wild self in someone else to be wild about us." His advice? "If you want to please the economist in me, send me cash. If you want to please my wild self (you know who you are!), use your imagination."

So next year, if you need a gift for a strict rationalist, consider cash. If you want to appeal to someone's wild self, you'll have to use your imagination. And if you're hoping to send a little something extra to the shareholders of Best Buy or the Gap or Tiffany, consider a gift card.

FILLING IN THE TAX GAP
April 2, 2006

This is the time of year when American citizens inevitably think about the Internal Revenue Service and, also inevitably, about how deeply they hate it. But most people who hate the I.R.S. probably do so for the wrong reasons. They think it is a tough and cruel agency, but in fact it is not nearly as tough and cruel as it should be.

The first thing to remember is that the I.R.S. doesn't write the tax code. The agency is quick to point its finger at the true villain: "In the United States, the Congress passes tax laws and requires taxpayers to comply," its mission statement says. "The I.R.S. role is to help the large majority of compliant taxpayers with the tax law, while ensuring that the minority who are unwilling to comply pay their fair share."

So the I.R.S. is like a street cop or, more precisely, the biggest fleet of street cops in the world, who are asked to enforce laws written by a few hundred people on behalf of a few hundred million people, a great many of whom find these laws too complex, too expensive and unfair.

And yet most Americans say they are proud to pay their taxes. In an independent poll conducted last year for the I.R.S. Oversight

Board, 96 percent of the respondents agreed with the statement "It is every American's civic duty to pay their fair share of taxes," while 93 percent agreed that everyone "who cheats on their taxes should be held accountable." On the other hand, when asked what influences their decision to report and pay taxes honestly, 62 percent answered "fear of an audit," while 68 percent said it was the fact that their income was already being reported to the I.R.S. by third parties. For all the civic duty floating around, it would seem that most compliance is determined by good old-fashioned incentives.

So which of these incentives work and which do not? To find out, the I.R.S. conducted the National Research Program, a three-year study during which 46,000 randomly selected 2001 tax returns were intensively reviewed. (The I.R.S. doesn't specify what these 46,000 people were subjected to, but it may well have been the kind of inquisition that has earned the agency its horrid reputation.) Using this sample, the study found a tax gap— the difference between taxes owed and taxes actually paid—of $345 billion, or nearly one-fifth of all taxes collected by the I.R.S. This sum happens to be just a few billion dollars less than the projected federal budget deficit for 2007; it also amounts to more than $1,000 worth of cheating by every man, woman and child in the U.S.

But most people *aren't* cheating. And when you take a look at who does cheat and who doesn't, it becomes pretty clear just why people pay their taxes at all. The key statistic in the I.R.S.'s study is called the Net Misreporting Percentage. It measures the amount that was misreported on every major line item on those 46,000 returns. In the "wages, salaries, tips" category, for instance, Americans are underreporting only 1 percent of their actual income.

Meanwhile, in the "nonfarm proprietor income" category—think of self-employed workers like a restaurateur or the boss of a small construction crew—57 percent of the income goes unreported. That's $68 billion in unpaid taxes right there.

Why such a huge difference between the wage earner and a restaurateur? Simple: The only person reporting the restaurateur's income to the I.R.S. is the restaurateur himself; for the wage earner, his employer is generating a W2 to let the I.R.S. know exactly how much he has been paid. And the wage earner's taxes are automatically withheld from his every check, while the restaurateur has all year to decide if, and how much, he will pay.

Does this mean that the average self-employed worker is less honest than the average wage earner? Not necessarily. It's just that he has much more incentive to cheat. He knows that the only chance the I.R.S. has of learning his true income and expenditures is to audit him. And all he has to do is look at the I.R.S.'s infinitesimal audit rate—last year, the agency conducted face-to-face audits on just 0.19 percent of all individual taxpayers—to feel pretty confident to go ahead and cheat.

So why do people really pay their taxes: because it is the right thing to do, or because they fear getting caught if they don't? It sure seems to be the latter. A combination of good technology (employer reporting and withholding) and poor logic (most people who don't cheat radically overestimate their chances of being audited) makes the system work. And while it sounds bad to hear that Americans underpay their taxes by nearly one-fifth, the tax economist Joel Slemrod estimates that the U.S. is easily within the upper tier of worldwide compliance rates.

Still, unless you are personally cheating by one-fifth or more, you *should* be mad at the I.R.S.—not because it's too vigilant, but because it's not nearly vigilant enough. Why should you pay your fair share when the agency lets a few hundred billion dollars of other people's money go uncollected every year?

The I.R.S. itself would love to change this dynamic. In the past few years, it has increased significantly its enforcement revenue and its audit rate, despite a budget that is only fractionally larger. A main task of any I.R.S. commissioner is to beg Congress and the White House for resources. For all the obvious appeal of having the I.R.S. collect every dollar owed to the government, it is just as obviously unappealing for most politicians to advocate a more vigorous I.R.S. Michael Dukakis tried this during his 1988 presidential campaign, and—well, it didn't work.

Left to enforce a tax code no one likes upon a public that knows it can practically cheat at will, the I.R.S. does its best to fiddle around the edges. Once in a while, it hits pay dirt.

In the early 1980's, an I.R.S. research officer in Washington named John Szilagyi had seen enough random audits to know that some taxpayers were incorrectly claiming dependents for the sake of an exemption. Sometimes it was a genuine mistake (a divorced wife and husband making duplicate claims on their children), and sometimes the claims were comically fraudulent (Szilagyi recalls at least one dependent's name listed as Fluffy, who was quite obviously a pet rather than a child).

Szilagyi decided that the most efficient way to clean up this mess was to simply require taxpayers to list their children's Social Security numbers. "Initially, there was a lot of resistance to the idea," says Szilagyi, now 66 and retired to Florida. "The answer I got was that it was too much like '1984.' " The idea never made its way out of the agency.

A few years later, however, with Congress clamoring for more tax revenue, Szilagyi's idea was dug up, rushed forward and put into law for tax year 1986. When the returns started coming in the following April, Szilagyi recalls, he and his bosses were shocked: seven million dependents had suddenly vanished from the tax rolls, some incalculable combination of real pets and phantom children. Szilagyi's clever twist generated nearly $3 billion in revenues in a single year.

Szilagyi's immediate bosses felt he should get some kind of reward for his idea, but their superiors weren't convinced. So Szilagyi called his congressman, who got the reward process back on track. Finally, five years after his brainstorm became the law, Szilagyi, who earned about $80,000 annually at the time, was given a check for $25,000. By this point, his idea had generated roughly $14 billion.

Which suggests at least one legitimate reason to dislike the I.R.S.: if the agency hadn't been so stingy with Szilagyi's reward back then, it probably would have attracted a lot more of the anti-cheating wizards it really needs today.

LAID-BACK LABOR
May 6, 2007

During the late 19th century, piano manufacturing was one of New York City's largest industries. Every right-minded American family, it seemed, wanted to fill its home with music. The advent of the player piano—a music-making machine that required zero talent—drove the boom even further. By the 1920s, some 300,000 pianos were being sold in the United States each year, roughly two-thirds of them player pianos.

But a pair of newer technologies, the radio and the phonograph, soon began to drive the piano into a deep disfavor that continues to this day. Last year, Americans bought only 76,966 pianos. That's a decrease of 75 percent over a period in which the population more than doubled. As much as people may love music, most of them apparently don't feel the need to make it for themselves. According to Census Bureau statistics, only 7.3 percent of American adults have played a musical instrument in the past 12 months.

Compare this with the 17.5 percent of adults who currently engage in what the Census Bureau calls "cooking for fun." Or consider that 41 percent of households have flower gardens, 25 percent raise vegetables and 13 percent grow fruit trees—even though just 1 percent of Americans live on a farm today, down from 30 percent in 1920. On a more personal note: one of the authors of this column has a sister who runs a thriving yarn store, while the other is married to a knitting devotee who might buy $40 worth of yarn for a single scarf and then spend 10 hours knitting it. Even if her labor is valued at only $10 an hour, the scarf costs at least $140—or roughly $100 more than a similar machine-made scarf might cost.

Isn't it puzzling that so many middle-aged Americans are spending so much of their time and money performing menial labors when they don't have to? Just as the radio and phonograph proved to be powerful substitutes for the piano, the forces of technology and capitalism have greatly eased the burden of feeding and clothing ourselves. So what's with all the knitting, gardening and "cooking for fun"? Why do some forms of menial labor survive as hobbies while others have been killed off? (For instance, we can't think of a single person who, since the invention of the washing machine, practices "laundry for fun.")

Economists have been trying for decades to measure how much leisure time people have and how they spend it, but there has been precious little consensus. This is in part because it's hard to say what constitutes leisure and in part because measurements of leisure over the years have not been very consistent.

Economists typically separate our daily activities into three categories: market work (which produces income), home production (unpaid chores) and pure leisure. How, then, are we to categorize knitting, gardening and cooking? While preparing meals at home can certainly be much cheaper than dining out and therefore viewed as home production, what about the "cooking for fun" factor?

In an attempt to address such gray areas, the economists Valerie A. Ramey and Neville Francis classified certain home activities as labor and others as leisure. In their recent paper "A Century of Work and Leisure," they employed a 1985 time-use survey in which people ranked their enjoyment of various activities on a scale of 0 to 10. Knitting, gardening and cooking were in the middle of the scale, with a 7.7, 7.1 and 6.6, respectively. These ranked well behind the three favorite activities—sex, playing sports and fishing (which scored 9.3, 9.2 and 9.1)—but firmly ahead of paying bills, cleaning the house and, yes, doing the laundry (5.2, 4.9 and 4.8).

But here's where it gets tricky. Ramey and Francis decided that anything at or above a 7.3 is leisure, while anything below is home production. (Knitting, therefore, makes the grade as leisure; gardening and cooking do not.) This leads them to calculate that we spend less time doing market work today than we did in 1900 but more time in home production. Men, it seems, have contributed mightily to this upsurge: in 1920, employed men spent only two or three hours a week on home production, but they averaged 11 hours by 1965 and 16 hours by 2004.

But how many of those home-production hours are in fact leisure hours? This, it seems, is the real question here: What makes a certain activity work for one person and leisure for another?

With no disrespect toward Ramey and Francis, how about this for an alternative definition: Whether or not you're getting paid, it's work if someone else tells you to do it and leisure if you choose to do it yourself. If you are the sort of person who likes to mow his own lawn even though you can afford to pay someone to do it, consider how you'd react if your neighbor offered to pay you the going rate to mow his lawn. The odds are that you wouldn't accept his job offer.

And so a great many people who can afford not to perform menial labor choose to do so, because—well, why? An evolutionary biologist might say that embedded in our genes is a drive to feed and clothe ourselves and tame our surroundings. An economist, meanwhile, might argue that we respond to incentives that go well beyond the financial; and that, mercifully, we are left free to choose which tasks we want to do ourselves.

Granted, these choices may say a good bit about who we are and where we come from. One of us, for instance (the economist, who lives in Chicago), grew up comfortably in a Midwestern city and has fond memories of visiting his grandparents' small farm. This author recently bought an indoor hydroponic plant grower. It cost about $150 and to date has produced approximately 14 cherry tomatoes—which, once you factor in the cost of seeds, electricity and even a nominal wage for the labor, puts the average price of a single tomato at roughly $20.

The other one of us (the journalist, who lives in New York) grew up on a small farm and was regularly engaged in all sorts of sowing, mucking and reaping. He, therefore, has little vestigial desire to grow his own food—but he is happy to spend hours shopping for and preparing a special dinner for family and friends. Such dinners, even if the labor were valued at only $10 an hour, are more expensive than a commensurate takeout meal.

Maybe someday the New York guy will get to cook a meal with some of the Chicago guy's cherry tomatoes. Add in another $32 for next-day shipping, and it might become one of the most expensive meals in recent memory—and, surely, worth every penny.

A Q&A WITH THE AUTHORS

Author Q&A's have great potential but often fail because of the canned and bland questions fed to authors by their publishers — or, worse, the fawning questions invented by the authors themselves. (*Tell us, were you brilliant even as a child?*) So let's put an end to that! We asked readers of our blog, www.freakonomics.com, to ask us what they wanted to know. As you'll see, they responded with vigor.

Q: How does your collaboration work? —Ryan

A: In a word, easily. The two of us have very different skill sets. Levitt is an academic researcher and Dubner is a writer. That doesn't mean that Levitt doesn't write; he does. And Dubner does research too. But if you were to spend a day looking over our shoulders (Levitt's in Chicago and Dubner's in New York), you'd find that Levitt spends most of his day feeding numbers into a computer while Dubner spends most of his day feeding words. That said, the nature of our collaboration on a given day is dependent on the nature of the material we are working on. We e-mail back and forth voluminously; we talk on the phone so much that our wives roll their eyes. In sum, we are more like a pitcher and catcher on a baseball team than, say, a right wing and a left wing on a soccer team.

Q: Can you tell us about subjects that you researched but didn't write about, possibly because the data didn't tell you anything, it was too controversial, etc. I'd like to hear what was left behind on the editing room floor. —Mickey

A: If you think we would leave something out because it is too controversial, you obviously don't know us very well! Maybe you will be convinced after reading our second book, *SuperFreakonomics,* where we write about prostitutes, terrorists, global-warming hysterics, and profit-seeking oncologists. There are countless research projects for which we couldn't find the right data, or where the results just turned out not to be very interesting. For every 10 research ideas, only 2 will turn into academic papers and only 1 will be interesting enough for a book like this. Some readers assume that we can go out and answer any question we want, but it doesn't work that way. The downside is that all kinds of fascinating subjects have eluded our grasp (so far); the upside is that readers know the stories we *do* tell are supported by data rather than just opinion or whimsy.

Q: Am I worse off for never having read *Freakonomics*? —Terry

A: Sadly, yes. Independent testing has shown that people who read *Freakonomics* have sweeter-smelling breath, better posture, and more interesting dreams. Also, women feel no pain during childbirth; male readers find that their sperm swim faster.

Q: Are you more concerned with presenting the average citizen a new way of looking at the world or with stimulating debate among people who are familiar with economics and its methods of analysis? —Christopher Luccy

A: Well, the obvious answer would be "both." But if we had to choose one, it would surely be the former. There are a million books that explain the principles of economics, and they are widely read, usually at universities. But those books explain what economics *is;* they don't really explain how to look at the world like an economist. While this latter goal may sound like something you wouldn't wish on your worst enemy, it can in fact be made bearable—as long you cover topics that the average reader is passionate about. Sumo wrestling, for instance.

Q: How much of the book's success do you believe can be attributed to your choice of title?

A: Levitt's sister, Linda Jines, came up with the title; she is the real creative genius in the family. It's hard to know how important the title has been, but our guess is ... *very.* On the other hand, as we write in the book, the name you give your child has no discernible effect on that child's life outcome. So should we expect the same from a book title? Perhaps not; a book and a person have different qualities. Still, it's worth noting that some commercial ventures have succeeded wildly despite having names that, at first, must have seemed a detriment. Do you really think the first producers of *Oprah* had an easy time with that name? And what about ESPN?

Q: Are there any baseball stats that, when compared over a period of time or based on age, show a strong suspicion of steroid use? —Joseph Rollo

A: We've looked in the data for evidence of steroid use, as have well-known baseball statisticians like Nate Silver (who is even better-known as the proprietor of FiveThirtyEight.com). It has proven hard to find anything that looks like the smoking gun that we see on teacher cheating or sumo wrestling. At this point, what's most likely is that the effects of steroids on a baseball player's performance just aren't that stark. Sure, they get mighty beefy while taking steroids, but a lot of the power hitters were hitting home runs even when they were scrawny rookies.

Q: Tell us about the criticism you have received from traditional/academic colleagues over *Freakonomics.*—J. Plain

A: Levitt's academic colleagues tend to react in one of two ways. The majority of economists thought about it like economists: the success of *Freakonomics* probably increased the number of students wanting to take economics courses, and since the supply of economics teachers is fixed in the short run, the wages of academic economists should rise. That makes economists happy. A second group of economists decided that if Levitt could write a book that people would read, surely they could too. So there has been a flurry of "popular" books by economists— some good, some not so good. And then, inevitably, there are a handful of economists who feel that he violated the secret handshake of economics by showing the outside world that what economists do really isn't that hard or complex. They will never forgive him.

Q: What will a gallon of gas cost in 2019? What implications will this price have on our culture? —Mike Thomas

A: Economists, like everyone else, are terrible at predicting the future. But in all likelihood, a gallon of gas in 2019 will cost about the same (when adjusted for inflation) as a gallon of gas in 2009. Even if we are running out of oil (which we probably aren't), we won't be running out that soon. Perhaps the government will have the good sense to put larger taxes on gasoline, which we've advocated for a long time because of what economists call the negative externalities of driving.

Q: What do bishops and tennis professionals have in common? —Stan

A: Comfortable shoes, unusual headgear, and a lot of love.

Q: Of the examples discussed in the book, which have gained the greatest traction in the popular/political discussion? —Rick Groves

A: There has been a lot of talk about the relationship between legalized abortion and the crime rate. And some governments have cited the low wages of street-level drug dealers as an incentive to young people to go legit. But on a day-to-day level, the part of the book that's probably spurred the most *change* is our discussion of real-estate agents. The standard fixed-commission, full-service Realtor model is gradually melting away. Even the White House weighed in, with the Real Estate Settlement Procedures Act, which is meant to increase transparency between Realtors and their customers.

Q: Why do you think that the U.S. Mint is still producing pennies if the cost of physically producing a penny is much greater than the value of the resulting penny? —Dutch

A: Don't get us started! Dubner has by now become a well-known penny hawk, telling anyone who will listen—including *60 Minutes*—that the penny is a beloved artifact that should finally be put out of its misery. It represents a massive waste of time and resources. One of its strongest supporters is the zinc lobby; did you know that modern pennies happen to be made of 97.5 percent zinc? The biggest reasons to keep the penny are inertia and nostalgia, but those aren't very good reasons. Dubner counsels his children to avoid pennies at all costs, even throwing them away if necessary. For this, he has been called un-American.

Q: Why are there so few economists in politics, as it is one of the most important issues in a country? Is it that they'd rather become professors, work in the private sector, become advisers or work in the Treasury, or do they think it is too compromising? —Neil

A: You ask an intriguing and important question. Many countries around the world have elected economists as president. In the U.S., however, economists generally do not fit into the political framework well. Why? One guess is that they are trained to think rationally and tell the truth about data. As any observer of U.S. politics knows, rationality and unvarnished data are practically forbidden on the campaign trail. Politicians (and, presumably, voters) are much more interested in emotion and rhetoric. That said, some administrations (Obama's, for one) hold economists in far higher regard than others.

Q: Who would win an arm-wrestling match between Dubner and Levitt? Golf? Tennis? Chess? —Kevin

A: Dubner would definitely win arm-wrestling, Levitt would win golf. Tennis and chess would probably be hard-fought matches. Note: they are both quite good bowlers.

Q: Some people buy a book because it is interesting and well written and some people buy a book because others are reading it. To what extent do you think the success of *Freakonomics* is due to the latter rather than the former? —Euclid

A: We have wondered the same. Books being what they are— not just stories and information, but stories and information *that people like to talk about with other people*—there is obviously an extra incentive to read what everyone else is reading. Our opinion is that of all the modes of book promotion (ads, reviews, interviews, etc.), none is so powerful as good word-of-mouth.

Q: What do you guys like to read (recreationally)? —Robb

A: Levitt admits to having the reading interests of a tweener girl, the *Twilight* series and *Harry Potter* in particular. Dubner's weak spot is sports, and newspapers (the old-fashioned kind, on paper).

Q: While many of the stories and conclusions in *Freakonomics* are fascinating, there seems to be no clear methodology or set of principles that profit-maximizing executives can use in managing their business. Have you ever considered distilling the lessons (such as they are) into a handbook for the manager interested in exploiting the "hidden side" of business? —Drew

A: Drew, have you considered becoming a literary agent? (Also, we admire your ability to simultaneously flatter and condemn.) Here are the facts. For reasons that remain unclear, our publisher initially called *Freakonomics* a business book. This led to certain expectations—nearly all of which, surely, were dashed the moment any credible businessperson read the book. You are right: we do not lay out any profitable methodologies at all. That said, in recent years Levitt has done a lot of research in the business arena, which we feel may someday yield a good book that does indeed explore the "hidden side" of business.

Q: How much is all the tea in China really worth? —Dave F.

A: About $1.5 billion. But just imagine how much more valuable it would be if, like marijuana, it were illegal. (Note to selves: corner the market on Chinese tea, then bribe the government to criminalize it.)

NOTES

The bulk of this book was drawn from the research of Steven D. Levitt, often done in concert with one or more collaborators. The notes below include citations for the academic papers on which the material was based; most of them are available for download at http://pricetheory.uchicago.edu/levitt/ LevittCV.html. We have also made liberal use of other scholars' research, which is cited below; we thank them not only for their work but for the subsequent conversations that allowed us to best present their ideas. Other material in this book comes from previously unpublished research or interviews by one or both of the authors. Material not listed in these notes was generally drawn from readily accessible databases, news reports, and reference works.

AN EXPLANATORY NOTE

XXI   THE ITALICIZED EXCERPT originally appeared in Stephen J. Dubner, "The Probability That a Real-Estate Agent Is Cheating You (and Other Riddles of Modern Life)," *The New York Times Magazine,* August 3, 2003.

INTRODUCTION: THE HIDDEN SIDE OF EVERYTHING

1–5   **THE FALL AND FALL OF CRIME:** The crime-drop argument can be found in Steven D. Levitt, "Understanding Why Crime Fell in the 1990's: Four Factors That Explain the Decline and Six That Do Not," *Journal of Economic Perspectives* 18, no. 1 (2004), pp. 163–90. / **1–2 The superpredator:** See Eric Pooley, "Kids with Guns," *New York Magazine,* August 9, 1991; John J. DiIulio Jr., "The Coming of the Super-Predators," *Weekly Standard,* November 27, 1995; Tom Morganthau, "The Lull Before the Storm?" *Newsweek,* December 4, 1995; Richard Zoglin, "Now for the Bad News: A Teenage Time Bomb," *Time,* January 15, 1996; and Ted Gest, "Crime Time Bomb," *U.S. News & World Report,* March 25, 1996. / **2 James Alan Fox's dire predictions** can be found in a pair of government reports: "Trends in Juvenile Violence: A Report to the United States Attorney General on Current and Future Rates of Juvenile Offending" (Washington, D.C.: Bureau of Justice Statistics, 1996) and "Trends in Juvenile Violence: An Update" (Washington, D.C.: Bureau of Justice Statistics, 1997). / **2 President Clinton's fearful comment** came during a 1997 speech in Boston announcing new anti-crime measures; see Alison Mitchell, "Clinton Urges Campaign Against Youth Crime," *The New York Times,* February 20, 1997. / **3–4 The story of Norma McCorvey/Jane Roe:** See Douglas S. Wood, "Who Is 'Jane Roe'?: Anonymous No More, Norma McCorvey No Longer Supports Abortion Rights," CNN.com, June 18, 2003; and Norma McCorvey with Andy Meisler, *I Am Roe: My Life, Roe v. Wade, and Freedom of Choice* (New York: HarperCollins, 1994). / **4–5 The abortion-crime link** is laid out in John J. Donohue III and Steven D. Levitt, "The Impact of Legalized Abortion on Crime," *Quarterly Journal of Economics* 116, no. 2 (2001), pp. 379–420. Other scholars have had disagreements with portions of the theory. See Ted Joyce, "Did Legalized Abortion Lower Crime?" *Journal of Human Resources* 39, no. 1 (2004), pp. 1–28; and the Donohue-Levitt response, "Further Evidence That Legalized Abortion Lowered Crime: A Response to Joyce," *Journal of Human Resources* 39, no. 1 (2004), pp. 29–49. See also Christopher L. Foote and Christopher F. Goetz, "Testing Economic Hypotheses with State-Level Data: A Comment on Donohue and Levitt (2001)," Federal Reserve Bank of Boston working paper 05–15 (2005); and, again, the Donohue-Levitt response, "Measurement Error, Legalized Abortion, the Decline in Crime: A Response to Foote and Goetz (2005)," National Bureau of Economic Research working paper, 2006.

5–8 **THE REAL REAL-ESTATE STORY:** The study measuring how a real-estate agent treats the sale of her own home versus a client's home is Steven D. Levitt and Chad Syverson, "Market Distortions When Agents Are Better Informed: A Theoretical and Empirical Exploration of the Value of Information in Real Estate Transactions," National Bureau of Economic Research working paper, 2005. / **6 The lax California auto mechanics** are discussed in Thomas Hubbard, "An Empirical Examination of Moral Hazard in the Vehicle Inspection Market," *RAND Journal of Economics* 29, no. 1 (1998), pp. 406–26; and in Thomas Hubbard, "How Do Consumers Motivate Experts? Reputational Incentives in an Auto Repair Market," *Journal of Law & Economics* 45, no. 2 (2002), pp. 437–68. / **6 Doctors who perform extra C-sections** are examined in Jonathan Gruber and Maria Owings, "Physician Financial Incentives and Caesarean Section Delivery," *RAND Journal of Economics* 27, no. 1 (1996), pp. 99–123.

8–11 **THE MYTH OF CAMPAIGN SPENDING** is told in greater detail in a trio of papers: Steven D. Levitt, "Using Repeat Challengers to Estimate the Effect of Campaign Spending on Election Outcomes in the U.S. House," *Journal of Political Economy,* August 1994, pp. 777–98; Steven D. Levitt, "Congressional Campaign Finance Reform," *Journal of Economic Perspectives* 9 (1995), pp. 183–93; and Steven D. Levitt and James M. Snyder Jr., "The Impact of Federal Spending on House Election Outcomes," *Journal of Political Economy* 105, no. 1 (1997), pp. 30–53.

12 **EIGHT GLASSES OF WATER A DAY:** See Robert J. Davis, "Can Water Aid Weight Loss?" *The Wall Street Journal,* March 16, 2004, which cites an Institute of Medicine report concluding that "there is no scientific basis for the recommendation [of eight glasses of water a day] and that most people get enough water through normal consumption of foods and beverages."

13–14 **ADAM SMITH** is still well worth reading, of course (especially if you have infinite patience); so too is Robert Heilbroner's *The Worldly Philosophers* (New York: Simon & Schuster, 1953), which contains memorable profiles of Smith, Karl Marx, Thorstein Veblen, John Maynard Keynes, Joseph Schumpeter, and other giants of economics.

1. WHAT DO SCHOOLTEACHERS AND SUMO WRESTLERS HAVE IN COMMON?

15–16   THE ISRAELI DAY-CARE STUDY: See Uri Gneezy and Aldo Rustichini, "A Fine Is a Price," *Journal of Legal Studies* 29, no. 1 (January 2000), pp. 1–17; and Uri Gneezy, "The 'W' Effect of Incentives," University of Chicago working paper.

18–19   MURDER THROUGH THE AGES: See Manuel Eisner, "Secular Trends of Violence, Evidence, and Theoretical Interpretations," *Crime and Justice: A Review of Research* 3 (2003); also presented in Manuel Eisner, "Violence and the Rise of Modern Society," *Criminology in Cambridge*, October 2003, pp. 3–7.

20   THOMAS JEFFERSON ON CAUSE AND EFFECT: *Autobiography of Thomas Jefferson* (1829; reprint, New York: G. P. Putnam's Sons, 1914), p. 156.

20–21   BLOOD FOR MONEY: See Richard M. Titmuss, "The Gift of Blood," *Trans-action* 8 (1971); also presented in *The Philosophy of Welfare: Selected Writings by R. M. Titmuss*, ed. B. Abel-Smith and K. Titmuss (London: Allen and Unwin, 1987). See also William E. Upton, "Altruism, Attribution, and Intrinsic Motivation in the Recruitment of Blood Donors," Ph.D. diss., Cornell University, 1973.

22   WHEN SEVEN MILLION CHILDREN DISAPPEARED OVERNIGHT: See Jeffrey Liebman, "Who Are the Ineligible EITC Recipients?" *National Tax Journal* 53 (2000), pp. 1165–86. Liebman's paper was citing John Szilagyi, "Where Some of Those Dependents Went," *1990 Research Conference Report: How Do We Affect Taxpayer Behavior?* (Internal Revenue Service, March 1991), pp. 162–63.

22–35   CHEATING TEACHERS IN CHICAGO: This study, which also provides considerable background on high-stakes testing, is detailed in two papers: Brian A. Jacob and Steven D. Levitt, "Rotten Apples: An Investigation of the Prevalence and Predictors of Teacher Cheating," *Quarterly Journal of Economics* 118, no. 3 (2003), pp. 843–77; and

Brian A. Jacob and Steven D. Levitt, "Catching Cheating Teachers: The Results of an Unusual Experiment in Implementing Theory," *Brookings-Wharton Papers on Urban Affairs,* 2003, pp. 185–209. / **24 The Oakland fifth-grader with the extra-helpful teacher:** Based on an author interview with a former assistant superintendent of the Oakland Public Schools. / **32 Cheating among North Carolina teachers:** See G. H. Gay, "Standardized Tests: Irregularities in Administering of Tests Affect Test Results," *Journal of Instructional Psychology* 17, no. 2 (1990), pp. 93–103. / **33–35 The story of Arne Duncan, CEO of the Chicago schools,** was based largely on author interviews; see also Amy D'Orio, "The Outsider Comes In," *District Administration: The Magazine for K–12 Education Leaders,* August 2002; and various *Chicago Tribune* articles by Ray Quintanilla.

35–36 THE UNIVERSITY OF GEORGIA BASKETBALL TEST was made public when the university released 1,500 pages of documents in response to an investigation by the National Collegiate Athletic Association.

37 THE CHICAGO BLACK SOX: Several readers of the original version of *Freakonomics* have declared that the White Sox came to be called the Black Sox not because of the gambling scandal, but for another reason entirely. This is how the explanation plays out on the user-generated encyclopedia wikipedia.org: "The term 'Black Sox' came about earlier in [1919], when [team owner Charles] Comiskey decided to make players pay for their own laundry. The players stopped doing their laundry in protest, and as their white stockings became soiled and dark, the writers tagged them with that nickname." As endearing as this explanation may seem, Levitt and Dubner found no support for it in the historical record.

38–43 CHEATING IN SUMO: See Mark Duggan and Steven D. Levitt, "Winning Isn't Everything: Corruption in Sumo Wrestling," *American Economic Review* 92, no. 5 (December 2002), pp. 1594–1605. / **38–39 There is a lot to know about sumo,** and quite a bit can be found in these books: Mina Hall, *The Big Book of Sumo* (Berkeley, Calif.: Stonebridge Press, 1997); Keisuke Itai, *Nakabon* (Tokyo: Shogakkan Press, 2000); and Onaruto, *Yaocho* (Tokyo: Line Books, 2000). / **42–43 Two sumo whistle-blowers die mysteriously:** See Sheryl WuDunn, "Sumo Wrestlers (They're BIG) Facing a Hard Fall," *The New York Times,* June 28, 1996; and Anthony Spaeth, "Sumo Quake:

Japan's Revered Sport Is Marred by Charges of Tax Evasion, Match Fixing, Ties to Organized Crime, and Two Mysterious Deaths," reporting by Irene M. Kunii and Hiroki Tashiro, *Time* (International Edition), September 30, 1996.

44 THE BAGEL MAN: Paul Feldman was looking for a research economist to take an interest in his data, and brought himself to Steven Levitt's attention. (Several other scholars had passed.) Levitt and then Dubner subsequently visited Feldman's bagel operation near Washington, D.C. Their research led to an article that was substantially similar to the version of the story published here: Stephen J. Dubner and Steven D. Levitt, "What the Bagel Man Saw," *The New York Times Magazine,* June 6, 2004. Levitt has also written an academic paper about Feldman's bagel operation: "An Economist Sells Bagels: A Case Study in Profit Maximization," National Bureau of Economic Research working paper, 2006. / **46** *The "Beer on the Beach" study* is discussed in Richard H. Thaler, "Mental Accounting and Consumer Choice," Marketing Science 4 (Summer 1985), pp. 119–214; also worth reading is Richard H. Thaler, *The Winner's Curse: Paradoxes and Anomalies of Economic Life* (New York: Free Press, 1992).

2. HOW IS THE KU KLUX KLAN LIKE A GROUP OF REAL-ESTATE AGENTS?

51–62 SPILLING THE KLAN'S SECRETS: This section has been substantially revised since the original version of *Freakonomics* was published, owing to the authors' discovery that Stetson Kennedy—in both his memoir, *The Klan Unmasked,* and in interviews with the authors— had misrepresented his role in personally infiltrating and attacking the Klan. (See page 240 ["Hoodwinked?" *The New York Times,* January 8, 2006] for a fuller explanation of this issue.) For general Klan history, see Col. Winfield Jones, *Knights of the Ku Klux Klan* (1941); David M. Chalmers, *Hooded Americanism: The First Century of the Ku Klux Klan, 1865–1965* (Garden City, NY: Doubleday, 1965); Wyn Craig Wade, *The Fiery Cross: The Ku Klux Klan in America* (New York: Simon & Schuster, 1987); and many others. The most relevant writings of Stetson Kennedy include *Southern Exposure* (Garden City, NY: Doubleday, 1946; republished in 1991 by Florida Atlantic

University Press) and *The Klan Unmasked* (Boca Raton: Florida Atlantic University Press, 1990), which was originally published as *I Rode with the Ku Klux Klan* (London: Arco Publishers, 1954). Also helpful was Ben Green, *Before His Time: The Untold Story of Harry T. Moore, America's First Civil Rights Martyr* (New York: Simon & Schuster, 1999). Stetson Kennedy's documents relating to the Klan, as well as the reports of "John Brown" and other related material, can be found in various archives, including the Schomburg Center for Research in Black Culture, a public library in New York City; the Georgia State University Library in Atlanta; and the archives of the Anti-Defamation League in New York City. Transcripts of the Drew Pearson *Washington Merry-Go-Round* radio program can be found at http://www.aladin.wrlc.org/gsdl/collect/pearson/pearson .shtml.

62–63 WHAT HAPPENED TO TERM-LIFE RATES? See Jeffrey R. Brown and Austan Goolsbee, "Does the Internet Make Markets More Competitive? Evidence from the Life Insurance Industry," *Journal of Political Economy* 110, no. 3 (June 2002), pp. 481–507.

63 SUPREME COURT JUSTICE LOUIS D. BRANDEIS writing that "Sunlight is said to be the best of disinfectants": See Louis D. Brandeis, *Other People's Money—and How Bankers Use It* (New York: Frederick A. Stokes, 1914).

63–64 THE BRAND-NEW USED-CAR CONUNDRUM: This thesis, and indeed much of what we think today about "asymmetric information," stems from a paper that George A. Akerlof wrote during his first year as an assistant professor at Berkeley in 1966–67. It was rejected three times—two of the journals told Akerlof that they "did not publish papers on topics of such triviality," as he later recalled— before being published as George A. Akerlof, "The Market for 'Lemons': Quality Uncertainty and the Market Mechanism," *Quarterly Journal of Economics*, August 1970. Some thirty years later, the paper won Akerlof the Nobel Prize in Economics; he is widely considered the nicest man to have ever won the award.

66–67 THE ENRON TAPES: As of this writing, the tapes could be heard on http://www.cbsnews.com/stories/2004/06/01/eveningnews/main 6_20626.shtml. See also Richard A. Oppel Jr., "Enron Traders on

Grandma Millie and Making Out Like Bandits," *The New York Times*, June 13, 2004.

67   ARE ANGIOPLASTIES NECESSARY? See Gina Kolata, "New Heart Studies Question the Value of Opening Arteries," *The New York Times*, March 21, 2004.

68–73   THE REAL REAL-ESTATE STORY, REVISITED: See Steven D. Levitt and Chad Syverson, "Market Distortions When Agents Are Better Informed: A Theoretical and Empirical Exploration of the Value of Information in Real-Estate Transactions," National Bureau of Economic Research working paper, 2005.

74   TRENT LOTT, NOT-SO-SECRET SEGREGATIONIST? The circumstances surrounding Lott's damaging comments are well summarized in Dan Goodgame and Karen Tumulty, "Lott: Tripped Up by History," Time.com/cnn.com, December 16, 2002.

74–77   THE WEAKEST LINK: See Steven D. Levitt, "Testing Theories of Discrimination: Evidence from *The Weakest Link*," *Journal of Law and Economics* 17 (October 2004), pp. 431–52. / **76 The theory of taste-based discrimination** originates with Gary S. Becker, *The Economics of Discrimination* (Chicago: University of Chicago Press, 1957). / **77 The theory of information-based discrimination** is derived from a number of papers, including Edmund Phelps, "A Statistical Theory of Racism and Sexism," *American Economic Review* 62, no. 4 (1972), pp. 659–61; and Kenneth Arrow, "The Theory of Discrimination," *Discrimination in Labor Markets,* ed. Orley Ashenfelter and Albert Rees (Princeton, N.J.: Princeton University Press, 1973).

77–82   THE ONLINE DATING STORY: See Günter J. Hitsch, Ali Hortaçsu, and Dan Ariely, "What Makes You Click: An Empirical Analysis of Online Dating," University of Chicago working paper, 2005.

82   VOTERS LYING ABOUT DINKINS / GIULIANI: See Timur Kuran, *Private Truths, Public Lies: The Social Consequences of Preference Falsification* (Cambridge, Mass.: Harvard University Press, 1995); also Kevin Sack, "Governor Joins Dinkins Attack Against Rival," *The New York Times,* October 27, 1989; and Sam Roberts, "Uncertainty over Polls Clouds Strategy in Mayor Race," *The New York Times,* October 31, 1989.

82–83 VOTERS LYING ABOUT DAVID DUKE: See Kuran, *Private Truths, Public Lies;* also Peter Applebome, "Republican Quits Louisiana Race in Effort to Defeat Ex-Klansman," *The New York Times,* October 5, 1990; and Peter Applebome, "Racial Politics in South's Contests: Hot Wind of Hate or Last Gasp?" *The New York Times,* November 5, 1990.

83 DAVID DUKE, MASTER OF INFORMATION ABUSE: Among the many helpful sources for this material were Karen Henderson, "David Duke's Work-Release Program," *National Public Radio,* May 14, 2004; and the exhaustive John McQuaid, "Duke's Decline," *New Orleans Times-Picayune,* April 13, 2003.

3. WHY DO DRUG DEALERS STILL LIVE WITH THEIR MOMS?

85–86 JOHN KENNETH GALBRAITH'S "CONVENTIONAL WISDOM": See "The Concept of the Conventional Wisdom," the second chapter of *The Affluent Society* (Boston: Houghton Mifflin, 1958).

86–87 MITCH SNYDER AND THE HOMELESS MILLIONS: The controversy over Snyder's activism was covered widely, particularly in Colorado newspapers, during the early 1980s and was revisited in 1990 when Snyder committed suicide. A good overview is provided in Gary S. Becker and Guity Nashat Becker, "How the Homeless 'Crisis' Was Hyped," in *The Economics of Life* (New York: McGraw-Hill, 1997), pp. 175–76; the chapter was adapted from a 1994 *Business Week* article by the same authors.

87 THE INVENTION OF CHRONIC HALITOSIS: The strange and compelling story of Listerine is beautifully told in James B. Twitchell, *Twenty Ads That Shook the World: The Century's Most Groundbreaking Advertising and How It Changed Us All* (New York: Crown, 2000), pp. 60–69.

87–88 GEORGE W. BUSH AS A MAKE-BELIEVE COWBOY: See Paul Krugman, "New Year's Resolutions," *The New York Times,* December 26, 2003.

88 NOT AS MUCH RAPE AS IS COMMONLY THOUGHT: The 2002 statistics from the National Crime Survey, which is designed to elicit honest responses, suggests that the lifetime risk of a woman's being the

victim of unwanted sexual activity or attempted unwanted sexual activity is about one in eight (not one in three, as is typically argued by advocates). For men, the National Crime Survey suggests a one-in-forty incidence, rather than the one-in-nine incidence cited by advocates.

88–89 NOT AS MUCH CRIME AS THERE ACTUALLY WAS: See Mark Niesse, "Report Says Atlanta Underreported Crimes to Help Land 1996 Olympics," Associated Press, February 20, 2004.

89– SUDHIR VENKATESH'S LONG, STRANGE TRIP INTO THE CRACK DEN: As
106 of this writing, Venkatesh is a professor of sociology and African American studies at Columbia University. /89–90 The biographical material on Venkatesh was drawn largely from author interviews; see also Jordan Marsh, "The Gang Way," *Chicago Reader,* August 8, 1997; and Robert L. Kaiser, "The Science of Fitting In," *Chicago Tribune,* December 10, 2000. / 91–95 The particulars of the crack gang are covered in four papers by Sudhir Alladi Venkatesh and Steven D. Levitt: "The Financial Activities of an Urban Street Gang," *Quarterly Journal of Economics* 115, no. 3 (August 2000), pp. 755–89; " 'Are We a Family or a Business?' History and Disjuncture in the Urban American Street Gang," *Theory and Society* 29 (Autumn 2000), pp. 427–62; "Growing Up in the Projects: The Economic Lives of a Cohort of Men Who Came of Age in Chicago Public Housing," *American Economic Review* 91, no. 2 (2001), pp. 79–84; and "The Political Economy of an American Street Gang," American Bar Foundation working paper, 1998. See also Sudhir Alladi Venkatesh, *American Project: The Rise and Fall of a Modern Ghetto* (Cambridge, Mass.: Harvard University Press, 2000). / 101 Crack dealing as the most dangerous job in America: According to the Bureau of Labor Statistics, the ten most dangerous legitimate occupations are timber cutters, fishers, pilots and navigators, structural metal workers, drivers/sales workers, roofers, electrical power installers, farm occupations, construction laborers, and truck drivers.

107 THE INVENTION OF NYLON STOCKINGS: It was Wallace Carothers, a young Iowa-born chemist employed by DuPont, who, after seven years of trying, found a way to blow liquid polymers through tiny nozzles to create a fiber of superstrong strands. This was nylon. Several years later, DuPont introduced nylon stockings in New York

and London. Contrary to lore, the miracle fabric's name did not derive from a combination of those two cities' names. Nor was it, as rumored, an acronym for "Now You've Lost, Old Nippon," a snub to Japan's dominant silk market. The name was actually a hepped-up rendering of "No Run," a slogan that the new stockings could not in fact uphold, but whose failure hardly diminished their success. Carothers, a longtime depressive, did not live to see his invention blossom: he killed himself in 1937 by drinking cyanide. See Matthew E. Hermes, *Enough for One Lifetime: Wallace Carothers, Inventor of Nylon* (Philadelphia: Chemical Heritage Foundation, 1996).

108   CRACK SLANG: The Greater Dallas Council on Alcohol and Drug Abuse has compiled an extraordinarily entertaining index of cocaine street names. For cocaine powder: Badrock, Bazooka, Beam, Berni, Bernice, Big C, Blast, Blizzard, Blow, Blunt, Bouncing Powder, Bump, C, Caballo, Caine, Candy, Caviar, Charlie, Chicken Scratch, Coca, Cocktail, Coconut, Coke, Cola, Damablanca, Dust, Flake, Flex, Florida Snow, Foo Foo, Freeze, G-Rock, Girl, Goofball, Happy Dust, Happy Powder, Happy Trails, Heaven, King, Lady, Lady Caine, Late Night, Line, Mama Coca, Marching Dust/Powder, Mojo, Monster, Mujer, Nieve, Nose, Nose Candy, P-Dogs, Peruvian, Powder, Press, Prime Time, Rush, Shot, Sleighride, Sniff, Snort, Snow, Snowbirds, Soda, Speedball, Sporting, Stardust, Sugar, Sweet Stuff, Toke, Trails, White Lady, White Powder, Yeyo, Zip. For smokeable cocaine: Base, Ball, Beat, Bisquits, Bones, Boost, Boulders, Brick, Bump, Cakes, Casper, Chalk, Cookies, Crumbs, Cubes, Fatbags, Freebase, Gravel, Hardball, Hell, Kibbles 'n Bits, Kryptonite, Love, Moonrocks, Nuggets, Onion, Pebbles, Piedras, Piece, Ready Rock, Roca, Rock(s), Rock Star, Scotty, Scrabble, Smoke House, Stones, Teeth, Tornado.

109   THE JOHNNY APPLESEED OF CRACK: Oscar Danilo Blandon and his purported alliance with the Central Intelligence Agency are discussed in great detail, and in a manner that stirred great controversy, in a three-part *San Jose Mercury News* series by Gary Webb, beginning on August 18, 1996. See also Tim Golden, "Though Evidence Is Thin, Tale of C.I.A. and Drugs Has a Life of Its Own," *The New York Times*, October 21, 1996; and Gary Webb, *Dark Alliance: The CIA, the Contras, and the Crack Cocaine Explosion* (New York:

Seven Stories Press, 1998). The U.S. Department of Justice later examined the matter in detail in "The C.I.A.–Contra–Crack Cocaine
Controversy: A Review of the Justice Department's Investigations
and Prosecutions," available as of this writing at www.usdoj.gov/
oig/special/9712/ch01p1.htm.

109   **GANGS IN AMERICA:** See Frederick Thrasher, *The Gang* (Chicago:
University of Chicago Press, 1927).

111   **THE SHRINKING OF VARIOUS BLACK–WHITE GAPS, PRE-CRACK:** See Rebecca Blank, "An Overview of Social and Economic Trends by Race,"
in *America Becoming: Racial Trends and Their Consequences,* ed. Neil J.
Smelser, William Julius Wilson, and Faith Mitchell (Washington,
D.C.: National Academy Press, 2001), pp. 21–40. / **111–12 Regarding black infant mortality,** see Douglas V. Almond, Kenneth Y.
Chay, and Michael Greenstone, "Civil Rights, the War on Poverty,
and Black-White Convergence in Infant Mortality in Mississippi,"
National Bureau of Economic Research working paper, 2003.

111–12   **THE VARIOUS DESTRUCTIVE EFFECTS OF CRACK** are discussed in Roland G. Fryer Jr., Paul Heaton, Steven D. Levitt, and Kevin Murphy,
"The Impact of Crack Cocaine," University of Chicago working paper, 2005.

4. WHERE HAVE ALL THE CRIMINALS GONE?

115–17   **NICOLAE CEAUȘESCU'S ABORTION BAN:** Background information on
Romania and the Ceaușescus was drawn from a variety of sources,
including "Eastern Europe, the Third Communism," *Time,* March
18, 1966; "Ceaușescu Ruled with an Iron Grip," *The Washington
Post,* December 26, 1989; Ralph Blumenthal, "The Ceaușescus: 24
Years of Fierce Repression, Isolation and Independence," *The New
York Times,* December 26, 1989; Serge Schmemann, "In Cradle of
Rumanian Revolt, Anger Quickly Overcame Fear," *The New York
Times,* December 30, 1989; Karen Breslau, "Overplanned Parent-
hood: Ceaușescu's Cruel Law," *Newsweek,* January 22, 1990; and
Nicolas Holman, "The Economic Legacy of Ceaușescu," *Student Eco-
nomic Review,* 1994. / **116 The link between the Romanian abortion
ban and life outcomes** has been explored in a pair of papers: Cristian
Pop-Eleches, "The Impact of an Abortion Ban on Socio-Economic

Outcomes of Children: Evidence from Romania," Columbia University working paper, 2002; and Cristian Pop-Eleches, "The Supply of Birth Control Methods, Education and Fertility: Evidence from Romania," Columbia University working paper, 2002.

117–19 THE GREAT AMERICAN CRIME DROP: As noted earlier, this material is drawn from Steven D. Levitt, "Understanding Why Crime Fell in the 1990's: Four Factors That Explain the Decline and Six That Do Not," *Journal of Economic Perspectives* 18, no. 1 (2004), pp. 163–90. / **118 James Alan Fox's "intentional overstatement":** See Torsten Ove, "No Simple Solution for Solving Violent Crimes," *Pittsburgh Post-Gazette,* September 12, 1999.

121 POLITICIANS WERE GROWING INCREASINGLY SOFTER ON CRIME: This and a number of related issues are discussed in Gary S. Becker and Guity Nashat Becker, "Stiffer Jail Terms Will Make Gunmen More Gun-Shy," "How to Tackle Crime? Take a Tough, Head-On Stance," and "The Economic Approach to Fighting Crime," all in *The Economics of Life* (New York: McGraw-Hill, 1997), pp. 135–44; the chapters were adapted from *Business Week* articles by the same authors.

120 INCREASED RELIANCE ON PRISONS: Concerning the fifteenfold increase in drug-crime prisoners, see Ilyana Kuziemko and Steven D. Levitt, "An Empirical Analysis of Imprisoning Drug Offenders," *Journal of Public Economics* 88, nos. 9–10 (2004), pp. 2043–66. / **121–22 What if we just turn all the prisoners loose?** See William Nagel, "On Behalf of a Moratorium on Prison Construction," *Crime and Delinquency* 23 (1977), pp. 152–74. / **122 "Apparently, it takes a Ph.D. . . .":** See John J. DiIulio Jr., "Arresting Ideas: Tougher Law Enforcement Is Driving Down Urban Crime," *Policy Review*, no. 75 (Fall 1995).

122–24 CAPITAL PUNISHMENT: For a full report on New York State's failure to execute a single criminal, see "Capital Punishment in New York State: Statistics from Eight Years of Representation, 1995–2003" (New York: The Capital Defender Office, August 2003), which is available as of this writing at nycdo.org/8yr.html. More recently, New York's Court of Appeals found the death penalty itself unconstitutional, effectively halting all executions. / **123 Executing 1 criminal** translates into 7 fewer homicides: See Isaac Ehrlich, "The Deterrent Effect of Capital Punishment: A Question of Life and Death," *American Economic Review* 65 (1975), pp. 397–417; and Isaac Ehrlich, "Capital Punishment and Deterrence: Some Further Thoughts and Evidence," *Journal of Political Economy* 85 (1977), pp. 741–88. / **124 "I no longer shall tinker with the machinery of death":** From Justice Harry A. Blackmun's dissenting opinion in a 1994 Supreme Court decision denying review of a Texas death-penalty case: *Callins v. Collins,* 510 U.S. 1141 (1994); cited in *Congressional Quarterly Researcher* 5, no. 9 (March 10, 1995). It should be noted that American juries also seem to have lost their appetite for the death penalty—in part, it seems, because of the frequency with which innocent people have been executed in recent years or exonerated while on death row. During the 1990s, an average of 290 criminals were given the death sentence each year; in the first four years of the 2000s, that number had dropped to 174. See Adam Liptak, "Fewer Death Sentences Being Imposed in U.S.," *The New York Times,* September 15, 2004.

124–25   **DO POLICE ACTUALLY LOWER CRIME?** See Steven D. Levitt, "Using Electoral Cycles in Police Hiring to Estimate the Effect of Police on Crime," *American Economic Review* 87, no. 3 (1997), pp. 270–90; Steven D. Levitt, "Why Do Increased Arrest Rates Appear to Reduce Crime: Deterrence, Incapacitation, or Measurement Error?" *Economic Inquiry* 36, no. 3 (1998), pp. 353–72; and Steven D. Levitt, "The Response of Crime Reporting Behavior to Changes in the Size of the Police Force: Implications for Studies of Police Effectiveness Using Reported Crime Data," *Journal of Quantitative Criminology* 14 (February 1998), pp. 62–81. / **125 The 1960s as a great time to be a criminal:** See Gary S. Becker and Guity Nashat Becker, *The Economics of Life* (New York: McGraw-Hill, 1997), pp. 142–43.

126–29   **NEW YORK CITY'S CRIME "MIRACLE":** The "Athenian period" quote came from an author interview with former police captain William J. Gorta, one of CompStat's inventors. / **127 The broken window theory:** See James Q. Wilson and George L. Kelling, "Broken Windows: The Police and Neighborhood Safety," *Atlantic Monthly,* March 1982. / **129 Bratton hiring more police in Los Angeles:** See Terry McCarthy, "The Gang Buster," *Time,* January 19, 2004.

130–
33   GUN LAWS: Concerning the fact that the United States has more
guns than it has adults, see Philip Cook and Jens Ludwig, *Guns in America: Results of a Comprehensive Survey of Gun Ownership and Use* (Washington, D.C.: Police Foundation, 1996). / **131 The gun-crime link:** See Mark Duggan, "More Guns, More Crime," *Journal of Political Economy* 109, no. 5 (2001), pp. 1086–1114. / **131 Guns in Switzerland:** See Stephen P. Halbrook, "Armed to the Teeth, and Free," *The Wall Street Journal Europe,* June 4, 1999. / **131 The impotent Brady Act:** See Jens Ludwig and Philip Cook, "Homicide and Suicide Rates Associated with Implementation of the Brady Handgun Violence Prevention Act," *Journal of the American Medical Association* 284, no. 5 (2000), pp. 585–91. / **132 Felons buying black-market guns:** See James D. Wright and Peter H. Rossi, *Armed and Considered Dangerous: A Survey of Felons and Their Firearms* (Hawthorne, N.Y.: Aldine de Gruyter, 1986). / **132 The gun-for-psychotherapy swap:** See "Wise Climb-Down, Bad Veto," *Los Angeles Times,* October 5, 1994. / **132 Why gun buybacks don't work:** See C. Callahan, F. Rivera, and T. Koepsell, "Money for Guns: Evaluation of the Seattle Gun Buy-Back Program," *Public Health Reports* 109, no. 4 (1994), pp. 472–77; David Kennedy, Anne Piehl, and Anthony Braga, "Youth Violence in Boston: Gun Markets, Serious Youth Offenders, and a Use-Reduction Strategy," *Law and Contemporary Problems* 59 (1996), pp. 147–83; and Peter Reuter and Jenny Mouzon, "Australia: A Massive Buyback of Low-Risk Guns," in *Evaluating Gun Policy: Effects on Crime and Violence,* ed. Jens Ludwig and Philip Cook (Washington, D.C.: Brookings Institution, 2003). / **133 John Lott's right-to-carry theory:** See John R. Lott Jr. and David Mustard, "Right-to-Carry Concealed Guns and the Importance of Deterrence," *Journal of Legal Studies* 26 (January 1997), pp. 1–68; and John R. Lott Jr., *More Guns, Less Crime: Understanding Crime and Gun Control Laws* (Chicago: University of Chicago Press, 1998). / **133 John Lott as Mary Rosh:** See Julian Sanchez, "The Mystery of Mary Rosh," *Reason,* May 2003; and Richard Morin, "Scholar Invents Fan to Answer His Critics," *The Washington Post,* February 1, 2003. / **133 Lott's gun theory disproved:** See Ian Ayres and John J. Donohue III, "Shooting Down the 'More Guns, Less Crime' Hypothesis," *Stanford Law Review* 55 (2003), pp. 1193–1312; and Mark

Duggan, "More Guns, More Crime," *Journal of Political Economy* 109, no. 5 (2001), pp. 1086–1114.

134– **THE BURSTING OF THE CRACK BUBBLE:** For a discussion of crack's his-
35 tory and particulars, see Roland G. Fryer Jr., Paul Heaton, Steven Levitt, and Kevin Murphy, "The Impact of Crack Cocaine," University of Chicago working paper, 2005. / **134 More than 25 percent of homicides:** See Paul J. Goldstein, Henry H. Brownstein, Patrick J. Ryan, and Patricia A. Bellucci, "Crack and Homicide in New York City: A Case Study in the Epidemiology of Violence," in *Crack in America: Demon Drugs and Social Justice*, ed. Craig Reinarman and Harry G. Levine (Berkeley: University of California Press, 1997), pp. 113–30.

135– **THE "AGING POPULATION" THEORY:** See Steven D. Levitt, "The Lim-
36 ited Role of Changing Age Structure in Explaining Aggregate Crime Rates," *Criminology* 37, no. 3 (1999), pp. 581–99. Although the aging theory has by now been widely discounted, learned experts continue to float it; see Matthew L. Wald, "Most Crimes of Violence and Property Hover at 30-Year Low," *The New York Times*, September 13, 2004, in which Lawrence A. Greenfield, director of the Bureau of Justice Statistics, says, "There is probably no single factor explanation for why the crime rates have been going down all these years and are now at the lowest level since we started measuring them in 1973. It probably has to do with demographics, and it probably has to do with having a lot of very high-rate offenders behind bars." / **135 "There lurks a cloud":** See James Q. Wilson, "Crime and Public Policy," in *Crime*, ed. James Q. Wilson and Joan Petersilia (San Francisco: ICS Press, 1995), p. 507.

136– **THE ABORTION-CRIME LINK:** For an overview, see John J. Donohue III
44 and Steven D. Levitt, "The Impact of Legalized Abortion on Crime," *Quarterly Journal of Economics* 116, no. 2 (2001), pp. 379–420; and John J. Donohue III and Steven D. Levitt, "Further Evidence That Legalized Abortion Lowered Crime: A Response to Joyce," *Journal of Human Resources* 39, no. 1 (2004), pp. 29–49. / **136 Abortion studies in Eastern Europe and Scandinavia:** See P. K. Dagg, "The Psychological Sequelae of Therapeutic Abortion—Denied and Completed," *American Journal of Psychiatry* 148, no. 5 (May 1991), pp. 578–85; and Henry David, Zdenek Dytrych, et al., *Born Unwanted: Developmental*

Effects of Denied Abortion (New York: Springer, 1988). / **137 The *Roe v. Wade* opinion:** *Roe v. Wade*, 410 U.S. 113 (1973). / **138–39 One study has shown that the typical child:** See Jonathan Gruber, Philip P. Levine, and Douglas Staiger, "Abortion Legalization and Child Living Circumstances: Who Is the 'Marginal Child'?" *Quarterly Journal of Economics* 114 (1999), pp. 263–91. / **139 Strongest predictors of a criminal future:** See Rolf Loeber and Magda Stouthamer-Loeber, "Family Factors as Correlates and Predictors of Juvenile Conduct Problems and Delinquency," *Crime and Justice*, vol. 7, ed. Michael Tonry and Norval Morris (Chicago: University of Chicago Press, 1986); also, Robert Sampson and John Laub, *Crime in the Making: Pathways and Turning Points Through Life* (Cambridge, Mass.: Harvard University Press, 1993). / **139 So does having a teenage mother:** See William S. Comanor and Llad Phillips, "The Impact of Income and Family Structure on Delinquency," University of California–Santa Barbara working paper, 1999. / **139 Another study has shown that low maternal education:** Pirkko Räsänen et al., "Maternal Smoking During Pregnancy and Risk of Criminal Behavior Among Adult Male Offspring in the Northern Finland 1966 Birth Cohort," *American Journal of Psychiatry* 156 (1999), pp. 857–62. / **139 Infanticide fell dramatically:** See Susan Sorenson, Douglas Wiebe, and Richard Berk, "Legalized Abortion and the Homicide of Young Children: An Empirical Investigation," *Analyses of Social Issues and Public Policy* 2, no. 1 (2002), pp. 239–56. / **141–42 Studies of Australia and Canada:** See Anindya Sen, "Does Increased Abortion Lead to Lower Crime? Evaluating the Relationship between Crime, Abortion, and Fertility," unpublished manuscript; and Andrew Leigh and Justin Wolfers, "Abortion and Crime," *AQ: Journal of Contemporary Analysis* 72, no. 4 (2000), pp. 28–30. / **142 Many of the aborted baby girls:** See John J. Donohue III, Jeffrey Grogger, and Steven D. Levitt, "The Impact of Legalized Abortion on Teen Childbearing," University of Chicago working paper, 2002. / **142 Abortion worse than slavery:** See Michael S. Paulsen, "Accusing Justice: Some Variations on the Themes of Robert M. Cover's *Justice Accused*," *Journal of Law and Religion* 7, no. 33 (1989), pp. 33–97. / **143 Abortion as "the only effective crime-prevention device":** See Anthony V. Bouza, *The Police Mystique: An Insider's Look at Cops, Crime, and the Criminal Justice System* (New York: Plenum, 1990). / **143 $9 million to save a**

spotted owl: See Gardner M. Brown and Jason F. Shogren, "Economics of the Endangered Species Act," *Journal of Economic Perspectives* 12, no. 3 (1998), pp. 3–20. / **143 $31 to prevent another *Exxon Valdez*–type spill:** See Glenn W. Harrison, "Assessing Damages for the Exxon Valdez Oil Spill," University of Central Florida working paper, 2004. / **144 Body-part price list:** Drawn from the state of Connecticut's Workers' Compensation Information Packet, p. 27, available as of this writing at wcc.state.ct.us/download/acrobat/info-packet.pdf.

5. WHAT MAKES A PERFECT PARENT?

147 THE EVER CHANGING WISDOM OF PARENTING EXPERTS: Ann Hulbert, *Raising America: Experts, Parents, and a Century of Advice About Children* (New York: Knopf, 2003), is an extremely helpful compendium of parenting advice. / **148 Gary Ezzo's "infant-management strategy" and sleep deprivation warning:** See Gary Ezzo and Robert Bucknam, *On Becoming Babywise* (Sisters, Ore.: Multnomah, 1995), pp. 32 and 53. / **148 T. Berry Brazelton and the "interactive" child:** T. Berry Brazelton, *Infants and Mothers: Difference in Development*, rev. ed. (New York: Delta/Seymour Lawrence, 1983), p. xxiii. / **148 L. Emmett Holt's warning against "undue stimulation":** L. Emmett Holt, *The Happy Baby* (New York: Dodd, Mead, 1924), p. 7. / **148 Crying as "the baby's exercise":** L. Emmett Holt, *The Care and Feeding of Children: A Catechism for the Use of Mothers and Children's Nurses* (New York: Appleton, 1894), p. 53.

149 A GUN OR A SWIMMING POOL? See Steven Levitt, "Pools More Dangerous than Guns," *Chicago Sun-Times*, July 28, 2001.

150–54 PETER SANDMAN ON MAD-COW DISEASE AND OTHER RISKS: See Amanda Hesser, "Squeaky Clean? Not Even Close," *The New York Times*, January 28, 2004; and "The Peter Sandman Risk Communication Web Site," at http://www.psandman.com/index.htm.

154 HOW MUCH DO PARENTS REALLY MATTER? See Judith Rich Harris, *The Nurture Assumption: Why Children Turn Out the Way They Do* (New York: Free Press, 1998); for a Harris profile that also provides an excellent review of the nature-nurture debate, see Malcolm Gladwell, "Do Parents Matter?" *The New Yorker*, August 17, 1998;

and Carol Tavris, "Peer Pressure," *New York Times Book Review*, September 13, 1998. / **155 " 'Here we go again' ":** See Tavris, "Peer Pressure." / **155–56 Pinker called Harris's views "mind-boggling":** Steven Pinker, "Sibling Rivalry: Why the Nature/Nurture Debate Won't Go Away," *Boston Globe*, October 13, 2002, adapted from Steven Pinker, *The Blank Slate: The Modern Denial of Human Nature* (New York: Viking, 2002).

158–61   **SCHOOL CHOICE IN CHICAGO:** This material is drawn from Julie Berry Cullen, Brian Jacob, and Steven D. Levitt, "The Impact of School Choice on Student Outcomes: An Analysis of the Chicago Public Schools," *Journal of Public Economics*, forthcoming; and Julie Berry Cullen, Brian Jacob, and Steven D. Levitt, "The Effect of School Choice on Student Outcomes: Evidence from Randomized Lotteries," National Bureau of Economic Research working paper, 2003.

160–61   **STUDENTS WHO ARRIVE AT HIGH SCHOOL NOT PREPARED TO DO HIGH SCHOOL WORK:** See Tamar Lewin, "More Students Passing Regents, but Achievement Gap Persists," *The New York Times*, March 18, 2004.

161   **THE BLACK-WHITE INCOME GAP TRACED TO EIGHTH-GRADE TEST SCORE GAP:** See Derek Neal and William R. Johnson, "The Role of Pre-Market Factors in Black-White Wage Differences," *Journal of Political Economy* 104 (1996), pp. 869–95; and June O'Neill, "The Role of Human Capital in Earnings Differences Between Black and White Men," *Journal of Economic Perspectives* 4, no. 4 (1990), pp. 25–46. / **161 "Reducing the black-white test score gap":** See Christopher Jencks and Meredith Phillips, "America's Next Achievement Test: Closing the Black-White Test Score Gap," *American Prospect* 40 (September–October 1998), pp. 44–53.

161–62   **"ACTING WHITE":** See David Austen-Smith and Roland G. Fryer Jr., "The Economics of 'Acting White,' " National Bureau of Economic Research working paper, 2003. / **161–62 Kareem Abdul-Jabbar:** Kareem Abdul-Jabbar and Peter Knobler, *Giant Steps* (New York: Bantam, 1983), p. 16.

162–68   **THE BLACK-WHITE TEST SCORE GAP AND THE ECLS:** This material was drawn from Roland G. Fryer Jr. and Steven D. Levitt, "Understanding the Black-White Test Score Gap in the First Two Years of School,"

Review of Economics and Statistics 86, no. 2 (2004), pp. 447–64. While this paper contains little discussion of the correlation between test scores and home-based factors (television viewing, spanking, etc.), a regression of those data is included in the paper's appendix. Regarding the ECLS study itself: as of this writing, an overview of the study was posted at nces.ed.gov/ecls/.

173   ADOPTIVE PARENTS WITH HIGHER IQS THAN BIRTH MOTHER: See Bruce Sacerdote, "The Nature and Nurture of Economic Outcomes," National Bureau of Economic Research working paper, 2000.

174   FINNISH LITERACY: See Lizette Alvarez, "Educators Flocking to Finland, Land of Literate Children," *The New York Times*, April 9, 2004.

176   A BOOK FOR EVERY TOT: See John Keilman, "Governor Wants Books for Tots; Kids Would Get 60 by Age 5 in Effort to Boost Literacy," *Chicago Tribune*, January 12, 2004.

178–79   THE INFLUENCE OF ADOPTIVE PARENTS: See Sacerdote, "The Nature and Nurture of Economic Outcomes."

6. PERFECT PARENTING, PART II; OR: WOULD A ROSHANDA BY ANY OTHER NAME SMELL AS SWEET?

181–82   THE STORY OF LOSER LANE: Drawn from author interviews and from Sean Gardiner, "Winner and Loser: Names Don't Decide Destiny," *Newsday,* July 22, 2002.

182–83   THE JUDGE AND THE TEMPTRESS: Based on author interviews.

184–85   ROLAND G. FRYER AND THE STUDY OF BLACK UNDERACHIEVEMENT: Drawn from author interviews.

185   THE BLACK-WHITE CIGARETTE GAP: See Lloyd Johnston, Patrick O'Malley, Jerald Bachman, and John Schulenberg, "Cigarette Brand Preferences Among Adolescents," *Monitoring the Future Occasional Paper* 45, Institute for Social Research, University of Michigan, 1999.

185–88   BLACK NAMES (AND OTHER BLACK-WHITE CULTURE GAPS): See Roland G. Fryer Jr. and Steven D. Levitt, "The Causes and Consequences of

Distinctively Black Names," *Quarterly Journal of Economics* 119, no. 3 (August 2004), pp. 767–805.

189–
90 "WHITE" RÉSUMÉS BEATING OUT "BLACK" RÉSUMÉS: The most recent audit study to reach such a conclusion is Marianne Bertrand and Sendhil Mullainathan, "Are Emily and Greg More Employable than Lakisha and Jamal? A Field Experiment Evidence on Labor Market Discrimination," National Bureau of Economic Research working paper, 2003.

190 YO XING HEYNO AUGUSTUS EISNER ALEXANDER WEISER KNUCKLES JEREMIJENKO-CONLEY: See Tara Bahrampour, "A Boy Named Yo, Etc.: Name Changes, Both Practical and Fanciful, Are on the Rise," *The New York Times,* September 25, 2003.

190 MICHAEL GOLDBERG, INDIAN-BORN SIKH: See Robert F. Worth, "Livery Driver Is Wounded in a Shooting," *New York Times,* February 9, 2004.

190 WILLIAM MORRIS, NÉ ZELMAN MOSES: Author interview with Alan Kannof, former chief operating officer of the William Morris Agency.

192 BRAND NAMES AS FIRST NAMES: Drawn from California birth-certificate data and also discussed in Stephanie Kang, "Naming the Baby: Parents Brand Their Tot with What's Hot," *The Wall Street Journal,* December 26, 2003.

193 A GIRL NAMED SHITHEAD: The woman who called the radio show to tell Roland Fryer about her niece Shithead might have been mis-informed, of course, or even outright lying. Regardless, she was hardly alone in her feeling that black names sometimes go too far. Bill Cosby, during a speech in May 2004 at the NAACP's *Brown v. Board of Education* fiftieth-anniversary gala, lambasted lower-income blacks for a variety of self-destructive behaviors, including the giving of "ghetto" names. Cosby was summarily excoriated by white and black critics alike. (See Barbara Ehrenreich, "The New Cosby Kids," *The New York Times,* July 8, 2004; and Debra Dickerson, "America's Granddad Gets Ornery," *Slate,* July 13, 2004.) Soon after, the California education secretary, Richard Riordan—the wealthy, white former mayor of Los Angeles—found himself under attack for a per-

ceived racial slight. (See Tim Rutten, "Riordan Stung by 'Gotcha' News," *Los Angeles Times*, July 10, 2004.) Riordan, visiting a Santa Barbara library to promote a reading program, met a six-year-old girl named Isis. She told Riordan that her name meant "Egyptian princess"; Riordan, trying to make a joke, replied, "It means stupid, dirty girl." The resultant outrage led black activists to call for Riordan's resignation. Mervyn Dymally, a black assemblyman from Compton, explained that Isis was "a little African-American girl. Would he have done that to a white girl?" As it turned out, however, Isis *was* white. Some activists tried to keep the anti-Riordan protest alive, but Isis's mother, Trinity, encouraged everyone to relax. Her daughter, she explained, hadn't taken Riordan's joke seriously. "I got the impression," Trinity said, "that she didn't think he was very bright."

199   A MUCH LONGER LIST OF GIRLS' AND BOYS' NAMES: Here lies an arbitrary collection of names that are interesting, pretty, uncommon, very common, or somehow quintessential, along with the level of education that they signify. (Each name occurs at least ten times in the California names data.)

SOME GIRLS' NAMES
(YEARS OF MOTHER'S EDUCATION IN PARENTHESES)

Abigail (14.72), Adelaide (15.33), Alessandra (15.19), Alexandra (14.67), Alice (14.30), Alison (14.82), Allison (14.54), Amalia (15.25), Amanda (13.30), Amber (12.64), Amy (14.09), Anabelle (14.68), Anastasia (13.98), Angelina (12.74), Annabel (15.40), Anne (15.49), Anya (14.97), Ashley (12.89), Autumn (12.86), Ava (14.97), Aziza (11.52), Bailey (13.83), Beatrice (14.74), Beatriz (11.42), Belinda (12.79), Betty (11.50), Breanna (12.71), Britt (15.39), Brittany (12.87), Bronte (14.42), Brooklyn (13.50), Brooklynne (13.10), Caitlin (14.36), Caitlynn (13.03), Cammie (12.00), Campbell (15.69), Carly (14.25), Carmella (14.25), Cassandra (13.38), Cassidy (13.86), Cate (15.23), Cathleen (14.31), Cecilia (14.36), Chanel (13.00), Charisma (13.85), Charlotte (14.98), Chastity* (10.66), Cherokee (11.86), Chloe (14.52), Christina (13.59), Ciara (13.40), Cierra (12.97), Cordelia (15.19), Courtney (13.55), Crimson (11.53), Cynthia (12.79), Dahlia (14.94), Danielle

* Concerning the teenage girl named Temptress on p. 183: judging from Chastity's poor showing here, it is doubtful that Temptress would have gained much benefit from being called Chastity.

(13.69), Daphne (14.42), Darlene (12.22), Dawn (12.71), Deborah (13.70), December (12.00), Delilah (13.00), Denise (12.71), Deniz (15.27), Desiree (12.62), Destiny (11.65), Diamond (11.70), Diana (13.54), Diane (14.10), Dora (14.31), Eden (14.41), Eileen (14.69), Ekaterina (15.09), Elizabeth (14.25), Elizabethann (12.46), Ella (15.30), Ellen (15.17), Emerald (13.17), Emily (14.17), Emma (15.23), Faith (13.39), Florence (14.83), Francesca (14.80), Frankie (12.52), Franziska (15.18), Gabrielle (14.26), Gennifer (14.75), Georgia (14.82), Geraldine (11.83), Ginger (13.54), Grace (15.03), Gracie (13.81), Gretchen (14.91), Gwyneth (15.04), Haley (13.84), Halle (14.86), Hannah (14.44), Hilary (14.59), Hillary (13.94), Ilana (15.83), Ilene (13.59), Indigo (14.38), Isabel (15.31), Isabell (13.50), Ivy (13.43), Jacquelin (12.78), Jacqueline (14.40), Jade (13.04), Jamie (13.52), Jane (15.12), Janet (12.94), Jeanette (13.43), Jeannette (13.86), Jemma (15.04), Jennifer (13.77), Johanna (14.76), Jordan (13.85), Joyce (12.80), Juliet (14.96), Kailey (13.76), Kara (13.95), Karissa (13.05), Kate (15.23), Katelynne (12.65), Katherine (14.95), Kayla (12.96), Kelsey (14.17), Kendra (13.63), Kennedy (14.17), Kimia (15.66), Kylie (13.83), Laci (12.41), Ladonna (11.60), Lauren (14.58), Leah (14.30), Lenora (13.26), Lexington (13.44), Lexus (12.55), Liberty (13.36), Liesl (15.42), Lily (14.84), Linda (12.76), Linden (15.94), Lizabeth (13.42), Lizbeth (9.66), Lucia (13.59), Lucille (14.76), Lucy (15.01), Lydia (14.40), MacKenzie (14.44), Madeline (15.12), Madison (14.13), Mandy (13.00), Mara (15.33), Margaret (15.14), Mariah (13.00), Mary (14.20), Matisse (15.36), Maya (15.26), Meadow (12.65), Megan (13.99), Melanie (13.90), Meredith (15.57), Michaela (14.13), Micheala (12.95), Millicent (14.61), Molly (14.84), Montana (13.70), Naomi (14.05), Naseem (15.23), Natalie (14.58), Nevada (14.61), Nicole (13.77), Nora (14.88), Olive (15.64), Olivia (14.79), Paige (14.04), Paisley (13.84), Paris (13.71), Patience (11.80), Pearl (13.48), Penelope (14.53), Phoebe (15.18), Phoenix (13.28), Phyllis (11.93), Portia (15.03), Precious (11.30), Quinn (15.20), Rachel (14.51), Rachell (11.76), Rebecca (14.05), Renee (13.79), Rhiannon (13.16), Rikki (12.54), Ronnie (12.72), Rosalind (15.26), Ruby (14.26), Sabrina (13.31), Sadie (13.69), Samantha (13.37), Sarah (14.16), Sasha (14.22), Sayeh (15.25), Scarlett (13.60), Selma (12.78), September (12.80), Shannon (14.11), Shayla (12.77), Shayna (14.00), Shelby (13.42), Sherri (12.32), Shira (15.60), Shirley (12.49), Simone (14.96), Siobhan (14.88), Skylynn (12.61), Solveig (14.36), Sophie (15.45), Stacy (13.08), Stephanie (13.45), Stevie (12.67), Storm (12.31), Sunshine (12.03), Susan (13.73), Suzanne (14.37), Svetlana (11.65), Tabitha (12.49), Talia (15.27), Tallulah (14.88), Tatiana (14.42), Tatum (14.25),

Taylor (13.65), Tess (14.83), Tia (12.93), Tiffany (12.49), Tracy (13.50), Trinity (12.60), Trudy (14.88), Vanessa (12.94), Venus (12.73), Veronica (13.83), Veronique (15.80), Violet (13.72), Whitney (13.79), Willow (13.83), Yael (15.55), Yasmine (14.10), Yvonne (13.02), and Zoe (15.03).

SOME BOYS' NAMES
(YEARS OF MOTHER'S EDUCATION IN PARENTHESES)

Aaron (13.74), Abdelrahman (14.08), Ace (12.39), Adam (14.07), Aidan (15.35), Alexander (14.49), Alistair (15.34), Andrew (14.19), Aristotle (14.20), Ashley (12.95), Atticus (14.97), Baylor (14.84), Bjorn (15.12), Blane (13.55), Blue (13.85), Brian (13.92), Buck (12.81), Bud (12.21), Buddy (11.95), Caleb (13.91), Callum (15.20), Carter (14.98), Chaim (14.63), Christ (11.50), Christian (13.55), Clyde (12.94), Cooper (14.96), Dakota (12.92), Daniel (14.01), Dashiell (15.26), David (13.77), Deniz (15.65), Dylan (13.58), Eamon (15.39), Elton (12.23), Emil (14.05), Eric (14.02), Finn (15.87), Forrest (13.75), Franklin (13.55), Gabriel (14.39), Gary (12.56), Giancarlo (15.05), Giuseppe (13.24), Graydon (15.51), Gustavo (11.68), Hashem (12.76), Hugh (14.60), Hugo (13.00), Idean (14.35), Indiana (13.80), Isaiah (13.12), Jackson (15.22), Jacob (13.76), Jagger (13.27), Jamieson (15.13), Jedidiah (14.06), Jeffrey (13.88), Jeremy (13.46), Jesus (8.71), Jihad (11.60), Johan (15.11), John-Paul (14.22), Jonathan (13.86), Jordan (13.73), Jorge (10.49), Joshua (13.49), Josiah (13.98), Jules (15.48), Justice (12.45), Kai (14.85), Keanu (13.17), Keller (15.07), Kevin (14.03), Kieron (14.00), Kobe (13.12), Kramer (14.80), Kurt (14.33), Lachlan (15.60), Lars (15.09), Leo (14.76), Lev (14.35), Lincoln (14.87), Lonny (11.93), Luca (13.56), Malcolm (14.80), Marvin (11.86), Max (14.93), Maximilian (15.17), Michael (13.66), Michelangelo (15.58), Miro (15.00), Mohammad (12.45), Moises (9.69), Moses (13.11), Moshe (14.41), Muhammad (13.21), Mustafa (13.85), Nathaniel (14.13), Nicholas (14.02), Noah (14.45), Norman (12.90), Oliver (15.14), Orlando (12.72), Otto (13.73), Parker (14.69), Parsa (15.22), Patrick (14.25), Paul (14.13), Peter (15.00), Philip (14.82), Philippe (15.61), Phoenix (13.08), Presley (12.68), Quentin (13.84), Ralph (13.45), Raphael (14.63), Reagan (14.92), Rex (13.77), Rexford (14.89), Rocco (13.68), Rocky (11.47), Roland (13.95), Romain (15.69), Royce (13.73), Russell (13.68), Ryan (14.04), Sage (13.63), Saleh (10.15), Satchel (15.52), Schuyler (14.73), Sean (14.12), Sequoia (13.15), Sergei (14.28), Sergio (11.92), Shawn (12.72), Shelby (12.88), Simon (14.74), Slater (14.62), Solomon (14.20), Spencer (14.53), Stephen (14.01), Stetson (12.90), Steven (13.31), Tanner (13.82), Tariq (13.16), Tennyson (15.63), Terence

(14.36), Terry (12.16), Thaddeus (14.56), Theodore (14.61), Thomas (14.08), Timothy (13.58), Toby (13.24), Trace (14.09), Trevor (13.89), Tristan (13.95), Troy (13.52), Ulysses (14.25), Uriel (15.00), Valentino (12.25), Virgil (11.87), Vladimir (13.37), Walker (14.75), Whitney (15.58), Willem (15.38), William (14.17), Willie (12.12), Winston (15.07), Xavier (13.37), Yasser (14.25), Zachary (14.02), Zachory (11.92), Zane (13.93), and Zebulon (15.00).

202   MOST POPULAR WHITE GIRL NAMES, 1960 AND 2000: The California names data actually begin in 1961, but the year-to-year difference is negligible.

204   SHIRLEY TEMPLE AS SYMPTOM, NOT CAUSE: See Stanley Lieberson, *A Matter of Taste: How Names, Fashions, and Culture Change* (New Haven, Conn.: Yale University Press, 2000). A Harvard sociologist, Lieberson is the acknowledged master of (among other subjects) the academic study of names. For instance, *A Matter of Taste* details how, from 1960, it was American Jewish families who first popularized many girls' names (Amy, Danielle, Erica, Jennifer, Jessica, Melissa, Rachel, Rebecca, Sarah, Stacy, Stephanie, Tracy) while only a handful (Ashley, Kelly, and Kimberly) began in non-Jewish families. Another good discussion of naming habits can be found in Peggy Orenstein, "Where Have All the Lisas Gone?" *The New York Times Magazine*, July 6, 2003; if only for entertainment, see *The Sweetest Sound* (2001), Alan Berliner's documentary film about names; and for an excellent visual overview of how any given name waxes and wanes in popularity, see http://babynamewizard.com/namevoyager/lnv0105.html.

204–5   BOYS' NAMES BECOMING GIRLS' NAMES (BUT NOT VICE VERSA): This observation is drawn from the work of Cleveland Kent Evans, a psychologist and onomastician at Bellevue University in Bellevue, Nebraska. A sample of Evans's work is available as of this writing at academic.bellevue.edu/~CKEvans/cevans.html; see also Cleveland Kent Evans, *Unusual & Most Popular Baby Names* (Lincolnwood, Ill.: Publications International/Signet, 1994); and Cleveland Kent Evans, *The Ultimate Baby Name Book* (Lincolnwood, Ill.: Publications International/Plume, 1997).

EPILOGUE: TWO PATHS TO HARVARD

210–11 THE WHITE BOY WHO GREW UP OUTSIDE CHICAGO: This passage, as well as the earlier passage about the same boy on pp. 156–57, was drawn from author interviews and from Ted Kaczynski, "Truth Versus Lies," unpublished manuscript, 1998; see also Stephen J. Dubner, "I Don't Want to Live Long. I Would Rather Get the Death Penalty than Spend the Rest of My Life in Prison," *Time*, October 18, 1999.

210–11 THE BLACK BOY FROM DAYTONA BEACH: This passage, as well as the earlier passage about the same boy on p. 157, was drawn from author interviews with Roland G. Fryer Jr.

ACKNOWLEDGMENTS

Jointly, we would like to thank two people who helped nurture this book: Claire Wachtel of William Morrow and Suzanne Gluck of the William Morris Agency. This is the third book that Stephen Dubner has written under their auspices; he continues to be grateful and, on occasion, awestruck. This was the first such book for Steven Levitt; he has been duly impressed. Many thanks also to the talented and supportive colleagues in each shop: Jane Friedman, Michael Morrison, Cathy Hemming, Lisa Gallagher, Debbie Stier, Dee Dee De Bartlo, George Bick, Brian McSharry, Jennifer Pooley, Kevin Callahan, Trent Duffy, and many others at William Morrow; Tracy Fisher, Raffaella DeAngelis, Karen Gerwin, Erin Malone, Georgia Cool, Candace Finn, Andy McNicol, and many others at the William Morris Agency. We would also like to thank the various subjects of this book (especially Stetson Kennedy, Paul Feldman, Sudhir Venkatesh, Arne Duncan, and Roland Fryer) for their time and trouble. Thanks also to the friends and colleagues who helped improve the manuscript, including Melanie Thernstrom, Lisa Chase, and Colin Camerer. And to Linda Jines, who came up with the title: nicely done.

Personal Acknowledgments

I owe an enormous debt to my many co-authors and colleagues, whose great ideas fill this book, and to all the kind people who have taken the time to teach me what I know about economics and life. I am especially grateful to the University of Chicago, whose Becker Center on Chicago Price Theory provides me the ideal research home; and also to the American Bar Foundation for its collegiality and support. My wife, Jeannette, and our children, Amanda, Olivia, Nicholas, and Sophie, make every day a joy, even though we miss Andrew so much. I thank my parents, who showed me it was okay to be different. Most of all, I want to thank my good friend and co-author Stephen Dubner, who is a brilliant writer and a creative genius.

—S. D. L.

I have yet to write a book that did not germinate, or was not at least brought along, in the pages of the *The New York Times Magazine*. This one is no exception. For that I thank Hugo Lindgren, Adam Moss, and Gerry Marzorati; also, thanks to Vera Titunik and Paul Tough for inviting the Bagel Man into the *Magazine*'s pages. I am most grateful to Steven Levitt, who is so clever and wise and even kind as to make me wish—well, almost—that I had become an economist myself. Now I know why half the profession dreams of having an adjoining office to Levitt. And finally, as always, thanks and love to Ellen, Solomon, and Anya. See you at dinnertime.

—S. J. D.

INDEX

"Understanding the Black-White
Test Score Gap in the
First Two Years of School"
(Fryer), 162
"Understanding Why Crime
Fell in the 1990's: Four
Factors That Explain the
Decline and Seven That
Do Not" (Levitt), 223
union busting, 53, 58, 59
University Press of Florida,
236

Venkatesh, Sudhir, 89–96,
100–102, 105–6, 221
voting, 233, 238–42

Wade, Henry, 4
Waksal, Sam, 65
Waldfogel, Joel, 249
Wal-Mart, 21, 100

Washington Merry-Go-Round, 60
Weakest Link, The, 11, 74–77, 81,
230
weapons of mass destruction, 88,
149
weather, 48
William Morris Agency, 190
Wilson, James Q., 135–36
Wilson, William Julius, 90, 94
Wilson, Woodrow, 52–53
women's rights, 88
WorldCom, 66
Worldly Philosophers, The
(Heilbroner), 14
World Series, 37, 122
World War, II, 53, 111

yakuza, 42
Yale University, 249

zinc, 266

About the Authors

Steven D. Levitt is a professor of economics at the University of Chicago and a recipient of the John Bates Clark medal, awarded to the most influential economist under the age of forty.

Stephen J. Dubner, a former writer and editor at *The New York Times Magazine,* is the author of *Turbulent Souls (Choosing My Religion), Confessions of a Hero-Worshiper,* and the children's book *The Boy with Two Belly Buttons.*

THE ITALIANS

THE ITALIANS

A FULL-LENGTH PORTRAIT FEATURING THEIR MANNERS AND MORALS

LUIGI BARZINI

A TOUCHSTONE BOOK
Published by Simon & Schuster
New York   London   Toronto   Sydney   Tokyo   Singapore

TOUCHSTONE
Rockefeller Center
1230 Avenue of the Americas
New York, NY 10020

First Touchstone Edition 1996

TOUCHSTONE and colophon are registered trademarks
of Simon & Schuster Inc.

Manufactured in the United States of America

10

Library of Congress catalog card number 63-17858
ISBN: 0-689-70540-9
ISBN: 0-684-82500-7 (Pbk.)

ACKNOWLEDGMENTS

PERMISSION *to quote is gratefully acknowledged to the following:* *Faber and Faber Ltd., for J. R. Hale's* England and the Italian Renaissance; *MacGibbon and Kee Ltd. and Monthly Review Press, for Danilo Dolci's* Waste; *Laurence Pollinger Ltd., the Estate of the late Mrs. Frieda Lawrence, and The Viking Press, Inc., for* The Collected Letters of D. H. Lawrence; *Martin Secker and Warburg Ltd., for Norman Douglas'* Siren Land; *and Thames and Hudson Ltd., for Paolo Monelli's* Mussolini.

THE *maps following page 352 were drawn by Joan Emerson.*

FOREWORD

*Past things shed light on future ones; the world was always of a kind;
what is and will be was at some other time; the same things come back,
but under different names and colours; not everybody recognizes them,
but only he who is wise and considers them diligently.*
                                              FRANCESCO GUICCIARDINI

*Is there any other country in Europe where the character of the people
seems to have been so little affected by political and technological change?*
                                              W. H. AUDEN
                    (in the introduction to Goethe's *Italian Journey*)

THIS BOOK does not pretend to be a scientific treatise. It is
no more ambitious nor accurate than the opening chapters of
a leisurely nineteenth-century novel in which the author
described at length the country in which his story would unfold, the
historical moment, and the people themselves. The reader of this
book, having read, can go to Italy and supply his own novel, with
whatever live characters he meets on the spot. He will have learned
more or less what to expect. Italy is still a country of limitless opportunities. It offers stage settings for all kinds of adventures, licit or
illicit loves, the study of art, the experience of pathos, the weaving of
intrigues. It can be gay, tragic, mad, pastoral, archaic, modern, or
simply *dolce*.

I have tried to set down only the most distinguishing features,
following the technique of the honest portrait painter, who puts on
canvas those traits which make the sitter the person he is and not
another. The sitter happens to be my country, and I have felt at times
like the man who does that most exacting of all things, the 'Portrait
of the Artist's Mother'. The Mother, in this case, is notoriously distinguished. Her past is glorious, her achievements are dazzling, her
traditions noble, her fame awe-inspiring, and her charm irresistible.

I have known her and admired her for a long time. I love her dearly.

As I grew older, however (like many sons of famous mothers), I became disenchanted with some of her habits, shocked by some of her secret vices, repelled by her corruption, depravity and shamelessness and hurt when I discovered that she was not, after all, the shining paragon I believed her to be when I was young. Still, I could have no other mother. I could not stop loving her. When I was writing this book, I did not want to hurt her feelings, I did not want to be unnecessarily cruel, I did not want to forget her good points; but, at the same time, I tried hard not to flatter her, not to be seduced by her magical charms or misled by my own sentiments. I was determined to do the most honest job of portraiture I possibly could.

*

This book was difficult to compile. It is notoriously easier to write about things and people one does not really know very well. One has fewer doubts. But to write about one's own country was a tortured enterprise. I knew too much. I saw too many trees. I sometimes could prove one thing or its contrary, with equal ease. I was embarrassed by the exceptions. I questioned every idea and watched every word. In my younger days sentimental patriotism was the fashion. In my anxiety to correct such prejudices, was I too eager to demolish sound and durable notions? I was afraid to be too conservative and, at almost the same time, too ready to follow new intellectual fashions, the rage among contemporary intelligentsia, to embrace seductive new theories which might be obsolete before the book appeared in print.

One of the sources of confusion was the absurd discrepancy between the quantity and dazzling array of the inhabitants' achievements through many centuries and the mediocre quality of their national history. Italians have impressively filled Europe and most of the world with the fame of their larger-than-life-size famous men. Italian architects and masons built part of the Kremlin in Moscow and the Winter Palace in Leningrad; Italian artists have embellished the Capitol in Washington. They have strewn churches, princely palaces, and stately villas all over Catholic Europe, especially in

Vienna, Madrid, Prague, and Warsaw; their influence on architecture was felt almost everywhere else, exterior architecture, to be sure, designed to impress and please the onlooker more than to serve strictly practical purposes. They have filled South America with ornate and rhetorical monuments to the local heroes.

Italy's smaller contributions to everyday life are so numerous as to go unnoticed. There would be no pistols but for the city of Pistoia; no *savon* in France but for the city of Savona; no faience anywhere but for the city of Faenza; no millinery but for the city of Milan; no blue jeans but for the city of Genoa, *Gênes*, where the blue cotton cloth was first produced, and no Genoa jibs; no Neapolitan ice-cream, no Roman candles, no Venetian blinds, no Bologna sausages, no Parmesan cheese, no Leghorn hens. Italians have discovered America for the Americans; taught poetry, statesmanship, and the ruses of trade to the English; military art to the Germans; cuisine to the French; acting and ballet dancing to the Russians; and music to everybody. If some day this world of ours should be turned into a cloud of radioactive dust in space, it will be by nuclear contrivances developed with the decisive aid of Italian scientists.[1]

---

[1] The list of the famous Italians is awe-inspiring. It is well to record them here, as they will scarcely be mentioned in the rest of the book, written with the presumption that the reader is well acquainted with them. Here are some of the main ones: the saints: Saint Francis, Santa Catarina da Siena, San Bernardino da Siena, San Luigi Gonzaga, Saint Thomas of Aquino. The sinners: the Borgia family (Spanish but acclimatized), Cellini, Caravaggio, Cagliostro, Casanova. The political thinkers: Dante Alighieri, King Frederick of Hohenstaufen of the two Sicilies (born in Italy, the inventor of the modern state, the 'state as a work of art'), Lorenzo de Medici (inventor of the 'balance of power'), Machiavelli, Guicciardini, Mazzini, Cavour. The military leaders: Giovanni dalle Bande Nere, Raimondo Montecuccoli (who led Austrian armies), Napoleon, Garibaldi. The admirals: Andrea Doria, Mocenigo, Morosini, Bragadin, Caracciolo. The scientists: Galileo Galilei, Leonardo da Vinci, Volta, Marconi, Fermi. The navigators: Columbus, Vespucci, the Cabots. The thinkers: Saint Thomas of Aquino, Campanella, Croce, Vico. The poets: Dante Alighieri, Boccaccio, Petrarch, Leopardi, Manzoni. The sculptors: Verrocchio, Donatello, Ghiberti, della Robbia, Cellini, Michelangelo, Bernini. The painters: Giotto, Botticelli, Fra Angelico, Leonardo da Vinci, Piero de la Francesca, Perugino, Michelangelo, Raphael, Titian, Tintoretto, Tiepolo, Modigliani. The musicians: Palestrina, Pergolesi, Monteverdi, Vivaldi, Rossini, Verdi, Bellini, Donizetti, Puccini, Toscanini. These are, of course, the names of first magnitude. The second and third category could easily fill a small city's telephone book.

There is no denying that all her geniuses made Italy great, one Italy, at least, the spiritual country, the land of culture, art, and ideas, of which only her best sons can be considered full citizens, as well as the distinguished foreigners who at all times felt themselves at home in it. Oddly enough, these great men did not make another Italy great, the concrete country to be found in almanacs and history books, the real Italy of past wars, invasions, treaties, political upheavals. In fact, it can be stated that many of these mental giants exercised little or no influence whatever.

Italians always loved a good entertainer who could stir their emotions and divert them from themselves; they were always delighted by a talented painter, musician, sculptor, architect, actor, dancer, as long as he did not engage their higher faculties. They respected and admired great scientists, especially if their discoveries and theories were abstract and incomprehensible. They endured and feared a forceful leader, but they always thoroughly enjoyed his fall. As a rule, however, most of them ignored, neglected, opposed, or derided disarmed prophets, philosophers, political and religious reformers, preachers, revolutionary scientists who proposed new and upsetting theories, men of outstanding stature in all fields.

It is true that in other countries great men have also occasionally been persecuted and put to death. Nowhere else, however, has this happened with the same discrimination, regularity, and determination. The majority of heroes in other civilized countries were allowed to live and flourish, to contribute to the power, prestige, and greatness of their native lands. They were, as a rule, not considered crackpots, deviations from the norm, but shining examples, impersonations of the national ideal, average men magnified, who indicated the path to follow. Italy instinctively neutralized all the men who tried to foist moral greatness on their countrymen. Nicolò Machiavelli was kept away from important affairs; Giambatista Vico, the father of modern thought, lived in a garret in extreme poverty; Galileo Galilei was persecuted for his ideas; Dante Alighieri, Giuseppe Mazzini, and many others went into exile. Some, like Tomaso Campanella, spent most of their lives in dungeons. A few of the worthiest were killed amidst the rejoicing of the populace, burned at the stake like Giordano Bruno and Savonarola, hanged like the patriots of the

Neapolitan Republic in 1799, stabbed and stoned by the crowd like Cola di Rienzo.

*

The coexistence of these two Italies presents some perplexing problems. Why did Italy, a land notoriously teeming with vigorous, wide-awake, and intelligent people, always behave so feebly? Why was she at all times so prone to catastrophes? She has been invaded, ravaged, sacked, humiliated in every century, and yet failed to do the simple things necessary to defend herself. This is not because the people shrank from fighting and dying. They have fought as many bloody wars as their more glorious neighbours, often under the foreigners' colours, and died in even greater numbers, the civilians massacred by foreign soldiery, the soldiers usually overwhelmed by superior enemies. A few wars they won, to be sure, but then mostly against other Italians and the Austrians. Perhaps the most difficult and deadly of all wars, a three and a half years' struggle in the snows of the Alps, they fought gallantly and, in spite of the Caporetto setback, finally won against not only the Austrians but the tougher Germans too. But most other wars they lost. It is absurd to think this is because the people are effete, cowardly, and too civilized. They are notoriously lively, brave, energetic. They can at times endure more and dare more than others.

Winning wars, after all, is the ultimate test not of the quality of single men but of their capacity to work together and accept common sacrifices. This is why the riddle which fascinated Machiavelli four hundred years ago is still endlessly debated among us: why did we not achieve national unity and a centralized government when other European nations did? Why did we not create a political régime of our own? It is possible to trace constant trends, too constant to be merely the result of coincidence, which have prevented Italians from coagulating into one nation: the rapid and enthusiastic acceptance of changing political fashions and of foreign conquerors which made all revolutions irresistible but superficial and all new régimes unstable; the art of living as if all laws were obnoxious obstacles to be overcome somehow, an art which made the best of laws ridiculously ineffective; the habit of treating whatever ruler was in command, local or foreign, as if he were corruptible, which soon transformed the most scrupulous and liberal ruler into a corrupt one; the certainty that the most inflexible government could, in the long run, be corroded from the inside. Most of the national governments we achieved at one time or another were therefore feeble, arbitrary, and inefficient, including our late totalitarian dictatorship, which was defined as a 'tyranny tempered by the complete disobedience of all laws'. Why were we so late in developing modern industries and free institutions? Why did we set about conquering colonies when all other imperial powers were on the point of losing theirs?

The qualities and defects which made us what we are fascinated foreigners, even though some of our characteristic habits were far from admirable. Travellers did not hide their contempt for us, since the end of the Quattrocento, to be exact. Yet they never stopped coming to Italy. Many begin to admire us today, listen to us, imitate us, and even envy us. Why? We are, of course, still great in the things which always came easy to us. We have improved, to be sure, in many fields, but not perceptibly in those which made us the object of foreigners' scorn in the past. We are not more honest, reliable, and law-abiding than we were, we are badly organized and badly governed. Our love life is still highly uncontrolled. Could it be that foreigners are no longer certain that their virtues are best? Or could it be that our vices have turned out to be desirable advantages in the modern world, qualities essential for survival? Did we or did the rest of the world change? And what exactly are the Italians' virtues and defects?

*

I know of no sure way to ascertain the Italian national character. There are no questionnaires for the dead. There are no authors to rely on. Descriptions of Italian habits and customs by Italian writers are very rare and seldom explicit. Few of them are trustworthy. Each writer had his own axe to grind, thesis to prove, course of action to propose, or spite to vent. Each wrote from his particular vantage point, the bias imposed by his century, class, province, education, political views, and luck in life.

There are, however, three or four small exceptions. There is an

essay by Giacomo Leopardi, the nineteenth-century poet, a remarkable man who managed to be objective in spite of the fact that he was
an aristocrat, a man of genius, and a hunchback, and lived in a dreary
provincial town; there are also revealing passages in Nicolò Machiavelli and Francesco Guicciardini; a few essays on Italian literature as
a key to national character by Francesco de Sanctis, a professor at the
Zurich Polytechnic one hundred years ago, and little more. Leopardi
himself had to admit: 'Italians do not write or think about their customs, as if they thought such studies were not useful to them.' There
are, of course, thousands of books by foreigners, but, among them,
there is only one real authority, Stendhal. John Addington Symonds
is, in my opinion, the next best, although blinded at times by his
stern moral views and his hatred for Popery. All others, for some
reason, either love us or hate us too much. Their best books on Italy
often contain brilliant flashes of intuition and some revealing truths,
in a clutter of clichés, superficial appraisals, supine acceptance of pre-
conceived notions, wrong information, and misspelled Italian words.

I have been helped, however, by the fact that, though Italians do
not write about their national virtues and vices, they talk about them
incessantly. The debate goes on in railway compartments, sidewalk
cafés and newspaper offices, on the most fascinating subject of all,
why are we the way we are? I have participated in such endless discussions all my life. I heard infinite theories and no conclusive
answers. I discovered, however, that we all instinctively agree that
some habits, traits, tendencies, and practices are unmistakably our
own. We call them *cose all'italiana*. The words are sometimes pronounced proudly, sometimes with affection, irony, compassion,
amusement, or resignation, very often with rage and contempt, but
always with underlying sadness.

What exactly are these *cose all'italiana*? They are things in which
we reflect ourselves as if in mirrors: a gratuitous *beau geste*, a shabby
subterfuge, an ingenious deception, a brilliant improvisation, an
intricate stratagem, a particular act of bravery or villainy, a spectacular performance. . . . Such *cose* may not be statistically prominent,
but they can happen only in Italy. They should not be taken lightly.
They are clues. By looking for them, following them, adding them
together carefully, the good and the bad, I slowly began to see a

pattern. They prove that there are things that come easy to us and others that are impossible. They clearly determined the course of past events. They will surely determine the future. Perhaps there is no escape for us. And it is this feeling of being trapped within the inflexible limits of national inclinations which gives Italian life, under the brilliant and vivacious surface, its fundamentally bitter, disenchanted, melancholic quality.

CONTENTS

THE ITALIANS

CHAPTER ONE

THE PEACEFUL INVASION

ITALIANS are pleased and perplexed. Every year since the end of the war they have seen the number of foreign visitors to their country increase at an incredibly rapid rate. The phenomenon has now reached unprecedented, practically inexplicable, and almost alarming proportions. In the 1950s the tourists numbered eight, ten, twelve million yearly. A little later, only yesterday, they were fifteen, seventeen, nineteen million. They have now passed the twenty million mark, a proportion of more than one tourist to every two and a half Italians, and the total is still growing. It appears that, if circumstances remain favourable, the travellers will reach thirty million within a decade, and will eventually match and even surpass the number of native inhabitants in the peninsula. Nothing daunts foreigners. Nothing frightens them. Nothing stops them. They arrive in a steady stream, by all forms of transport and even on foot, by day and night, from the sea or via the Alps. What is but a small trickle in the winter months grows in the spring to the size of a stream, and, in April, May, and June, turns into a monsoon flood, breaking all dikes, covering everything in sight. It begins to recede in September. It never completely dries up.

People come from all parts of the five known continents, from the old established nations of Europe and America and from the newly founded ones in Africa and Asia. The largest number come from the north, the vast, democratic, bourgeois, industrial north of Europe and America. Some now also come from Russia, in some ways the most northerly of all countries, organized parties of sightseers, behaving like military units traversing a dangerous territory inhabited by treacherous natives, as diffident and self-contained as Xenophon's Greeks marching across Asia Minor. Russian tourists all wear the

same box-like clothes, as new as those of provincial newly-weds, and
ankle-length raincoats. They look well-fed, self-satisfied, and well-
behaved. They appear eager to acquire as much culture, in all its
forms, as rapidly and cheaply as possible. They have a disturbing
resemblance to the diligent German tourists at the beginning of the
century, the solid subjects of William II.

There are many travellers who, in order to obey the urge that
drives them south, abandon their own countries, whose delights and
tourist attractions are being advertised and celebrated all over the
world. What do they seek that is better than what they left behind?
Not many Italians willingly travel abroad in any direction, north,
south, east or west. They always feel more or less exiled and unhappy
in alien lands, and honestly believe the attractions of their homeland
to be most satisfying. They are the first victims of the famous charm
of Italy, never satiated with her sights, climate, food, music and life.
Familiarity never breeds contempt in them. Neapolitans, for instance,
after many thousand years, still gaze with the same rapture on their
native landscape, eat *spaghetti alle vongole* as if they had never tasted
them before, and compose endless songs dedicated to the immortal
beauty of their women and their bay. Those Italians who travel
abroad are, as a rule, the privileged—Milanese industrialists and
Roman princes who have adopted foreign ways, cabinet ministers,
diplomats, newly-weds—and the disinherited who go looking for
work. They are usually all equally homesick abroad; the rich and the
poor look for *caffè espresso*, a good Italian restaurant, wherever they
go, and sigh for the day of their return.

At the high tide of the tourist season, from early June till late September, visitors fill every empty space available in Italy. Trains,
buses, boats, restaurants, churches, museums, Greek and Roman
ruins, chapels, concert halls, historic landmarks, and famous belve-
deres, whence romantic landscapes (two stars in the guide books)
can be admired, are packed to capacity with foreigners. One literally
finds them everywhere, often at one's table, unknown friends of
friends, sometimes even in one's bathroom and bed. They also fill a
couple of universities, Perugia and Urbino, set aside for them, where
they study the language, imbibe the Latin sun-drenched culture,
make love, go swimming, and feed themselves cheaply on pasta, olive

oil, tomatoes, and garlic. American universities sometimes hold summer sessions, in art appreciation, history of civilization, and related subjects, in some ancient villa on a hilltop near Florence with a view over the whole city, or a *palazzo* on the Grand Canal. Swedish and Norwegian workers' clubs have purchased wooded strips of deserted Italian coastline, where they have built their own club-houses and recreation centres.

There are sultry days in July and August when the cities, emptied by the natives, are almost completely taken over by the swarms of dusty and perspiring foreigners. During the siesta hour, when even the carriage horses sleep under their straw hats, the relentless tourists finally slow down. They bivouac everywhere. They recline on park benches, kerbstones, the stone brims of fountains, or ancient ruins. They place their heads over their crossed arms on café tables for a siesta among the empty bottles, the dirty napkins, and the recently purchased souvenirs. They then really look like a tired and bedraggled army after a fatiguing battle, who have occupied a city abandoned by their fleeing enemy. They have conquered. The place is theirs.

I am not talking here of the minority, the experienced foreigners who know why they come to Italy and what Italy is. Many have come here before and know their way about, others have never been here but somehow know what to do and what they want. They all avoid the heat and the dust, seldom visit the obvious places but, when they have to (the obvious places are often the most desirable), they go at convenient hours, when the crowd is away and the air is cool. They wear ordinary clothes, the same as everybody else. Some are in love with nature, others with art, culture, archaeology, or music. Some like meeting people and making friends, others discover little-known beaches or unexplored islands. There are those who make lengthy detours, to see some little-known masterpiece, and those who like food and wine and know the *trattorie* which only few natives and no foreigners have yet discovered. There are many who speak the language well. These easily disappear in the background. They do not interest me here. There is nothing peculiar about them. I am talking of the vast majority of tourists, the millions driven by some unknown urge.

They are so punctual and numerous that their mass arrival, in the eyes of ordinary Italians, appears as irresistible as a natural event, as ineluctable as the seasonal return of migratory birds, swallows, quails, or partridges, driven by instinct; or as an anthropological phenomenon like the migration of nomadic tribes seeking green pastures for their herds. The impression is heightened by the fact that many of these travellers look somewhat alike to Italian eyes. They dress in garishly-coloured clothes, much as the members of the ancient barbaric hordes once did and as the Gipsies and Berbers still do. A great number of Germans, Scandinavians, Britons, and Dutch have pink skins, which the sun seldom succeeds in tanning a decent brown but reddens to the tender colour of *prosciutto* or covers with freckles. They perspire freely in the heat, under their nylon shirts. They wear barbaric sandals. They have dark glasses over their eyes and their heads are bare or covered with cheap straw hats on whose brims are printed or embroidered the names of cities, sanctuaries, beaches, islands, or other famous landmarks.

There is something mysteriously significant about the behaviour of many of them. A mild frenzy takes most of them and transforms them once across the Italian border. It resembles the irresistible excitement which captures some living organisms and makes them forget themselves and everything else, when, like salmon going up-stream, they obey some deep and secret impulse of Nature; or the intoxication, the gentle and sweet delirium, which makes all honey-mooners quietly mad everywhere in the world and honeymooners in Italy doubly so, both because they are on their honeymoon and they are in Italy. Like all newly-weds, in fact, many ordinary travellers seem deliciously drunk with new illusions and hopes. The sedate professional man, the sober shopkeeper, the loyal employee, the rigorous scientist, the stern educator, the tidy housewife, the bespec-tacled spinster, the innocent maiden, the virtuous wife, the resigned husband, all behave as they probably never dared to behave before and as they probably would not behave publicly in their native habitat. More exactly, they behave as if they had shed the rôles assigned to them and the personalities bestowed on them by Nature, because such rôles and personalities had suddenly become repugnant and alien to them; or as if all the rules of the game of life had been changed or suspended. Some seem strangely deprived of all, or part of, their customary discernment, of their powers of control and discrimination, and of the scepticism, diffidence, prudence, suspicion, and fear necessary for survival in most countries. They get into all sorts of scrapes. They make friends with all sorts of people. They look at all things with indulgent and dewy eyes, apparently ready to love, admire, understand, or, at least, excuse and forgive almost everything, the good, the bad, the indifferent, the repugnant. They are often easily swindled, but many do not always mind if they are.

Most of these visitors from Northern Europe drink vast and indiscriminate quantities of wine. They drink, with equal good-natured enthusiasm, anything at all: costly vintages from famous vineyards, raw wines still smelling of sulphur and wooden staves, sweet and syrupy wines made for people who know little about such things. It is, for some curious reason, the first thing Germans and Austrians do, as soon as they cross the Brenner pass on their southward trip. They stop the car at one of the many wineshops which line both sides of the valley road, just beyond the border, as frequent as the petrol stations. Each *osteria* has a wrought-iron hanging sign, a terrace in the quivering shadow of a leafy pergola, checked table-cloths, waitresses in *dirndl*, everything designed in a tasteful fairy-story style, a style which is a mixture suited to the geographical and psychological spot, half German and half Italian, half Walt-Disney-Tyrolean and half *Il Trovatore* or Palio-di-Siena-Medieval. On the Brenner road, German and Austrian tourists behave as the Americans did under prohibition, when they rushed for the first bar across the Canadian border. There is no obvious explanation for this phenomenon. There is no scarcity of cheap wines, local or imported, in Germany and Austria. Perhaps these people are trying to quench not a physiological but a psychological thirst. This may be an unconscious magic rite; they drink wine as if it were a potion necessary to acquire a new personality, or they drink it as one drinks champagne on New Year's eve, on the stroke of midnight, to celebrate the crossing of a spiritual border and to inaugurate new hopes and a new life.

With equal indulgent enthusiasm, these summer visitors indiscriminately enjoy all kinds of doubtful attractions, things they probably shunned at home. They listen with the same breathless rapture and delighted smiles to the best opera singing in the world at Rome, Milan, or Spoleto, and to wheezy village bands, to impeccable Vivaldi quartets and to tinny dance orchestras. They eat the dainty food of famous chefs with the same pleasure with which they devour gross peasant dishes, mostly composed of garlic and tomatoes, or fisherman's octopus and shrimps, fried in heavily scented olive oil on a little deserted beach. They buy vast quantities of souvenirs to take home, smart things they cannot find elsewhere, cheap trinkets made in Japan, costly masterpieces, tawdry imitations.

Many try to speak Italian. A few creditably manage this in a short time. Others think they do. Things seem, of course, more significant and enjoyable when expressed in the native language. A spade is only a spade, a *Shaufel* but a *Shaufel*, but a *badile* cannot help being a pagan, Mediteranean, intoxicating *badile*. Some study lists of words phonetically spelled in handbooks. Some pick them up in random conversations. They also try hard to gesticulate wildly as they speak. They usually manage it in the style of amateur comedians playing an Italian character. They laugh loudly and converse with everybody, the people at the next table, travelling companions in the trains, the waiters, the beggars, the street singers, the cicerones, anybody in sight, with the same good-natured lack of discrimination with which dog lovers pet any dog.

The men, many men at least, those of all ages who have a natural bent for that sort of thing, admire and pursue Italian girls. It must be said that the Italian girls and young women, for reasons nobody knows for sure, are now more disturbingly beautiful than they have ever been in men's memory and perhaps in history, certainly more attractive and desirable than the models of the most famous statues and paintings in the past; Botticelli's 'Venus', Titian's 'Sacred Love', and Raphael's 'Fornarina' would not make anybody turn around in the streets. Italian girls are more attractive, and approachable, not only than in the past but also than in many other countries today. Feminine beauty, before the war, like prosperity, seemed to be a privilege reserved to rare local cases, but widespread among many foreigners, especially Americans. Smart Italian young men of the time anxiously awaited the disembarking of the American girls in the spring, well-shaped, well-washed, well-dressed, and incredibly long-legged, who always looked as if they really arrived from another and younger world. They were healthy, witty, free, and unafraid. Now our women, too, have somehow surprisingly acquired long and shapely legs; they have lovely and pert faces, overbearing breasts, thin waists, and harmonious behinds like double mandolins. But, more than this, they have simple, unembarrassed, friendly manners: they can say tender words with heart-breaking candour or, at times, prettily pronounce unprintable ones.

Foreign men, it is true, have always pursued women in Italy. The courtesans of Venice and Rome during the Renaissance were much appreciated. The Carnival season in Rome and Venice was for centuries merely an excuse to chase masked girls through the streets. Now the hunt has acquired a more determined, almost desperate, character. Many visitors are fascinated by the girls to the point that they often lose all powers of coherent speech and judgment: they are bewitched by the girls' sinuous and provocative walk, their inviting and hospitable ways, their smart clothes which often look as if they are sewn on them, or, more especially, their tiny two-piece bathing suits. Foreign men sometimes follow some specially provocative specimens in the street like hungry dogs following butcher boys delivering meat. Striking up an acquaintance is not always difficult, in a *caffè* or on the beach. Many men easily, too easily perhaps, find their way to some girl's bedroom. Some of these always fall deeply in love. They earnestly want to get married. They want to bring back a living souvenir of the land of sunshine and amiable ways to their gloomy countries. At the end of every summer, there are men who threaten suicide (a few kill themselves), for the love of a beautiful woman, with whom they can scarcely talk, and who would possibly discredit them and make them unhappy if she became their wife.

Many foreign women think Italians are irresistible. The men too have a long-established reputation. Some are indeed irresistible. Their charm, skill, lack of scruples, and boldness are proverbial. Most of them always feel free as birds, even the married ones, or those who are deeply in love or engaged. Many are disposed to make love at the drop of a hat, anywhere, in a car, on a beach, behind a bush, on mountain summits, under water, or even in a bed, during the day or at night. They are not too difficult to please, young or mature men, fat or lean, peasants or city playboys with Maserati cars. They seldom waste time. All that a woman has to do in many cases is throw a meaningful glance across a café table, smile cryptically to herself, wave a hand, or put an unlighted cigarette in her mouth and look vainly for matches in her handbag. The better men take just a little more effort to attract. Naturally, some women, the ugly ducklings with flat chests, the middle-aged who still feel young at heart, the lonely and well-preserved grandmothers, all come to Italy with the hope of enriching their lives with the souvenir of an Italian love affair, a pagan romance under the stars, by the sea, accompanied by guitar music. There are even inexpensive camps, collections of straw huts on lonely beaches in Southern Italy and on the islands, founded by foreign institutions, dedicated to the meeting of neglected and impecunious foreign women and eager Italian men, whatever men the primitive surroundings provide, fishermen, sailors, soldiers, and unemployed farm-hands, with brilliantine in their curly hair and flashing smiles.

*

Many foreigners come back the next year. Some come back more and more often. Some stay a little longer, every time, and decide to live in Italy for a spell. A few eventually discover to their dismay they can no longer leave. They cannot help feeling there is something cowardly in the decision to live here for ever. Their sensations have been well described long ago by Nathaniel Hawthorne, a tourist in Rome, who watched himself gradually turning into an expatriate: 'The years, after all, have a kind of emptiness,' he wrote, 'when we spend too many of them on a foreign shore. We defer the reality of life, in such cases, until a future moment, when we shall again breathe our native air; but, by and by, there are no future moments; or, if we do return, we find that the native air has lost its invigorating quality, and that life has shifted its reality to the spot where we have deemed ourselves only temporary residents. Thus, between two countries, we have none at all, or only that little space of either in which we finally lay down our discontented bones.'

How many of these transplanted foreigners are there in Italy today? A few hundred thousand? One million? Nobody knows.

Some are inconspicuous. They are the *Italianizanten*, in love with the place, those who have always been here and who know why they are here. A special mental disposition, an elective affinity makes them honorary Italians. A few of them are more Italian than the Italians themselves: they know more about the country, its literature, its manners, its past history, its hidden treasures, and its possibilities than many natives. Those who interest me are the others. The most conspicuous are naturally the rich, the millionaires from turbulent South American countries afraid of revolutions, the successful artists, the Hollywood actors, the dilettanti rentiers, the world-weary aesthetes with Swiss bank accounts.

They spend a season, a few years, or a lifetime in a house in Florence or in some stately Medicean villa overlooking the town, among priceless paintings and frescoed walls (like Queen Victoria, the Brownings, Mark Twain, Bernard Berenson, Aldous Huxley). They rent a *palazzo* on the Canal Grande, complete with gilded gondolas and liveried gondoliers (like Lord Byron, de Musset, Ruskin, Wagner, Barbara Hutton, and Cole Porter). Or, like a character out of a Henry James novel, they settle in the *piano nobile*, the noble first floor with the high-ceilinged rooms, in some Roman *palazzo*. Some prefer to inhabit quaint and dramatic houses, perched on hilltops, overlooking the sea or a lake (like Shelley at Lerici; Axel Munthe, Norman Douglas and Krupp von Bohlen in Capri; Gorki in Sorrento).

The rich come because, understandably, they want to avoid paying heavy income tax at home, or have their fortunes riddled by death duties. Others want to go on living opulently, surrounded by servants, as the rich have always done, and as it will be possible to do in Italy for but a few years more. The *nouveaux riches* crave the reassurance of noble surroundings. All of them want a maximum of visible splendour with the minimum possible outlay of money. But there is something more. Many clearly want to withdraw from the rude turmoil of active life, to preserve and cherish a romantic illusion about themselves, their excellent taste, genius, beauty, and rank, which could be shattered by unkind confrontations in their own country. They pathetically want not to be contradicted by facts.

Then there are the poor expatriates. They greatly outnumber the rich, and they increase yearly. Many of them, as they were in past centuries, are artists, some are good artists, others are the struggling young, the old failures and the young hopefuls, the successful and those who will never amount to anything; they know it, and do not care. Italy suits them, a country in which one may work, decant one's own and other people's ideas, experiment, meet stimulating people and generally develop latent possibilities. There are all kinds: writers, painters, dancers, musicians, actors, sculptors, poets, or followers of new and as yet unnamed arts. Some are mere dabblers, dilettanti, people whose love for art is much greater than their modest capacities and talents, who somehow eke out a living in artistic surroundings, on the margin of the art world. For all these, Italy is the world's timeless refuge, the river bank on which to withdraw from the rapidly rushing stream.

The inartistic impecunious are perhaps more numerous than the artists. They are of all sorts. There are German war widows, decrepit French courtesans who live on the prizes of love games of a forgotten era, Indian Army colonels, pensioned Scandinavian school teachers, American grandparents who dislike Southern California, misfits, déclassés, divorcees of all nations, and all kinds of beachcombers. Many live in the big cities, where they often rent tiny furnished flats in decrepit houses or artists' studios. They avoid the busy industrial centres and the brazenly new and anonymous blocks of flats. They prefer Italy picturesque, poor, and decrepit. There is comfort in decay. Many also prefer the historic hill-towns, the villages perched on mountain tops, the tiny fishing ports along the coast, the rocky islands. Some of the delightful spots impecunious foreigners discovered in past generations, like Capri, Ischia, Ravello, Taormina, or Bordighera (where Edward Lear lived his last years and wrote his last limericks), have now become very famous, expensive, noisy, and overcrowded. But there are always others, new unspoiled ones.

The impecunious wear shabby but picturesque clothes, sometimes cook their own meals, sometimes board with peasants or fishermen, or eat in a cheap *pizzeria* or wineshop for a few lire. Ordinary food is as good as in provincial France or as it once was in China. Most of these poor foreigners say they came to Italy mainly because the climate is milder and the money goes further than anywhere else. What they like, of course, is not only low prices and sunshine but a place where indigence looks like modest affluence by contrast with the surrounding poverty, where poverty can be worn with dignity, as it is not noticeable or embarrassing. Lack of wealth, in fact, is seldom the object of pity or contempt among ordinary Italians. It is considered the natural condition of man. Poverty is a private matter, like religion, politics, or other qualities, habits, and vices, not to be questioned. What these people look for, in other words, is the Italians' traditional indifference to other people's personal appearance and idiosyncrasies, poverty among them, and indifference which verges on indulgence and sometimes on encouragement.

The Italy of these foreigners, both rich and poor, is mainly an imaginary country, not entirely corresponding to the Italy of the Italians. The expatriates often do not really pay attention to, see clearly, or like the Italy of the Italians. Many know too few natives, to begin with, and see them too fuzzily to understand them and their problems. The poor foreigners mostly meet servants, hotel concierges, waiters, shopkeepers, an artisan or two, the postman, and sundry hangers-on. The rich also meet bright members of the local café society, the Italians who speak foreign languages, have travelled abroad, sometimes have foreign relatives, and drink whisky. Few ever know the great mass of the people. These foreigners treat natives kindly enough: many mistake the amused and indulgent manners with which the Italians treat them, which sometimes approach the condescension with which one treats children, for courtesy and sympathy.

The problems of contemporary Italy are too disturbing and too difficult to understand; local political events have always seemed mysterious and negligible. Before the war, many who disliked the Fascist régime nevertheless thought it was a harmless and picturesque buffoonery, 'good enough for the natives'. After the war, there were some who believed that a little Communism 'would do the Italians good'. Ezra Pound's ideas about Mussolini and his government, before and during the war, are perhaps the most illustrious example of this kind of utter but honest confusion. There is also a minority who heartily dislike the Italians. These think that the beautiful scenery, which is the stage setting of their own dream life, is incongruously cluttered up by millions of extras, men, women, boisterous children, and ruined by *vespas*, fluorescent lighting, noise, modern constructions, pretensions and complications of all kinds. The country most of these foreigners really inhabit is the tiny Italy of the expatriates, made up of a few celebrated quarters of the ancient cities, some towns, villages, famous landscapes, three or four islands, where they consort mostly with people like themselves.

Many find, at one point, like Hawthorne, that they can no longer leave this practically non-existent country. They can no longer face the harsher world where they came from, where they see things perhaps too clearly, and where every word in their familiar language has a precise meaning. They have become hopelessly addicted to the amiable and mild ways of Italy. Many also have nobody left to go back to. They cling to their little lair, the view of the sea from the hill, the view of the Coliseum from the window if you turn your neck far enough to the right, the view of the Grand Canal, the roofs of Florence, the decayed villas of Rapallo, a clutter of antiques they picked up during the years, and their set habits. Italy is filled with people growing old, who can no longer think of leaving, living alone, comforted by a cat or a dog, waited on by a servant, an honest person at times but often enough an unscrupulous maid who feeds her family with what she steals. A day comes when these old people grow ill and helpless, far from the familiar sights and sounds of their youth, self-exiled for reasons which have become dim in their memories, in an alien place which they never really saw as it is and quite understood. At the end, they wait for death, some of them still dressed in gaudy and youthful resort clothes, surrounded by foreign sights and people who have somehow become the necessary props and conventional supporting characters of the imaginary drama of their lives. Many die every year and are buried hurriedly in the corner of an Italian cemetery reserved for heathens or heretics; some bodies are shipped home to practically unknown and indifferent relatives. Many die without having really discovered why they chose to live the last years of their lives in Italy, of all places.

*

Many idle expatriates are not old but young. They do not seek a princely life of splendour at reduced rates, modest and easy comfort, or the slightly cowardly peace without competition and adverse criticism which Italy can afford. They do not want to nourish illusions about themselves, pursue unusual inclinations, or prepare themselves for a future of glory. Many of them are not weak and desperate but vigorous, hopeful, lively, and healthy. On late summer afternoons in Rome, when the sea breeze, or *ponentino*, cools the leaden air, these young foreigners of both sexes, uncombed, sun-burned, wearing crumpled cotton clothes and dusty sandals, the men sometimes looking strangely feminine and the girls strangely masculine, crowd the stairway of Trinità dei Monti on the Piazza di Spagna.

They lean against the old travertine stone balustrade, sit or lie on the steps, and wait. For what or for whom do they wait? Without knowing it, they occupy one of the spots where, in past times, one hundred years or so ago, other youths met, lazy artists' models waiting for a job. There, on the Spanish steps, sat holy monks with white beards, brigands, pilgrims with their scallop shells, and beautiful *contadine* in their costumes, prepared to pray at some painter's wayside shrine, off-duty bandits with conical hats and bushy beards, Holy Families appropriately grouped. There were theatrical assassins, Judases, Bacchuses, young Saint Johns, shepherds in cloaks of goatskin or buffalo hide, looking like antique satyrs, white-bearded Eternal Fathers, and fierce-eyed peasants from the hills. Without knowing it, these young foreigners also occupy one of the spots where, before the artists' models, thieves, murderers, and other desperate people, pursued by the Papal gendarmes, once found inviolable asylum. According to an ancient privilege, they could not be arrested as long as they did not stray from there.

The contemporary youths have an improbable appearance of make-believe like the models of old, and look, in their shabby and crumpled clothes, as if they, too, had run away from home and were seeking some sort of asylum. They also are left alone by the Italian authorities, to do and dress as they please, as if they were protected by some ancient privilege. From what unnamed and unknown modern crimes and horrors are these young foreigners fleeing? What mysterious emptiness in their souls is filled by merely standing on Italian soil?

CHAPTER TWO

THE ETERNAL PILGRIMAGE

ALL THIS IS, of course, very old, so old it could be considered part of the very nature of things. Its beginnings go back to the dawn of time, to the days when Saturn, the father of all the gods, after being deposed and humiliated by his son Jupiter, fled from Olympus. He is said to have found refuge in Latium, the territory embracing the yet unfounded city of Rome, where he became king and ruled in the golden age. He, too, was a disillusioned refugee trying to forget misunderstanding, ingratitude, and defeat. Italy is still known in poetical jargon as *Saturnia tellus*, Saturn's land. *Saturnalia*, the week in December dedicated by the Romans to the expatriate god, the first of all their foreign guests, was, significantly enough, the feast when everything was permitted, all laws could be violated, and the world was turned upside down. Schools were closed, no war was declared or battles fought, poor men gave orders to the rich, slaves insulted their masters, thieves could not be molested, and the timid seduced haughty women.

Immortal and mortal foreigners, armed and unarmed, alone and in vast numbers, have sought a Saturnian interlude in Italy as far back as men can remember. The Barbarians came, in the declining days of the Roman empire, in great hordes, apparently driven by a desire for peace, stability, rich plunder, new pasture-lands, and, above all, by the pathetic and provincial hope of somehow acquiring the graces, accomplishments and respectability of decadent and effete Roman citizens, and to be taken for Romans. Northern travellers came to the Holy City even before being baptized, like the fair English youths Pope Gregory the Great once met in the forum, when he was still a simple priest. *Angeli non Angli*—they are Angels and not Angles—is the famous pun he made on that occasion.

Through the obscure centuries of the remote Middle Ages, pious travellers never stopped coming, following each other like ants along the decaying imperial roads, the Aurelian, Cassian, and Flaminian ways, on foot, on horse, on mule-back. All roads at that time truly led to Rome. Kings, lords, commoners, clerics, bishops, monks, saints, vagabonds, adventurers, bandits, knights, merchants, scholars, were all pilgrims to Rome. They all wanted, before they died, to behold the seat of the Universal Church and be blessed by the Pope himself, Christ's vicar on earth. Language was no barrier then. All Christians spoke Latin. They devotedly thronged famous basilicas and miraculous shrines, attended Pontifical functions, listened to world-renowned preachers, prayed to venerated images and sacred relics. They were not yet interested in the memory of ancient times, and no one bothered to gaze on the awe-inspiring ruins of imperial Rome. In fact, the more devout were horrified by what they believed to be the remnants of the works of Satan himself or the handicraft of damned souls. Were not the heathen gods but the disguises of the Devil?

Through the later Middle Ages German emperors and military leaders often came down at the head of their iron-clad armies. They came only incidentally to pray; above all they wanted to impress the Popes and the Italians with their power, to plunder and raze rebel Italian city-states, reward their loyal friends and allies, the Ghibellines, and destroy their enemies, the Guelphs. They could as easily have gone somewhere else. They could, for instance, have picked a quarrel with the Sultans of Turkey or the Grand Dukes of Muscovy, they could have pursued the Teutonic Knights into the Baltic, or followed Alexander's itinerary to the Indies, thus changing the whole history of Europe and the face of the world. Most of the time they preferred travelling south, as if attracted by a magnet, over the snow-clad Alps, down the narrow and rocky peninsula, among treacherous and unpredictable people, who did not understand and like them, where the plunder was slim at best, because they, like all Germans, were fascinated by the name of Rome and all it still evoked, so fascinated that they called themselves 'Roman', not 'German' Emperors, and their emperor Caesar, Kaiser. They felt that they could not legitimately rule unless crowned, like Charlemagne, by the Pope himself, in Saint Peter's, and in the name of a ghostly empire which had disappeared centuries before.

The emperors were also fascinated by other things, of which they were scarcely aware and which they seldom mentioned. Being solid northerners, they were attracted and repelled by all that which was to attract and repel so many northerners in future centuries; they liked the mild climate but feared it, as they liked but feared at the same time the Italians' elegant life, easy pleasures, adaptable morals, intricate reasoning, wines, women, the harmonious landscapes, the feeling of being immersed in history and ennobled by it. They were thrilled by one of the pleasurable sensations Italy always gives visitors from the north, that of feeling morally superior to the natives. The emperors carried away all kinds of souvenirs, the clever workmanship of the contemptible Italians. All conquerors did that down the centuries. Napoleon stole the bronze horses from Saint Mark's, which the Venetians themselves had taken from Constantinople; Hitler and Goering filled railway trains with the best *objets d'art* they could find.

The crusaders, too, travelled through Italy on their way to the Holy Land. It was the shortest route. On their way back, Richard Coeur de Lion spent an uncomfortable winter in Messina; Guy de Montfort hacked the young Henry of Cornwall to pieces as he clung to the altar in the cathedral of Viterbo. Traders later came to buy the goods which arrived from the Orient, spices, precious stones, silks, and Arab stallions. Others, still later, during the Renaissance, came to learn the newest arts of bankers and merchants, how to handle and multiply money, keep books, exchange and speculate on merchandise and gold. Chaucer came twice on business as a diplomatic representative for his king, and went perhaps as far as Padua, on his own, to meet Petrarch. Bishops came to confer with the Pope; theologians, jurists and scholars to study with famous masters at Bologna; horsemen to perfect the art of schooling horses. Knights drifted south in search of adventure. Sir John Hawkwood is perhaps the most illustrious of them all, the early prototype of a different kind of nordic expatriate, who flourished in Italy through the centuries and is still flourishing, the professional man or businessman who makes a fortune because he is reputed by the Italians to be duller and more honest than his local competitors, their own compatriots.

Sir John Hawkwood arrived in 1360. When the peace of Bretigny interrupted the King of England's hundred years war against the French, he found himself unemployed. He had been at Crécy; had gained the favour of the Black Prince; had enjoyed the luxury of inhabiting splendid castles commandeered with all their inhabitants, servants, kitchen and cellar; had known the love of beautiful and accomplished continental ladies. Like all wartime temporary gentlemen, he was reluctant to put on civilian clothes; he disliked the prospect of returning to his native Essex and his trade as a tanner. He felt somehow attracted by Italy. He crossed the Alps over the Mont Cenis Pass, at the head of a group of mounted men who called themselves the White Company. They were quickly snapped up by local princes to fight their little wars. From this unimportant beginning, the White Company went on to fight for wealthier and more powerful patrons. Their leader was celebrated as Giovanni Acuto, by no means because of his mental sharpness, but because the word *acuto* was the nearest the Italians could come to the original pronunciation of his name.

He was tall, ruddy-faced, blue-eyed, slow of movement, taciturn and brave. He was believed to be a sound man, not too expensive, who tried to carry the day as best he could, without unnecessarily losing too many of his own soldiers, but reckless with the lives of his enemies, a man who never betrayed his masters, one of the few reliable and reasonably honest *condottieri* of his times. The Pope gratefully made him Signore di Bagnacavallo, or Lord Horsebath, a good title for an English cavalry man. He successfully ended his career as permanent commander-in-chief of the army of the Republic of Florence, a solid and enviable position.

Accurate descriptions of some of his battles have come down to us. They are well conceived and diligently executed military operations. His English soldiers served him well. They fought better than their opponents, also because they fought with a youthful desire to win which was then considered unusual and dangerous. The White Company were the first well-drilled, uniformly armed, disciplined, spit-and-polish troops ever seen in Italy. Contemporary astonishment is described by Filippo Villani, the chronicler:

'They were all young men and therefore hot and impetuous, quick with weapons, careless of safety. In the ranks they were quick and obedient to their superiors, yet in camp, by reason of their unrestrained dash and boldness, they sometimes lay scattered about in disorderly and incautious fashion. . . . Each had one or two pages and some had more. When they took off their armour, the pages set to polishing them, so that when they appeared in battle their arms seemed like mirrors and were therefore so much more terrible . . . Bound and compact, with lowered lances, they marched with slow steps towards the enemy, making a terrible outcry, and their ranks could hardly be pried apart.' Villani concluded sadly: 'They succeeded rather by the cowardice of our people than because of their own valour.'

The Florentines, Machiavelli pointed out, trusted Sir John and did not fear he would enslave them, as many *condottieri* had enslaved other free cities, because they did not believe the Englishman was astute enough to do it. He lost in the end. He had stipulated with the Republic that after his death an equestrian statue should be erected to him in the Duomo. He died in 1394. The expensive statue was reduced to a cheap fresco, very high over the door, and so badly done that Paolo Uccello had to repaint it years later.

*

Travel to Italy, in the old days, was, for the solitary private man, always risky and adventurous. Many found their unmarked graves at the side of the road. Death, however, when met on a pilgrimage to Rome, was recognized as meritorious by the Church, sufficiently so to alleviate a lengthy punishment in Purgatory. The mortal dangers began on the Alps. The paths were often erased by sudden snow storms or avalanches. Even the guides lost their way at such times. Some of them were unreliable rascals, who robbed and killed their clients. Dead bodies of travellers always cropped up in the spring, as soon as the high snow had thawed. Avalanches were the next great menace. To find and restore their buried victims, hospices were built along the main passes by religious orders. The monks kept stores of wood and food, good beds, warm blankets, brandy, and sturdy dogs, who could sniff out a live body several feet under the snow. Avalanches were so much part of the necessary emotions of the trip that until just before the Alps were finally pierced by railway tunnels sporting Englishmen would stop in suitable spots and fire pistols at the mountains, in order to disturb the still air and cause the snow to slide down from the high peaks. A mountain crossing without avalanches was thought to be as insipid as a sea crossing without sighting a whale or meeting a hurricane. Bold travellers were sometimes buried alive with their luggage and companions as the result of their own successful scientific experiments.

Bandits awaited travellers along the roads in the plains. Those who were not ambushed, robbed and killed on the way, were sometimes murdered in their beds by greedy innkeepers. It was prudent therefore to appear as poor as possible, in order to avoid arousing the rapacity of all sorts of people, including travelling companions. All kinds of subterfuges were employed. Vespasiano da Bisticci, the Florentine Renaissance bookseller, relates one of them: 'William Gray (later Bishop of Ely) was a student in Cologne.... When the time came for him to leave for Italy it was necessary to order his departure with the greatest caution, because he was reputed to be a very rich man, and one who might pay a high ransom; moreover, there were many in Cologne who were on the watch for his leaving, designing to attack him somewhere on the road. Also the road was full of minor barons, and travel was dangerous. From the reports which were brought to him he decided on a plan by which he might travel in safety. It seemed best to him that he should feign illness, and should call the physician to visit him every day and then unknown, with a single companion, should steal away in the garb of Irish pilgrims. Meantime he arranged that the physician for the next seven or eight days should visit his apartment regularly.'

Then there were local wars to avoid. Travellers always tried to gather information about who was fighting whom on the road ahead. It was a tricky business. News was seldom available and not very reliable when it was. Italian politics were always puzzling to foreigners, as they still are today. Wars broke out unexpectedly. Fronts shifted without warning. Allies became enemies overnight and vice versa. Travellers often found themselves suddenly in the middle of a battle and disappeared without leaving a trace, dead among the dead. Others met a victorious army rejoicing, the soldiers drunk with looted wines, or met a defeated army mourning its losses, the soldiers just as drunk on looted wines. Both were equally dangerous. The lucky or obstinate foreigners who did not die or disappear on their way sometimes met their doom when peacefully resting and enjoying the sights and pleasures of some Italian city. Large numbers of them, down the centuries, were murdered by ruffians, killed in duels by gallant gentlemen they had picked a quarrel with in an inn, or died of some unknown disease. At best they were jailed for being without means of support after being robbed.

A sea voyage was often even more dangerous than the overland trip. At times, storms wrecked the ships, or crews mutinied in order to loot the cargo and to rob the passengers. Not infrequently the ship was boarded by Muslim pirates and all hands were taken prisoner. It is impossible to say how many good Christians on their way to Rome spent the rest of their lives as oarsmen on Turkish galleys or obscure slaves in North Africa and the Orient. Their families never knew they were still alive and prayed for their souls. Only a few, now and again, managed to send word of their survival and be ransomed. They sometimes returned to freedom and their families as broken old men, unwanted by wives who had forgotten them and found other consolations. As late as 1805, sailing from Genoa to Sicily, the ship on which Washington Irving was travelling was seized by a privateer and boarded by a crew of desperadoes with rusty cutlasses, pistols and stilettoes. This incident understandably predisposed the American author to see bandits everywhere when he set foot on Italian soil. The pirates released him after seeing the letters of introduction to distinguished people the young traveller bore on his person. Pirates were not snobs, easily impressed by high rank and famous names, but rightly feared the revenge of the well-connected more than that of the unknown poor.

Travellers who chanced on an uneventful journey had other troubles to worry about. Beds were rare, in Italy, as everywhere else in Europe. They were usually stinking and crawling with insects. Bed sheets and blankets were dirty with the sweat and grime of all the people who had slept in them for months or years. Guests of both sexes and of all ages and degrees of cleanliness were usually forced to share the few beds available. There were no glass panes in the windows until late in the seventeenth century. (Montaigne continually grumbled in his diary about the cold draughts in his rooms, which the wooden shutters were usually inadequate to keep out.) The food was bad, often nauseating. As late as the eighteenth century, Smollet still complained that 'the inns are enough to turn the stomach of a muleteer' and 'the victuals... cooked in such a manner to fill a Hottentot with loathing'.

There was as yet no way to heat houses in the winter except for an occasional fireplace and brazier. Murray's *Guide for Southern Italy*, in its 1858 edition, still found no great improvement in the little provincial inns since the Middle Ages. It says: 'In the remote districts the *osterie* are as bad and comfortless as they were in the time of Montaigne, except that the wooden shutters have mostly been replaced by glazed panels. The traveller . . . who can make his own omelette, and instruct the *padrona* how to cook a dish of ham and eggs, will find these commodities in the highland villages, where even milk and butter are rarely to be met with.' Local cookery must indeed have been repulsive, if English amateur efforts were to be preferred to it.

To hire a horse, a carriage, a servant, a guide or a room was a tricky, difficult and sometimes even dangerous business. This continued to be true until very recently. Murray's 1858 Guide still advised travellers to make 'their bargains with the landlords on their first arrival. All foreigners make it a rule to adopt this precaution, and for this reason they not only pay about a third less than English travellers, but escape the annoyances and delays of disputed bills.' Another nineteenth-century guide-book for northern travellers warned: 'Whenever you engage your place [on a coach], always stipulate for a front seat, and by all means reduce your bargain to writing, and then have it witnessed by a public notary.' Recourse to local police, in remote as well as more recent times, was a risky business. Often the policeman preferred to help the dishonest countryman with whom he had to live the rest of his life, rather than the guileless foreign traveller, whom he would never see again.

Nevertheless travellers never stopped coming. In spite of inconveniences and contretemps, draughty windows, cold rooms, rutted

roads, verminous beds, poisoned food, robbers, bandits, and murderers, braving tornadoes, avalanches, earthquakes, wars, marauding armies, Muslim pirates and obscure diseases, more people certainly undertook the trip to Italy during the Middle Ages than to any
other country. Religion was undoubtedly the strongest single moving
force. Pilgrims came to Rome at all times and seasons but they
especially thronged the Eternal City during holy years, at fifty-year
intervals, when blessings and indulgences were particularly plentiful.
An average of two hundred thousand of them were present every day
during the first holy year of all, when the practice was inaugurated,
in 1300. During the second holy year, in 1350, Matteo Villani, the
chronicler, estimated that a total of one million two hundred thousand
people entered the city's gates. Those are impressive figures, even if
inaccurate. Many were probably Italians from nearby provinces, but
a substantial number arrived from farther afield and from abroad.

Rome offered unique advantages to the believer. And yet the
journey was not strictly necessary. There were other ways to gain
Paradise, cheaper, quicker, and safer ways to wash away sins and
achieve a state of grace. One could travel to a nearby sanctuary, anywhere in Europe, pray to the same God, obtain the same or almost
the same indulgences and be back safe and sound in a matter of days.
Or one could do even bettter: one could lead a godly life, practise
the principal virtues, and achieve sanctity without leaving one's
village. The trip to Rome was, if not superfluous, not indispensable
from a religious point of view.

The quest for eternal salvation, indeed, gradually ceased to be the
only justification for the trip. Visits to shrines, sanctuaries, miraculous images; attendance on Pontifical ceremonies and rare festivals;
the absolution of specially grievous sins, or the liberation from
sacred ties, the privileges which could only be obtained in Rome,
never ceased to be among the principal reasons for many people
leaving home. They still are. But their paramount importance slowly
faded as the years advanced. More and more holy buildings began to
be visited not only for the reverence and edification they inspired
but also for their profane new elegance, the wealth and perfection of
the decorations and the works of art adorning them. Pictures of the
Madonna were increasingly admired not only for the renown of their

supernatural powers but also for the excellence of their workmanship, the fame of their painters and the beauty of the models.

For the first time in centuries art became something to be appreciated for itself. In fact, religious art was only partially dedicated to the praise of God and His Saints. It was also dedicated to the praise of man, woman, beauty, the pleasures of life on earth, colours, sunshine and hard work. Behind the shoulders of the Virgin or some bearded Father of the Church, the Italian painter joyfully depicted a miniature town or a well-cultivated landscape, so small that only from a very short distance could all the details be discerned, the walls, towers, churches, streets, the artisans at work, the ships in the river, the ladies on the balcony, the children, the barking dogs, the gaily coloured clothes drying in the sun, the ploughman and the hunter. Many nordic travellers who lagged behind the times apprehensively thought they detected a slight odour of sulphur and brimstone about art and life in Italy, the 'odour of unsanctity'. They still detect it today. The country was in fact slowly acquiring that pagan, slightly irreverent, sacrilegious reputation which it was never to lose. The reputation did not repel visitors. In fact, the danger of losing their souls attracted as many of them as the hope of gaining everlasting salvation.

*

It is not surprising that more people came during the impious Renaissance than during the pious and severe Middle Ages. Italy had become the richest, most dazzling, cultured, irreverent, and intelligent nation of Christendom. Italians had transformed the universe, or, at least, man's ideas about the universe and his place in it. They had started a revolution which was to transform Europe during the following centuries. Humanism, or the study of man's achievements, involved the acceptance of man's immense capacities for good and evil, his virtues, foibles, his nature split between the animal and the angelic. Within a few years, amazing new inventions, discoveries, and techniques were made or adopted. New activities produced incalculable and unimaginable wealth, which, in a chain-reaction, sparked off other new activities, producing yet more wealth; geographic discoveries, daring scientific experiments, ingenious commercial and banking devices, and intellectual speculations all managed to multiply the available financial resources. Wealth also encouraged the refinement of manners, supported schools and academies, made life easy for poets, painters, sculptors and scholars.

There was a thrilling darker side, too. John Addington Symonds wrote: 'Beneath the surface of brilliant social culture, lurked gross appetites and savage passions, unrestrained by medieval piety, untutored by modern experience. Italian society exhibited an almost unexampled spectacle of literary, artistic, and courtly refinements, crossed by brutalities of lust, treason, poisonings, assassinations, violence. . . . Steeped in pagan learning, emulous of the manners of the ancients, used to think and feel in harmony with Ovid and Theocritus, and at the same time rendered cynical by corruption, the educated classes lost their grasp upon morality. Political honesty ceased almost to have a name in Italy. The Christian virtues were scorned by the foremost authors and the ablest thinkers of the time, while the antique virtues were themes for rhetoric rather than moving-springs of conduct.' Symonds knew the matter well. He was rich, in bad health, and was ordered by his doctors to spend a long time in Italy where he studied the Renaissance in order to write his monumental work. His private life was a struggle between the principles of the Anglican Church and his own 'gross appetites and savage passions', above all his inclination for the love of effeminate young men. He died in Rome, alone, in a hotel room, and was buried in the Cimitero degli Inglesi, not far from Keats. Few people were at his funeral. Among them, his young Swiss valet was seen weeping copiously.

Nothing of any importance could be undertaken anywhere in Europe at the time without first travelling to see what the Italians had lately been up to and what they had recently discovered or invented. Painters, architects, sculptors, as well as shipwrights, doctors, theologians, engineers, astronomers, jurists, mathematicians, scientists, and scholars arrived uninterruptedly from abroad. English literati came to learn how to write poetry in their own tongue and to copy new models of composition. Merchants plied back and forth among market towns, leading caravans of loaded mules on better and slightly safer roads than before. Note was taken of all the novelties seen, of the new fashions. Thomas Coryat wrote, in 1611, describing to his uncouth countrymen one of the things that had dazzled foreigners for more than a century: 'I observed a custom . . . that is not used in any other country that I saw in my travels. The Italians and also most strangers that are commorant in Italy do always at their meals use a little fork when they cut the meat. . . . The forks are for the most part made of iron or steel, and some of silver, but those are used only by gentlemen. The reason for this is that the Italian cannot by any means endure to have his dish touched with fingers, seeing all men's fingers are not alike clean.'

A few inns had by then become more hospitable. The best was in Urbino, built by the duke, perhaps the first comfortable hotel of the modern age. An anonymous Frenchman described it in 1578: 'It is the best and most extensive in Italy. There are forty bed rooms, all on the same floor, and all opening on the same long gallery. There are also five or six dining rooms, which are very beautifully decorated as if the building were a nobleman's castle.' Everybody came, who was anybody. The universities were filled with foreign young men. Some studied hard, and all had a rollicking time. Wealthy and powerful northern fathers sent their sons to Italy to acquire some knowledge of Italian, which was the language suited for diplomacy, court life, love, and intrigue; they were following the Emperor Charles V's maxim: 'I speak Spanish to God, Italian to women, French to men, and German to my horse.'

Young men were sent to learn one thing above all, how to become perfect gentlemen. The model had been invented and perfected by the Italians of the time, and it was widely copied. 'To be a gentleman,' wrote Symonds, who was one, 'meant to be a man acquainted with the rudiments at least of scholarship, refined in diction, capable of corresponding or of speaking in choice phrases, open to the beauty of the arts, intelligently interested in archaeology, taking for his models of conduct the great men of antiquity rather than the saints of the Church. He was also expected to prove himself adept in physical exercises and in the courteous observances which survived from chivalry. To this point the awakened intelligence of the Renaissance, instructed by humanism, polished by the fine arts, expanding in genial conditions of diffused wealth, had brought the Italians at a period when the rest of Europe was comparatively barbarous.'

*

Even after the Reformation had swallowed many great countries in the north of Europe, travellers did not stop coming. They found Italy once more transformed. Within a few fateful decades, at the end of the fifteenth century and the beginning of the sixteenth, ruin, defeat, and ignominy had followed pride and splendour. Foreign armies had fought on her territory, the proudest cities had been occupied and sacked. The Catholics still came to be comforted and strengthened by the old faith. Many still came to study. Most foreigners no longer expected to be edified and instructed, and to bask in the brilliance of a flourishing civilization. They came to look upon things in Italy with amusement, condescension, or contempt, to gape with horror at the abyss in which the country had sunk. She was for many of them the devil's own country. As J. R. Hale, the English historian, puts it:

'Enforced by geographers' opinion of the effect of the climate on character, the idea that the quick, crafty Meridional peoples were milking the slower stolid Septentrionals had become a plaintive obsession. Machiavelli was judged by an age that expected to find subtlety and cunning in the hot South. And it became a fixed idea, in spite of travellers' accounts of the general sobriety of Italian customs, that the Italians did not even turn the money they cozened out of the Northerners to good use, but squandered it on fantastic dress and curious vice. The *Inglese Italianato* mocked God in foreign-bought ribbons that led straight from the tailor to the bawdy house and the pit. The traveller who had mastered the arts of dressing and making a bow would probably bring back as well the arts of atheism, whoring, poisoning, and sodomy.'

A great part of Roger Ascham's famous treatise *The Schoolmaster*, published in London in 1570, was dedicated to warning guileless youth against the irresistible seductions of Italy. If a young English gentleman incautiously went there without a prudent tutor, he pointed out, he would inevitably fall into 'popery and filthy living'.

'Some Circes shall make him, of a plain English man, a right Italian.'
Thomas Palmer, writing in 1606 an essay on foreign travel, pointed
out that, as far as Italy was concerned, it was safest not to go there at
all. Italians would teach the honest northerner such arts as stiletto
stabbing, poisoning, intriguing, and treason. In John Webster's two
plays, Italian characters poison their victims in four ways: by the
leaves of a book, the lips of a portrait, the pommel of a saddle, and an
anointed helmet. The number of Italian traitors, cheats, pimps, spies,
and murderers in nordic literature becomes practically endless from
that time on. The parade starts with the many cowardly and crafty
killers in the Elizabethan theatre, continues in the Gothic novels,
nineteenth-century historical romances and the more recent inventions of Baron Corvo, and practically reaches our days with the
Mediterranean murderers and Sicilian gangsters of contemporary
detective stories and films.

Nevertheless such sinister warnings did not discourage many
travellers. Either they wanted to witness or experience such debased
debauchery personally, in order to develop the proper horror for it,
or they thought that Italy, even in her degenerate condition, could
still enrich their culture and exercise their intelligence. Young
Englishmen dared everything to follow Richard Lassels' advice, 'to
season their minds with the gravity of that nation which has civilized
the whole world and taught mankind what it is to be a man'. Italy
was irresistible. Milton himself was troubled by doubts on the real
reasons why he had undertaken the trip to a country a virtuous and
religious man should have carefully shunned. 'Why Italy?' he asked
himself. 'Was it that, like another Saturn, I might find a hiding place
in Latium?' He answered his own questions a little defiantly, as if
afraid of not being believed: 'No. It was because I well knew, and
have since experienced, that Italy, instead of being, as you suppose,
the general receptacle of vice, was the seat of civilization and the hospitable domicile of every species of erudition.'

*

The eighteenth century saw no diminution in the number of travellers. Their justification, however, for making the journey was a
novel one: they wanted to improve themselves and thought that

nothing could beat a trip to Italy for that purpose. A lengthy visit to Venice, Florence, Rome, and Naples was believed to be an indispensable part of a man's education, the necessary completion to his studies, a real *voyage philosophique*. After the Holy Italy of the Middle Ages, the Unholy Italy of the Renaissance, the Italy of Ostentation, Corruption, and Superstition, we had the Italy Propaedeutic, or the World's Finishing School. It was also, in a way, a status symbol. Doctor Johnson, for instance, believed that 'A man who has not been in Italy is always conscious of an inferiority, for his not having seen what is expected a man to see.' Like most other people at the time, the Doctor thought that a man acquired moral stature and authority if he saw not what he liked or what interested him but what public opinion commanded him to look at.

The man who stayed at home might not have been inferior to the returned traveller, but nevertheless felt so in himself and was thought so by others. To be rid of this inferiority, he had only to transport himself and his things many miles, follow a recommended itinerary, roughly equivalent to the one which pilgrims to Rome had followed from time immemorial, post letters home with well-known post marks, fill a diary with wonderful experiences, strange encounters, natural catastrophes and, like Boswell, the description of the comely women who had consented to sleep with him. Many felt so superior on their return that they were practically unrecognizable. Italy had gone to their heads. They affected Italian mannerisms, carelessly dropped Italian words in their conversation, sang arias from the operas, wore ornate clothes, and sighed for the only country where they could be happy.

The best results could be obtained by following the routine, as prescribed by the guide-books, and omitting none of the sights indicated. Those were always the same. The century spurned all the products of the Middle Ages and the early Renaissance as ugly and worthless. It liked only a limited number of relatively recent *palazzi*, statues, churches, and paintings. The style of the late sixteenth century was considered supreme. Raphael and Guido Reni, the 'divine Guido', were the greatest painters who ever lived. Together with art, the traveller was not to miss the natural beauties, the famous Italian views described by poets and painters: the snowclad Alps, the lakes, the fever-infested Campagna, the gulf of Naples. 'Of all the countries in the world,' enthusiastically wrote an English author at the time, 'Italy is the most adorned by the arts. Of all the countries in the world, she has the least need of them.'

After Art and Nature, a traveller had to dedicate his devoted attention to the remnants of ancient buildings, those very ruins which were ignored by all until a few years before. Education, Self-Improvement and Culture could be imbibed only by direct contact with what was left of the monuments of Roman antiquity, the historical landmarks and the scenes of mighty events. Some of these spots were of doubtful authenticity, to be sure, some of the sights mere tourists' traps, such as the alleged ruins of Cicero's villa at Formia, Virgil's tomb at Naples, or Nero's tomb on the Cassian way near Rome. Still, they obtained their effect on people who thought they were genuine. Many were undoubtedly authentic. The traveller would stand watching the celebrated landscapes, the shores of Lake Trasimeno and the plains of Cannae (where the Carthaginians defeated the Romans), the Appian way or Mount Soracte (described by Horace), the beach near Gaeta (where Cicero was knifed to death), Capri (where Tiberius spent his abominable last years), and fill them with the ghosts of his imagination. People stood in silence, their heads bared, on the spot in the Forum where Caesar had been slain, or in the Coliseum where so many Christians had been devoured by lions.

The concentration on art, nature, and the remnants of Roman antiquity was perhaps one of the reasons why the rest of the Italian scene seemed to interest travellers so little. They watched the contemporary life of the people with the absent-minded detachment with which Egyptologists consider the mores of fellahin in Egyptian villages. The people crowding the streets in their colourful costumes were seldom described and then only as if they were not really alive, but quaint wooden puppets in a vast *Presepio*. Stendhal shrewdly noted the Englishman's unawareness of contemporary Italians: 'Many English people,' he wrote, 'limit themselves to reading, in every spot, the descriptions left by Latin poets, and go away cursing the Italian manners, which they only know from mixing with the lowest classes.' Most of them concentrated on the masonry.

In a letter written to his mother, Gray wrote from Rome as if the city was deserted: 'As high as my expectation was raised, I confess the magnificence of this city infinitely surpassed it. You cannot pass along a street but you have views of some palace, or church, or square, or fountain, the most picturesque and noble one can imagine.' Only the memory of antiquity could add interest to a contemporary scene. A traveller wrote: 'See where that wretch is strumming his mandoline. It is perhaps the place where a virtuous father killed his child rather than see her handmaid to an Emperor's lust!'

Guide-books provided scanty information on contemporary Italy but furnished many ready-made extracts from Greek and Latin authors, in the original texts, suitable for each historical spot. Translations of the Greek fragments were provided in footnotes but not of the Latin quotations. Gentlemen were supposed to read fifty or sixty hexameters or a massive chunk of archaic prose without help. Diaries and letters home, to north Europe, England, the Russias and America, were filled with ample quotations cribbed from the guide-books and great thoughts, some of them original, which the sights of Italy always inspired in pensive travellers. The stones and walls, overgrown with wild figs and fennel, made them meditate on the frailty of human greatness and inspired some to higher achievements. 'It was at Rome, on the 15th of October, 1764, as I sat musing amidst the ruins of the Capitol,' remembered Gibbon, 'while the barefooted friars were singing vespers in the Temple of Jupiter, that the idea of writing the decline and fall of the city first started to my mind.' Only dead Italians were deemed worthy of attention, the longer dead the more worthy.

The eighteenth-century Italy of foreigners' desires, the country of dead languages, dead Italians, and mute stones, was never so dissimilar from the Italians' Italy. Of course, travellers could not help also seeing the gay, profane and corrupt reality, which was all around them. It did not disturb them. It shocked a few. It seduced many. They enjoyed it. They had a wonderful time. But few would admit they had come principally for the fun of mingling with such contemptible people. Theirs was an earnest quest for knowledge, only rarely interrupted by inevitable interludes of immorality. It is interesting to note that this fictitious Italy, the Pedagogic Museum, was perhaps the invention of one man more than any other. It was he who authoritatively closed visitors' eyes to what was really going on around them and concentrated their attention exclusively on the worthy things which would inspire them with great thoughts. He was, naturally enough, an antiquarian, a Puritan, a converted Protestant, born in Prussia. He worked in Rome all his life, busy with his intellectual construction; he never confessed even to himself that he lived there also because life was enchanting, morals laxer, the wine cheap and people paid little attention to the private weaknesses of solitary erudite gentlemen. It is instructive to review his life, as he is the prototype of many expatriates who followed in his footsteps.

His name was Johann Joachim Winckelmann. He came to Rome as a young man in 1735, was converted to the Catholic faith, was befriended and encouraged in his artistic studies and his religious zeal by friendly high prelates. He was quickly promoted to the rank of abate. An abate wore priestly clothes, which made him inconspicuous in Rome, but was not technically a priest. Cardinal Alessandro Albani, a wealthy amateur who filled one of Rome's most sumptuous villas with priceless masterpieces, became his patron. As the cardinal was practically blind, he especially needed the young Prussian's help for the purchase of paintings; statuary he could touch. The Villa Albani is still intact today as the cardinal and the abate furnished it.

Winckelmann felt a profound repulsion for the southern sensuality which was rampant everywhere and tainted everything. He preferred the frigid chastity of Roman statuary, the harmonious but cold lines of classical architecture. To test his powers of resistance to earthly temptations, he used to lie in bed for hours with Margherita Guazzi, the shapely Italian wife and model of his friend and countryman, the painter Raphael Mengs. The abate and the lady, naked in the heat of the Roman summer, carried on elevated conversations on cultural subjects. The experiment, while meritorious, was not as difficult as it sounds. Winckelmann preferred, to the knobby and often unharmonious prettiness of women, the smooth beauty of adolescent boys, so much nearer to the perfection of his beloved Greek statuary. This preference of his only rarely made his life difficult. It usually went unnoticed. Once, though, his tender friendship with a winsome *castrato*, the popular singer of *soprano* rôles in operas, provoked a scandal. The Vatican, where Winckelmann was employed as librarian, disapproved. His patrons were jealous. The liaison had to be dropped.

The Prussian abate was the first man to have seen, measured, studied, caressed, catalogued, and classified so many statues from Greek to Roman times, practically all those to be found in Italy, which were then almost all that existed. He was among the first to travel as far south as Paestum to visit the ruins of the Greek temples, facing the sea on the lonely beach, amidst wild roses and herds of water buffaloes, where no man dared to linger after nightfall for fear of the marsh fever. He was also a constant visitor to Pompeii, which had been discovered a few years before and was still mostly concealed under its blanket of ashes; and to Herculaneum, which was then a dark underground city, to be reached through tunnels dug under the houses of Portici, and to be seen by torchlight.

His theories about beauty and art were finally compressed in his *Geschichte der Kunst des Altertums*, which marked a revolutionary break from past ways of thinking. It was the birth of a new discipline, the history of art. Either his enthusiasm and scholarly pursuits mysteriously changed the taste of his contemporaries, or Providence had put him on this earth with his own unique preferences and novel ideas at the proper time. The fact is that he originated the Neo-Classic style. Greek sculptors, according to him, had reached ultimate perfection, beyond which man could not go. They had observed and reproduced idealized human forms at their best, Praxiteles by measuring his many exquisite concubines, Pheidias by visiting the gymnasium daily, where he studied naked athletes at their games. In the art of painting, curiously enough, the abate, like most of his contemporaries, thought only Raphael had approached the Greek sculptors' perfection. Of all later painters, only one German could be compared to the Italian master, his friend Mengs. (Mengs was, of course, not very good: just a diligent and scrupulous eclectic, who, as he himself explained, mixed 'the expression of Raphael, the colour of Titian, and Correggio's wonderful harmony of light and shade'. Winckelmann compared him to the bee, who 'culled various sweets from different flowers and made its honey sweeter'.)

Perfection, for the Prussian abate, was stately and harmonious form, almost anonymous in its regularity, unmarred by individual traits, frigid, devoid of emotions and showing no explicit sexual characteristics. The fact that human beings in the streets of Rome often happened to be more beautiful than the insipid Greek models or Raphael's vapid Madonnas did not disturb him. He believed living people's beauty to be only apparent. They were beautiful in a wrong and meaningless way, therefore not beautiful at all, only agreeable, pleasing, pretty. Nobody knows how far his revolution towards Greek canons in art and love would have gone had he lived longer. He died, a victim of his proclivities, at the relatively early age of fifty-one in a dingy hotel in Trieste, on his way back from Vienna, where he had been received with great honours by the Empress Maria Theresa and his friend and patron, Prince Kaunitz, the Imperial Chancellor. He was murdered by a scullery boy of eighteen, whom he had invited to his rooms to show some ancient medals of rare design. The boy was later found roaming the countryside with the medals in his pockets. He was tried and hanged.

What Winckelmann had done in the realm of visible art, another man probably did in literature, a good friend of his and Mengs', Johann Wolfgang von Goethe. The poet liked pretty girls all his life. At seventy-three he complained to his friend Chancellor Müller: 'I don't feel well perhaps because I am at present in love with nobody and nobody is in love with me.' In his Italian journey he left no petticoat unturned. He arrived in Rome in 1786, when thirty-seven years of age. Winckelmann's books were his guide through classical Rome, taught him to overlook all the Baroque and contemporary buildings, illustrated the principal statues in private and public collections and fanned in him an ardent love for ancient ideals.

All Winckelmann's teachings strengthened Goethe's vague conceptions, which he had come to Italy to perfect. The trip had been on his mind for years. He had dreamed of it as a break from his past, a symbol of revolt against the nordic romanticism of *Sturm und Drang*. Once in Rome he translated the calm, passionless, Olympic aesthetics of the converted abate into literary, poetical, philosophical, and moral rules. The contact with the unruly country somehow taught him that everything in art and life was to be the result of control, a show of man's mastery over accident, excesses, storms of passion and chaos. 'Certainly,' he wrote, 'people out of Rome have no idea how one is schooled here. One has to be born again, so to speak, and one learns to look back upon one's old ideas as upon the shores of childhood.' Everything, he discovered, must have a law and a form. *Gestalt* (Form) and *Gesetz* (Law) were to curb Nature. *Gesetzlichkeit*, or the essence of legality, was to reign supreme. All forms of disorder, whether created by God, Michelangelo, or Shakespeare, were equally to be deplored and avoided.

All this Pheidian harmony, frigidity, restraint, and immobility, all this nordic love for legality, all this contempt for disorderly passion and the untrammelled expression of human weakness and instincts, Goethe and many other foreigners after him sought in Italy, of all places, the very same country where the natives obeyed exactly opposite rules; they gave themselves to the unconfined sway of passions, the uncurbed expression of instincts, *joie de vivre*, freedom from dull duties and stupid laws, indulgence for all human frailties. Which was Italy? Goethe himself must have had doubts. In one of his first days in the country he asked an innkeeper at Torbole, near Venice, where the bathroom or *cabinet d'aisance* was. The man vaguely pointed to the courtyard. Where exactly in the courtyard, the German poet insisted. The answer was, '*Ma da per tutto, dove vuole.*' ('Wherever you wish, anywhere.') This was no *Gesetzlichkeit*; this was scarcely an example of man's mastery over the disorder of Nature.

We now suspect that travellers of the late eighteenth century and early nineteenth century unconsciously came to enjoy the interludes of fun among the live Italians more than the lessons of ancient history among the dead Italians. Few foreigners would admit it to themselves. Very few tried to analyse the nature of the particular pleasures they found in watching the Italians live their noisy lives, mingling with them, and accepting their lax rules and indulgent habits. This sense of liberation which they experienced was, first of all, a distinct physical sensation they felt the moment they passed the frontier, a muted excitement, a quickening of the senses. What its cause was nobody dared explore.

Stendhal thought it was principally due to the climate. He

describes the feeling: 'It is certain that the climate alone produces a nervous and inexplicable effect on arriving foreigners. When the army corps commanded by Marbot, after having crossed Germany, in 1806, arrived in the Venetian Friuli, a new spirit seemed to overtake those fifteen thousand Frenchmen; the harshest characters appeared to have become sweet; everybody was happy; in everybody's soul spring had taken the place of winter.' It is to be noted that the climate of Friuli, the northernmost part of the Venetian provinces, differs but little from the climate of the southernmost German provinces across the border, which the French soldiers of Marbot had just left.

Shelley more or less agreed. Meteorology was his explanation too. 'No sooner had we arrived in Italy,' he wrote, a few days after crossing the Alps, 'than the loveliness of the earth and the serenity of the sky made the greatest difference in my sensations.' He later confirmed his first impression in the preface to *Prometheus Unbound*: 'The bright blue sky of Rome and the effect of the vigorous awakening Spring in that divinest climate and the new life with which it drenches the spirit even to intoxication were the inspiration of this drama.' It was perhaps natural that visitors from the gloomy north should be more impressed by sunshine and (as Goethe put it) 'moonlight brighter than daylight' and more easily inclined to think that the light and climate prepared the mind for the enjoyment of many other enchantments. Heinrich Heine once in Italy reminded himself: 'Our German summers are but winters painted green. . . . The very sun wears a flannel coat. . . . In this yellow flannel sunshine fruits do not ripen. . . . Confidentially speaking, the only ripe fruits we have at home are cooked apples.' Russian poets thought of little else. Apollon Nicolayevich Maykov wrote enthusiastically: 'Under that fiery sun, in the roar of a waterfall, inebriated you said to me: "Here we can die together, the two of us".' Gogol noted: 'Who has been in Italy can forget all other regions. Who has been in Heaven does not desire the Earth. Europe compared to Italy is like a gloomy day compared to a day of sunshine.' 'I was born here,' he proclaimed to his friend the poet Zhukovsky. 'Russia, Saint Petersburg, the snows, the nasty people . . . all this has been but a bad dream.'

Germans and Scandinavians naturally dedicated to the sunshine

and warm weather of Italy a flood of second-rate poems and a few
of their best. But it is curious to note that travellers from milder
climates, the French, for instance, who were certainly not starved for
a sight of the sun, were also impressed. Chateaubriand wrote to his
friend de Fontanes, in a famous letter: 'You have undoubtedly
admired, in Claude Lorrain's paintings, that light which seems ideal
and more beautiful than in nature? Well, it is the light of Rome!'
Alfred de Musset wrote of the 'enchanted sky, so pure that a sigh
rises to God more freely than in any other place on earth'.

Whether caused by the sun, the climate, the sky, the light, or by
anything else, the sensation was a powerful, almost an overwhelming
one, often strong enough to change a man's life. Macaulay incredu-
lously recorded: 'I had no idea that an excitement so powerful and
agreeable still untried by me was to be found in the world.' Henry
Adams remembered later: 'Italy was mostly an emotion and the
emotion naturally centred in Rome. Rome, before 1870, was seductive beyond resistance. The month of May 1860 was divine. . . . The
shadows breathed and glowed, full of soft forms felt by lost senses.'
'Rome is beautiful, wonderful, magical,' Ibsen wrote in 1866, 'I feel
an extraordinary capacity for work and the strength of a giant-killer.
I kept struggling with my poem, "Brand", for a whole year, before it
took shape clearly. Then one day I strolled into Saint Peter's and
there I suddenly saw in strong and clear outlines the form for what
I had to say.' On his first day in Rome, in 1869, Henry James confided to his diary: 'At last, for the first time, I live.'

Under the influence of this sensation, Italy did not seem to many
a land like all others, created by the same God, but a masterpiece
made by Him in a moment of special felicity, each mountain shaped,
each lake designed, each tree planted, and each shoreline etched in
the exact way to achieve some particular poetic or pictorial effect.
Anatole France suspected the existence of another God, a better
artist. 'But look, darling,' he wrote in *Le Lys Rouge*, 'look again. What
you see is unique.' (What the characters were seeing was Florence
from the Fiesole heights.) 'Nowhere else is Nature so subtle, elegant
and fine. The God who made the hills of Florence was an artist. How
could it be possible that this violet hill of San Miniato, so purely
and firmly designed, be by the author of the Mont Blanc?'

There was also in many voyagers the Proustian temptation to compare everything to a figment of the artistic imagination. They sought to attribute every landscape to the appropriate painter, every real person to the writer who could have invented him, every sensation of the soul to the poet best suited to express it. This was more than a literary trick. Faced with the Italian scene many experienced in the past and still experience today the heightened emotions which only great art usually imparts. It is as if Italy were not only the home of Art but an immense and elaborate *objet d'art* herself. 'Thou art the garden of the world,' wrote Byron, signifying by 'garden' something planned and carefully laid out by an artist with the precise intention of delighting and amusing human beings.

'There is only one country in Europe,' noted Alexander Herzen, the Russian revolutionary millionaire, 'which can give you a feeling of peace, which can make you shed tears not of disgust and disillusionment but of delight, and that country is Italy.' The words are obviously more suited to describe the impression produced by great music, tragedies or immortal poetry than those produced by a foreign country. The 'feeling of peace' and the shedding of delighted tears are among the unmistakable signs of Aristotle's catharsis at work. Many were tempted to think that the translation of everyday scenes into durable masterpieces was far easier in Italy, where the distance between nature and art was shorter, and more easily bridged than in less picturesque and more familiar parts of the world. Wordsworth regretted having discovered this quarry of practically ready-made poems too late for profit: 'My mind has been enriched by innumerable images,' he deplored, 'which I could have turned to account in verse and vivified by feelings; earlier in life they would have answered noble purposes in a way that now are little likely to do.'

The delusion that art and nature were one in Italy irritated Byron, who had been one of the principal victims of it, when he sensed it in others. Thomas Moore tells this revealing story of his meeting his great friend in Venice after a long separation. 'We stood out on the balcony, in order that, before daylight had quite gone, I might have some glimpse of the scene which the Grand Canal presented. Happening to remark, in looking at the clouds, which were still bright in the west, that "what had struck me in Italian sunsets was that peculiar rosy hue"—I had hardly pronounced the word "rosy" when Lord Byron, clapping his hand on my mouth, said with a laugh, "Come, damn it, Tom, don't be poetical".'

*

The rapture and delight were not pure. They were often mingled with other sensations, different, disturbing and alarming. There was, for example, the bitter pleasure of pitying and despising the Italians. They were oppressed by corrupt, inept, and avaricious tyrannies. Still, one could not help thinking that they deserved them. They seemed to lack all the virtues which had made other people great. They were dirty. Their clothes, houses, and streets were dirty. They were incredibly noisy. They were deceitful. They were improvident. Their misfortunes seemed to be the natural result of their lack of virtue and their lack of virtue, in turn, the inevitable consequence of their misfortunes. There was no easy way to break the vicious circle. Ruskin, who loved Italy with more passion than he loved his wife, wrote to his father in 1845: 'Take them all in all, I detest the Italians beyond measure. . . . They are Yorick's skull with the worms in it, nothing of humanity left but the smell.' In *Mornings in Florence*, he complained: 'In the streets . . . you never hear a word uttered but in rage, either just ready to burst, or for the most part explosive instantly: everybody—man, woman, or child—roaring out their incontinent, foolish, infinitely contemptible opinions and wills, on every smallest occasion, with flashing eyes, hoarsely shrieking and wasted voices—insane hope to drag by vociferation whatever they would have, out of man and God. . . . Look at the talkers in the streets of Florence, being essentially unable to talk, they try to make lips of their fingers. How they poke, wave, flourish, point, jerk, shake fingers and fist at their antagonist . . . impersuasive and ineffectual as the shaking of tree branches in the wind.'

Walter Savage Landor, who spent long years in Florence, wanted little to do with the same Florentines. 'I visit none of them,' he declared firmly. 'I admit none of them within my doors. I never go to the gaming house, to the coffee house, to the theatre, to the palace, to the church.' The natives so irritated him, in fact, that he sometimes kicked and punched labourers who worked in his house and

garden, and once threw out his landlord, who had come to his rooms
with his hat on. D. H. Lawrence, many years later, felt an overwhelming repugnance for 'city' Italians, the bourgeoisie. 'Then I got
to beastly Milan,' he wrote to Lady Cynthia Asquith, on October 23,
1913, 'with its imitation hedgehog of a cathedral and its hateful city
Italians, all socks and purple cravats and hats over the ear.' A few
days later he added: 'I loathe and detest the Italians. They never
argue, they just get hold of parrot phrases, shove up their shoulders
and put their heads to one side, and flap their hands. And what is an
honest man to do with them?'

And many asked themselves whether Italy was really as beautiful
and pleasant as one's misled senses led them to believe, or whether it
was a mirage. Was one the victim of some devilish trick done with
emotional mirrors? The puzzled defencelessness of a moral gentleman from the north was eloquently described by Hawthorne:

'When we have once known Rome, and left her where she lies, like
a long decaying corpse, retaining a trace of the noble shape it was,
but with accumulated dust and fungous growth overspreading all its
more admirable features—left her in utter weariness, no doubt, of her
narrow, crooked intricate streets so uncomfortably paved with little
squares of lava that to tread over them is a penitential pilgrimage, so
indescribably ugly, moreover, so alley-like, into which the sun never
falls, and where a chill wind forces its deadly breath into our lungs—
left her, tired of the sight of those immense seven-storied, yellow-
washed hovels, or call them palaces, where all that is dreary in
domestic life seems magnified and multiplied, and weary of climbing
those staircases, which ascend from a ground floor of cookshops,
cobblers' stalls, stables, and regiments of cavalry, to a middle region
of princes, cardinals, and ambassadors, and an upper tier of artists,
just beneath the unattainable sky—left her, worn out with shivering
at the cheerless and smoking fireside by day, and feasting with our
own substance the ravenous little populace of a Roman bed at night
—left her, sick at heart of Italian trickery which has uprooted whatever faith in man's integrity had endured till now, and sick at stomach
of sour bread, sour wine, rancid butter, and bad cookery, needlessly
bestowed on evil meats—left her, disgusted with the pretence of
holiness and the reality of nastiness, each equally omnipresent—left

her, half lifeless from the languid atmosphere, the vital principle of which has been used up long ago, or corrupted by myriads of slaughters—left her, crushed down in spirit with the desolation of her ruin, and the hopelessness of her future—left her, in short, hating her with all our might, and adding our individual curse to the infinite anathema which her old crimes have unmistakably brought down— when we have left Rome in such a mood as this we are astonished by the discovery, by and by, that our heart strings have mysteriously attached themselves to the Eternal City and are drawing us thither- ward again, as if it were more familiar, more intimately our home, than even the spot where we were born.'

That Italy possessed a magic power to weaken foreigners' resis- tance to temptation was discovered by many, who were also shocked to realize, like Hawthorne, that the process did not displease them or fill them with remorse, but gave them a feeling of resignation, accep- tance, and repose. Bulwer Lytton, for instance, wrote: 'Clime that yet enervates with a soft Circean spell, that moulds us insensibly, mysteriously, into harmony with itself. . . . Whoever visits thee seems to leave earth and its harsh cares behind—to enter the Ivory Gate into the Land of Dreams.' Art, too, the ennobling pursuit of the more earnest visitors, the main purpose of the pilgrimage for many of them, inevitably also came under suspicion. Was it not sometimes merely an excuse for profligacy and loose living? Hawthorne was tortured by this doubt. 'Every young sculptor,' he wrote in *The Marble Faun*, 'seems to think that he must give the world some speci- men of indecorous womanhood, and call it Eve, Venus, a Nymph, or any name that may apologize for a lack of decent clothing. I am weary even more than I am ashamed of seeing such things. Nowadays people are as good as born in their clothes and there is practically not a nude human being in existence. An artist, therefore, cannot sculpture nudity with a pure heart, if only he is compelled to steal guilty glimpses at hired models. The marble inevitably loses its chastity under such circumstances.'

CHAPTER THREE

THE FATAL CHARM OF ITALY

WHAT THEN is this fatal spell of Italy? Sometimes it seems almost possible to measure it exactly—just as the scientist measures the refraction of light in water by observing the angle at which a stick appears bent in it—by comparing the difference between a traveller's enraptured recollection of his personal experiences and more sober and objective accounts of the same events. Take, for instance, Lord Byron's letters home on his first stay in Venice. What wonderful women he described, all young, all in love with him, all incredibly beautiful, some *ragazze* from humble families, some proud *contesse*. They all visited his famous apartment in the Palazzo Mocenigo or his special *garçonnière* at Santa Maria Zobenigo, in an endless cortège, sometimes fighting with each other for his attentions.

He wrote to his friends in London:

'I have fallen in love . . . fathomless love. My goddess is only the wife of a Merchant of Venice, but then she is pretty as an antelope, is but two and twenty years old, has the large, black Oriental eyes, with the Italian countenance, and dark glossy hair. . . . Then she has the voice of a lute and the song of a Seraph (though not quite so sacred), besides a long postscript of graces, virtues, and accomplishments. . . . But her great merit is finding out mine: there is nothing so amiable as discernment.' 'A Venetian girl, with large black eyes, a face like Faustina's and the figure of a Juno—tall and energetic like a Pythoness, with eyes flashing, and her dark hair streaming in the moonlight—one of those women who may be made anything. . . . I am sure if I put a poniard into the hands of this one, she would plunge it where I told her—and into me if I offended her. . . .'

41

Then take Shelley's sober description of Lord Byron's same love life in Venice:

'The fact is that the first Italian women with whom he associates are perhaps the most contemptible of all who exist under the moon, the most ignorant, the most disgusting, the most bigoted. Countless smell so strongly of garlic than an ordinary Englishman cannot approach them. Well, Lord Byron is familiar with the lowest sort of these women, the people his gondolieri pick up in the streets. He associates with wretches who seem almost to avow practices which are not only not named, but I believe seldom even conceived in England. He says he disapproves, but he endures.'

What then is this fatal spell? What dulled Byron's sense of discrimination? It made a severe, dutiful, middle-class naval hero, Horatio Nelson, forget his virtuous wife, the honour due to his uniform, the respect due to His Majesty's Minister to the Court of Naples, and fall in love with the worthless and fascinating Lady Hamilton. It gave middle-aged and resigned people the sensation of being, if not young again, at least daring and pleasing to others, and the illusion that they could still bite the fruits of life with their false teeth. At the same time, the spell drove a few sinners to an existence of prayer and penitence. It made and still makes unwanted people feel wanted, unimportant people feel important, and purposeless people believe that the real way to live intelligently is to have no earnest purpose in life. This fatal spell is very old. It can be traced back to the most remote antiquity. It is still one of the forces to be reckoned with in the modern world, a force that somehow helps to shape the lives of multitudes. It is easy today to show that it was the search for this unique quality in Italian life, for a sensation which gave strength and urgency to all others, which enticed people here, rather than all other motives, because millions now come for all the reasons which attracted them in the past, reasons so contradictory as to exclude and cancel each other.

Many, of course, are still in quest of holiness or the reassurance of religion. Not all of them are Catholics. There are Protestants, Jews, Buddhists, and Moslems, not to speak of agnostics and atheists, at all Papal audiences. Thousands of non-Catholics are granted private audiences and special Apostolic benedictions, in which they do not officially believe, but which they fervently welcome. They buy rosaries and holy medals for their friends. Many are tempted to forget past theological controversies, envious of the unquestioning and peaceful faith of the Catholic masses. Non-Catholics often admit that they receive, from their visits to Rome and the sight of the Holy Father at close quarters, a spiritual uplift which is often stronger than that experienced by Catholics, who are accustomed and therefore inured to such ceremonies. The Pope has once again become a great spiritual leader, a symbolic figure, the moral head of all the forces of good against evil.

Catholics, of course, undertake the voyage not only to see him but also to visit the traditional places of worship, the great basilicas, sanctuaries, shrines, and also to gain indulgences. Catholics and non-Catholics flock to Assisi, where the poetic memory of Saint Francis is still fragrant and where Giotto's frescoes depicting his life are well preserved. They go to Loreto, where the Holy Virgin's cottage can still be seen, brought through the air by angels from Asia Minor. Pilgrims sometimes visit Saint Michael's sanctuary on Monte Gargano, the spur of Italy. It was founded in a deep cave, where the Prince of Angels appeared in the eleventh century to Norman knights on their way back from the Holy Land. Others go to Syracuse, in Sicily, where a new, inexpensive, and ugly bust of the Virgin, a mass-produced article currently sold in all department stores in Italy, is known to have wept, a few years ago, shedding abundant tears which, according to the chemical analysis of the municipal administration, contained all the ingredients of real human tears.

There is now a special rush to the village of San Giovanni Rotondo, in Apulia, not far from Saint Michael's cave. Non-stop buses leave Rome for the once obscure hamlet every day during the tourist season. People go (as so many have done in past centuries) to worship a living saint. He is Father Pio da Pietralcina, a bearded Capuchin. He lives a simple and holy life. Since 1918, he has been blessed with the stigmata on feet, hands and ribs. Those on his hands he keeps modestly hidden under mittens. Stigmata, to be sure, are only the first signs of sainthood and not the surest nor worthiest of all. Even some Protestants and heretics have been known to have had them. The Church does not acknowledge their validity; it does not consider Padre Pio a saint because of them. Surer signs of sanctity, of course, are levitation, ubiquity, an exceptionally ascetic life and miracles.

Father Pio does not fly. It is perhaps the only saintly feat he has not yet performed. But he is renowned for ubiquity and miraculous cures. Without ever leaving his convent cell, he has appeared a number of times simultaneously to trustworthy witnesses miles from each other and carried on conversation with all of them. Once a well-known cardinal even saw him kneeling in Saint Peter's, in Rome, lost in prayer. He has become visible in the bedrooms of the sick and dying, in prison cells and hospital wards, after his help had been invoked. When he cannot go (apparently his personal appearances are not without some limitations), he sometimes sends a strange perfume in his stead, which pervades the whole room and is smelled by everybody present, including the incredulous, reminding them invariably of fresh wood violets. It is the well-known 'odour of sanctity', described by many authorities since the early Middle Ages. Many of the despairing people who invoked him were cured of mortal and sometimes incurable diseases, as numerous doctors' certificates testify, or were freed from distress and anguish.

The little town of San Giovanni Rotondo is now the centre of feverish activities, some of them questionable, exploiting his name and presence. The Church takes a diffident view of most of them, warns the faithful against possible exploitation, and periodically sends inspectors to report on what is going on. There is a large hospital, financed with foreign money. There are inns, hostels, restaurants, shops selling all kinds of relics and mementoes, shady intermediaries who promise anybody a meeting with Father Pio and even a miracle, for a little extra money.

He himself seems unconscious of all this and takes no part in it. He says mass very early in the morning, as he has always done, in front of a vast crowd, which includes one-day tourists, pilgrims seeking grace, sufferers asking for a release from their sufferings and many devout followers who have left everything behind to live near him in poverty. The mass celebrated by him lasts more than an hour, as he pronounces every word with clarity and great devotion, and sometimes loses himself for long minutes in rapture. He exchanges words, after mass, with a few people who have obtained a meeting with him. His conversation is good-humoured and witty, not at all the forbidding sayings of an ascetic or mystic saint, but rather those of a good country priest of peasant extraction, which he is.

Among his followers there is a former American bomber pilot. During the last war, on his way back from a mission in the Balkans, he wanted to jettison the unused bombs before landing in Foggia. Over San Giovanni Rotondo, as he was on the point of opening the hatch, an immense figure suddenly appeared in the clouds, almost a cloud itself, the figure of a bearded monk, with upraised arms, imperiously commanding him not to drop the bombs. The pilot, greatly impressed, could not help obeying. Several years later, when his adventure was almost forgotten and was nothing more than a dubious after-dinner anecdote, he happened to read about Father Pio in an old magazine. Suddenly he understood the meaning of what he had seen and what had happened to him. He came to Apulia, met the holy friar, and was converted to the Catholic faith.

*

Perhaps just as many people still come for exactly opposite reasons. Italy to them is one of the last countries in the Western world where the great god Pan is not dead, where life is still gloriously pagan, where Christianity has not deeply disturbed the happy traditions and customs of ancient Greece and Rome, and where the Renaissance has not spent itself. Religion, they point out, is but a thin veneer over older customs. Many of the saints, venerated as powerful protectors of this or that village, are, in fact, but the local gods disguised. Sometimes their names give them away. On the flanks of Mount Aetna, in Sicily, for instance, people worship a 'Santa Venerina', who, among other gifts, has the power to make barren women fertile, like the Venus of old, *Venere* in Italian. And is there not a relation between the name of the patron saint of Naples, the venerated bishop Januarius, whose dried-up blood becomes liquid twice a year, whose relics many times stopped Vesuvius' lava at the very gates of the city during the fiercest eruptions, and the Roman protector of all portals and doors, Janus? The Church, they say, knows or suspects all this, but, in its great wisdom, allows it to go on, since it does not interfere with fundamental doctrines. It takes almost as much work and bother to unmake a saint as to make one. Only two lost their rank recently, after years of priestly research and deliberation. One was the old and glorious Saint George, protector, among many things and places, of the Republic of Genoa and of the Kingdom of England, the saint whose image is on every golden sovereign. The other was Saint Philomena, an erudite mistake of the early nineteenth century, born of the misreading of an old inscription.

Foreigners come to Rome to taste *la dolce vita* in Via Veneto, in night clubs, in villas on the Via Appia, in film studios, or artists' ateliers in Via Margutta. Some play nymph and faun on solitary beaches, in secluded caves and woods, where they can bathe in the nude, drink the wine, eat simple food with their hands, consort with *contadini* and fishermen, living close to nature and in harmony with the vagaries and caprices of human instincts. For these people, Italy is the world's earthly paradise, where sin is unknown, man is still a divine animal and all loves are pure; the right milieu for legal, illegal, natural, seminatural, unnatural or merely bizarre honeymoons, affairs, liaisons, and escapades.

To Italy come the mature ladies who still feel young inside and long to renew the thrills of their adolescence, and mature gentlemen who pine for the love of uncomfortably young girls. To Italy flock ladies or gentlemen in pairs of the same sex, middle-aged couples who settle down somewhere to the regular routine of bourgeois housekeeping: one shops, the other cooks, one washes, the other mends the socks or stockings, and they both shine the silverware. Or the lone men on the prowl who find it easier and safer to seduce penniless peasant boys, sailors or firemen in Italy than elsewhere.

Others are longing for things that have kept their natural flavour, those simple flavours which industrial civilization is now supplanting with conventional ones. They like the guileless wines, the local cheeses which are unknown a few miles away, the freshly-picked fruit warmed by the sun; the sea urchins, split in half with a rusty knife when still dripping salt water, and eaten with a few drops of lemon juice; the *pane casareccio*, or home-baked bread; the passion of the hairy peasant girls smelling of healthy sweat. These people above all relish what they believe are the simple and genuine emotions of the

Italians who are apparently unashamed of them and seldom try to hide them. There is a tense, dramatic quality, a shameless directness, about the Italians which is refreshing to foreigners accustomed to nordic self-control, to feigned or real frigidity. These people still seek, like Stendhal, 'that combination of love, sensuality, and sincerity' which apparently still characterizes the race. Here 'a man who plays a rôle is as rare . . . as a natural and simple man in Paris', and, one might add, anywhere else in the northern hemisphere. They also believe with Stendhal that 'music lives only in Italy', together with other sensual arts, and that 'in this beautiful country one must only make love; other pleasures of the soul are cramped here. Love here is delicious. Anywhere else it is only a bad copy.'

*

Italy is today again the teacher of many arts. Italians have maintained, or have newly invented, a variety of crafts and skills which are still rare and precious in the contemporary world. Foreigners learn the art of carving marble, training show horses to jump, racing Grand Prix cars, making pitiless films about sex-mad and disinherited characters in the slums, designing special bodies for elegant automobiles, designing shirts, clothes, shoes, and all sorts of contemporary gadgets, designing modern buildings in the *bravura* style of Pier Luigi Nervi, the great master of concrete structures. Young pianists from all over the world, severely selected, study free with Benedetti Michelangeli, the mysterious Italian maestro, in a castle which he keeps near Turin. Young opera singers, composers, directors, and conductors work hard in winter as apprentices at the Rome Opera and put on their graduation shows in the main theatre at Spoleto, at the end of the year, when Gian Carlo Menotti is not using it. Art students live and work in the ancient and glorious Academies which many foreign nations keep for the purpose. Some are supported by the West: the American Academy on the Janicular Hill, the French Villa Medici in Trinità dei Monti, the Belgian, West German, Spanish, and Danish Academies, here and there in the city. Others are still surprisingly kept by Marxist popular democracies and by the non-committed nations: the Hungarian, Polish, Rumanian and Egyptian Academies.

Some of these pupils eventually finish by doing things *alla Italiana* more conscientiously than the natives and beating them at their own game. It happens almost every year at the Rome horse show, when foreigners riding with the Italian jumping style beat the local champions, or at Monza, when the foreign drivers drive their Ferraris or Maseratis to victory ahead of their local rivals. For many more expatriate residents, Italians are pupils, as they have often been in the past. Television and musical comedy choreography is the monopoly of the young and well-paid Americans. Russian émigré choreographers and scene designers work in many opera houses and theatres. American film directors make vast historical potboilers in Technicolor for Italian producers. There are branch offices of American universities where business management and public administration are taught to the natives with missionary zeal. American Quakers roam the countryside teaching illiterates how to read and write. Soviet theoreticians and organizers occasionally give a hand to the local Communists. German technicians, engineers, and chemists, and American management consultants work in Italian factories. English and American advertising firms have offices in Milan and Rome. Swiss graphic arts experts, Hungarian and Spanish football coaches are widely employed. All these people, like Sir John Hawkwood of old, find life pleasant and invigorating, even if their Italian pupils sometimes seem obstinate in their ways and do not improve easily.

*

Perhaps few things illustrate the contradictory character of the motives driving some foreigners to Italy better than the contrast between snobs and non-snobs. The snobs come here, as they have come for several centuries, as to their own paradise. Italy is the happy hunting ground of the newly rich and the insecure name-dropper. These can easily re-create a life of long ago, a life of royal splendour which would be impossibly expensive and pretentiously ridiculous in their home towns. Furnished palaces with historical names can be leased in no time. Nobody wants them. Liveries can be bought or hired within a few hours, servants engaged by the day or the year to fill them, including an impressive *maggiordomo* and good cooks. In an emergency all this can be staged overnight by specialized firms. A number of important-sounding guests, with names going back to the Crusades or related to famous Popes, can be gathered with a little patience but no special difficulty. Such people, like characters in nineteenth-century novels, still have practically nothing to do, wear their clothes well, and have impeccable manners. They have little money, regal tastes, and like being expensively entertained. Sometimes invitations to some of the biggest affairs are broadcast all over Europe and the United States. Women journalists and gossip columnists from as far away as London, Chicago or Hollywood flock in to describe the dinner or the ball with glowing phrases. Such things usually leave the Italians cold. They are not even mentioned in the local press.

The non-snobs flock here to enjoy the company and the relaxed attitude of the inhabitants, completely indifferent as they are to status symbols. The tiring game of extracting social recognition from others and expensively impressing the world with one's own fortune, name or rank, is played by a relatively small minority of Italians, mostly people with foreign ties or blood, who ape foreign manners and have been educated abroad, or brought up in Italy, years ago, by Edwardian nannies from England. Madame de Staël discovered long ago that Italians as a rule were not impressed by titles and appearance. Being rich, noble by marriage, and famous, she could not hide a certain irritation. She complained: 'Distinctions in rank have little effect in Italy. . . . People are hardly susceptible to aristocratic prejudices, and as society considers itself the judge of nothing, it permits everything. . . . There is no *salon*, there are no little daily devices with which to shine.' Stendhal also pointed out that 'a marquise of the highest nobility may be the friend of a simple drawing teacher. . . . Vanity is but one of the passions, far from being the ruling one. . . . A man living on an income of fifteen hundred francs speaks to a man who has an income of six million as simply as he would to an equal. This would be thought incredible in England.'

J. P. Morgan the elder died in Rome, at the Grand Hotel, where he stayed at least once a year. He came principally to eat in small *trattorie*, where nobody knew who the fat American gentleman with the bulbous nose was, and to roam the streets at night, endlessly talking, as he could not do in New York or London, to one of his dearest friends, the impecunious Italian journalist Salvatore Cortesi, about the meaning of life, death, love and God. At the beginning of the century, the charm of places like Capri and Taormina, before they were improved and transformed into ordinary and expensive resorts, was the moral and social equality of all, which, at the time, could not be enjoyed anywhere else. Russian revolutionaries, millionaires from Germany and the United States, English lords, penniless painters, poets, or vagabonds, local loafers, peasants, sailors or fishermen, all dressed alike in the same cheap cotton clothes, often ate in the same *osterie*, drank the same wines, wasted the time in idle talk together and led the same kind of life.

Important people still find today the refreshing restful pleasures of obscurity and simplicity. The King of Sweden, together with his family, pursues his hobby, which is archaeology. Dressed in old clothes, without attracting attention, he digs for Etruscan tombs in search of little bronzes and pottery. The Queen of the Netherlands has built herself a simple cottage by the sea, at Porto Ercole. Bettina, the widowed friend of Aly Khan, bought herself a piece of the coast of Sardinia. While the famous enjoy the pleasure of being ordinary mortals for a change, obscure people find a different kind of satisfaction: they escape from the torture of being obscure in places where others enjoy the limelight. They also relish an added attraction. In little picturesque villages, still known only to few, but which may become celebrated ten or twenty years from now, in places where the great go about in shabby clothes and speak to everybody, it is usually easier for the simple foreigner to be taken for the great or the equivalent of the great and to strike up acquaintances which would be difficult or impossible anywhere else.

*

Many of the historical reasons for coming to Italy are entirely imaginary. The Holy See, to be sure, is only to be found in Rome, Vesuvius in Naples, the ruins of Pompeii at Pompeii, the art treasures of Florence in Florence, but some of the other very important attractions can also be found elsewhere. They are often more conveniently situated, sometimes the equal of, or better than, those in Italy. Take the climate, for instance, sung by poets through the centuries, at all times one of the principal pretexts for the voyage. 'Sunny Italy,' foreigners used to say. The definition was obviously created by the English, the Russians, and the Scandinavians, people whose native weather was irremediably bad, the worst in the civilized world. What these people meant was that in Italy, surprisingly enough for them, the sun shone in summer. The sun of course shines in summer in many other places, too. How many poor northerners fell victims to this misleading *lieu commun*, who, suffering from an affliction of the lungs, were sent to Rome, Florence, or Pisa, to spend the winter, where they declined and perished in the rain, sleet, cold and humid air? Among the victims of this prejudice we can also reckon hundreds of imaginary characters in nineteenth-century novels. Oswald, Lord Nelvil, the preposterous hero of Madame de Staël's *Corinne*, was one: he had to leave his native Edinburgh, because 'his health was perturbed by a deep sensation of pain, and the doctors, fearing his lungs were attacked, had ordered him the air of the Midi'. He did not improve.

In fact, the climate of Northern Italy is about the same as that of most continental European countries. Milan and Turin are colder in winter than Copenhagen, warmer in summer than Valetta or Algiers. Central and Southern Italy have about the same climate as other Mediterranean countries, milder on the coast than inland, not as good as in Hong Kong or in the Crimea. Winter is undoubtedly more comfortable in Egypt, Florida, the Sahara, the oases of Libya, Morocco, and Algeria. Rome notoriously has one of the most unpleasant weathers of all, *scirocco* for almost two hundred days a year, a sultry southern wind which fills the sky with low, grey, dampish clouds, makes mildew blossom almost everywhere, puts liverish stains of humidity on the walls, makes people feel weak, impotent, irascible, their heads filled with cotton wool. Norman Douglas, who named a book after it, called the wind 'the withering blast whose hot and clammy touch hastens death and putrefaction'. Venice is under a dreary rain most of the autumn, winter, and the beginning of spring. There is no sadder atmosphere in the world, especially when the wind turns south-east and the city smells vaguely of rotten cabbages and stagnant waters. Oscar Wilde, who was there on such a day, and rode in a black gondola, said dejectedly that he had felt as if he had 'travelled through sewers in a coffin'. The city inspired mostly thoughts of death to Thomas Mann.

Or take another of the traditional reasons for the trip, good food. As a rule, food is good in Italy. It is always beyond reproach in a few famous restaurants and *trattorie*; very rarely it is mediocre, almost never bad. It has character. It is seldom ambiguous or pretentious. Things frankly smell, look, and taste as they should, every component sharply differentiated and true to its nature. No velvety sauce dims their appearance or their flavour. Everything is eaten fresh and in its proper season, when it is at its absolute best. No fruit or vegetable comes from a hothouse, with the damp paper taste of artificial products. Nothing is picked before its time and allowed to ripen in storage. Nothing is frozen, nothing is chemically preserved. The colours are gay: the yellow of the *risotto alla milanese*, the red of tomato salad or spaghetti with tomato sauce, the green of broccoli, the white of Tuscan beans, the bishop purple of boiled octopus, the gold of *fettuccine al doppio burro* are all clean hues, as pure as the colours of flags or children's crayons. Pizzas are painters' palettes ready to portray a summer sunset. The wines are resplendent like jewels when the sun shines through the glasses: no subtle nuance betrays the vigour of their tints or their bouquets.

A good meal is good in Italy, better in fact than anything one gets in more efficient countries in the north, better than in Spain, infinitely better than in Greece. But food and wines, it must be admitted, are not quite as good as in France. Italian cuisine merely presents Nature at its best. French cuisine is a challenge to Nature, it subverts Nature, it creates a new Nature of its own. It is an art. What does it matter that Italian wines are exactly what the juice of particular grapes becomes after fermentation, the products of diligence, when the French ones are often creations of genius, wise mélanges of various crus, some vulgar and some extremely rare, manipulated by experts? They undoubtedly manage such things better in France.

Or take the ruins. Some of Italy's ruins are admittedly unique. There are perhaps more Greek temples still standing on their original

pillars and more Greek remnants of all kinds in Southern Italy, the
Magna Graecia of old, than in all of Little Greece. But there are older
and sometimes more famous and awe-inspiring monuments strewn
all over the world, from the jungle of Yucatan to Ankhor Vat, from
the desert of Mesopotamia to Iran, from Egypt to India. Great
palaces, museums, celebrated masterpieces can be viewed and admired in many places, all over the world, as good as and sometimes
better than those in Italy, from Spain's Escorial and El Prado to
Leningrad's Winter Palace and Hermitage. Or take art. Contemporary
art is livelier and more arresting in Paris and New York. There an
ambitious young artist can not only study but make himself known
and a collector has a wide range to choose from. La Scala is undoubtedly the greatest opera house in the world. But good opera can
be seen and heard in Vienna, London, and New York, and good sym-
phonic music can be found in Vienna, Munich, Berlin, Düsseldorf,
Cologne, Frankfurt, Paris, London, New York, Boston, and a score
of other American cities, not to speak of the Soviet Union. Ballet is
bad in Italy. It is infinitely better in Moscow, Leningrad, New York,
London and even Copenhagen.

Is it spectacular landscapes, majestic mountains, iridescent bays,
waterfalls, coquettish lakes, pretty islands that travellers think they
cannot do without? Of course, natural beauty and famous views are
abundant in Italy. Such things, however, are not unknown elsewhere.
Nature is usually more inspiring even in the United States, wherever
man has not meddled with it. Italy has no century-old woods, which
turn all sorts of hues in the autumn, from gold to crimson, as they do
in upper New York State or in New England; Italy has no canyons
and no deserts. Rio de Janeiro, Istanbul and Hong Kong are as
beautiful as the bay of Naples. The Alps look just as impressive from
the opposite slopes in France, Switzerland and Austria. Other mountains are as tall, steep, craggy; some are more remote, wild and unattainable. Lakes surrounded by wooded slopes can be counted by
the hundred in other parts of Europe, many as pretty as the Italian
ones. Waterfalls are romantic, to be sure, but puny and slender in
comparison with the best in Africa and America. Italian rivers
are little brooks when measured against the four or five mighty
rivers of the rest of the world. Islands? The Greek islands are

more numerous, wilder, more remote and warmer all the year around.

Some confess that it is *la dolce vita* which attracts them. Only the name is new. The sweet life has always attracted travellers, to Venice in the months of the famous Carnival and elsewhere at different times of the year, down the centuries. But is *la dolce vita* really more *dolce* in Italy than elsewhere? Is it more *dolce* than in Paris, for instance, Las Vegas, New York, Munich, or Hollywood? Comparisons are impossible. Unfortunately gay life is something that cannot always be found by travelling to definite spots in the world. It is often a quality a man carries with him, a capacity to provoke light-hearted adventure wherever he goes. Many visitors are disappointed in Rome, when they discover that life can be as prim and proper there as it was back home, or as it is for most Romans.

Is Italy, then, as some claim, the ideal place to enjoy the inefficient and lax enforcement of laws, a refuge from the tyranny of income tax and other fiscal impositions? The world is filled with pleasant little republics or principalities where the well-to-do foreign resident is respected and considered beyond the pale of the law, and where a good friend in the right place or a gift in time to an official will save a lot of trouble. As for the pure avoidance of taxes, there are better places than Italy. The rich Italians themselves prefer Switzerland to their own country. Monte Carlo, Luxemburg and Liechtenstein are celebrated hiding places for conspicuous fortunes. Or do these foreigners want the flattering comfort of a warm-hearted, hospitable, obliging, willing, picturesque and skilful populace, ready to supply craftsmen, artisans and sycophants with little trouble? Such endearing people exist in many countries, everywhere, in fact, where an ancient and refined civilization has decayed without yet giving birth to a local version of modern industrialized society.

Obviously such explanations are only good as far as they go. People do not always, of course, expect to find in Italy the absolute best. Sheer superiority does not interest them as much as the special quality which imbues everything, animate or inanimate, in Italy and nowhere else. It is vulgarly known, in tourist bureau advertising, as 'the charm of Italy': it notoriously adds value and interest to obvious attractions, it makes them all better here than elsewhere, just as salt makes ordinary tastes sharper and clearer. Even sorrows become precious. Heinrich Heine noted: 'Simply letting yourself live is beautiful in Italy. In these marble *palazzi* sighs have a more romantic echo than in our modest brick houses; in the shade of these laurel bushes it is more pleasant to weep than under our gloomy fir trees; it is sweeter to day-dream following the shapes of Italian clouds than under the ash-grey dome of a German sky, a work-day sky in which even clouds take on the solemn and sulky expression of little burghers and yawn with boredom. . . . What is, after all, pleasure if not an extraordinarily sweet pain?' What is it? 'The charm of Italy,' concluded Stendhal, 'is akin to that of being in love.' He should have known what he was talking about as he had dedicated most of his life to a painstaking study of both subjects. The two, love and the charm of Italy, are similar and complementary. One intensifies the other. Love in Italy is notoriously more satisfactory. Italy seen through lovers' eyes is more enchanting.

Is Italy love? Or is Italy, as some say, art? Like the Italian scene, art, too, can be intoxicating, can transform people, can transport them far from themselves, can be delightfully aphrodisiac. 'Art,' says Walter Pater, with words which could be applied equally to Italy and to love, 'gives nothing but the highest quality to your moments as they pass.' But can an ancient country, a peninsula stretching from the Alps to the Mediterranean, filled with fifty million busy people and their historical problems, be seriously compared to a delicate sentiment, to a primeval urge, or to the highest flowering of the human spirit? Can geography be mixed up with psychology or with aesthetics?

*

Henry James suspected that the pleasure of Italy was inseparably tied to the human element, the people who had created the landscape almost with their own hands in the course of so many centuries. It was for him, 'the incomparable wrought fusion, fusion of human history and moral passion with the elements of earth and air, of colour, composition, and form; that constitute her appeal and give it supreme heroic grace'. He stopped one day in the dull little town of Velletri, south of Rome, for a few aimless hours. It was a dreary place. There was nothing to see. And yet he was fascinated. 'There was a narrow raised terrace, with steps, in front of the best of two or three local cafés,' he wrote, 'and in the soft enclosed, the warm waning light of June, various benign contemplative worthies sat at disburdened tables and, while they smoked long black weeds, enjoyed us under those probable workings of subtlety with which we invest so many quite unimaginably blank (I dare say) Italian simplicities. The charm was, as always in Italy, in the tone and the air and the happy hazard of things, which made any positive pretensions or claimed importance a comparative trifling question. . . . We lay at our ease in the bosom of the past, we practised intimacy, an intimacy so much greater than the mere accidental and ostensible: the difficulty for the right and grateful expression of which makes the old, the familiar tax on the luxury of loving Italy.'

Others felt this undeniable link between the people and the attraction of the place, between the people's moods, habits, looks, approach to life and the pleasure of Italy. William Dean Howells, the *Italianizant* who had chosen, as a prize for having written the campaign biography of Lincoln, to be appointed consul in Venice, noted: 'It was their lovely ways, far more than their monuments of history and art, that made return to the Florentines delightful. I would rather have had a perpetuity of the *cameriere's* smile when he came up with our coffee in the morning than Donatello's San Giorgio, if either were purchasable; and the face of the old chambermaid, full of motherly affection, was better than the façade of Santa Maria Novella.' He loved 'the delightfully natural human beings one could always be sure of in this land of human nature unabashed'. 'It is their manners as a whole,' Stendhal noted, 'their natural ways, bonhomie, the great art of being happy which is here practised with this added charm, that the good people do not know that it is an art, the most difficult of all.'

It is not quite true, of course. The Italians know that everything in their country is governed by their experience, the product of their industry, imbued with their spirit. They know that there is no need, really, to distinguish or to choose between the smile on the face of a *cameriere* and Donatello's San Giorgio, between the 'composition and classicism' and landscaped hill about Florence. They are all works of art, the 'great art of being happy' and of making other people happy, an art which embraces and inspires all others in Italy, the only art worth learning, but which can never be really mastered, the art of inhabiting the earth.

*

This, finally, is the ultimate motive, the one that gives strength, urgency and validity to all other motives, the answer to Milton's question, 'Why Italy?' People still come as they came for centuries because they are attracted by a certain quality in Italian life. Whether they know what it is or not, it somehow quickens their blood. It still gives them a Saturnian feeling of liberation. Italians around them seem to understand things which still perplex other people, to have explored short cuts, a few of which are a trifle shabby and questionable, but useful to avoid life's roughest spots. They seem to be trying to work out a sure *système* to break the bank of history. The *système* is not quite perfect. It seems to work well only when the stakes are low but it warms people's hearts and gives them the illusion of cheating fate. The Italians seem happy. They show a porpoiselike eagerness and zest in everything they do which are contagious. One of Goethe's travelling companions tried to teach him the secret: 'Why think?' he told the young poet. 'Man must never think. Thinking makes you grow older. Man must have many things, a great confusion, in his head.' One must allow contradictory tendencies to proliferate, one must cultivate opposite ideals, one must follow reason alone, one must not fret over the imperfections of life on earth. One must carry on. The pleasure of Italy comes from living in a world made by man, for man, on man's measurements.

CHAPTER FOUR

THE IMPORTANCE OF SPECTACLE

THE extraordinary animation is what strikes one at first, the vigorous ant-hill life of the natives. Streets, squares, market-places teem with people, noisy, elated, gay, energetic, busy people. There are uniformed *carabinieri* watching everything and everybody through half-closed eyelids, fat priests strolling slowly, peasants dressed in rough velvet clothes, smart young soldiers on leave, housewives carrying heavy shopping bags, desperate youths with long hair and blue jeans, swarms of pretty girls and children playing between everybody's legs. Ladies lower little baskets on a string from a fourth-storey window, in the manner of anchorites from the top of Egyptian pillars, for the postman to put the mail in, or the baker his bread. Begging monks pleadingly push little wooden boxes under everybody's nose. A hunchback sells lottery tickets, 'last numbers left, sure to win'.

Ladies come out of shops to check the colour of some material in the full light of the sun. Vendors extol the advantages of their wares in loud voices (watermelons are always 'good to eat, drink, and wash one's face with'). Craftsmen carry on their work in the open air, in front of their shops, and sing or chat with passing friends: mechanics dive under disembowelled cars, cobblers hammer shoe leather, carpenters polish table-tops with the sweeping gestures of a conductor directing an *adagio cantabile*. A waiter changes table-cloths and snaps each in turn in the sunshine with a twist of his wrists. Sometimes a religious procession goes by: a musical band and *carabinieri* in full uniform, with red and blue feathers over their cocked hats, precede chanting priests in lace surplices, girls in white veils, little boys with angels' wings attached to their shoulders, and the chief priest under the ancient velvet canopy, uncertainly held aloft over his head by devout gentlemen. Or a funeral may pass: prancing black horses, their harness decorated with black plumes and silver ornaments, a glass-enclosed hearse surmounted by a flight of golden wooden angels, more black feathers and sundry symbols of eternal life, followed by weeping relatives and friends.

Carts, shop-windows and stalls are loaded with vegetables, flowers, fruits, toys, clothes, shoes and fishes in the colourful confusion and disarray of gifts pouring out of a cornucopia. There are white cauliflowers in the north, green cauliflowers in Rome, and purple in Catania; short and green *zucchini* everywhere or white and six-foot-long *zucchini* in Naples, artichokes with thorns on the Riviera and without thorns in the south. There are pyramids of oranges, some sliced to show the bloody flesh preferred by Italians. There are fishes: coral pink mullets, cuttlefish made of glistening alabaster, long swordfish or tunafish in Sicily, sleek sturgeons near the mouth of the Po river, soles along the Adriatic, entangled octopus still writhing in agony. The *salumerie* windows are worthy of the brush of a *natura morta* painter from Bergamo, a city distinguished for its food and a school of painting completely dedicated to it: triumphal arches of *prosciutti*, *mortadelle* hanging from the ceiling like Venetian lanterns, festoons of *zamponi*, *caciocavalli*, and *provoloni*; *mozzarelle* swimming in milk, pillars of Parmesan cheese wheels painted funeral black, large jars of olives, mushrooms in oil, pickled cucumbers, barrels of anchovies in brine.

Everything is displayed everywhere, in dramatic and artistic disorder. Flowered cotton material is unrolled from its board and thrown at the observer as if in anger. Spaghetti in sheaves are tied at the waist with white, red, and green patriotic ribbons. *Fiaschi* of wine or olive oil are decorated with medals like war heroes. In the butchers' windows, pale calves' heads, with eyes closed and lips curled in secret merriment, hold a lemon or a carnation between their teeth in death-defying insouciance. Even a hernia truss, shown in the window of an orthopaedist's shop, bedecked with little flags and colourful ribbons, becomes a gay and desirable object.

The noise is usually deafening. People chat, whistle, swear, sing, curse, cry, howl, weep, call to each other and shout, carrying on

elaborate discussions or delicate negotiations. Mothers murmur endearing baby words to their little children and ask bystanders to be
witnesses to their darlings' charm and pigheadedness. Other mothers
call their sons from top-storey windows with voices carrying to the
next province. Bells clang with deep bronze notes from the top of the
belfry above, drowning every other sound. Somebody is always
practising the cornet or the trombone. At times the same popular
song or famous operatic aria comes apparently from everywhere,
from radios in every shop, from the open windows of apartments,
from under the tables in the café, from the pockets of clients, from
the abdomens of passing housewives. *Vespas*, cars, motorcycles,
trucks go by with roaring engines.

The air is in fact filled with so much noise that one must usually
talk in a very loud voice to be understood, thereby increasing the
total uproar. Lovers sometimes have to whisper 'I love you' to each
other in the tones of newsboys selling the afternoon papers. Italians
on their death beds, in rooms facing especially noisy squares or
streets, are known to have renounced leaving their last wishes and
advice to weeping relatives, being too weak to make themselves
heard. It is, however, a gay and happy noise, magnified by the stone
walls, the absence of greenery, the narrowness of the streets. It goes
on from dawn to the small hours of the night, when the last strollers
stop under your bedroom window to debate a fine point of politics or
the personality of a common friend, both speaking at the same time
at the top of their voices.

The show can be so engrossing that many people spend most of
their lives just looking at it. There are usually café tables strategically
placed in such a way that nothing of importance will escape the
leisurely drinker of *espresso* or *aperitivo*. Reserved old ladies peer
unseen at the spectacle through the wooden slats of green-painted
blinds. Nothing escapes their sharp eyes; they draw deductions from
every detail: a woman's purchases, a girl's new dress, a new smile
on the face of a young man, a strange car from out of town, a boy's
whistle to a third-storey window. There are free benches or little
walls in the sun for the elderly. There are balconies along the façades
of all houses, as convenient as boxes at the theatre. You can place an
armchair there, or stand leaning on your elbows, and see the days,

the years or your whole life go by, as you watch a cavalcade with thousands of characters and hundreds of subplots.

What makes all such scenes more intensely fascinating is perhaps the transparency of Italian faces. Conversations can be followed at a distance by merely watching the changing expressions of those taking part in them. You can read joy, sorrow, hope, anger, relief, boredom, despair, love, and disappointment as easily as large-printed words on a wall poster. Undisguised emotions, some sincere and some feigned, follow each other on an Italian's face as swiftly as the shadows of clouds over a meadow on a windy day in spring. A waiter taking an order for lunch, for instance, will show the following series of moods in quick succession: (1) bored obsequiousness and professional courtesy, as he hands a menu to the new client; (2) resignation, as he whips out his pencil and keeps it poised on his pad waiting for the usual, dull, unimaginative order; (3) slight curiosity, if the client looks thoughtful, coughs and asks a few pertinent questions; (4) incredulous attention, if the client shows himself really difficult to please, somewhat circumspect in weighing possible choices; this may be followed by (5) a look of alertness, eagerness and pleasure if the client proves himself a knowing expert, or by (6) a return to the bored obsequiousness of the beginning if the order turns out to be, after all, the ordinary thing.

Reading facial expressions is an important art in Italy, to be learned in childhood, perhaps more important for survival than the art of reading print. Spoken words may be sometimes at variance with the grimaces that accompany them. The words should then be overlooked. Only the face counts. Italians are often disconcerted, unhappy and lonely in the north of Europe, and seldom know what is going on, surrounded as they are by blank faces on which little can be read and that little seldom exciting. They wrongly conclude that, as the people show no feelings, they have no feelings worth showing. The proverbial impassivity of the English is believed to be a definite proof of coldness and insensibility. The Italians' excessive facility to express emotions is, strangely enough, a drawback for actors. Perhaps they are too richly endowed by Nature: they have more natural gifts and talent than necessary. Their florid acting turns too readily into hamming when not under rigid control. The best spend years to unlearn what many of their foreign colleagues have to learn. Orson Welles once acutely observed that Italy is full of actors, fifty million of them, in fact, and they are almost all good; there are only a few bad ones, and they are on the stage and in the films.

*

Then there are the gestures. Italian gestures are justly famous. Indeed Italians use them more abundantly, efficiently, and imaginatively than other people. They employ them to emphasize or clarify whatever is said, to suggest words and meanings it is not prudent to express with words, sometimes simply to convey a message at great distance, where the voice could not carry. In the hurried world of today gestures are also employed more and more as time-saving devices. Motorists no longer slow down and waste precious seconds to shout intelligible and elaborate insults to each other or to pedestrians, as they used to do but a few years ago. Now they merely extend one hand in the general direction of the person to whom they want to address the message, a hand with all fingers folded except the forefinger and the little finger. It conveys the suggestion that the other man does, should or will shortly wear horns, in other words be cuckolded by his wife, fiancée or mistress. A few gestures are as arbitrary and conventional as the deaf and dumb alphabet or the sign language of American Indians. Most of them, however, are based on natural and instinctive movements, common to the majority of men, certainly common to all Western men, elaborated, intensified, stylized, sharpened, made into art. Like all great traditional arts, this one too can generally be understood by the inexperienced at first sight.

The mimicry is not, as many think, always exaggerated and dramatic, emphatic contortions of arms and body, rolling of eyes, convulsive agitation of hands and fingers. Probably the acting of opera singers, directly derived from the Italians' natural mimicry, spread this erroneous impression. The best gestures are often so economical as to be almost imperceptible. Sicilians, for instance, are known to convey a vast range of grave and sometimes mortal messages practically without stirring a muscle of their faces or moving their hands. For them, a slowly raised chin means 'I don't know' or, more often, 'Perhaps I know but I will not tell you.' It is the answer policemen always get when questioning possible witnesses of a Mafia killing which took place in front of hundreds of people in a busy market square. It is also the answer a harmless stranger gets from diffident Sicilian peasants when he asks the way to the nearest village.

The extended fingers of one hand moving slowly back and forth under the raised chin means: 'I couldn't care less. It's no business of mine. Count me out.' This is the gesture made in 1860 by the grandfather of Signor O.O. of Messina as an answer to Garibaldi. The general, who had conquered Sicily with his volunteers and was moving on to the mainland, had seen him, a robust youth at the time, dozing on a little stone wall, in the shadow of a carob tree, along a country lane. He reined in his horse and asked him: 'Young man, will you not join us in our fight to free our brothers in Southern Italy from the bloody tyranny of the Bourbon kings? How can you sleep when your country needs you? Awake and to arms!' The young man silently made the gesture. Garibaldi spurred his horse on.

The lifting of one single eyebrow means, 'I'm ready to take what decisions are necessary.' The slow closing of both eyes in an otherwise immobile and expressionless face signifies resignation in front of the inevitable, acceptance of a difficult and unpleasant duty, as, for instance: 'We warned him again and again. The man is stubborn. He does not want to listen to reason. We will do our duty.'

One of the most economical and eloquent of Sicilian gestures I saw one day in the lobby of the Hotel des Palmes, in Palermo. A man entered from the street. He obviously wanted everybody to know immediately, beyond doubt, that he was a gentleman, *un gran signore*, a man of means and authority, accustomed to being attended on. He looked around as if searching for a friend among the people loitering in the room, took off his overcoat, held it at arm's length for a fraction of a second, and, without bothering to see whether a servant was at his side, dropped it. A real *signore* always has somebody ready to receive his coat when he takes it off. He never needs to check. The coat, of course, did not drop to the floor. A bell-boy was there to catch it.

Strangely enough, no serious study has ever been made of the subject. One man alone, that I know of, a priest and antiquarian from

Naples, Canon Andrea de Jorio, attempted to catalogue the gestures of his countrymen. He began by trying to read a meaning in the scenes painted on Greek vases and Roman frescoes or depicted in mosaics and bas reliefs collected in the Bourbon Museum in Naples. He asked himself what these gods and mortals would be saying if they were modern Neapolitans and what a contemporary deaf Neapolitan would make of their mimicry. To begin with, he identified and collected hundreds of such signs from life around him, described them, had them drawn and engraved by an artist, then catalogued and double-indexed them. After many years, in 1832, he published the result of his life-work in one thick volume, dedicated to Frederick William of Hohenzollern, hereditary Prince of Prussia. The slightly misleading title is *La mimica degli antichi investigata nel gestire napoletano* (The Mimicry of Ancient People Interpreted Through the Gestures of Neapolitans).

The interpretation of the ancient people's mimicry fills only a short section. The bulk is dedicated to a practically complete and unique list of all the signs necessary to express anything, or almost anything, in Naples and elsewhere, without opening one's mouth. It is a very rare volume. It is not included in bibliographies, encyclopaedias, lists of rare books for sale, or catalogues of Italian libraries. It is unknown to specialists and scholars. The only copy I know of is in my hands. I stole it from the library of an old and unsuspecting English gentleman.

A glance at the contents proves how natural, easily understood, universal, and timeless such gestures really are. As they have changed little since 1832, it is probable, as the Canon tried to demonstrate, that they may still be more or less what they were in ancient times. Take the chapter headed 'Rage, anger'. It lists ten principal ways of silently expressing such emotions. They are, to quote only the headings and not the elaborate descriptions: (1) 'biting one's lips'; (2) 'biting one's hands and single fingers'; (3) 'tearing one's hair'; (4) 'scratching one's face'; (5) 'firmly enclosing one fist in the other hand and rubbing it with such force that the joints crack'; (6) 'gnashing one's teeth with wide open lips'; (7) 'moving one's lips with a shuddering, nervous rhythm'; (8) 'stamping the ground with violence'; (9) 'beating palm against palm, as if to applaud, once or twice only, with force'. The only gesture not easily understood is number 10, 'pretending to bite one's elbows'. It is the pantomime of an Italian idiomatic saying. It means, in words, 'I will do anything to avenge myself, even the impossible, of which biting my elbows is a hyperbolic example.'

The chapter headed 'No, denial, negation' lists thirteen ways of expressing the same concept, ranged in a scale of growing intensity. The first and simpler ones are: 'raising one's eyebrows as far as they will go and in one quick motion'; 'turning one's face away from the object that is being refused'; 'moving one's head to left and right'; 'lifting one's lower lip over the upper, or lowering one corner of the lower lip'. The erudite Canon only listed nine ways of demonstrating 'love', all chaste. His eyes were probably averted from the more provocative examples, to be seen in abundance all around him, in the Neapolitan streets, in his day as they are now.

Often enough, a simple gesture, accompanied by suitable facial expressions, takes the place not of a few words but of a whole and eloquent speech. This, for instance: imagine two gentlemen sitting at a café table. The first is explaining at great length some intricate question which interests him, perhaps how the world will shortly be changed for the better by some new and impending development. He may be saying: 'This continent of ours, Europe, old, decrepit Europe, all divided into different nations, each nation subdivided into provinces, each nation and each province living its own petty life, speaking its incomprehensible dialect, nurturing its ideas, prejudices, defects, hatreds. . . . Each of us gloating over the memories of the defeats inflicted by us on our neighbours and completely oblivious of the defeats our neighbours inflicted on us. . . . How easy life would become if we were to fuse into one whole, Europa, the Christendom of old, the dream of Charlemagne, of Metternich, of many great men, and, why not? the dream of Hitler too. . . .' The second gentleman is listening patiently, looking intently at the first's face. At a certain moment, as if overwhelmed by the abundance of his friend's arguments or the facility of his optimism, he slowly lifts one hand, perpendicularly, in a straight line, from the table, as far as it will go, higher than his head. Meanwhile he utters only one sound, a prolonged 'eeeeeeh', like a sigh. His eyes never leave the other

man's face. His expression is placid, slightly tired, vaguely incredulous. The mimicry means: 'How quickly you rush to conclusions, my friend, how complicated your reasoning, how unreasonable
your hopes, when we all know the world has always been the same
and all bright solutions to our problems have in turn produced more
and different problems, more serious and unbearable problems than
the ones we were accustomed to.'

*

The extraordinary animation, the vivid colours, the disorderly abundance of all God's things, the military uniforms and clerical robes,
the expressive faces, the revealing gesticulation, the noise: these are
among everybody's first superficial impressions in Italy, anywhere in
Italy, in the north as well as the south, in big cities as well as in
sleepy villages, in modern centres as well as in decrepit and miserable
hamlets forgotten by history. There are, of course, deep regional
differences, of which the traveller becomes aware little by little. A
cattle fair at Lugo in Romagna, not far from Bologna, is obviously
not the same as a cattle fair in Paestum. Lugo is a medieval town near
the mouth of the Po river, with a brick-red castle and old baroque
churches, at the heart of bountifully fertile lands criss-crossed by
canals and ditches. The farmers there are big and fat, with red,
shining faces, brown hair and light-coloured eyes. The cattle are
well-fed, happy, and heavy. Paestum, at the mouth of the Sele river,
south of Salerno, is the centre of a hitherto sterile and arid plain,
once cursed with malaria, which has been only partly reclaimed and
irrigated since the end of the war. The peasants are swarthy, lean,
with burning black eyes and shining white teeth. The cattle are small
and bony. Still, the cheerful and good-natured fervour, the feverish
activity are the same in both places.

Or take Rome. Via Veneto is one of the great streets of Europe, one
of the principal thoroughfares of a great capital. In reality, it is the
enlargement of the *corso* of any Italian small town. On both sides are
café tables crowded with customers who watch the strollers going
back and forth, at apéritif time or after the theatre. Among the
strollers are herds of tourists, Italian and foreign, and, against this
anonymous background, the habitual native characters. One can

learn to recognize a few by sight, after a while, and follow their lives through months and years. There are the lean, the ambitious and handsome young men, who arrive one day from the suburbs or the provinces with one suit on their back and a few lire. They manage to make a few drinking friends, meet one powerful person, meet his mistress, gain his confidence, gain her favours, meet a few more powerful persons through them, and slowly rise, like gas bubbles of putrefaction in a muddy marsh. You can check their rising practically day by day. First they buy another suit, then a second-hand car, a few better suits, the first expensive car. In the end, they sport the smartest clothes on the Via, the most beautiful and bejewelled women, a glib and condescending manner, and the fastest and most glittering cars. How long does it take? Sometimes just the time to introduce a millionaire to an independent film producer and a pretty actress, or a high government official to a contractor of public works.

There are the defeated and shabby old men (how smartly and insolently they wore their uniforms, boots, and decorations when they were young, under Mussolini, how quickly they disappeared for a time after the war), who now try to hide their decay, loneliness and flabby bellies. There are flocks of unknown starlets (some arrive daily fresh from the country), who walk back and forth hoping to be noticed by one of the new great directors. After a while, they merely hope to be noticed by any old director, maybe the kind that makes historical potboilers in colour for the South American and Middle Eastern markets, who will offer them two or three days' shooting, with one or two close-ups, and a few spoken lines. In the end, most of them only hope to be noticed by just a man, a solitary man with the price of a good dinner on him and maybe a little *cadeau* in the morning. Some end by jumping from their boarding-house windows. You recognize their faces in the newspapers the next day and learn their names for the first time. A few become world-famous: they stop coming to Via Veneto, except two or three times a year, and then only surrounded by friends, photographers and women noticeably not half as beautiful as they. The old actresses, often drunk (how lovely and frail they were only yesterday), come more often, accompanied by insolent young lovers. There are hundreds of female and male prostitutes; photographers for the better scandal and blackmail magazines waiting for a world-wide celebrity to show up drunk, to quarrel with a friend and be arrested. They are often satisfied. There are black market pedlars of contraband cigarettes or dope, actors' agents, pimps, or simple Roman bourgeois taking the air. One can follow many parallel lives, in Via Veneto, an episode at a time, year after year, with no effort, by merely sitting at a café table, as one does in the main street or in a *piazza* everywhere in Italy.

Even where Italy is superficially less like Italy and more like any other nordic European country, an acute observer cannot fail to discover some of the national characteristics under the alien surface. Milan, for instance, the steel and glass capital of industry, commerce, and finance, here and there looks like Zürich, Düsseldorf, or Madison Avenue. The crowds look well-fed, well-dressed, purposeful, efficient and busy. People rush about with a frown on their faces as if they had but a few minutes to find a doctor and save a human life. They sometimes gulp food at snack bars without sitting down. The business men you interview are often glacially uncommunicative, laconic and reserved. They do not move their pale hands and roll their eyes when they speak. They manage world-wide enterprises, compete with the Japanese and the Germans, launch bright new projects, build dams and bridges in Africa and Asia, talk about millions of dolars. The buildings where they work are higher than anything in Europe, more daring and modern than those in New York.

Is this Italy? you ask yourself. Then you walk about the city and explore the older quarters, the forgotten squares where the housewives do their shopping. Or you discover the Galleria. It is the crossing of two streets at right angles, glass-covered like a Victorian hothouse, in the centre of the city. Café tables line both sides, filled with leisurely customers observing the people going by, as in Piazza San Marco, in Via Veneto, in Via Caracciolo in Naples, or in hundreds of other streets. Loiterers discuss grave matters and wave their hands to emphasize some important point. Some are opera singers without a job, waiting for an engagement to drop from the sky, to sing *Rigoletto* or *Trovatore* in the provinces, abroad, in South America, anywhere. Other strollers are visibly from the country, red-faced, fat, solid. They are farmers and brokers who have gathered there on certain days of the week to trade grain, ever since the Galleria was built almost a hundred years ago. They buy and sell actively and shrewdly, shaking hands to close each deal, and marking it down in their little notebooks. You can tell who wins or loses by watching their faces. The noise and the gestures fill the empty space. Or you may wander down Via Monte Napoleone, a short street of elegant and expensive shops, at apéritif time. Handsome and well-dressed young men stroll there with feline steps, to look disdainfully at women; handsome and well-dressed women stroll languorously to look at and be looked at by men. Brand-new *gran turismo* cars, each one a unique model, the most costly in the world, go by slowly or are parked along the kerb. Here again you can follow what goes on by watching faces. You can recognize the newly-born flirtation or the tired old liaison; the hopeful girl pursuing the bored man; the eager youth in attendance on the mature and wise beauty.

When you observe things more closely, in Milan, even the things which want to appear foreign, extremely efficient and modern, the powerful businessmen, the aerial skyscrapers reflecting the passing clouds in their hundreds of windows, the elevated autostrade running along on concrete crutches, the complex industrial plants apparently invented by mad engineers or science-fiction writers, you begin to notice that many things are a little too much and too emphatically what they are supposed to be. In fact Milan, in its newer quarters, is a little more like Zürich, Düsseldorf, and Madison Avenue than Zürich, Düsseldorf, or Madison Avenue themselves. You are in Italy after all.

*

The fact that everybody, or almost everybody, seems to be doing his job with whole-hearted dedication and enthusiasm is what impresses travellers next. This does not mean that Italians do everything with efficiency, speed and thoroughness. They do not. They merely do it with visible pleasure, as if work were not man's punishment. Often in other countries, one is waited on by people who obviously believe they were destined for better things but were forced by cruel fate to accept a degrading occupation, so degrading in fact as to bring them in contact with repulsive people like you. This never happens in Italy. Nobody is rude to strangers. Nobody looks bored, surly or mutinous. This discovery gives you a pleasant feeling. It also puzzles you, after a while. Is it really true, you ask yourself, that Italians escape from the common lot? Can it be that they are happy, each doing in life exactly what he wants to do, what his hopes conceived for him, what Providence put him on earth to achieve?

The evident delight and eagerness with which things are done are contagious. Cheerful faces surround you as soon as you cross the border. Cheerful customs inspectors wave away technicalities connected with the *carnet de douane* of your car or the cigars in your suitcase. Cheerful porters carry your bags. In the hotel a cheerful concierge or director finds you a room in a full house as if you were his own dear cousin, cheerful waiters suggest in a low voice not to take the fish today, as if they were really interested in your health. You begin to think that everybody, no matter how humble, degrading, or insignificant his position, has, after all, a dignity all his own, the dignity of the man who does not envy anybody and finds himself at ease with his conscience.

Take the singers of Neapolitan songs in the open-air restaurants. Many have no voice, a rough musical ear, a bad memory for words; they barely make a living with what money the customers toss them; they sometimes feed themselves with warmed-up left-overs from the kitchen. But they sing with incredible gusto. They improvise variations, infuse sweet sentiment in the languorous passages, become effervescent and sprightly in the gay ones, spin out long notes through their round little mouths, as if they were real tenors. They choose the proper song for each table: little dance tunes for the young, lonesome love laments for the solitary couples and old numbers for the aged and nostalgic, exactly as if they were highly-paid entertainers under steady contract. Or take the majestic and motherly ladies who oversee public lavatories in parks or restaurants. They graciously open doors, hand you soap and towels as if they were flowers, exchange a few courtly words, and finally accept a modest tip with a queenly nod and a smile. What better way to spend one's life, they seem to think, than amidst the shining porcelain, the roar of many waters, the perfume of such delicate soaps, in contact with such distinguished people?

In previous centuries, foreign sculptors in Italy were always carried away by the skill, humility and eagerness of their marble-cutters, the men who translated their rough clay models into lasting stone and often improved them. In the same way, in Rome, today, foreign film directors, sober and efficient men in their homelands, often incapable of any sustained flights of imagination, are known to become intoxicated and to acquire a weird feeling of omnipotence when working with their local collaborators, a court of compliant assistant directors, cameramen, stage designers, architects, builders of sets, mechanics, carpenters, and electricians. The meekest soon discovers himself almost turning into a Tiberius, Nero or Caligula, a divine autocrat giving impossible and capricious orders to devoted slaves. He finds that anything, anything at all, which would take months of haggling elsewhere, can be done at once, in a matter of hours. There are apparently no obstacles to the free expression of his ideas, no petty chicanery from the front office, no financial difficulties, no trade union rules to hold up his inspiration. Finally he can prove himself the great artist Providence intended him to be.

The script can be revised, improved, enlarged at any time, whenever a good idea strikes him, even on the spur of the moment, on the set, while shooting. New sets can be ordered for scenes invented during a sleepless night, disrupting whole schedules. Episodes can be whipped up to exploit some bit of natural scenery the director has seen in the country or to employ the undiscovered talents of a little blonde girl he has met at a party. There is an enthusiastic feeling of improvisation which makes the work exciting. Sometimes a good suggestion comes from the make-up man or an electrician perched with his lights under the roof, and is immediately adopted. 'This is the stuff the *Teatro dell'arte* was made of,' says the delirious director. Every new idea, new turn in the plot, or new scene he suggests is welcomed with cries of enthusiasm from the Italian collaborators, who rush about feverishly giving immediate orders. '*Che ci vuole?*' they say, which means that nothing is impossible.

These people naturally do not dislike to see their precarious jobs prolonged, perhaps indefinitely. A morning shooting often turns into a whole day, sometimes goes on all night, if necessary, without interruptions and without anybody complaining. No one seems to remember he needs food and sleep and has a home, a family and a bed to go back to. In this way a film scheduled to be finished in six weeks often takes three or four months. A few are never finished. Only rarely do these happy improvisations and new ideas manage to improve a film. Many, in the end, turn out to be too long, slow, involved, amateurish and incomprehensible. A lot of work must be done to them, back home in the cutting room, to shorten them; often a voice off-screen must be added to explain the inexplicable jumps in the narration. Not a few Napoleonic directors have found their Waterloo in Rome.

Even ordinary foreigners, who have nothing much to do, who while away their time and their income as agreeably as possible, become fascinated by the opportunities and ease of Italian life. As they rent a house, hire a servant or two, order a suit and a few shirts, have a few pieces of furniture made by a cabinet maker on the basis of a vague sketch on the back of an envelope or a picture in a magazine or look for some rare antique, they are inevitably carried away by everyone's docile and enthusiastic collaboration. They begin to discover a new kind of freedom. One can order anything, or almost anything, made or done, and it costs no more, or only a little more, than what one has to accept from superior powers in other countries. Life is malleable, a soft, yielding matter which can be shaped to any form. Possibilities seem infinite and inexhaustible. Any whim can be satisfied, provided one has money, and it does not take too much money, at that. One can really express oneself in Italy.

Take the prostitutes. Experienced travellers, and the Italians themselves, naturally enough, believe that no professional courtesan in Europe beats the Italian. She has qualities all her own. She is often soft-spoken, gentle, at times even slightly timid and a little awkward. She appears anxious to please. She can be motherly, sisterly, wifely and also, suddenly, turn into a shameless bacchante, a delirious and skilful voluptuary. She has inherited from her immemorial past the knowledge of a great number of delicate refinements, but hides her art under an engaging appearance of embarrassed clumsiness. *Ars*, she has learned from the ancient Romans, even if she cannot say it with the old words, *est celare artem*. Great art must be guided by an invisible technique; it must seem the spontaneous blossom of the moment's mood and impulse.

Money seems not to be her immediate aim in life, as it does not seem to be the aim of all great artists. Of course, she does what she does for a few thousand lire. But somehow she gives the impression that, a few times, this time especially, the payment is a pure formality, a gross necessity. The perfection of her performance seems to be her real aim, and pleasure, the delicate pleasure of effortless love, pleasure for herself, of course, but also the pleasure she reads on a man's radiant face. What she apparently wants above all is to create a moment of pure and fragile illusion. At the end, she will toss the money away without counting it, and perhaps waste a few precious minutes talking to the client as if to an old friend. She will show him a picture of her little son, whom she keeps in the country with her peasant mother. She will notice a spot on the man's coat and take it off with benzene. She may pass a carnation through his button-hole. Often enough, her last kiss on the doorstep will be surprisingly chaste and affectionate, by no means perfunctory or lascivious. There is nothing hard, nothing commercial, nothing arid about her. She is a proud girl.

The traveller (after gathering these superficial impressions, before really plunging deeply into Italian life) is at first tempted to conclude that what he has been told and has read was all wrong. Italians are transparent people, he thinks, incapable of dissimulation and hypocrisy. He dives with joy and relief into this new and heady atmosphere, even though he cannot easily define the various elements which compose it. Only later he begins to suspect that there may be, with all this, a theatrical quality which enhances but slightly distorts all values.

CHAPTER FIVE

ILLUSION AND CAGLIOSTRO

CLEARLY, then, the surface of Italian life, often gay and playful, sometimes bleak and tragic, has many of the characteristics of a show, a show in both meanings of the word. It is, first of all, almost always entertaining, moving, unreservedly picturesque, self-explanatory, animated, and engaging, as all good shows are, secondarily, all its effects are skilfully, if not always consciously, contrived and graduated to convey a certain message to, and arouse particular emotions in, the bystanders. Only the dull can refrain from smiling, gaping, or wiping a tear from their cheeks, as the case may be. Only the stupid can misinterpret the patent meaning of what they see.

The staging of scenes and the expression of sentiments inevitably tend to become more elaborate when the public is present. Watch an Italian mother fondle her baby. If she is alone, she is tender and solicitous like any other mother, in a matter-of-fact way. As soon as somebody enters the room, she will immediately enact a tasteful impersonation of Mother Love. Her face will suddenly shine, tears of affection will fill her eyes, she will crush the infant to her breast, sing to him, fondle him and make up poetic pet names. An Italian will often utter grave and sincere words (dictated by wrath, jealousy, the defence of his interests and dignity, or passionate love) and, at the same time, look out of the corner of his eye to check the impression he is making on his public.

The striving for effects, which can often be perceived in things made by God, is always present in those made, adapted and corrected by man: in the tiny and timid smile of a begging child; in the vast and majestic façade of a famous church or palazzo; in the green glass carafe of red wine on a pink table-cloth near two yellow lemons by

74

the dark blue sea. The old bearded fishermen who sit on the sea wall smoking their clay pipes look ready to be photographed in colour for a travel poster. The forsaken appearance of a Sicilian village square, with its immense baroque church, the lounging unemployed men, the cadaverous donkeys, is a concrete dramatization of doom and hopelessness. The chrome and glass geometry of a northern industrial town is an equally concrete dramatization of efficient modernity.

The first purpose of the show is to make life acceptable. Life in the raw can be notoriously meaningless and frightening. Italians feel uncomfortable when surrounded by nature. They have for centuries cut down ancient woods where the pagan deities found their last refuge and solitary majestic trees. They long ago invented ways to force vegetation to obey their will: they pruned bushes into sculptured forms, they created gardens which were as similar to green cities as possible. Gabriele d'Annunzio, who was perhaps more Italian than any other Italian, spent the last years of his life passionately uprooting trees and bushes in his beautiful garden on Lake Garda (planted years before by a nature-loving German) to put in their place stone pillars, stone walls, marble arches and allegoric statuary. He even transported and installed among the flower beds the iron prow of a first world war torpedo boat. Italians long ago devised ways to make water design harmonious arabesques in fountains. The art of teaching horses apparently impossible things, which is still cultivated in Vienna by the *Spanische Schule* riders, was perfected in Naples by a man named Pignatelli almost four hundred years ago.

Dull and insignificant moments in life must be made decorous and agreeable with suitable decorations and rituals. Ugly things must be hidden, unpleasant and tragic facts swept under the carpet whenever possible. Everything must be made to sparkle, a simple meal, an ordinary transaction, a dreary speech, a cowardly capitulation must be embellished and ennobled with euphemisms, adornments and pathos. These practices were not (as many think) developed by people who find life rewarding and exhilarating, but by a pessimistic, realistic, resigned and frightened people. They believe man's ills cannot be cured but only assuaged, catastrophes cannot be averted but only mitigated. They prefer to glide elegantly over the surface of life and leave the depths unplumbed.

This eternal search for shallow pleasures and distractions, this dressing up at all costs of reality could become cloying and revolting if they were not accompanied by *garbo*. *Garbo* is another Italian word which cannot be translated exactly, as it describes a quality particularly necessary and appreciated here. It is, for instance, the careful circumspection with which one slowly changes political allegiance when things are on the verge of becoming dangerous; the tact with which unpleasant news must be gently announced; the grace with which the tailor cuts a coat to flatter the lines of the body; the sympathetic caution with which agonizing love affairs are finished off; the ability with which a *prefetto* gradually restores order in a rebellious province without provoking resentments. Without *garbo* a rousing patriotic speech would become rhetorical, a flamboyant declaration of love sickening, an elaborately adorned building loathsome, a florid musical composition unbearable. *Garbo* keeps everything within the boundaries of credibility and taste.

It is impossible not to be enchanted and fascinated by the show. In Italy a man is never alone with his thoughts, always feels himself immersed in humanity, everything around him is clear and open. Such picturesque performances by natural elements, landscapes, human beings and architecture constitute a kind of perpetual entertainment. Everything tells its own pathetic story. You are anxious to hear the next instalment. Nobody ever becomes surfeited with these delights. Even the natives cannot bear to be away from them for long. When they emigrate, they choose, if they can, to surround themselves, in the new country, with their own countrymen, familiar noises, gestures and facial expressions. They sometimes settle in dramatic landscapes resembling those they left behind, as they did generations ago in California. Neapolitans think other people die when they see Naples: what is certain is that the Neapolitans themselves decline visibly when they leave it.

Foreigners are doubly affected. They have never felt such a heady sensation. Like the inexperienced watching their first film, they are taken in by the life-like shadows and carried away by the emotions evoked; they suspect there must be a trick somewhere, but do not bother to discover it. They seldom ask themselves why life in Italy should be so moving, why the Italians should be the actors, playwrights, choreographers, and *metteurs-en-scène* of their own national drama; they just enjoy the show. Once foreigners begin to understand that things are not always exactly what they look like, that reality does not have to be dull and ugly, they are no longer the same. This sensation is important. It is a discovery which has influenced more than ordinary travellers. It has subtly transformed great writers who have come in contact with Italy and, through them, the spirit of Europe. The new animation which was felt in the work of men like Chaucer, Milton, Goethe and Gogol, on their return, or even of men who never left home, like Shakespeare and Pushkin, and who knew about Italy from hearsay, was due only in part to the fact that these writers may have studied the language, imitated literary models, adopted new techniques, but, above all, that they had become aware of the exhilarating Italian secret, that life can be ennobled as a representation of life, that it can be made into a work of art.

*

Polite lies and flattery can be utilitarian on occasion but, most of the time, must be honestly classified among the devices disinterestedly designed to make life decorous and agreeable. They are the lubricants that make human relations run more smoothly. Flattery somehow makes the wariest of men feel bigger, more confident, and therefore more indulgent, generous and almost magnanimous. It is so common in Italy as to go practically unnoticed. One breathes it as one breathes the scent of violets in woods in the spring, without recognizing exactly what it is that gives one such a delicate sensation. Everybody is constantly being vaguely praised by everybody else. A decrepit man is always told he looks years younger; any old hag that she is beautiful, more beautiful this year than last, today than yesterday, tonight more than this morning. Almost imperceptible flattery is in the eagerness with which your orders are obeyed, or the obsequiousness with which your advice is sought in matters in which you have no particular experience. It is in the use of academic or other titles; people affix them to your name, as if to prove that you so visibly deserve such honours that it is impossible you have not been awarded them. A middle-class man is called *dottore* in his youth and becomes a *commendatore*, or *knight commander*, when over forty. Ordinary letters are addressed to the 'most egregious', 'illustrious', 'celebrated', 'eminent', 'renowned' Signore, or simply to N.H., the abbreviation for *Nobil Uomo*. Tailors praise your build. Dentists exclaim: 'You have the teeth of an ancient Roman!' The doctor cannot help remarking that he has rarely encountered an influenza as baffling as yours. The antique dealer, the jeweller, the waiter, the butcher, everybody will exclaim that your taste is exquisite, that it is a pleasure to serve you, that they would not sell what you are buying to anybody and certainly not at the ridiculous price you are asked.

Naturally nobody takes such transparent homages seriously. Nobody, for instance, pays attention to the implicit flattery contained in every-day greetings. A friend of mine was saluted in Naples (the capital of hyperbolic and meaningless flattery) with the simple and courteous formula: 'Sir, consider me the last button on the livery of your last lackey.' What could be more tasteful? My friend, not being a Neapolitan, was taken aback. He did not know what to say. He mumbled incoherent monosyllables. The correct answer to that one, of course, is: 'Sir, the last button on the livery of my last lackey is of diamonds.'

Most polite lies, like flattery, are too transparent really to further the liar's interest. When the shoemaker convincingly says, one hand on his heart, 'Of course, sir, you will have your new shoes on Thursday, without fail. Do not worry!' he is aware that he cannot fulfil his promise. The shoes will not be ready on time. But he is lying not for himself. He is lying for you. He wants you to feel at peace until Thursday, at least, warmed by the hope that your shoes will arrive. Norman Douglas long ago derided this kindly habit. He wrote (in *Siren Land*): ' "Can you supply me with something to eat, fair Costanza?" "How not? Whatever you command." Whatever you command: fairy-like bubbles of southern politeness which, when pricked, evaporate into different macaroni.' It cannot be denied that in the few minutes preceding the appearance of the macaroni, as in the few days before Thursday, the expectation has added something to a man's life.

Even instruments of precision like speedometers and clocks are made to lie in Italy for your happiness. The instrument in your car always marks a figure which is between ten and twenty per cent above the actual speed at which you are travelling. It is meant to make you feel proud of your automobile and your driving skill, but also to make you slow down sooner than you would otherwise and possibly save your life. The clocks on railway stations are all five minutes fast; everybody knows it, of course; and yet travellers, who would arrive on time even if they walked, are stupidly encouraged to quicken their step. Only foreigners are sometimes discouraged sooner than necessary and miss their trains. The electric clocks on the trains themselves, on the other hand, are often a few minutes slow, to give passengers the illusion they arrive on time when they are late, or a little ahead.

*

Transparent deceptions are constantly employed to give a man the most precious of all Italian sensations, that of being a unique specimen of humanity, a distinct personality deserving special consideration. An Italian considers it a duty to cultivate such illusions in fellow human beings, but, above all, he considers it a duty to himself. Nobody in Italy ever confesses to being 'an average man'; everybody persuades himself he is, sometimes for intricate and improbable reasons, one of the gods' favoured sons. This sensation can be bolstered up not only with words but in many other ways. Take the matter of theatre tickets. To pay the full price for a theatrical performance is equivalent to admitting that one is nobody, has no friends and enjoys no particular powers. It is not surprising that Italian theatres are half-filled with non-paying customers and the other half with customers who pay a reduced price. (People who hold free tickets are known as *Portoghesi*, not because the natives of Portugal are especially addicted to the habit, but because, several centuries ago, a gala performance given in Rome in honour of a Portuguese mission was swamped by Romans who, as they entered, brazenly declared themselves Portuguese.) Similarly nobody pays the full price for railway tickets. All kinds of people travel free; most of the others enjoy vast discounts; only a few *grands seigneurs*, foreigners or naive Italians pay the full fare. This naturally

creates complicated problems of accounting. It has been calculated
that, if everybody paid, all fares could be halved.

Northern Italians love to tell the following joke about the Neapolitans' compulsion to make anybody feel a privileged person. It is the
story of a Milanese buying a stamp in Naples. He walks out into the
street carrying a letter, looking for a tobacco shop where stamps are
sold, when he meets a Neapolitan acquaintance, who immediately
grasps the situation. 'You want a stamp?' he says. 'You know where
to buy it? Anywhere? How silly of you. It is lucky you met me. You
must be careful these days. I know a good place, the best place in
town—what am I saying?—in all Southern Italy. An old-fashioned
tobacconist. He is honest, reliable, not one of those money-mad
modern tobacconists. I will take you to him.' As he enters the shop,
leading the Milanese, he winks visibly and addresses the man behind
the counter: 'Giuseppe, this is a friend of mine, from Milano, who
must be served with all due consideration. This is his problem. He
wants a stamp, a thirty-lire stamp, for a most important letter which
must be mailed immediately. I told him only you could give him
entire satisfaction. Have you still some of those good thirty-lire
stamps, those very good ones, which you sold me last week? Let him
have one, please, one of the best.'

Less needy Italians successfully conceal the same ingratiating technique under a cloak of professional impassivity. Suave businessmen
from the north confidentially offer some of their clients exceptionally
encouraging deals, fabulous opportunities in profitable ventures,
at particularly favourable conditions, 'just for you'. In reality
most of these things are as difficult to obtain as thirty-lire stamps for
thirty lire.

*

The show however is not always purely disinterested. It is often
enacted also for the promotion of the actor's interests and those of his
family, friends, and protégés. How many impossible things become
probable here, how many insuperable difficulties can be smoothed
over with the right clothes, the right facial expressions, the right
mise-en-scène, the right words? With them anybody at all can quickly
gain the attention, benevolence, and sympathy of the public at large

or of a single important person. Alastair Reid, at a meeting of literary men gathered at Formentor, in 1962, to award two prizes to unknown writers, admired this particular technique. 'The Italians held forth,' he wrote, 'with such persuasive eloquence that no one could bear to impose on them the time limit of seven minutes that had been agreed on. (On one occasion, Vittorini stopped dramatically in mid-phrase to observe that he had outrun his time. "Go on, go on!" cried the bedazzled throng, and he did for a good ten minutes more.) Their every appearance was a performance, their every utterance a stylist's delight.' (The Italians that year managed to have one of the prizes awarded to one of their candidates, a struggling young woman writer, a protégée of Moravia.)

Sometimes the show is put up by a whole city, which wants to appear either prosperous or miserable, as the occasion requires. Rome was made to appear more modern, wealthy, and powerful with the addition of whole cardboard buildings, built like film sets, on the occasion of Hitler's visit, in 1938, in the fashion of Potemkin's villages. (Trilussa, the dialect poet, wrote a famous epigram on the occasion: *Roma de travertino, refatta de cartone, saluta l'imbianchino, suo prossimo padrone*, or 'Rome of travertine, re-made with cardboard, greets the house painter who will be her next master.') Hitler was notoriously impressed. Sometimes the show is put up by the whole country. After the war, Italian officials rushed to New York, some to describe the hunger, poverty, ruin and hopeless desperation of Italy, in order to get free grants of grain, cotton, coal, oil, and other raw materials from the American government, while others rushed to New York to describe an entirely different picture, the feverish activities, the new hope, the eagerness, the upsurge of energies, the fervid initiatives, the faith in the future of their countrymen, in order to get ordinary loans. Sometimes the same men were entrusted with both missions. When passing from one office to another, or from a party with government officials to another party with private bankers, they quickly changed facial expressions and tone of voice. Of course, they never lied. Both pictures were true.

*

Such behaviour was recommended long ago by one famous book. Few Italians, it is true, ever read it. Perhaps the author's teachings sank so deep into his countrymen's conscience that they are now part of their very nature, or, more probably, he, being Italian, merely codified what everybody more or less knew then and would still know centuries later. The book, by Baldassar Castiglione, is *Il libro del cortegiano*, printed in Venice in 1528. It was translated into English soon after as *The Book of the Courtier*; it became famous as the perfect guide for young members of the English Establishment practically until Edward VII's times. Castiglione teaches many accomplishments necessary to win and keep the favours of one's masters and to get ahead in the world: how to be at home in the tilting yard, the banquet-hall, the ladies' boudoir and the council chamber.

He was well suited to write such a treatise. His father was a wealthy count. His mother belonged to the almost royal house of Gonzaga. Born in 1478, at Casatico, in the duchy of Mantua, he was very carefully brought up and became a man of varied accomplishments, in all of which he was good but in none of which he was uncouth enough to excel: he was a soldier, politician, scholar, diplomat, author of renowned Latin poems, sportsman, art critic, and connoisseur, *homme à femmes*. He was at home in the principal courts of Europe. He visited London, in 1506, to accept the investiture of the Garter from Henry VII, as proxy for his master, the duke Guidobaldo d'Urbino. He was a friend of the best-known figures of his day, including Raphael, who painted his portrait, which now hangs in the Louvre. His advice is always practical and shrewd.

This is what he has to say, for instance, about facing dangers at war, in the language of his English translator: 'Where the Courtier is at skirmish, or assault, or battle upon the land, or in such other places of enterprise, he ought to work the matter wisely in separating himself from the multitude, and undertake the notable and bold feats which he has to do, with as little company as he can, and in the sight of noble men that be of most estimation in the camp, and especially in the presence and (if it were possible) before the very eyes of his king or great personage he is in service withall: for indeed it is meet to set forth to the show things well done.'

Castiglione is a gentleman and does not invite his reader to shirk his duty. A man, however, must not waste his heroism: he must undertake whatever dangerous task 'he has to do', seeing to it, with *garbo*, that his performance is not confused among many others, but staged well in sight of a choice and influential public, so that his daring shall not be in vain and his courage shall not go unrewarded. Are the arts of the courtier really honest? Castiglione reassured his reader that the skills he teaches, if properly employed, are not necessarily dishonourable: they are no more dishonourable than the dexterity with which the better sportsman defeats his opponent in a match ('Will you not say also that he who beats his fellow . . . at fencing . . . beguiles him because he has more art than the other?') or than the ability of the talented jeweller, who makes a precious stone 'much fairer' by setting it properly ('Will you say that the goldsmith deceives the eyes of them that look at a jewel?').

The devices are not always animated by the ignoble desire to deceive and bedazzle observers. Often, to put up a show becomes the only pathetic way to revolt against destiny, to face life's injustices with one of the few weapons available to a desperate and brave people, their imagination. To be powerful and rich, of course, is, for an individual as well as a nation, more desirable and satisfactory than to be weak and poor. Italians know it as well as anybody else. For some reason it has always been extremely difficult for them, individually and nationally, to conquer power and wealth. What were they to do? They staged an almost perfect imitation of the real thing. In normal times, after all, when there are no conflicts, power and the show of power can be considered equivalent. The mere shadow of power, if convincingly projected, can be as frightening as power itself. By its use, one may gain a few years or decades of tranquillity, and that is all one wants. In a crisis, of course, only real power can defend one. But crises are rare, seldom come unannounced, and can be delayed or avoided by a tactful change of policy. This is a risky game. It may last a certain length of time, perhaps a very long time, but not forever. At some point, real power destroys make-believe power and everything ends in catastrophe. But the show is better than nothing, better than the supine acceptance of immediate defeat.

Similarly, it is infinitely better to be rich than to seem rich. But if a man or a nation does not have the virtues and opportunities necessary to conquer and amass wealth, what is he or it to do? The art of appearing rich has been cultivated in Italy as nowhere else. Little provincial towns, capitals of tiny principalities in past centuries, like Lucca, Modena, Parma, Mantua, Ferrara, boast immense princely palaces, castles, vast churches, and stately opera houses, all disproportionate, sometimes ridiculously so, to the size of the principality, its means, and its population. There were in Naples penniless aristocratic families who could not afford carriages: they only owned the doors, with their coats of arms splendidly painted on them, which they attached to hired coaches on the rare days when they needed to parade in public. There were, here and there, decayed families who saved every lira, living in but a few rooms of their *palazzi* and eating boiled potatoes with the servants in the kitchen, in order to throw a big ball on one day of the year. The gilded salons were then thrown open, thousands of candles illuminated the gloom, flunkeys hired for the day stood in ancient liveries on the marble stairways holding silver candelabra in red peasant hands, two orchestras alternately filled the air with melodies, the champagne flowed freely. There are still today gentlemen buried in obscure country villages, where they manage what estates they have left, who emerge once a year, to go to Monte Carlo, Paris, or Biarritz for a few days, where they stay in the most celebrated hotels, dine with bejewelled ladies, entertain fabulously wealthy guests, are entertained in turn, tip lavishly, and then go back to their hiding places for another year of skimping.

One must bear this in mind even today, when the country has reached, for the first time in history, an unwonted opulence. Italians wear good clothes, drive shining cars and fill expensive restaurants. New companies erect stately steel and glass buildings for their head offices. Some of these people (not all, of course) own little more than the clothes on their back, the part of their car they have already paid for and the money with which to buy their expensive meals. Some of the companies dedicate a large part of their financial resources to the construction and the decoration of their resplendent new offices. Sociologists have recorded that the first expenditures made by the illiterate non-skilled workers in the South, when they get their first steady job in centuries, are strictly dedicated to superfluous and gaudy purchases: wrist watches, radios, television sets, and fancy clothes. Apparently the things they want above all are the show of prosperity and the reassurance they can read in the eyes of their envious neighbours. Only later do they improve their houses, buy some furniture, blankets, sheets, pots and pans. The last thing they spend money on is better food. Better food is invisible.

*

The suspicion that what surrounds one in Italy may be a show can be disturbing. It perplexes Italian adolescents, who have had a sheltered education, when they grow up. The pleasure foreigners feel at first is embittered, when they prolong their stay, by doubt and diffidence. Foreign diplomats in Rome disconsolately say: 'Italy is the opposite of Russia. In Moscow nothing is known yet everything is clear. In Rome everything is public, there are no secrets, everybody talks, things are at times flamboyantly enacted, yet one understands nothing.' To avoid making mistakes, some people conclude too hurriedly that everything here is only make-believe, nothing is ever what it looks like, and one can never trust appearances; everything then takes on a double outline as it does to a drunken man. These cautious people are just as easily misled as the naïve. Appearances in Italy are not always illusory. Is the young man less in love with his young lady if he courts her in a dramatic way? Is the man who watches the public's reaction from the corner of his eye less dominated by wrath, jealousy or love? Is the Sicilian village less miserable because it looks so evidently miserable? Is the army less powerful if it is pompously paraded? Not necessarily, of course, not always. In fact, the thing and its representation often coincide exactly. They may also coincide approximately, or may not coincide at all. There is no sure way of telling.

*

Take a very common example, the embarrassment of a pretty foreign girl who meets her Italian lover in an Italianate garden or a gondola under the moon. The man softly murmurs reassuring and entreating words into her ears. Meanwhile his hands seem animated by a life of their own. They caress her, attract her near him, tickle her hair at the nape, and boldly slip under her dress. His cheeks brush hers. He becomes more ardent, voluptuous and commanding. He is difficult to resist. What can she make of the performance? What is he, really? He may be an honest lover like any other, perhaps a little more skilful. He may be, at the opposite end of the scale, an accomplished performer, a complete impostor. He may also be anything in between. Reality and representation may differ by a mere hairbreadth, like the two images in a camera telemeter. He himself often does not know where truth ends and invention begins. He may sincerely think he is in love but may only be a lukewarm and temporary *innamorato* carried away by emotions and his ability. Or he may have found the challenge to his skill or daring too strong to resist in an especially difficult situation, matched with a particularly virtuous woman. Or he may be desperately in love. Whatever his feelings, his performance is almost always delightful, moving and tactful. Only rarely it may be irritating. The poor girl can only give in within reason, play her own rôle, keep her head, and enjoy the show.

One does not have to be a pretty woman, a diplomat, or a businessman to meet the problem. Ordinary sightseers face it. Everything must be interpreted in a similar fashion. Monuments, to begin with. The biggest in Italy is dedicated to Victor Emmanuel II, the Father of His Country, in the Piazza Venezia, in Rome. It is, obviously, and visibly, what it purports to be, the massive tribute of a grateful people to the king and military leader responsible for their liberation and the foundation of the Italian unified national state, in 1861. Its grandiose architecture is an early twentieth-century, or Belle Époque, copy of Roman Imperial style. We must overlook the fact that, since it was inaugurated in 1911, hundreds of film sets have aped its example and numberless *papier maché* reproductions of the same colonnades and tympana have somewhat spoiled the original effect for us.

Then one examines it a little more closely. Why was such a huge pile erected in the very heart of ancient Rome, on the most sacred of the seven hills? Why was it not built in a park, outside the city, on a less revered height, possibly on Monte Mario? Why does it conceal and practically swallow the Campidoglio? Was the sight of the famous hill disturbing to the pride of modern Italians? (One knows, of course, why the marble is so irremediably white. It is not the traditional stone of Rome, travertine. It was quarried near Brescia, in North Italy, for the good reason that the prime minister of the time, Zanardelli, was from Brescia.) Why is its style so self-consciously imperial?

By and by one begins to perceive another monument, underneath the first. The excessive size of the construction, its position, its architecture reveal the insecurity which surrounded the patriotic minority who managed to achieve Italian unity and tried to strengthen it against almost overwhelming opposition. They clearly wanted to celebrate a National Hero to cancel out many of the heroes of the past, a patriot to obliterate all non-patriotic Italians, a king to annul all republican partisans of the Risorgimento. If Victor Emmanuel II had not existed, or if he had not been as brave and generous a king as he was, one suspects the governing élite of the time would have invented him, attributing to him the Plutarchian virtues he should have possessed. In the end, one concludes that the monument is not only the sincere tribute of a grateful people to the memory of their great king, but also the theatrical representation of such a tribute.

Or take some of the churches. Take the biggest and most revered of them all, Saint Peter's. It is undoubtedly an impressive place of worship. All of the greatest artists since the Renaissance laboured to make it so. Michelangelo was one of its architects. All the paraphernalia and personnel necessary for ritual communication with the deity are abundantly available. Grandiose ceremonies are staged periodically, according to a very ancient liturgy, dedicated to the revealed mysteries and holy traditions of the Roman Catholic Church. Hundreds of unbelievers are converted yearly within its walls. Thousands of believers are confirmed daily in their faith and comforted. But, when one compares it to other churches, elsewhere, and to a few very old small ones in Rome itself, one finds it perhaps too ornate, mundane, rhetorical, and vast to conciliate the intimate emotions usually connected with religious fervour.

One can pray there only with some difficulty. One is distracted by the colours of the rare marbles, the complicated architecture, the miniature perfection of the sculptures, the gesticulation of the statues, the celestial music, the coming and going of herds of indifferent sightseers. One begins to understand, at a certain point, that it is not only a great basilica, a place of worship, the seat of the Holy Roman Church, but also the dramatic representation of all this. One discovers that it is not merely designed to inspire religious emotions but also to impress the onlooker with the power, the majesty, the wealth and the solidity of the Church and, therefore, the glory of God himself. If you then happen to come across one of the secret storehouses where the necessary decorations and machines for the various ceremonies are kept, you cannot escape an irreverent conclusion: Saint Peter's is also God's own holy playhouse.

*

The search for the secondary level of everything Italian becomes a game, at a certain point. Is the hungry beggar in the street real or a good imitation? How much is Signor A, the celebrated contemporary politician, whose picture daily appears in the press, a real statesman, and how much, instead, the skilful impersonation of one? How truly is Signor B a great novelist, Signor C a great actor, Signor D a great film director, Signor E a great poet? Of course there is no simple answer. Most of these eminent gentlemen may be, in their particular callings, what they seem. They certainly are, at the same time, and in varying degrees, good impersonations. A few may be clever impostors, some, on the other hand, may be even greater than their public character; others may be great but in a different way.

D'Annunzio, for instance, lived like a Renaissance prince, was a voluptuary surrounded by borzois, a gaudy clutter of antiques, brocades, rare Oriental perfumes and flamboyant but inexpensive jewellery; dressed like a London clubman; preferably slept with duchesses, world-famous actresses, and mad Russian ladies; wrote exquisitely wrought prose and poetry; rode to hounds. His politics were of the extreme right. In reality he was a penniless provincial character of genius, the son of a small merchant from Pescara.

Alberto Moravia, on the other hand, wears turtle-neck sweaters and shabby clothes; often writes the awkward language spoken by uncultured people, freely employing words children are punished for pronouncing; publicly escorts unemployed starlets, unknown lady poets just out of school, and the daughters of metal workers and bricklayers. His politics are of the extreme left. In reality he is the son of a wealthy bourgeois family, decently brought up according to the rigid standards of the first decades of this century (there are pictures of him in Little Lord Fauntleroy and sailor suits), who could easily live on the income from his properties, inherited from his father, who was a hard-working construction engineer.

Both men, d'Annunzio and Moravia, are extraordinary writers, both typical representatives of their respective generations. Both tried to become spokesmen for a class and a kind of life which was not theirs. The perfection of these performances is such that it is usually almost impossible to determine at first sight how close the real and fictitious characters are to each other. An exact valuation often takes some time. Meanwhile one must behave with caution.

*

This is, it must be admitted, more or less true in many other countries. It has been true at all times. There have always been eminent men who played their own rôles with skill. Impersonation has been an essential part of the métier of mighty personages in all epochs. Nero died thinking he had been a great actor playing the rôle of a Roman Emperor. Louis XIV was proverbially faithful all his life to his duties as a showman. Many men managed to persuade the crowds of their own greatness; others only the more naïve, from a distance, and not for long. Great historical events often took the form of ceremonial display. There have always been monuments and edifices which were at the same time what they were and representations of themselves. Take the old castles, anywhere in Europe: how much strictly military value had they and how much were they designed to impress the enemy with their impregnability?

This is also true in Italy. But there is a fundamental difference. In other parts of the world substance always takes precedence and its external aspect is considered useful but secondary. Here, on the other hand, the show is as important as, many times more important than, reality. This is perhaps due to the fact that the climate has allowed

Italians to live mostly outside their houses, in the streets and *piazze*; they judge men and events less by what they read or learn, and far more by what they see, hear, touch and smell. Or because they are naturally inclined towards arranging a spectacle, acting a character, staging a drama; or because they are more pleased by display than others, to the point that they do not countenance life when it is reduced to unadorned truth. It may be because the show can be a satisfactory *ersatz* for many things they lack, or because they love, above all, a good actor who can stir them, a good dramatic situation which can make them feel the emotions only art can evoke well. Whatever the reason, the result is that at all times form and substance are considered one and the same thing. One cannot exist without the other. The expression is the thing expressed.

This reliance on symbols and spectacles must be clearly grasped if one wants to understand Italy, Italian history, manners, civilization, habits, and to foresee the future. It must by no means be overlooked by anyone who does not want to delude himself. It is the fundamental trait of the national character. It helps people to solve most of their problems. It governs public and private life. It shapes policy and political designs. It is, incidentally, one of the reasons why the Italians have always excelled in all activities in which the appearance is predominant: architecture, decoration, landscape gardening, the figurative arts, pageantry, fireworks, ceremonies, opera, and now industrial design, stage jewellery, fashions, and the cinema. Italian medieval armour was the most beautiful in Europe: it was highly decorated, elegantly shaped, well-designed, but too light and thin to be used in combat. In war the Italians themselves preferred the German armour, which was ugly but practical. It was safer.

Inevitably Italians are tempted to applaud more those performances which stray dangerously farthest from reality, those which make do with the scantiest of materials, those which do not even pretend to imitate existing models and still manage to be effective, convincing, stirring or entertaining. Take imitation marble. Since the earliest days local craftsmen have been unique in their ability to counterfeit the real thing. Half the marble one sees in churches or patrician *palazzi* is in fact but smooth plaster deceptively painted. It is not necessarily always cheaper than the real thing: at times it can be infinitely more expensive and inconvenient. Of all the imitation marbles, Italians appreciate more those which really imitate nothing at all, but create a combination of colours which never existed in nature. What is specially prized is the daring of their makers, their Promethean challenge to God.

The word for such dexterity is *virtuosismo*. The greatest of all, Nicolò Paganini, often finished playing his most complicated sonatas after breaking all the strings of his violin except one. Down the centuries, Italian *virtuosi* have been famous for having produced floods of *trompe l'œil*, *trompe* the mind, and *trompe* the heart. They have filled libraries with admirable love poems inspired by no vulgar passion but by a highly developed ability to make harmonious and technically perfect combinations of words. They can write impeccable essays proving the absolute opposite of what everybody knows is the truth; impeccable scientific papers knowingly based on slightly spurious data; historical studies in which the facts disagreeing with the author's thesis are carefully neglected. Some criminal lawyers take special pride in having those clients acquitted who they know are really guilty.

Many see through the deception and yet applaud the adroitness of the performer. It takes a great man to do such things. Anybody can make an omelette with eggs. Only a genius can make one without. *Virtuosismo* is not necessarily an empty display of ability. It often has a practical value. Take warfare during the Renaissance. As it was practised abroad, it consisted of the earnest and bloody clash of vast armies. He who killed more enemies carried the day. In Italy it was an elegant and practically bloodless pantomime. Highly paid *condottieri*, at the head of picturesque but small companies of armed men, staged the outward appearance of armed conflict, decorating the stage with beautiful props, flags, coloured tents, caparisoned horses, plumes; the action was accompanied by suitable martial music, rolls of drums, heartening songs and blood-chilling cries. They convincingly manœuvred their few men back and forth, pursued each other across vast provinces, conquered each other's fortresses. Victory was decided by secret negotiations and the offer of bribes. It was, after all, a very civilized and entertaining way of waging war. It often left matters as undecided as warfare practised elsewhere, but cost less in money, human lives and suffering.

Italians have been suspected of duplicity in every epoch. They are believed to excel in such disreputable and dubious fields as diplomacy, the conduct of intrigues, fraudulent speculations and the organization of swindles. Severe foreigners point out that the arts of political deception were codified by the Italians and that some of the most famous international adventurers were Italians—such names as Giacomo Casanova and the Count of Cagliostro are often quoted to prove the point. These accusations are old, so old that some go back to the Middle Ages and some probably to earlier times, rooted in racial and religious prejudices and misunderstandings. But there is some truth in some of them.

It must be admitted, first of all, that the virtues of the Italians, like those of other peoples, may at times degenerate into their corresponding vices. The parsimony of the French easily turns into avarice; the reserve of the English into deaf and dumb isolation; the animated activity of the Americans into senseless agitation. It is not surprising, therefore, that the possession of a knack to correct and embellish the appearance of life may at times tempt some Italians to utilize it to mystify their neighbours for their own private advantage. But something always prevents an Italian from achieving a lasting, world-wide, stupendous swindle. He is usually the victim of his own machinations. Italian adventurers, founders of counterfeit religions and dishonest financiers on a large scale are few and insignificant when compared to those born in other countries. None of the internationally famous scandals of the past is connected with an Italian name. John Law was a Scotsman; no Italian was involved in the South Sea Bubble, the speculation in tulip bulbs in the Netherlands, the scandal of the Panama Canal company shares in Paris at the end of the last century, the Stavisky case in France between the two world wars or the growth and collapse of the empire of Kreuger, the Swedish match king.

There is no doubt that the Italian Giacomo Casanova had the qualities for a career as an international adventurer and swindler, comparable to the best foreign examples, but it can be proved that what prevented him from reaching ultimate success was, curiously enough, his most typical Italian characteristics. He was tall, handsome, with a spacious forehead and a Roman nose, the looks of a gentleman, and an air of authority about him. He was untiringly vigorous and healthy. He was also clever, wrote well and fluently, played several musical instruments, spoke and wrote several languages with ease, Italian and French with elegance. He had read a great deal, quoted glibly from the Latin and Greek classics and contemporary authors; he could converse as an equal with philosophers, poets, and novelists. He visited Voltaire to dispute with him on some minor point. He pleased women at first sight, women of all ages and conditions, and usually succeeded in rendering them helpless and defenceless in front of his pressing entreaties. His physical capacity to satisfy the most exacting mistress by renewing his homages to her a practically unlimited number of times through the night and the following day, with only short *entr'actes* between the exertions, is not as surprising as the feat of psychological endurance: he was never bored, never embittered by experience, sincerely admired one woman after another, and slipped into bed at a moment's notice with the fat, the lean, the young, the old, the dirty, the *soignée*, the lady, the chambermaid, the strumpet, the nun, always admirably animated, till very late in life, by the same schoolboyish eagerness.

He spoke in a very persuasive manner and often impersonated any character he chose. 'My secret is simple: I always say the truth, and people naturally believe me,' he lied in his memoirs. His truths were, to say the least, improbable and, at times, blatantly absurd, yet most people trusted him for a time. He had no scruples of any kind, in any field, to embarrass him. He died penniless, alone, far from his native land. He was saved from destitution by a charitable friend, Graf Waldstein, who gave him a dreary job as librarian in his castle at Dux, in Bohemia. The great adventurer's last years were embittered by humiliating squabbles with the Graf's servants, who played backstairs tricks and practical jokes on the defenceless old man.

*

The other notorious Italian adventurer usually mentioned in the same breath with Casanova, was born Giuseppe Balsamo but called himself Count Alessandro di Cagliostro (Cagliostro was the family name of a married aunt who had been his godmother). His success is almost inexplicable. He is described as short, fat, ugly, dark-skinned, unwashed, with a sullen and suspicious expression on a vulgar face. He was arrogant, rude, boastful and given to outbursts of frantic rage. He had no known mistress. He was a faithful husband. Practically illiterate, he spoke only one language really well, the Sicilian dialect, and all others with a heavy Sicilian accent. 'There is,' wrote Lavater to young Goethe, 'nothing seductive about him.' Goethe was so interested in the famous charlatan that, when he was in Palermo, he went out of his way to prove to himself beyond doubt that the Count of Cagliostro and Giuseppe Balsamo were the same person. (Cagliostro had denied it and was to deny it to his end.) He searched for the family and found them to be poor, honest, God-fearing people, in a spotlessly clean kitchen. Cagliostro's mother plaintively asked the young German poet, if he should ever meet her son in the North, to remind him that he still owed money to her since the last time he had been home, years before, when he had pawned some of her jewellery and had never redeemed it. 'We are told,' the relatives said to Goethe, 'that Giuseppe has made a fortune and now lives like a very rich man. What luck would be ours if he returned here and took care of us!' It was the candid expression of an aspiration which is still universal in Sicily—to be supported by a rich relative.

Giuseppe Balsamo was born in Palermo in 1743. He entered a convent where the good brothers, who dedicated their lives to healing the sick, taught him the rudiments of medical arts which were to be useful to him later in life. He ran away after a while and grew up in the streets, making ends meet by practising many illegal trades. He dabbled in the primitive magic practices of the poor and illiterate, who obscurely still preserved pre-Christian and Moslem traditions and beliefs. He sold potions, made incantations, evoked demons, prepared amulets, told the future, healed the sick and endeavoured to kill his clients' enemies from afar for a small price. Above all he practised an art for which he had a special talent and which he went on perfecting all his life: he reproduced any signature with such perfection that he often deceived the original signer, and could counterfeit all sorts of difficult documents. In 1768 he decided Palermo had nothing more to teach him and left to seek his fortune in the world.

He emigrated to Rome where he met and married Lorenza Feliciani, the daughter of a small artisan. Lorenza was so beautiful as to be practically irresistible. She was still described as 'seductive' by sober and reliable witnesses twenty years later. What his unsavoury and repellent aspect had prevented him from attempting he could now do with the aid of his wife. Smiling Lorenza attracted and reassured wealthy men. Some slept with her and paid her well, some merely basked in the radiance of her beauty. They were all fleeced by her husband. Cagliostro sometimes feigned terrible attacks of jealousy and blackmailed some customer (in London he blackmailed a married Quaker with no difficulty), but more often he just placidly counted the money coming in. (It was not an unusual practice at the time. The husband of a well-known eighteenth-century ballerina used to say: '*Les cornes c'est comme les dents. Ça fait mal quand ça pousse et puis l'on mange avec.*') At the same time, he continued to practise his own arts.

The young couple travelled through Europe, as all good adventurers had to. Everywhere they lived in luxury and were encouraged and aided by the rich and important friends Lorenza soon gathered around her: in Saint Petersburg it was Potemkin himself who protected them. Wherever he stopped, Cagliostro organized a lodge of a Masonic rite of his own invention, the 'Egyptian Order', which possessed magical secrets no other order had ever heard of. All his wife's friends were usually enrolled with elaborate ceremonies. Among the many advantages of the order was the possibility of purchasing from the Grand Copht, the leader himself, one of his two famous elixirs. The first, the less expensive brand, merely stopped a man's age at the moment he took the first sip; the second managed to turn time backwards and rejuvenated the customer by a matter of ten, twenty, or thirty years, according to the dose. The success of the two potions was immense. Cagliostro filled Europe with his bottles.

He himself, as he liked to point out, was living proof of the success of his secret formulæ. He was thousands of years old. He remembered everything he had seen in his centuries-old life. He would reminisce about the construction of the Pyramids, the Roman emperors he had met, and what Jesus Christ had told him. No great personage of the past escaped his friendship. He was probably the greatest name-dropper in history. The manufacture of his elixirs was among his lesser activities. He conducted magic rites and experiments of all kinds, turned lead into gold in front of sceptical audiences, communicated with superior spirits, healed the sick, and foretold the future. Some of this was pure quackery. Some, however, showed him to possess mysterious, metapsychical powers of sorts. He really healed many sick clients and a few of his prophecies came true. Fleeing from France in 1785 he predicted the revolution, the destruction of the Bastille, and the coming of 'a great Prince who would reform religion'.

Cardinal de Rohan was convinced that he had seen him actually manufacture gold in the cardinal's own palace in Strasbourg and construct from tiny stones a huge diamond worth 25,000 livres. 'He will make me,' proclaimed Rohan, 'the richest man in Europe', and placed a marble bust of the magician, inscribed with the words 'The divine Cagliostro', on the staircase of his country palace at Saverne. In Paris, a city notoriously hospitable to quacks, he and his wife had a great success. Lorenza adopted the name of Serafina and pretended to be an ageless spirit from another world. He cured wealthy patrons and crowds of paupers who waited for him at the gate of his house every morning. Unfortunately, his friendship with the gullible cardinal involved him in the famous affair of the Queen's necklace. As a result, he and Lorenza were locked in the Bastille. Being innocent of this particular crime, he was quickly able to prove it; the Cagliostros were freed, but obliged by the police to leave Paris immediately.

This incident was the beginning of the end. The couple meandered once again through Europe, but without success. The old charm was gone. He had become too notorious. Too many people thought he was a humbug. The couple ended up in Rome, almost twenty years after leaving the city. This was his final mistake. He failed as a healer; the Romans were neither as ill nor as gullible as the Parisians. He tried, as a last resort, to set up a Roman lodge of his famous Egyptian Order. He invited all the best people, including high prelates, to an introductory meeting at the Villa Malta. (The villa is next to the Villa Medici. It belonged to the Knights of Malta, later became the residence of Prince von Bülow, who was German ambassador in Rome in 1914, and is now owned by the Jesuit Order.)

A sceptical eye-witness, the abbé Lucantonio Benedetti, has left us a minute description of Cagliostro's last desperate effort to ward off ruin. The count, short, thick-set, dark, appeared sitting on a tripod, like the Sybil of old, and gave what probably was his set speech for such occasions. 'It is fitting that I reveal who I am, that I open up my past. . . . I see the endless desert, the giant palms project their shadows on the sand, the Nile flow quietly, the Sphinxes, the obelisks, the columns rise majestically. Here are the wonderful walls, the temples rising in great numbers. . . . It is the sacred city, Memphis. . . . The victorious king is entering the gates, Thotmes III the Glorious, after having defeated the Syrians and the Canaanites. . . . *Io vedo*. . . . But now I am in another city, here is the sacred temple where Jehovah was adored. . . . The new god has vanquished the old. . . . I hear voices, people are acclaiming the prophet, the son of God. . . . Who is he? He is the Christ. Ah, I see him, at the wedding feast of Cana, turning water into wine. . . .'

The abbé added: 'Here he gave a great cry and jumped from his tripod. He shouted: "He was not the only one to perform that miracle. I will show you. I will reveal to you the mysteries, nothing is unknown to me, I know all, I am immortal, antediluvian. . . . *Ego sum qui sum.*" ' He proceeded to add a few drops of magic liquid into a carafe of water and turned it into wine ('sparkling like Orvieto', the abbé duly noted), which he declared to be the famous Falerno of the ancient Romans. 'A few people tasted it and called it excellent,' the abbé wrote, who did not touch it. The count then spoke of other secret powers he possessed and of his magic elixirs. He distributed samples of elixir number one to a few elderly gentlemen in the audience, whose eyes immediately shone and whose cheeks became pink. (The abbé wrote in his diary: 'The elixir had about the same visible effect of a good glass of Montefiascone.')

Finally, he gave the demonstration of his power to transform small diamonds into big ones. He borrowed a ring from the French ambassador, the same Cardinal de Bernis who had been Casanova's friend in Venice and Paris, put it in a crucible, poured various liquids and powders over it, spoke words which he said were Egyptian and Hebrew, and finally handed the cardinal his ring with a stone more than twice the original size. 'The cardinal cried out that a miracle had been performed,' wrote the abbé Benedetti, 'but I believe the second ring had nothing to do with the first and that the second stone was but a piece of rock crystal.'

The meeting was a failure. Cagliostro was arrested and imprisoned in Castel Sant'Angelo, by order of the Holy Office, not for being a swindler but for impiety, heresy and practices offensive to the Church and the Christian religion. His wife turned witness for the prosecution, to save her neck. He was tried and sentenced to death. The sentence was later commuted to life imprisonment. Cagliostro was locked in a small cell in the impregnable castle of San Leo, near Rimini. He died a short time before the French revolutionary armies, who had invaded the Papal states and were liberating all the prisoners of the Papal tyranny along their way, could reach him.

*

An old English lady I knew, who spent most of her life in Rome, used to wag a finger and say: 'There is some Cagliostro and some Casanova in every Italian, even in those you'd suspect the least.' The fact, which, of course, did not displease her, is not entirely exact. Casanova and Cagliostro, it is true, could not have been born elsewhere. Their adventuorous lives were, in a way, a retaliation all'Italiana against a world that had made them poor, powerless, despised, and members of a nation that offered to them at the time, only a life of poverty, buffoonery, and sordid humiliation. They also had the common Italian defect, that they could not employ their particular gifts to construct something solid, to transform their lives in a stable way, to conquer durable honours, wealth, prestige, and power, as adventurers from other lands would have done.

Something always stopped them. They practised their art for art's sake. They distributed treasures with the same ease with which they amassed them. They were contented with but the appearance of success. Their careers, however, belong to Europe and not to Italy. They had to go abroad to find customers in sufficient numbers. Their achievements depended in part on the absence of other Italians in their entourage and among their customers. Their victims could only be foreigners. The credulity of their easy public spoiled them in the end and made them over-confident. Their *virtuosismo* led them astray. They overreached themselves, making their stories more and more daringly incredible. That is why, every time they touched Italian soil, they came to grief: Casanova was once jailed in Venice and twice forced to flee, Cagliostro met his final defeat in Rome. Both of them were not such good Italians as those who never left the country, lived a quiet life, and used their powers in a discreet and inconspicuous way, without ending up in prison or in a solitary cell in a remote castle, leaving a spotless name and a tidy fortune to their descendants. Not to become notorious is the most important rule.

These are (to sum them all up) the most easily identifiable reasons why Italians love their own show, why they prefer often to live in their own ambiguous world of make-believe, among *papier maché* reproductions of reality, flowery but insincere words, in the penumbra of half truths, among the convulsive gesticulations of unfelt sentiments and emotions. First of all, they do it to tame and prettify savage nature, to make life bearable, dignified, significant, and pleasant, for others and themselves. They do it, then, for their own private ends; a good show makes a man *simpatico* to powerful people, helps him get on in the world and obtain what he wants, solves many problems, lubricates the wheels of society, protects him from the envy of his enemies and the arrogance of the mighty. They do it to avenge themselves on unjust fate.

In difficult times, under bloody tyrannies, the show can also be used as a defence. It is, often enough, the only defence. During the last few months of the last war, when Italy was the battle ground of foreign armies and divided by civil war, I was living on a lonely part of the coast of Tuscany, near Porto Santo Stefano. Allied bombers rained bombs on us night and day. During a lull, a German navy captain and some officers came to pay me a visit: they carefully looked over the house to see if there was anything suspicious, talked obscurely among themselves, finally relaxed, sat down, and drank some wine. I drank with them. The captain sighed and said: 'You don't know, sir, how insidious life in Italy today can be for men like us. Everybody, literally everybody you meet can be an enemy, a deadly enemy.' I said nothing. He went on: 'Not everybody is like you, sir. I can see from your face that you wish for the victory of your country and its German allies. There are many, you will not believe this, who want our defeat, but there is absolutely no way to tell them apart from the others.'

I was left speechless. The captain was honestly disconsolate. The fact that the Italians did not go around carrying large signs, reading 'Loyal ally of Nazi Germany' or 'Despicable traitor wishing for the defeat of his country and its allies', seemed to him incredible. How could he really tell friends from foes? Was he a mind reader? How could he reward the good Italians and shoot the others on sight, when they all smiled to him in about the same way, talked mildly about the weather and the war, expressed the same vague hopes in speedy victory and peace, lifted their glasses to Mussolini and Hitler, and looked about as honest and reliable as all Italians did to a good German? In my case, obviously, he felt he could rest secure. Why? He did not know I was on a Fascist government list of suspects to be arrested on sight and possibly shot (such lists were long and had practically no importance in the front lines; they often lay forgotten in their unopened envelopes). He could not know that I had been busy with underground work and was at the time giving partisans all the help I could. How could he, if I did not tell him?

The case, I admit, is too extreme to be used as a typical illustration. The captain, without a doubt, was less perspicacious than most of his countrymen. He might also have been tired, confused by the incessant bombings, dejected and frightened. He might have been stupid. Still, his sincere and heart-breaking lamentations will remain with me as the most memorable example I have ever encountered of a northerner's bewilderment in front of the complexity of Italian life. His words also proved to me, incidentally, how thoroughly Italian I was, in spite of my foreign travels and education, since I was able, practically without speaking, to convince a poor, guileless, candid Nazi that I was openly and firmly on the side of the Axis.

CHAPTER SIX

THE OTHER FACE OF THE COIN

BEHIND the turbulent and picturesque agitation of Italy, behind the amiable, festive, and touching spectacle, behind the skilful performances, real life is something else. It can be sordid, tragic, and pitiless. It is often an anguished, sometimes a mortally dangerous game. It is always difficult. The cradle of every newly-born baby is surrounded by a number of evil and all-powerful genii, determined to make his existence a miserable one. He must try to ward them off and to defeat them, if he can, when he grows up. His is a desperate job, with only a few and feeble good influences to help him.

The first of the evil spirits is poverty. Italy is still a very poor country today, poorer as a whole than any other western European country except Spain. (The average standard of living has been calculated to be at present about what it was in the United States in 1914, in France in 1924, and in Britain in 1927.) The Mezzogiorno is still by far the most miserable region. In spite of the vast sums invested by the government over the past decade, the poverty of the Meridionali as a whole is still only a little less acute than that of the population of North Africa. The majority of them still manage to eat only enough to stave off death; it is an improvement, of course, on what they could afford in the past. In the newly-built factories, the management compels the workers to consume one square meal a day in the canteens to be sure they have absorbed an adequate amount of calories and are strong enough to carry on their work. It is well-known that, should they be allowed to lunch at home, they would eat practically nothing, as they would have to share their food with many famished relatives. Then there is the shoddy poverty of most of the northern industrial slums; the melancholy and concealed poverty of better-paid workers, the more modest employees, and the lower middle class in general, who often save every lira in order not to conquer status symbols but to give their sons a superior education and allow them to go to the university; their sons' angry poverty, the cultural proletarians, who earn less than unskilled workers as teachers, municipal doctors or veterinary surgeons in country towns and villages, petty bureaucrats, police officials, trade union organizers, and party hacks.

There is the poverty of the decayed and proud aristocrats, owners of once prosperous lands ruined by price drops, agrarian reform or foreign competition, the poverty of the dispossessed élites of yesterday and the day before. All these *déclassés* join with the cultural proletarians to form the cadres of the fanatic mass movements of the extreme left and the extreme right. Even where there is no actual poverty, among reasonably prosperous people, there is always the fear of its possibility which casts its gloomy shadow over everything. The rich tend to behave as if wealth were a precious medicine in times of epidemics. Many cling pathetically to it and defend it by every means, legal or illegal.

The second of the evil genii is ignorance. Millions of people, between ten and thirty per cent of the population, are still illiterate. The figure varies according to the definition of illiteracy. Is a man who cannot read and can write only his name literate or illiterate? Is a man who went to school but forgot everything, or who can only occasionally make out a few familiar words on a wall poster, literate or illiterate? Even the undeniably literate are seldom very proficient. Fewer newspapers per million of the population are sold in Italy than in any other country of western Europe. The cultured minority itself, as a rule, still possesses only an old-fashioned, provincial and inadequate culture.

Practically nobody, except cabinet ministers, journalists, diplomats, businessmen, a few scholars, and the rich, has the possibility of travelling abroad to study foreign habits and compare foreign countries with their own. The widespread ignorance of real conditions in the rest of the world feeds unjustified prides and prejudices, excessive admiration or absurd contempt for foreigners. The new politicians, improvised since the end of the war, have mostly been compelled to become real experts in one art alone, the most difficult of all, that of getting themselves elected by an inconstant electorate and of jockeying for high position within their parties, in Parliament, and in the government. They have all been frenziedly occupied with day-to-day chores, signing thousands of letters every day, conferring, flying to international conferences, travelling through the provinces, making speeches of all kinds for all occasions; too busy not only to make a serious examination of the national problems, to devise modern solutions for them, to survey the wheezy functioning of the State apparatus, and to analyse the causes of its decay, but even at times to read the newspapers. These are read for them by underlings, who cull a few paragraphs for their perusal. Political business is carried on mostly by ear.

The most erudite Italians, the university professors, the depositors of the nation's culture, lack funds to purchase books and to carry on simple scientific experiments. University laboratories are ridiculously inadequate, the libraries pitifully small and out of date. The salaries being offensively tiny, professors must make a living. They take on extra jobs, as consultants for business concerns, or as practitioners of the professions they teach, doctors, economists, lawyers, geologists, engineers, surgeons. This becomes their main activity. Their academic rank, the 'prof.' on their visiting cards, merely serves them to earn bigger fees. They have little time for anything else also because they must live where they make their money and commute to the provincial cities where they have their chairs. They lecture and run. Many keep abreast of progress abroad by desultorily reading specialized magazines. Only a few heroic ones somehow manage to study seriously, find the money necessary to carry on their scientific research, become world authorities in their field and win Nobel Prizes. Even the Church is alarmed at the low level of erudition of the ordinary clergy and the parish priests, whose worldly and theological knowledge is often much below that of their French and German colleagues.

The third evil spirit is injustice. There are too many laws in Italy. A tropical tangle of statutes, rules, norms, regulations, customs, some hundreds of years old, some voted last week by Parliament and signed this very morning by the President, could paralyse every activity in the land, stop trains, planes, cars, and ships, shut every shop, industrial plant, hospital, school, and office, if they were suddenly applied. The late Luigi Einaudi, Italy's foremost economist and ex-President of the Republic, calculated that, if every tax on the statute books was fully collected, the State would absorb 110 per cent of the national income. It has been proved that the laws, being so numerous, contradictory and ambiguous, could allow a determined government to carry out any kind of revolution, of the extreme left or the extreme right, by merely selecting a few appropriate statutes and applying them to their ultimate consequences. Nobody knows how many of them are still valid, nobody knows for certain what some of them really mean. Often, not even recourse to the records of what the law-makers said, years before, when debating them in Parliament, reveals their significance and precise purpose. They are generated in a continuous stream by a curious Italian superstition: when things go wrong, problems are baffling, and nothing else avails, a new law is usually passed, often too difficult and complicated to be applied properly, in the hope that it will have thaumaturgic affects, that it will act like an incantation and ward off that particular evil. Some, of course, are useful. A few are good. Many useless or unpractical ones have been forgotten, 'abrogated by desuetude' is the technical term, but all can be suddenly rescued from oblivion, dusted, and used at any time for the benefit of a powerful group, as weapons for the destruction of its enemies.

Courts do very little to disentangle the confusion. Few Italians in their right mind expect anything but erratic justice from them. The current rule is never to sue when one is in the right. It is too risky. One should go to court only when one knows one is in the wrong and on the defensive. 'The judge,' experts explain, 'may easily make a mistake and award you the verdict. And anyway, the controversy will drag on for years, from one postponement to the next. Your opponents may lose patience and come to a compromise.' Trials last interminably, also because the judges are few, badly paid, with practically no staff to help them. They are usually intelligent, erudite and honest men, who somehow try to cope with mountains of legal papers literally threatening to bury them; they pile up daily on their tables, chairs, the floors of their dingy offices, along the walls, and rise to the height of a tall man. The magistrates have no secretaries, often no telephones. Second-hand typewriters are bought by the clerks with their own money, and used surreptitiously, as the law says that all documents should be written in long hand, with steel pen and ink, in order to be valid.

In a solemn speech in January 1963, one of Italy's highest magistrates complained that many judges in Rome lacked an office of their own, lacked desks, lacked chairs. The dearth of chairs was especially bothersome as lengthy proceedings could not be carried on standing up. Most controversies are settled privately by an agreement between the lawyers. Creditors often accept ruinous settlements, a token sum or a small part of what is owed them, rather than wait years for a larger amount. '*Pochi, maledetti, e subito*', is the rule, or 'few lire, damned, and on the spot'. Even such substitute arrangements are expensive. Poor people can scarcely afford them. They often prefer to be the victims of an injustice, submitting to obvious wrongs, and forget the whole thing, rather than go to all the trouble and expense of litigation. Some day, they hope, should the opportunity arise, they will get even somehow with their enemies. One never knows; '*Dio non paga il sabato*,' they say, 'God does not pay on Saturday'.

Bureaucracy should, of course, interpret and administer many of the laws. Bureaucrats should, as a start, at least know what the laws are. But they are badly paid, badly chosen, badly organized and badly treated. As a rule they are impatient, overbearing, hurried, ignorant, indifferent to other people's problems, insolent, and sometimes corrupt. There are a few, however, without whom the State apparatus would stop functioning altogether, who are intelligent and efficient. They know no better than the others what the laws are, but devise short cuts through the tangle of red tape and obsolete regulations; they keep the masses of paper slowly moving; they manage to solve some problems. There are two or three in every large bureau, who cheerfully do everybody's work. The others place their hats on the hat-stand, to prove they have not left the building, and go for walks, go home, or to another and better-paid job. The few good ones are obviously not enough. Things inevitably get delayed. Claims for damage done by Garibaldi and his Redshirts to property in Sicily in

1860, for instance, were still being paid in 1954, ninety-six years later, in lire which had lost all value and meaning, to heirs who barely remembered the reason why they were entitled to receive such pitifully small sums of money. Nobody thanks the good bureaucrats for their zeal, and they are not rewarded for their efficiency. State regulations say that all salaries are fixed solely according to seniority; the few good employees, their many bad and indifferent colleagues, all follow the same predetermined career from beginning to end; they get the same rises on the same day, are promoted and named *cavaliere* at the same time, and are pensioned at the same age. Nobody can ever be fired for inefficiency. A bureaucrat can only be fired for the most scandalous and flagrant crimes, like robbing the safe, purloining funds, or killing the *capo ufficio*.

Italians of all classes (unless they are important people with powerful friends) spend a substantial part of their time standing in angry queues, in front of office windows, or waiting endlessly merely to have some simple right recognized. What their rights are, nobody knows for sure. Uncertainty is used, in Italy, as *instrumentum regni*. The Republic has multiplied the bureaucracy of the old Kingdom, partly because the tasks of the modern State have increased, but also in order to give steady jobs to many supporters of the parties in power. When the country is separated into little self-governing regions, as the constitution commands, each little sovereign region will then have its own little government and will pass its own complicated laws. Each will be legitimately entitled to float loans, pile up debts, organize its own offices and regulations. The number of bureaucrats and queues will increase proportionately.

Fear is the fourth evil spirit. It is the offspring of the others, of poverty, ignorance and injustice, but more powerful, far-reaching and harmful than all of them. Fear lurks in every fold of Italian life, even where one does not suspect it. There is the fear of the lowly, the poor and the down-trodden, for their overbearing masters; the fear of the high-born, the mighty and the rich for their unreliable and mutinous subjects and the fear on two fronts of the middle class for both the mighty and the explosive masses. Fear silently settles almost all questions, exasperates political decisions, fans discontent into raging revolts. It dominates many men's lives, distorts characters, robs a firm man of his will, an honest man of his virtues, a free man of his independence, a sincere man of his love for truth, a proud man of his dignity, an intelligent man of logic and consistency. It forces many a loyal man to betray his friends and his convictions. It kills all hopes and teaches sordid resignation.

Italians first of all fear sudden and violent death. The vigorous passions of a turbulent and restless people are always ready to flare up unexpectedly like hot coals under the ashes. Italy is a blood-stained country. Almost every day of the year jealous husbands kill their adulterous wives and their lovers; about as many wives kill their adulterous husbands and their mistresses; fathers or older brothers kill the seducers of defenceless and guileless virgins; virgins kill the men trying to rape them; desperate young lovers commit suicide together in pairs, or separately one at a time. This steady massacre, inspired by love, which has been going on for centuries, has surely cost more lives than the many pestilences and catastrophes which have ravaged the country, and the wars fought on Italian soil.

Money, honour, prestige, politics and the desperate struggle for power or survival also exact their daily human sacrifices. Dismissed workers kill their employers; ruined businessmen kill themselves or their competitors; angry tax-payers kill the tax-collector; failed students kill their teachers; Mafia men kill their rivals, stool-pigeons, policemen and bystanders. Fascists kill Communists and Communists kill Fascists; rioting workers kill policemen and strike-breakers with stones, clubs, steel pipes wrapped in newspapers or stevedores' hooks; policemen kill rioting workers. Veteran Communist leaders are frightened by the violence of the younger men who, when called upon to stage a peaceful demonstration, smash everything in sight, overturn trams and cars, viciously beat up innocent bystanders, and get themselves senselessly killed.

The world of vice also demands its daily victims. Street-walkers are found dead with silk stockings wound tight round their necks or knives stuck in their ribs, on their unmade beds or in country lanes; fatherly homosexuals are found in public parks with their heads smashed in and pockets turned out; on deserted beaches, naked call-girls are found at dawn drowned in a few inches of water. Prostitutes kill their pimps, whom they usually primly call '*il mio fidanzato*', my fiancé; pimps and dope-peddlers kill each other over territorial disputes. Thousands die every year in the most devastating and spectacular car crashes in the western world. Others die in train accidents. Then there are recurring earthquakes, floods, landslides, tidal waves.

Even when violent death is not lurking in the shadows, when things look pleasant and peaceful and life seems secure, prosperous and easy, an Italian must remain on the alert and move with circumspection. The country is about as large as California, but less fertile and less endowed with natural resources. The inhabitants are incredibly numerous, fifty million of them. The competition at every level and in every field is intense, ruthless, and without pause. Jobs of all kinds were few until very recently. Now ordinary jobs are plentiful, but the good ones are still scarce. Those most sought after are still very rare. There is, as a result of all this, not much elbow-room. The country has often been compared to 'a plate of soup surrounded by too many spoons'. It is no wonder that table-manners are as bad as they are.

An Italian learns from childhood that he must keep his mouth shut and think twice before doing anything at all. Everything he touches may be a booby-trap; the next step he takes may lead him over a mine-field; every word he pronounces or writes may be used against him some day. He must also pay attention to the unknown people who may be photographed in a group with him at some ceremony or on an outing; at a later date the picture may turn out to be the damaging proof of complicity with scoundrels or of compromising political allegiances, and may eventually destroy him. In the last two years of the Fascist régime, prudent journalists, who did not dare or could not afford to leave their jobs, stopped signing their articles and bitterly said, '*Chi si firma è perduto*' ('Whoever signs is lost'), which was the paraphrase of one of Mussolini's arrogant slogans, '*Chi si ferma è perduto*' ('Whoever stops is lost'). Those who either defiantly signed their Fascist articles to the end or left their jobs for jail or the underground movement were not few but they were especially brave.

An Italian must know how to take care of himself and his kinsfolk

in the most outlandish circumstances and foresee all future emer-
gencies. Peasants somehow knew exactly what to do in front of
approaching armies, during the last war. 'Cattle and women up the
mountains,' they ordered as their forefathers had done so many times.
He must know that he must count only on himself alone. The
moment he relaxes and thinks good times are here to stay, he is lost.
Good times have never lasted long in Italy.

Fortune is notoriously fickle and history restless. '*Pourvou que ça
doure*,' Madame Letizia Bonaparte used to mutter in her Corsican
accent, when her son Napoleon ruled all Europe. Rachele Mussolini
repeated the same concept in different words and a Romagnuol
accent, during the twenty years of her husband's fortune. The old
king, Victor Emmanuel III, used to look with gloomy diffidence at
the vast crowds gathered to cheer him and said to his aide-de-camp
that about the same number would come to his execution and would
cheer just as lustily. He could never forget that his father, the 'good
king' Umberto, was shot and killed in 1900 by a man called Bresci,
an Italian anarchist from Patterson, New Jersey.

Fear has taught Italians to go through life as warily as experienced
scouts through the forest, looking ahead and behind, right and left,
listening to the smallest murmurs, feeling the ground ahead for
concealed traps, taking notice of signs on the bark of trees, of broken
twigs, and bent grass. Perhaps one of the best examples of their
capacity to come out alive from the most difficult ordeals is the life of
Palmiro Togliatti, the Communist leader. In the twenties, after
Mussolini marched on Rome, he went into exile and was sent to
Moscow as the Italian party representative in the Comintern. He
lived in the Hotel Lux, in Gorki Street, with all the international
leaders. He worked daily with the heroes of the Russian revolution,
Zinoviev, Bukharin, Stalin, Molotov, Trotski. They all befriended
him, the inconspicuous, little, bespectacled Italian, whose only
known weakness was running after the young girls who arrived from
the West, couriers or secretaries. He never left Moscow, except once
to go to Spain during the civil war and several times to Paris.

At the end, he emerged as one of the few survivors of his generation, the most authoritative interpreter of Marxism-Leninism in the
West. All the others who sat with him in the Comintern were dead,

most of them killed by Stalin, some by their disorderly and adventurous lives, only a few by simple old age. The circumspect and taciturn Togliatti, the son of the administrator of a State-owned orphan asylum for the sons of low bureaucrats on the island of Sardinia, was one of the few endowed with the knowledge necessary for survival. He knew which way the ideological wind was going to blow, who was going to be the next boss, who was really powerful and who only seemed to be, what friends to drop, what enemies to acquire, what snares to avoid. The arts of the ill-paid and insecure Italian cultural proletarian were more than a match for the Asian cunning, ruthlessness and cruelty in the top echelons of international Communism.

The rich and powerful are naturally afraid for their fortunes, privileges, honoured positions in society and, often enough, for their lives. They are so timid and insecure that most of them are always tempted to follow a demagogue who promises them solid and enduring security. This is nothing new. In the Middle Ages, the wealthy, known as the *popolo grasso*, or the fat people, were always the target for the hatred of the poor, known as the *popolo minuto* or *popolo magro*, the minute or lean people. The fat ones organized parties, ruthlessly played power politics and hired murderers to free them of their enemies. They built their *palazzi* as strong as fortresses. Still today the doors of some of these ancient mansions, now occupied mostly by harmless banks, insurance companies, government bureaus or foreign embassies, can be barricaded in a matter of minutes; the ground-floor windows are defended by stout iron grills; easy passage to the roof could allow men to pour boiling oil or molten lead on assailants; inconspicuous slits are predisposed here and there for the careful aiming of crossbows and guns. To the left of the main entrance of the Quirinale, which was once the Popes' seat as temporal sovereigns, later the King of Italy's royal palace, and now the President's official residence, there still stands a strong round tower, made of red bricks, with sufficient louvres cut in the thick walls for a well-aimed concentration of fire on an attacking crowd, if the need should again arise.

Wealthy Italians also know that they must always be ready for any emergency. A new law could suddenly expropriate some of their

property or all of it. A revolution may break out. They must be prepared to flee the country at any time. This has happened in the past
and may happen again: throughout the centuries exiles from some
city-states filled other Italian city-states, plotting endlessly for their
return at the head of friendly armies. The Liberals and Democrats
returned from exile with the Piedmontese armies during the Risorgimento, when the country was unified, in the nineteenth century; the
anti-fascist émigrés returned with the Allied armies at the end of the
last war. In 1944 many, compromised by Fascism or afraid of a
revolution, fled abroad or hid in convents and came back only when
things became safe again. Many are ready to go today: they keep
yachts in nearby ports or will make for the Swiss border in their fast
cars at the first rustling of the leaves.

The fear of the rich is nothing to that of the poor. They have no
protection, no private armies, no treasures at home or abroad, no
palazzi, no influential friends. They have but their miserable jobs
and their lives to lose. They do not like the way things are run and
have been run for a long time, but they are also frightened by change.
Even the revolutionaries are afraid of revolution: they talk and write
truculently of the next blood bath but do little to bring it about.
Stalin sneered at Togliatti for his timidity and once said to Tito:
'Togliatti will never start a revolution. Look at him. He is a lawyer, a
professor.' He thought the Italian was the best man in the Comintern
to write subtle and astutely worded documents and no more. The
poor know that they are the first victims of any crisis or disturbances,
even of those of their own making. When Fascism collapsed, after the
fury of the first few days, when Mussolini, his mistress, and many
members of his last government were shot, few of the great and
famous personages were arrested, tried, and executed, but thousands
of unknown little men were killed at random or arrested, put in concentration camps, tried and condemned to death as directly responsible for starting the war and provoking the ruin of their country.

*

Fear can also be detected behind the Italians' peculiar passion for
geometrical patterns, neat architectural designs, and symmetry in
general, which is part of their love for show—mainly the fear of the

uncontrollable and unpredictable hazards of life and nature; fear and also its shadow, a pathetic desire for reassurance. This compulsive predilection for regularity can be seen everywhere. It is only rarely utilitarian and seldom satisfies strictly functional needs, as almost always it is merely meant to please the eye and comfort the heart. Fruit and vegetable dealers spend precious minutes of the morning building fragile pyramids of their wares which they will have to demolish in the course of the day. The new maid will stubbornly remove every piece of furniture in your room from its accustomed place, every morning, to satisfy her ideal of symmetrical decorum. She will arrange the bibelots on the mantelpiece until it will look like the parody of an altar. Old gardens leave nothing to chance and unbridled nature. Their complicated patterns of hedges, gravel walks, fountains, statues, always strictly symmetrical, often puzzle the visitor, because they can only be fully admired by people flying over them in balloons, who see them as elaborate tapestries.

Streets, *piazze*, avenues, public parks, *corsi* have been planned in rigid symmetry; almost identical churches, like Chinese *potiches*, flank the opening of an avenue, several streets converge on the same obelisk or monument, similar or identical fountains beckon to each other at the two ends of a long *corso*. The cultivated countryside is always unnecessarily neat. Saplings in newly-planted woods are always set in military rows. The same obsession with regular patterns can also be traced in invisible things, in absurd rules and regulations which balance prohibitions to this group with prohibitions to that one; in the elaborate outlines of scholarly treatises, in the organizational charts of government bureaus and military units. The greatest Italian literary masterpiece, Dante's *Divina Commedia*, is so well-ordered that students reading it must buy a plan showing the exact position of Hell, Purgatory and Paradise. It is composed of an introductory canto and three parts, each of thirty-three cantos, each ending with the same word, '*stelle*'.

The word for this is *sistemazione*. To *sistemare* all things is considered to be the foremost, perhaps the unique, mission of man on earth. *Sistemare* and *sistemazione* cannot be exactly translated. The latest dictionary bravely attempts a few well-meaning suggestions, as inaccurate as random artillery shots. *Sistemare* means, according to its authors, 'to arrange, regulate, settle', and *sistemazione*, naturally enough, 'regularization, arrangement, settlement'. The English terms are not colloquial and are mainly used in official prose, editorials and scholarly dissertations. The Italian words are, on the contrary, as common as bread and cheese. They occur in everyday conversation. To begin with, *sistemare* means to defeat nature. Italians *sistemano* mountain torrents, marshy land, wild animals, spoiled children and unruly populations. '*Ti sistemo io*' is a much abused threat. It means, 'I will curb your rebellious instincts'.

The words are also often used in the sense of 'conquest of security'. *La sistemazione*, or, more frequently, *una sistemazione*, any kind of *sistemazione*, is the dream of most Italians. It does not necessarily signify hard work, responsibility, good wages, and the possibility of getting ahead, but often nothing more than a mediocre but durable position, protected from unforeseen events, with a predictable career, some moral authority, and a pension at the end. (The advice of a dying Roman father to his sons is famous. 'My sons,' he said, 'you must all try to have an occupation in life. Life without an occupation is contemptible and meaningless. But always remember this: you must never allow your occupation to degenerate into work.') Fathers all over Italy want to *sistemare* their sons, mothers want to *sistemare* their daughters, with good and steady husbands, not too rich or handsome, as rich and handsome husbands do not take easily to a definite *sistemazione*. The girls themselves, the pretty girls in bikinis who win beauty contests on summer beaches, and the ugly ones, clothed in black cotton smocks down to their ankles, who work in offices, do not often dream, like girls in other countries, of a career in the films, the intoxicating love of muscular gentlemen, a wealthy and nomadic existence. They prefer *una sistemazione*. International courtesans as well as tired street-walkers want to *sistemarsi* where their past is unknown, they can pose as widows and respectably bring up their illegitimate children. Industrialists often dream of being able to *sistemare* competition, by establishing strong cartels and iron-bound agreements. The royal government before the war used to *sistemare* the colonies: pioneers, gamblers, adventurers, soldiers of fortune and speculators were strictly forbidden to go there.

The passion for *sistemazione* is also curiously common among the rebellious non-conformists and the outlaws. The *bandito* Giuliano, who flourished in Sicily just after the war, gave proper military titles to his henchmen and was surrounded by a primitive but rigid etiquette. *Poètes maudits* and avant-garde writers, painters, and film directors who shock the world with their daring, often marry good cooks and good housekeepers, who raise their children well and try to save money; the food they eat is never avant-garde. After the March on Rome, in 1922, almost all the Blackshirts, rebels who sang blood-curdling songs about their contempt for death, the authorities, laws and conventions ('Life thou art my friend, death thou art my mistress'), brandished hand-grenades, daggers and machine-guns, and had skulls and bones embroidered on their chests, had one main ambition, besides establishing a new régime, that of becoming regular bureaucrats, with a good and steady salary and a pension in the end. It was nothing new. In 1860, when the Redshirts of Garibaldi reached Naples, after having miraculously liberated all of Sicily and Southern Italy in a few months, many of them also demanded to be *sistemati* in the regular army. Some of the brave partisans who heroically contributed to the defeat of the Germans in Italy also requested to be enrolled as policemen, firemen, soldiers or bureaucrats, as soon as the war ended.

*

Some of this national obsession can also be found, in various degrees, in the ideologies of the political parties most popular in Italy, those which have obtained the largest percentage of votes in every election since the war. They are, reading from left to right, the Communists, the Socialists, the Christian Democrats, and the Fascists, or, as they prefer to call themselves, the *Movimento Sociale Italiano*. Together, these now represent about 85 per cent of the electorate. None are especially interested in freedom. Fascists, Communists, and left-wing revolutionary Socialists notoriously deride liberty as a silly and sentimental weakness of their enemies, a *petit bourgeois* prejudice, which can be utilized to provoke disorders, to disrupt the functioning of the State and carry on preparations for their particular revolutions with greater ease. Christian Democrats and right-wing

Socialists, on the other hand, praise liberty, mention it a number of times in every speech, exalt it in their anthems and marching songs; the Christian Democrats even have its Latin name inscribed on their escutcheon, '*Libertas*'. But when these parties' ideals are analysed, they appear so confined by limitations, provisos, theological preoccupations, controls, class prejudices and arbitrary shackles, that one must conclude they are really wary of liberty, want only a little of it, at best, safely diluted, and, at times, none at all.

All mass parties of right and left (and a good many Christian Democrats) dream of different but all equally stable futures, with little or few surprises; societies in which people will be divided along well-defined horizontal strata, as neatly as the oranges and apples in the fruit and vegetable dealers' pyramids, each man knowing where his place is and will be, from his birth to the end of his life; decisions of every kind, private, moral, cultural, economic, political, taken by wise leaders who alone know what is good for the country, as they alone possess all the information; leaders selected not by the blind and haphazard choice of the voting booth, but, more intelligently, through the secret intrigues, the infighting and the ruthless struggles of power politics.

The people, these parties promise, will no longer have to worry about abstract ideas, policies, intricate and technical problems, of which they know little and in which they are not interested, anyway. Bureaucracy will do most of the work. Naturally enough, Italians who vote *en masse* for these parties are too wise not to know that such ideals might presumably function in more efficient and disciplined countries but never in their own. They know that, should one of these parties gain absolute power, it would at most be able to super-impose on Italian reality a shining façade of new buildings, parades, uniforms, celebrations, mass meetings, speeches and slogans, under which the shoddy life would imperturbably go on, the clever ones making money and having an easy time, all others carrying on as well as they can. It has happened a number of times in the past and would almost certainly happen again. They also know that the idea of en-trusting the future entirely to bureaucracy, if reasonable in other countries, is madness in their own, where the bureaucrats have always shown themselves the least able to run anything efficiently, honestly, and equitably. Nevertheless, the hope of defeating fear, the mirage of a final *sistemazione* to end all *sistemazioni*, the dream of constructing a perfect and everlasting *papier mâché* State, is so fascinating that they keep on voting for the same mass parties election after election.

CHAPTER SEVEN

COLA DI RIENZO OR THE OBSESSION OF ANTIQUITY

THERE ARE, throughout Italian history, many characters who personify the national reliance on make-believe as an instrument of policy. But only one of them can be considered the Italian hero in all his perfection, who possessed all the typical attributes in their utmost purity. These are: literary, artistic, vague and contradictory ideas, practically unrelated to the contemporary world; the vast ambition to dominate all Italy, to re-establish the Empire and, in the end, to dominate the rest of Europe; the dream of building a 'new State', inspired by ancient history, in which peace, law and virtue would prevail; a genuine love for his people, his country and their glorious past, a love so intense it could be confused with self-love, as if he identified himself with Italy and the Italians; and the desire to avenge his people's ruin and humiliation, which he attributed solely to the wickedness of others. This man recklessly flung challenges to all the great powers of the day, tried to awaken his countrymen to a new sense of their mission, and dragged them reluctantly into wars neither he nor they were prepared to fight.

At first he frightened enemies, comforted friends, aroused the admiration of some of the best contemporary minds, and enchanted the multitudes. He was the greatest orator of his times, carried on all public business from a balcony, addressing himself to the crowds massed in front of him. He seemed irresistible. His principal device was showmanship: the use of symbolism, pageantry, ceremonies, parades on horse and on foot, uniforms, sonorous titles for himself and his followers. He was driven once from power. Brought back by foreign soldiers, he was killed, in the end, by the very people he had tried to make great and powerful. His body was hung from the feet, head downwards, in a public square, mocked and jeered by the same people who had praised him as their saviour and applauded him only a few days before. His name was Cola di Rienzo, or Nicholas son of Lawrence.

He was born in Rome, in 1313 or 1314, in the Regola quarter, near the church of Saint Thomas, hard by the Ghetto. His father was an innkeeper, his mother a washerwoman. (Mussolini's father had been a blacksmith at first but later opened a wineshop. Garibaldi's mother had been a washerwoman.) Cola liked to think he was of better blood than the rest of his family. He boasted he was the bastard son of Henry VII, the emperor who had been visiting Rome at the appropriate time and had been a guest at Lorenzo's inn, incognito, for a few days. Cola's bearing and appearance confirmed his pretensions. As a young man he was handsome, bore himself with dignity, spoke persuasively, enlivening his speech with suitable quotations and poetic images. 'On his lips,' says the contemporary chronicler, 'laughter had a fantastic quality'. He was brought up in the country, at Anagni, after the death of his mother, by some relatives, but came back when he was twenty, a brooding youth, lost in the contemplation of ancient ruins, the reading of Latin inscriptions, and the interpretation of freshly unearthed statuary.

He collected antiquities, especially cammei, some of which he later mentioned in his writings: the portraits of Scipio, Caesar, Metellus, Marcellus and Fabius. He read what classic authors he could find, Livy, Sallust, Cicero, Seneca and Valerius Maximus. He also studied the Bible. Till the last days of his life, he knew by heart whole passages from all these books. The pagan writers and the Christian texts and legends formed in his self-taught mind a strange confusion of medieval mysticism and Roman glory. He often spoke to the people, at random, gathering them around him in the streets, and stirring them with the evocation of their past and their present humiliation. 'Where are now these Romans?' he would exclaim. 'Their virtue, their justice, their power? Why was I not born in those happy times?'

The times could not have been sadder. Rome was in a desperate condition. It had been abandoned by the Popes in 1305, after Clement V had preferred to settle in Avignon rather than face his own rebellious subjects. No effective government was left in the city. Without law, the people, high and low, defended themselves as best they could from robbers, arsonists, rapists and murderers. Each of the great noble families had a fortress in the town and impregnable castles in the surrounding territories. The Orsini owned Castel Sant'Angelo and dominated the quarters around Monte Giordano, Pompey's theatre, and Campo dei Fiori. The citadel of the Colonnas was near the church of the Holy Apostles, by the Quirinale hill, where they still live today; they dominated the Corso all the way to the Piazza del Popolo. They all maintained private armies of horse and foot soldiers, led by sons, grandsons, and other relations. They imposed their own law and order within their jurisdiction, fighting interminable wars among themselves. When things went well, they lived in Rome with great pomp, but when the odds were against them, or when the sultry *scirocco* became oppressive, they retreated to the country, with all their women, children, treasures, cattle and retinues.

Poor Romans without means purchased protection and peace by giving their allegiance to the noble family ruling over their part of the town. When a Roman moved, he shifted his loyalties with the furniture. Humble commoners had to serve in the little private armies, from time to time, but could always ask for help, when necessary, to defeat an attack or, if aid was slow, to avenge a wrong and carry out retaliation. Of course, human life had little value. Women were raped, houses burned down, convents raided, cattle abducted, money stolen as a matter of course. Every morning corpses were swept from the streets and thrown into the Tiber with the refuse. The physical condition of the buildings was just as desperate. The Basilica of Saint John Lateran was roofless; the Milvian bridge in ruins, destroyed by the Orsini who owned and controlled the only other bridge, near Castel Sant'Angelo; the belfry of Saint Peter's had been devastated by lightning; many churches, bridges and papal *palazzi* were abandoned in various degrees of decay, damaged by fire, old age, the weather, sacking and the repeated pilfering of stonework, statuary and tiles.

In 1342, young Cola, the promising orator, was sent by his countrymen to Avignon as a member of an embassy to the Pope. He harangued

Clement VI, pointing out that as long as law and order were in the hands of those who had least interest in defending them, the unruly barons, the city would know no peace. He was especially keen on the subject, as he had recently lost a brother, killed by unknown murderers, and this private grief had turned his thoughts to the ills of the city. His vigorous words in defence of the people did not please the members of the baronial families who composed the rest of the embassy and whose relatives were among the members of the papal court. He was thrown out into the streets, in disgrace, and lived in Avignon a few months as a pauper. But his brilliant ideas, his ornate mind, his culture and his eloquence seduced the poet Petrarch, who was more or less in love with the same dream, that of reviving the glories of the past and re-establishing in Rome the capital of united Italy and of all Europe. The two men strengthened each other's convictions and became life-long friends. Thanks to Petrarch's intercession, and the fact that the old Pope had died in the meantime, Cola returned to favour, was named an apostolic notary and sent back to Rome.

His job was one which most Italians fancy: he had a steady income of five gold florins a month, some authority, underlings to do the real work and time to pursue his private studies. Cola walked about, met all sorts of people, meditated on the causes of the decay of Rome, denounced them, made beautiful speeches that moved his hearers to tears. He refused to write with a goose quill, as he thought it was beneath the dignity of an apostolic notary, and had a pen made for him out of silver, possibly inventing the first metallic pen in history. Above all, he cultivated a following among the common people, the tradesmen, the merchants, the petty bourgeoisie, the low clergy, the intellectuals, tied together loosely by their admiration for the leader and dissatisfaction with existing conditions.

He called himself at the time, 'the tribune of widows, orphans and the poor'. He was possibly also the inventor of the political cartoon: he often had pictures painted on suitable walls, depicting complicated allegories, to drive home some particular point, each female figure clearly labelled Rome, Christendom, Italy, Religion, the Empire and so forth. Noblemen often invited him to dinner in their town forts, to make him talk of their sins. One night, at the house of

Giovanni Colonna, he boasted: 'One day I shall be a great lord or emperor.' Then, pointing to each in turn, he went on: 'I shall imprison you, behead you, quarter you, torture you and hang you.' They all laughed uproariously when he said these words, not suspecting that that was exactly what he was going to attempt to do before long.

The night of Saturday, May 9, 1347, he spent in the church of Sant'Angelo in Peschiera, listening to twenty masses dedicated to the Holy Ghost. In the morning he emerged bare-headed but fully armed. The impressive pageantry was carefully staged. Surrounded by his armed companions and protected by a hundred hired soldiers, preceded by four flags, he marched on the Campidoglio, the seat of the nominal and ineffective government of the city, a few minutes away. The first flag, dedicated to liberty, was red (it was perhaps the first appearance of a revolutionary red flag in history) with gold-embroidered letters and figures, Rome sitting on two lions, holding the globe in one hand, a palm in the other, and the legend *Roma caput mundi*. The second flag was white, dedicated to justice, with Saint Paul wearing a crown and carrying a sword. The third was also white, with Saint Peter holding the keys, symbols of concord and peace. The fourth was the banner of Saint George, so old and ragged it had to be carried in a wooden box on top of a pole.

The cortège, soon joined by loafers, street urchins, beggars and inquisitive Romans, arrived on the hill and occupied the building by surprise. Nobody was defending it. Most of the noble families had heard about the secret plot but thought it was a comical invention of the mad notary, not to be taken seriously. The most powerful, the Colonna clan, was out of town. They had gone *en masse* to Tarquinia to procure wheat which was scarce at the time. Stefano the elder, the head of the family, who was then about eighty years old, returned at full speed, a few days later. When he heard the news, he disdainfully said: 'If this madman continues to bother me, I shall have him thrown from the windows of the Campidoglio.'

Cola went to the Campidoglio balcony, after seizing the building, and spoke. He was surrounded by armed men, his flags, relatives, henchmen and followers. He made a memorable speech on the wretchedness of Romans, their past glories and the urgent need to establish a firm government. The crowd roared its approval. He then asked one of his relatives to read aloud the new constitution, which he had prepared. Finally he stepped forward and asked the people who they wanted to elect as the head of the new state. 'You,' they shouted, waving their arms frantically.

He immediately got down to business. He first assumed a high-sounding title, 'Nicholas, the severe and merciful, tribune of liberty, peace and justice, liberator of the holy Roman republic'. Then he organized a people's militia, of 360 horse and 1,300 foot, civilians from all quarters of the city who were to rush with their arms to the Capitol when they heard the great bell boom. He proceeded to hang robbers and murderers, including a few prominent noblemen, and decreed that henceforth no private forts and fortified emplacements were to be tolerated within the walls, that all noble families were to be held responsible for the safety of wayfarers along the roads crossing their lands and that they were forbidden to give asylum to bandits and criminals of any kind. All bridges, narrow passes, gates and fortified emplacements in Rome itself were to be manned by the people's militia. Those that were not considered necessary were to be demolished.

Whoever did not obey his orders was to be exiled to his country estates and was never to set foot in Rome. Two weeks later, to make sure, he summoned all heads of noble families to his presence. Most of them appeared. He received them dressed in a scarlet cloak over his armour, the symbol of his newly-acquired authority, and led them to an altar in front of which he had placed the insignia of the Church. He asked them all to swear over the Bible and a consecrated host that they would avoid all aggression against him, his government, his soldiers and the people at large. They gave their oaths, thus accepting implicitly the end of feudal rule, the restoration of the 'republic', the legitimacy of his authority and the validity of the new constitution. He made the anti-feudal revolution obvious to all when he prohibited commoners from giving oaths of allegiance to noble lords, putting escutcheons on private houses or shops for their protection, and addressing noblemen as My Lord, or *Mio Signore*.

Things went well enough for a time. 'Never perhaps has the energy and effect of a single mind been more remarkably felt than in the sudden, though transient, reformation of Rome,' noted Gibbon, who was born a few centuries too soon to witness similar sudden and equally transient reformations of Rome. 'A den of robbers was converted to the discipline of a camp or convent: patient to hear, swift to redress, inexorable to punish, his tribunal was always accessible to the poor and stranger; nor could birth, or dignity, or the immunities of the Church, protect the offender or his accomplices.' An anonymous contemporary chronicler understandably exaggerated when he wrote: 'The woods began to rejoice that they were no longer infested with robbers; the oxen began to plough; the pilgrims visited the sanctuaries; the roads and inns were replenished with travellers; trade, plenty and good faith were restored in the markets; and a purse of gold could be exposed without danger in the midst of the highway.'

Cola, after a few weeks of peaceful rule, finally began to reveal a little more of his plans. His first aim was to unite all Italy into one great federation under his leadership. This he proceeded to do not by waging wars or carrying on vast political intrigues but by correspondence, so to speak, by sending swift and trusted messengers with noble letters in eloquent Latin prose to the governments of the many Italian cities, republics and small principalities. These men travelled on foot, unarmed, carrying a white stick in their hand for recognition, and were welcomed almost everywhere with great demonstrations of joy. Friendly and respectful, but evasive, answers soon began to be received, followed by ambassadors of princes and free cities. The low-born notary assumed more and more the dignity of a legitimate official sovereign and power began to corrupt him. His titles became more sonorous and florid, and embraced more and more territory as the time passed. He was known at this time as 'Nicholas, severe and merciful, deliverer of Rome, defender of Italy, friend of mankind, and of liberty, peace and justice, tribune august'.

He rode a white horse about the city, a privilege reserved for popes and royal princes; his clothes were of white silk embroidered with gold, the papal colours; in front of him walked one hundred foot soldiers from his own native quarter, Regola; over his head flew always the great banner of the republic, designed by him, a sun with a circle of stars and a dove with olive branches. He went once to

Saint Peter's with great pomp and people came from all quarters to line his route and admire him. The cortège was preceded by a detachment of his cavalry, well-dressed and armed, then came officials of his government, followed by a man carrying a cup of gold, then more cavalry, musicians on horses with silver trumpets and tymbals, and heralds. One man carried a naked sword, another threw gold and silver coins to the populace, with an assistant on either side holding bags filled with money, something which had been seen before only when emperors entered Rome.

The tribune rode alone, dressed in half yellow and half green velvet lined with fur. In his right hand he carried the rod of justice, a sceptre of polished steel, crowned with a globe and a cross of gold which enclosed a small fragment of the true cross. Behind him a man kept the great banner raised over his head. At his sides fifty men from the village of Vitorchiano (the faithful allies of Rome who still today take part in all municipal ceremonies) walked, dressed in furs, carrying halberds, and looking, as a contemporary witness says, 'like armed bears'. A cortège of friends and supporters came last. At about the same time, his plebeian relations all changed names and professions; his uncle, a barber, dressed like a knight and called himself Messer Rosso. In July Cola began dating his missives according to a new era, Year One of the Restoration of the Roman Republic. He went no further, as his rule lasted only seven months, from May till Christmas, 1347. Mussolini, who imitated this practice six centuries later, was able to go farther. He proudly wrote, on a photograph he gave a journalist three days before his death, 'Anno XXIII E.F.' or Fascist Era.

The first really ambitious show Cola staged was to celebrate his acceptance of knighthood in the church of Saint John Lateran, on August 1. It was a bizarre show, as it was weighed down by too many allegories at the same time: it was to surround him with the mystic medieval halo of ecclesiastical consecration, to make him a nobleman, and, at the same time, to revive imperial Roman memories; but especially it was meant to establish, with the greatest solemnity, a turning point in history, a revolution in contemporary political principles, a new age. An interminable cortège went from the Campidoglio to the old basilica on July 31, through streets decorated with flowers, arches of foliage, and precious tapestries, between vast applauding crowds. Jugglers entertained the onlookers, street singers sang songs, poems were declaimed by popular poets, musicians blew trumpets, played drums and strummed lutes. Cola led the procession on his white horse, followed by ecclesiastical, civil, and military dignitaries in rich clothes, each group with its own banner. Cola's wife came on foot, attended by gentlewomen: flowers were strewn in front of them. Some of the foreign ambassadors changed their clothes several times along the way, throwing what they discarded to the populace.

When the parade reached the church, everybody was dismissed until the next day. The tribune disappeared from sight. Inside he took a ritual bath in the porphyry sarcophagus in which, legend says, the Emperor Constantine was miraculously cured of his leprosy by Pope Sylvester. This was considered at once a shocking sacrilege and was later used as one of the charges for Cola's excommunication; he merely meant it as a symbol of his new power, which drew its confused strength from Christian, feudal and ancient Roman roots. He then lay down on a luxurious state-bed, prepared near the high altar (one leg gave way under his weight; the incident was taken as an omen of bad luck), and slept till morning.

The following day he was knighted with a pompous ritual of his own invention. At the end, he showed himself to the people from the balcony in a majestic attitude, wearing an imperial purple robe with gold spurs (the mark of knighthood and noble birth) and carrying a naked sword. Back in the church he finally revealed to his guests and the public the meaning of the celebration and for the first time disclosed his political plans in their entirety. Rising from his throne, he proclaimed in a loud voice: 'We summon to our tribunal Pope Clement, and command him to reside in his diocese of Rome. We also summon the sacred college of cardinals. We also summon the two pretenders, Charles of Bohemia and Louis of Bavaria, who style themselves emperors.[1] We likewise summon all the electors of Germany to inform us on what pretence they have usurped the inalienable rights of the Roman people, to elect the lawful sovereign of the

---

[1] They were both claiming, at the time, to be the one and only legitimate emperor; one was supported by German feudal chiefs and the other by the Pope.

empire.' Unsheathing his new sword, he brandished it three times in three directions, repeating 'This too is mine!' each time.

The revolutionary significance of his words and gestures could not be clearer. He wanted nothing less than to re-establish Rome as the official capital of the world, *caput mundi*, make the Roman people once more arbiters of their own destiny, and revive the Roman empire in its ancient form. He wanted the Pope reduced to the subordinate position of bishop of the eternal city and head of a worldwide spiritual organization, and no longer to be temporal sovereign of his Italian possessions; he branded both emperors as usurpers, since only the Roman people could elect a legal one. And who could he be? He could only be one man, the present head of the Roman republic, the people's choice, in other words, himself, Cola, the son of Lawrence the innkeeper. Without visible force with which to fight and defeat his enemies, he had at one stroke challenged all the available powers of the day, the Roman nobles and feudalism, the Pope and the Church, Germany, and the Empire.

Later that day he offered his guests and the Roman citizens one of the largest and most expensive banquets ever seen in those days of chronic famines. The Lateran Palace had been transformed for the occasion: walls had been torn down, new stairways built, courtyards, porticoes and rooms spread with tables, eighty kitchens installed to prepare all kinds of elaborate food. Red wine flowed from one and water from the other nostril of the bronze horse of the equestrian statue of Marcus Aurelius, which was then in front of the Lateran Palace and was still believed to be the statue of Constantine, the first Christian emperor. In the middle of the main dining-room an immense cake was built, shaped like a castle, from whose windows and doors new dishes appeared as if by magic.

A subsequent day was appointed for another dazzling show, his coronation. That ceremony too was overloaded with fantastic meanings: it adopted some of the features from the traditional coronation of poets on the Campidoglio and some from the coronation of ancient Roman heroes when they were carried in triumph through Rome. Six crowns were successively placed on Cola's head by six eminent priests, representing the gifts of the Holy Ghost, which then apparently numbered only six and not yet seven. A ruffian in ragged clothes tore each crown except the last from his head as soon as it was placed there. He too was a badly remembered relic of the past (in the old days, the soldiers and the people were free to jeer and address irreverent remarks and insults to the military leader who was being carried in triumph), and symbolized the impermanent quality of all worldly honours. The last crown made of silver, which the ragged pauper did not take away, was placed on his head by the prior of the Hospital of the Holy Ghost (it still exists; its telephone number is 652257) who also handed him a sceptre. Finally, old Goffredo degli Scotti, the nobleman who had knighted him a few days before, gave him a silver globe on which was a cross and said: 'Most high tribune, accept and exercise justice, give us peace and liberty.'

That day Cola's ambitions reached their maddest point. Not content with having ideally conquered, for the time being, a position higher than the Pope's and the Emperor's, he dared to compare himself to Jesus Christ. In a little speech he alluded to his age, thirty-three, the age of the Saviour at His death, as a sign that for him too a great fate was in store. A holy monk, who had been one of his supporters, wept bitterly at this and said: 'Now is our master cast down from heaven. I never saw a man so proud. By the aid of the Holy Ghost he has driven the tyrants from the city without drawing a sword. Why is he so arrogant and ungrateful to the Most Holy?'

All the preceding weeks the chancery had been working frantically, preparing letters for foreign princes of ever-ascending rank, and studying their replies. Cola even sent an embassy to the King of England and one to the King of France directing them to stop the war between them, as it had been doing 'great damage to all Christendom'. A third letter was sent to the Pope in Avignon, commanding him to reconcile the two sovereigns without delay. An embassy arrived from King Louis of Hungary, asking Cola to intervene in his favour in a difficult family quarrel: his brother, King Andrew, husband of Queen Joan of Naples, had been murdered and he asked for permission to cross the Roman territory with his army in order to avenge the wrong done to his family. Another embassy arrived from Queen Joan, almost at the same time, asking the tribune to protect her and to intercede on her behalf with the King of Hungary. Cola promised to do what he could, inserting in his replies admirable and rare quotations from the Bible. To and from all Italian cities went messages, in preparation for a solemn congress of lawyers to be convened in Rome, which would proclaim in erudite juridical terms the rights of the Roman people (all Italians had, meanwhile, been made honorary Roman citizens). Once the supremacy of the city was clearly established by a congress of eminent lawyers, lawyer Cola had no doubt that nobody would ever dare challenge it.

To consolidate his rule, he invited all the heads of the noble families to dinner. Old Stefano Colonna, at the table, felt the hem of the tribune's dress, and said with contempt: 'It would be better for you to wear the honest clothes of the common people rather than this pompous apparel.' Cola became furious, had them all imprisoned, ordered the great hall decorated with red and white hangings (the colours suitable for a sentence of death), summoned the executioner and sent a priest to confess the prisoners. (Stefano Colonna refused the administrations of the confessor, disdainfully saying he was not yet ready to die.) But then Cola, as usual, became frightened at what he was about to do and changed his mind. He set them all free in exchange for a pledge not to break the peace, gave them gifts, said it had all been a joke and led them in mounted procession through the city as a public sign of reconciliation. This was the fatal mistake that destroyed him. The contemporary chronicler knew it as well as the people when he said: 'This man has lighted a fire he will not be able to put out.' (The chronicler drove the point home with an earthy proverb, which cannot be printed here in English: '*Che vale petere e poi culo stringere? Faticasi le natiche.*') From that day on, the feudal chiefs of Rome knew they could not trust Cola and had better call their soldiers to arms, man their castles and prepare for war.

The war eventually destroyed him. The Roman nobles were the key to his designs. He was forced to fight them to keep his power in Rome. Without the support of Rome he would lose the support of the outlying districts. Without those, his ambitions in Italy were ended. Without a united Italy he could not face the Pope or the Emperor or bend either to his wishes with the aid of the other. He fought a desultory and amateurish war against the noble families, with some incidental successes, but could not hope ever to destroy his enemy, comfortably ensconced in so many fortified towns, far from the city.

The people, in the end, tired of his madness, his expenses, his inconclusive warring, the pomp, the ceremonies, the show, the empty eloquence, and the scarcity of food, longed for the bad old days, before the 'new State' was established, the days which suddenly seemed peaceful and prosperous in retrospect. They mutinied. Scared by an unimportant but noisy street riot, without trying to defend himself and his government, he left the city at the head of the few soldiers who had remained faithful to him. It was December 5, 1347.

Cola returned seven years later, on August 1, 1354, at the head of a mercenary army led by two French captains, the brothers Monréal. He had wandered through Europe as a pilgrim, finally visited the emperor in Prague, who promptly imprisoned him as a dangerous revolutionary and heretic and sent him in chains to the Pope. In the end, after much writing of eloquent Latin letters and much skilful debating, he gained the emperor's trust and friendship and the Pope's pardon. He was sent back to Italy with the papal legate, the Spanish cardinal Gil d'Albornoz, who was to reconquer and pacify the papal states for the Church. Cola offered to go ahead of the main army to Rome where he had heard the people were anxiously awaiting him. In fact he was acclaimed as the liberator. The Roman cavalry welcomed him along the road, at Monte Mario, waving olive branches. The people of the city cheered him, 'as if,' says the chronicler, 'he were Scipio Africanus.'

He was led once more to the Campidoglio through streets decorated with tapestries and with gold and silver ornaments. He spoke again from the balcony and again the people waved their arms and shouted his name. But he was no longer the same man. He was flabby and fat. 'In the society of Germans and Bohemians he is said to have contracted the habits of intemperance and cruelty,' says Gibbon. 'Adversity had chilled his enthusiasm without fortifying his reason or virtue.' He had become avaricious, cowardly, suspicious and cruel. He often had his enemies, or those he suspected of being his enemies, condemned to death after a mock trial, sometimes only in order to confiscate their wealth. He again waged insensate and inconclusive wars against the well-fortified barons, as he had done seven years before, until he had again spent all his money, the mercenary soldiers were on the verge of mutiny, and the people of Rome once more ready to revolt. He imposed heavy taxes on them, spent public money freely for himself, his friends and his mad schemes and did nothing to prevent trade from languishing and famine from tormenting the city. On October 8 sporadic riots broke out. The people were shouting 'Viva il popolo!' They gathered at the foot of the Capitol hill, crying 'Death to the traitor Cola!'

Cola was at first unimpressed. He refused to have the bell of the Commune sounded and went on the balcony to reassure and placate the crowd; dressed as a knight, with the great banner of the republic as usual over his head, he lifted his arm, asking for silence in which to speak. The shouting increased. Stones were thrown at him. His hand was pierced by an arrow. He hurried back into the building, frightened and undecided on what to do next. He repeatedly and mechanically put on his helmet as if meaning bravely to face the revolt in arms with his men, then took it off as if to change his clothes and flee. Meanwhile the people were setting fire to the palaces: flames were already devouring the wooden stairway. Cola finally made up his mind. He entrusted his life to his acting ability. He took off his armour, cut his beard with scissors, painted his face black, put on the old clothes of a gardener, took on his back a mattress, to protect himself from flying embers, and sneaked out of the building.

He had already passed the last door, and was mingling with the crowd, shouting in heavy peasant dialect, 'Down with the traitor!' and 'Let's go upstairs to steal, there are many things there!' when somebody saw the golden bracelets still around his wrists and the rings on his fingers. He was recognized and killed. His dead body was struck time and again with pikes, spears, lances and pitchforks, then dragged along the Corso, to San Marcello, where it was hung by the feet. Two days and two nights it was left there, stoned and spat upon by jeering boys, until it was finally burned near the ruins of Augustus's mausoleum over a bonfire of dried thistle.

*

It was easy for Gibbon to dismiss Cola as just another 'mixture of the knave and madman'. We now know better. Mad knaves abound at all times in all countries, but few, very few indeed manage to leave their permanent marks on history. To do that they have to be more than just insane adventurers, although, as a rule, they must be that, too. They must, also, be the unconscious and docile instruments of the gods, unknowingly attuned to the secret harmonies of the universe, somewhat like the people who, the Neapolitans say, can 'dare i numeri', give numbers; these are usually old monks, beggars, idlers, ragged women, rag-pickers who do not know and could not tell you what numbers will be extracted the following Saturday in the national lottery but somehow infallibly indicate them. You must follow them and observe them closely. A few casual words or absent-minded actions of theirs, if properly interpreted according to ancient methods, may at times reveal the correct answer and enrich you.

Men like Cola are unconscious interpreters of their times and have an intuitive and prophetic understanding of what their countrymen long for. You must ignore their explanations, which are often ridiculous. You must watch them. Listen to them talk to the crowds. They speak as if they are giving words to the crowd's own dumb sentiments. They awaken an echo in men's hearts. They drive them to great deeds. People willingly die for such men, good people who do not like to die and would not die for simple knaves and madmen. Men like that somehow identify the great themes history is going to propose like dowsers feeling secret veins of water underground. Cola's ideas were a disorderly and laughable hodgepodge. But inadvertently he managed to put his finger on most of the great motifs which would dominate Italian history for centuries and most of which still dominate it today.

He sensed the necessity for popular government, justice (or the same law for every man), good administration, order, liberty and the end of bloody feudal anarchy, not so much because it was bloody and feudal, but because it was inefficient. He wanted to give Italy a unified government five centuries before the Italians managed to do so. He learned what so many were sadly to learn later to their cost, that every time a man was to attempt to solve the Italian political problem he risked heresy and excommunication. Cola understood that Italy had to be unified and strong in order to fight on two fronts, against the foreign oppressors, the Germans' imperial authority on one side, and on the other, the Church's political power and the

Popes' temporal aspirations. He was considered by many enthusiastic scholars, centuries later, to have been one of Italy's earliest patriots, a prophet of national ideals, a forerunner of the Risorgimento, second only to Dante, Petrarch, and Machiavelli.

Cola was Italian. He spoke eloquently, wore handsome clothes, invented flags, staged the most tremendous feats and ceremonies of his day, sent elegant letters to all and sundry, put his trust in fragile juridical formulas and historical precedents, but neglected to build a real republic, with a real army, appoint good captains, secure sufficient funds for military campaigns, draw up suitable plans for defeating or intimidating his enemies. He never for a moment suspected that it was not enough to build a life-like persuasive façade. The façade and reality, for him too, were one and the same thing.

As a result, his achievement had the practical flimsiness and spiritual durability of a work of art. That is why, perhaps, he appealed mostly to artists, to such men as Byron (who dedicated a part of *Childe Harold* to him), Bulwer Lytton (who wrote the novel *Rienzi, the Last of the Roman Tribunes*), Richard Wagner (who composed the opera *Rienzi*), and Gabriele d'Annunzio, who spent precious hours compiling Cola's biography, the only historical work he ever did. Cola also appealed to other 'knaves and madmen' of destiny. In Napoleon's carriage, as he trundled his way back from Moscow, there was a copy of a book called *Conjuration de Nicholas, dit de Rienzi*, by the abbé Jean Antoine du Cerceau, printed in Paris, in 1733.

CHAPTER EIGHT

MUSSOLINI OR THE LIMITATIONS OF SHOWMANSHIP

Nobody knows his servants as badly as their master; nobody knows his subjects as badly as their ruler; because they do not show themselves as they do to others; they always strive to disguise themselves and to seem different from what they truly are.

FRANCESCO GUICCIARDINI

A N OLD socialist from Bologna, Aldo Parini, a modest man, who had been a good friend of Benito Mussolini in the early days, asked to see him just before the last war. Il Duce received him at the Palazzo Venezia. Parini had nothing to ask for himself; he had a job, and was no longer interested, he said, in politics. He pleaded with the dictator, however, to help some of their ancient comrades, brave and honest men who had fought, with them, the socialist battles at the beginning of the century, and who were now penniless, unable to get a job, and persecuted by the police. Could he not give orders to leave them in peace so that they could make a living? Could he not perhaps assign the oldest and poorest of them a small pension out of secret funds? Mussolini liked playing the magnanimous and generous prince. He reassured his old comrade that all he was asking for would be done, and took down the names of the needy socialists. Then he started talking about things in general.

'He was dressed in a white linen suit. It was summer. His face was sunburned,' the old socialist told me years later, after Mussolini's death. 'He swaggered, made faces, pushed his chin forward, bent his knees, hands on hips, as cavalry officers used to do, all in good humour. He recalled some forgotten mutual friends. He boasted about the achievements of his régime. I said nothing. Then he told me: "You are a stubborn fool, not becoming one of us. Why don't you join the Fascist Party ?" I felt that if I had said yes, I was tired of living apart from the rest of my countrymen, he would have given me a party card then and there. It would have solved many problems. I wanted, however, to be true to my youth, and said no, I was happy as I was and needed nothing. He insisted. Finally I blurted out what was in my mind. I said: "This régime of yours, I am afraid, will end badly. Such things always do. Benito, you'll die like Cola di Rienzo." At these words, which I meant seriously but said in a facetious tone, Mussolini made one of his grimaces, expressing mock horror, then laughed and looked at his hands, spread out in front of him, fingers wide apart, the thick and short hands of a peasant. What he said I will never forget. He said: "I wear no rings, you see. It will not happen to me." '

*

Mussolini was born at Dovia di Predappio, near Forlì, in Romagna, on July 29, 1883. His father was a blacksmith, an ardent revolutionary (a 'primeval socialist', as somebody called him), who named his first-born son Benito after Benito Juarez, the Mexican leader of the rebellion against Maximilian; his mother was a long-suffering schoolteacher. He was brought up hating the Church, the army, the king, the *carabinieri*, the law, the rich, the well-educated, the well-washed, the successful, any kind of authority, all the things he was later to defend, and to hate at times even the proletarian revolutionaries who disappointed him: he often called them 'socialist noodles'. He was a turbulent boy, determined to be first in everything, proud, quarrelsome, boastful, superstitious and not always very brave. A friendly biographer wrote: 'He picked quarrels for the sake of the fight; when he won at games he wanted more than the stake, when he lost he refused to pay.' He was expelled from two schools for having knifed two school-mates. Many of his companions hated him. A few loved him dearly, almost fanatically, and followed him as their leader. Old men in Romagna still remember his harsh childish charm, his winning smiles, and his fierce loyalty to his friends and followers. He was always persuaded that a great destiny was reserved for him. 'One day,' he said to his mother when he was still a boy, 'I will make the earth tremble.' He did.

He became a school-teacher in 1901. The following year he fled to Switzerland to avoid conscription: it was at the time a duty for a serious revolutionary. In Lausanne he tried, once or twice, actually to become a member of the working class by getting a job as a labourer but discovered that he did not like hard work. He much preferred reading revolutionary literature and talking. He read voraciously and indiscriminately, mostly pre-Marxist or non-Marxist rebels, including Nietzsche, Sorel and Schopenhauer. Of Marx he apparently read only the Manifesto. He preached indiscriminate violence—atheism, class warfare, the 'myth of the general strike', and revolution for revolution's sake—to his countrymen, mostly poor immigrant bricklayers, who were so impressed they elected him secretary of their trade union. He sought the company of other revolutionaries who were at the time mostly Russian nihilists, anarchists, and social democrats. They called him familiarly Benitushka; he called himself more dramatically an 'apostle of violence'.

He never washed, shaved seldom, wore his thinning hair long on his neck and lived wherever he could. Once he inhabited an abandoned packing case under a bridge together with a young girl. The police watched him and arrested him several times. Angelica Balabanova, the Russian socialist, befriended him and was charmed by him for a time. She understood that, under the blustering, blasphemous and rebellious talk, he was a timid man, uneasy when in the presence of people he suspected to be his social or intellectual superiors. In reality he watched himself playing the great rôle he was inventing as he went along, hamming at it with gusto; no earnest revolutionary in Switzerland at the time was as visibly frightening as he was. Certainly not Lenin, who diligently impersonated a little professor.

Mussolini returned to Italy in 1904; an heir had been born to the king and so an amnesty had been granted. He became a village school-teacher, served in the Army as a *bersagliere* (he turned out to be a good soldier, after all), earned a new diploma as teacher of French in high schools, and did odd jobs as a journalist, socialist agitator and organizer. He began to improve his oratory, slowly developing a technique which was to make him one of the best and most moving speakers in Italy. He paid little attention to the logic and truth of what he said as long as it was energetic and stirring. His gestures had rhythm and vigour. He used short, staccato sentences, with no clear connection between them, often with long and dramatic pauses, sometimes changing voice and expression in a crescendo of violence and ending in a tornado of vituperations. When his audience was carried away by his oratory he would sometimes stop and put to them a rhetorical question. They roared their answer. This established a sort of heated dialogue, through which the spectators became involved in decisions they had no time to meditate on. By means of violent writings and incendiary eloquence, he rose in the socialist party organization until, by 1912, he was made editor of the party organ, *Avanti!*

He was a very successful editor. The paper's circulation rose from 50,000 copies to 200,000 under his leadership. The rôle of the journalist was one of the few in his life he did not have to act, because he really was one, perhaps the best popular journalist of his day in Italy, addressing himself not to the sober cultured minority, but to the practically illiterate masses, easily swept by primitive emotions. Those very qualities which made him an excellent rabble-rousing editor made him a disastrous statesman: his intuitive and superficial intelligence; his capacity to oversimplify and dramatize; a day-by-day interest only in the most striking events; a strictly partisan point of view; the disregard for truth, accuracy, objectivity and consistency when they interfered with his aims; the talent for doing his job undisturbed by scruples, doubts or criticisms; and above all, an instinctive ability to ride the emotional wave of the day, whatever it was, to know what people wanted to be told, and by what low collective passions they would more easily be swept away. If the Italians had been a newspaper-reading public like the English, *Avanti!* would have easily reached a circulation of two or three million copies. As it was, 200,000 was considered a miracle.

He went to live in Milan with his family, which consisted of his common-law wife Rachele (socialists at the time refused to acknowledge the existence of Church and State and got 'married' without a civil or religious ceremony) who was the very young daughter of his father's mistress, and his little girl, Edda, who looked like him, two large black eyes in a pale and bony face. He was only a little better dressed than the 'apostle of violence' of his Lausanne days. He still washed seldom, shaved only twice a week, wore the same suit until it fell to pieces and neglected to tie his shoe-laces. He made strange grimaces when he talked, used violent and unprintable words, had an impatient temper, but managed, as he had done in his schooldays, to attract faithful friends and fanatical followers, some of whom clung to him to the end.

There was something about him that startled and fascinated almost everybody, including some of his enemies. Most people who knew him well, who spoke frequently with him, who worked for him, were the victims of this inexplicable charm. Men literally fell in love with him as if he were a woman, unreasoningly and blindly, ready to forgive him everything, his rudeness, his errors, his lies, his pretentiousness, his obstinacy and his ignorance. One of the men who had worked for him since 1914, Manlio Morgagni, committed suicide in July 1943, after writing these words on a piece of paper: 'Il Duce has resigned. My life is finished. Viva Mussolini!' He also attracted many women. He treated them roughly, as he had the peasant girls of Forlì, sometimes taking them without preliminary explanations on the hard floor of his study or standing them up against a wall. Only a few of them sensed his timidity, his lack of security, his desire for admiration and affection. Those lasted some time. The others, mesmerized and frightened, were soon dismissed.

My first impression of him, years later in 1932, during some army manœuvres, was a disturbing one. He wore a white yachting cap, a wing collar, the double-breasted jacket of a businessman, greygreen army breeches, and black boots. He looked like a circus performer in off hours. Perhaps his clothes were meant to symbolize the multifarious variety of his interests: horses, business, the sea, the economic life of the nation, and the army. He looked small, thick, rude, and stubborn. I remember the large ivory-coloured bald head, the bulging black eyes in the pale face, the protruding jaw, the yellow teeth set wide apart (a sign of good luck, according to popular belief), a little potato-like excrescence on his cranium, and the large black mole under his chin. He moved his arms and legs as a wrestler does to make his clothes fit better.

I wrote in my diary: 'He is the engineer at the throttle, we are the passengers on the train. Will he always be able to see if the bridges ahead are still standing or have been washed away? Let us hope for the best.' It is true that I had not been exposed to his charms as I had not talked to him. I had merely watched him for days, from a short distance, at army observation posts. He was, of course, playing the rôle of the man with an indomitable will 'whom,' large black letters on village houses proclaimed at the time throughout Italy, 'neither God nor man will bend.' In reality, he was, as he had always been, obstinate, deaf to criticism, self-willed, suspicious, but also erratic, undecided most of the time, prone to adopt the most recent opinion he heard. He was trying to hide his irresolution and fear. This I was too young and inexperienced to know. I took him at his face value.

He had certainly been irresolute during the fateful summer of 1914. Italy was tied to the Austrian and German empires by the Triple Alliance. The right wing, the conservatives, the general staff, the business and financial interests and the government were in favour of maintaining strict neutrality. The younger people, avant-garde artists, trade unionists, anarchists, students, republicans, democrats, nationalists, the hot-heads of the right, and the more moderate socialists, were all, for different reasons, in favour of war on the side of France and Great Britain. Socialist doctrines, as usual, were no certain guide. Workers should have been against a bourgeois, capitalist war, but they also had a theoretical duty to encourage a catastrophe which would have accelerated the proletarian revolution. The editor of *Avanti!* at first repeated the old slogans: 'Down with war! Down with armaments! Long live the international brother-hood of workers!' He denounced war-mongers. He organized a referendum among his readers: 'Are you for war or peace?' He headed one of his violent articles: 'Who drives us to war betrays us.' But then the journalist in him wavered, when he felt he would lose followers by supporting the cautious government policy. Pacifism was unpopular with those he wanted to lead, the younger generation of rebels. After a few months, on October 18, 1914, without taking orders from or consulting the party leaders, he published an editorial urging war. He was immediately dismissed from his job and expelled from the party in a stormy session. He walked out crying dramati-cally: 'You hate me because you cannot help loving me!'

With foreign and Italian money, he started a new newspaper of his own, *Popolo d'Italia*, which came out on November 14. He immediately managed to gather behind him more followers than he had had when editing *Avanti!* and more readers. Italy entered the war on May 24, 1915. He also went to war, when his class was called, and served well as a corporal in the *bersaglieri*, until he was wounded. (It was noticed that he went about Milan on crutches long after they should have become useless.) After the war, when the frail structure of Italian political unity was endangered by civil strife, economic difficulties and the collapse of the existing method of government, he used his paper to give vent to all the passions, to rally all the hotheaded veterans of all parties who found it difficult to go back to dull civilian pursuits, the very young men who felt they had been cheated by not having been in the war, and all those who had wanted a revolution, any kind of revolution, so long as it was not a socialist and Marxist one. On March 23, 1919, in Milan, he founded something called *I Fascii*, a vague but determined organization which adopted a fiery and contradictory programme, so contradictory in fact that it attracted dissatisfied and restless men from the right and the left, anarchists and conservatives, businessmen and artists. Arturo Toscanini was one of them. The confusion of the programme reflected the disorderly but brilliant mind of the leader, his lack of principles and his perennial irresolution. Here and there, in other cities, in the provinces, in towns, in villages, bands of young men sprang up, to fight socialists and communists in the streets. The movement quickly found conservative support. Street fighting became a common occurrence.

Mussolini was generally considered the truculent and arrogant leader of all this, the man who rode the storm. In reality, he was secretly reluctant as usual and devoured by doubts; but he put up a good front. The expression on his face was resolute. He scowled and clenched his teeth. His working table at the *Popolo d'Italia* was covered with an arsenal of weapons, hand-grenades, pistols of various calibres, muskets, knives. (He loved weapons until late in his career. In the waiting-room of his study in the Palazzo Venezia there were often a couple of duelling pistols and a couple of duelling sabres, to intimidate his visitors.) His articles bristled with insults for the cautious and timid. He often wore a black shirt, like his followers.[1] He wrote arrogant articles, heaping insults on grave and prudent statesmen, challenging his enemies to fight, forecasting the most glorious future for the party. But he never took a personal part in a street brawl. Manœuvring behind the scenes, skilfully keeping all doors open, he negotiated with the socialists and the conservatives, at the same time as he was fighting them both; with the monarchists and the republicans; with the government and the opposition. His genius was proved above all by the fact that he maintained himself at the head of a mass party composed of many different factions, always managing to defeat all his possible rivals, until practically the very end, twenty-five years later.

None of this was visible from a distance. His public figure was one thing, the fearless leader braving danger at the head of his fighting men, his private figure was another, known only to few. (The discrepancy was naturally known to his wife, Rachele, who later used to complain to him, as one of his sons told me many years ago: 'You bend forty million Italians to your will but you are not able to make your own sons obey you.') His vacillating character was well-known to the leaders of the party who decided to march on Rome, in October 1922; Balbo told him: 'We are going, either with you or without you. Make up your mind.' He remained prudently behind in Milan while the Blackshirts straggled through the rain into the capital, without meeting any opposition. He arrived the next day in a Wagons-Lits compartment, after he had been summoned by the king for consultations. He presented himself at the Quirinale symbolically attired in a tight morning coat he had borrowed, spats and a black shirt, a blend of tradition and revolution. He said: 'Your Majesty must excuse me for wearing a black shirt, but I have just returned from the battle which we had to fight, fortunately without shedding any blood. . . .'

*

[1] The Italian habit of wearing a shirt of a distinct colour as a political uniform was started by Garibaldi in Montevideo in 1843, who dressed his Italian Legion, then fighting for the independence of Uruguay, with an old stock of unsold red shirts made originally for slaughter-house workers. Black shirts had been used in Italy by workers in the railways, steel mills, and machinery shops.

There is a disturbing mystery about Mussolini's career. He was dictator of Italy for about two decades, exactly from October 28, 1922, till July 25, 1943. Two decades is almost the time lag between two generations, the years necessary for schoolchildren to become mature men, and for mature men to become old. He himself was thirty-nine when he took power and sixty only a few days after he had to relinquish it. In the end, he was leading a country different from that in which he conquered power, a new country which he had shaped according to his wishes, organized according to his theories, staffed by men educated and selected by him and his lieutenants. His powers were limitless: where his legal prerogatives ended, his undisputed authority and immense personal prestige began. He ran the only political party officially in existence, so capillary and widespread that it interfered with the daily habits of millions of people from dawn to dusk and even later at night (he wanted Italians to produce more and more children and granted advantages and prizes to large families), and from the cradle to the tomb. He decided the contents of newspapers, books, magazines, radio programmes, films, encyclopaedias. He had no opposition to contend with.

He was sole legislator, judge, censor, policeman, ambassador, general. He was the Head of the Government, President of the Grand Council, President of the Council of Ministers, and, at one time or another, occupied most of the seats around the council table himself. He was on and off, for years, Minister of the Interior, of Foreign Affairs, of the Army, the Navy, and the Air Force; he managed economic affairs as Minister of Corporations. The ministries he did not run he controlled indirectly. Everything was conceived by him as a preparation for the ultimate test, the biggest world war ever seen, which he did little to avoid, foresaw with accuracy years before, and practically welcomed. The armed forces he led as commander-in-chief had been organized, trained, and armed by him for the conflict; they were supported by the economic and industrial organization he had shaped with that sole aim in view; encouraged by the propaganda machine he had invented and run for two decades; led by him during the war, through successive strategic moves, conceived and decided by him and by generals of his own choosing.

He was practically defeated by one man alone, himself. He found himself impotent in front of the overwhelming enemies he had evoked, and of the arrogant ally he had encouraged and cultivated, with the scarce resources he himself had predisposed, the industries he had encouraged, and the weapons he had designed and built. He was left in the lurch by himself as Foreign Minister (his grasp of the world situation had been highly over-optimistic), as Minister of the Armed Forces (he had chosen the wrong commanders, strategies and weapons), as Minister of the Interior (he underestimated the will of the Italian people to suffer and die for a war they did not understand), as Minister of Propaganda (he had believed his own newspapers), and as Head of the Fascist Party (he glibly thought he had worked out all the answers to the riddles of the modern world).

Italian artillerymen in the Western Desert fired Austrian guns of first world war vintage, built by the Skoda works in 1908 or thereabout, against the very modern American and British models. Mussolini lacked raw materials, fuel and food to fight a long war, and he lacked merchant ships with which to supply the far-flung theatres he had chosen to fight in, since many Italian ships in foreign waters, not having been informed about their country's entry into the war, were immediately impounded. His tanks were small, weak, slow, tinny affairs, which could be pierced by machine-gun fire; he had chosen them because they were cheaper and, for the same price, he could have more of them. He said they were faster than the heavier models, more 'attuned to the quick reflexes of the Italian soldiers'. He had no aircraft carriers. His planes were good but too few to count; he could not replace them fast enough. They were clever toys, elegant models laboriously made by hand by ingenious mechanics for peacetime reviews, rather than industrial products which could be turned out fast enough to produce results. His navy, which had somehow managed to run itself for years, was relatively efficient, but certainly not big and advanced enough to stand up to the combined strength of the fleets he attacked. It lacked radar and, what is worse, it never suspected such an invention existed, which made Italian ships sitting ducks for the British, at long range or at night.

The army was at first disciplined and in good spirits. The cliché of Italian soldiers running away was not true in the beginning. The men sacrificed themselves even after it was amply clear the whole thing was a macabre and hopeless joke. Of course, nobody likes fighting against overwhelming odds. The men tried their best, armed as they were for a short colonial adventure against disarmed backward people, but certainly not to face the biggest, richest, most numerous and advanced armies in the world. The navy sacrificed its ships and one half of all officers in the desperate attempt to save its honour. What was missing in Italy was often not the courage or the will to fight but any kind of serious plans and organization behind the fighting men.

Even if the experiment had not ended in catastrophe, historians would probably have wondered at the curious scarcity of concrete achievements during the twenty years of Fascist rule. What had Mussolini really done with his time? He promoted public works, to be sure, built harbours, railways, roads, schools, *autostrade*, monuments, aqueducts, hospitals, irrigation and drainage networks, public buildings, bridges and so forth. Some of these things were good and useful: they were admired and envied by friends and enemies. And yet, in retrospect, the result of all this activity seems meagre. To get the exact measure of his achievements one must, first of all, subtract from the total all that would have been accomplished by any government in his place. It is difficult to believe that, without a dictator, dirt roads would not have been covered with asphalt, as they were all over Europe at the same time. Some marshes had been reclaimed, aqueducts and railways built, industries promoted in Italy by the liberal governments before the Fascist *coup d'état* and, even before them, by the Bourbons of Naples and by the Popes' inefficient governments. When all the projects which, hypothetically, would have been undertaken anyway are subtracted from the total, Mussolini's contributions, while still important, shrink perceptibly. They shrink a little more when one considers how many projects were plain mistakes, decided for political and spectacular reasons rather than the hope of practical results; and how much money disappeared into the pockets of dishonest contractors. As a result the sum total of the Fascist achievements in this field seems out of proportion to the noise surrounding them, their fame and their moral cost.

In reality, behind the scenery of modernization and industrial investments, millions of Italians still lived a life of prehistoric squalor, and most of the fundamental problems of the country had been left practically untouched. One Mussolini really solved, peace with the Church. A few problems had somehow solved themselves, with the passage of time. Of some others only the visible symptoms had been attacked, never the deep-seated causes, too complicated and dull to interest a flashy, amateurish, hurried and journalistic leader. The problems which only a dictator could solve, the really hard ones, were left intact or became more serious and ingrained, problems like illiteracy, the Mafia, malaria, banditry, the social and political backwardness of the southern provinces, unequal distribution of income, primitive agriculture and an inadequate industrial structure.

His approach to many of the great contemporary difficulties was somewhat optimistic and facile. The very first instructions I received, in 1930, when I joined the *Corriere della Sera* bureau in London, were: 'Do not mention the world economic crisis.' They were his own words relayed to all journalists, his own way to settle one of the greatest difficulties of the times. I remember asking myself what would have happened if the Italian press had stopped mentioning the Atlantic Ocean: would Italians have drowned trying to go to New York on bicycles? When I went to Sardinia, a few years later, I was told I was to write about anything, anything at all, except two things, bandits and malaria. They were then the two most important phenomena of life in the island. They could easily be kept out of newspapers. But, I wondered, how could they be avoided in official documents and statistics? They were not, of course. They only had different names. The bandits were called *latitanti*, or fugitives from justice, and malaria was *febbre intermittente*, or intermittent fever. While urgent problems went unsolved, a number of imaginary ones were invented yearly and brilliantly eliminated: Italians were forbidden to shake hands (only the Fascist salute was allowed), foreign words were abolished from street signs and ordinary usage (the Pensione Milton of Rome became Miltone), and the *lei*, the formal address in the third person singular, was strictly prohibited by law and abolished in all grammars.

What is the explanation for the inaction and ineffectiveness of Fascism, and why did it fail? Mussolini was not stupid. He was shrewd, quick to learn, wary, astute. He could grasp a complex situation in a few minutes, face resolute opponents with success, usually take what intuitive decision any situation required. Perhaps he did not work hard enough. The suspicion came to me one day, many years ago, in Rome. I had given a lift to a soldier in my car. 'Where to?' I asked him. 'Palazzo Venezia,' he said. I asked him why. He explained simply that he was from the same town as Mussolini's office cook, and that he had to deliver a package her people had given him. 'Do you ever see Il Duce?' I asked idly. I, of course, saw him often, as a journalist, but only at formal ceremonies, surrounded by his retinue, and in uniform. 'Oh yes,' said the soldier calmly. 'I see him all the time. He is always in the courtyard, talking to drivers and the doormen.' I was stunned. I had probably stumbled on one of the darkest state secrets of the time. We now know that the light in his study was kept on until very late at night even when he was not there, which was often, to give people the illusion that he was sleeplessly attending to their welfare. Even so, he worked hard enough.

He liked work. He knew everything that went on in Italy (he got his first news report in the morning from the chief of Police and the general commanding the *carabinieri*), knew everybody (important people and people who wanted to be thought important went to see him several times a year), was kept *au courant* of the smallest secrets (telephones were tapped not only to defeat the enemies of the régime and to uncover the devious plans of foreign emissaries, but also to provide him with gossip), read everything that was easy to read, newspapers, magazine, books, saw every film, and met all the distinguished foreigners who went through Rome. If he was not the great statesman he wanted to appear, he certainly was a good politician, busy with the numberless chores of his calling, and a good journalist, keeping abreast of every development gathering information for future use.

The explanation of his failure is perhaps that he was not a failure. He lost the war, power, his country, his mistress, his place in history, and his life, but he succeeded in what he had wanted to do since he took power. It was not to make his country safe and prosperous. It was not, obviously, to organize Italy for a modern war and for victory. He had dedicated his life just to putting up a good show, a stirring show. He had managed to do it extremely well. He should not be compared to Cromwell, Washington, Cavour, Bismarck, or Talleyrand, but to men like Ernesto Rossi and Tommaso Salvini, the eminent actors, and to P. T. Barnum. He was a flamboyant interpreter of heroic rôles in the style of great nineteenth-century tragedians or operatic baritones. Paolo Monelli, the author of the best life of Mussolini, wrote: 'The Italians saw in him only the tenor for whom they raved as they had years before for Caruso and Tamagno. As one does with tenors, they enjoyed his good long notes and the melody without paying any attention to the words, but, if they had listened more carefully, they would not have been surprised by the catastrophe later. He had announced it.'

He played a versatile and multifaced rôle, that of Mussolini, a heroic mixture of the Renaissance *condottiere*, cold Machiavellian thinker, Lenin-like leader of a revolutionary minority, steely-minded dictator, humanitarian despot, Casanova lover, and Nietzschean superman. He added later to his repertoire the Napoleonic genius, with well-known results, and, just before he died, the socialist renovator of society. He was none of these things. In the end, like an old actor, he no longer remembered what he really was, felt, believed, and wanted. Ugo Ojetti, an erudite art critic, writer and man of taste, who liked him, used to say in the thirties: 'I cannot help thinking, when I see him, how much his face must ache at night when he retires.' That he was conscious of playing rôles all the time could be discerned by any attentive observer: he walked, strutted or strode like a tragedian wearing an ancient costume; he pivoted on one spurred boot heel as if he were always trailing a long purple cloak behind him. He never tired but never looked at ease.

His success seemed incredible. He was more popular in Italy than anybody had ever been and probably will ever be. His pictures were cut out of newspapers and magazines and pasted on the walls of poor peasant cottages, at the side of the Madonna and Saint Joseph. Schoolgirls fell in love with him as with a film star. His more memorable words were written large on village houses for all to read. One of his collaborators exclaimed, after listening to him announce from the balcony that Ethiopia had been conquered and that Rome had again become the Capital of an Empire, in May 1936: 'He is like a god. . . .' 'Like a god? No, no,' said another. 'He *is* a god.'

I remember him, one day, during military manœuvres in the Langhe, in 1932, walking through a vast bare plain of yellow stubble surrounded by distant green hills, trees, and the steeples of village churches. Peasants came running from all sides, red-faced, panting, to see him, touch him, shout to him. One of his secretaries followed him with a leather envelope, the exact size of thousand-lire bills, to hand banknotes to the more miserable with the gesture of a gambler dealing out cards. Soon enough Mussolini was leading a parade of thousands of frenzied and gesticulating followers. He showed no expression on his face except the usual wooden determination. Mothers lifted babies high for him to see and possibly to touch, as they had done to kings in the Middle Ages. At one point a few nuns came running, their long black veils flying in the wind, carrying baskets of freshly-picked peaches to offer him. He accepted their homage without thanking them, without turning his head or smiling, and handed the fruit to his retinue. Nobody who saw it will ever forget the sight of city squares filled with crowds listening to him; the heads were as close together as tesserae in a mosaic, all eyes turned to one focal point, the balcony or stand from which he was speaking. It was an ominous and frightening sight.

We laugh now when we see him in old newsreels. Possibly his showmanship was like some wines which do not last or travel well, but which are excellent when consumed the year they are made in their native surroundings. His technique was flamboyant, juvenile, ridiculous, but highly effective: it pleased his public, the plebeian and illiterate masses from which he had sprung, the patriarchal Italians of the villages and the countryside who longed for the ancient peace they had lost with the industrial revolution and the first world war; the 'bigoted and reactionary' *petite bourgeoisie*, as Mario Missiroli called it, who wanted to attend to their little affairs and let other people worry about vast problems; the half-baked intellectuals and the frustrated nationalists who felt humiliated, born and living in a third-rate country with a first-rate glorious name, a country easily beaten by less glorious but more efficient rivals. His technique was obviously not meant for men of taste and culture. In Italy these were, anyway, a minority which did not count; many, like Benedetto Croce, their leader, firmly resisted the régime; many faced death in

exile or life imprisonment; many collaborated with it, either intimidated and frightened or ready to exploit what opportunities the
régime offered.

The job had been an easy one in the beginning. There was practically no gap between the spectacle and reality. Many things were
being done. Some of the easier problems were effectively dealt with.
The country was improving. Living conditions were getting better.
He had inherited a good bureaucracy from the previous governments. He was then still ready to listen to good advice. Later the job
became more and more difficult: the international situation grew
more menacing and complicated. The gap between the flamboyant
representations, the ceremonies, the fiery speeches and the plain and
ugly facts widened dangerously. After twenty years of dictatorship,
people did not know he was not really solving any problems. People
were drugged by propaganda and stirring shows. Most of them had
lost or forgotten the capacity to judge things independently. Those
who were alarmed at the way things were going consoled themselves
by thinking that he was always there, in the Palazzo Venezia, the
'sleepless one', working hard, seeing to it that nothing irrevocably
bad would happen. His reassuring face looked at everybody from
each wall, from every film screen. Many secretly trusted him to
avoid a real show-down, a catastrophe. Had he not made Italy a
first-rate power, well-armed, well-commanded, feared by her
enemies? Was he not the greatest man ever born in Italy? Was he
not, like all of them, no fool?

*

Trying to find out what really happened, one gets lost in a complex
psychological labyrinth, bewildered by an Italian play of mirrors
reflecting each other's distorted images. There is no doubt, to begin
with, that Mussolini deceived the people. He used deceit as a tool to
govern with. The thing is not deplorable in principle. All great
statesmen have had recourse to occasional distortions, misinterpreta-
tions and outright lies. Mussolini merely lied more than all other past
statesmen, a little more than some of his contemporary competitors,
less than Hitler anyway; he enjoyed a monopoly and was able to
multiply his lies by making good use of the newest communication

techniques. His slanted views and fabrications filled newspapers, posters, the radio, the film screens, many books, magazines, and even the conversations between people who did not know each other very well. After such unprecedented mass attacks, it is not surprising that the majority of his captive audience believed most of what he wanted them to believe.

He was not entirely a ruthless and cold-blooded souls-engineer, a push-button politician who heartlessly manipulated people's emotions, beliefs, hopes, in his own interest, to further his schemes. He could be described as such only when he tried to convince his people of things he knew were utterly false; this happened often enough, but not always. He, too, was an Italian. He, too, loved a good show, enjoyed a good military parade, was comforted by a naval review, or strengthened by a vast ocean-like meeting in a city square. He, too, believed his own slogans. He, too, was amazed by the fake statistics, thrilled by empty boasts, stirred to tears by his own oratory. He, too, confused appearances for reality, the veneer for the solid wood. Truth, for him also, was what it looked like and what most people liked to believe.

His show was necessarily always new and startling. Only by keeping his public interested, thrilled, puzzled, frightened and entertained, could he make them forget the sacrifice of their liberty and their miserable poverty, unite a solid majority of them behind him, dishearten and divide the opposition, assure internal order and international prestige. Obviously, the choice of a sober policy imposing real sacrifices and a stern discipline, the admission that difficulties could not be annulled by the use of words, sleight-of-hand tricks and optimistic communiqués, but needed a lot of grim studying, careful planning, and hard work, would have probably cost him his job. He was not the man to conceive such a dreary programme, anyway, or to carry it through. Boredom would have destroyed him. Therefore one may say that not all his performing was his own, dictated by his caprice. Much of it was demanded by the people themselves; most of the time he had to give them also the lies they expected, the myths they wanted badly to believe in, in a critical and dramatic phase of their history, just as the character he impersonated was not wholly of his own choosing, but also one many Italians had been expecting, the impersonation of their secret longings, and which placated their obscure anxieties. Signs proclaimed all over Italy: 'Duce, you are all of us!' It was, in a way, true.

He could not help being corrupted by his own spectacle and people who surrounded him. Roman emperors all began to deteriorate the day they were raised to the imperial dignity. Many great leaders in the past, drunk with their own great importance and vast intelligence, thinking themselves infallible, surrounded by sycophants, eventually stumbled and committed a fatal mistake. At one point, they all took too big a risk. Napoleon attacked Russia and Hitler tried to fight two wars on two fronts. But Napoleon and Hitler commanded the most efficient and powerful military machines of their times, which had hitherto defeated all their enemies. They both had a reasonable chance; they both came close to winning, against heavy odds.

Mussolini never had a chance. It is true, he thought the war was almost over when he entered it, in June 1940; he counted on the aid of his mighty ally in an emergency; he trusted his intuition and his luck. But any reasonably prudent dictator should also have been prepared for unforeseen circumstances. He was not. He should have known that Germans sometimes lost wars and that they had an even chance of losing this one if it lasted long enough. He had suspected it, for a while, in the beginning when Italy was still neutral, and knew it at the end. He explained to friends and collaborators. 'Germans, of course, are militarists, not soldiers. They are going to lose. If they had as much political as strategic genius, they would have been the masters of the world centuries ago.' What he never knew was what every military attaché in every foreign embassy in Rome knew, that Italy was ridiculously and tragically unprepared. What blinded him?

He never even suspected that practically nothing was behind his show. He never knew how really weak, disarmed and demoralized the country was. He honestly thought he could play a rôle with his ineffective army, his servile generals, his Biedermeier guns, his toy planes, his tin tanks, and his ramshackle industries. This is an inexplicable state of affairs. He was no fool. He was not mad. While a little worn out and prematurely aged by his intense life, his love affairs (Claretta Petacci had come into his life in 1936, when he was 53 and she 24), and his bad health (he suffered from nervous stomach

cramps, which gave him great pain in moments of crisis), he was on
the whole still well aware of what was going on. He was badly informed, that is all. But he wanted to be badly informed. He knew
nothing about Italy's military preparations. He had kept himself in
the dark. He had been deceived by himself. But he had been aided by
his ministers, his generals, the shows, the parades, the mass meetings
and the people.

He had tried, from time to time, in the beginning, to pierce the
curtain of official obsequiousness and official half-truths and deceptions. As long as his brother Arnaldo was alive (he died in 1931) and
as long as he saw some outspoken old friends and collaborators, he
was not yet dangerously detached from reality. But gradually the
heady atmosphere of high position got the better of him. Somehow
he was not capable of protecting himself from its deleterious effects.
The master of make-believe could not always detect make-believe
when practised by others on him. This, of course, is the heart of the
matter. His resistance to deception, which was never very strong,
gradually dwindled and eventually disappeared altogether. When
people warned him against adulation, he shrugged his shoulders. In
one of the first months of his government, in 1923, an old ambassador
returned from Geneva, where he had represented Italy at a meeting
on the control of poison gases. As the venerable gentleman entered the
younger man's room, Mussolini did not look up from his desk and went
on writing. Finally, after long minutes, he lifted his eyes from the
paper and, jutting his chin forward, asked disdainfully: 'What are the
most dangerous gases, ambassador?' The ambassador gravely
answered: 'Incense is the most lethal of all, your excellency.' He was
soon put on the retired list. As the years went by, Mussolini became
completely addicted to the artificial paradise he had created for
others. He needed bigger and bigger doses of flattery and deception
each year. In the end the most sickening and improbable lies, as long
as they adulated his idea of himself and confirmed his prejudices,
seemed to him the plain and unadorned expression of objective
truth.

All great personages, of course, are surrounded by fawning courtiers. Flatterers are especially common in Italy, where the people
have always employed such arts offensively, to gain advantages,

destroy rivals, and conquer power and wealth; and defensively, as the squid uses ink, to blind and confound powerful men, dictators and tyrants. But most great personages are aware of the danger surrounding them. All men in authority, in Italy, any kind of authority, even village mayors, know that the smiles, the praises, the gifts, the applause are not for them but for their rank. Most of them manage to protect themselves from disaster. Mussolini never learned. He was too convinced of his own infallibility. He liked only the men who did not warn him of the dangers facing him and never tried to tell him the truth. As a result the only people approaching him were the best flatterers of the kingdom. They were not all dishonest. Some were just fools who believed what they said. Some desperately hoped that what they said was true, that he really was the greatest man alive and that all would turn out for the best in the end. They flattered him also to reassure themselves. Others were just unscrupulous crooks.

In the end he lived within a private imaginary world of his own. The cities he visited had been carefully prepared a long time before his arrival: he was shown only the things and the people that would please and comfort him. Everything else was efficiently hidden. He did not know the enthusiastic crowds cheering him were reinforced by regiments of black-shirted policemen and by thousands of extras brought from the provinces the day before. He did not know that some of the new buildings, public works, or villages he opened were abandoned and began decaying the following day, that some of the aqueducts never carried water, and that all the numberless divisions he was passing in review were more or less always the same few, transported here and there.

The technique was so smooth that it even deceived Hitler. Preparations for his visit in 1938 went on for six months. All Italy was to show the German dictator a new face. Nothing was to be left that was 'nineteenth century, homely, familiar'. The country was transformed. Streets where the parades were to pass were redesigned and reconstructed like film sets, houses were painted and decorated along the railway line from the Brenner to Rome. The soldiers taking part in the reviews had been hand-picked. Most of them were to be blue-eyed and tall, to show the visitors that Italians, too, were Aryans. (Only the king could not be changed, to Mussolini's annoy-

ance. He was very small and not impressive. He was, strangely
enough, the only nordic one of them all, with so much Austrian and
German blood in him, showing through his light blue eyes.) The
parading soldiers were armed with all the weapons existing in the
country. They were all dressed in brand-new uniforms.

It is well known that Hitler's favourable opinion of his partner, of
Italian military preparations, and the people's devotion to the régime
and to the Axis, made him commit several miscalculations, one of
which probably cost him the war. He believed, in the end, that he
lost the Russian campaign because he had started four weeks too late;
he was four weeks late because he wasted time to rescue the Italians
bogged down in Albania, in their ill-prepared attack on Greece. If
this were true, Mussolini could be considered the greatest negative
military genius the world has ever seen, who defeated two great
nations single-handed, his own and Germany.

Il Duce enjoyed the show more than Hitler did. He always
chuckled when he read the writings on house-walls, as if the words
were really the expression of the people's will. He also read with
relish the reports of ambassadors from abroad, strictly announcing
the things he wanted to believe. He read his own newspapers with
great pleasure. It was easy to fool him. Once, during the war, he
looked at some figures in a report, pretending to be the total number
of new guns his army possessed, and protested. There were not that
many new guns in Italy. He knew. His Under-secretary for War, an
astute general, quickly replied: 'No, Duce, there has been a mistake.
These are the guns our industries are planning to produce in the
near future.' He was reassured.

*

Mussolini fell from power on July 25, 1943. The Allied armies had
invaded Sicily only a few days before. All overseas possessions were
lost. The Italian army had been destroyed in Russia, in the Balkans,
and in Africa. Italy was battered and paralysed by mass air-bombard-
ments. The Germans themselves were only carrying on defensive
retreats, economically, sparing whatever resources and men they had
left. All the big Fascist chiefs took part in a fateful meeting of the
Grand Council, presided over by Il Duce, who looked tired, haggard,

and senile. He made an objective, or almost objective, exposition of the situation, showing that he had kept a good journalist's superficial grasp of things to the end, in spite of all, but talked as if he were talking of other countries, other wars, other leaders, other times. His henchmen demanded that the command of all armed forces be turned over to the king. Mussolini pleaded with them, cajoled them, threatened them, pointing to some files, presumably filled with compromising secrets, which he had on the table beside him, pleaded with them to respect his old age. ('I shall be 60 in a few days,' he said.) Finally he acquiesced. He accepted his demotion.

The following day Victor Emmanuel received him in his private villa and ordered his arrest. There was no Fascist revolt when the news spread. No faithful followers rose in arms. Nobody kept the Fascist oath: 'I swear to defend the revolution with my blood.' Nothing happened. The show was over, that was all. The dictator had been defeated by the Italians in the most costly way for them, but the only way. The people rejoiced tumultuously. Mussolini was transported here and there, to some islands at first, then to a resort hotel in the mountains of Abruzzi he had built for skiers, in search of a place the Germans could not reach. The Germans found him anyway, in spite of the fact that there was no road to the hotel and only a cable railway connected it with the lowlands. They used gliders. Mussolini arrived at Hitler's headquarters in East Prussia, thanked his liberator, donned his old uniform, and was named president of a puppet régime, the Fascist Republic of North Italy.

His headquarters were on Lake Garda, comfortably on the direct road to the Brenner Pass, in case of sudden retreat. His last few months of life were dismal. He knew everything was lost, he was a failure, his régime had plunged Italy into the wrong war, at the wrong time, with practically no weapons; and those few moral and material resources which existed, including the heroic courage of thousands of men, were squandered in insensate expeditions dictated by an amateur strategist's desire to show to his ally that he, too, was a master-mind. Sometimes he tried to find alibis: the fault was the Italians', he said, their soft character, their dislike of vigorous action; they were not the descendants of the ancient Romans but of foreign slaves, mongrels, serfs. He dreamed of a return to power, when he would take revenge on all his enemies, made possible by the secret weapons which the Germans had prepared. He paid practically no attention to current affairs, read many books, wrote an enormous quantity of insignificant articles, essays, apologias, memoirs, including some for children's publications. He was interested in but one thing, the position he would have in history. Jesus Christ, Napoleon, Caesar? he asked his visitors guardedly. He never mentioned Cola di Rienzo. He never mentioned Barnum, either. He visited Claretta Petacci in a little villa nearby almost every day. He was sick, weak, and dispirited. He knew the end had come.

The end indeed came on April 25, 1945. The Germans had signed a secret armistice with the Allies, behind his back, and were giving themselves up to the Allies as prisoners of war. He tried to negotiate his own armistice through the Archbishop of Milan but soon realized he had no power and no other open possibility than that of giving himself up. He had counted on the loyalty of the people of Milan who had cheered him in the streets with practically the old enthusiasm only a few months before in January, and had wildly applauded a speech he had made in a theatre. But the people were now all against him. It was dangerous to stay in the city. He decided to escape with a handful of faithful followers to Valtellina or to Switzerland. To the end, as usual, he vacillated and could not make up his mind. How should his adventure finish?

Like Cola he was undecided: heroic death or bourgeois escape? Valtellina is a narrow Italian valley which penetrates into Swiss territory like a wedge; it can be defended on a small front by few men, as it is protected to the left and right. He could easily make a last stand there, with a few companions, or, if he changed his mind, reach foreign soil with only a few hours' march through the mountains. In the end, like Cola, he decided to trust his art as an actor: to disguise himself and flee. He made up his mind to go directly to Switzerland, without wasting time in more futile and bloody heroics, carrying all his money and all his most useful documents, those he would employ to frighten Allied statesmen and to defend himself if he were tried as a war criminal. He was found and arrested by partisans on the road going north along the shore of Lake Como, hiding in a German truck, dressed in the heavy coat of a German petty officer and a German helmet. Claretta Petacci was arrested with him.

They were both shot against the ornate gate of a pompous villa, the next morning. The woman had tried to shield his body and was mown down with him. The money and documents disappeared for ever. The bodies were taken to Milan and hung, like Cola's, feet high, from a petrol station roof, alongside those of all the other Fascist chiefs caught and killed on the same road, on their way to Switzerland. Thirteen years before he had told Emil Ludwig: 'Everybody dies the death that corresponds to his character.' He had deluded the people, that was his crime. But his fatal error was that he had not known that the people were also deluding him. They led him to the catastrophe which was the only way they knew to get rid of him.

CHAPTER NINE

REALISM AND GUICCIARDINI

THE PROBLEM the people faced under Fascism was as old as Italy: how to survive and possibly prosper in the midst of corruption, civil wars, revolutions and foreign invasions, under bloody tyrants and their greedy courtiers, without the protection of the law. Most of the methods evolved by the Italians are unsatisfactory. They are partial solutions at best. A few individuals manage to prosper in a decaying world, but the better they fare the worse the world becomes. And yet what is a man to do? He cannot change his countrymen. He cannot choose the times he is born in. He is powerless to deflect the tides of history. He can only try to defend himself from their blind violence, keep his mouth shut and mind his own business. The greatest Italian authority in these arts is Francesco Guicciardini, lawyer, diplomat, statesman, historian and thinker from Florence, who tested and refined them during his busy and successful life. He confided his experience in a secret notebook, *I Ricordi*, which was only published centuries after his death. It is the best handbook yet written for navigating in treacherous times. It is still invaluable today.

Montaigne, no mean practitioner himself of the related French arts of *savoir faire* and *savoir vivre*, called him, affectionately, '*mon Guichardin*'. Even Machiavelli, whose name has become proverbial as that of the heartless codifier of the Italian rules of the game, paid homage to his rival, for whom he felt not only the highest esteem, a rare sentiment among competitors, but also admiration, friendship, and even love. 'I love Messer Francesco Guicciardini, I love my fatherland more than my soul,' he once wrote. He could not go higher, as he loved his little fatherland, Florence, and his large fatherland, Italy, literally more than his own soul.

The two men have been compared repeatedly through the centuries. The parallel is almost irresistible. After all, they were both Florentines, born in the same city at about the same time (Machiavelli in 1469 and Guicciardini in 1482); both started young, when the popular republic of Florence employed them as ambassadors; both pursued political careers, and were fascinated by the technique of governing men and achieving power. Both, in the end, were defeated and chose to retire to their country estates, where they studied, wrote historical works and meditated on history's immutable and mysterious laws; both reached the conclusion that men and things were what they were and that all reasonable plans of action had to start from that assumption. The two friends believed that the pursuit of success was an absolute imperative, for individuals as well as states, the only sensible goal for action. 'He who has no position in life,' Machiavelli wrote, 'cannot even get a dog to bark at him.'

In spite of these superficial similarities they were profoundly different. Machiavelli, the older man, kept some of the youthful illusions of an earlier and happier age. He was an artist, above all, who wrote perhaps the most beautiful, lean and muscular prose in all Italian literature, at times bitter, biting, ironical and light, at other times solemn, grave and sonorous, but always limpid. He lived an irregular, almost bohemian life. He was a brilliant failure, never really managing to achieve his ends: he never made love to the women he wanted, satisfied his ambitions, reached the top in his political career and was never taken seriously as a thinker during his lifetime. He died penniless: he never even succeeded in persuading the republic of Florence to pay his arrears and to reimburse him for his expenses. He never managed to get his immortal works published. He was the permanent victim of political changes: he had made no headway when Florence was democratically ruled by the people; but, when the despotic Medici came back to power, he was arrested and tortured with four turns of the rack as a suspect republican; later, when the republic was once more restored, he was wrongly considered with suspicion and excluded from public business as a supporter of the Medici. Such is the fate of very intelligent men who are, however, not intelligent enough to conceal their intelligence and lull other people's fears and suspicions to sleep.

Machiavelli was, in reality, too much of a dreamer and an optimist to achieve practical results. He thought there were sure ways to solve the Italian national problem; he believed history could be re-routed, fate averted, the people changed, of course not by means of moral teachings, crusades, reforms, and prayers, but of realistic expedients and devices. He thought (just as Stendhal was naïvely to believe, three hundred years later, that all the ills of Italy would vanish the day a bicameral parliamentary system was adopted) that a militia of conscripted citizens, which would do away with the need for mercenary armies led by corruptible *condottieri*, would make the country invincible. (This proposal was rejected by the more experienced Guicciardini, when he was governor of the Romagna, as too abstract and dangerous; he thought that nobody could stop the citizens, once armed, from making war on each other.) Machiavelli hoped, above all, for the coming of a Great Leader, a superman who could perform the miracle of uniting Italy and ruling over her with a firm hand, and could keep foreign armies and local enemies at bay by the employment of all the arts and tools of contemporary statesmanship, poisons, deceit, terror, bribes, spies, and, when necessary, justice.

Guicciardini was no light-minded artist. He led no bohemian life. He entertained no illusions. Born a wealthy patrician, he was well brought up and educated. His virtuous youth had been spent, as he himself wrote, 'without corruption, levity, or waste of time'. His only known vice was women, for whom he had a long and persistent, though secret, weakness, women of all conditions and ages. (He never liked his wife, whom he had married for political reasons and always left at home.) He seemed so aloof, reserved and forbidding, that he provoked the hatred of all who knew him only superficially. He had learned his first lessons in the art of surviving and prospering in treacherous times from his father Piero. Piero was unsinkable. He managed to have a good reputation, but not so good as to frighten others; he managed to get appointed to high positions but not high enough to provoke envy and criticism. He had always felt the wind turning with sufficient anticipation to prepare himself without vulgar haste. He flourished under all régimes, popular and aristocratic, democratic and tyrannical.

Francesco had the same keen sense of political meteorology and managed to float just as surely most of his life, through some of the most complicated and deadly convulsions of Italian history, perhaps with even more dignity and ease than his father. To float, to prosper, to wield power were his only aims. He occupied some of the highest offices in the country with dignity, reaching almost regal powers. He acquired a solid reputation, seriously cultivated historical and political studies, and enlarged his private fortune. He got everything he wanted by honest means, not courting powerful personages, or courting them so discreetly as to be undetected. 'I always allow appointments to run after me and not vice-versa,' he disdainfully wrote. This was due to luck, his character and upbringing, his uncanny knowledge of human nature, and his ability and prudence which made him a desirable man to employ by anybody in difficult posts. Even those who hated him still admired him: 'Messer Francesco,' wrote Benedetto Varchi, the Florentine chronicler who loathed him, 'besides his wealth, his degree of knowledge, besides being governor or lieutenant of the Pope, was also famous for the practical knowledge he possessed of human actions, which he discussed and judged with great perception.'

These, briefly, were the stages of his rapid career. He was a struggling lawyer of twenty-nine when the republic of Florence appointed him ambassador to the King of Spain. In 1515, when he was thirty-three, he was sent by the republic to greet Pope Leo X, another Florentine, formerly Cardinal Giovanni de Medici. Leo, who had a keen nose for able men, took him into his favour and three years later appointed him Governor of the rebellious cities of Reggio and Modena. In 1521 Parma was added to his rule. The young and inexperienced democrat from Florence knew enough to surround himself with princely pomp, an impressive retinue, and escorts of cavalry and foot soldiers whenever he appeared in public. He was an efficient governor. He acted ruthlessly against all rebel subjects, not only those who sided with the emperor and were, therefore, open game, but also against those who sided with the pope, had friends at the Roman court, and could make the governor's life difficult. He disarmed everybody, arrested and tortured suspects, whatever their rank, executed robbers and murderers, generally enforced law and order, paved the main streets with stone, and balanced the budget. The Pope who succeeded Leo (after the short reign of another) was also a Medici, Clement VII; he named forty-one-year-old Francesco Governor of the vast province of Romagna and, three years later, Lieutenant-General of the papal armies.

In 1531 he was promoted to the Governorship of Bologna, the most important of all the papal Lord-Lieutenantcies. After the death of Clement, in 1534, he resigned and came back to Florence, to play local politics as a faithful henchman of the Medici family. With his support, Alessandro de Medici conquered power. He was a cruel, stupid, avaricious and dissolute tyrant, who ordered most of the pretty girls and handsome matrons of Florence to be brought to his bedroom, and was hated by everybody, including Guicciardini, who nevertheless served him loyally. Alessandro was murdered. Messer Francesco then used all his political skill and influence to bring to power another tyrant, the young Cosimo de Medici, belonging to a cadet branch of the family, and procured for him from Charles V the imperial title of 'Grand Duke', thus destroying the very name, if not the memory, of Florentine republican liberties.

This was his only mistake. Cosimo was a boy of seventeen, much addicted to sports and frivolous pursuits. Guicciardini thought he would just amuse himself with the 12,000 gold florins which were to be paid to him every year and leave matters of state to him. (Benedetto Varchi graphically describes Messer Francesco's unconsciously revealing his secret designs: 'Lowering his face and raising his eyes, Guicciardini said: "Twelve thousand gold florins—*è un bello spendere*, a nice enough sum to spend!"' The gesture would be still good for the villain in an Italian opera or costume film.) What Guicciardini did not know was that Cosimo was a political *enfant prodige*, a precocious teenage statesman. With decent modesty and becoming show of deference, the inexperienced youth had used the circumspect and shrewd veteran, one of the greatest politicians of all times, as his ladder to mount the throne, and then kicked the ladder away.

Guicciardini retired decorously to his villa near Arcetri, called *Il Finocchieto*, the fennel patch, to oversee his peasants, improve his wine, study, meditate, sum up his experiences, and write some of the best books of history in Italian literature. He died of a stroke at the age of fifty-eight.

What is striking and instructive about Messer Francesco is the wide discrepancy between his personal thoughts and beliefs, and his public acts. What is even more striking and instructive is the fact that he was not surprised or troubled by the discrepancy which he placidly accepted as one of the facts of life. He never allowed his private intimate convictions to interfere with the business on hand. He was, for instance, privately a devoted and religious man, honest and honourable, brought up strictly within the Catholic faith. In his youth he had even thought of becoming a priest. He wanted religion to return to ancient piety and moral zeal. As a good Christian, he despised the temporal power of the Popes, which had transformed the Vicar of Christ into a worldly princeling playing dirty Renaissance politics. He denounced in his secret notebook the corruption which power, wealth and ambition inevitably furthered among priests. Yet he served two Popes' unholy schemes and helped consolidate and enlarge the material domains of the Church.

He calmly explained in his *Ricordi*:

'No man hates the ambition and avarice of priests more than I do; for these vices, odious in themselves, are most unseemly in men who make a profession of living in contact with God. . . . My position under several Popes has compelled me to desire their aggrandisement for the sake of my own profit. Otherwise, I should have loved Martin Luther like myself—not that I might break loose from the laws which Christianity . . . imposes on us, but that I might see . . . villains . . . forced to live either without vices or without power.'

Although he hated tyranny above all, he did nothing to free Florence from tyrants and helped to destroy the city's liberty forever. He merely expressed his disapproval of tyrants in his journal and went on with the task in hand. He was too wise to allow himself to dream and to hope. Could he trust the men who plotted to re-establish free institutions? Of course not. Francesco sadly wrote:

'Do not take too seriously most people (not all of them, of course) who preach the advantages of liberty, because, if they hoped to find an advantageous position in a tyrannical state, they would rush there by the quickest post. In almost all men, the concern for their own interest is stronger than love of glory and honour.'

And:

'I do not blame those who, enflamed by love of country, defy dangers to establish liberty and popular rule, though I think that what they do is extremely risky. Few revolutions succeed, and, when they do, you often discover they did not gain you what you hoped for, and you condemn yourself to perpetual fear, as the parties you defeated may always regain power and work for your ruin.'

One had to learn to live with tyrants. Here are a few hints on how to prosper under them.

'No rules are useful when living under a bloody and bestial tyrant, except perhaps one, the same which is useful in times of plague: flee as far as you can. But when the tyrant is obliged to be relatively moderate and respectful, out of caution, necessity, or political convenience, a wise man must try to appear capable and courageous, although for the time being resigned to things as they are. . . The tyrant will then flatter him, not to offer him any cause to desire a different government. This the tyrant would not do if he knew the man to be restless, for if he thought there was absolutely no way to keep him quiet, he would think only of how best to kill and put him out of the way.'

'I believe that a good citizen and patriot should maintain good relations with the tyrant not only for his own saftey, but also for the benefit of everybody else. By seeing the tyrant often and gaining his trust, he may at times favour a good initiative and forestall a bad one. Those who blame this behaviour are mad. It is best, however, not to be among the tyrant's most intimate confidants. Thus you enjoy the advantages of his power and, when he meets his ruin, you will not be swept away with the rest.'

Prudent behaviour inevitably involves some dissimulation. How should a moral man envisage this necessity? Here is Messer Francesco meditating on this eternal problem:

'Everybody likes open, truthful and frank persons. To be open, truthful and frank is a noble and generous thing, although often harmful. On the other hand, dissimulation and deception are useful and often indispensable, because of the evil nature of men. These arts are, however, despised and hated by everybody. Therefore I do not know which behaviour to choose. I would suggest truthfulness should be ordinarily preferred, without abandoning deception altogether. That is, in the ordinary circumstances of life, use truthfulness in such a way as to gain the reputation of a guileless man. In a few important cases, use deceit. Deceit is the more fruitful and successful the more you enjoy the reputation of an honest and truthful man; you are more easily believed.'

The Guicciardini basic formula is this: 'Those men conduct their affairs well who keep in front of their eyes their own private interest and measure all their actions according to its necessities.' It is the way to survive and prosper in treacherous times. He added that unfortunately too many short-sighted men 'think that their interest lies mainly in the accumulation of wealth and not also in keeping a good reputation and a good name'. Messer Francesco knew better. He knew that without some renown and respect a man could amass riches but rarely preserve or increase them. He also knew that the lofty ideals he cherished would not interfere with his personal success only if he considered them his own private prejudices. He could speak of piety, honour, liberty, justice, morality, and the hope to see Italy freed from foreign oppressors to a few trusted friends, teach them to his children and grandchildren, write about them in his notebooks, within the four walls of his house, behind locked doors. But his decisions in the world were never to be dictated by a desire to change it. He could be compared to a seasoned captain who naturally would prefer to sail over a smooth sea, driven by favourable breezes in the right direction, but is prepared to adapt himself to whatever conditions will prevail. To arrive safely with any weather is his only goal. *Navigare* is a word employed often in the metaphorical sense, meaning to cut the sails and set the course according to the prevailing political winds, knowing that it is beyond man's power to change them. When Giovanni Musco, the Sicilian dialect comedian, was asked by Mussolini whether he was a Fascist he answered cryptically: '*Marinaio sugno*, I am a sailor.'

*

Italians do not need to read Guicciardini. In fact few of them ever do. They learned long ago to beware privately of their own show and to be sober and clear-eyed realists in all circumstances. They mind their own business. They behave with circumspection, caution and even cynicism. They are incredulous: they do not want to be fooled by seductive appearances and honeyed words. They cannot afford to be carried away by emotions. They keep them under control. This does not mean that they are cold people. When it is safe to do so, they enjoy genuine and unrestrained emotions as well as anybody. But they know that the free expression of genuine emotions is a luxury for the privileged, often a dangerous and expensive luxury. Only saints, heroes, poets, gentlemen of means, foreigners, madmen, and the poor, who have nothing to lose, can afford to give way to their emotions. Ordinary people must usually choose between the un-restrained expression of counterfeit emotions and the controlled expression of real ones. Though they have forgotten one of their old proverbs, which Lord Chesterfield quoted to his son, they still obey it; they keep *volto sciolto e pensiero stretto*, an open countenance and closed thoughts, for the same reasons that the façades of their houses are often cheerfully inviting but their front doors are always double-locked.

Like anybody else, they, too, would naturally prefer the world to be different: an Arcadia where the sheep could lie with the wolf, where everybody could say and write what he thought, and men were all brothers. But they know that those who delude themselves are almost sure to meet a bad end: they know the world is an ugly and pitiless place, and adapt themselves, without useless recriminations, to its inviolable laws. They good-humouredly make the best of their lot, whatever it may be, as soldiers do in a solitary outpost sur-rounded by the enemy, who grumble, shirk unnecessary dangers, make their dug-outs comfortable, adorn them with pictures and flowers, hoping for salvation but also resigned to death.

Only few Italians find solace in actual rebellion. Not all of the many members of the Communist party want to start a revolution. Most of them want to enjoy the privileged status of revolutionaries in a frightened capitalist society. Those few who want to set up a Marx-ist state know sadly that their revolution, as Guicciardini pointed out, would not modify the fundamental injustices of life. Revolt, anyway, gets one nowhere, tears one away from safe and anonymous obscurity, and makes one's life unnecessarily difficult. In the most favourable circumstances, on the rare occasions when it is successful, it may eventually improve one's great-grandchildren's lot, but almost never one's own. This is why many Italian rebels and revolutionaries always were and still are the best of men, more disinterested and worthy of admiration than others. Most people in Italy, in fact, believe that the *condition humaine* is a sentence without pardon and amnesties, that original sin cannot be washed away, that man cannot easily change his fate and that, in the end, he must pay for whatever relief he may gain with other and worse troubles.

For all these reasons they tend to be concrete people, never allowing their imagination to stray too far, preoccupied with concrete problems, situations, men and things as they are. They cultivate tangible pleasures, the pleasures of the senses, and, when they can, those, just as substantial, which wealth and power afford. The imperative which they implicitly obey in all their decisions is *non farsi far fesso*, not to be made a fool of. To be *fesso* is the ultimate ignominy, as credulity is the unmentionable sin. The *fesso* is betrayed by his wife, buys gold bricks, falls for deceptions and intrigues, and often accepts the wolf's invitation to lie down with him. The *fesso*, incidentally, also obeys the laws, pays the taxes, believes what he reads in the papers, keeps his promises, and generally does his duty. Fortunately, there are still enough *fessi* in Italy, mostly in the north, to keep the country alive; without them everything would probably stop; and yet few admire or praise them. Their number is therefore diminishing. Nobody knows what will happen when they disappear altogether.

This intense preoccupation with solid, measurable, sensible reality is readily perceived by anybody having even a superficial acquaintance with Italian life. It can be read in the ambiguous political decisions of every day, in the astute way in which business negotiations are conducted. It can also be confirmed simply by overhearing the conversation at the next café table, in a train compartment, or in any waiting-room. Average Italians talk mostly about what many other people talk about, food, money, the art of fornication, work, clothes, appearances, amusements, how to defend oneself from the schemes of rivals and the rigours of the law. Only the very young talk about art, virtue, justice, dreams, liberty, and ideals. The emphasis is always on the solid, the down-to-earth, the material, with a wealth of precise and substantial details. The people they describe are seldom virtuous, disinterested and generous; the loves, seldom pure and spiritual. The characters they mention, living politicians or dead historical figures, are always blandly accused of all sorts of crimes, homosexuality, adultery, the seduction of minors, corruption, nepotism, treason, cowardice, the plundering of public funds, or, the worst crime of all, stupidity. Why was a certain man appointed to a certain post? The last explanation they accept is that he may be capable of fulfilling some of its functions. It pleases them to think that it is because he is somebody's brother-in-law, has come across documents which would ruin the man who appointed him, belongs to an all-embracing secret society, or made love to a powerful man's mistress.

After the war, for instance, everybody tried hard to find a suitable answer to the puzzling problem: why was the United States showering billions of dollars on their country? Communists were certain that it was part of a master-plan to impoverish, starve, enslave, and destroy the Italian proletariat. Non-Communists could not make up their minds. Were the Americans mad? Many possible explanations were debated and discarded. At the end, most people said: 'Why should they, who won the war, enrich us, who lost it? They must have their own reasons. Whatever they are, there is no doubt the Americans are serving their own interests. Therefore, there is no need for us to be grateful to them.' There is a large part of reality which the realistic Italians never really grasp; there are many things they do not see for being too clear-sighted.

*

A few years ago a small English family rented an unpretentious villa near Florence. They had modest means, no ambitions, and tranquil ways. The father was a scholar, read a lot, and wrote an interminable book. The wife took good care of her two children, cultivated her garden, and typed her husband's manuscript. Florence and its surrounding hills have been a traditional refuge for people like them, studious and mild-mannered Anglo-Saxons who found life in their countries too hectic and exhausting. This particular family settled down comfortably: they liked the landscapes, the simple *contadini*, the long walks in the country. They were happy.

A maid helped them with the household duties, Elvira, a simple peasant girl, whom they treated as one of them. They taught her to read and write and to brush her teeth twice a day. As the months passed, the girl began visibly to swell. One day she could no longer postpone confessing what they had already guessed, that she was expecting a child. She wept copiously, tore her hair, told them she was not worthy of their trust, that they would be right to dismiss her and send her out into the street. She said she wanted to die, that she had to die, in any case, as she had no place to go, and her own father would kill her if he found her out. Her lover, the cause of her condition, had emigrated months before, and could not be traced; there was absolutely no way to get him back to marry her.

The Englishman consoled her as best he could, his wife took her in her arms, the children embraced her. The couple assured her that, according to their more modern and enlightened views, it was no shame to be an unwed mother, just a *contretemps*, and that she was not the first nor the last to whom such an accident had occurred. She was to stop worrying, it was bad for her. From then on they were going to take care of everything. She would stay in the house, do whatever light duties she could, look after her health; in the end the child would be born in a good clinic in Florence, at their expense, and then both mother and baby could come back and live with them for ever after. The Englishman even generously proposed that he be godfather and his wife godmother at the christening, if the difference in religion did not prevent it. The maid dried her tears and smiled.

When she returned with her baby, the Englishman sent for her father, told him what had happened, reassured him, explained that everything was all right, and invited him and the whole family for the *festa* of the christening. At the end of his little speech he looked benignly on the old peasant, feeling justly proud of being ready to alleviate other people's sorrows with his modest means and to do what he could to make poor Elvira and her baby secure and happy.

He was also understandably proud of showing this simple Tuscan *contadino* how generous and civilized the English could be in such matters. Maybe the lesson would not be wasted, maybe it would be remembered in similar cases in the future, and help modify the harsh and primitive local customs.

The old man looked grim and suspicious, as he listened to the foreigner's halting words with the strange accent, shook his head, and said nothing. Of course, he was too intelligent to believe the incredible fairy stories he had been told. Why should an Englishman, obviously a very wealthy and well-born gentleman, want to take care of that shameless and lying strumpet, Elvira, who should be better dead than alive to dishonour her family, as everybody would agree who knew anything about life? Why, then, had the Englishman not kicked her out of his house? Why had he spent all that good money on fancy doctors, a room in an expensive clinic, chicken broths, talcum powder, and diapers? Why did he want to go on spending more? Why did he want to be godfather? And, above all, why did he waste time telling him all that noble nonsense?

There was, obviously enough, but one true explanation. Anybody could guess it. The Englishman was the father of the newly-born baby. Elvira had probably seduced him, as she was perfectly capable of doing, the shameless *puttana*, or he had taken Elvira into his house to sleep with her. One could understand his reasons, one could even sympathize with him, when one looked at his bony English wife. What a stupid or immoral woman she must be, the peasant thought, to be willing to be godmother to her husband's bastard child, to the fruit of a sinful relation! The ways of foreigners are mysterious. Still, he concluded, whatever had happened, there the matter was and he had to do what was right. He nodded curtly and left.

The following day legal documents began raining on the poor English household. The Englishman, it appeared from the stilted prose, was being sued by Elvira's father for a very large amount of money, money for damages, money to assuage outraged feelings and redeem the dishonour and discredit to the family, money to assure the child and his mother adequate means for life, more money to pay the lawyers and, eventually, the courts. Obviously, Elvira's family considered that they had acquired the right to live comfortably from that day forth on the misfortune and disgrace of the poor girl. The Englishman left the whole matter in the hands of lawyers, gave up the villa, dismissed the maid, and hurriedly departed with his wife and children.

*

This obvious predilection of the Italians for the solid, the all-too-human, the comprehensible, the pleasurable; this constant suspicion of the honourable, the unworldly, the chivalrous, and the noble; this persistent fear of emotional traps; this concentration on private interests and disregard for public welfare; this certainty that all things, no matter how alluring, will end up badly, all these have been constant characteristics of Italian life since time immemorial. They are ancient mental precautions and expedients, unconsciously accepted by almost all, developed by the people in order to get through life unscathed. Numerous foreign scholars, who found them confirmed by abundant examples from the literature and the art of centuries, concluded that these were not expedients but perennial traits, an immutable part of the very nature of the people. The erudite John Addington Symonds, for example, dedicated to this preference several eloquent passages in his *Renaissance in Italy*. 'When we complain,' he wrote, 'that the Italians are deficient in the highest tragic imagination, that their feeling for nature lacks romance, or that none but their rarest works of art attain sublimity, we are but insisting on the realistic bias which inclined them to things tangible, palpable, experienced, compassable by the senses. . . . Realism, preferring the tangible and concrete to the visionary and abstract, the defined to the indefinite, the sensuous to the ideal, determines the character of their genius in all its manifestations.'

Norman Douglas even thought, curiously enough, that Italians were so preoccupied with practical matters that they became oblivious to pure beauty, the beauty of their own land in particular. 'There are wondrous tints of earth, sky, and sea, in these regions,' he wrote in *Siren Land*, speaking of Capri and the nearby coast, 'flaring sunsets and moons of melodramatic amplitude that roll upon the hilltops or swim exultingly through the aether; amber hued gorges where the shadows sleep through the glittering days of June, and the mad summer riot of vines careening in green frenzy over olives and elms and figs; there are tremulous violet flames hovering about the sun scorched limestone, sea mists that climb in wreathed stateliness among wet clefts, and the sulphurous gleams of a scirocco dawn when fishing boats hang like pallid spectres upon the skyline: there are thousands of joys like these, but the natives do not see them, although, to please foreigners, they sometimes pretend to. . . . The coils of muscle about the shoulders of some stripling as he strains himself to raise a heavy limestone block; a young girl whose swelling form gives promise of fruitful maternity; a waving cornfield, a shower in May, a dish of fat roasted quails—all this is legitimately *bello*: but mountains are mere hindrances to agriculture, unsightly protuberances upon the fair face of the earth; land-caves are useful for storing hay; sea-caves blue or green, for sheltering boats in the rain; the sea itself with all its choral harmonies, is merely a place where fishes are caught.'

*

This attachment to the solid, the substantial, and the real is particularly evident in the old *novelle*, the most typical product of Italian literature, the tales which Shakespeare and other northern poets ransacked for their plots. There are thousands of them. The very word *novella* is concrete. It does not mean story, a fiction of the imagination, a poetic invention, but news, actual news, reports of events which really took place, anecdotes in the life of rich, powerful and famous persons, information received from distant places. Foreign writers were as justified in borrowing ideas for their plays and poems from them as contemporary authors are in borrowing plots from the newspapers. The events in the old *novelle* do not take place in a misty and legendary atmosphere, among vaguely defined and shadowy characters, virtuous knights and noble maidens, driven by honourable motives, as in the stories which were written at about the same time, the late Middle Ages, in other parts of feudal Europe. There are real people in the Italian stories, merchants, monks, artisans, shopkeepers, and princes, human beings of solid flesh and sound appetites, who speak the quick and colourful dialects of the market place and the wine shop.

The lesson the reader drew was not meant to edify him. He did not learn to shun sin, to combat evil, to protect the weak, to control his base instincts, to respect the virtues of others, to reform the world, and prepare himself for salvation in after life; he learned mainly to protect himself from deceit, treachery, the arrogance and the cunning of others; to profit by their weakness, to see through their hypocrisy, and to enjoy the good things in life: the lusty wenches, the blushing maids, the good food, the good wine, the gay companions, and the victorious battles against feebler enemies. The cruel and ruthless ways of the world are accepted as unchangeable. They are seldom judged. The poor in spirit, the gullible, the naïve, the betrayed husband, in other words the *fessi*, are derided. Their sorry fate is considered not only inevitable but just and proper. The rich in spirit, the clever and strong men who use their gifts without scruples or charity, always come out on top, the object of the author's and the reader's admiration and approval. Only a few princes are allowed to be magnanimous and generous. All others live, win, or lose, strictly according to the rules of the game as the Italians understood them at the time and understand them, more or less unchanged, today.

Practically without interruption, through the years, Italians have continued to create works of art dedicated mainly to the praise of the strong and the powerful and the derision of the weak and defeated, or dedicated to the glory of the flesh, and the harmonious and perlaceous beauties of the naked female body; some of these works were coarse, ribald, bawdy, others delicate, thinly veiled, and allusive. Even when these artists tried their hands at more elevated subjects, their real tendencies ineluctably cropped up. In many of their Madonnas one can read the pleasure the painter has found in the fresh look of a pretty peasant girl, rather than his piety. Raphael's Madonnas are portraits of his voluptuous mistress, the baker's daughter, called *La Fornarina*, whose insatiable appetite for love was one of the causes of his early death. In great and more ambitious poems dedicated to religious and epic themes, the noble sentiments easily sound sugary and conventional, the language stilted, and the images contrived and literary. Only when the poets describe the fury of battle, palpable objects, villainous infidels, earthy delights and human passions are they at ease and convincing. How much more comfortable many authors feel in the many irreverent and satirical parodies they wrote of the noble and inspiring poems fashionable in the rest of Europe!

Italians also liked to compose cynical comedies of intrigue and deceit, closely following ancient Roman models so coarse they could not be produced unexpurgated even today. The best of these plays were composed by Nicolò Machiavelli, deriding men of the Church, bourgeois conventions, jealous husbands, and the virtue of women. It is odd that such a great historian and political thinker should waste his time writing pornographic farces, but not as inexplicable as it sounds. Many eminent men of the time, high prelates, statesmen and scholars, dedicated their spare time to the composition of obscene poems in Latin or Italian. Then Machiavelli's plays are not as morally distant from his great books, the *Commentaries on the Decades of Livy* and *The Prince*, as one would think. They are all inspired by failure, disappointment and bitterness: the private failure of an extremely clever man who never managed to become important, the public failure of an extremely clever and civilized nation, his own, which never achieved the unity and discipline necessary to defeat illiterate foreign invaders.

In his political works he challenged, for practical purposes, the validity of lofty and disinterested motives in the conduct of public affairs; in his comedies, he challenged the validity of similarly lofty and disinterested motives in the conduct of private affairs. In both fields, like all good Italians, he played safe: he trembled lest he be made a fool of, a dupe, fatally led to wrong conclusions and a bad end by honourable ideals. He felt much more secure believing that *le pire est toujours certain*, or, as he himself would have said in good Tuscan, *il peggio non è mai morto*. He preferred to take it for granted that all sovereigns were cruel, crafty, and ruthless; that all priests and monks were libertines, whoremongers, gluttons and rapacious money-grubbers, and all women harlots. He considered that he was, at the most, wrong only a very few times, hardly ever.

From the end of the eighteenth century to the end of the nineteenth, Italian writers at last dedicated their genius to something more worthy than the colourful description of worldly pleasures and the activities of men and women pliably and readily adapted to the worst in the world. Finally some authors appeared who believed the Italian people could rebel against their dreary and ignominious lot, correct their national defects, and work to better their moral and material conditions. These poets and novelists exalted spiritual values, religious faith, noble ideals; they praised patriotism, strength of character, courage, honesty, justice and truth. Some foresaw the resurrection of the ancient virile virtues of the people and the spiritual renovation of Italy. Their resounding poems and historical novels, as well as Verdi's heroic music, accompanied a vast moral, political and military upheaval, the revolution of the Risorgimento, the conquest of national independence and unity.

But with the end of the old century and the beginning of the new, after the smoke of battle had cleared, Italians began discovering that they were more or less the same as they had always been, that those who had really believed in the Risorgimento had been a small minority. The ancient traits began to reassert themselves, the old outlook to reappear in print. Writers went back to trusting only the palpable and measurable. Giovanni Verga, the Sicilian novelist, described the harsh avarice of peasants and fishermen as they strived to amass *la roba*, or wealth, in order to become bourgeois in the new liberal State. D'Annunzio felt patriotism no longer as a youthful and clean passion, but as an excuse for bloody, ornate and decadent adventures. Above all he believed in all kinds of physical pleasures, the feel of a panting horse at a gallop between his knees, a swim at dawn in the sea, rare perfumes, the killing of enemies in battle, and the endless delights of women's bodies. The old tradition continues. A few famous Italian writers of today (and some of the best films, which are partly inspired by them) have paid as much attention as their forefathers did to the solid aspects of life and have shown the old familiar suspicion of the ideal and noble. Some of these men have described the pleasures of lust, greed, and ambition with the ancient gusto, sometimes reaching daring refinements which even the Renaissance had not known.

When you consider, however, other contemporary works of art you are tempted to believe that Italians are for the first time no longer what they have always been. These are the leaden avant-garde novels, macabre paintings, disconsolate films and joyless poems which the best critics admire. The old fear of being made a fool of by illusions has now become an obsession. The search for truths which will not betray a man, modest truths if need be, has now reached a dead end. Obviously nothing much is left for a man to believe. Not yesterday's noble ideals, the love of country caricatured by the Fascists, the love of honour, honesty, morality, integrity derided by the current mores; not the hope of a better future in which not even the Communist dare believe any longer. Nothing is left because the last refuge of all Italians, his own *particulare*, his strictly private interest, the pursuit of concrete and measurable things, has been discredited for the first time. These newest Italians apparently do not even believe in the ultimate and fundamental Italian certainty, the flesh. In fact, fornication has, for the first time in centuries, become a tedious and almost repellent diversion in some of the best current Italian novels. Nothing is left, then, than *la noia*, the boredom which Moravia has so acutely analysed. But then you listen to people talk in cafés, watch them diffidently buy fish or fruit in an open-air market, watch them rapturously listening to sonorous band-music, watch old men smile to an unknown pretty girl in the street. . . . You are immediately reassured. The Italians are the same.

CHAPTER TEN

THE PURSUIT OF LIFE

LET us consider the solitary Italian, whoever he may be, at the moment he is actually born, on the day, that is, when he realizes that things are seldom what they seem, words not always what they sound like, and most of what he learned in school, in the army, or from his elders, and what he read in many grave books, is complete nonsense. On that day he understands that he will surely come to grief if he carelessly tries to live according to the rules he has been taught, like a blind man groping his way in a room in which the furniture is not where he expects it to be. The rules he has been taught are noble rules. They are probably useful to regulate life in other countries, those immaculate, well-ordered and prosperous countries of the north he has heard about. There, Italians believe, the same law is valid for the weak and the powerful; all officials are incorruptible; the inhabitants are honest, truthful and splendidly defenceless because they have no reason to fear one another. There, Italians believe, taxpayers gladly pay all their taxes without cheating; jobs are always awarded to the best man; medals to the real heroes; the labels of bottles always correspond to their contents, flowers and vegetables always come out as depicted on the seed-envelopes. There life is wonderfully easy. It is a different matter in Italy.

A moment of revelation comes, it must be admitted, practically to everybody and not to Italians alone. A day comes when men of all nations understand that life can be pitiless and ugly. Each has his own way of reaching maturity. Some need the imperceptible passing of the years. It takes but a tiny incident for others; like the shaking of a kaleidoscope it precipitates an abrupt change of the picture. Or it may be a great event that awakens him: he sees his country defeated and humiliated, and his leaders revealed as loathsome fiends or irresponsible imbeciles; he discovers that some of the principles he was taught as eternal were but empty words and that he himself was but a puppet in the hands of cynical realists.

The struggle between what should be and what is, hypocrisy and sincerity, make-believe and reality, notoriously goes on everywhere. Things are nowhere done exactly as the naïve or the young imagine. There is, at all times and in all countries, a behind-the-scenes brutal truth which shocks the uninitiated when they discover it; great decisions are never entirely noble; great leaders in all fields are by no means as witty, handsome, magnanimous and far-sighted as their official biographies make them out. As Lord Acton (who saw such things clearly, as he was born in Naples, the grandson of a Neapolitan prime minister) put it in a letter to Gladstone's youngest daughter Mary: 'Most assuredly, now as heretofore, the Men of the time are in most cases unprincipled and act from motives of interest, or passion, or prejudice cherished and unchecked, of selfish hope and unworthy fear.'

It is, however, possible for an ordinary non-Italian, at normal times, when the whole structure does not collapse on his head, never to wake up and to live his whole life wrapped in consoling illusions, affectionately attached to all the dear nonsense of childhood, revering the proper ideals and heroes. Nothing much happens to him. He may just wonder once in a while why unjust men should be rewarded and honoured more than he, but the matter does not embitter him unduly. In Italy no one can afford to delude himself. The most obscure and unambitious individual will be derided, swindled, betrayed if he does not clearly know his way about. The lower his condition the more vulnerable he is and the quicker he must recognize the real rules governing life in order not to prosper but merely to survive. Only after he has learned them, life will become simple, human, pleasant, easy, rich with many opportunities, and satisfactions more rewarding than life in many other countries. Such rules, of course, are not written anywhere. They are suggested by proverbs, humorous mottoes on ash-trays, innuendoes, winks, or shrugs of the shoulder. Few Italians can avoid learning them, however, as they are taught by fear, humiliation, deception and defeat. These things are

met earlier in life and more frequently in Italy than in many other
countries.

*

Poor illiterate boys from the slums and starving children from southern villages obviously know all they need to know even before they
begin to speak. Those who never learn to read have a clear un-
cluttered mind: they do not have to forget what others have to learn.
How old are the little boys in Naples who steal bags from parked
cars and procure prostitutes for sailors on shore-leave? They are
born decrepit. The eight-year-old boy who was kidnapped by the
Mafia, a few years ago, with his grandfather, one of the great Sicilian
landowners, knew, without being told by anybody, that he must show
no fear, see nothing, hear nothing, and later remember nothing of
what had happened to him.

Many boys acquire their wisdom in school: they quickly learn how
to get ahead smoothly, how to defeat rivals while retaining their
friendship, how to pass examinations without working too hard.
They know which sentiments to express in their essays in order to
please the teacher. The penniless university graduates with their
worthless law degrees who, every year, swarm north to Rome,
Milan and Turin are as wise as members of the Soviet élite:
they know the technique of getting a small foothold in some obscure
office, through a relative or friend, manœuvre their way to a better
position, surpass their competitors, please whoever is on top at the
moment, and patiently crawl from one mediocre job to a better one,
until they achieve their purpose. Half the Italian bureaucracy is composed of such men. By these arts southerners in the north gradually
conquer commanding positions in private business and industry.
Most of them are intelligent and useful men, who work well and
deserve the jobs they would not have if they ignored the technique of
conquering them.

There are many apparent exceptions, men who seem not to need
the arts of getting on: great artists, scholars, scientists, who live
among abstract ideas, theoretical problems and imaginary characters,
as well as the few rich people who have inherited wealth and manners, the gentlemen. But even they when they want really to get

ahead, preserve or enlarge their wealth, authority and status, defend themselves from envious rivals, or when they are devoured by ambition, must sooner or later learn. The real exceptions are found elsewhere. There are a few men of great moral stature, stern and obstinate men who play a lone hand, refuse to pay attention to the rules or who make their own. They struggle on, in the face of hostility or criticism, in their own way, win or loose. Most of them have always lost. They still lose today. A minority, however, manage to triumph somehow, from time to time, as some did in the past. They are the great men of Italy, whom the Italians seldom like when alive but honour when dead. They are considered not quite *simpatici*, because they follow their own stern principles and not the *convenances*.

*

Among the few who learn last are the best educated Italians. They therefore can be considered, at times, less Italian than their countrymen, less able to understand what is going on and speak for their country. They discover Italy with a shock. Take the distinguished Neapolitan general Carlo Filangieri, Prince of Satriano and Duke of Taormina, who was born in 1784 and died in 1867. He was the son of Gaetano Filangieri, one of the outstanding political philosophers of the eighteenth century. Educated at Prytanée, the French military school, he fought brilliantly under Napoleon at Ulm, Marienzell, Austerlitz and Burgos, and under Murat, King of Naples, as his *maréchal du camp*, reaching the rank of general in 1815. He could not bear to hear his countrymen insulted. (He once killed the French general Franceschi in a duel, for merely having called the Neapolitans *bougres*.) On the other hand, he knew exactly what life was like in his native country. He left these words for his son: '*Credimi: per chiunque ha un po' d'onore e un po' di sangue nelle vene è una grande calamità nascere napoletano*' ('Believe me, for any one who has a little honour and a little blood in his veins, it is a great calamity to be born Neapolitan'). By *napoletano* he meant a subject of the King of Naples, a southern Italian in general.

Or take another distinguished example, Massimo d'Azeglio. He was a Piedmontese marquis, well brought up, well educated, honourable, intelligent, a man of the world, a patriot. He became a renowned painter, a novelist of note, an excellent cavalry officer, aide-de-camp to the king, and his prime minister from 1849 till 1852. He married Alessandro Manzoni's daughter and was one of the patriots of the Risorgimento. He knew Italy well. When a very young man, in 1820, he first came to Rome, where he met many foreign travellers, including some distinguished English ladies.

He wrote in *I miei ricordi*:

'With foreigners I experienced a sensation of humiliation so painful that from their friendship came to me more bitterness than satisfaction. I was ashamed of being an Italian! . . . The cold behaviour of the English . . . the tranquil and self-confident pride that could be seen on their countenances . . . looked as if they were intended for me, to make me feel my inferiority, to make me understand that when a nation is the prey of anybody that takes it, when it allows all sorts of people from the four quarters of the world to come to it to amuse themselves, just as hunters migrate to regions where the game abounds, then those who belong to such a nation can be tolerated among foreigners, but cannot be considered their equal, ever.'

The bitter words of Carlo Filangieri and Massimo d'Azeglio are notable because of the eminence of the two men, and also because they were written and printed. Usually such comments were said in private. Giovacchino Rossini, the composer of the *Barbiere di Siviglia* and inventor of a famous steak, used to say to his intimates: 'Thank God for the Spaniards. . . . If there were no Spaniards the Italians would be the last people in Europe.'

Clearly the reactions of the well educated are more vigorous and their deception is more profound. As they reach the day of the awakening later than their illiterate compatriots, and are more articulate, they can usually also define and describe their thoughts with greater clarity. On that day, to begin with, they already know what everybody should know everywhere: that life is fundamentally a merciless game; that man should find his protection in the warp and woof of society; that curbs on man's instincts constitute the essence of civilized living. Without such protections man is alone in the world, as alone as a beast of prey or as the prey itself, waiting to be devoured.

These people, however, also discover that all official institutions are weak and unstable in Italy: the law is flexible and unreliable, the State discredited and easily dominated by powerful persons or groups, and society (as conceived elsewhere) has little influence. And yet, somehow, life around them flows easily: man is not always devoured by man; people do defend themselves; the daily work is done; the country can be considered civilized, in fact it is among the most civilized in the world, although admittedly enjoying a peculiar civilization of its own. Man is by no means alone here. He is immersed in humanity. He is aided, comforted, protected in many ways. In fact, life can often be gay, animated and satisfying. It is, anyway, all these things for those who do not insist upon abstract and impartial justice, or expect the legal apparatus to function smoothly. Life for resigned and disenchanted people appears to be no more cruel than in better organized countries, or, at least, not cruel and unjust in the same manner. It is as if the people themselves tried to compensate with their own good will for the lack of rigid rules and legal protections. Genial toleration, sympathy for other men's weaknesses, the feeling of intimate complicity among people secretly fighting the same enemies, a vast and indiscriminate indulgence often bathe all things in a tepid bath of benevolence and soften all harshness. Moral preoccupations seldom cast their gloomy shadows. While the official machinery of collective life is omnipresent (there are policemen in five different uniforms, innumerable forms to fill, stamped papers to be used on all occasions, permits required for the smallest activities, hundreds of law books, and stately government buildings in practically every other street), nothing essential really depends on it. How do Italians really function?

The first basic thing an educated Italian discovers is that feudalism as a moral conception was alien to Italy, and never deeply influenced Italian life. Its external and concrete aspects were naturally accepted, as many foreign fashions always are here, but even they were soon adapted to local tastes and conditions, and transformed into something useful and comprehensible. Chivalry, for instance, was turned mainly into a polite pastime for the upper classes. Only its picturesque trappings were eagerly adopted, the elaborate escutcheons, the titles, the elegant courtesies, and the spectacular tournaments. But its moral precepts were generally ignored. There is no local equivalent to the oath which King Arthur administered to his knights, there is no Italian Bayard, *chevalier sàns peur et sans reproche*.

Fewer Italians, in fact, obeyed the highest call of the age of chivalry, actually leaving wives and castles to redeem Christ's sepulchre from the Infidels' possession, than gentlemen from any other nation. The men of Pisa, Amalfi, Genoa and Venice, the four sea-republics, shrewdly made money as contractors and merchants in the Crusades. The Venetians, in particular, habitually rented their ships on charter for the crossing of the Mediterranean to the knights from Germany, England and France, and often craftily routed military operations to where they would do most good to the interests of the Venetian republic, towards the conquest of ports and islands which could be used later as bases for a leisurely commercial penetration into the Levant.

The Italians were also naturally impervious to most of the ideals which made the medieval world go round: unswerving loyalty to one's chief, allegiance to one's sovereign, and *noblesse oblige*, or the sense of duty towards dependents, inferiors, the weak and defenceless. Foreign words like honour, *honneur*, *Ehre* cannot be translated exactly. The Italian nearest equivalent *onore* is misleading: it mainly means something bestowed from outside, esteem or reverence, rank, dignity, distinction, and almost never 'a fine sense of and strict allegiance to what is due or right (1548)', as the Oxford Dictionary puts it. Machiavelli, for instance, complains: '*Gli uomini non sanno essere onorevolmente tristi*', or 'Men do not know how to be wicked in an *honourable* way'.

All this could have little importance were it not for the fact that the modern world still functions on the remnants of the feudal code. It would go to pieces without them: there could not be powerful nations, governments, armies and navies, solid military alliances; there could not be vast organizations of any kind, financial combines, or great industries; there could not be sporting competitions without a certain amount of Teutonic chivalry, what little of it, anyway, has percolated down to the nineteenth-century bourgeoisie and finally to us. Reverence for truth, fair play, respect for laws, rules, and regulations; respect for one's opponents; capacity to work in teams; willingness to apply to oneself and one's friends the same rules one applies to all others; loyalty to one's convictions and faith, loyalty to one's party, class, school, country, these are the virtues which not only made the Crusades possible and kept together the mighty empires of old, but still manage somehow to hold modern empires together.

The contemporary capitalistic world is still almost incomprehensible to most Italians, who admire, envy and imitate, often very successfully, its outward aspect, its power, and its practical products, but miss its moral character. They even doubt if it exists at all. Many current rules of fair conduct strike the Italians as pure nonsense. Take the English saying 'never kick a man when he is down'. They do not believe anybody really obeyed it. They know a man should not be kicked if he is old, if he is strong and can immediately kick back, if he can later avenge himself, if he has powerful friends or relatives, if he could be useful some day in any way, or if a policeman is watching. But why not 'when he is down'? When else, if you please, should one kick a man more advantageously? When more safely and effectively? A famous handbook on how to play *scopa*, the most common Italian card game, written in Naples by a Monsignor Chitarella, begins: 'Rule Number One: always try to see your opponent's cards.' It is a good concrete practical rule.

There is, it must be admitted, one small remnant of the age of ancient knights which has been preserved intact in Italy. It is a handbook published for the first time in 1887 and reprinted eighteen times, until practically yesterday. A dog-eared copy is to be found in the library of many middle-class Italians of a certain age. It is seldom a copy which they themselves bought, but one they borrowed in a hurry, years before, and never gave back. One usually needs the book immediately, in an emergency, perhaps in the middle of the night or on a Sunday. It is on rare occasions still used today.

It is called the *Codice cavalleresco italiano* or Italian Code of Chivalry, written by one Jacopo Gelli, a cavalry colonel from Leghorn; it teaches one how to behave when involved, in any capacity, in a dispute among gentlemen. Nothing is left to chance. Every minute variation has been foreseen. No rule has been arbitrarily made up, the author points out, who claims to have merely recorded the customs already valid among honourable men. It naturally begins with definitions: a gentleman is 'the man who, out of a refined moral sensitivity, does not believe that the laws . . . are sufficient to protect his honour, and imposes on himself the rigid observance of special rules which are called the laws of chivalry'; honour is determined from outside, *all'Italiana*; it is defined as 'the esteem and consideration which an honest person has been able to gain in public opinion through his actions, always in agreement with natural and civil laws'. 'The sentiment of honour must dominate all other considerations in a gentleman. It is, however, a vulgar prejudice that the honour of a gentleman can be measured by the number of duels he has fought.'

A man may lose his quality of a gentleman (and become an inferior kind of person, who cannot ask for satisfaction after having been insulted) if he violates ordinary laws; he can also be disqualified by a jury of professional gentlemen for adequate technical reasons, which are laid down. Offences are graduated in a scale of intensity like earthquakes or typhoons. The most serious, fourth degree, are those 'which touch the family'. Controversies started by the highest offences can be terminated only with open letters of abject apologies or a proper duel. Meticulous instructions follow on how to organize all kinds of proper duels.

Loopholes, of course, abound. Gelli points out that the first duty of seconds is not to see that one of their principals kills the other at any price but, if at all possible, to settle the matter without recourse to arms. This is difficult to arrange, as neither party ever wants to apologize. There are, however, several catches. The most widely used is Article 9: 'When the offensive act was not provoked or justified, or when it was caused by an erroneous valuation of facts or by misunderstandings, a solution by way of an armed encounter must be excluded.' What insult cannot be said to have been determined by 'an erroneous valuation of facts'? At the end of the volume are many letters, ready prepared, for the use of all participants, a letter from the offended who charges two friends to defend his interests, a letter of challenge to the offender, known as *cartello di sfida*, and models for sundry other documents.

The book is useful in a practical way. It contains the experience of centuries and indicates tactful and dignified means for solving intricate and annoying disputes which ordinary laws and normal procedures leave unsolved or aggravate. It is obvious that such matters can be handled better by third parties, who examine them and debate them with cool heads, than by the actors themselves. Nobody ever gets killed. If Oscar Wilde had challenged the Marquis of Queensberry, with the aid of this handbook, instead of suing him in court, he would have lived a long and industrious life, almost reaching the day in which his tastes had become openly accepted, respected in good society, and useful in the world of literature and art.

But discussions between four polite friends would easily draw out until doomsday (neither group usually wants to admit defeat and offer satisfactory excuses), were it not for one threat, the highly improbable but real possibility of placing the two gentlemen involved, naked to the waist, on a lawn, at dawn, weapons in hand, surrounded by the proper paraphernalia and personnel. This now happens very rarely, once every three or four years, but cannot be excluded. The threat is not only a vague one to the life of the protagonists. As duelling is strictly forbidden by law, the seconds, the doctors, and the expert who directs the encounter are also liable to end up in jail. This slight preoccupation for their own liberty inevitably quickens the seconds' decisions and facilitates most peaceful settlements.

A friend telephones excitedly, to tell you that he is in trouble; you meet him and a friend of his, the other second, to examine the terms of the dispute; you hurriedly thumb through the nearest copy of Gelli in order to study the possibilities available; you copy the suitable letters at the end of the book (there are only forty-eight hours in which to challenge the offender); you do all this and you cannot help smiling inwardly at the ludicrous and archaic procedures, terminology, and complications. I have a few times been the second of friends (journalists are traditionally supposed to be experts in the matter) and, speaking the proper lines and doing the proper things, have always felt as if I were taking part in a bad costume play.

But when, side by side with the other second, both dressed in dark suits as if for a christening or a board meeting, I have handed the offender the letter I had just copied, and, as he read it and tried excitedly to answer something, stopped him with the traditional formula, 'I'm sorry, we cannot listen to anything you say. Please name two of your friends with whom we two will be glad to talk. We'll be waiting for them all the afternoon. Goodbye,' I could not help feeling, in spite of the preposterous words and the pompous and embarrassing gestures, that the moment still preserved a small and remote solemnity.

I once had to hand such a letter to a Communist journalist in a busy *caffè* in Rome, among the cries of rushing waiters, the hiss of the espresso machines, and the chattering of the clients. (We had not much time before the deadline and that was the only appointment I could get with him. We had lost precious hours debating with experts whether a Communist could be considered a gentleman, something on which Colonel Gelli had nothing to say.) He came in from the rain, shut his umbrella, saw us from far away, smiled, waved to us, and came over, saying 'Are you mad? Why did you have to see me before sundown?' He laughed as he took the letter, not thinking what it could be, perhaps suspecting some sort of stupid joke. Then he read the stilted and antiquated words and became very pale and very grave. Obviously, even for him the little ceremony had some vestigial meaning left. The party did not allow him, in the end, to fight the duel. He regretfully had to disqualify himself.

Colonel Gelli's is admittedly an obsolete and silly way of settling disputes. And yet it survives not only because it may be still useful at times. There is another reason. The gentlemanly way of settling quarrels according to the code of chivalry has lasted in Italy longer than anywhere else because it agrees with one of the deepest national traits. It is one more way of disregarding official laws, rules, statutes, State-appointed authorities, and to regulate matters according to a private concept of right and wrong, traditional precepts, and the help of one's friends.

*

Very few then are the rules which can help an Italian plot his course and steer a safe line in a country which has never really accepted the moral teaching of feudalism, and in which society, the law and the

State have feeble powers. He must defend himself. He begins early by being his own school-teacher (most schools are inadequate) and professor (universities are poor, backward and badly run). Later he must be his own journalist (published news of internal affairs can be so biased that to rely on them is to court disaster), his own literary, film, art, and dramatic critic (reviews rarely reflect the worth of the film, book, or drama, but a number of factors, the personal relation between author and critic, their respective political parties, relative ages, philosophical bias, and so forth), his own strategic expert in times of war (nobody will tell him who is winning and when to run until too late), and his own fiscal expert (to distinguish which are the taxes to be paid fully, which only in part, and which to be ignored altogether). He must at times be his own lawyer, policeman and judge. In short, his security depends not on the combined exertions of his countrymen to which he should add his own but mostly on his individual capacities and native shrewdness.

He soon discovers that he can occupy in society only whichever position he can conquer and defend with his personal authority. His authority depends on many factors, his capacity, talents, energy, determination, but ultimately on his ability to intimidate his enemies and, if the need should arise, to destroy them. There are many ways of doing this in Italy, almost as many as there are *milieus*. In convents, bishoprics, or the Vatican, the means are almost imperceptible; a cold stare, a curt nod, a Latin pun followed by an inaudible chuckle, an obscure article on a small theological point or a compliment bestowed for the wrong reasons may suffice. In the business world and in politics a man can be slandered, cuckolded, demoralized, cut off from powerful contacts, blackmailed, pushed to the verge of ruin, or driven to suicide. In some sections of Sicily, to destroy a man may literally mean to have him blasted off the face of the earth or silently poisoned.

All these techniques need power. There must be power behind the seemingly mild words, the obscure menaces, the decision to cut a man off from the sources of his livelihood. Without power all threats would be risible and bombastic gestures. Nobody can hope to live without power, not necessarily a great and frightening amount of it, but as much as is indispensable for the job in hand, neither more nor less, proportionate to one's needs. A cabinet minister behind his desk and the *usciere* introducing visitors to his presence both dispose of what power is necessary for their respective positions, otherwise neither would be where he is.

This necessity forces each man to obey, in the daily struggle for existence, roughly the same rules which have dominated international relations at all times. Each Italian must learn to face problems with the detached technique with which sovereigns and statesmen determine policy. Few decisions are allowed to be influenced by sentiments, tastes, hazards or hopes, but usually by a careful valuation of the relative strength of the contending parties. The choice between one alliance or another, between hostility or peace, resistance to the last breath or immediate surrender, are the result of a realistic estimate of the forces each side can marshal.

This is one of the reasons why, when negotiating even the smallest deal, Italians must always look at each other's faces. They read in their opponent's eyes (or catch in his voice and choice of words) the signs of his stubborn decision or hidden timidity. They can thus decide when it is safe to increase one's demands, when to stand pat, and when it is more prudent to retreat and accept the other man's conditions. Capitulation, of course, must be done with *garbo*, the retreat (for which a door has always been kept ajar) disguised with ingenious and flattering explanations. People are so unconsciously expert at this difficult art that few describe it. This necessity inevitably has its drawbacks. It slows down and complicates all kinds of transactions. Nothing serious can ever be decided by correspondence. People must travel to look at each other. But it has some advantages: Italians, for instance, were naturally gifted diplomats in the days when diplomacy was still a responsible and exacting trade.

This must be kept in mind by anybody trying to fathom the real reasons for some puzzling Italian decisions, or to foresee some future Italian move. Like all statesmen, after Italians have realistically gauged the relative weight of conflicting parties, they fight a weaker enemy and join a winner. Such rules of conduct make conflicts of all sorts last a shorter time in Italy than elsewhere. The number of worthy and heroic people willing to go on fighting on the side which they believe is right but which public opinion knows will succumb in the end is necessarily small. The rules make some decisions, turning points in history, or revolutions inevitable much too soon, when they could still be avoided, prevented, or deflected. It also often makes their results superficial, unstable and insincere.

Power, personal power, is the key.

CHAPTER ELEVEN

THE POWER OF THE FAMILY

THE first source of power is the family. The Italian family is a stronghold in a hostile land: within its walls and among its members, the individual finds consolation, help, advice, provisions, loans, weapons, allies and accomplices to aid him in his pursuits. No Italian who has a family is ever alone. He finds in it a refuge in which to lick his wounds after a defeat, or an arsenal and a staff for his victorious drives. Scholars have always recognized the Italian family as the only fundamental institution in the country, a spontaneous creation of the national genius, adapted through the centuries to changing conditions, the real foundation of whichever social order prevails. In fact, the law, the State and society function only if they do not directly interfere with the family's supreme interests.

Italy has often been defined, with only slight exaggeration, as nothing more than a mosaic of millions of families, sticking together by blind instinct, like colonies of insects, an organic formation rather than a rational construction of written statutes and moral imperatives. There were times in her past, and even in recent, almost contemporary history, when the State was at its lowest and weakest, impoverished and defeated, and yet the inhabitants were feverishly active, happy and prosperous. Some gloomy writers compared the joyous activity of the people and the impotence and disruption of the official institutions at those times to the merry swarming of worms on a corpse. Conversely, there were times, rare times, when the interests of the coalition of families coincided with those of the State, and Italy seemed to foreign observers to be a solid, efficient and powerful nation.

This is, of course, nothing new, surprising, or unique. In many countries and among many people, past and present, where legal authority is weak and the law is resented and resisted, the safety and welfare of the individual are mainly assured by the family. The Chinese, for instance, in their imperial days held the cult of the family more praiseworthy than the love of country and the love of good. This is why the Communist régime of Mao Tse-tung tried to stamp out the family, recognizing it as its most powerful opponent. Similarly, wherever the Jews were allowed to settle in Europe, they outwardly conformed to the local laws and impositions, but in their hearts obeyed only their religious rules and the immemorial code of their family life, which allowed them precariously to survive persecutions.

It is therefore not surprising that the Italians, living, as they have always done, in the insecurity and dangers of an unruly and unpredictable society, are among those who found their main refuge behind the walls of their houses, among their blood-relatives. Italians have, after all, many points of contact with the Chinese: the Chinese, too, love ceremonies, feasts, elaborate rites, deafening noise, fireworks, and good food; love children and produce many of them; their art is also highly decorative and ingenious but not always deep; they fashion lovely things by hand, and are astute negotiators and subtle merchants. The Italians are also, in many ways, similar to the Jews: the Jews have the same disenchanted and practical outlook; are among the few people who laugh at their own foibles; they entertain a wary diffidence for other people's noble intentions and always look for the concrete motives hiding behind them.

There is, however, this fundamental difference between the Italians and most other people who use the family as their private lifeboat in the stormy seas of anarchy. Anarchy in Italy is not simply a way of life, a spontaneous condition of society, a natural development: it is also the deliberate product of man's will, the fruit of his choice; it has been assiduously cultivated and strengthened down the centuries. The strength of the family is not only, therefore, the bulwark against disorder, but, at the same time, one of its principal causes. It has actively fomented chaos in many ways especially by rendering useless the development of strong political institutions. This, of course, brings up a complex problem: do political institutions flourish only where the family is weak, or is it the other way around? Does the family become self-sufficient only where the political institutions are not strong enough? However it may be, political institutions never had much of a chance in Italy. The people gave birth to but a few of them: they had to import most of them ready-made from abroad, from time to time, feudalism, the centralized monarchy, the constitution, the bi-cameral system, liberalism, democracy, socialism, as they are now threatening to borrow the Communists' régime prefabricated from Soviet Russia.

The family was also invincible because it was the sacred ark in which Italians deposited and preserved against alien influences all their ancient ideals. It clearly preserved the national character from contamination. The Italy of the families is definitely the real Italy, the quintessential Italy, distilled from the experiences of centuries, while the Italy of the laws and institutions is partly make-believe, the country Italians would like to believe was or will be but know is not. Will all this continue? Will all régimes the Italians give themselves in the future be inevitably corroded and destroyed by the family? Is this belief the reason why Italians are always compliantly ready to experiment with new political ways and why so many of them do not fear revolutions? Will anarchy ever end in this country? Will the family always predominate? This is, of course, the central riddle of Italian history and political life.

*

What follows is a simplified picture of the Italian family as it is supposed to be, an ideal model drawn for the edification and instruction of the reader. Of course, he is too intelligent not to realize that things are seldom as perfect and typical as this in real life, just as no human body corresponds to the coloured images in anatomy text-books. There are in Italy, too, broken families, dissensions, secessions, rifts, and interminable feuds among relatives; in Sicily, members of the same family often crouch behind prickly-pear hedges with hunting rifles in their hands, waiting to kill each other; in Lombardy, members of the same family almost invariably contest their grandfather's will, with the aid of expensive lawyers and all kinds of chicanery, from one court to another. The excessive tenacity, however, with which relatives fight each other at times proves that they are struggling against their very instincts: even when feuding, they cannot help feeling an almost irresistible urge to conform to ancient precepts and an unusually deep sense of remorse when they violate them.

The majority of families manage to be as faithful to the perfect pattern as possible. Usually the best examples are found among the more old-fashioned people, those who are perhaps more Italian than others, peasants, fishermen, landowners, and petty bourgeois from the small towns, and the provincial and more rigorous aristocracy. Southerners of all classes preserve the traditions almost intact, with more tenacity than northerners. In the industrialized north and in the café society of the big cities, the bad examples set by other countries are being increasingly imitated. And yet even the deviations are superficial. No Italian does, without hesitation and remorse, many things Americans, Englishmen and Frenchmen do as a matter of course. He cannot, for instance, lightly abandon a wife who is the mother of his first-born male child.

The family extracts everybody's first loyalty. It must be defended, enriched, made powerful, respected, and feared by the use of whatever means are necessary, legitimate means, if at all possible, or illegitimate. Nobody should defy it with impunity. Its honour must not be tarnished. All wrongs done to it must be avenged. All enemies must be kept at bay and the dangerous ones deprived of power or destroyed. Every member is duty-bound to do all he can for its welfare, give his property if needed, and, sometimes, when it is absolutely inevitable, sacrifice his life. Men have spent their last penny to save a relative from bankruptcy. The family should by every means be safeguarded from runs of bad luck, the disastrous effects of political mutations, and economic crisis. For this, at least one representative must be a member of the party in power and another of the opposition. A well-run family must split in all civil wars. It must be made to prosper for generations, possibly till the end of time. There must be children, of course, lots of children, especially sons who can carry on the name. Nothing should be spared to produce them. Everything is done for them in Italy. They are the protagonists of Italian life. Their smallest wishes are satisfied. A crowd will always gather around a pretty baby. Humble parents go without food, clothes, and comforts in order to pamper their sons, and to see that they go to school and reach a higher rung in the social ladder. The climbing is not hurried, it is done in successive waves, one generation after the other, till the highest pinnacles are reached.

One fundamental point which escapes most foreigners must be understood and remembered. Most Italians still obey a double standard. There is one code valid within the family circle, with relatives and honorary relatives, intimate friends and close associates, and there is another code regulating life outside. Within, they assiduously demonstrate all the qualities which are not usually attributed to them by superficial observers: they are relatively reliable, honest, truthful, just, obedient, generous, disciplined, brave, and capable of self-sacrifices. They practise what virtues other men usually dedicate to the welfare of their country at large; the Italians' family loyalty is their true patriotism. In the outside world, amidst the chaos and the disorder of society, they often feel compelled to employ the wiles of underground fighters in enemy-occupied territory. All official and legal authority is considered hostile by them until proved friendly or harmless: if it cannot be ignored, it should be neutralized or deceived if need be.

There have been men in Italy who, in wars not of their liking, often did only what was necessary merely to return alive to their homes and no more, men who could be technically accused of cowardice; the same men often face, when it becomes necessary, in peacetime, almost unbearable sacrifices and mortal dangers for the sake of their parents or children. Fathers, brothers, sons, grandsons (mostly from the south and the islands, but frequently also from the more advanced north) daily risk death to protect their women from outrage and themselves from dishonour. Many of these champions of family respectability end up in prison for life, but with a clear conscience. They carry themselves proudly, head high. They know they have done their duty and have obeyed one of the few valid laws they recognize. They also know that their relatives will take care of their women and children for as long as it will be necessary.

*

The obligation to provide one's family with the wealth and power necessary to defy the centuries explains many peculiar Italian habits, including the custom of ancient Popes of elevating their nephews and kinsmen to high position and enriching them. It is easy now to sneer at nepotism. It should, however, be studied without malevolence. Kings and Popes, like all Italians, unquestionably owed their first loyalty to their families. But a king, as a rule, had many advantages: he came from a family which was already illustrious, powerful and wealthy, and had many useful connections and ramifications; he did not usually have to worry about conquering his throne and knew his eldest son would inherit it as a matter of course and, after him, his eldest son's eldest son; a king usually had plenty of time and opportunities to promote his relatives' interests, enlarge the family's domain and fortune; furthermore, he was surrounded by a traditional élite of experienced men trained to serve him faithfully.

A Pope was, on the other hand, in a difficult position. He usually reached power when already an old man, a decrepit old man at times. He was in a hurry: he had to do for his kinsmen, within a few years, before it was too late, what most royal families had taken centuries to achieve. His people needed practically everything: they were usually obscure, provincial and poor. He did not know what would happen to them after his departure. He had, of course, the power to confer sonorous titles on them all, but titles are worthless without capital and properties. The men surrounding him were adequately loyal but not to him. They served the Holy Father, whoever he was, and would serve his successor just as loyally. Like all *novi homines* in a tight spot the Pope could count only on his blood relations: they knew their fortunes were tied to his.

All this explains the almost unseemly hurry and the apparent lack of scruples with which many otherwise virtuous Popes, within a few days or hours of their election, provided for their relatives' welfare. Their efforts were usually successful and had long-lasting effects. The great noble families of Rome (few of them of Roman origin) are still the descendants of the Pontiffs. Many of them still manage to be among the richest, amply enjoying the fruits of ancient favours and plunders. Even the unlucky who received worthless land in the Campagna, picturesque pasture-land amidst ruined aqueducts, are now also immensely wealthy: their estates have in this century become priceless property within the city limits.

We possess a few reliable details respecting the incomes of Papal nephews during the sixteenth and seventeenth centuries, when nepotism was already on the wane. They were recorded by Venetian ambassadors, who, being businessmen, were interested in figures. Saint Charles Borromeo, a nephew of Pius IV, was made cardinal at twenty-two years of age, with excellent results, as he was a great and holy man, and was reasonably believed to have enjoyed revenues amounting to 50,000 scudi a year, which he gave to the poor or spent on the endowment of holy institutions. (The Princes Borromeo are a Milanese family. They still enjoy ample means. They live in their own *palazzo*, the Palazzo Borromeo, in the Piazza Borromeo, in Milan.) Giacomo Buoncompagno (the family now spells the name Boncompagni), the bastard son of Gregory XIII, received an estate of 120,000 scudi, while two cardinal nephews of the same Pope had each about 10,000 scudi a year. (The Boncompagni still own *palazzi*, landholdings, and villas. The last of their *palazzi*, a nineteenth-century imitation of the antique, is now the U.S. Embassy in Via Veneto.)

Sixtus V Feretti enriched Cardinal Montalto, his nephew, with an ecclesiastical income of 100,000 scudi. Clement VII Aldobrandini bestowed on two nephews, one a cardinal and one a layman, revenues of about 60,000 scudi apiece in 1599. He is computed to have hoarded altogether for his family a total of about one million scudi. (The Aldobrandini are still among the most affluent in Italy. They own, among many properties, the famous villa in Frascati, where they live today, built for the cardinal nephew, with vast terraced grounds overlooking Rome in the distance. In its gardens Henry James spent 'ineffable hours'. It was requisitioned during the war by the Germans as General Kesselring's headquarters.) Paul V Borghese was believed to have given to his relatives nearly 700,000 scudi in cash, yearly revenues of 24,000 scudi in funds, and 268,000 in revenues from various offices. (The Borghese are still one of the four or five leading families of the Papal aristocracy, connected with other notable clans all over Europe. They still own the Palazzo Borghese, known as the *cembalo di Roma*, or Rome's harpsichord, because of its curious form.)

Cardinal Ludovico Ludovisi, nephew of Gregory XV, had a reputed income of 200,000 scudi, and the whole Ludovisi family (which has merged with the Boncompagni who are now called Boncompagni-Ludovisi) obtained 800,000 scudi in *luoghi di monte*, or Papal government bonds. The fortunes of the Barberini go back to two nephews of Urban VIII, who were said to have enjoyed revenues of about half a million scudi a year. Their total gain from the pontificate reached the record sum of 105,000 scudi. The Barberini were among the most avid of all papal families. They built castles, stupendous villas, and one *palazzo*, in the Piazza Barberini, designed by Borromini and Bernini, the most famous contemporary architects.

The most illustrious example of how an Italian, reaching a commanding position (and therefore becoming, whatever his age, the head of the family), sees to it that all his relatives are taken care of, is that of the Bonapartes. Napoleon was a *homo novus* if there ever was one, who, like most Popes, knew he could trust only his blood relations and often not even them. As soon as he was able to, he made adequate arrangements for his brothers, sisters, in-laws, and stepson. His older brother Joseph was made King of Naples for a time and later promoted King of Spain; his younger brother Lucien, who mistrusted Napoleon, was made Prince of Canino, a rich fief north of Rome, in the Maremma; his sister Elisa was married to Prince Felice Bacciocchi and was first given the Duchy of Lucca and later the Grand Duchy of Tuscany; his brother Louis became King of Holland; his sister Pauline married Prince Camillo Borghese; his sister Caroline married Joachim Murat, who was appointed King of Naples; his brother Jérôme, who had married the American beauty Elizabeth Patterson of Baltimore, had to divorce her and marry the not very pretty Catherine of Würtemburg to become King of Westphalia; his stepson Eugène de Beauharnais was an excellent viceroy of Italy.

Less illustrious examples of this tradition can be quoted to this very day. To disseminate relatives in key positions (like sentries in outposts around a fortified camp) not only assures them all good incomes but also guarantees the family from possible attacks. The habit still persists sporadically even in Papal families. Pius XI Ratti merely made his only nephew a count. John XXIII Roncalli did absolutely nothing to improve the status and revenues of his peasant brothers and his working-class nephews. 'They are the relatives of the Pope,' he said simply. 'They dine with me once a year. That should be enough for them.' On the other hand, the nephews of Pius XII Pacelli were made princes (not by him, to be sure, but by King Victor Emmanuel III, to save embarrassment to their uncle), and placed in command of vast business corporations in which the Church has dominating interests. A perusal of current reference books will contribute any number of contemporary examples: brothers, brothers-in-law, sons, sons-in-law or cousins of prominent politicians in the Christian Democrat party are ensconced in comfortable and rewarding positions in State-controlled or nationalized organizations, industries and holding companies, posts for which they seldom had a particular training.

At least one great political leader managed to amass, since the end of the last war, a private fortune comparable to those of Papal families of old, one of the largest in the country. He put it together shrewdly, using his political power, and quickly, within a few years, fighting against time, as he too was an old man. He did it with a clear conscience, clearly for his sons' future and not for himself: he was too near death to want more from life, but they were yet too young to be placed in important and rewarding positions of their own. To be sure, the tradition is also followed in privately controlled business in Italy, as it sometimes is in other countries; it is also widespread in the minor establishments. There are Government bureaus, modest little offices, tawdry hospitals in the provinces, especially in the south, where important places are occupied by people with the same surname or somehow related to those with the same surname. Often, the only way for an ambitious man to succeed is to marry one of the daughters of the men at the top.

Marriages are naturally important, as decisive for the promotion of the influence and prosperity of an ordinary family as they were in royal families of old. Many sons and daughters of prominent political leaders are married to each other, hostages in each other's camp, thus secretly complicating the work of political commentators, who sometimes cannot unravel apparently inexplicable situations unless they know the invisible ties binding the various politicians, not as heads of internal factions, but as fathers-in-law of each other's offspring. Stern fathers no longer oblige rebellious daughters to sacrifice themselves for the family, as Victor Emmanuel II was forced to do in 1859, with his younger daughter, Princess Maria Clotilde, who was to wed Prince Napoleon Bonaparte, known as Plon-Plon, a fat, middle-aged and dissolute man, before Napoleon III would declare war on Austria and help her father conquer Lombardy. Compulsion is rarely necessary nowadays. Somehow, a well-brought-up young lady naturally desires in a man exactly the qualities that will improve her family's fortunes. A young man will look more attractive to her because of his relatives' power in the very world in which she was brought up, business, politics, the armed services, bureaucracy, the universities, or even criminal life.

The great Mafia families of Sicily, for instance, are as intricately bound to each other by a network of old and recent marriage ties as old aristocratic families in the Almanach de Gotha. Only lately has the U.S. Narcotics Bureau become aware of the significance of such connections among immigrants and started exploring them; it diligently drew up genealogical charts of the most notorious families of Sicilian extraction in the United States underworld and discovered that everybody was everybody else's son-in-law, grandfather, stepson, great-uncle, first, second, or third cousin, godfather or godmother, and so forth. Some of these clans in the United States form compact interlocked groups, their descendants intermarrying continuously; others have looser but still solid connections and share some common business interests. Like European powers in the eighteenth and nineteenth centuries, they combine to preserve peace or to make wars, offensive wars to destroy common rivals or conquer new territories for expansion, defensive wars to preserve intact their spheres of influence; negotiate and conclude truces and solemnly sign peace treaties.

*

The Italian male, the head or heir of the family, is justly famous the world over for his manliness. He jealously defends his independence. No woman submits him to her will. His pride is clearly visible. Watch him promenade down the *corso* of any small town at sunset, or on Sunday morning after mass. How cocky he looks, how close fitting are his clothes, how triumphantly he sweeps his eyes about, how condescendingly he glances at pretty girls from the corner of his lowered eyelids! He is visibly the master of creation.

And what is woman? She was obviously placed on earth to amuse and comfort him, as decorative and unimportant as the dumb girls who aid the magician to do his tricks on the stage. Like all inferior people, like negroes in former colonies, she must by every means be kept in her place, for her own sake, above all. When she does not become the victim of seditious propaganda, she can indeed be pleasant and useful. She is also happier. She knows it, too, and she is grateful to her master. Whenever she starts giving herself airs, she must immediately be taught a lesson. 'A woman,' says an old Italian proverb, 'is like an egg. The more she is beaten, the better she becomes.'

Naturally Italians commiserate with other people who have not been able to subjugate their women or who have allowed them to run rampant. See how tormented and unsatisfied their women are, they say, who feel no rein on their necks and are allowed to do things which were not meant for them! Look at foreign husbands, they say, who treat their women with awe, sometimes with fear, as if they were carnivorous animals: how obedient these men are to their women's whims, and, as a result, how spoiled, intractable, and unhappy their women become! It is rumoured that these husbands hide nothing of their own private lives and thoughts, account for every hour of their days and every penny they make, and even have to ask permission to go out some night with harmless men friends. How much more in accordance with Nature's laws and the will of Providence things are in Italy and how grateful is the Italian woman to be treated as she is!

She knows practically nothing of her husband's private life. Has he a mistress? Has he two? Does he go from one regular liaison to another or does he have several at the same time? She is troubled by no doubts. She is only rarely jealous: few suspicions touch her. She trustfully waits for his return home and is happy with whatever he tells her. As for herself, she knows she must be very careful and not so much as look at another man. If she did, she would deserve severe punishment, repudiation, and, frequently enough, death. She knows her place in the immutable order of things, as the wives of southern peasants do, who carry heavy weights on their heads and walk for miles behind their men sitting astride the family donkey. At the end of a summer day, southern Italian families sit on the road in front of their door-steps *a prendere il fresco*, to enjoy the cool air. The men smoke, the women knit, and talk among themselves. The men invariably sit facing the street and nod to friends going by, the women sit with their faces decently turned to the house-wall and see nothing but plaster and stones. Only the brazen hussies, who will surely meet bad ends, turn their heads to the street, from time to time.

*

All this, of course, is mostly nonsense. It is the official cant which inexperienced travellers describe in their diaries. Do Italian men believe it? Many do. Most of them, however, harbour secret doubts and fears. A moment comes when every one of them is struck by the fact that most of the women he has affairs with are somebody's wives and that it is not, therefore, materially possible for all the husbands in Italy to stray from marital fidelity while none of the wives do so. There is no escaping the fact that each day a substantial number of proud Italian males, jealous, suspicious, overbearing, proud men, are being made *cornuti*, and become the object of scorn and ridicule. And this has obviously been going on for centuries.

Appearances, as always, are misleading. Men outwardly behave as if matters were permanently ordered according to immutable and unquestioned customs. Women are willing to play the rôle of second-class members of humanity; they patently act as if they really were but fragile, docile and adaptable creatures. Behind the façade things are different. What is the truth? It would be imprudent and dishonest to generalize too sweepingly. There is not one reality but an infinite range of realities, varying with the section of the country, the social class, the background and the individuals, each reality sometimes changing day by day, merging into another; slippery, ambiguous, many-faceted realities all. This, however, can be said for sure, that there is in Italy a neat and permanent division of prerogatives between the sexes. The man is the titular head of the household but by no means the absolute monarch. He is in charge of general policy, definitely responsible for war and peace and for relations with the rest of the world. The wife is officially a subordinate figure, in charge of humbler duties, but her sphere is largely undetermined and wide-ranging.

The arrangement gives no overwhelming authority to either. It gives the woman the greater moral responsibility. It is only thanks to her that households function smoothly. But the centuries have taught her to make her husband forget how important she effectively is. She usually manages things in a subtle, almost imperceptible, way; she assuages his feelings; she avoids open contrasts but generally has the last unspoken word. She keeps her place, of course. She would obviously lose her ascendancy if she forgot it. Her place may be the kitchen (in lower income families), the drawing-room and boudoir (for the more affluent), and, for all, the double-bed at night, but, whatever it is, it is a position of great power. Men run the country but women run men. Italy is, in reality, a crypto-matriarchy.

Things could not be otherwise. Everybody's status, security, and welfare, depend on power. The first source of power is the family. The strength of the family is determined by many factors—wealth, connections, alliances, prestige, rank, luck—but, above all, by its inner cohesion and ramifications. These are in the hands of women everywhere in the world and in Italy in a special way. Women engineer appropriate and convenient marriages, keep track of distant relations, and see to it, at all times, that everybody does the suitable thing, suitable, that is, not for him and his happiness, but for the family as a whole.

Italian women are aware of their importance. They know that without them the whole structure would collapse like a house of cards within a few hours. They are ant-like in their incessant and un-daunted efforts. Days and nights are dedicated to their duties. They devote the same zeal, enthusiasm, and spirit of sacrifice to their families which heroes and heroines dedicate to King, Leader, Flag, Fatherland, Constitution, Revolution, Seven-Year Plan and which saints of both sexes dedicate to the greater glory of God.

While the struggles and martyrdoms of patriots, revolutionaries, and saints have justly been celebrated by many, nobody has ever even tried to describe the vast, obscure, courageous, and awe-inspiring activities of Italian women of all times to keep their men on their feet, their families safe and the country functioning at all. Very few of these women have reached celebrity. (One of the few is Countess Teresa Confalonieri Casati of Milan. Her husband, who had plotted for Italian independence against the Austrian government, was arrested, tried, and condemned to death in 1823. She travelled to Vienna, to kneel at the feet of the Emperor, asking for mercy. She was successful. Her husband was reprieved and imprisoned for life in the Spielberg fortress, in Bohemia. She never exchanged letters with him. She died without seeing him again.)

How many unsung sisters, wives, daughters, mothers, aunts, grandmothers have been mixed up in the tormented lives of Italian men? How many women have secretly given their every thought, their beauty, their hopes, their health, their serenity of mind, for the protection and welfare of their families through so many centuries of convulsions, invasions, defeats, famine, massacres? How many had to lie, carry on intrigues, manœuvres, plots, or forayed far afield to gather precious informations or to conquer useful allies or hostages of some kind? Many nobly gave their lives, either drop by drop, through the years, or at one stroke, if it was necessary. How many of them dared to kill? How many accepted a life of shame? How many have slipped into the cold bed of a powerful person, under every régime, not certainly always for their pleasure, but in order to secure promotion for their husbands or their fathers? What more can a woman do for her family?

*

The fact that woman is the predominant character of Italian life, even if not the most conspicuous, can be read in many small signs. Almost as many popular songs are dedicated every year to *La Mamma* as to voluptuous hussies or romantic beauties. '*Mamma mia*'! is the most common exclamation. What other people call for their mother in time of stress or danger? Do the Germans say '*Mutter*', the French '*Maman*', the English '*Mother of mine*', when faced by a disappointment or an emergency? Wounded Italian soldiers in front-line dressing stations moan '*Mamma, mamma, mamma*', almost inaudibly, like hurt children. '*Mamma,*' say men condemned to death as they wait for the firing squad to fire. The

next most common exclamation is '*Madonna*', which is a supernatural equivalent, as *La Madonna* is the universal symbol of
suffering and self-sacrificing womanhood.

The Church itself happily encourages this national tendency.
Jesus Christ shares, in Italy, His supreme place with His Mother, on
almost equal footing. There are perhaps as many churches dedicated
to her, in her many manifestations, attributes and specializations, as
to Him. The most popular, revered and frequented sanctuaries are
hers, famous shrines, the Madonne di Pompei, di Loreto, del
Rosario, del Carmine, del Divino Amore. There are more miraculous
images of her than anyone else, some wafted on the waves from the
East, in ancient times, by supernatural means, a few painted allegedly
by Saint John the Evangelist, and many done by the great
Italian masters. They are especially helpful in the solutions of particular feminine problems: spinsters pray to them to find a good husband, sterile wives to become pregnant, unhappy wives to give them
back their husbands' love, mothers to cure the incurable diseases of
their children. Most Italian men are also personally consecrated to
Mary: they have Maria among the names given to them at christening. Mary is one of the saints officially entrusted with the protection
of Italy. There is at least one day dedicated to her every month, feast
days observed not only by the Church but also by Government
offices and private business. The whole month of May is her own
month, and, at intervals, whole years are consecrated to her.

It must be remembered that Italians were so attached to the cult of
the Virgin Mary, so reluctant to neglect her, that they consented, also
for her sake, that the unity of Christendom be dismembered by the
Protestants, who did not deem her worthy of so much attention. The
national devotion to *La Madonna* helped at all times to make re-
unification of all Christians extremely difficult or almost impossible.
It is principally the pressure of the Italian faithful and the zeal of the
Italian clergy which prodded the Church to proclaim dogmas concerning *La Madonna*, codifying and sanctifying traditions and
legends dear to the hearts of simple people.

*

Italian men are justly suspicious and jealous of their women. It is one of the foremost masculine duties. The stability and good name of the family notoriously depend more on the wife's faithfulness than on her husband's. Italian laws are clear on the subject: adultery committed by a woman is a punishable crime, adultery committed by a man is not, unless it is accompanied by scandalous and outrageous behaviour. Italian history is studded with famous examples of the determination with which husbands, brothers, and sons punish their women for sins which cast discredit or ridicule on their names. Practically every morning the newspapers are still filled with gruesome tales of the kind. Nevertheless the women show no sign of being afraid of punishment.

Fine examples of this tendency are particularly abundant in the sixteenth century, that most Italian of all centuries. Take, for instance, the case of beautiful Donna Pellegrina Bentivoglio, who was killed in Bologna in 1598, by order of her husband, Count Ulisse. She was unjustly suspected of having committed adultery. Four masked assassins cut her to pieces, in broad daylight, together with two ladies-in-waiting and her coachman, and left the remains on the road. In 1590, in Naples, Don Carlo Gesualdo, son of the prince of Venosta, assassinated his wife, Donna Maria d'Avalos, in his palace, with his own hands, together with her lover, Don Fabrizio Carafa, Duke of Andria. In 1577, in Milan, Count Giovanni Borromeo, a cousin of Cardinal Federigo and of Saint Charles, a most devout man, stabbed his wayward wife, Countess Giulia Sanseverino, at table, during dinner, with three mortal wounds.

Or take what happened to the Massimo family. It is surely one of the noblest and oldest in Rome, whether it is actually descended from the Roman Fabii and Fabius Maximus, Hannibal's conqueror, as they claim, or not. Lelio, the head of the house at the time in question, had six robust sons, all of gigantic stature and herculean strength, by his first wife, a Savelli. After their mother's death, in 1571, their father fell in love with a girl of inferior status—in birth, breeding and past life—to what was proper for a Roman prince at the time. She was a certain Eufrosina, born not far from Gina Lollobrigida's birthplace, in Ciociaria, who had at one time married a man named Corberio. Her remarkable beauty had already attracted the

attention of Prince Marcantonio Colonna; he had lost his head and
murdered her husband, so that he could bring the attractive widow
to Rome and establish her in his house as his mistress. To take her
away from Colonna, Massimo had to offer more: he married her.
This was obviously an insult to the honour of the family, which his
sons could not endure. On the night of her wedding, in 1585, they
refused to welcome her in the house. The next morning, five of them
entered her bedroom and shot her dead. Only one of the six did not
take part in the murder. Lelio blessed him and cursed the others.
After a lapse of a few weeks the old man followed his wife to her
grave, killed by a broken heart. The blameless son Pompeo grew up
to continue the great line of Massimo. (His contemporary descend-
ant, Vittorio, shows the milder blood he had inherited: he married
Dawn Addams, the film star, by whom he has a son, but desiring to
divorce her, unlike his ferocious ancestors, he avoided bloodshed
and went to court.)

Fathers' maledictions being still effective at the time, old Lelio
Massimo's were not hurled in vain. The five sons all met bad ends.
The first, Ottavio, was killed by a cannon ball at sea, fighting the
Turks. Another, Girolamo, who found refuge in France, was shot in
an ambuscade while making love to a noble lady. A third, Alessandro,
a soldier in the troops of General Farnese, was shot dead near Paris.
A fourth, Luca, the only one arrested in Rome for the murder of his
stepmother, was released on the plea that he had avenged the honour
of his family. He died, however, poisoned by his own brother, Marcantonio, in 1599. Marcantonio was arrested on suspicion of having
killed him, and imprisoned in the Torre di Nona, where he confessed
his guilt. He was beheaded in the little square before the bridge of
Castel Sant'Angelo.

*

As the centuries progressed, only the lower classes preserved these
severe traditions intact. They are practically the only ones who still
jealously preserve them today. Among the well-born, manners became gradually milder and more indulgent. Wives entertained their
lovers with increasing generosity and insouciance. Husbands
necessarily had to deal with the problem of *corna* in a more realistic,

civilized, and less bloody fashion, otherwise more than half the adult population would probably have been exterminated. Some of them (like Count Guiccioli of Ravenna, justly famous as the accommodating husband of Lord Byron's lady love, the great poet's 'last attachment') even managed to keep a good temper, a good appetite and make friends with their wives' lovers, who, after all, were taking a load off their shoulders. The witty Count Papadopoli, the husband of a famous nineteenth-century Venetian beauty, is another good example. Sleeping one night at her side, from the creaking, breathing, and snoring he heard he realized that one of her numerous lovers had been surprised by his arrival and had found refuge under the bed. The count said nothing. In the morning, when coffee was served to him, he lowered one hand with a full cup and, without looking, asked politely: 'Do you take it with sugar or without?' He thought one whole night spent on the floor, directly underneath his mistress's husband, was enough punishment for any man.

There is the case of a jealous and moral gentleman, who disliked being cuckolded, but managed to avoid it without harsh words and bloodshed. He was Baron Bettino Ricasoli, born in 1809, a religious man, dedicated to politics and serious studies in his favourite field, agriculture. He was by no means handsome. In fact he was extremely cross-eyed, but had a tall and lean figure, and carried himself with a military and proud bearing. He was appointed prime minister in 1861, the second prime minister of united Italy, after the death of Count Cavour, but lasted only a short time in this post, as he incessantly quarrelled with the king, Victor Emmanuel II, who was as aristocratically stubborn as he was.

One night, when he had been married only a few months, Bettino, who had been nicknamed *Barone di Ferro*, or Iron Baron (such unbending characters are not necessarily admired in Italy, where *souplesse* is prized above all; the sobriquet has a derisive quality it would not have elsewhere), took his young wife Anna Bonaccorsi to a ball in Florence. There the poor lady was briefly and perfunctorily courted by a young man, who danced with her a few times. The husband immediately told her: 'We must leave, my dear.' He escorted her to their waiting carriage, sat down next to her, and told the coachman: 'To Brolio.' Brolio was the family seat, a lonely and gloomy castle, lost in barren and sterile hills, where none of the Ricasoli had lived for ages. The couple rode in silence through the snow, until dawn, he in his black evening clothes, she shivering in her ball dress. They lived in Brolio for practically the rest of their lives.

To while away the time he reconstructed the manor, which now looks as if it had been dreamed up by Sir Walter Scott or designed as a background for *Il Trovatore*. He also experimented with planting different qualities of new vines and producing wines with improved processes. (One must have patience and a firm character for such pursuits. It takes approximately five years for a man to taste the first product of a new combination of grapes he has planted.) The baron came across a pleasing mixture of black and white grapes, Sangiovese and Malvasia, and a way to make them ferment in two successive waves, which imparted a novel taste to the *cru*. The wine became popular, was copied by the vineyard owners of the region, the Chianti, and acquired, in the end, a world-wide fame. One of the best Chiantis is still the Ricasoli, of which the Brolio Castle is the choice and most expensive variety. Thus the baron managed to preserve the sanctity of the family, his wife's name and his honour unblemished, to amass a fortune, and to enrich his neighbours, all at the same time.

*

Also in Italy modern life is eroding the splendid solidity of the family. The change could clearly have serious consequences. If the family weakens, will anarchy reign supreme? Or will Italians finally develop a suitable respect for public authorities and institutions? The family seems no longer what it used to be, everywhere but especially in the industrial centres of the north. Naturally the phenomenon is more noticeable there, as the north is closer to the rest of Europe and is the section where the transformation of society is being spurred on by industrialization and the gradual spread of affluence. Northern Italians often live in tiny flats, separated from relatives by vast wastelands of masonry and congested streets, as far apart as if they lived in distant regions. Relatives see each other at ever longer intervals and some of them inevitably get lost and forgotten. Young people want to have their own independent lives, tastes, studies, ambitions and friends, and to live apart from authoritarian parents. Some of the more old-fashioned rites are gradually disappearing, or are performed with little smiles of condescension and irony.

Divorce is beginning to be adopted as an upper-class custom. Of course there is still no divorce on the law books, and there never will be. Not only is the Church against it, but the people themselves rightly consider it a barbarous and ruinous institution; the necessity to preserve some solid bulwark against the impermanence of things will always prevent its adoption. Not even the wildest anarchists and left-wing revolutionaries dared to propose it in the past. The Communists today angrily deny they are contemplating it. After all, as everybody knows, the principal purpose of married life is not the impossible satisfaction of adolescent love dreams, not the achievement of romantic ecstasy, not the perfect fusion of two souls, but the foundation of a new family and the reinforcement of existing ones. It is naturally desirable that husband and wife be happy in each other's company, but it is not indispensable. One thing is, however, imperative, that, should one or both of them be tempted to stray from fidelity, he, she, or both manage things in such a way as not to endanger a permanent structure and ruin other people's lives. Erring husbands or wives should by all means give his or her partner all possible chances to deceive himself or herself. Lack of precautions (even transparent ones), the habit of leaving open letters everywhere, or an adolescent urge not to keep secrets and to confess everything, are considered dangerous tendencies which must be repressed.

In Genoa, a few years ago, there lived a middle-aged married banker of steady habits who loved a pretty woman, the wife of a man of modest condition. The banker did not like the emotions of clandestine meetings in rented rooms. He preferred seeing his mistress at leisure in her own comfortable home. When he visited her in the evening, he always said to her husband: 'My dear friend, I have a hunch that this number will win at roulette tonight. Would you mind going down to the club and place this sum of mine on the proper spot?' The husband always went. He came back after two hours and said that, alas, the number had not come up and that he had lost the money. This went on for years. Brutal moralists would have derided this pleasant little ceremony, and blurted out the shocking truth, that the husband regularly pocketed the money, was a low scoundrel making a living on his misfortune, and that his wife was a low strumpet. Brutal moralists would have spoiled this delicate and civilized arrangement by demanding that the wife openly confess her wrongs, the husband divorce her, and the banker abandon his wife and children to marry his mistress, thus ruining two families at the same time.

Now, however, many people want brutally to get divorces at all costs, so as to be able to marry again. As a result, *ersatz* divorces of sorts have been devised by ingenious lawyers, for those couples who cannot obtain an annulment of their religious bonds. After the war, for instance, by legal subterfuges, many marriages were dissolved in countries which had reciprocal treaties with Italy making court sentences in one country also legal, in certain cases, in the other. Few Italian tribunals, however, dared to accept the validity of the foreign decrees. At one time, however, a stubborn old judge made them all valid for a few years, until he retired. He freed thousands of unhappily married couples. This lone loophole has now been closed by more explicit legislation and stringent regulations, but other methods are being explored. These divorces are naturally easier for unknown and obscure people, who do not interest newspaper readers and do not provoke wide scandals. Film stars, well-known politicians, and popular singers have to go without. But when there is no way out, when no chicanery is possible, more and more people now take the law into their own hands and set up house with new partners, without the benefit of the municipal authorities and the clergy.

This, of course, has happened before. It has always happened. But there is a difference between what went on and what is going on now. The illegal couples are no longer left alone, like lepers, to live a solitary and almost clandestine life. They are not considered outcasts, like Anna Karenina and Vronsky. They are accepted, invited everywhere, looked upon with compassion and commiseration, encouraged as the innocent victims of a cruel and medieval legislation. The lady is usually called by the name of her lover, out of courtesy. By means of legal tricks of various sorts, their children are also illegally given the man's family name. Such liaisons are now almost

entirely respectable, so respectable and solid, in fact, that many of
these unmarried ladies and gentlemen begin to have love affairs on
the side.

*

As in the past on many occasions, the Italians now seem eager, even
anxious, to adopt many foreign fashions. Family discipline is visibly
relaxing. Does all this really mean that Italy is changing? Behind the
frivolous appearances, behind each family's closed doors, a silent,
stealthy, and tenacious struggle is going on to preserve the substance
of the old ways. The struggle is going on within the very heart of
each individual Italian. The outcome, of course, will be presumably
what it has always been, a pleasing show of liberal broadmindedness
which will not entirely correspond to the invincible reality behind it.
The naïve and superficial observers will notice that 'Italy is no longer
the country she has been for centuries', that many Italians are now as
'modern' as anyone else, and that a 'deep revolution' has definitely
transformed their lives. Deeper and experienced observers will know
better. Of course, something of the new ideas will stick, something
not quite essential. But the spirit of the old ways will survive somehow. An Italian will still choose to stand by his family, in a crisis,
against the *carabinieri*, the police, the courts, public opinion, and
even, at times, his own conscience, because the family has for so long
been the only reliable vessel on a sea of troubles, which will always
float to safety with all its crew and contents. Things may change, to
be sure, but they are changing very slowly, or not changing at all; as
in shabby old provincial hotels in Italy only the façade and the entrance hall are being renovated while the rest is left intact.

Reassuring signs of the family's undimmed power in the most
modern and affluent *milieus* are still abundant. Take the seven
brothers C. of Genoa (there were eight but one of them died in a car
accident). Together they own shipping lines, olive oil refining plants,
various other industries, enterprises, and organizations worth several
billion lire. To preserve the family solidarity, by common agreement,
each of them owns nothing more than the clothes on his back and
those on the backs of his wife and sons, plus the furniture in his
house. Everything else is common property. Even the cars belong to

a pool and are summoned by telephone when necessary. The brothers consider the patriarchal arrangement the best possible in order to carry on complex, vast, and privately owned enterprises with the least friction. Or take younger brothers in great Sicilian households. In Sicily, the power of the older families still largely depends on the prestige of an inherited title and the income from inherited land. Italian law does not recognize titles and imposes an equal distribution of a large part of the inheritance among all the children. To avoid seeing the common property divided among too many rivulets and vanish within one or two generations, there are younger brothers who, like lay monks, do not marry, or, when they marry, refrain from begetting children, so that the family fortunes, titles, prestige, and authority will go on undiminished to the next generation.

Other examples could easily be quoted; they are to be met with in every conversation, business deal, news item; they are the very core of Italian life. This, for instance, happened not long ago. A literary prize was offered to the author of the best first book of the year. Among several candidates one was specially favoured. He is a brilliant young man who had published by far the best book and had become well known practically overnight. He is the son of a distinguished man of letters who happened to be a member of the jury awarding the prize. The father, who was a scrupulous gentleman, was embarrassed. He did not want to sit in judgement on his son's work. He did not want to condemn his son's rivals. He did not want to dim his son's almost certain victory with suspicions of favouritism and nepotism. He therefore decided not to participate in the jury that year and wrote a dignified letter to his colleagues. He did not explain his scruples (any explanation would have had to include the admission that he thought his son might win, and that explanation too could have been interpreted as a form of pressure). He therefore refrained punctiliously from indicating that his son was in any way worthy of the prize and suggested two or three other names, names of writers obviously not half as good.

One or two of the judges proposed the son. He did not get the award. The argument that defeated him had no answer in Italy and was accepted by all as final. When one of the judges said: 'We must be mistaken about him. He must not be as good as most of us think,

THE POWER OF THE FAMILY

for not even his father thought he deserved the prize. He never even mentioned him in his letter,' they all solemnly agreed. How bad must this son have been, the judges thought, if his own father had not had the courage to do his duty, what his heart dictated, and had been done since time immemorial?

CHAPTER TWELVE

HOW TO SUCCEED

THE Italian family, this Macedonian phalanx of strict fathers, self-sacrificing mothers, doting grandparents, spinster aunts, in-laws, pimply adolescents, and swarming children, with its unwritten code and stern discipline, can be compared to a ship sailing over dark and treacherous waters infested by invisible and ruthless enemies. The ship does not sail alone: it is usually surrounded by a vast convoy which ensures its safety. The convoy is the organization (legitimate or illegitimate), to which the family loosely happens to belong. It is the group, clan, political party, *camarilla*, sect, trade union, association, open or secret, formed by people with more or less analogous backgrounds, hopes, fears and needs.

There is, to be sure, one substantial difference between such an arrangement and real-life sailing in wartime. The family follows a formation only as long as it promises safety and prosperity. Whenever the captain judges it prudent, the ship will stealthily but unhesitatingly abandon the convoy for another more convenient, less exposed one; perhaps, in an emergency, even an enemy convoy. At rare times, the family will sail alone, for a while at least, waiting to see which side in a battle will show signs of coming out on top, which side offers more objective chances for survival.

Of course similar alliances flourish in every country. They manage to dominate most human activities everywhere. Everywhere, in fact, it is useful to be 'in' in order to succeed in life. All over the world, it is indeed difficult to get ahead without the consent of entrenched côteries. Some of the most famous groups, it is true, are not as powerful as people think; some are pure fiction, or have but a shadowy and imaginary existence; a few are often nothing more than obsessions in the minds of the defeated, who use them to justify their own lack of success. Many, however, undoubtedly do exist; a few have undeniably left their marks in history, like the Masons and the *bouilleurs des crus* in France; the *Grosse Generalstab* in Germany; the Southern slave-owners, the Wall Street bankers in the United States; the English Establishment; and the Soviet Politburo. Some are really as strong and influential in the world of today as people believe. Contemporary art fashions, to mention one instance, are determined by a small group of dealers in Paris and an inner circle of museum directors throughout the world. Nevertheless, no matter how powerful these groups may be anywhere else, they seldom have the far-reaching importance they always had and still have in Italy.

In Italy, powerful groups know no other limit to their power than the power of rival groups. They play a free-for-all game practically without rules and referee. Of course the law is allegedly supreme; the apparatus of a quasi-modern State is visibly omnipresent, with its props, cast of characters, costumes, titles, and institutions, but there are important differences between such dignitaries and organizations and what they are elsewhere. Each branch of the State machinery in Italy is in reality a mighty independent power which must struggle sometimes for its existence, and usually for the prosperity of its protégés and subjects against all other rival branches of the State machinery: they fight savagely at times, but more often surreptitiously, exactly like private pressure groups, for a larger place in the sun, a bigger cut of the budget, more employees, a higher rank and wider prerogatives for their leaders.

When necessary, public institutions join hands to fight, without the particular advantages which the law should give them and armed only with the power they can marshal, all kinds of private groups, defeat them when they are weak, or come to some sort of arrangement when they are strong. The *Polizia* and the *Carabinieri* have been carrying on a running feud for more than a century. (The unusual existence of two rival police forces many Italians believe to be one of the best safeguards of their liberty. One always keeps watch over the other.) In western Sicily the two police forces have carried on a running fight with the Mafia for more than one hundred years. From time to time the Mafia allied themselves to the *Polizia*, or the *Polizia* allied themselves with the *Carabinieri*. When the two joined forces against the outlaws, they managed occasionally to predominate for a time, not because they represented the law but because they happened to be stronger. This fact, that the State does not necessarily have all the odds on its side, must be remembered if one wants to understand the fine points of such struggles as that between customs guards and smugglers, the Ministry of Labour and trade unions, the Ministry of Finance and the reluctant tax-payers, the Ministry of Public Instruction and the teachers and students, the Ministry of Industry and the industrialists.

The Prime Minister himself must have private backing of his own if he wants his orders to be obeyed, backing within his own party, within the bureaucracy, and within the Church, or of one of the powerful factions within the Church (if he is a Christian Democrat), as he can scarcely depend on his constitutional authority alone. There were a few honourable though inexperienced ministers, just after the war, who did not remember all this (they had been in jail or abroad during Fascism and had lost contact with practical affairs) and gallantly tried to impose their will on reluctant and rebellious bureaucrats or on the people without the proper support and alliances. All of them ended up completely isolated in their offices, bewildered and impotent men. Their telephones seldom rang, only close friends and relatives visited them, nobody told them what was going on, and the office boys even neglected to supply them with stationery and to fill their ink-stands with ink. In Italy even the Law, any law, changes meaning and purpose according to the power of the person who applies or violates it; taxes tend to become milder and more easily evaded for the powerful and the well-connected (the terms were synonymous with the rich and well-born, they now mean mostly people personally controlling many votes). Everything, in short, turns out to be, in the end, not a balancing of legal rights but a confrontation of pure power.

*

Some sort of protection is therefore necessary for everybody. Even the little man with no ambitions needs ample help merely to be left alone. The Italian historical weather has always been notably unstable. In practically every generation, tidal waves of political change batter all obstacles and wash the scene clean of everything that does not have a deep enough foundation or is not tied to something solid. Here generosity is notoriously considered a form of weakness; there is little pity for the beaten enemy; the opposition does not openly wait its turn but always vanishes from the earth and goes underground, perhaps only to reappear in the light of day after a generation or two. Century-old institutions disappear; the old élites are uprooted; raw new leaders must learn the job as they go along (a few always start by accumulating their own private fortunes); solid pillars of society are transformed overnight into dangerous subversives; text-books have to be re-written; old traditions, virtues, beliefs are banned and new ones take their place with bewildering rapidity, frequency and confusion.

In these upheavals, even the obscure and harmless men who obey the law and mind their own business are in danger. The slow and stupid men, the honourable men of firm character who are loyal to their ideals and consider it unworthy to adapt themselves to the new circumstances, and the isolated men without friends are inevitably washed away by the raging breakers. A few honest men emigrate, some sacrifice their lives, liberty or property; many go into hiding and live obscurely without prestige, authority and power. The great majority knows better. Events never surprise them. Just as men facing the violent surf join hands in a chain in order not to be carried away, Italians must at all times attach themselves to a strong group of friends. They never know when the next historical storm will break. They only know that those who stand alone are lost.

*

Italians are not, as foreigners believe, individualists. They loyally serve in their own organizations, which are very rarely the official ones. This was recognized, among few others, by Antonio Gramsci, the acute and erudite hunchback who founded the Italian Communist Party in 1921. He left many notes, reflections provoked by his random reading, jotted down in cryptic form while hopelessly ill in Fascist jails. This is one, freely translated and abbreviated: 'It is being affirmed, with complacency by some and with scorn and pessimism by others, that the Italians are a "people of individualists". A few say "fortunately", others say "unfortunately". Are the Italians really individualists? Is it really individualism that makes the ordinary people ignore politics today and made them ignore the interests of the nation as a whole in the past? Is this the reason that made them repeat: "Let France come or let Spain [it is all the same], as long as we eat"? The fact that one does not participate in the life of the community or the State does not necessarily mean that he lives a lone life, the splendidly isolated life of the proud man who counts only on himself to create his own economic and moral world. It merely means that, rather than joining political parties and trades unions, Italians prefer joining organizations of a different type, like cliques, gangs, *camorras*, *mafias*. This tendency can be observed both among the lower and the higher classes.'

Gramsci, of course, innocently believed all this to be the fatal result of capitalism, in spite of the fact that he knew the phenomenon was far older than capitalism, practically as old as the Italian people themselves, and that, curiously enough, it was almost unknown or did not prevail in the more progressive nations, where capitalism was really strong. He sincerely believed, however, that communism was the only cure, and that, once all the means of production were public property, the Italians would all become law-abiding citizens. He had to cling to his faith in spite of contrary evidence and doubts: to do otherwise was to admit that all his work and sacrifices had been in vain. We know better. Recent experiences show that Italians carry on in the same old way in any form of economic organization. In fact, the more economic activities the State controls the more people rely on friends and accomplices for their protection and to safeguard their power and property. Nothing is as clique-ridden in Italy as a nationalized industry. Gramsci himself did not live to see his own small and heroic party turned, after the last war, into just another vast mutual-aid association *all'italiana*, directed only vaguely by ideological orthodoxy but mostly by agile opportunism.

*

The cliques, camarillas, mafias, cabalas, or as the Italians often call them, *consorterie*, as well as the more honourable but just as un-official organizations to which the people entrust their security are not always chosen consciously. Sometimes a man happens to be born in one of them. In the past, he found himself the subject of a prince, the citizen of a tiny republic, the member of a historical party, like the Guelphs and the Ghibellines, or a family clan, like the Montagues and Capulets. He somehow knew from birth (nobody needed to tell him) that he was bound to help all other members and had the right to exact help from them. Such spontaneous formations still exist. Southerners in the north, for instance, or northerners in the south automatically behave like members of a secret society and extend brotherly aid to each other on sight. Such bonds are so strict that people who would naturally be enemies back home (born in rival towns or in rival quarters of the same town) immediately become allies and accomplices in alien surroundings. Italians of all regions, north or south, obey the same moral obligations when they meet abroad. They recognize each other without speaking. They do not have to speak. They communicate with imperceptible gestures and are ready on sight to do practically anything for each other.

Their instinctive recognition and feeling of complicity could be compared to the sympathy and attraction which sadly draws together men addicted to secret vices, as if being Italian and living the Italian way were also some kind of secret vice, a crime against nature. The same feeling binds almost all Italians under a foreign tyranny perhaps more strongly than the inhabitants of any other country in the same predicament. The French, the Dutch, the Danes naturally tried to help each other against the German occupation during the last war. None however were trained so well by history to violate all laws, to understand each other at a glance and to combine their efforts against the occupying authorities as the Italians. They already knew all the tricks. Only a tiny and unreliable minority sided with the Wehrmacht. The great majority spontaneously and immediately behaved as if they were all long-lost cousins. Anybody anywhere could find refuge without fear in the first farm house he came to. He knew that the peasants would cheerfully defy death to feed and shelter him. The same privileges were extended to the Allied escaped prisoners, as many of them can testify, not only because of the ideals they represented, but also because they, being persecuted by the Germans, had somehow become honorary Italians.

More often a man must choose what group to join. The range is rarely very wide; nobody is entirely free; his background, tastes, class, talents, character, ambitions will narrow the field still further. There often is, however, a moment in a man's life in which he must take a chance and make up his mind. Some of the associations he can join are old, powerful and nation-wide. Some are village groups. Within the vast associations, there are again other cliques, one inside the other like Chinese ivory balls, among which a man must skilfully find his way.

One, the oldest and the largest of all, containing all sorts of subsidiary factions and bodies, is the worldly organization of the Church, honourable, virtuous, far-reaching, powerful and omnipresent, a State within the State. It obeys its own laws, it offers infinite possibilities, it protects and aids loyal followers, it solves all kinds of problems, it promotes prosperity and security of good men in all kinds of circumstances. It has notoriously always made official life in Italy precarious and feeble. It can afford the timid man a safe life (he can become a parish priest or a monk). It can afford the ambitious man plenty of opportunities (he can become a Vatican diplomat, the confessor of sovereigns and statesmen, the general of a religious order; the head of a Catholic university or publishing house, a high prelate dominating all sorts of spiritual or worldly spheres, a cardinal invested with wide responsibilities, even the Pope himself). A layman, too, can lead a sheltered and happy life with the aid of the Church. It can accompany him, step by step, from birth to death, assuring him a good job and a steady career, protecting him from the envy of rivals, procuring for him, at times, worldly success, fame, political power, and wealth.

The Church is a world in itself, the most labyrinthine and complicated of all human organizations. From the outside, to the stranger, it looks monolithic. Inside it is an entanglement of factions politely and almost imperceptibly fighting each other for the greater glory of God: the Pope and his private advisers against the Curia, the Curia against the bishops, liberal against conservative bishops, all bishops against the lower clergy, the religious orders against the priests, the religious orders among themselves, all tenaciously struggling for supremacy. The lay Catholics are also divided into a bewildering number of groups, from the extremely wealthy Knights of Malta to the Catholic Action and the disinherited left-wing workers' organizations.

Or, until a few years ago, a man could entrust his prosperity to the Masons. They were in Italy a powerful and secret organization (also divided, like the police, into two rival branches) which, until the first world war, furthered many careers and probably controlled most of the highest positions in the Italian State. It protected its adherents in all walks of life. The Masons were anti-clerical and fought the Church's influence in all fields, in politics, the academic world, the armed forces, and business enterprises. They have now practically lost all their power. There are still today many similarly vast institutions, none, however, as powerful and far-reaching as the Church or the Masons of old, which a man can join for protection: political parties, coalitions of economic interests, cultural cliques of all kinds. A man can also become at the same time a member of several associated and kindred groups: he can be, for instance, a protégé of the Jesuits or of the left-wing Catholic Action, a good Christian Democrat politician, and the director of a nationalized industry; he can be a member of the Communist Party in order to control one of the camarillas in the world of art and culture which the Party dominates.

A man can also join smaller groups, of which there are thousands, some less honourable than others, some outright criminal, all powerful in their respective spheres of influence, down to the Sicilian village Mafia. When dealing with an Italian it is always prudent to know exactly where his loyalties lie, to what clique, association or party he belongs, who protects him, who are his friends, and from whom he derives his power. Naturally there are no handbooks listing such indispensable information. The man will often hotly deny his allegiance. Some bodies (the Masons of old, the democratic parties under the Fascist régime, a few financial combinations today) are secret. Nevertheless, the information is usually not difficult to ferret out. Everybody knows.

One of the reasons why a man will deny his allegiance is that, while it is indispensable to belong to some group or *consorterie*, it may became dangerous and compromising in troubled times. It is, therefore, a good rule never to be too conspicuous. One should always try not to be the standard-bearer; one should accept only solid and secondary positions, one should avoid being known as the follower of one man or the absolute champion of one idea. Nobody knows when the next historical storm will break and when what was accepted formerly as an advantage may become a disastrous liability overnight. One should always leave open doors behind one. This is also one of the reasons why one should always try to have friends among one's opponents. (The thing is easy, because there are many among one's opponents who obey the same rule.)

When, in April 1940, a *commissario di polizia* arrested me for being a dangerous enemy of the Fascist régime, he was inordinately polite. While I waited at the Questura to be interrogated, he sent for a good dinner from the nearest *trattoria*, sent to my house for clean shirts, a change of clothes, and some money, and warned me veiledly about what was best to say and not to say when questioned. He courteously drove me in his car to the Regina Coeli prison. I thanked him and asked him why he had been so kind. He frankly said: 'One never knows. Maybe you'll be able to do the same for me, some day.' (The régime was still very powerful and unchallenged at the time. Italy was still neutral. Germany looked likely to win the war. The *commissario* was carefully buying insurance against a most improbable event.)

A few years later, during the last few months of the war, the Fascist chief of Grosseto, the province in which I lived at the time, sent for me. Italy was then divided. In the south were the legal government, the king, and the Allies; in the north were the Germans, the quisling government and Mussolini. Grosseto still belonged to the north. The Fascist chief kept me waiting for hours in his office, while he dispatched the business on hand. He made me watch him giving orders to hide cattle from the Germans who wanted to requisition them, orders to give shelter to partisans and to warn others of a forthcoming raid. In the end he turned to me and said: 'I hope you will some day be able to tell all you saw and heard today to a court of law.' I did, after the war, in Perugia. He got thirty years.

Plain speaking is often a dangerous practice. Obscurity is the rule in almost all fields. Most newspaper editorials, art criticisms and political speeches are, as a rule, clothed in elegantly ambiguous prose. One must not make unnecessary enemies. One never knows when one's widely accepted and non-controversial opinions will turn out to be compromising and daring. One conceals one's thoughts, unnecessarily at times, because, for one thing, to conceal them is never dangerous while to reveal them might be so. There are often, of course, less discreditable reasons. Concealment in difficult times may be the only way to protect one's liberty, both one's inner liberty, in which things may be thought as one wishes, and one's practical, ordinary, everyday freedom of action. This is the kind of prudence the citizens of Communist countries well know.

This theory has largely been explored, among others, by a dis-tinguished Italian novelist, essayist, and political writer, Guido Piovene, in a recent book entitled *La coda di paglia*, or *The Tail of Straw*. (A 'tail of straw', an old Italian metaphor, supposedly prevents the man who has it from going too near a fire; it is made up of the compromising facts in his past life, which he wants to have forgotten, and which therefore gravely limit his possibilities in the present. He is always afraid somebody will discover buried secrets and divulge them to discredit him.) Piovene was recently attacked by the press because he is now a sincere anti-Fascist and a Communist sympathiser, in spite of the fact that, under Mussolini's dictatorship, he wrote a few articles extolling the dictator's literary style and praising his anti-semitic policy, and had volunteered for the Spanish war on Franco's side. It must be admitted that he had gone too far. Few intelligent men in their right senses went so far. It was not necessary. People managed to get on well and even reach important positions without once praising qualities which Il Duce did not possess and never thought he had, and policies which he himself secretly despised, as they reminded him of his subservience to Hitler. Piovene defends himself by pointing out that perhaps his actions were not strictly necessary, but that their gratuitous quality is his best excuse. He did what he did not merely to preserve his personal liberty but, he claims, also to discredit the régime. He relied on what he calls 'the melancholic faith of hypocrisy'.

'Mine was the experience of bad faith in times of tyranny,' he writes, without however explaining why he is now so eager to renew that hideous experience by siding with the Italian Communist Party in most controversies. 'I do not even pretend that my bad faith was always a conscious one,' he wrote. 'This would have required a strength of character, a coherence, a courage in mendacity, an almost perverted form of sincerity, which are as difficult to achieve as self-sacrifice. . . . I administered to myself tiny drops of conviction not to despise myself too much.' (This, incidentally, is the difference between men like Piovene and Guicciardini. Guicciardini did not want to be deceived. He had the strength of character to prosper in a world which he knew was irremediably wicked and execrable.)

'Being made of infinite duplicity,' Piovene continues, 'the Fascist period appeared to me "psychological" in the extreme, and I mean by this a period in which man could fabricate for himself complicated intellectual instruments in order not to see the simplest truths: man then shut himself within himself and invented deceptions. There was another kind of mystification in my writing. It happened that, while at work, I entered into a state of contemptuous rage which prevented me from moderating my language and drove me far beyond the point at which I should have stopped; I would exaggerate my prose in such a preposterous way that anybody endowed with the least common sense should have seen through it. The justification was: this article is so stupid that I cannot even consider it mine. I had the illusion of cutting it away from myself and attributing it to some idiot rhetorician I had hired for the job. Thus such absurd comparisons came to my mind, as those between Mussolini and Shakespeare or even between Mussolini and Pascal. I could have just as easily written Parmenides or Lucretius. I wanted to escape as far as possible from plausible comparisons.'

Unfortunately, Piovene's deliberately hyperbolic and ridiculous comparisons did not at the time strike the unsuspecting reading public in the way that he now likes to believe. Most people then thought that there must have been some similarity after all between Mussolini and Pascal or Shakespeare, since a well-known critic said so in an authoritative newspaper. Others, the anti-Fascists, thought Piovene was one more toady of the régime. Only his intimate friends knew the truth, that he despised the Fascists; that he was not particularly eager to acquire advantages but merely wanted to avoid troubles; and that he was so inexperienced in such games that he overshot the mark by an unbelievably wide margin.

In spite of his claim to speak for his generation, Piovene cannot be considered entirely typical. It is true that he did then and he now does side with the party that presumably can assure him the greatest peace of mind. This is admittedly what the majority of Italians are at all times supposed to do. But there are a few points that set him apart. He commits the ultimate sin: he confesses, analyses, and discusses his choices in the open, attracting on himself all sorts of abuse from left and right. He thus squanders away what advantages he might gain by his arts. He also never manages to deceive himself or others completely. And he never got anything out of his adaptability.

An old story illustrates this point, a story the Italians invented at the time of the Berlin blockade, when a third world war looked a matter of weeks away and NATO did not yet exist. The Russians (the story goes) one day suddenly attacked Western Europe with overwhelming forces. Local defences were immediately pulverized. The United States naturally were unprepared to offer ready help. They needed the usual number of years to make up their minds, manufacture the equipment and train the men. The Russians therefore easily went unopposed from the Elbe to Gibraltar in a few days, conquered the British Isles, and organized all the occupied territory according to their political prejudices.

They set up Communist régimes and exterminated all anti-Communists. In due time, years later, the Americans landed, defeated the Russians and liberated Europe. New free governments were organized, who proceeded to shoot all Communists. At the end, the continent was practically uninhabited. Only handfuls of Britons, Frenchmen, Germans, Dutch and so forth were left in the vacant spaces and the empty cities. Italy alone was overcrowded. In Italy almost fifty million people were left alive. They had obviously remembered one of their old proverbs, which says 'Brave men and good wines last a short time'.

Or take another bitter story, an older one, also invented by the Italians themselves in the twenties, when the Fascist régime was but a few years old. The Secretary of the Fascist Party visits a large factory, accompanied by the obsequious company director. At the end of the tour all the workers are massed in the yard to listen to a speech. Before addressing them, the Fascist chief looks them over proudly from his podium, and asks the director: 'What are these people's politics?' The director answers: 'One-third of them are Communist, one-third Socialist, and the rest belong to several small parties.' The Fascist's face turned livid. 'What?' he cries. 'And how many of them are Fascist?' The director reassures him quickly: 'All of them, Your Excellency, all of them.'

Many Italians, in reality, are not technically opportunists: they do not find it difficult to weave in and out of political parties, conceal their thoughts, accept and repeat whatever official ideas are being imposed from above merely because they want to avoid risks; they do all this also because they are sceptical. They believe that all ideologies are equally right and wrong, that there is no abstract solution to their problems, that the world can somehow be made to function under whatever political institutions seem easier to accept at the moment, because all of them will always function defectively in Italy, where they have all failed, at one time or another, and will all fail sooner or later. They think a bad republic is no better than a bad monarchy; a corrupt socialist State is no improvement on a corrupt capitalist State. They know Communism would be an Italian travesty of Communism. They believe there is no panacea for their ills.

*

The simple skills necessary merely to survive are not difficult to learn. They are, after all, not exclusively Italian but roughly common to all insecure societies, with, however, untold local refinements and subtleties which cannot be matched elsewhere. Italians become such deft masters, so early in life, in these arts, that they are usually unaware of their existence. As a result, life flows smoothly, conflicts are concealed or attenuated to the point that foreigners once believed they lived here in a heavenly country, almost the best in the world, an Arcadia where nothing harsh ever happened, where people were happy, cheerful and friendly. Some still believe it today.

Let us recapitulate, for the sake of clarity, these elementary rules: one must cultivate one's family, entertain as many useful friends and as few dangerous enemies as one can, and therefore perfect the art of being obliging and *simpatico* at all times and at all costs. One should always be on the *qui vive*, watch the horizon for the smallest cloud and people's faces for the smallest variation of mood; one should join a powerful group, sail with a safe convoy; one should beware of History.

On the negative side these are the things one must avoid: one should never be too conspicuous, daring, confident, explicit, trusting, credulous; one should not officially embrace definite opinions, nor be out of step with the crowd. Above all, one should remember at all times that conflicts are not decided on the basis of the law, abstract considerations of justice or the relative merit of the contestants, but most frequently by a pure confrontation of power. Might is not only very often right, but might is often the equivalent of beauty, culture, intelligence and charm as well. No harm will come to the man who diligently does all these things. No harm but, of course, nothing really good either.

The skills necessary to do more than just survive, the skills indispensable to achieve even a modest success, are infinitely more difficult to define and to teach. The Italians who practise them and reach even a small commanding position are admirable indeed, larger-than-life heroes who can operate among their own countrymen, people who can see through every trick and know how to defend themselves in all circumstances. The virtues necessary to become the head of anything, in Italy, head of a convent, a municipal kennel, a vegetable market Mafia, a secondary railway station, or the mayor of a mountain village, are such that could, in most other countries, easily make a man foreign minister, the alcove favourite of the queen, the chief of staff, or the president of the republic.

There are, of course, no infallible recipes, no tested instructions which can be applied by anybody with the certainty of getting results. Every case is a different one. Like all great artists, most successful men in Italy seem to obey a few general rules but in reality develop their own particular techniques, exploit their own unique talents, adapt themselves brilliantly to the milieu and the circumstances. The general precepts, like those governing all arts when described in popular handbooks, seem deceptively easy to follow. There is nothing esoteric about them. They are approximately the same to which ambitious men have resorted whenever competition was rife, competitors were numerous, ruthless and intelligent, and the positions to conquer were scarce and strenuously defended, in places like Louis XIV's Versailles, Wall Street in its heyday, or Hollywood in the good years.

But courtiers, speculators, and Hollywood arrivistes were rarely condemned exclusively to seek high position and fame in their respective bear pits. They were free, as gamblers are who choose to suffer in a hell of their own making, but who can always leave the green table. There is a final quality about such things in Italy. If a man has a modest ambition and wants to improve his lot, he has no alternative. He knows he must not count merely on his worth and talents; he must compete in a game without rules; the man who wins is the best man exclusively in the art of inventing new ways to paralyse or destroy his opponents; there are no side-lines, no benches to retire to, no sponges to throw in, no ways to escape. The whole nation is one vast battlefield. Most prizes are modest. The risks are mortal.

These, then, are some of the deceptively obvious rules. Rule One: choose the right companions. In order to succeed, a young man must not only join a large and powerful group but also, once in, worm his way to the top, become one of the influential élite, one of the leaders, or even the solitary chief, if he can, in order to use the whole group to serve his own purposes. It is clearly impossible for any man to do so alone. He must have an *entourage* of his own: he must choose a smaller group inside the large group, join it, and eventually influence it. He must recognize, at the start, which of the various existing cliques presents the best chances. Roughly speaking, there is usually a clique of older men well-entrenched in commanding positions who can defend themselves and who allow only their own friends to prosper, and a clique of ambitious young men determined to oust the older men and take their places. The choice of which faction to side with is a difficult and delicate one. Romantic and sentimental prejudices must naturally be overlooked. One cannot afford to make mistakes, as it is almost impossible to change places later, when the outcome is clear, without paying a heavy price.

Rule Two (perhaps the most important of all): choose the right protector. All inner cliques are usually dominated by a few influential men, sometimes by one leader. In all fields there are a few authorities. Any young man who wants to excel must attach himself to the proper mentor, become his aide-de-camp and use him for his own purposes. There are thousands of ways for a young man to seduce a more mature man, just as there are thousands of good ways to seduce women. In this field, too, a man must remember that art is not enough: no seduction is ever a thoroughly cold-blooded one, or one which goes against natural affinities. Women and older men are seldom fools. There are women who cannot be seduced, just as there are older men who, for fear of being stabbed in the back, prefer to surround themselves with inept and stupid followers, aspirants who will never amount to anything. Mussolini only liked subservient and incapable underlings. As a rule, women favour men they have a natural inclination for and who offer them something in return for their love; protectors prefer young men who have something in common with them, who share more or less the same ideas, who admire them and imitate them. The choice therefore falls on few of the many aspirants. Still, the use of the art to get oneself noticed and selected must never be entirely overlooked. Art must always be employed to accelerate and facilitate the natural course of nature.

It is curious that, such being the fascinating complications and psychological subtleties of the game, such being the stakes for which it is necessarily played by everybody at all levels and ages, a vast literature, based not on the commonplace pursuits of love and the all-too familiar intricacies of amorous dalliances but on pure ambition, does not exist, a literature dedicated to the heart-breaking courtship of elderly protectors, the penetration of closed cliques, the infinite manœuvres and labyrinthine intrigues, the conspiracies, the plots and counterplots necessary to prosper even modestly in Italian life. Of the two emotions moving men, love and ambition, the latter undoubtedly is the more vigorous, longer lasting, more varied, and presents more dramatic possibilities. As a matter of fact, only two famous novels are dedicated to such matters, against an Italian background, both written by foreigners: *La Chartreuse de Parme* by Stendhal, and *The Cabala* by Thornton Wilder.

How does a young man proceed? He must be around as much as

possible, to begin with. He must be seen. He must be available. This is one of the reasons why the waiting-rooms of powerful men are always crowded with people offering their services and asking for favours, sometimes merely waiting for hours in order to speak to the leader for a few minutes, walk a few steps with him, offer him a match or a cigarette, hold his coat, do whatever will attract his attention and put them in a favourable light. This was deplored by Count Cavour who used to say: 'The worst of Chambers is always to be preferred to the best of antechambers.' In fact the power of a man in any particular period can be measured exactly by the number of people surrounding him. A few favoured ones follow him in the street, anywhere he goes, or on longer trips whenever he travels. Such hangers-on are still known as *clienti*, in the south, from the Latin term used to describe them in old Roman days, *clientes*, people who offer their services and demand aid, protection and advice.

An old politician in Benevento used to hold court, every morning, like a king of old under a tree, in the barber's shop, sitting on the throne-like chair, with his face covered with lather and a towel draped around his shoulders, while the barber shaved him. It was an unforgettable scene. A noisy crowd surrounded him, proffering petitions, asking for help, jobs for grown-up sons, subsidies, pensions, in a great confusion, while a few henchmen defended him from the bolder assailants. The Jupiter-like old man listened, nodded, called every one by name, laughed and gave orders. The practice is not as visible nor as picturesque in the more modern centres. Nevertheless, the great men of business, finance, industry and science in the north are just as much surrounded and courted by *clienti*, though in a more discreet way.

Flattery, of course, utilitarian flattery, has always been the principal way to get attention, to conquer affection and to get ahead. Perhaps the most heroically successful example in history of one poor and friendless Italian promoting at one stroke, with but a few words (four, to be exact), the business on hand and his own career for the rest of his life, is to be found in the memoirs of the Duc de Saint-Simon. (Success in this instance was facilitated by the fact that the powerful man to be flattered was a foreigner, definitely an easier man to seduce than an Italian.) The incident happened near Parma in

1706. The Duke of Parma, Saint-Simon relates, feared that the French armies fighting the Austrians in his territories would ravage them, and wanted to ask the French commander, the Duc de Vendôme, to move his soldiers a few miles away.

The negotiations appeared especially delicate and difficult. Vendôme was known to be a hard man to convince. He was erratic and capricious. A bastard of royal blood, he was, like most royal bastards, suspicious and touchy. He was furthermore stubborn, clever, lazy, insolent and greedy. He was proud of being a homosexual and paraded his minions and favourites; slept together with his dogs and never disturbed his bitches when they delivered themselves of their puppies in his bed; ate vast quantities of food, mostly rotten fish, which he especially relished, but vomited almost immediately into a basin in front of his guests, without interrupting the conversation. He always used rough and soldierly language; he received his visitors and carried out the business on hand always sitting on his *chaise percée*.

The Duke of Parma decided to send an ambassador who could impress the French commander: the Bishop of Parma, a dignified and tactful old man, in his purple robes, followed by a young abbé. The prelate was treated like everybody else. After listening to a few rough jokes and watching some scandalous scenes, he left in a huff. But the clever abbé, one of the most ambitious men ever born in Italy, stubbornly stayed on. 'Knowing well who was Vendôme,' Saint-Simon writes, 'he decided to please him at all costs in order to conclude the business on hand according to his master's wish. . . . Vendôme treated him as he had done the bishop. *Il se torchait le cul devant lui.* At this sight, the abbé exclaimed "*O culo di angelo!*" and ran to kiss it.' The matter was concluded quickly in a satisfactory way. The abbé, the son of a modest gardener, attached himself to Vendôme, became his adviser, and eventually followed him to Spain. There the abbé became the confidant of the king and queen and was appointed prime minister. A few years later he was named a cardinal by the Pope. He made himself the arbiter of Europe, deciding war and peace among the great powers. His name was Giulio Alberoni.

*

How, then, can Italy function so splendidly at times in a highly competitive and merciless world? How can so many Italians do their work reasonably well when they and their leaders are seldom selected according to objective capacities, talents, and experience, but mostly through their flair for intrigue? How can any kind of organization function at all when riddled with favouritism and clogged up with flattery? How can so many things be done well, so many industries compete with more efficient and tenacious rivals in the international markets, and life apparently flow so smoothly and gaily? Why, if what is described in the preceding pages is true, do Italians not fail at everything they try? What is the secret?

The answer is complex. To begin with there are definite fields in which the Italian rules of advancement are suspended. Only strictly capable men reach the top in surgery, for instance. For some reason, Italians do not mind entrusting their national life to incompetent and intriguing generals, but refuse to entrust their personal lives to inept surgeons. For analogous reasons, they do not encourage bad opera singers, conductors, ballerinas, courtesans, actors, film directors, cooks, tailors and pilots. These people get ahead strictly on their merit.

It must also be remembered that, at times, men who care enough for their work and have the extra energy needed to excel, easily master the procedure necessary to reach the top as an indivisible part of their job. Without subtle arts, they could not begin to develop their possibilities, and all their latent capacities would go unused. They acquire such arts as part of the necessary knowledge, just as they acquire manners and learn to read and write. Their talent puts them in an advantageous position. Talent is, after all, one of the sources of power. Then, as I have explained, older men and cliques prefer to promote the fortunes of men who will be useful to them, men who unite ordinary talents to the skills necessary to further themselves, and often these young men objectively deserve promotion. Finally, in most private enterprises, Western competitive habits struggle with the Italian traditional ways and often prevail. In the top echelons and very big business, of course, where problems are not concerned with technique and efficiency but with pure power, the chiefs emerge in the old-fashioned Italian manner; only in the lower echelons and smaller business concerns do the men who get ahead tend to be strictly those who get results.

The unbearable pressure of free competition, this selection which heartlessly favours only uncouth and rough persons whose only merits are those of passing tests, doing their job well and knowing their business, is naturally resented by most Italians. What kind of a life is that, they ask, in which a man must relentlessly fight for his position and not bask secure in the protection of powerful friends? This is one of the reasons why all kinds of rigid organization of economic life find favour in Italy. The people liked their guilds in the pre-industrial world, which regulated every trade and occupation from apprenticeship to the tomb; Fascism, before the war, which prevented all competition as dangerous to the State and surrounded the country with impassable tariff barriers; and any kind of Socialism today, as long as it allows ambitious men to get ahead as they have always done, using the protection of powerful relatives, personal charm, a facility for flattering people, and a keen eye for favourable openings.

CHAPTER THIRTEEN

THE PROBLEMA DEL MEZZOGIORNO

AT this point the reader has been told practically everything that can help illuminate the Italian landscape for him and dispel many shadows. He has all, or almost all, the clues, and should be able to work things out for himself. He will recognize pathetic and picturesque scenes for what they are and not what they appear to be. Some of the obscure, contradictory and incomprehensible events of past history or contemporary politics, whose actual significance is vainly debated by honest and baffled experts, will unfold and reveal their secret nature, like Japanese wooden flowers put in water. Foreign diplomats and journalists, recently arrived in Rome, may attribute with ease a precise meaning to equivocal official pronouncements, to apparently clear proclamations of political aims and to subtle and puzzling manoeuvres. Italophiles will know precisely what they are in love with and why. Not every little detail will be thoroughly clarified, to be sure. There will always be mists in the dells. A few facts, characters, events and problems, a few mass emotions and upheavals, in the past and the present, will always defy interpretation. Not all of Italy is *all'italiana*. Life never entirely corresponds to rational and logical man-made schemes.

There will be times when the reader will be mystified. He may even be misled by a too rigid and unimaginative application of the keys to Italian living. He must remember that, while things may not always be what they seem to a naïve onlooker, they are not always or entirely what cynical and realistic observers believe. It may happen that the foreigner dismisses some disinterested gesture, some sincere declaration of friendship and affection, and some selfless heroic act as nothing more than show. He may take a tidal wave of collective enthusiasm for a pure spectacle without significance. He may be rudely surprised by the truth. General Léon de Lamoricière, for instance, commander-in-chief of the Papal Armies, formed by French, Irish, Swiss, German and Belgian volunteers, challenged the Royal Italian Army of Victor Emmanuel II to battle at Castel-fidardo, on September 8, 1860, proudly pronouncing the famous last words: '*Les Italiens ne se battent pas*,' 'Italians can't fight'. He knew. He despised them. He had seen them in battle. The Italians trounced him soundly. The Papal domains were lost for ever that very day. And how many observers declared in 1922 that Fascism was but a straw fire which would not last three months? There is every reason why foreigners should be misled by their own caution when the Italians themselves, who know all about the rules governing their conduct, have, down the centuries, so often been deluded, frustrated and paralysed by their own fear of deceiving themselves.

*

The application of some of the principles already outlined can, for instance, clarify the ancient and puzzling *Problema del Mezzogiorno*, or the profound difference between the Two Italies, the North and the South. There is no doubt that all Italians, observed from a distance, have a family resemblance. They all come more or less from the same stock, have predominantly dark hair, dark eyes and vivacious expressions. They have been shaped by similar historical vicissitudes and have developed or sharpened the same talents in order to survive. They all love life and enjoy a good show. They are all similarly wary of the law; they all pursue their type of happiness *alla* Guicciardini, the advancement of their private welfare, or *il particulare*, at the expense of society; they must defend themselves, their family and *consorteria* against the treachery, envy, hatred of men; they use the family as an ark to outlast natural calamities, historical convulsions, and political upheavals. Unlike the inhabitants of better organized nations, they have to rely on their private virtues and public vices, their adaptability, charm, intelligence, shrewdness, the use of their personal power.

All this is the same in the North as in the South. But there is a difference. The difference is important: it is one of the causes of the slower development of the southern economy, in the past century, and of the more rapid growth of the northern economy. It has so far defeated all attempts to bring the two standards of living more or less onto one level. It will always misdirect the spending of at least a part of the vast sums of money the government invests in the South. There is even a danger that the mutual mistrust and misunderstanding which separate the Two Italies may be strengthened and that national unity, which was always fragile at best, may become more unstable than in the past.

The private aims of southerners and northerners are, of course, more or less the same. The northerner, however, thinks that there is one practically sure way to achieve them: the acquisition of wealth, *la ricchezza*. Only wealth can, he believes, lastingly assure the defence and prosperity of the family. The southerner, on the other hand, knows that this can be done only with the acquisition of power, prestige, authority, fame. The northerner of whatever class, therefore, is perpetually trying to acquire wealth in its various forms. He wants a job, a good job, a better job; he wants land, capital, credit, industrial shares, houses, technical and scientific knowledge and expensive and rare university degrees, which assure him better-paid employment and advancement; he brings up his children with these aims in mind, educating them to become well-paid technicians, engineers, specialists. He undergoes any sacrifice in order to gain material advantages for himself and his family. He wants a rich wife, rich daughters- and sons-in-law, rich friends. He is similar to the French bourgeois, almost a pure *homo economicus*.

The southerner, on the other hand, wants above all to be obeyed, admired, respected, feared and envied. He wants wealth too, of course, but as an instrument to influence people, and, for that, the appearance of wealth is as useful as wealth itself. In the South, the little peasant, the illiterate day labourer, the olive-tree pruner, the sulphur miner, as well as the landed proprietor, the noble member of exclusive clubs, the *nouveau riche* owner of recently founded industries, all will cultivate the gratitude of powerful friends and relatives, the fear of their enemies, the respect of everybody, and the reputation of their families.

In Naples and in Milan there are, for example, wholesale fruit and vegetable merchants. They belong more or less to the same class of people. They have roughly the same education. They pay dues to a local association of *grossisti*, which belongs to a national confederation. They may meet at national congresses and even at European Market congresses. They probably know each other and nod when they meet. They consider themselves colleagues in a vague way. Here all similarities cease.

The Neapolitan usually tours the countryside with his henchmen, bullying and protecting peasants in his well-defined sector, and forcing them to sell their products only to him at the prices he fixes. He defends his territory and his vassal farmers from the encroachment of competitors. He carries a gun. He shoots straight. He can kill a man if necessary. He can command killers. As everybody knows that he can enforce his will and defend his power by killing his opponents, he never, or almost never, has the need to shoot. If the farmers were to refuse to sell at his price, he can leave their produce to rot in the field. The farmers never refuse because nobody else would dare buy their products in competition with him. A superficial observer, of course, would not know what exactly was going on, what were his real relations with the farmers and retailers, and would notice none of the invisible threats and fears. Farmers, dealers, henchmen, retailers, competitors, all smile, joke, exchange pleasantries, drink wine, shake hands. They appear to be the best of friends. Only rarely something goes wrong, and the police find an unexplained corpse in a country lane. The culprits are seldom identified. Nobody usually gets killed, however, in Naples, if he is careful and plays the game.

The Milanese is an entirely different kind of man. He resembles his foreign colleagues more than his Neapolitan or Sicilian competitors. He carries no gun, is followed by no henchman, rarely sees the farmers he buys from, almost never tours the countryside. He sits in a modern office, surrounded by dictating machines, graphs on the wall, brisk secretaries. His business is carried on by telephone, with brokers and buyers in Germany, France or Switzerland, by the carload or the trainload, peaches from Verona, apricots from Naples, oranges from Sicily, grapes from Apulia, spring potatoes or cabbages from Tuscany. His only aim is to ship more and more refrigerated railway trucks abroad, filled with more and more of the fresh produce foreigners consume, at the highest possible prices. He naturally makes a lot of money, in good years one hundred or one thousand times more than his Neapolitan colleagues. But the Neapolitan does not mind. He is not unhappy about it. He wants other things than money, rarer and more satisfactory things. He wants to be well known (his sinister nickname must be recognized in the whole province); to be feared (policemen, at times, must forget they saw him go by); to be powerful (politicians must beg for his help at election time). He also wants to be loved (he will redress wrongs and protect unimportant people asking for his aid).

This, of course, is a didactic simplification, an example chosen to prove a point. Nothing is quite so simple in real life. There is no definite moral frontier between the two sections. Not all the South is purely southern, nor is all the North only northern. One finds men in northern Italy who apparently want to increase their power, authority, prestige and rank above anything else. Likewise, it is easy to find hundreds of people, in the South, who seemingly forgo all preoccupations of prestige in order to amass a lot of money. When observed closely, however, these exceptions usually confirm rather than confute the general rule. Frequently, in fact, the northerner who seems to pursue power does so only because power will generate more money, and the southerner who apparently seeks to increase his fortune really wants the added prestige which wealth brings him. There are, for instance, well-known politicians from the North, in Rome, who use their eminent position in the government in order to enrich their families; and southerners who amass possessions in order to become deputies, under-secretaries and cabinet ministers. Generally speaking, southerners tend to make money in order to rule, northerners to rule in order to make money.

The difference may not be identifiable in every individual but is always discernible in the two societies. It permeates every detail. It strengthens the contrasting characteristics of the Two Italies. It widens the gap. Official Italy, in the course of one hundred years, has apparently succeeded merely in unifying names, labels and titles, but not reality. Take a *prefetto*, the functionary appointed by the central government to rule over a province. He is always a southerner: only a southerner likes a badly paid job with power, honours and high protocol precedence. He rates the title of *Eccellenza*, like a bishop, a papal prince or an ambassador, and sits very high at any table. Nothing would be more misleading than to think that the *prefetto* in a northern province has any resemblance to his colleague in the South. In the North he is an inconspicuous bureaucrat. Few remember his name. In the South he is the ruler, a social leader. He goes to banquets, weddings, funerals, and christenings. He is surrounded by courtiers and sycophants. His word, a mere suggestion on the telephone, or a wish whispered as to himself, is law. He can still sometimes swing elections for the government. When he goes by, in his black car, people bow low and take their hats off.

It is pointless to pass judgment on either of these two societies, to determine which is more civilized, which is more likely in the long run to provide the 'greatest good for the greatest number'. There are obviously more material advantages in the North, but they do not compensate for the dangers of spiritual impoverishment, the crude hedonism, the infantile cultural and emotional life, the dreary levelling, the discipline, which are inseparable from an industrialized society. The southerner, on the other hand, employs all his faculties keenly in the daily struggle, he frequently overwhelms his competitors, he enjoys, at times, the pleasures of victory. He has time to pursue idle and wasteful passions. His life is often more intense, human, nearer nature and natural instincts. But these advantages may not compensate him for its squalor, poverty, hopelessness, insecurity and injustice.

It is worth considering what great benefits southerners have contributed to past Italian achievements. A people wholly dedicated to the rational and scientific pursuit of pure wealth inevitably becomes dull. Civilization and the graces of life flourish best where there are dedicated and intelligent people, who cheerfully accept mediocre living conditions for the sake of more satisfactory occupations and who prefer dignity, fame, authority, prestige or ease of conscience to mere money: scholars, poets, artists, novelists, saints, philosophers, jurists, eccentrics, spendthrift aristocrats. The Mezzogiorno has produced the majority of such characters in Italian life. Italy's debt to them is great. Some of the best novels in contemporary Italy were written by southerners. Italy's greatest playwright, Pirandello, was born in a place aptly called Chaos, near Agrigento, in Sicily. Her greatest philosopher, Croce, and one of her greatest poets, d'Annunzio, were born in the Abruzzi. The State was cheaply run for decades, by generally able and honest southern bureaucrats. The universities were, and are, staffed mainly by southern professors. Her colonies were administered, her courts were manned predominantly by southerners. The Sicilians formed a nucleus of the Foreign Service, where they excelled. Some of the principal publishing houses dedicated to unprofitable culture were in Bari, Naples and Messina. They kept the Italian soul alive in the dark times of the Fascist dictatorship.

The fact that many southern traits and habits may be classified as typical of an 'agrarian', 'feudal', or 'pre-capitalistic' society is only a partial and misleading, though tempting, explanation. It assumes that southerners would be northerners if only they were surrounded with the proper political and economic structures. This is not the case. Industries, for instance, were founded at both ends of Italy at about the same time, the beginning of the nineteenth century. After the unification, under theoretically identical conditions, they declined in the South and flourished in the North. It was said authoritatively that the industrial decay was due to the fact that the South was feudal. The North, of course, was just as feudal. It was said that it was due to the fact that the South had been ruled for centuries by oppressive foreigners: most of the North had been ruled equally by oppressive foreigners.

It was also said that the North was nearer to foreign markets. In reality it was separated from them by the Alps while the South did not lack good and conveniently located ports. Neither the North nor the South had coal mines and cheap sources of raw materials. It is believed that southern Italians were the victims of northern bureaucracy, impoverished by Piedmontese or Lombard competitors. In reality, the unified State administration quickly became predominantly southern. The political parties were soon also run by southerners. They were the men who really knew how to reach the top. Cabinet ministers, deputies, high officials did what they could to help. The decisive reason is another: the industrial revolution was not congenial to the inhabitants of the Mezzogiorno. They instinctively felt that the gains were not worth the sacrifice. They felt happier at other pursuits.

*

They had clung to their way of life, through thick and thin, in the past, sometimes heroically fighting the invaders and their novelties, sometimes accepting defeat, ignominy, poverty and desperation, in order not to betray their own nature and traditions. Like the Spanish, they sometimes carried on savage guerilla warfare in their mountains; at other times, like the Chinese, they seemed docilely to adopt foreign ways, in order to neutralize, digest and transform them into something unrecognizable, something of their own. The *Code Napoléon*, for instance, was introduced at the time of the First Empire by two French kings, Joseph Bonaparte and Joachim Murat. After a few years it had been so modified by local usage and interpretation that French lawyers could not recognize it. Even railways were adapted to the ways of the South. Tracks in northern Italy unimaginatively followed the shortest and cheapest routes between cities. In the South, they meandered all over the landscape sometimes in order to pass in front of obscure hamlets where a powerful person was born or owned a country residence, sometimes to lengthen the mileage and enrich the contractor responsible for the construction.

Southerners naturally cannot reconstruct the happy days of long ago, when Ferdinand II reigned, the Bourbon king who spoke dialect and knew his people's foibles. He died in 1859. He used to boast: 'My kingdom is an island, protected by salt water on three sides and holy water on the fourth.' Cold northern winds sweep the land now. Foreign ways are introduced freely. The people must make believe they are like all others. Many of their ancient virtues have now officially become vices. They do not feel at ease among the new techniques of production. They are often beaten and humiliated by duller competitors, who ignore the fine points of the art of living. They cannot resign themselves to becoming *homines economici*, stupidly bent on making money. Yet, at the same time, they cannot endure their condition of 'inferior' or 'backward' people. They are proud of their past. This is the psychological heart of the *Problema del Mezzogiorno*.

*

The *problema* is nothing new. One hundred years ago, it was clearly apparent that the South deserved immediate attention. Cavour's dying words, a few months after the proclamation of the new kingdom, were dedicated to the *poveri napoletani*. In his last delirium the Prime Minister said: 'North Italy has been established. There are no longer Lombards, Piedmontese, Tuscans, Romagnuols, we are all Italians, but there are still the Neapolitans. Oh! There is a lot of corruption in their country. It is not their fault, poor people. They have always been so badly governed. It was the fault of that rascal Ferdinand. We must bring morality to their country, educate the children and the youth, create nurseries and military schools. We must not dream of changing the Neapolitans by insulting them. They ask me for government posts, decorations, promotions. They must work, they must be honest, and then I will give them knighthoods, promotions, decorations. But above all we must allow them no transgressions. Government employees must not be suspected. I will govern them with liberty and will show what ten years of liberty can do in that beautiful country. . . .'

Special laws, special projects of public works, special credits for business ventures, special appropriations for the South have been a constant feature of Italian policy since the beginning of this century. Giolitti and Mussolini dedicated some of the best years of their lives to satisfying the South's claims to particular attention. Since 1950, the new democratic republic has spent in the South more than double what had been spent in the previous half century, and will possibly go on spending a large percentage of the State revenue. Progress has been immense. Nevertheless the old ills are still present.

*

A short journey through any part of southern Italy by train or car will bear out the truth of this. Wherever he goes, the visitor will see a larger number of public structures and buildings erected with public money than in the North or in any other country in Europe. He will see first, chronologically speaking, the Cyclopean structures of his great-grandfather's time, erected by the first Bourbons, Joseph Bonaparte, and Joachim Murat, at the end of the eighteenth century and the beginning of the nineteenth. He will then see the incredible amount of construction done by Ferdinand II. All this still constitutes the majority of basic works: roads, harbours, government buildings, hospitals and schools. Then he will recognize the more familiar and modest buildings of the early Victor Emmanuel III era, the years before the first world war, followed by the more numerous, lavish and 'imperial' attempts of Mussolini to perpetuate his name and the fame of his régime in perennial marble and concrete. Lastly, he will see the glittering new buildings erected by his contemporaries, the Christian Democrat governments of this post-war period.

Each epoch shows a state of disrepair naturally proportionate to its age. In the suburbs of Naples, for instance, some of the oldest factories, built at the beginning of the century, are literally falling down. The plaster is peeling from the walls. It is sometimes impossible to read the name of the firm painted on the façade, obliterated by the sun and dust. Rotten roof-beams bend under the weight of moss-encrusted tiles. Doors hang from rusty hinges. The courtyards are littered with refuse, dilapidated machinery, weather-beaten packing cases, tin cans. The factories still run, of course. Somehow, on the verge of collapse, the wheels turn. The reason is that economic criteria are considered secondary. The factory is seldom a strictly money-making enterprise. It is not meant to function efficiently. Its shoddy products are probably cheap enough to sell on the market, but cheap because the capital came largely from public funds and not loans; the company enjoys special tax facilities, interest is kept low, and little money is spent on modernization, upkeep or renovation. Wages are (or were until a short time ago) lower than elsewhere, miserably low, in fact.

The factories built by the Fascists are somewhat better, if only because they are newer. Even so, they show no sign of improvements and no attempt to keep up with the times and technical progress. The recent post-war factories, dramatically ultra-modern, with plastic roofs and painted in the bright dazzling colours of sherbets,

strawberry, peach, pistachio nut, are still in relatively good condition. Even here, however, flakes of plaster and large spots of
moisture reveal their dubious future.

This is generally true also of agricultural establishments. Sometimes, near the bright new villages of the *Enti di Riforma* (the State
agrarian reform and development organizations which split up the
large landholdings into small farms) are the villages of similar State
enterprises built back in Fascist days. They are now abandoned.
(Most of the new ones are also uninhabited, make-believe villages
because southern farmers anyway prefer to live not on the land but in
nearby towns.) The old houses have been allowed to decay. No
money is spent on their upkeep. They look like the crumbling ruins
of some distant and forgotten historical era, disorderly agglomera-
tions of huts and hovels, their roofs sprouting with weeds and wild
fig bushes. Occasionally, the roof has caved in, or has been blown off,
and the flora proliferates on the walls and the floors. Often doors,
windows, roof beams, sills, and other movable parts have been stolen.
The ruined houses of Pompeii and Herculaneum, in the care of the
Ministry of Public Instruction, are in far better condition and look
newer.

This disregard for upkeep is revealing. Even today the law enabling
the *Cassa del Mezzogiorno* to spend billions of lire on the development and modernization of the country contains no provision whatever for maintenance. The older generation, watching the decay of
expensive projects, sadly called the region the 'Cemetery of public
works'. The definition is still often used today.

The predominance of psychological and uneconomic motives is
confirmed by other signs. Often the old or new structures are
noticeably too elaborate, massive and expensive for the wretched town
and village they serve. On both the Tyrrhenian and Adriatic coasts
the traveller's eyes will rest on large harbours, equipped with granite
or concrete breakwaters, quays, and adequate storage facilities.
Many of these secondary ports are usually empty and silent, no more
than sporadic havens for the odd fishing smack when the *buriana*
blows. Likewise one comes across immense post offices where only a
few letters and postcards are sent or received weekly by a small population of semi-illiterate peasants; or monumental school buildings

sheltering a tiny number of children, which naturally cannot be properly heated or cleaned with the miserable sums of money allotted for the purpose. A *carabinieri* barracks in Bari, built by the Fascist régime, on the waterfront, in a location more suitable for a luxurious block of flats or a hotel, is loaded with statuary, sculptured ornaments, statues and columns, which can clearly add nothing to the efficiency of a police station.

This waste is often explained away as 'foresight', the preparation of suitable conveniences for, and the stimulation of, future growth. This is sadly contradicted by the fact that the local population and local activities have, in frequent cases, dwindled instead of increased. Nothing happened before the war and now most of the younger men emigrate, seeking employment in the North. Naturally, there are exceptions, cases of public expenditures which succeeded in creating chains of connected initiatives and investments out of nothing, but these are not many, they are usually strictly functional, and seldom dictated by a desire for prestige. It is not always that the organ manages to create the function. Many such constructions, very old, moderately old, new, or glaringly new, remind one at times of the stately imperial buildings of the Raj in old India, isolated signs of alien power and splendour.

The psychological and spectacular purpose of many of these structures is finally proved by their siting. In Palermo, for instance, there is a brand-new power station, an impressive structure built since the war. (Palermo is specially prone to display investments. After it was conquered by Garibaldi and his thousand Redshirts, in 1860, and became part of the new Kingdom, the city urgently built two opera theatres, both bigger than San Carlo in Naples, la Scala in Milan, and the Opéra in Paris.) The power station was not placed away from the public gaze, behind a hill, suitably masked so that the ugly buildings and high smoke-stacks could be forgotten, and the smoke and fumes become less obnoxious. It has been proudly placed near the harbour, in the heart of the city, thus ruining one of the most beautiful sights of all Italy, a famous panorama dear to ancient poets and painters. It has been placed in precisely the spot where in ancient days a cathedral would have been erected, consecrated to the local patron saint, or, even earlier, a marble temple dedicated to a tutelary god or to Zeus himself, a monument, that is, to whatever power the century believed could endow the city with untold benefits.

Such behaviour, sociologists justly point out, is not typical of southern Italy but of poor men everywhere, who waste what money they can get on superfluous, luxurious and showy things, while skimping on the necessary. Small backward republics, in Africa, or Latin America, which squander their meagre resources on marble monuments to the Founder and neglect building a sewage disposal plant, adequate schools or a hospital, knowingly or unconsciously are doing all they can to increase poverty, illiteracy and disease. When, however, this is done by citizens of an old European nation, many of them noted for their brilliant intelligence and culture, who have all the necessary economic knowledge, in contact with more progressive examples a few hours away, it can be considered no longer the result of blind sociological reflexes but a deliberate choice.

*

The South is no longer the same. It is changing daily, it is being developed, it is improving. The changes have been brought about by an infinite number of factors, only a few of them manœuvred by man. The South is no longer King Ferdinand's 'island': it is part of a contemporary nation, part of Europe, part of the modern world; it has not been sheltered from history and protected from the influx of world-wide trends. The large amounts of money spent in the last few years could not help having an influence. Some of the money at least was well-spent. The rest could not somehow help modify the local scene, even if not always in the direction desired.

Even war has changed things. Southerners have done their duty in strange and distant lands, from 1866 to 1945, in North Italy, the Alps, the deserts of North Africa, Spain, the plateaus of Ethiopia, Albania, Greece and Russia. Many of them also visited India, Great Britain, Germany and the United States as prisoners, during the last war. All people bring back from wars a secret resolution to lead different and more satisfactory lives, and southern veterans were no exception. Emigration of labour to North and South America and to the rest of Europe, which has been going on since the end of the last century, provoked a steady return flow of money, experienced and enriched emigrants, new ideas, new habits, and restlessness. For a century and a half, able and intelligent men from the middle classes emigrated, mostly to North and Central Italy, where they and their descendants now occupy leading positions. Southern soldiers brought back northern wives. The films and television forced the inhabitants of obscure mountain villages to gaze upon an idealized, bourgeois, well-washed, polite, law-abiding and well-fed image of the outside world. Finally the sudden and vigorous upsurge of economic activities in the last few years could not help having its effect. Unemployed and unskilled workers are now going north *en masse*. Those who remain behind obtain steadier employment and higher wages.

The change is visible. Factories rise along the main roads and the railways. More are being built. A few new industries have a difficult time, of course. They were built in a hurry, with no clear ideas, not enough credit, not enough experience, sometimes by dishonest operators. Others produce something which is produced better and cheaper elsewhere. The South believes not in specialization but in emulation. Many plants, however, are flourishing. They are the factories which nature decreed should be built in that particular spot, because of objective reasons. Some of these were erected by northern firms, taking full advantage of the legislation facilitating economic enterprises in the South, and run by northern managers. Others, like the immense steel works in Taranto, were willed and financed by the State. There are now flourishing industrial centres, here and there, comparable to those of northern Europe. A stretch of coast between Syracuse and Augusta, in Eastern Sicily, where the Greek city of Megara is believed once to have been, and where until lately there were only contorted olive trees and flocks of sheep grazing, in front of the wine-dark sea, now looks like Newark, New Jersey, or Galveston, Texas, the plains crowded with chemical factories, aerial tanks, yellow, red, and blue pipes, and intricate metal structures rising in the sky.

New quarters in decrepit cities everywhere look like Brazilia. The very delirious audacity of the architecture reveals, as it does in South America or in Nehru's India, a secret fear of appearing behind the times, anchored to ancient habits, left behind by the march of progress. Even the faces of the people have changed in the cities and more prosperous towns. The women are freer and more smartly dressed. The crowds look better fed and clothed. Street urchins wear shoes. Beggars have disappeared. Eating habits have changed. The younger people are taller and straighter than their fathers: they are determined not to eke out a living, as their ancestors have always done, no longer to resign themselves to the will of God, the favours of the mighty, the caprice of fortune, and the everlasting *miseria*.

Yet, in spite of all these considerable and sometimes incredible improvements, it would be foolhardy to conclude that the *Problema del Mezzogiorno* is definitely on its way to a solution. To begin with, the immense poverty is too old and too deeply rooted really to have disappeared. It has been mostly swept under the carpet. Its pressure still underlies everything. Most of the improvements and moderniza- tions can be observed around a few chosen cities, a few favoured sites, and the most fertile agricultural sections. Everywhere else, where the casual visitor from the north does not usually go, around the corner from a prosperous scene, a stone's throw from the resplendent new hotels, factories or workers' housing projects, a short walk up the hills, almost everywhere in the countryside, the *miseria* is still supreme. It is better *miseria*, often comforted by new, modern con- veniences, a road, a public telephone, sometimes an aqueduct, sewers, a new cemetery, a doctor twice a week, a midwife in residence, a *miseria* tempered perhaps by the distribution of American surplus flour and condensed milk to the children, free medicines to the desti- tute, but *miseria* nevertheless.

Even if it were to disappear, however, the problem would still not be solved. Even if the process of modernization should continue, if everybody had a roof over his head, enough to eat, relative security, medical care, an elementary education and a steady job, the moral aspects of the *problema* would not vanish. The malaise and the rest- lessness, the feeling of being the victims of historical injustice and the prey of other people's greed, the desire to revolt and break away from the centralized government of Rome would go on.

Southerners, of course, naturally want to live better lives, at about the standard of the average Western European, and to solve some of their most urgent material problems. They want all this but they also want something else. They want to see the gap between North and South dwindle. They want to live as well as northerners. Anything else is not acceptable. Anything else is dishonourable, damaging to their pride. They do not understand why their nordic countrymen, obviously less clever than they, should have such splendid living conditions, such wonderful factories, such awe-inspiring hospitals, and so much money, and why such things should be less impressive in the South.

Southerners will never be placated, and the *problema* buried, until the real and imaginary differences can be erased. There are a number of reasons why this is not easy. To begin with, a part of every lira spent to improve the South goes to the North. From the North come the engineers, the specialists, the managers, the contractors, the skilled workers for many jobs. From the North comes practically all the machinery for new plants and installations, even the humble pump necessary to irrigate a tiny plot of land. From the North, finally, come almost all the consumer goods, shirts, shoes, clothes, furniture, radios, television sets, and motor scooters which southerners increasingly can afford. In fact, even if some of these things are now manufactured in the South, the fact is kept secret, as southern buyers think it is safer and more honourable to wear or consume things made in Milan.

Take the *cassate alla siciliana*. It is a delicious iced cake, a Sicilian speciality, the ultimate result of tradition that goes back to the Arabs, a thousand years ago. In the North, the *cassate* are but poor and shoddy imitations. Sicily now consumes an enormous number of *cassate* industrially produced in Milan. The local product can now be found only in a few old-fashioned *pasticcerie* or cafés. The Milan product has more prestige. It is advertised on television. It can be ordered in any quantity. It is delivered by refrigerated truck to the smallest mountain village. It costs little enough. It is sanitary.

If the Sicilians ever got round to starting a *cassate* factory they would undoubtedly invade Milan with their better product and eventually the rest of Europe and the world. They do not do this, perhaps, because they can seldom set up a financial company big enough for the job. (Nobody in the South likes to be a minority stockholder. Everybody wants to be the boss. Nobody trusts his partners very far.) Southerners, then, do not like to produce what they do best: they prefer to make more prestigious things like steel, machinery, ships, and, if they could, cars. They also submit too easily to the authority of the North, even in cases, like that of the *cassate*, where their own superiority is universally recognized and indisputable.

There is a final reason, the fundamental reason. Southerners think mainly in political, not economic, terms. Even a *cassate* factory could rise in Sicily only through the initiative of some government bureau, the will of an influential cabinet minister, the intervention of an archbishop, or the decision of a political party. Most southern initiatives, in the past centuries, were the king's. They still are. Politics determine what plants will rise and where, what money shall be allotted to them, and which people will run them. It is the slower and duller northerner, without imagination, who has to rely on his own initiative, and is compelled to do things privately, on his own. As a result the race between the southern and the northern economies is uneven. It is a race between a puppet manœuvred by wires from above and a living man. Inevitably, the northern economy is more vigorous and adaptable. It is run by people mostly selected through competition, guided by experience, spurred on by the hope of gain. While the South progresses by feet, the North progresses by miles.

*

As long as the southerners do not really want just prosperity but moral equality with the northerners, they will go on spending most of their efforts and money only incidentally on purely economic aims but mainly on the display of newly-acquired or not yet acquired modernity, power and prestige. Some of their new factories will go on being monuments, not instruments to produce wealth but demonstrations that the city or region is to be considered no longer backward but modern and progressive, among the most modern and progressive in Europe. Such investments naturally do not produce exemplary economic results. Nor do they produce the required psychological effect. They do not bridge the gap between the North and the South. They increase it. Slowly, a few at a time, southerners are reluctantly discovering the bewildering fact that only investments dictated by hated northern criteria can, in the long run, produce stable southern results, the psychological, spectacular, and political effects required. They alone can, in the long run, really solve the *Problema del Mezzogiorno*. The great majority of southerners, of course, have not yet discovered this dreary and disappointing truth. Most of them, however, are the victims of the eternal Italian delusion, of confusing reality with the representation of reality, in their effort to solve an unsolvable problem: how to produce in the Arcadian past of the Bourbon kings and consume in the contemporary world of cheap and abundant industrial goods.

CHAPTER FOURTEEN

SICILY AND THE MAFIA

G OETHE was right when he wrote: 'Without seeing Sicily one cannot get a clear idea of what Italy is.' Sicily is the schoolroom model of Italy for beginners, with every Italian quality and defect magnified, exasperated and brightly coloured. Sicilians, for example, have a genius for *sistemazione* or giving order to chaos: how many of them were law-givers, how many the first in history to indicate a new mode of expression, a new vision of reality, a new conception of the world and man? Archimedes, Stesicorus (whose future eminence as a poet was foretold when a nightingale perched upon his lips and sang), Empedocles and Theocritus (the inventor of pastoral poetry), in the remote past, and, more recently, Bellini, Verga, Pirandello and Lampedusa are obvious names. In the island, the Italian propensity for pomp, pageantry and spectacle becomes convulsed, superhuman, almost grotesque in its magnificence, stupendously overloaded with superfluous ornaments. There is no more elaborate Baroque in all Italy than that of the churches and *palazzi* of Ragusa, Comiso, Noto and Syracuse, ingeniously carved out of the local golden sandstone.

Everywhere in Italy life is more or less slowed down by the exuberant intelligence of the inhabitants: in Sicily it is practically paralysed by it. The intelligence of Sicilians is so exorbitant, in fact, that some of it had always to be exported. Their capacity to grasp situations with lightning speed, invent a way out of intricate tangles, gauge exactly the relative power of contending parties, weave wonderfully complex intrigues, coldly control their smallest acts, emotions and words, but, when it is safe, abandon themselves to generous enthusiasms, their capacity to do all these things is such that they often bewilder continental Italians as easily as continental

Italians surprise foreigners from the north of Europe. The islanders are all so expert, in fact, that they neutralize each other. The simplest project, something which could be carried out anywhere else by means of a letter and a couple of conversations, becomes among Sicilians an enterprise of heroic proportions, each participant inventing diabolical schemes of his own to get the better of his opponent and, at the same time, foresee all possible schemes which his opponent will try to employ. The result is almost always the immobility of two wrestlers of equal strength, the melancholic immutability described by Lampedusa, the 'feeling of death'.

The Sicilians' best virtues, like those of most Italians, are obviously not those of the anonymous organization man of today, but those of the ancient hero fighting, with his little group, the rest of the world. If the native of the mainland is often capable of gallantry and disinterested behaviour, the Sicilian can reach unbelievable heights of fortitude, generosity, selflessness and fearlessness. He can even accept death with open eyes or deal death impassively, without hesitation or regret, whenever he thinks there is nothing else to do, in defence of his particular, strictly Sicilian ideals. If most Italians manage at times to weave skilfully in and out of written laws, most Sicilians appear to avoid them all completely. They are the supreme masters of this skill, recognized by all Italians as the unbeatable champions.

*

Each man's individual rank is determined by the amount of fear he can generate, by the halo of fear that surrounds him. This is especially true in Western Sicily, where fear is the naked fear of death, but it is more subtly and imperceptably true everywhere in the island. The elusive techniques developed through the ages to acquire status by scaring and intimidating an ever larger number of people are loosely known as the 'way of the Mafia'. The word Mafia notoriously means two things, one, which should be spelled with a lower-case 'm', being the mother of the second, the capital letter Mafia.

The lower-case mafia is a state of mind, a philosophy of life, a conception of society, a moral code, a particular susceptibility, prevailing among all Sicilians. They are taught in the cradle, or are born already knowing, that they must aid each other, side with their friends and fight the common enemies even when the friends are wrong and the enemies are right; each must defend his dignity at all costs and never allow the smallest slights and insults to go unavenged; they must keep secrets, and always beware of official authorities and laws. These principles are shared by all Sicilians, by the upright gentleman and the petty thief, the penniless prince living in his dusty *palazzo* or the heroin smuggler with relatives in the United States, the erudite scholar lost in his researches and the illiterate sulphur miner. These principles are also carefully preserved among Sicilians living in the rest of Italy and abroad. In fact, a Sicilian who does not feel these compulsions should no longer consider himself a Sicilian. In this sense, *mafioso* is anybody bearing himself with visible pride. 'What a *mafioso* horse!' Sicilians will exclaim when seeing a prancing stallion, well-caparisoned, with arched neck, dilated nostrils and fiery eyes. They obviously do not mean the horse is a member of a deadly secret society.

Mafia, in the second and more specialized meaning of the word, is the world-famous illegal organization. It rules over only one part of Sicily: its threats are terrifying in Palermo, Partinico or Agrigento, but are ignored in Messina, Catania and Syracuse. It is not a strictly organized association, with hierarchies, written statutes, head-quarters, a ruling élite and an undisputed chief. It is a spontaneous formation like an ant-colony or a beehive, a loose and haphazard collection of single men and heterogeneous groups, each man obeying his entomological rules, each group uppermost in its tiny domain, independent, submitted to the will of its own leader, each group locally imposing its own rigid form of primitive justice. Only in rare times of emergency does the Mafia mobilize and become one loose confederation.

Nobody knows how many *mafiosi* there are. Only a minority of Sicilians are technically *mafiosi*, in the criminal sense of the word. Many do not honestly know whether they are *mafiosi* or not. Western Sicilians must, as a rule, entertain good relations with the Mafia in their native village or city quarter. They have to live there, they must protect their family, job, property or business, and want no trouble. The Mafia is for them a fact of life, one of the permanent conditions of existence, like the climate, the average rainfall or the local patois. It is often impossible to draw a neat dividing line between *Mafiosi* and non-*Mafiosi*.

Take the good friars of Mazzarino, who were recently arrested and tried for having acted as messengers between the Mafia and its intended victims, men who were being blackmailed. The pious fathers patiently explained to the non-Sicilian court that they were by no means to be considered advisers, instigators or accomplices of the criminals. They had only done their best to persuade the intended victims, to whom they brought the Mafia's blackmail message, that it was safer to pay, and pay quickly, in order to save their lives. Were not one or two men, who had stubbornly overlooked the advice, subsequently found dead in solitary country lanes? Yes, of course, the monks had written some of the messages themselves, but only because the *mafiosi* were illiterate and did not own a typewriter.

Furthermore, the friars pointed out that they were by no means responsible for the conditions of law enforcement in Mazzarino. They were not policemen. They took for granted that there were extortionists and potential victims, moneyed men whose only safety was in conforming with the Mafia's demands, and men who could live and prosper out of the fear they could evoke in others. The monks explained they were only doing their duty: they had avoided unnecessary bloodshed. Was theirs not a charitable mission? (The monks were found guilty, nevertheless, and given long prison sentences.)

Everybody, of course, knows (although such things are never admitted openly) that the trouble the Mafia defends one from is almost always contrived and controlled by the Mafia itself. Everybody knows that the tributes he is paying to the local boss could be compared to a tribute to a powerful feudal baron. Everybody is resigned. But the relationship between the Mafia and its victims is not limited to the collection of money. A day always comes when the Mafia also needs some favour in return. On that day, a man discovers he can no longer refuse. A businessman finds he must give a job to an ex-convict, a banker extend a loan to a risky customer, a farmer shelter some unknown men for a few days in a barn without asking questions, an honest man remember distinctly something he never knew or forgets something he saw. All these people gradually get so enmeshed in the net, in the hope of avoiding trouble, that they cannot free themselves.

Take another example. A political candidate needs votes; the Mafia can provide as many as he wants in certain districts; he accepts them with some misgivings. Many outstanding politicians have done so, after all. Why should he not? Orlando, perhaps the highest Italian authority on constitutional law, the Sicilian who was prime minister of Italy in 1918, at the end of the first world war, and, one year later, one of the Big Four at Versailles, with Lloyd George, Woodrow Wilson and Georges Clemenceau, had always welcomed Mafia aid. In the first free election held in Italy after the last war, in 1946, a large canvas sign was put up in Partinico, near Palermo, a notorious Mafia stronghold, where he had been elected for the first time in 1897. It said: 'Vote for Vittorio Emanuele Orlando, *l'amico degli amici*, the friend of friends.' It could not have been more explicit. Everybody knew who the 'friends' were.

When a candidate is elected anywhere in the world he must show some gratitude to his electors. He must do things in return for their votes, things he may not always like. What successful candidate does not, after all, run small errands for his constituents? In Sicily he may have to recommend highly unsuitable men for a good job, write letters to cabinet ministers in defence of shady characters, get a man out of jail, block some public works project (like the construction of an aqueduct) which endangers the power and revenue of some *amico* (the owner of springs of water) and so forth. Does this practice of using the Mafia and doing them favours necessarily make a man a member or an accomplice? Moralists think so. Sicilians are uncertain. They define such men, men who can keep a secret, do favours, accept favours, but also have power and authority of their own, not derived from the Mafia, but which make them useful to the Mafia at times, merely as *uomini rispettati*, men who exact respect from others and who should not be harmed.

Obviously the whole thing is confusing. The two Mafie are closely related. The second Mafia could not flourish if the first were not widespread. A man could scarcely prosper and get to the top in the second if he were not a master of the first. It is difficult to know exactly where one begins and the other ends. They often overlap. The phenomenon has deep roots in history, in the character of the Sicilians, in local habits; its origins disappear down the dim vistas of the centuries.

*

Nobody really knows what the word means, where it came from, where the thing originated, and why the capital-letter Mafia turned out the way it did. Sicilians mention the word reluctantly, and only to make themselves understood when talking to mainland Italians or to foreigners. They prefer to call it the *onorata società*, or honoured association, or some other name. The members are usually known as *gli amici*, the friends, or *gli amici degli amici*, the friends of friends. Sober businessmen in Palermo use a brisk, modern, businesslike term, when mentioning the influential Mafia men they occasionally turn to for help in a difficult predicament: they call them *uomini qualificati*, qualified men, specialists.

This much is known of the Mafia's origins: for centuries landowners used to set up private little armies of their own to defend their families and estates from marauding bandits. There were few roads, the island was wretchedly governed by rapacious foreigners, revolt against alien laws and institutions was endemic. These so-called *compagnie d'armi* maintained some sort of primitive justice by drastic means: as they had no courts of law and no prisons they had to punish the smallest crime with the death sentence. Justice was conceived as something innate in man: wrongs were righted, the weak defended, robbers punished, the outraged virgins married off to their seducers, according to what was, in reality, a rough peasant version of the code of chivalry which the Norman invaders had brought to the island in 1070, and which had been kept alive by the *teatro dei pupi*, the puppets' theatre, frequented by grown-ups as well as children, dedicated to the noble feats of Charlemagne's knights.

Even today the more traditional Mafia men try to maintain the fiction that they are not ordinary criminals but the enemies of criminals; that they do not commit crimes but are sometimes regretfully compelled to employ force in order to finance themselves and to enforce their law, which, after all, they explain, has been for centuries the only valid law in Sicily, the only defence against anarchy. In effect, the visible lives of the old high-ranking Mafia men are generally spotless. They are good fathers, good husbands, good sons; their word is sacred; they fastidiously refrain from having anything to do with spying, prostitution, drugs, or dishonest swindles. They never betray a friend. They are always devoted churchmen, who give large sums to the local parish or to the deserving poor. Many have sisters in convents and brothers in holy orders. When considering the *società*, one must not forget this remnant of the Middle Ages, this cherished rhetoric which is not wholly fictitious. It is important. It distinguishes the Sicilian Mafia from strictly criminal organizations or plain rackets, as the American so-called Mafie really are. It also furnishes a noble alibi tn honest men for their occasional collaboration.

Most leaders of *compagnie d'armi*, like the sheriffs in Western films, found it convenient at times to recruit new men among the bandits themselves, usually the older bandits who tired of life in the woods, wanted stability and longed for the respectability of family life. They were the only men around who did not fear taking risks. The dividing line between law-breaker and law-enforcer became more and more indistinguishable. It was easy for men to pass from one group to another and back again. The *compagnie d'armi* degenerated. It was tempting for them, so far from any control, to come to a working agreement with their enemies, the outlaws, so that all could co-exist and prosper peacefully. If the bandits played the game, and did their robbing and killing in other territories, they were well taken care of; if they wanted trouble, they were destroyed.

The landowner was usually far away, in Palermo or in Naples. If he was on the spot and he discovered that his guards were the accomplices of the bandits, he was quickly placed in a distressingly awkward position. He had no choice. He had to accept the will of his men. They protected him, his family, his castle, his cellars and granaries, did they not? What did he care if they played havoc at times with his neighbours' possessions? His guards could impose their will on him. In return for their services, he naturally had to pay them a share of the crops (did one not always do that with governments?), overlook their crimes, defend them from the official authorities with his influence, and see to it that they were never punished for the outrages, kidnappings, extortions, robberies, and murders which they committed elsewhere.

The primordial and arcadian form of the Mafia with its mixture of ruthless brutality and noble sentiments still exists in Sicily wherever large estates survive. The foreign heir or buyer of an isolated estate is soon told, in a confidential, mysterious, courteous but intimidating manner, that to avoid trouble, he had better hire a certain local man as an overseer, without asking too many questions. The man usually turns out to have spent a few years in prison for robbery, arson or murder. Foreigners, in this case, include Sicilians from the east of the island. The native heir or buyer does not have to be told. He knows. He does what is necessary or sells the land to whoever is allowed to buy it from him at whatever price the *amici* decide. If the new owner is so foolish as not to understand the message, he soon grasps its implications: his vines are cut down overnight, his woods and haylofts set on fire, his sheep and cattle stolen, and perhaps one of his children is kidnapped. The police confess themselves impotent and kindly advise him to do what he was told. If he does, he will be *rispettato*: he will be honoured, served hand and foot, surrounded with feudal courtesies, loudly praised everywhere. Unknown men will take their caps off and bow low when he passes. His life will be more than safe: it will be downright paradisiacal.

Other Mafie now exist, more modern, lucrative and powerful. Most of them specialize in exacting a tribute from all sorts of economic activities. There are the cattle and pasture Mafie; citrus grove Mafie; water Mafie (who control the scarce springs, wells, irrigation canals); building Mafie (if the builder does not pay, his scaffolding collapses and his bricklayers fall to their death); commerce Mafie; public works Mafie (who award contracts); wholesale fruit, vegetable, flower, and fish markets Mafie, and so forth. They all function more or less in the same way. They establish order, they prevent pilfering, each in its own territory, and provide protection from all sorts of threats, including the legal authorities, competitors, criminals, revenue agents, and rival Mafia organizations. They fix prices. They arrange contracts. They can see to it, in an emergency, that violators of their laws are surely punished with death. This is rarely necessary. Most of the time the fact that they can condemn any man to death is enough to keep everybody toeing the line.

The supreme heads of these separate organizations are often well-to-do bourgeois, respected lawyers, renowned surgeons, or country proprietors. They have spotless records. Their manners are ingratiating, they use diplomacy rather than force, speak in a low voice and prefer to employ old-fashioned forms of address: '*Bacio le mani*, I kiss your hands.' Their politics are conservative, often reactionary: they resent all social progress which inevitably endangers their power. They want to keep things as they are. They always side with whatever government exists at the moment, as it is only from the government that they can obtain favours. They are *simpatici*. They have to be.

*

The first nucleus of the Mafia is the family. Some families have belonged to the *società degli amici* from time immemorial, each father leaving the domain to his eldest son as naturally as a king leaves his kingdom to his heir. A father always takes part in confidential negotiations with the eldest son at his side. The latter never speaks. He looks, listens, and remembers everything, in case the older man were suddenly killed. Some new families emerge from nothing. Like all new people, they must struggle with the older families, survive, and slowly assert themselves. As the years go by, they accumulate henchmen, vassals, and property, establish solid relations with land-owners, businessmen, politicians, policemen and other Mafia families. Their rank is determined, at first, by the number and fear-lessness of their male members and, later, by the number of useful connections they establish. In one village several Mafia families can co-exist as long as they do not compete in the same field of activity: each of them must work its particular sector and all of them be ready to unite against a common threat.

A group of powerful families, belonging to the same district, pursuing identical or related activities, sometimes finds it convenient to form a stable union which is known as a *cosca*. It is the second step in the organization. The *cosca* is not an alliance between equals: it is kept together by the recognized supremacy of one family and the leadership of its head. The word *cosca* itself comes from a corruption of the dialect term for artichoke: a composition of separate leaves forming a solid unit. The *cosca* maintains good relations with other *cosche* dedicated to different pursuits. With competing *cosche* it usually comes to a working agreement: boundaries are established, territories defined, pacts negotiated and respected. Only rarely do the *cosche* have to wage war on each other. The war takes the traditional form of all feuds: a man from one group is killed, another from the rival organization is later murdered in revenge, a third is found shot in a country lane, a whole family is exterminated in return, and so on, for years, until the original cause of the feud is practically forgotten.

A feud which cost hundreds of lives almost a century ago, between the *stoppaglieri* of Monreale and the *fratuzzi* of Bagheria, is still remembered. One of the *fratuzzi*, Salvatore d'Amico, who had lost all his family, at one point turned informer. He told the police all he knew and then said: 'I shall die killed by the Mafia. Neither you nor all the police in the Kingdom of Italy will be able to save me.' Eleven days later he was found riddled with bullets, with a cork in his mouth, the symbol of the *stoppaglieri*, and an image of the Madonna del Carmine, the symbol of the *fratuzzi*, on his chest. The two fighting *cosche* had forgotten their enmity for the time strictly necessary to punish him. He had committed what is the ultimate crime for all Mafia men: he had talked to the authorities. This is known as *infamità*. (The man who had betrayed the bandit Salvatore Giuliano was killed a few years ago in the Ucciardone jail of Palermo with a poisoned cup of coffee.)

Many *cosche* pursuing identical or similar activities often join in an alliance called *consorteria*. The group also recognizes one *cosca* as supreme and its leader as everybody's leader. This happens spontaneously, almost gradually, when the *cosche* realize that one of them is more powerful, has more men, more friends, more money, more high-ranking protectors and relations than any of the others, could do untold damage to anybody defying its will and could benefit all those who collaborate and submit. All of the *consorterie* in Sicily finally form the *onorata società*, or the Mafia. It is, as has been said, a fluid and incoherent association, with vague boundaries.

There are all sorts of degrees of affiliation: a family may operate as a unit without necessarily joining forces with other families, a *cosca* may carry on its business for years without joining other *cosche*, and a *consorteria* of *cosche* may dominate its territory independently of the island association. A sort of Mafia patriotism, however, unites all members: they know they owe all possible support to any *amico degli amici* who needs it, for whatever reason, even if they have never heard of him, provided he is introduced by a mutual *amico*. Most Mafia men of any importance know hundreds of colleagues of all ranks. The great leaders meet, follow each other's activities from afar, and evaluate exactly each other's worth, as eminent men do in all walks of life. A few chiefs become especially renowned all over Sicily, for their particular qualities of sagacity, prudence, ruthless resolution, and for their successes. In the end, as a matter of course, one man is acknowledged as the most respected, trusted, and revered of all. He can generate more fear than anybody else. He is the head of the Mafia.

There are no exact rules for choosing him, no statutes, no elections, no conclave of big chiefs, no electoral body. What meetings take place are informal. In the old days, of course, in the last century, he always had to fight his way to the top and destroy his most dangerous rivals. The process was wasteful: it took years and cost hundreds of valuable lives. Nowadays he almost always emerges peacefully. His peers usually have known for years he was the best among them. At times, for brief periods, there has not been a single head but several equally revered candidates, a sort of *sede vacante*, an *interregnum*. Business, of course, goes on as usual. The chief is soon found. He is not indispensable anyway. His power is only absolute over his *consorteria*; it is nominal in the rest of the island. He does not give orders, draw up plans of action, conduct negotiations in the name of the Mafia with political powers or foreign agents. At times he may be called upon to settle a dispute, end a feud or define a boundary; very rarely he declares war against rebels in the name of the whole Mafia.

*

Legendary and still revered above all in Sicily is the name of the late Don Vito Cascio Ferro, perhaps the greatest head the Mafia ever had, who reigned from the end of the last century till the late twenties. (Don is the corruption of the Latin *dominus*. It means a little more than *signore*. It is used for noblemen, gentlemen of means, priests, and Mafia leaders.) Don Vito was born in Bisacquino, near Palermo, the son of illiterate peasants. He quickly emerged as a young man of great qualities. There was a natural aura of authority about him: people of all kinds found themselves obeying him and asking for his advice and consent for their projects without knowing why. Don Vito was the first to adapt the archaic and pastoral ways of the country Mafia to the twentieth century and the complex life of a relatively modern city. He organized all crimes, from the largest deals down to the chicken thefts and the purloining of brass coins from alms boxes in the churches. All criminals were more or less indexed in his memory and that of his henchmen; they were all licensed by him, could do nothing without the *società*'s consent, and incidentally without giving the Mafia the customary cut.

Crime there had to be, of course, as there was in every country under every régime. But in the well-ordered world of Don Vito it had to be disciplined, channelled, intelligently employed on occasion for useful purposes, and made to pay taxes. Crime was, after all, only one of the many activities of man. All of them, without exception, were chartered by the Mafia, paid a tribute to the Mafia and could be conscripted, in an emergency, to defend the Mafia's interests. For the first time in Palermo even beggars were no longer the victims of occasional abuses and impositions by petty criminals, but were enrolled in a regular organization and, like all businessmen, had to contribute a regular percentage, no more nor less, of their daily collections, to the *amico* in charge of their sector.

Discipline was such that, when a *uomo rispettato* from the country, an important politician from Rome, or a distinguished foreign guest of Sicily was robbed by mistake within Don Vito's jurisdiction, he gave an order and, in a matter of minutes, the suitcase, the watch, the wallet or the lady's jewellery was returned with apologies. Palermo was not Catania, in the east of the island, where there was no Mafia to control things and anarchy prevailed. Everybody knows what happened there to Mussolini's hat in 1923. It was a disgraceful incident. The dictator, an *uomo rispettato* if ever there was one, had arrived to visit the city and to confer with the authorities about its urgent needs. He shut himself up in the *prefettura* with the *prefetto*, the chief of police and prominent local personalities, for a long meeting. At the end he asked for his hat, a bowler hat. At the time he still dressed like a well-born clubman on the race course, wearing spats, morning clothes, and carrying a stick. Il Duce's hat could never be found. It had been stolen by some irresponsible and unknown petty thief or souvenir hunter.

Discipline in Palermo itself is today no longer what it used to be. A few years ago, after the last war, an English lady friend of the late Prince Don Raimondo Lanza di Trabia missed her expensive fur coat. The prince reassured her, sent for Don Vito's successor, and ordered him to return it. The Lanzas are one of the first families in Sicily. They arrived one thousand years ago, fought at the side of Frederick II of Hohenstaufen, King of Sicily and Emperor, in the thirteenth century. Lanzas have been advisers to kings and emperors, viceroys, generals, and admirals. Don Raimondo's late father was one of the aces of Italian aviation in the first world war. The family owned thousands of acres of land, whole towns, rivers, castles, *palazzi*, and villas. They could demand absolute *rispetto* in Sicily. The Mafia leader apologized humbly and quickly produced all the fur coats stolen in Palermo within the last few days. The lady's own was not among them. It had been stolen by a free-lance, an unknown man, perhaps a stranger from the mainland, who did not fear the *amici*.

Don Vito brought the organization to its highest perfection without undue recourse to violence. The Mafia leader who scatters corpses all over the island in order to achieve his goal is considered as inept as the statesman who has to wage aggressive wars. Don Vito ruled and inspired fear mainly by the use of his great qualities and his natural ascendancy. His awe-inspiring appearance helped him. He was tall, spare, elegantly but sombrely dressed. A long white beard made him resemble a sage, a New England preacher of the last century, or a respected judge. (He was practically illiterate.) His manners were princely, his demeanour humble but majestic. He was well loved by all. Being very generous by nature, he never refused a request for aid and dispensed millions in loans, gifts and general philanthropy. He would personally go out of his way to redress a wrong. When he started on a journey, every mayor, dressed in his best clothes, awaited him at the entrance of his village, kissed his hands, and paid homage, as if he were the king. And he was a king of sorts: under his reign, peace and order were preserved, the Mafia peace, of course, which was not what the official law of the Kingdom of Italy would have imposed, but people did not stop to draw too fine a distinction.

He admitted having killed one man in his long life, only one, and not for money, but for the honour, prestige, and preservation of the *società*. The man had challenged the Mafia as a whole and had to be killed personally by Don Vito and nobody else. He was Giuseppe Petrosino, the head of the Italian squad of the New York Police Department who had come to Palermo in 1909 to study the relations between the *onorata società* and the Black Hand organization among Sicilian immigrants. Petrosino was not Sicilian and did not know the Sicilian ways: he was from Padula, in the province of Salerno, and emigrated to the United States in 1873, when thirteen years old. He thought he was safe as nobody knew of his arrival except the police. Don Vito shot him a few hours after his landing, in the street, in the Piazza Marina, in front of the courthouse.

Don Vito was arrested in 1926, for the first and only time, by *prefetto* Mori, a tough policeman whom Mussolini had charged with the task of destroying the Mafia. Mori waged relentless war on the *società*, employing Mafia-like methods, disregarding all written laws, striking terror in the heart of everybody. He succeeded for a time. Don Vito easily established his authority over the whole prison, as a well-loved general does when incarcerated in a concentration camp among his soldiers. Order and discipline reigned there for the first time. He settled all quarrels and helped the inmates with their private troubles. He sent subsidies to the families of needy prisoners, sent rich dowries to the daughters of *amici* who were getting married, and generally continued to conduct his business from his cell as well as he could in such difficult times. He died in prison, of a broken heart. Until a few years ago one could still read a few words he had carved with a knife on the wall of the corridor of the Ucciardone prison. Prisoners read the sentence and nodded their approval long after his death. Like most memorable sayings of great men, this too expressed a platitude. It said: 'Prison, sickness, and necessity reveal the real heart of a man.' It is still considered a great honour today for an imprisoned Mafia man to occupy the cell in which Don Vito lived the last years of his life.

*

It is surprising to discover that a man belonging to the Mafia does not know he is doing wrong. This is approximately the way he sees things. Order has to be preserved. Justice must be assured. Unfortunately, men being what they are, it is often necessary to enforce the will of the Mafia by means of violence. At times, one is also unfortunately compelled to finance the operations of the law-enforcing *cosche* by means of extortion, robbery and blackmail. Do not many organizations fighting an unjust or foreign government do the same? People get hurt, of course, but only because they are stubborn. It is often admittedly difficult to restrict the use of such methods to legitimate purposes. There are deplorable abuses. Power corrupts. All Mafia leaders are tempted by their power. Some yield and come to a bad end. The good ones do not. They are able to control their greed. The good ones are unfortunately getting scarcer. Things are no longer what they were in Don Vito's time. The Mafia is losing sight of its traditional aims, more and more of its men seem bent in violating the old rules merely to make money for themselves by all possible means. Discipline is lax. It is not so much the Mafia's fault as the times'. Similar trends are visible everywhere in the modern world. All men are today inclined to serve their private interests and forget moral duties. Nevertheless, good Mafia men still exist. The breed has not disappeared. They want, above all, to be helpful to others. This they consider their mission in life.

This is how one of them sees himself:[1]

'This is the way I was born, signor Danilo. Whenever somebody asks me to do him a favour, I do it, because Nature made me that

[1] A verbatim confession, recorded by Danilo Dolci and printed in his book *Waste*: it has been slightly abridged here.

way. . . . A man comes and says: "I have a quarrel with Tizio. Could you please help me settle it?" I call the person mentioned, or I go to see him, according to the case, and make the two men come to an agreement. It is a power I have. I am neither vain nor ambitious. I open my arms wide to all kinds of men. I cannot say no to anybody. The trouble is never such that I should deny myself. There is a feeling of duty which compels me to aid others. Often, of course, one gains people's gratitude, one makes friends, many friends, and opportunities arise when one can demand some favour in return. . . . Things follow each other, one after the other, in life. . . . My name has spread. . . . All sorts of people ask me how to vote. They feel it is their duty to ask for instructions, in order to show their gratitude for what I have done for them. They are in the dark, they do not know what to do, and want to please me. . . . Tomorrow, for instance, I must leave the threshing, my cattle, all my things, in order to go to Agrigento. I have been asked to recommend a student to his teachers, so that he may surely pass his examinations. You see how things are?'

Obviously the teachers are going to give the student pass marks, no matter how ignorant and dumb he may prove to be. They are not fools. They too want to be on the right side of the Mafia man. Who knows when they will need him? He may help one to be promoted or transferred to a better residence. On the other hand, to displease him would be dangerous and, above all, pointless. Many practically illiterate boys will be promoted that same day in the same school, recommended by all sorts of important men. Why not one more? And so it goes, one favour begetting another, one favour creating the gratitude of the favoured who know they will have to do something in return when required, maybe give their votes to one particular candidate. A successful politician in Palermo or Rome can do them many favours. An illiterate chicken-thief in an obscure village can be asked to render a little service to a powerful gentleman, a small matter like purloining a compromising document or shadowing somebody. A killer can be ordered to kill a man. It is an endless chain secretly held together by fear, ostensibly held together by ties of gratitude, friendship and honeyed compliments. This is why the *mafiosi* call themselves *gli amici, gli amici degli amici* and see themselves as a vast benevolent mutual-aid association, only at times reluctantly compelled to destroy stubborn enemies and to violate official laws, in order to preserve the welfare of their members.

*

A man who considered himself, above all, a benefactor to society, a good Sicilian patriot, and a good Catholic, was Don Calò Vizzini, the last head of the Mafia who could be compared with Don Vito Cascio Ferro; he was not as great as Don Vito, of course, who will remain a shining example for all times, but he was great enough. Don Calò was born in Villalba and died in the same place at seventy-seven years of age, in 1954. His funeral was worthy of a prince. There were bands, lines of priests and monks chanting and swinging censers. There were ink-black horses drawing the hearse, mounds of flowers, and thousands of peasants all dressed in black. There were women crying, old men with red eyes, and children wailing. All the village authorities participated; more authorities came from Agrigento and Palermo; politicians came from all over eastern Sicily and from as far as Rome. Mournful orators pronounced ornate eulogies, extolling the dead man's virtues: he had been the poor man's friend, he had never left a request for help unheeded, he had been selfless and disinterested. The traditional sign nailed at the top of the church's main door ended with the simple words: 'He was a *galantuomo*'. *Galantuomo* means an honest man, a man of his word, a man of character, a reliable man, but also a man of property: he left approximately two billion lire worth of sulphur mines, land, houses and sundry investments. He was also well-connected, for an illiterate peasant. One of his uncles had been a bishop and one of his cousins, titular Bishop of Noto, was the revered founder of the monastic order of *Maria Santissima del Carmelo*. Two of his brothers were priests, one of them a Monsignore.

Don Calò's power, while never equalling that of Don Vito Cascio Ferro, had been great. Nobody has yet succeeded, so many years after his death, in knitting the Mafia together again into one unit as he had done. When you saw him (I knew him well) you could not imagine the amount of fear he could generate. He looked harmless. He was small, slightly bowed by rheumatism, dressed in the velveteen suit of a well-to-do farmer, with a cloth cap on his head. His manners were mild and courteous. Only his eyes gave him away. They were grey-brown, wide awake, watchful, intelligent. It was instructive to see him leave his house in the morning. Villalba's *piazza* is like a little stage, ready for *Cavalleria Rusticana* to begin, with the church on one side, various *palazzi* and shabby houses all around. Don Calò would punctually come out of the little door on the square at matins and peacefully walk back and forth, his hands clasped behind his back, conversing with his brother the Monsignore.

From the shadows along the walls and the tiny side-streets emerged people who had arrived earlier, some from far away, and were wait-ing to talk to him. They were peasants, old women with black veils on their heads, young *mafiosi*, middle-class men. They all walked along with him in turn, explaining their problems. He listened, then called one of his henchmen, gave a few orders, and summoned the next petitioner. Many kissed his hand in gratitude as they left.

A little later he would sit at the café table, on the *piazza*, and carry on the business of the day while drinking *espresso*, an elderly farmer or cattle dealer like many others. He would nod as somebody reported an entangled business affair or proposed a plan of action. He rarely smiled. Only once in a while he would place his hand on another man's shoulder, as if to reassure, strengthen or console him. His magnanimous and protective manners, the respectful salutes of passers by, the retinue surrounding him, the humility of the people approaching him, the smiles of gratitude on their faces when he spoke to them, all reminded one of an ancient scene, a prince holding court and administering justice in the open air. Of course, the many victims of his reign were not visible, the many corpses found riddled with bullets in the countryside during more than half a century, the widows weeping, the fatherless orphans.

Don Calò's authority was strengthened by the American Army. When the U.S. forces landed in Sicily he was immediately nominated mayor of Villalba and given ample powers. He disposed of military vehicles and supplies. It was said that he had served the Americans well, before their landing, furnishing information to their emissaries, and getting the whole Mafia network ready to collaborate with them. How much truth there was in the rumours it is hard to tell. What is known is that, under the Allied occupation, he resumed all the powers which he had lost under the Fascist régime and reconstructed the *società* as it had not been for a long time, ever since *prefetto* Mori started sending *mafiosi*, including Don Calò himself, to prison or exiling them in one of the forlorn islands along the coast. He ruled, from the day the first American soldier arrived in Villalba until the day of his death, according to the old rules, with an iron hand. He was informed of literally everything that went on in his district (to supply information is one way to gain a man's gratitude), and of most things of importance that went on all over Sicily. No great business transaction was done without his consent. He was, like most old men, extremely conservative in his political views. He supported the Christian Democrats and fought all revolutionary novelties.

The communists and trade union organizers were his personal enemies. He considered them competitors, leaders of rival Mafie. When Girolamo Li Causi, the veteran Communist hero of Sicily, wanted to hold an open-air meeting in the *piazza* of Villalba, Don Calò sent word advising him against it. 'It is unsafe,' he said. Li Causi naturally knew what the mild warning meant. Being a stubborn and proud man, who respected no authorities, not even that of the *amici*, he came anyway and spoke to a small scattered crowd. At one point his speech was cut short by rifle fire: Don Calò's men were shooting at him and his listeners from the roof tops. The small crowd dispersed in a hurry. A few people were wounded including Li Causi himself, in one knee. He was left at first alone lying in the empty *piazza*. Suddenly a shadow crossed his body, an old man bowed over him and, in the silence, asked in a colourless voice: 'Can I do anything for you?' It was Don Calò himself.

*

There are Americans who believe that criminal groups in their country belong to the Sicilian Mafia, are in effect overseas branches of the main organizations, and that they are all directed by orders from Palermo. This myth is shared even by some naïve American criminals of Italian descent, who learned it by reading the newspapers. They sometimes land in Sicily believing not only that they belong to the *società* but that they have a high rank in it. At the most they are *uomini rispettati*, like all moneyed foreigners. Soon enough most of them discover to their dismay that they are considered merely strangers by the real *amici*. One of these gullible Americans was Lucky Luciano. When he arrived in Palermo, deported from the United States, the police official who had to watch his movements said: 'He believes he is a big shot in the Mafia, the poor innocent man.' Lucky Luciano went around with powerful leaders, entertained them, and visibly treated them as friends. They swindled him out of fifteen million lire by persuading him to invest money in a caramel factory. The partnership was rigged in such a way that the more money the factory made the more Lucky Luciano lost. Thus was the mastermind of the American underworld treated in his native island by the real Mafia.

The theory of a world-wide conspiracy with headquarters in Italy is also difficult to eradicate because it is comforting and plausible. It helps explain away mysterious events, accounts for unaccountable loyalties and alliances, and is very useful to justify the curious impotence of some American police organizations. The real nerve centres of the criminal groups are far away, across the seas. The head of the dragon must be cut first. And that is not the job for Americans but for Italians, foreigners, unreliable people, speaking an incomprehensible lingo.

The theory also has deep psychological roots. The international conspiracy of dark, treacherous and devious men, who use secret and unfair methods to achieve their purposes and beat fair-haired and chivalrous opponents, resemble other international conspiracies of dark and cunning men, the Jewish Bankers or the Jesuits, with secret headquarters in faraway countries. Such an organization, of course, does not exist. In order for it to exist and function it would have to be disciplined and centralized. It would be dangerous but easy to discover, penetrate, and destroy. The reason why the real Mafia cannot be fought efficiently is that it is many things at the same time but not one tight and well-run organization. It is a many-headed dragon which can continue to live for a long time with no head at all. And why, anyway, should the Mafia be able to give orders in the United States when it has no influence whatever in Catania, only a few miles away?

There is, however, some foundation for the American myth. The many Sicilian immigrants to the United States undoubtedly brought with them the lower-case mafia. They felt gallant Sicilian sentiments within their breasts and many still do. Many still keep track of their family in the old country and visit them. As all relations must, they help each other in moments of need. Many rich Americans give money for an orphanage, a hospital, a school, an aqueduct to their fathers' native villages. Some send subsidies to relatives or pay for young Italian cousins to go to school at their expense. A few of these Americans, belonging to the criminal classes, have particular needs. Occasionally an escaped gangster finds shelter for a short time in the farmhouse of distant relatives. He does not stay long, of course: he can be easily spotted and he never likes the primitive living conditions. A Sicilian escaped criminal will naturally be helped by his relatives to land clandestinely in the United States, be provided with money and false papers. They would help him in any case, even if he were honest, as long as he was in need. (One of Salvatore Giuliano's henchmen with relatives in Boston was discovered in Texas, safely serving in the United States Air Force under an assumed name.) Cousins or friends collaborate to smuggle drugs out of Palermo to American ports, but such traffic notoriously goes on in every port of the world: heroin is carried to the United States in ships of all flags by men of many nationalities, and not by Sicilians alone. There are relationships of all sorts between Sicilian criminals and American criminals of Sicilian descent, but they are haphazard, spontaneous, disorganized relations, and scarcely amount to an international conspiracy. Clearly no order from Palermo can decide vital matters in the United States underworld.

*

Sicilian immigrants to the United States found themselves surrounded by an alien and hostile society. They had to cope with an incomprehensible language, puzzling customs, rigid laws, and what they considered an oppressive régime. They felt cut off, for reasons they did not quite understand, from access to the good things in life, wealth and authority. They clung to what could give them protection and comfort, the Church, the family, and their ways. They soon discovered that the arts their people had developed in the old country to neutralize alien laws were also useful in the new. The forefathers had beaten the Arabs, the Normans, the Anjou kings, the Spanish, the Austrians, the Bourbon kings, and the Piedmontese; the descendants endeavoured to employ the same means to survive and prosper in America. That they felt themselves a minority on the defensive is borne out by one of the names of their criminal organization, *Cosa Nostra*. It means 'our own affair, something which must be guarded from intruders'. In fact, they discovered that the ancient arts were far more useful in America and went farther. The Americans were generally trustful, unprepared to defend themselves from guile, often unwilling to fight for what they considered small stakes.

All Sicilians in the United States, among whom the criminals were a small minority, followed the same old rules, the only ones they knew anyway, a sharpened version of those all Italians follow. They are not *per se* dishonest, but they can be employed effectively for the achievement of dishonest ends. Of course, the rules are best in fields like politics and big business where power is a predominating factor, less useful where personal capacity rather than pressure is indispensable. They helped many honest Sicilians in the United States and their descendants to reach higher and higher rungs in the social ladder.

In order to beat rival organizations, criminals of Sicilian descent reproduced the kind of illegal groups they had belonged to in the old country and employed the same rules to make them invincible. The convicted American gangster, Joseph Valachi, once explained the facts of life of the Sicilian village, probably as old as Mediterranean civilization, the principles guiding Homeric kings and heroes in their decisions, to a Senate committee and an awe-struck twentieth-century television audience. He patiently pointed out that an isolated man was a dead duck in the American underworld; that he had to belong to a family, his own, or one which accepted him; that families were gathered in large groups, the groups in alliances, and the alliances in a loose federation called *Cosa Nostra*, governed by an unwritten code. When he spoke, officials of the F.B.I. exposed diligently-designed graphs illustrating the ramifications of *Cosa Nostra* families. He revealed that the organization was, more or less, what it had been in Sicily sixty years ago, before Don Vito Cascio Ferro reformed it. It still needs a lot of killing to preserve a precarious peace and to determine who is to be Numero Uno. He also revealed that the Sicilian criminals in America had abandoned the feudal pretences of their fathers. They no longer pretended to be interested above all in peasant justice for the oppressed; they were interested in dollars, and made money in activities which the older men would have considered unworthy of them, brothels and drugs.

His view of things was partial. It could be compared to a panorama of Napoleonic history as seen by an infantry corporal. War is the extension of policy by other means in the Mafia too. Valachi knew nothing of the long negotiations between leaders, the plans they conceived, the truces they had enforced and the successes they achieved without shedding blood. All he knew was what happened when war broke out, the gunmen marched and rebel factions had to be wiped out. He did not know the real triumphs of *Cosa Nostra* were the silent and unsung ones, when the money flowed in peacefully. More and more, in fact, the leaders abandon criminal activities, manage to infiltrate more or less legitimate business, like gambling, or some really legitimate business, where they establish a monopoly. The monopoly, if closely scrutinized, shows the old arts at work. Nobody dares compete with them because they can destroy a rival, in many ways, and, if need be, have him wiped out. Such men Valachi never met. Even the F.B.I. does not know all their names and, if it did, could pin nothing on them. They live far from their activities, legal or illegal. They contact one or two trusted lieutenants to control a vast sector, deal in cash, never use the telephone, travel seldom, give money to charities, and lead unimpeachable private lives.

*

There is no denying that the Mafia in western Sicily is fundamentally a criminal organization, which causes great suffering among the people, condemns a majority of them to a primitive life of shame, squalor, poverty, hunger and fear. It fights and prevents almost all possible progress. Nobody wants to invest his money and improve things when the will of unknown persons can arbitrarily stop all his activities and ruin him at a moment's notice. Only a few *uomini rispettati*, who come to an agreement with the *amici*, dare to do so, and they have to pay a price. Not even a fearless and disinterested politician can triumph against ruthless rivals, if they are supported by such a vast network of powerful friends and accomplices.

The Mafia, however, is not this alone. If it were only a criminal organization, bent merely on robbing and killing for money, it would provoke a wave of resentment; it could be fought and destroyed. It is believed to be also a spontaneous way, developed by the people themselves through many centuries of misrule, to administer a rough and archaic form of justice, a way to keep one kind of peace and ensure the safety of the inhabitants, an *ersatz* of legal government. To defeat it, the State should first make the Law supreme. Sicilians should be made to feel that they are safe to confide in the police. Things being as they are, the police cannot guarantee anybody's immunity, while the *amici* can, and furthermore can also bestow other untold benefits.

The situation is worse now than it ever was. The Mafia is rapidly degenerating. It is a cancer which destroys all healthy tissues. It is the exaggerated, cancerous form of the milder disease prevailing in all Italy. The art of living, of defending oneself with one's own power, of supplementing the defectiveness of the State with one's own private virtues, corrupts, in the end, all forms of sound government, obstructs the functioning of all legitimate organs, and makes the correction of defects in the government apparatus almost impossible.

CHAPTER FIFTEEN

FORNOVO AND AFTER

*What was this beautiful land in the midst of which [Charles VIII's sol-
diers] found themselves, a land whose princes poisoned while they smiled,
whose luxuriant meadows concealed fever, whose ladies carried disease
upon their lips? To the captains and the soldiery of France, Italy already
appeared a splendid and fascinating Circe, arrayed with charms, surrounded with illusions, hiding behind perfumed thickets her victims
changed to brutes and building the couch of her seductions on the bones of
murdered men. Yet she was so beautiful that, halt as they might for a
moment and gaze back with yearning on the Alps that they had crossed,
they found themselves unable to resist her smile. Forward they must
march through the garden of enchantment, henceforth taking the precaution to walk with drawn sword, and, like Orlando in Morgana's park,
to stuff their casques with roses that they might not hear the siren's voice
too clearly. It was thus that Italy began the part she played through the
Renaissance for the people of the North. 'The White Devil of Italy' is the
title of one of Webster's best tragedies. A white Devil, a radiant daughter
of sin and death, holding in her hand the fruit of the knowledge of good
and evil, and tempting the nations to eat: this is how Italy struck the
fancy of the men of the sixteenth century. She was feminine and they
were virile; but she could teach them and they could learn. She gave
them pleasure; they brought force.*

J. A. SYMONDS (*Renaissance in Italy*)

THE year 1492 is one of the notorious watersheds of history.
In that year Columbus discovered America; Cardinal
Roderigo Borgia was elected Pope and took the name of
Alexander VI; Spain became a nation by the conquest of Granada
and directed her unspent impetus to foreign fields; Lorenzo de'
Medici, *Il Magnifico*, died. These were all irreparable disasters for
Italy. The discovery of America (followed a few years later by the
opening of the Indian seas) diverted world commerce into new
channels; Alexander VI made the German reformation and the
English schism inevitable; Spain's consolidation prepared the way

276

for the domination of Europe by Charles V, King of Spain, Archduke of Austria, and Emperor of the Holy Roman Empire; the death of Lorenzo destroyed the fragile construction of balancing alliances, built by him, which had kept Italy at peace and safe from foreign attacks.

That same year Charles VIII of France, who had just come of age, received secret emissaries from Italy. They had been sent by Ludovico il Moro, Lord of Milan, a treacherous man, who thought he would try on the inexperienced young king one of the perennial ploys of Italian politics, that of inviting a foreign potentate to Italy to fight one's enemies. Ludovico's enemy of the day was, for complicated reasons, the King of Naples. The secret emissaries proposed to Charles the conquest of Naples, offered to finance his expedition, and assured him free passage through north Italy on his way south. Charles had been selected because he had a feeble claim to the throne of Naples. (All kings, of course, have feeble claims to practically all thrones. King Victor Emmanuel III of Italy, for instance, had vague pretensions to the throne of the Stuarts, and also called himself to the end, in official documents, 'King of Cyprus and Jerusalem'.) The Milanese emissaries never hoped their absurd and dangerous proposal would get more than a half-hearted welcome. Why, after all, should the King of France, who had many important things to attend to, risk his power, wealth and life so far from home for such a puny prize?

'Providence,' says J. A. Symonds with solemnity, 'deigns frequently to use for the most momentous purpose some pantaloon or puppet, environing with special protection and with the prayers and aspirations of whole peoples a mere mannikin. Such a puppet was Charles VIII.' This is the way Guicciardini describes him: 'From infancy he had been weak in constitution and subject to illnesses. His stature was short and his face was ugly, if you except the dignity and vigour of his glance. His limbs were so disproportionate that he had less the appearance of a man than of a monster. Not only was he ignorant of liberal arts, but he hardly knew his letters. Though eager to rule, he was in truth made for anything but that: for while surrounded by dependants, he exercised no authority over them and preserved no kind of majesty.' This dim-witted and deformed king usually did what his sycophants and counsellors wanted him to do. They were, in Guicciardini's words, 'men of low estate, body-servants for the most part'.

Charles did not laugh in the emissaries' face. He did not reject their proposal as a deadly trap and lock them up in prison. He listened attentively to their words. In fact, the more he thought of it the more he liked the idea. The reason was that it fitted in with an old dream of his own, inspired by his youthful reading of fashionable romances. He wanted to defeat the Infidels, conquer Constantinople, and be crowned the Roman Emperor of the East. To do that he could use Naples, its army, fleet, treasure, and handy ports. Of course, he had France to think of first. The country was restless, the army weak, the treasury empty; foreign enemies threatened every border. Before he started on his Italian venture, Charles bought peace from England with Ludovico's money; appeased Emperor Maximilian by the concession of a few vital provinces; gave Ferdinand of Spain (a relative of the King of Naples) the strong places in the Pyrenees, the key of France's defences, as prize for his neutrality. Once he had made his country absolutely defenceless, he proceeded to take every able-bodied man away from it. He gathered a new army, concentrated stores and ships in the ports of Genoa and Marseilles, and began moving south to Lyons. This was in 1494, 'a year', says Guicciardini, 'most unfortunate for Italy, the very first of our disastrous years'.

The coming invasion was regarded in Italy with uneasy fascination. Only a few people thought Charles was mad and was courting disaster. He would stretch his communication lines to a dangerous point, they said, and, once he was deep in Italy, his way back to France could easily be cut and his army destroyed. Many prepared themselves to welcome the French. In Florence, the friar Savonarola, divinely inspired though widely off the mark, preached of Charles as *flagellum Dei*, the scourge of God, appointed to regenerate the Church and purify the founts of spiritual life. A large number of Italians, as they were to do on numerous successive occasions, convinced themselves that the foreign invaders were coming really to rid them of their bad governments and of their dishonest rulers, and to set up model régimes in which worthy natives would finally hold the principal posts. The vast majority were just frightened. They could not help shuddering at the thought of what the impending arrival of the 'barbarians' might bring upon them. They admitted that whatever calamities were in store, they deserved them. In fact, Ludovico il Moro had done no more, in the view of many of his countrymen, than bring down by a breath, as it were, the avalanche which had been long impending.

The princes of Italy, led by the King of Naples, hurriedly started intense diplomatic activity to form a defensive alliance. They visited each other, kissed, exchanged special ambassadors, letters, gifts and orders of chivalry. They swore solemnly they would be true to each other to the end, whatever that was going to be. They drew up excellent military and political plans. They appeared full of confidence. Italy had the best generals, more money, troops, supplies and weapons than France. Military art had no secrets for the Italians. Furthermore, they were fighting on home ground, close to their stores, on terrain they knew foot by foot. They arranged to place bodies of soldiers in strategic spots, where they would do most harm. In spite of the fact that, on paper, the odds were with them, they did not feel at ease. Next to the King of Naples, Pope Alexander was most frightened: he dreaded the assembly of a Council which might possibly depose him from the throne he had bought by simony. So strong was his terror that he even sent ambassadors to the Sultan of Turkey, imploring him for aid against the most Christian King, but Bajazet II was too far off and too busy to be of use.

The defensive plans could easily have been successful if they had been adhered to. But that absolute agreement which is necessary for the execution of any large and effective scheme, always difficult to preserve in any alliance, was impossible among Italians. Nothing, in fact, turned out exactly as planned. Some leaders, of course, were brave, but could do little by themselves. Some were simply inept. Many were sceptical: after more than a century of bloodless battles and parade campaigning, mainly decided by bribes, they thought the French were going to be only a little more difficult than Italians. Others were just careful. What, they reasoned, if Charles was going to win, after all, and decided to punish those who had fought too valiantly against him? One never could tell what barbarians would

do. Would it not be better, then, these wise men thought, to put
their money on both *pair* and *manque*, to be on both sides at the same
time? They had to think of their families. Many princes surreptitiously sent emissaries to the French camp or made friends with
French courtiers, while they carried out their orders with studied
slowness and without enthusiasm.

Charles VIII left Vienne, in the province of Dauphiné, on
August 23, 1494, with 3,600 men-at-arms, the flower of French
chivalry, 6,000 Breton archers, 6,000 crossbowmen, 8,000 Gascon
infantry, 8,000 mercenary Swiss and German soldiers. He crossed
the Alps at the Montgenèvre pass, without striking a blow, arrived
safely in the plains below, and entered the city of Asti on September
19. The trip could not be done more quickly today on good roads, in
peacetime, by men on foot or on horseback. Neither Piedmont nor
Montferrat (the first Italian principalities he crossed) stirred to hin-
der him, for a reason which was typical of Charles' luck. The two
ruling princes were children at that time, the Duke of Savoy was
twelve years old and the Marquis of Montferrat fourteen. Their
mothers and guardians quickly made terms with the French, to
avoid trouble, and allowed them a free passage.

From then on it was but a promenade to Naples. The Neapolitan
fleet sailed too late to effect a desired rising in Genoa and stop the
French supplies from landing. The Neapolitan troops sent north
never went further than Cesena, on the Adriatic. Other allied armies
were retarded, enfeebled, and divided by the necessity to stop and
fight small wars and mutinies. Venice played a watchful game; she
aimed to intervene, when everybody else was exhausted, on the
side of the winner. Piero de' Medici of Florence, who held the
Apennine passes and could have stopped the invaders with little
effort (he held the line on which weak and defeated Kesselring easily
kept the mighty Allied armies at bay in the winter of 1944), rode as
fast as horses would carry him to the French camp and delivered to
Charles the keys of all his mountain fortresses, and also those of
Sarzana, Pietrasanta, Pisa, and Leghorn. This relieved the French of
the difficulty of forcing their way along a narrow plain, hemmed in
on one side by the sea and on the other by a high and abrupt mountain range. At the news, the Florentines rose in fury against their

lord. When Charles entered the city, on November 17, it was a free republic once again. The people cheered him as their liberator.

He rode, armed at all points, to the palace of the Medici and told the elders he had come as conqueror and not as a guest. He asked for huge sums of money. Money had been one of his persistent worries. He never could have enough. The Florentine secretaries refused his terms. He peevishly insisted. Then Piero Capponi snatched a paper on which they were written and tore it before his eyes. Charles, who had kingly dignity, warned him: 'We shall sound our trumpets.' Capponi answered: 'We will ring our bells.' At the sound of the tocsin each house would have been turned into a fortress, the streets barred by iron chains, and every quarter would have poured forth men by the hundreds. Charles covered his disappointment with a bad pun in Italian. '*Ah, Ciappon, Ciappon,*' he said, '*voi siete un mal Ciappon.*' The 'bad capon' did not ring his bells, after all. Florence agreed to pay Charles 120,000 florins on condition that he move on.

He reached the Porta del Popolo, in Rome, on December 31, 1494. At three o'clock in the afternoon began the entry of the French army. It was nine at night before the last soldier and the last carriage defiled through the gates, in the glaring light of torches and *flambeaux*. The people cheered themselves hoarse. '*Francia, Francia!*' they cried. The spectacle was indeed magnificent. There were gigantic Germans and Swiss flaunting plumes and emblazoned surcoats, the chivalry of France with silk mantles over their armour and gilded corselets, the king's Scots guard in their strange tartan uniforms, the terrifying German *landsknechte* with their scythe-like halberds. The people cheered also because they hoped the Pope and all his family would soon come to a bad end. Alexander VI prudently shut himself up in Castel Sant'Angelo. How would the conqueror deal with him? At Charles' side were the Cardinals Ascanio Sforza and Giuliano della Rovere (later Pope Julius II), urging him to summon the Council. But one of the king's trusted courtiers, a certain Briçonnet, managed to turn the destinies of Rome, the Borgia family, the Church and all Christendom. The husband of the daughter of the king's silversmith, the father of five children, Briçonnet wanted badly, for some reason, to become a cardinal. He convinced Charles that he should compromise.

The king abandoned the idea of the Council in exchange for money, a few fortresses, a red hat for Briçonnet, the Pope's son Cesare and Djem, the brother of the Sultan of Turkey, as hostages. (How Djem happened to be in Rome is a long story. The Sultan wanted his brother dead but strangely enough did not want to kill him or have him killed in Constantinople. He sent him to the Pope, to keep at a yearly pension of 40,000 ducats, with the secret understanding that Djem would soon be done away with. Nobody wants to see a guest die who pays 40,000 ducats a year. The Muslim prince enjoyed excellent health for a time at the Roman court, where many courtiers and prominent members of the household were killed every week. He died, however, probably poisoned, soon after he became the guest of Charles. It was thought that Alexander, in the end, had preferred to keep faith with the Sultan rather than with the King of France.)

After a month's stay in Rome, he was welcomed, cheered and fêted by the Neapolitans who are always delighted by a change of masters. As he had done everywhere else, Charles dedicated himself to pleasure. He enjoyed dances, tournaments, feasts, banquets, and the love of the most beautiful, ardent and well-born ladies of the city. Soon enough (as all the conquerors of Naples did after a while), he began boring and irritating the people. With his posturing he made himself *antipatico*. He exacted enormous tributes and distributed all profitable offices, titles and fiefs of the kingdom among his retinue.

On May 17 he managed to cover himself with ridicule. He rehearsed what he hoped would be the crowning triumph of his expedition by parading the streets dressed as the Emperor of the East, with the robes and the paraphernalia he had invented for his coronation in Constantinople. He carried an orb in one hand, a sceptre in the other, and a large crown on his head. (Such premature performances bring bad luck, as all Neapolitans know. What happened, for instance, centuries later, to Mussolini, when he shipped his favourite white horse by plane to North Africa in preparation for his entry as a conqueror in Alexandria? He never entered Alexandria, lost North Africa, and barely managed to get the horse back alive.) A few days after this ill-omened exhibition, news reached Charles that behind his back the Italians had formed a league and were making earnest preparations to cut his retreat and crush him. Naples was obviously becoming a trap. He decided to return home as fast as he had come.

Italian patriots, who had suffered seeing their country trampled and humiliated, aware of what would surely follow if the King of France was not severely punished for his daring, had somehow managed for once to get most of the princes, the Pope, Milan, Florence and Venice to agree to put an army together and challenge the French. Brave people openly spoke of the 'war of Italy against her enemies', of the 'liberty of Italy' which they had to defend, as if 'Italy' really existed, and was not merely, as the Military and Sovereign Order of the Knights of Saint John always properly called this country, 'the Italian language'. But in Italy patriotism has rarely been the predominant moving force. Most members of the league joined it not merely for love of their country but because it looked like the safer, or less unsafe, thing to do at the moment. It was obviously dangerous to back the King of France, at this point, or aid him with one's neutrality. He was at the end of his resources and possibly of his luck. Where could he go from Naples, practically at the dead end of Italy's narrow peninsula? He was no longer the same man: he did not behave as a victorious conqueror should. His decisions were increasingly erratic. He had little money left. His army was tired, discontented, and decimated by syphilis, the new dread disease which the Spanish had brought back from America, and which the French had met in Naples. Alexander Borgia, who was witty, had said that the French had conquered Italy with lumps of chalk and wooden spurs, because they rode unarmed in slippers and sent couriers ahead to mark the doors of the most comfortable houses in which to spend the night. Obviously, the achievements of their conquest could be as easily effaced as the chalk marks they had left behind. It was clearly more prudent in 1495 to join the league.

*

The army of the Italian league met the French in north Italy, near the village of Fornovo, on July 6, 1495. Fornovo is on the river Taro, at the northern end of the Cisa pass across the Apennines, between Sarzana and Parma. The place was chosen because the French had passed through it on their way to Naples and it was thought they would pass it again on their way home. Near Fornovo the road along the river-bank begins to straighten out and to descend gently to the plain below, after having meandered for many miles through narrow gorges, between precipitous walls of rock. Upstream, the valley would have been a good place for an ambush; downstream, it was wide and flat enough for the manœuvring of cavalry squadrons and the evolutions of foot soldiers, yet narrow enough to constrict all movements within a well-defined battlefield.

The French numbered about 9,500 fighting men, most of them weary with long marches, insufficient food, and weakened by disease. They were afraid of the approaching encounter (they were experienced enough to know that their position was desperate), disheartened because they had to abandon their conquests without honourable reasons, and, having not fought for a long time, had lost the old zest for battle. Their opponents numbered about 30,000 men, all fresh, well-armed and well-provided. They were confident of victory. The Italian-born among them (the overwhelming majority) knew they were fighting a decisive battle for their country, win or lose, all or nothing, on their home ground, against an inferior enemy who had humiliated them all. In command was one of the best generals of the time, Francesco Gonzaga, Marquis of Mantua, surrounded by the men of his family and by a few expert and trusted condottieri. Gonzaga had chosen the spot and the time. He had drawn up a clever and apparently unbeatable plan of battle.

The French advanced carefully that morning, knowing they were to meet the enemy at any moment. They were prepared for the usual, the frontal attack which the medieval military technique considered the only form proper for gentlemen. They sent their baggage, supplies, provisions, impedimenta, including the royal treasure (a caravan of between 5,000 and 6,000 loaded mules), to the hills parallel to the road, so as not to be encumbered by them during the fight. In the vanguard they placed 350 heavily armed knights, what was left of the flower of the French chivalry, followed by the Swiss infantry, 3,000 men in their typical formation, marching shoulder to shoulder in a solid square bristling with long and sharp spears. The rest of the army, personally led by Charles, followed at regular intervals. The

Italians were to be broken up by the French knights, then dispersed by the sturdy Swiss, decimated by the king's guard of Scottish archers and French crossbowmen, and finally given the *coup-de-grâce* by the rearguard of 300 French men-at-arms.

Gonzaga was too clever to do exactly what the French imagined he would do. A frontal attack, of course, might have assured him the victory, as he had numerical superiority, but at a heavy cost in human lives. He preferred a different plan, something new and unusual, which Captain Liddell Hart calls the 'indirect approach' and was employed by all the great victorious generals in history. For this, too, the Italian commander awaited the enemy where the valley widened and there was room to move. This is what he planned. As the French carefully filed in formation along the road on the left bank of the Taro, the Italians were to pin down the vanguard (as he expected) with repeated attacks of light cavalry units. While this was going on, two columns of heavy cavalry, led by Francesco Gonzaga in person and by his best *condottiere*, Bernardino Forte-braccio (whose name fittingly means Strongarm), were to go swiftly up the opposite (or right) bank in a surprise move; they were to ford the river simultaneously at two points, attack the French flank, spread panic, break up their orderly formation, drive them against the side of the hills, cut the column in sections, and massacre each separately. Unfortunately things did not exactly work out as planned. This is what really happened.

The French vanguard was pinned down, for a time at least, by the Stradioti (the swift light horsemen which Venice had recruited and trained in Dalmatia and Albania to fight the raids of the swift light Turkish horsemen across the border). The Stradioti, armed only with scimitars, were not meant to last long against the heavy cavalry and the Swiss. They were ordered only to harass the enemy and to disengage quickly. The time they afforded Gonzaga and Fortebraccio for their enveloping moves was short. But the unusually heavy rains had raised the level of the river that day and had made the fords impassable. Gonzaga tried vainly to cross where he was supposed to do but lost many men and horses, who could not swim encumbered as they were by steel armour, and were washed away by the rushing waters. He made several stubborn attempts, which took up precious time, and finally decided to try once more farther up-stream, where the valley was narrower, the river shallower but more impetuous.

His difficulties immediately revealed his plan to the French. They saw the threat to their flank, turned to face it and prepared for the attack. Many of Gonzaga's men managed, in the end, to reach the right bank, but only at the same ford which Fortebraccio's men were using. As a result the two columns got inextricably entangled. Then they found another unexpected obstacle, an almost unsurpassable barrier, a deep canal with steep and slimy banks of clay which fed water to a mill. More knights and horses were lost. More precious minutes were wasted. At this point, the French, who had rearranged their formation, attacked the Italians, to take full advantage of their difficulties, with the desperate courage of men fighting for their lives, far from home, their backs to the wall.

Within a few minutes the fighting became a disorderly massacre at close quarters, the bloodiest battle that had been seen in Italy in two centuries. The lances broke and the men hacked at each other with swords and pikes. What was left of the Gonzaga and Fortebraccio contingents charged time and again, wildly crying, 'Alla morte! Alla morte!' and 'Italia! Italia!' The ground was quickly strewn with dying and dead men and horses. Knights who had lost their mounts fought on foot. At one point, in the confused mêlée, Gonzaga sighted Charles fighting desperately at the head of a small group of men (Charles was a brave and able soldier, trained in tournaments). The Italian gathered a few men and charged once more. This could have been the turning-point. He knew it. But when he was on the point of capturing or killing the king, Gonzaga's horse was wounded and he was dismounted. Fortebraccio had been killed a few minutes before. Charles was saved. Gonzaga was left practically alone, on foot, to do what he could merely to save his own life.

The final result was disorderly and confused butchery, complete chaos. When night came, Charles managed to sneak away, with whatever troops he had left, quickly reached Asti and crossed the Alps. Nobody pursued him. Four thousand dead men were left on the battlefield, two-thirds of them Italian.

*

Fornovo is the turning-point in Italian history. The distant consequences of the defeat are still felt today. If the Italians had won, they would probably have discovered then the pride of being a united people, the self-confidence born of defending their common liberty and independence. Italy would have emerged as a reasonably respectable nation, capable of determining her own future, a country which adventurous foreigners would think twice before attacking. Nobody would have ventured lightly across the Alps, for fear of being destroyed. The European powers would have been discouraged from endlessly quarrelling over Italian politics and from cutting slices of Italian soil, with their defenceless and laborious inhabitants, in order to placate dynastic rivalries and satisfy everybody's greed. The history of Italy, Europe, and the world would probably have taken different tasks. The Italian national character would have developed along different lines. The voices of patriots would not have been mocked but respectfully heeded. When unity and independence finally came in the nineteenth century, the old habits were set. They could not change easily—De Commynes records that the fighting proper lasted at Fornovo for a quarter of an hour, the pursuit and the killing of the routed Italians three quarters of an hour more. Thus the destiny of Italy for centuries was gambled away in fifteen minutes.

Why did the Italians lose at Fornovo? Certainly not because they were cowardly. It was the kind of battle they understand and in which they always fight valiantly, a battle in defence of their country and their own honour, against a hated foreign enemy. The odds were on their side. All contemporary reports agree that the men engaged had shown themselves as brave as the French and had faced death heroically even after they realized all hope was lost. There were other reasons for the defeat, which historians never tired of analysing.

First of all, the will of God. Charles had been lucky ever since he had left France, as lucky as a child or a drunken man. Innumerable times he had squeezed through terrible dangers without realizing it. His army could have been stopped, decimated, or destroyed by any one of many causes, avalanches in the Alps, the timely arrival of a body of troops at a mountain pass, the resistance of a single fortress, the revolt of the loyal peasants. His luck was so scandalous that many people (Guicciardini among them) thought the expedition was divinely sustained and guided. The words '*Dieu montrait conduire l'entreprise*', or 'God seemed to lead the enterprise', recur many times in the *Mémoires* of De Commynes, who had accompanied the king as political adviser. It never rains in July in Italy. It is the month when the countryside is parched, the fields become as hard as city streets, the springs dry up, the cattle show their ribs, and rivers are reduced to small rivulets. The Taro was swollen and impetuous that day as it usually is for only a few weeks in winter. Gonzaga's plan, depending as it did on the swift simultaneous crossing of the river at two points, was, first of all, clearly defeated by Charles' luck and the weather. The ground was spongy, soft, and slippery, bad for all heavy cavalry but decidedly worse for horsemen attacking than for those on the defensive.

The daring novelty of the complex Italian plan undoubtedly contributed to the disastrous conclusion. Gonzaga chose the more difficult terrain downstream also because he could better deploy and move his men about, taking full advantage of his numerical and mental superiority to the French. He had forgotten, however, that, in the kind of battle he had envisaged, in order to execute manœuvres in the open, and eventually to change plans to face unexpected events, he had to have, first of all, a docile instrument in his hands, homogeneous troops, ready and capable to obey orders or to improvise their own movements as the need arose. What he had instead was a random collection of contingents, brought together at the last minute for the encounter, variously trained, experienced, armed and reliable. When things went wrong each body of troops did what it thought best: some rushed to the fray and died, some ran away, some gathered booty, and some waited patiently to be told what to do next or to see who was going to win. Undoubtedly those who sacrificed themselves were many; the Venetian company of infantry commanded by Gerolamo Genova, to mention one unit, did their duty: they rushed where the fighting was heaviest and lost two hundred men out of three hundred. On the other hand, there is no doubt that the Milan contingent of Ludovico il Moro spared themselves, for lack of orders but probably also for political reasons.

But even if the army of the league had been a uniform, docile and disciplined instrument, Gonzaga could not have utilized it. He had planned a modern battle but had taken part in it as an old-fashioned medieval leader. He plunged into the fray, charged time and again at the head of his men, looking for victory or death. He should, of course, have remained safely, to one side, on a hillock, in order to observe the course of the events with calm, and take the only decision which could have saved the day: send the reserves where they would do most good at the opportune moment. This he could not do. Most of the time he was isolated, in contact with but a few men around him, too busy saving his own life and killing Frenchmen to think of the battle as a whole. He was never able to modify his earlier orders and to adapt his plans.

Contemporary chroniclers pointed to the defection of the Stradioti as the principal cause of the defeat. This is, after the rain, the favourite explanation of Italian historians, because it assuages wounded national pride. Where were the Stradioti, after they had stopped harassing the vanguard? They disappeared from view. They had sighted the train of mules with the French baggage on the hills and had started in pursuit. At that tragic moment, when the arrival of one more fresh squadron could have won the battle, the Stradioti were gathering booty: it was valued at 300,000 ducats and included the king's helmet, his sword of office, his seals, part of his archives, the Dauphin's portrait, the portable altar, and several holy relics.

Duodo, their surviving commander, was immediately arrested, tried, and demoted. He defended himself with ability: he was the first to point out, at his trial, that Gonzaga should not have lost himself in the fighting but should have kept to one side, in order to control the reserves. It is to be remembered that the Stradioti were what they were, irregular troops, trained for one kind of war only, the swift hit-and-run raids against enemy camps, caravans, and cavalry. The principal objective in such wars had always been the enemy's treasure, including women, slaves and cattle. The Stradioti followed their instinct and did what they had always done. Being foreigners and mercenaries, serving the republic of Venice for money and a share of the booty, they were not sentimentally involved in the final outcome anyway. What else were they expected to do?

Perhaps the Italians were defeated by their virtues and vices. They had united too late. They should have fought Charles the year before, on his way down and not on his way back. They had wasted twelve precious months with diplomatic manœuvres and exquisite intrigues. When they finally made up their minds and decided to crush the French, they could hurriedly put together only a patchwork collection of random military units. The troops arrived at Fornovo almost on the eve of the encounter, too late in fact for Gonzaga to consider ambushing Charles in the mountains. More men arrived even later, in the days following the battle. The decision to fight where the valley widened was also influenced by non-military motives *all'italiana*: Francesco admitted he tried to keep as close to Parma as possible; he did not trust Parma and was afraid the Parmensi would attack his rear.

Finally Gonzaga's personal virtues and vices were also determinant. He was the best general in Italy but not as good as he himself thought. He designed a battle also to show off his *bravura*. His plan was defined recently by an Italian expert, Piero Pieri, as '*una esasperazione di virtuosismo tattico*'. Obviously, the marquis was keeping an eye out for his own personal aggrandizement. He had yielded to the inveterate Italian temptation of exploiting a national crisis to become a great historical figure, cheered by the multitude, covered with immortal glory. For this, he could not stay to one side and watch the others fight. He needed to show off his own valour, that of his family, and that of his Mantua men-at-arms. They all fought with great courage. Most of them died. In the end Francesco thought he had won. Was he not left in possession of the terrain? Had he not captured the enemy's treasure? Had he not forced the King of France to flee? Back in Mantua, he had a church built to thank God, called it the *Chiesa della Vittoria*, and had a gold medal struck bearing the words '*Ob restitutam Italiae libertatem*', or 'For the re-establishment of Italian liberty'. Note the word *Italiae*, which showed how aware the contemporaries were of the national significance of the battle. Everybody else, however, knew they had lost the battle, the war, and the liberty of Italy.

*

Charles VIII's expedition could be compared to the Opium War which the English fought against the Chinese Empire in the nineteenth century. It too was a comparatively mild affair, unimportant as such things go. It too started a chain reaction of unpredictable events and opened the way for a long period of foreign interventions, bloody conflicts, civil wars and revolts. The English (like the French of Charles VIII) showed the world the impotence of a great nation, the immense booty which could be gathered with little danger, the passive weakness of the over-civilized inhabitants, their incapacity to work in cohesive and coherent bodies, their readiness to resign themselves pliantly to the ways of rough, brutal and resolute invaders. The ruin and the humiliation of great peoples, the Italians and the Chinese, proud of their past achievements, fanned nationalism, a hidden hatred of the foreigners, so obviously inferior to the natives in culture, *savoir faire* and the arts, a xenophobia without which many succeeding events could not be easily explained. It sporadically burst out in savage and bloody revolts, followed by periods of supine and servile resignation. The ultimate consequences of all this reach to the present day. Fascism and the Boxers' rebellion, the Communist victory in China and the strength of Communism in Italy, all have many roots, some of them in distant, half-forgotten defeats and the desire for revenge.

The European powers, however, brought to China an entirely dissimilar culture, based on science, organization, and modern weapons; they brought to Italy a more backward but recognizable form of the common culture. Undoubtedly Francesco Gonzaga was a better general than Charles. Only the foreigners' determination on the battlefields, their courage and discipline, were their own, the virtues of people who could unite behind their leaders. The weapons and the stratagems employed by the French and all the other invaders who followed them had been invented and perfected by the Italians, and this made their humiliation infinitely more bitter. The war in China provoked the final collapse of a decrepit Empire, the end of a civilization which had not developed the means with which to defend itself. The European invasions of Italy, on the other hand, while destroying her supremacy in war and politics, spurred the Italians to greater efforts in the fields left open to them, those in which they were unchallenged. Some of their greatest triumphs in the arts and the newly-born sciences were achieved while the wars were still going on. Decline came later.

*

What happened after Fornovo is intricate and tragic. Even the diligent old *Encyclopaedia Britannica* groaned under the burden of having to clarify subsequent events to its readers and gave up. Its eleventh edition (Cambridge, 1911, Volume XV, page 41), sadly says: 'It is impossible in this place to follow the tangled intrigues of the period.' Practically all the available armies of Europe came to Italy in the thirty-odd years after 1495. The Austrians, the Germans, the Burgundians, the French, the Flemish, the Spanish, the Hungarians and sundry others marched down the Alps or landed from their ships. Even the Swiss abandoned their peaceful valleys and their prosperous cows for the Italian battlefields, under everybody else's flag as mercenaries, or their own, to get on to a good thing; the Swiss have a notorious instinct for safe business opportunities. Everybody formed everlasting alliances with everybody else in turn, broke them, formed new ones, marched, countermarched, fought, made peace, and resumed fighting again. At times, when reading the detailed chronicles of those decades, one's head reels and one is reminded of the closing scenes of old silent film comedies, the free-for-all drunken brawls in which everybody slugged everybody else regardless.

The foreigners won or lost in turn. The Italians always lost. When things were going well, they had to supply everybody with food, fodder, lodgings for men and animals and bags of gold coins. Things went well only sporadically. Most of the time the inhabitants were robbed of their possessions and massacred, their women were raped, their fields ravaged, their farm-houses demolished, their stores emptied, their wine barrels shot through, their churches desecrated, their cattle slaughtered, their beautiful cities sacked, dismantled and burned. Bands of marauding deserters, the scum of Europe, roamed the countryside. Hunger and the plague spread like stubble fire. Italians who were not killed at home, in their native towns and villages, found death on every battlefield. Not a skirmish was fought in which they were not among the victims, as actors on both sides and innocent bystanders.

The local princes and republics, unable to form another military alliance among themselves to defend their country, always joined this or that coalition of foreigners, to spite their personal rivals, and sent their subjects in droves to fight and die in innumerable and incomprehensible little side-wars. The Italians who enrolled as mercenaries in other people's armies thought life in camp was better than life anywhere else. What happened in the last eighteen months of the second world war—the Allies of all colours fighting the Germans, the fascists fighting the anti-fascists, the cities turned into rubble, starving children begging, women selling themselves for a piece of bread, men being deported, tortured, killed by the S.S., hunger, despair, corruption and disease spreading—continued after Fornovo for more than thirty years. Nobody seemed to be strong enough to put an end to the senseless destruction.

In 1527, after thirty-three years of bloody troubles, a new Imperial army marched on Rome. Mustered at random, it included German *Landsknechte* who were fanatical Lutherans, recruited with the hope that they would show extra zeal against the Pope, Spanish soldiers who were fanatical Catholics and Italian mercenaries. It was led by the Constable of Bourbon, a traitor to the King of France. Like all Charles V's soldiers, these were not paid; they paid themselves by exacting levies and sacking cities. The Constable was killed as he approached the walls of Rome with a ladder, in a fog, on May 6, 1527, two hours before sunset. Benvenuto Cellini boasted in his *Memoirs* that he had killed him with his own crossbow. No serious historian believes him. The shot was but one of few. There was no resistance. The walls were scaled, the gates opened and Rome conquered in a matter of hours.

For nine months the city was abandoned to the lust, rapacity and cruelty of thirty thousand men without an authoritative commander to check them. The Pope, Clement VII, imprisoned in Castel Sant'Angelo, saw, day and night, the smoke billow from new fires in every quarter of the city, heard the wailing of women and the groans of tortured men mingled with the jests and the songs of drunken soldiers, and murmured to himself the words of Job: 'Because it shut not up the doors of my mother's womb nor his sorrow from mine eyes.' All Europe was shocked by the horrible tales. For months on end, men were being put on the rack to make them reveal the hiding place of their money; women of all conditions and ages, including the nuns, were being raped by lines of jeering men; priceless art treasures were destroyed or dispersed forever; high prelates were kidnapped for ransom and dragged through the streets dressed in precious holy vestments, mounted backwards on donkeys, in sacrilegious parody. The churches were despoiled of all precious or non-precious objects: holy relics and books were thrown in the streets with the garbage and the rotting corpses. Not even the dead were safe. Julius II's tomb was prised open and his ring stolen from his dessicated finger. The Catholics behaved as viciously as the Protestants, the Italian soldiers as viciously as the foreigners, the Roman populace as viciously as the conquerors.

*

The sack of Rome, the distant consequence of the defeat at Fornovo, was the catastrophe from which Italians never recovered, the trauma which left its indelible marks on their national character. Not one of them ever doubted that it had come about through their own faults. Why had no leader found the energy and courage to stop the motley and disorderly Imperial army on its drunken way south? Why did the people not rise in revolt against the foreign rabble?

The sack of Rome has no exact parallel as an example of national humiliation. It cannot really be compared to the event which first comes to mind, the fall of Paris in 1940. The Paris of the Third Republic was also the most splendid and glorious city in Europe, the storehouse of priceless wealth accumulated through many centuries, the library of the world, the depository of all that was best in old and new arts, the habitat of distinguished men. But Paris was not destroyed and sacked. It emerged intact from its ordeal. It awed its conquerors. The barbarians crowded the museums, filled the concert halls and the Comédie Française, honoured the dead French cultural heroes while they tortured living French patriots. Rome, on the other hand, was spared nothing. There was no mercy for it. Its glorious past, its majestic ruins, the terrible memory of its greatness, the masterpieces filling *palazzi* and basilicas, the treasures filling libraries and coffers did not protect it from one single abuse. In fact, all its qualities (like the beauty of most of its women, the virtue of some, and the great dignity of a few), made the rape the more irresistible.

But Rome was something infinitely more than Paris in 1940. Rome was also God's seat on earth, the rock on which Christ had established His Church, the centre of a vast spiritual Empire of which all Christians had been subjects until a few years before. Those who laid hands on it did more than perpetrate an ordinary outrage: they committed an irreparable sacrilege. To see their sacred city being defiled, as the Italians did, without being able to lift a finger to avert its doom, was more than a proof of their military and political impotence: it was the betrayal of their moral and spiritual inheritance. The destruction of the city, like the destruction of Jerusalem, was taken to be a clear sign of the wrath of God in retribution for the vices and the sins of the people. It destroyed their soul. It weakened irremediably their pride and their will to live as one nation, because Rome, like Jerusalem, was also the symbol of their national existence. Italians had not achieved unity, but had always felt themselves to be a nation nevertheless formed, not like others, by kings, soldiers and statesmen, but by churchmen, poets, artists and philosophers. This spiritual country which Italians loved desperately had a capital which was Rome, not the stone Rome on the banks of the Tiber, but the ghostly city to be found in books and legends. It had bewitched Dante, Cola, Petrarch. It was to bewitch all great Italians in the future. Rome was the great mother, the womb from which everything Italians held dear had come, without whose possession they could find no peace. Its loss was irreparable.

*

The Emperor Charles V emerged from the fighting as the sole winner. The noise of battle died. The dust settled. He imposed on Italy a heavy Pax Hispanica. The Italians resigned themselves to their state. Nothing could be done against him. He lived far away: nobody could poison him, plot against him, deceive him, trap him; no league could be formed with foreign allies to fight him. He was more powerful than anybody had ever been: he had the greatest navy, the biggest army, more allies than anybody, the largest treasure ever gathered, overseas possessions so vast that there was as yet no map of them. On his empire, as everybody knew, the sun never set. In 1530 he was also elected Emperor of the Holy Roman Empire.

He graciously consented to be crowned at the hands of the Pope at the same time Emperor and King of Italy. The gold crown of the King of Italy, called the 'iron crown' because it is said to contain one of the true nails of the Cross, of remote antiquity (it probably belonged to Constantine), was kept in the Duomo of Monza, near Milan, where Queen Teodolinda of the Longobards had left it. (It is still there.) It was seldom used. It was never moved far from Monza. The crown of the Empire was kept in Saint Peter's, in Rome. Previous emperors (the first had been Charlemagne in 800) had been crowned there or in Saint John Lateran. But Charles could not spare the time to stop in Monza and then go on to Rome. He disdainfully said that he was not accustomed to run after crowns but to have crowns run after him. He gave orders that both be brought to Bologna, which was halfway between Rome and Monza, and Clement VII meet him there. The Pope accepted meekly. In July 1529 the emperor commanded Andrea Doria to meet him in Barcelona, crossed the Mediterranean in a rough passage of fourteen days, landed in Genoa, and proceeded to Bologna.

The meeting of Pope and Emperor was one of the terminal events of Italian history. With pomp and pageantry it established the moral hegemony of the Church and the material dominion of Spain over a large part of Europe. The ceremony closed a miraculous age of unrivalled intellectual splendour and immense suffering in Italy, and inaugurated a new era, a period of more than three centuries of subjection to foreign rulers, during which it can be said that Italy had no history of her own.

Great preparations had been made in Bologna. There was no money, of course, after the events of the past years. The people were gloomy and hostile. It was noticed that when the Pope entered the city none of the population had responded to the cries of *Viva Papa Clemente!* raised by his attendants. The Pope and his court wore mourning. After the sack of Rome they had sworn never to shave and to wear their beards unshorn in memory of their past sufferings. Yet the municipality and the nobles of the city managed somehow to get enough money together to give the emperor a memorable welcome. Illustrious guests flocked from everywhere. All the great princes of Italy were present. The Pope was attended by the most illustrious cardinals, high prelates from the Curia and the sees. The emperor was followed everywhere by a cortège of courtiers from Spain, Italy and Germany, ambassadors from England, France, Scotland, Hungary, Bohemia and Portugal.

Veronica Gambara threw her apartments open to the numerous men of letters: the poets Bembo, Mauro and Molza could be seen in conversation with witty Berni, learned Vida, stately Trissino and Marcantonio Flaminio. Giovio and Guicciardini were there. What still remained in Italy of Renaissance splendour, wit and fashion, after the sack of Rome, the ruin of her wealthiest cities, and thirty-five years of continuous wars, was concentrated in a sunset blaze of festivities, games, *conversazioni*, banquets, balls.

Francesco Mazzola, called *Il Parmigianino*, painted Charles attended by Fame who crowns his forehead while an infant Hercules hands him the globe. Titian received the honour of several sittings. His life-size portrait of the emperor in full armour, seated on a white charger, has been lost. Others remain. Charles was so pleased with Titian that he personally picked up a brush the painter had dropped, made him a knight, and appointed him painter to the emperor with a regular pension.

People observed that Charles and his suite in their excursions through the streets of Bologna always wore the Spanish habit. While Italians were dressed in the bright and gay colours fashionable at the time, in silks, borcades, velvets, laces, and woollen cloth, of red, green, yellow, pink, blue, the Spanish wore black suits with black silk stockings, black boots or shoes, black velvet caps adorned with black plumes. The gloom was brightened by buttons of jewellery, and, on Charles' breast, by the chain and the hanging lamb of the Order of the Golden Fleece. The Spanish were pale men who never smiled. Charles was seen to smile only once, at a lady who had thrown a flower at him from a balcony. Such slight details would not deserve attention were it not for the fact that Italians, as they have always done, quickly discarded their varied and brilliant clothes and adopted the conquerors' fashion, the funereal black of the Spaniards. It seemed as though the whole country had put on mourning for its servitude to foreign tyrants, for its loss of liberty. The very faces of the people, in the following generation, as we see them in portraits, took on an expression of sadness and despondency corresponding to their black garments. A poet noticed the change and wrote:

> Black robes befit our age. Once they were white;
> next many-hued; now dark as Afric's Moor,
> night-black, infernal, traitorous, obscure,
> horrid with ignorance and sick with fright.

> For very shame we shun all colours bright,
> who mourn our end—the tyrants we endure,
> the chains, the noose, the lead, the lure—
> our dismal heroes, our souls lost in night.

The reader does not have to be reminded that black was also the official colour of the Fascist régime. Mussolini was dressed in black from head to foot and so were all his ministers.

CHAPTER SIXTEEN

THE PERENNIAL BAROQUE

WHAT happened to Italy is what usually happens to old ladies who were once famous beauties. Just as they relinquish only reluctantly the gestures, curls, witticisms and fashions of their sunset years, Italy still clings to the manners and ideals of the two centuries which followed the coronation of Charles V. This must be kept in mind by anybody trying to understand anything about this confusing country, past events, current developments, art movements, political evolutions, or by anyone wanting to peer into the clouded crystal-ball of the future. He must not allow himself to be deceived (so many things in Italy are perfect *trompe-l'oeil*). He must look beneath the surface. He will then discover that Italian reality is generally still a Baroque reality.

Baroque is a mysterious term. Some scholars (Benedetto Croce among them) believe that it derived from an artificial word (b-a-r-o-c-o) invented by medieval scholars to teach dull pupils a particularly intricate form of logical reasoning, the fourth mode of the second figure of the syllogism, to be exact. Others think it is the old trade name for the oddly-shaped monstrous pearls still known as *perle barocche* in Italy. The two hypotheses are not in contradiction. Somehow the term came to be used metaphorically to describe anything pointlessly complicated, otiose, capricious and eccentric, similar to rarely used syllogisms or irregularly bulging pearls: twisted theories, elliptical and over-ornate poetry, elaborate and guady architecture. Later it came to define a whole period in history, the Baroque era, in which Baroque men thought Baroque thoughts, led Baroque lives, surrounded by Baroque art. The age had a more than casual resemblance to our own.

With the Baroque era, all kinds of things which had been lax, spontaneous, comfortable and haphazard before, became rigid, uniform and somewhat inhuman all over Europe. Absolute monarchs flattened out all rivals and ruled practically without opposition; great kings joined in vast but changing alliances, a slow game of dynastic musical chairs. The minor principalities and republics were left without real responsibility and autonomy. They were robbed of their dignity and became impotent, unwilling and embittered vassals. The danger of little wars decreased but the fear of vast conflagrations involving the whole world was ever present. Centralized power developed the instruments for efficient rule: laws were codified and enforced, bureaucracy became powerful and quickly proliferated, with its archives, forms to fill in, rites, and the authority to punish all those who did not submit to it. The little liberties consecrated by usage, the privileges of dignitaries, guilds, towns, universities, religious orders, professions or any individual who disliked being pushed around, were worn thin until only a vestige was left. Man was left practically alone before the will of his sovereign.

All economic activities which were not prohibited were strictly controlled. The king held monopolies of the main indispensable products, which he alone could export or import. Taxes rained down with unprecedented severity to support the armies and the heavy machinery of government. Stable and pyramidal hierarchies were established in all fields. The armies, no longer amateur collections of men chosen at random, happily bent on arson, pillage and rape, acquired organizational charts, uniforms, an iron discipline and a well-defined chain of command. Authorities determined once and for all the only correct spelling of words and rules of grammar, as well as the unbending etiquette of court and private life. Cities were no longer the spontaneous and untidy products of man's needs, passions and tastes: they were designed by the king's architects. The king demanded straight and wide avenues and large squares. Of course, he wanted the Baroque prestige of a great and ornate capital, but also easy passage for his troops to quell riots. Beauty itself, the most elusive of all qualities, was codified down to minutiae. Religious life was strictly regimented. Gone were the wild debates and revolts of the preceding age in both Catholic and Protestant countries.

Morality was imposed, dogmas and principles were defined, rites standardized. In both camps orthodoxy was sternly defended. Free thinkers and heretics were persecuted and burned in Rome as well as Geneva. Miguel de Servetus, the Catalan physician and theologian, was condemned to death in the same month by the Sorbonne and the Calvinists.

Society appeared formed of two main layers. At the top there were a few *grands seigneurs*. At the bottom the vast ragged, picturesque and powerless crowds. The *grands seigneurs* derived their power mostly from the favours of the king and from the revenue of their land. They were encouraged to live lavishly, on their estates or at court, and not to dabble in trade, banking, politics, or scholarly pursuits. Cosimo I de Medici, to avoid trouble, forced the great banking and trading families of Florence to invest their capital in country estates and rewarded them with sonorous titles. Titles were much sought after. The nobility cut off from responsibilities inevitably became overbearing, inept and dull. The populace was kept ignorant, poor, superstitious, harassed by tax-collectors, religious authorities, bureaucrats and soldiers. At times the poor broke out in bloody but short-lived and unprofitable riots. Most of the time, they were kept happy in their misery by the distribution of alms, the sale of cheap flour, the splendid performance of public spectacles and the clubs of policemen. The show was all important. This is why the Baroque age is still unsurpassed in the breathtaking beauty of public buildings, churches, parks, residences and cities. It was not an accident that all great architects of the day were also famous scenic designers. Historical events were, whenever possible, staged like sumptuous theatrical productions.

Behind the splendour, the agitation, the shouting, the roll of drums, the flutter of flags and the roar of guns, under the impeccably rational order of the era, lay a heavy feeling of futility and tedium. Men took refuge in distractions which took many forms: secret revolts against all conformism, open or invisible struggles for liberty or its substitutes, the search for free expression of man's unemployed talents in some interstice between forbidden fields. Men travelled to the far end of the world, fought savages, founded colonies, entertained dangerous political thoughts, volunteered in their own or other people's armies, joined new religious cults, the more outlandish and persecuted the better. Others lived, outside all known laws, lives of licentiousness, violence, profligacy, debauch and crime. This is the other face of the Baroque era, the more Baroque face of Baroque life.

*

When the times turned to Baroque, Italy found herself surprisingly at ease for a defeated, dismembered and oppressed country. She took to Baroque with a vengeance. She looked, in the end, more Baroque than any other Baroque country of Europe. She set the style. Her discoveries, *divertissements*, techniques and designs were eagerly imitated. Rome became the world capital of Baroque. This was because Baroque life utilized fully many of the people's latent talents, tastes and inclinations, but also because the elements of Baroque life, oppression, tedium and revolt, were stronger in Italy than anywhere else. While regimentation in other countries had noble justifications, was imposed allegedly to defend national unity and prestige, and to submit all to a common purpose and the supremacy of the law, in Italy it was imposed externally, by two cosmopolitan powers, Spain and the Church, for external reasons, in their own interest and for their own advantage.

Spain was a mighty empire which ruled Italy like one of her many colonies through viceroys and satellite princelings. The Church, as a temporal body, was a small Italian state, one of many, perhaps more bankrupt, corrupt, disorganized, ridden with bandits than most of the others, as ridiculously impotent as any to carry out an independent policy of its own. But it was also an immense spiritual empire, holding sway in every Catholic country, distributing slices of the American continent as if it were its own property, drawing incalculable strength from the loyalty of Catholic princes and the faith of the Catholic multitudes. The foremost of Catholic princes was His Catholic Majesty the King of Spain, the most fanatically devoted to the Holy See were the Spanish people. The two empires buttressed each other. Each of them endeavoured to employ the other to make up for its weaknesses: the Church made use of Spanish soldiers to enforce its decrees and defend Catholic unity; Spain exploited the spiritual hegemony of the Church to keep the people docile. All the time, like all good allies, they struggled for supremacy. The Church won in the end. It always does.

The difference between Baroque in Italy and that in other countries could be compared to that between Communism in the satellite republics, mechanically imposed by foreign armies after a defeat, and Communism in the Soviet Union, the product of the Russians' tortured genius, of their passionate love for their unfortunate country, and of their perennial self-pity. The outward forms of the régime were more emphatic in Italy, the declarations of faith unnecessarily forceful. There was, at the same time, something vaguely degrading and contemptible about obeying the will of the local authorities, as there now is in any eastern European country; and secret revolt, sabotage, insubordination, anarchy, and lawlessness were considered meritorious and manly. Like all oppressed people, the Italians were forbidden to think, act, work and fight for themselves. Responsible jobs were in the hands of foreigners and of faithful servants of the foreigners, the collaborators. For the ordinary natives there were idle and frivolous occupations, insignificant and servile work or the pursuit of private greatness.

The situation grew more and more explosive as the decades passed. The people, notoriously the most restless, unruly, talented in Europe, found themselves with but a few narrow and secondary fields in which to give vent to their energies. The rulers, Spanish viceroys and petty princes, were more avaricious, dull-witted and ignorant than most other rulers, but also more insecure and frightened; nowhere was the populace purposely kept more hungry, superstitious and illiterate; nowhere else was it entertained more lavishly with spectacles and dazzled more expensively with ostentatious architecture. Nowhere else, at the same time, were so many people plagued by a feeling of futility, more anxious to take revenge on their oppressors, more desperately eager to explore unusual ways to escape.

*

The Italians did not face the challenge of the outside world as, for example, the Japanese did when their turn came, in the nineteenth century. The Japanese easily understood their ancient civilization was a decorated paper-screen, too flimsy to defend them. They went to school. They drilled themselves in Western skills, aped Western ways, adopted foreign uniforms, routines, laws, methods. They became so good that they beat the West at its own game. The Italians did the opposite. They were too proud to admit they had to learn from others. And what could these barbarians teach them who had taught the world? Of course the barbarians had gained military glory and political supremacy over Italy. But what did these short-lived advantages amount to when compared to the Italians' triumphs in the arts and the sciences, which challenged the centuries? What were the ephemeral political structures the foreigners set up when compared to the greatest flowering of the Italian political genius, the result of the Italians' devoted collaboration with God Himself, the Holy Roman Catholic Church, which was to last eternally by divine will? The Italians went on cultivating the very virtues which made them invincible, in their own eyes, but which had also made them the foreigners' too easy victims.

Many capable Italians dedicated themselves to the urgent job of shoring up and defending their tottering Church. Some were the holy men the Church needed at the time, saints like Charles Borromeo and Roberto Bellarmine. All the great Popes of the era (some were among the greatest in history) were Italian, as well as most of the famous cardinals, theologians, writers, scholars, preachers, educators, heads of religious orders, who practically constructed, within a few decades, a brand new Catholic church. These men were serving God, to be sure, but, at the same time, Italy, or what was, after all, the greatest Italian institution left standing after the débâcle, the only one which could still awe and dominate foreigners. This, of course, was nothing new. The Church had been, since the early Middle Ages, the rallying point of the Italians against the menace of imperial power. When a town was on the verge of being conquered by a victorious enemy, who threatened to abolish its liberties and rob it of its wealth, the people turned to their bishop, made him the head of the government for the time being, and sent him out to start negotiating with the enemy, to obtain more tolerable conditions. Even after the second world war, the Italians instinctively turned to the Church. They had been defeated, their country had been invaded, their own national state had collapsed, disease and hunger were spreading, and a bloody revolution looked inevitable. The Pope's Rome obviously wielded at all times a world influence infinitely superior to their own.

Other contemporary Italians went on stubbornly with the work in which they had a head start over all rivals, the arts and the sciences. It was after the sack of Rome and the coronation of Charles V in Bologna that Michelangelo painted 'The Last Judgement' in the Sistine Chapel and planned the Cupola over Saint Peter's, Cellini cast his 'Perseus' for the Loggia dei Lanzi in Florence, Palladio raised San Giorgio from the sea in Venice, Titian painted some of his greatest masterpieces, and Sansovino designed some of his most famous buildings. There was, however, something about their work which distinguished it from what they themselves had done but a few years before, a complacent dwelling on fantastic forms, perhaps, an excess of technical skill, a tortured exaggeration, a new kind of *bravura*. When the giants of a past age died, new men almost as good kept up their work. There was an endless procession of them. Tintoretto was born in 1518, Paolo Veronese in 1528, Caravaggio in 1573, Guido Reni, the painter whom our grandfathers believed to have been the greatest of all Italian painters, the 'divine' Guido, in 1575. The Caracci family team of eclectic painters came to Rome from Bologna in 1595. And Pietro da Cortona, Il Guercino, Salvator Rosa, Magnasco followed, a cavalcade of hard-working, versatile, prodigiously fecund artists. They were no longer the sedate and pious craftsmen of an earlier age. Most of them were slightly mad: they went around booted, spurred, with swords and poignards at their sides, like adventurers, and often had to run for their lives after having murdered somebody in a brawl.

Sculptors and architects were in great demand. They reached heights of excellence never seen before. Men like Bernini, Borromini, Juvara and their followers filled Rome with hundreds of *palazzi* and churches, studded the panorama of the city with new and daring cupolas, built Saint Peter's and the colonnade in front of it, and gave Rome the face it has today. Many went around Italy, or roamed abroad, from capital to capital, building royal palaces, basilicas, cathedrals, and gardens, planning cities, designing avenues, vistas, *piazze* and fountains, until they dropped dead. In everything they did was the same love of dramatic and bewildering effect, which became more and more theatrical as the years passed, the same unprecedented and daring use of technique, the same perfection in all details. It was not an accident that their genius was also dedicated principally to the Church, to the glorification of its triumphs over the infidels and the heretics, through the most spectacular and pyrotechnical display of *virtuosismo* ever seen. Many of these artists were deeply religious: Michelangelo had become obsessed with the salvation of his soul; Carlo Dolci was determined to paint only subjects which might provoke religious ecstasy; Luca Giordano would not travel to Spain without his personal confessor. Others found solace in serving God and also Italy, poor unfortunate Italy.

It was inevitable perhaps that Baroque Italians should invent theatrical forms which were to dazzle the world for centuries. The age was one of display, make-believe and emotions; the only reality was that of the imagination. Ingenious artists designed stage-sets of miraculous splendour and built stage-machinery to produce incredible effects, storms at sea, floods of real water, flying birds or angels, instantaneous changes of décor, fantastic panoramas stretching apparently to infinity. The *Teatro dell'arte* was started in Florence by a company of bored actors who called themselves I Gelosi in 1575. They were tired of repeating night after night the same old words written by the author. They invented their own lines and business as they went along, following a tenuous plot. They were brought to Paris by Catherine de Medici for her wedding, and had an immediate tremendous success. They, and other companies imitating them, soon took Europe by storm.

People everywhere laughed at the famous masks: Arlecchino and Brighella, the astute servants; Pantalone, the rich merchant worried by taxes and greedy relatives; Doctor Balanzon, the parody of all learned men and physicians; Captain Spaventa, the cowardly and boastful soldier. People wept real tears at the pathetic sentiments expressed by Colombina, the pretty maid, or Rosaura, her young and unhappy mistress, and their lovers. The *Teatro dell'arte* influenced all European theatres. Words percolated from the *Teatro* to all common languages. 'Zany' became an English word in 1588—it means John in Venetian dialect; Zani was a variation of Arlecchino. When a Soviet Russian today wants to say that what he is showing you is not a *papier mâché* structure built to deceive foreigners but the real thing, he earnestly assures you it is not *trovarobe*. *Trovarobe* was the man employed to 'find things', to be sure that all the props needed were on the stage at the right time; later he became the stage-manager, responsible for the scenery and the illusions.

Music is notoriously the consolation of oppressed and frightened people. It is the one art in which one can be safely sincere in danger-ous times. This Heinrich Heine understood: 'To poor enslaved Italy,' he wrote in his *Reisebilde*, 'words are not allowed. She can only describe the anguish in her heart through music. All her hatred against foreign oppression, her enthusiasm for liberty, all the anguish at her own impotence, her longing for her past greatness, pathetic hopes, watching, waiting for help, all this is transposed into her melodies.' Before Baroque Italians could find a refuge in music, however, they had to invent it. The man who not only started Italian music on its glorious way but also had to save the newly-born creation from immediate death was Palestrina. The clerical authorities of the times looked upon singing in churches with dis-taste. This was inevitable, as most of the choirs sang holy words to ribald tunes of foreign importation, suggesting the tavern, the dancing room and the brothel. Masses bore the titles of the popular melodies on which they were founded, names more suited for con-temporary perfumes than religious tunes: '*A l'ombre d'un buissonet*', '*Baise-moi*', or '*Adieu, mes amours*'. The very explicit words of love ditties and obscene ballads rang out often during religious services, squalled by the tenor, while the bass sang an '*Agnus Dei*' or a '*Benedictus*'. The scandal could not be tolerated any longer. The Council of Trent, in its twenty-second session, on September 17, 1562, decided to 'exclude from churches all such music that intro-duced anything impure or lascivious'. Could music suggest anything but the impure and lascivious? Pius IV appointed a congregation of eight cardinals to look into the matter.

It was known that four of them were determined to ban all music from the churches. Giovanni Pier Luigi, called Palestrina from his birthplace, was asked to break the deadlock. He was instructed to compose something which had never been tried before, an original mass in sober ecclesiastical style which would inspire strictly holy thoughts. If he failed, as everybody thought he would (Cardinal Charles Borromeo, the Pope's nephew, personally told him so), the choral establishments of the Pontifical Chapel and all other church musical organizations would be disbanded and music excluded from religious services. Palestrina had an apparently simple but almost impossible task. He was to invent a new form of art or to behold the ruin of his own life and the lives of all his colleagues. He composed the now famous 'Mass of Pope Marcellus'. The cardinals heard it, were placated and convinced. Church music was saved for ever in its new form. Italian music was founded at the same time. What if Palestrina had not succeeded? The mind staggers.

At about the same time, a private academy of scholars, dabblers and artists gathered regularly in the Palazzo Vernio, in Florence, for the avowed purpose of reviving the musical declamation of the Greeks. The quest was, of course, vague and visionary. Nobody knows how the Greeks sang. No Greek music came down to us. The Florentine *dilettanti* had only a dim intuition to guide them, the belief that the ancients had read dramatic verse with musical intonations. As the alchemists vainly searching for the philosopher's stone initiated modern chemistry, the Palazzo Vernio friends invented something entirely different from what they were looking for, Opera. One of them, Claudio Monteverdi, developed the *recitativo*, in his *Orfeo*. It was the acorn from which all the operas in history grew. The new theatrical form, decorated with all the artifices, the scenery, the theatrical effects and the costumes of the era, had an immediate success.

Behind it all, however, behind the splendour and ingeniousness of everything, was a tragic feeling of despair, a spiritual frustration so intense as to be embarrassing. Behind religious art, for instance, behind the monumental stateliness of church façades, the unbelievable *virtuosismo* of the engineering, the convulsed agitation of the decorations, the tortured emphasis of all details, the epileptic gestures of the statues, the fluttering of stone cloaks in perennial hurricanes, the exasperated emotions on the faces of painted saints, there is little intimate religious feeling to be seen, but something else, a pathetic preoccupation with proclaiming beyond all possible doubt the victory of the Church over all its enemies and with convincing the world of its invincible supremacy. Behind most of the ornate, eloquent, erudite prose of the time there was little truth and practically no significance: only specialists read it today. Poetry invented new rhythms, new ways of employing words, new and marvellous metaphors; it entertained, cajoled, caressed, and flattered the reader; it evoked lascivious and impossible pleasures. It reminds us of those great machines built at about the same time, vast aviaries filled with wonderfully variegated birds moving their wings and singing melodiously: they look alive but are merely the product of man's cold inventiveness; they repeat themselves endlessly.

Everything, in fact, was done not for itself alone but principally for the effect it would produce. For two centuries or more an immense number of men of genius dedicated their incredible talents to the national belief that the show is, *faute de mieux*, a good substitute for reality: they filled the world with masterpieces in order to find compensation for the insecurity, emptiness, disarray, impotence and despair of their national life, to forget their humiliation and shame, to forget their collective guilt. It was a frenzied search for consolation and revenge against the crude and overbearing foreign devils. The Italians never succeeded in the end in affirming their own kind of greatness. They were always laughed at. Their achievements were thought to be suspicious, inferior, as if they lacked a manly character. As Croce says, 'Italians lost whatever reputation they had for the earnestness of their intellectual production; their talents gave them the name of excellent actors, singers, composers, decorators, versifiers. They were praised as a "*popolo d'artisti*", or "a people of artists", at times despised as "charlatans" and "clowns".'

*

Some Italians did not resign themselves to impotence, perhaps many more than one imagines. These odd men disliked being entertained, distracted, dazzled, and benefited: resented being kept in ignorance, deceived and exploited. They hated being obliged to depend on the art of living (which is notoriously nothing more arcane than the art of gaining favours from dull, ungrateful and capricious masters) to make a living. One occasionally gets a glimpse of these men's unhappiness. This is what an earnest writer, Battista Guarini, wrote disconsolately to a friend, after receiving the appointment of poet at the court of Ferrara: 'I strove to transform myself into another man, and, like a play-actor, to assume the character, manners and emotions of a past period. Mature in age, I forced myself to appear young; exchanged my melancholy for gaiety; affected loves I did not feel; turned my wisdom into folly, and, in a word, passed from philosopher to poet.' Croce says: 'He who knows the documents of the time does not always see in them serenity and gaiety. One is tempted to affirm that even laughter had been lost, good healthy laughter; men created it artificially by means of burlesque poetry, academic fancies, and heroic-comic poems, games of words rather than spontaneous expressions of joy.'

Proud Italians felt the shame of not being ruled by laws, the protagonists of their national life and arbiters of their destinies, the humiliation of watching the servile and contented condition of the people around them. 'Italy, who had given birth to apostles and martyrs in earlier centuries,' Croce explains, 'and would beget more later, during the Risorgimento, did not produce any in the Baroque age, because such men cannot exist when there is lazy tranquillity and resignation in the spirit.' There were not many apostles and martyrs, perhaps, but there were many men who suffered because there were none, and found the lack of purpose and the emptiness of their lives unbearable. Many of them emigrated. Even if Italy had no history of her own, individual Italians tried to become historical characters. Some became diplomats and statesmen for foreign sovereigns, like Cardinal Mazarin. Some served in other countries' armies. Italian engineers directed the works at the siege of Antwerp and in the siege of La Rochelle. Alessandro Farnese became one of the great generals of Philip II of Spain and led armies in Flanders and France. Gabriele Serbelloni, a Milanese, defended Malta from the Turks, became a Spanish general in Flanders with the Duke of Alba, fought at Lepanto on the 166th galley, called *La Donzella*, on the extreme left, as master-general of the artillery for the Christian fleet against the Turks. Raimondo Montecuccoli from Modena com-

manded the imperial armies against Turenne at the battle of Sass-
bach and wrote treatises on the military arts (he believed in small,
well-drilled, light and fast-moving armies). The kingdom of Naples
was considered by the Spanish an inexhaustible reservoir of soldiers
and officers: thousands of them fought all over Europe and the
Americas. Many became renowned Spanish generals.

That these men were fighting for something more than a stipend
and a part of the booty was shown by their extreme touchiness in
matters relating to the national honour. They were perennially
challenging foreigners (mostly French) who ridiculed the bravery
and loyalty of the Italian soldiers. The memory of such chivalrous
encounters (which the Italian usually won) is kept alive in Italy:
schoolchildren have to study them. The French, of course, have
forgotten them. The first of such pathetic combats took place in
1503 and is known as the *Disfida di Barletta*. Italian knights under
Prospero Colonna had joined the Spanish under Consalvo de Cor-
doba to fight the French for the possession of Apulia. A French
captain, called La Motte, was captured and taken to the Spanish
camp. At dinner he derided the Italians as cowardly and treacherous, adding that he, with a handful of Frenchmen, was ready to
meet any equal number of Italians on the field, at any time. The encounter took place in a lonely spot between Andria and Corato, thirteen Frenchmen against thirteen Italians, on February 13. The
Italians unsaddled all their opponents and were declared winners.
Nobody was killed. A stone tablet twenty feet high was raised on the
spot to celebrate the event in noble Latin words. French Napoleonic
soldiers overturned it one night in 1805; it was proudly set on its
feet again by the local population after Waterloo. It is still there,
lost in a vineyard, to remind Italians that, even when things
looked darkest, all was not lost.

Another similar challenge took place in 1636, in the plains of
Crevacuore, near the Tessin river, in northern Italy. There were two
squads of thirty men, this time, and they were to fight until all those
on one side had been killed or incapacitated. The Italians took the
lead. But when their success looked almost assured, all the French
soldiers who were watching the encounter joined in. To avoid the
danger of a vast and disorderly battle the officers on both sides

stopped the fighting. The French commander later apologized for the unchivalrous behaviour of his men. No monument was raised. For centuries there have been countless duels between individual Italians and foreigners for the same reasons. As late as the beginning of the nineteenth century, the Neapolitan Carlo Filangieri challenged and killed a French general who had offended the Neapolitans. On February 19, 1826, in Florence, the exiled Neapolitan general, Gabriele Pepe, challenged the secretary of the French Legation in Tuscany, the poet Alphonse de Lamartine, who had called Italy 'the land of the dead, *la terre des morts*' in a poem. Lamartine was wounded, embraced his opponent, and confessed chivalrously to having been wrong. Pepe became a well-known figure in Florence and finally made a living giving Italian lessons to foreigners. The last of such noble encounters was fought by Victor Emmanuel of Savoy-Aosta, Count of Turin, a cousin of King Victor Emmanuel III. He challenged a French prince, Henri d'Orléans, who had written a few articles for *Le Figaro*, from Ethiopia, in which he had ridiculed the Italian colonial army. The duel was fought at Vaucresson, near Versailles, on August 15, 1897. Henri d'Orléans was slightly wounded.

*

Many learned writers have attributed the final warping of the national character during the Baroque era solely to ecclesiastical influence. Benedetto Croce pointed out: 'Those very Italians who, a while earlier, had been accused of being the children of Machiavelli were now thought to be the disciples of . . . the priests.' The old Neapolitan philosopher clearly smiled at the contradiction. How could this be? Machiavelli was a notorious *mangiapreti*, or 'priest-eater', the opponent of Vatican policy, the author of ribald satires against clerical corruption. How could the people have changed so radically in such a short time? The thing was patently absurd. Of course Croce was right. He was also wrong. The problem is an intricate one. Only political pamphleteers and journalists can dare give it a clean-cut, black and white, answer. It is impossible for anybody else to disentangle the snarled skein.

In fact sixteenth-century Italians can be considered the disciples of both Machiavelli and the Church. Machiavelli, after all, had not made up his theories out of the air, but had deduced them from the contemporary events in his country, the behaviour of his country-men, and his own built-in prejudices. He never forgot his Catholic upbringing, and his anti-clericalism sprang more from his love than from hatred of the Church: he pilloried only unworthy priests and bad monks. Churchmen, too, could at the same time be accused of obeying Machiavellian rules, which, after all, represented the com-mon sense of the era, just as eighteenth-century Americans, even those who never heard of Franklin's *Poor Richard's Almanack*, could be said to follow its precepts. In other words, all of them, Machia-velli, the people, the Popes, the native cardinals, the Curia, and the native priests, were Italian; all were sons of their land and of their times. The Church can rightly be considered the mother of the Baroque age but also its daughter, the teacher of the Italian people at the time but also their disciple. Was the Italian character really warped because of this? Or was the Church's worldly policy not un-duly influenced by Italian native habits?

*

Never had the forces of the Devil been so close to victory. The Church was fighting deadly internal and external threats. The inter-nal threats were infinitely more dangerous and more difficult to deal with. After all, the external enemies were well-known, recognizable and could be squarely fought. They were the self-proclaimed rebels, the schismatics, and the heretics. The internal enemies were less easy to identify: they were the indifferent, the incredulous, the materialists, who preferred a few earthy joys in the hand to eternal bliss in the bush. They were superstition, ignorance, corruption, nepotism, simony, careerism, and the disintegration of ecclesiastical discipline. Above all, the Church had to beware also of its good friends, the misguided and enthusiastic faithful who, wanting to cure all ills indiscriminately and in a hurry, risked spreading new and more malignant heresies and causing its final collapse. Things had indeed come to a bad pass if Cardinal Gaspare Contarini himself, a man of undaunted faith and solid doctrine, had to admit: 'I cannot hide my indignation that some of the most illustrious Catholic cities are tainted with moral plague and loose ways to such a point that many monasteries designed to shelter virgins dedicated to God have now been turned into brothels. Can there be anything more abject and infamous?'

We know how the Church, at the time of the Council of Trent, managed miraculously to triumph over all its enemies. It reformed itself, established a new discipline, eradicated many lax and corrupt habits, restored and revived religious faith, stopped the progress of schismatics and heretics, and emerged stronger and greater from the ordeal Rome assumed an air of exemplary behaviour. Gravity of manners, visible signs of piety, a composed and contrite face, ostentation of orthodoxy became fashionable. Sinners had to adopt the famous rule, '*Si non caste tamen caute*', 'If not chastely at least prudently'. Like all institutions desperately fighting for survival, the Church had to employ energetic means, some of them ruthless and cruel. In order not to be destroyed by its enemies it had to destroy them first, even if, with them, went a number of innocent bystanders. The Holy Inquisition was introduced from Spain, a larger index of forbidden books was promulgated, and the multiform activities of the vigorous and enterprising Jesuits encouraged.

The Holy Inquisition filled its prisons with suspects. 'At Rome,' writes a shocked resident in 1568, 'some are daily burned, hanged or beheaded. Places of confinement are filled to capacity and new ones must be built.' He was, of course, carried away by his emotions. Prisons were probably indiscriminately packed for many years but we know that the actual victims were not many. They were a handful of heroic and stubborn men, Antonio Paleario, Giordano Bruno, Pietro Carnesecchi, and a few others, among whom was one lone Englishman, who was burned to a crisp on August 5, 1581, for grossly insulting the host. Only in a few cases, in the provinces, was extreme vigour displayed. One of the rare important massacres occurred in 1561 near Cosenza, in Calabria, where a colony of about 4,000 Waldensian heretics was practically wiped out. They were killed by sword, fire, famine, torture, imprisonment or were hurled from the summits of high cliffs. A few survivors were sent to row in Spanish galleys.

It must be remembered that Italians, as a rule, find slaughter stupid and repugnant: through the centuries they were more frequently massacred by landing Muslim pirates or foreign invaders than vice versa. They were massacred indiscriminately by the German army during the last few months of the last war but never massacred Germans indiscriminately. There were never witch-hunts and pogroms in Italy. There could never be a Saint Bartholomew's Night in Rome. Some Italians have few objections to the private killings of one's enemies, when the circumstances demand it, but all of them consider the legal death penalty useless and cruel. (There is no death penalty in the law-books today.) The people's dislike of legal persecution and their kind hearts make them indiscriminately help all victims of the authorities: they feel irresistibly drawn to bandits, fugitives from justice, escaped convicts, as well as political refugees. In 1943, 1944 and 1945, at the peril of their lives, they sheltered anti-Fascists, American and English prisoners of war. They saved thousands of Jews from annihilation in eastern Europe by hiding them from their German allies, smuggling them to safety or providing them with false documents.

It is not surprising, therefore, that many sixteenth-century thinkers of doubtful orthodoxy were saved by the aid of their countrymen. Only a few were Italian Protestants. Most of them (like innumerable anti-fascists under the late dictatorship) were warned in time of their forthcoming arrest, perhaps by the very officials who were charged with arresting them. Some were clever enough to feel disfavour in the air, and did not wait for their doom; some managed to satisfy superior authorities with timely concessions and an outward display of conformism. Others ingeniously explained that a scientific thinker could hold one set of opinions as a philosopher and a completely different set as a Christian. Their motto was the celebrated '*Foris ut moris, intus ut libet*', or 'The façade must conform to the style of the day, the interior to one's choice'.

This is how Clelio Calcagnini, professor of *belles lettres* at Ferrara, explained the rules in a letter: 'There are things which it is safer to suppress and conceal rather than to bring before the common people. . . . Now, when the decrees of the Fathers and long usage have introduced other modes, what necessity is there for reviving antiquated practices which have long fallen in desuetude? Let us

then, I pray you, allow these things to rest. Not that I disapprove of
their being embraced by scholars and lovers of antiquity, but I
would not have them communicated to the common people and those
who are fond of innovations, lest they give occasion to strife and
sedition. . . . Wherefore, in my opinion, the discussion of many points
ought to be confined to the initiated. I must deem it safest to "speak
with the many and think with the few".' It is well known that many
'spoke with the many and thought with the few' throughout later
Italian history. They did so also under the late dictatorship. Benedetto Croce managed to write and publish his work for twenty years
in spite of Fascist censorship, because his writing was obscure,
learned and appealed to a minority. Mario Missiroli, the great
political journalist of the time, used to say to the younger men who
considered him a maestro: 'Do not fret about the freedom of the
press. Freedom of the press, after all, is necessary only for bad
writers.' A good writer can always find a way to convey seditious
thoughts cryptically to the initiated.

*

The forces of the Inquisition could not be directed, as in Spain,
against masses of heretics but only against a few reckless leaders, and
less often against men than books. Dangerous books were confiscated,
destroyed, burned, their owners imprisoned and tried. Bookshops
went out of business, printers stopped printing. Guards at the fron-
tiers diligently searched travellers for hidden publications. All this,
as usual in Italy, was at first done with a flamboyant show of
thoroughness. The psychological effect was immediate and devastating. Prudent people turned in suspicious books and denounced
others who still kept theirs. Even a man like Latino Latini, a scholar,
a protégé of the Vatican, was alarmed. He wrote to a friend in 1559:
'Have you not heard of the peril which threatens the very existence
of books? Here there is no one who for many years will dare write. . . .
As you love me and yourself, sit and look at your bookcases without
opening their doors, and beware lest the very cracks let emanations
come to you from the forbidden books of learning.'

Fra Paolo Sarpi, the learned theologian of the republic of Venice,
called the Index 'the finest secret device ever invented for applying

religion to the purpose of making men stupid', and desperately warned all his friends abroad not to try to smuggle books to him, since they would be found. Forbidden books, however, never stopped coming. A few, as they are now in the Soviet Union, were allowed in for the needs of scholars who could not otherwise refute their false doctrines. Controls became lackadaisical in time, and very lax. As people become more confident, forbidden books were brought in by important persons (whose baggage went unchecked), obscure travellers, pilgrims, merchants, books bound sometimes with the covers of harmless publications, hidden in ships' holds, or mixed with merchandise. Some treatises were copied by hand and circulated and even printed clandestinely.

This has to be kept in mind, before one can determine the real effect of the Index on Italian life in the Baroque era: only a tiny minority of the Italian people read books nowadays and only a few hundred learned specialists read them in the sixteenth century; the book readers never had much influence on their countrymen, anyway, most of whom live in an out-of-doors, speaking, and not an indoors, reading, civilization. Still, the effect of the prohibition was stifling, because the great majority of peace-loving and reasonable men were too easily intimidated. The 'finest secret device' made few men stupid who did not want to become stupid, but undoubtedly encouraged many in their natural inclination for ignorance and the art of shamming correct sentiments and the beliefs approved by the superior authorities.

*

Nothing in Italy appeared more Baroque-Italian than the Company or Society of Jesus. Strictly speaking, of course, it was by no means an Italian institution. It had a soul of Spanish steel. It was invented in 1539, as everybody knows, by a Spanish *hidalgo*, soldier, disciplinarian, a born leader of men, who imbued it with the stern, heroic, and obstinate qualities and prejudices of his people and his class, Don Iñigo Lopez de Recalda, Lord of Loyola and Oñaz, commonly known as Saint Ignatius Loyola, aided by a handful of Spanish and French priests. The first Italian disciples joined him only at a later date. Nevertheless the Society brilliantly identified, interpreted and encouraged the main aspects of Italian Baroque life: conformism, spectacular opulence, dazzling shows, and the ingenious evasion of obnoxious laws.

No lay or ecclesiastical body of Christians had ever been more dedicated to regimentation, more tightly disciplined, rationally organized, systematically run, and successfully standardized. The fathers were instructed in blind obedience to their superior, 'who stood in the place of God', without reference to his wisdom, piety, or discretion. Their general was closely controlled by subordinates he could not dismiss. All Jesuits were interchangeable cogwheels in a vast machine; they spoke all languages and could fit in anywhere. They infiltrated every nook and cranny and dominated society. They were taught to be 'all things to all men'. They influenced the Church, the private lives of obscure millions and the decisions of princes. Similarly, no other institution satisfied so brilliantly the Italian craving for spectacle and opulence and for the emotions which only a good show could produce.

What we know as Baroque style was created by the Society's architects, the good fathers who designed the first Jesuit churches in Rome. It was called the 'Jesuit style' when nobody yet remembered syllogisms or deformed pearls. It is still distrusted and disliked by Protestants and northern Catholics, because it reeks too much of the Mediterranean. The Jesuit churches were designed to envelop the faithful in a dreamlike atmosphere, an intoxicating feast of *son et lumière* and fragrant incense fumes. Never had ornaments been so sumptuous, or marble of all colours, gold and silver been so lavishly employed. Baroque make-believe reached unprecedented heights: marbles were cut on soft folds to imitate velvet or damask, plaster was painted to imitate marble, and not all the gold was gold.

Was the very essence of Baroque style not its perpetual effort to delude and delight? Croce called it '*la ricerca dell'inaspettato e dello stupefacente*,' 'the search for the unexpected and the stupefying'. '*E' del poeta il fin la meriviglia*,' 'It is the poet's aim to astonish the crowd', wrote the greatest poet of the times, who used words as deceptively and decoratively as the architects used marbles, Giovanbattista Marino. The Jesuit churches rang with entrancingly sweet music, and their pulpits with studied eloquence, the like of which had never been heard before, a revolutionary departure from the dreary and scholastic rebukes of other priests, an ornate and honeyed eloquence which stirred the faithful with ineffable sentiments. The Jesuits' churches were crowded when many others were empty.

In the confessional their advice was eagerly sought in all kinds of complex difficulties. They soon became the fashionable professors of the art of directing souls. 'Their purpose is not that of corrupting morals,' admits one of their most implacable opponents, Blaise Pascal. 'This is not their plan. But they do not have as sole aim that of reforming them. This would be bad politics.' They elaborated an elastic yardstick, casuistry, to measure the moral value of human actions, by which they were able to reassure, guide, persuade sinners without frightening them. 'Thus,' Pascal bitterly commented, 'they preserve all their friends and defend themselves against all their enemies.' And Fra Paolo Sarpi, who also hated the Society, wrote in one of his letters: 'The Jesuits have so many loopholes for escape, pretexts, colours of insinuation, that they are more changeful than the sophists, and, when one thinks to have caught them between thumb and finger, they wriggle out and vanish.'

There is no doubt, however, in the mind of their severest opponents and critics, that the fathers themselves allowed no casuistry to mar their own conduct. They led saintly lives. No breath of personal scandal ever touched them. At a time when most of the clergy had sunk into a moral and intellectual slough, the fathers won respect for themselves and for priests in general by their own modesty, dedication, scholarship, earnestness and the unimpeachable purity of their lives. Casuistry was only for the common people.

Pascal was right in a way. They firmly believed they were the only ones who could save the Church from disaster. They saw themselves as a body of soldiers facing overwhelming enemy forces. The comparison goes back to the military mind of the founder. The very name he gave his order, *Compagnia*, was that of the bands of soldiers following a *condottiere*. He said that the ancient monastic communities were the infantry of the Church, whose duty was to stand firm, while the Jesuits were its light horse, capable of moving swiftly and manœuvring. Like all light horse (like William T. Sherman's column, commandos, the *bersaglieri*), they were to penetrate deep behind enemy lines, explore, reconnoitre, gather information, capture hostages and prisoners, do as much damage as they could, and carry out whatever job presented itself with whatever means were available.

Ignatius' military mind also realized the unique strategic value of Italy. He knew that the decisive battles for the salvation of the Church, like most terrestrial battles for European supremacy, were to be fought south of the Alps. Elsewhere the Church could gain influence, power or authority: in Italy it could be saved or lost forever. Therefore he diligently concentrated most of his good men and his best efforts in Italy, and established his headquarters in Rome. The Society devised weapons and tactics for the particular job on hand, and adapted its approach to the local environment. It invented ingenious ways to edify, amuse, instruct, frighten, beguile and dominate Italians as it found them. It created schools everywhere, the best schools of the age, free schools for poor but clever children, expensive schools for the well-born, manned by competent scholars, so that the ruling élite of the following generation would have a Jesuit background; but, at the same time, spread culture and erudition. It made use of many Italian corrupt proclivities, but also employed the Italians' abundant intelligence, artistic talents, religious feeling, and pride in their Church.

The Society succeeded fully. Within a few years, it practically conquered the people's soul and controlled Italian society. While it never lost its stern Spanish character, it appeared so Italian to foreigners, so much the typical expression of the times and the place, that it had to face much opposition. The hostility it provoked abroad was greatly increased by the older hostility Italians had always aroused. And, vice versa, the Society made the life of the Italians more difficult, because the suspicion that had surrounded them for centuries was aggravated by the current belief that they had become the disciples of the Jesuits.

*

There are Italian writers, who, filially anxious to find outside causes for their country's many catastrophes, believe that the long Spanish domination in southern Italy and Milan, and their influence every-where, are the origin of some of our apparently incurable ills. There is some truth in this. The Spanish, for instance, entertained a feudal contempt for useful and productive occupations. We still see, all over the south, that men of rank today consider doing nothing a sign of distinction, and idleness a status symbol. They are known as *galantuomini*. They may live on miserable pensions, or the trifling income from a few fields of broad-beans which they let: they may be definitely poorer than the baker, the owner of the petrol station or the store-keeper; but they wear a collar, a tie, a coat, a hat; they carry a cane; sit on the wicker chairs of the club on the pavement of the main street to watch people go by; they talk politics and read newspapers. They treat common people with disdain. No trade or business sullies their hands. A *galantuomo* does not go to court to defend his honour. Like a Spanish *hidalgo* he takes the law into his own hands.

As the government apparatus has been run mostly by southerners, generally coming from the *galantuomini* class, these Baroque pre-judices have more or less permeated all official Italy in the last one hundred years. Common people are treated with contempt in all government offices. Taxes are as a rule still like those imposed by Spanish viceroys, haphazard, arbitrary and crushing for everybody, but especially punitive for those who show enterprise and produce things. Most officials and politicians believe that economic life is an evil which should be strictly controlled by the authorities, like a treacherous river, and the more it is regulated the better for every-body. Many of these people still dream of an orderly State in which the king owns practically everything, holds monopolies of all prin-cipal products, assures a miserable livelihood for everybody, but dis-tributes particularly ample bounties to his friends. Often, nowadays, this Spanish Baroque dream is fashionably hidden behind Marxist formulas: the king is the Socialist or Communist state and the king's friends are the party apparatus.

The idle *galantuomini* (and, to a lesser extent, most other Italians) still like pompous titles and all sorts of honorary attributes. This foible too is definitely a Spanish importation. The oldest of all Italian nobility had no titles whatever: the Venetian aristocrats, some of whose illustrious families went back to the decline of the Roman Empire, were simply known as *Nobil Uomini*, or noble men. It was only after the Austrians annexed Venice in 1815, that they were awarded the title of counts, to give them a proper place at court. The patricians of the Republic of Genoa were officially allowed to call themselves *marchesi* only when travelling in Spain, England and France, where such things were important. The old kingdom of Naples, on the other hand, swarmed with titles. The President of the Dijon parliament, the severe Charles de Brosses, noted in 1740: 'The populace is rebellious in Naples, the bourgeoisie vain, the high nobility ostentatious, and the lower nobility greedy of titles. . . . Titles have been given to anyone who wanted one and this has given rise to the common saying: "*E' veramente duca ma non cavaliere*" (or "He is really a duke but not a gentleman"). The butcher who used to serve us personally before now serves us only through his helpers, since he has been made a duke.'

Titles wear out in the course of time, and lose value like coins. Nowadays the simplest man anywhere in Italy would consider it only natural to be called *dottore*, whether he ever went to the university or not; to be addressed as a mere lord, or *signore*, a title also introduced by the Spaniards, is practically offensive. A lowly Member of Parliament, like the author of this book, is addressed as *Onorevole* not only in his official capacity, in the Chamber of Deputies, but also by waiters and car-park attendants. The very form of address, the third person singular, which embarrasses most people learning the language, is also a Spanish left-over. It is a conventional way of talking not directly to a man but to his aura, so to speak, to a shadowy person, *la sua signoria*, his lordship. *Signoria* being feminine requires all adjectives and pronouns in the feminine gender, even in the case of males, thus engendering suspicions and confusions in foreigners. '*Come sta lei?*' for instance, usually rendered as 'How are you?', literally means 'How is she?' or 'How does this other and invisible female person fare?' With this desire for titles and empty honours went the Spanish Baroque passion for personal exhibition, ornamentation and affectation, which is still common. As a great Baroque poet, Battista Guarini (a northerner from Ferrara), complained: 'Ours is an age of appearances and one goes masquerading all the year.'

There is no doubt that some of these Spanish traits retarded or prevented progress: the disregard or contempt for the economic facts of life, the preoccupation with non-essentials and with the outward aspect of all things, the hope of bettering one's conditions not through one's efforts but through the favour of the mighty, the belief that the king (or whoever takes the king's place) must take care of all. Is it really the Spaniards' fault that these habits lingered so long after they had left? Why is it that none of the great Spanish virtues took root? And why should the Spanish domination have left such indelible traces in Italy, and more particularly in the old Kingdom of the Two Sicilies, when it made practically no mark in other European provinces ruled from Madrid at the same time? Why, to quote one example, are the Flemish and the Dutch so enterprising, modest in their appearance, industrious and thrifty? Why do most Milanese rely on their own initiative, are proud to be their own masters, and favour, as a rule, an untrammelled economy?

Obviously it is difficult to draw simple conclusions. There is no doubt that the Spanish and the Church helped shape the Italian national character during the Baroque era. There is no doubt, either, that the bent it received at the time was irremediable. But the Spanish and the Church inevitably encouraged only the characteristics which were more congenial to the Italians themselves, probably the traits the people would have developed anyway. The Spanish and the Church were not arbitrary inventions of a demigod. It was the Italians' defeat, or the fact that they could not govern themselves and satisfy the first elementary necessity of a self-respecting people, that of keeping foreign enemies out, which had created a power vacuum. The Spanish were sucked into it. The Church was not an alien machination forcing an alien way of life on a reluctant people. We now know that no domination will last and be effective if it is imposed by force alone. It must be accepted by some of the people, at least, as the genuine expression of their hopes and illusions. The Church went about its sacred, eternal and universal mission with Italian prudence, *savoir faire*, and intelligence. It was manned by Italians. It could not help embodying also some Italian ideals. It would not have had its success otherwise. The will of the people also determined the intensity and depth of the political and moral domination. The Spanish viceroys, and the local quislings, after all, were as overbearing and greedy as the Italians allowed them to be. The Church was all-pervading because it had to shoulder responsibilities which the Italians had thrust upon it. There is no final answer to the problem.

CONCLUSION

THE Baroque Era might have perplexed men of an earlier generation. It has unfortunately few secrets for us. We know regimentation when we see it: the suffocating oppression of economic control, the compulsion of the affluent mass society, the paralysing embrace of paternalism, the degrading influence of bloody and stupid totalitarian régimes. We now smile at what were once considered horrifying rigours. The old governments look relatively mild and ineffective to us compared to modern models; the *grands seigneurs* were rarely capable of really ignoble deeds on a vast scale; even the worst of kings wanted to be called magnanimous by posterity; man in most countries might have been defenceless before his sovereign, but the laws had man-sized holes in them, the police had no machine-guns, radio, telephone and telephone-tapping equipment. They did torture people, but we doubt if the techniques of which they were so proud were half as good as those perfected by our contemporaries. Baroque oppression, however, looked redoubtable in its day. It was new. It was frightening and stifling. And men behaved all over Europe as we have seen them behave with our own eyes, as they do in all ages in similar circumstances.

Oppressive regimentation does not come unwanted and undeserved, like floods and pestilences. Its establishment is always facilitated, sometimes provoked and often welcomed by its beneficiaries or victims after periods of anarchy and troubles. Without it, men devour each other, trade and industry decline, life itself comes to a stop. It affords familiar advantages. It imposes a truce of sorts, makes trains run on time, gives the illusion that business can go on during political alterations, keeps the lower classes in their place. Its order looks like order but it is often but a *trompe-l'oeil*. It is a smooth-polished surface covering multicoloured reality, a slab of clear glass over the stormy surface of the sea. Deep problems remain unsolved and some become gangrenous. At the end they usually provoke a catastrophe.

Oppressive regimentation begins inconspicuously with the imposition of restrictions almost everybody gladly recognizes as necessary and overdue. It proceeds with the imposition of a set of approved ideas and uniform standards of behaviour. Unless checked in time, it ends up by controlling everything. Controls are at first visible and external. Soon they grow inside men, as invisible and pernicious as cancer. Many people persuade themselves that they do what they do of their own free will, that they are living in the best of all possible worlds. Everything is decided by an Olympus of revered supermen, or by one omniscient and omnipotent supreme person. What could be better? A man learns to be grateful for every largesse or concession from above. He learns to love and admire his masters. He believes the current slogans because so many of them, after all, reflect his own prejudices. He forgets himself in the mass-spectacles and the stirring ceremonies. He is proud of serving superior purposes and obeying an historical mission. He must be careful, of course. He must keep his mouth shut. He must never do anything unusual. He must accept hypocrisy and deceit as wise rules of behaviour and teach his children the use of flattery, ambiguity, evasion and duplicity. After all, his main business is to survive. But there are men who know or vaguely feel at times that they are prisoners in an ornate concentration camp. As only a few are capable of horrifying cruelties and abject cowardice, only a few are capable of selfless abnegation and heroism. Most of the discontented, however, secretly long for the lost age of Saturn, avoid the most unpleasant spots, try to find evasions and consolations.

On the surface, Italians submitted to Baroque regimentation more easily and eagerly than other people, in order to receive benefices from above, to be entertained and dazzled. They heartily took part in the public spectacles and the private little shows. They skilfully employed flattery, ambiguity, evasion. They also had no choice. Revolt was impossible. Who could ever hope to weld all the little Italian states together in order to forge one instrument to chase out the foreigners? It was unthinkable. Being realists, they recognized the fact that somebody had to be in command, and it was not a bad arrangement to allow foreigners and quislings to do this unpleasant job, exact taxes, levy troops, and attract the hatred of the governed. Laws were indispensable. They made life not only possible but also enjoyable. They were in a way like the hedges in a steeple-chase course. How could the clever men take the lead and win if there were no obstacles to keep the weaker men behind? How could one circumvent laws if there were none?

Under the surface the Italians invented ways to defeat oppressive regimentation. As they could not protect their national liberty in the field of battle, they fought strenuously to defend the liberty of the individual and his family, the only liberty they understood anyway. This necessity honed the single man's private virtues to an edge unsurpassed anywhere else. As Vittorio Alfieri boastfully wrote (and Stendhal and Garibaldi after him, using his very own words): 'The plant man grows in Italy second to none.' Single men, in the heart of their families, developed superior qualities. Added together, millions of them, they always amounted to no more than a weak, gullible and foolish mob. In peace-time, many achieved world fame in their fields. In war-time, many became invincible heroes, like the knights who defeated the French at Barletta, or the naval officers and sailors who, during the last war, penetrated the harbour of Alexandria underwater at night to torpedo British warships at their moorings. But the Italian nation never managed to solve its elementary problems and the Italian armed forces rarely succeeded in defeating their enemies. Italy has never been as good as the sum of all her people.

The people not only defeated their rulers but also managed to invent splendid and melodramatic ways of making each humble or ignoble hour as bearable and satisfying as possible. This is the reason why their manners, food, houses, cities, love-life are so delightful. This is also why their art, or most of it, is principally designed to give the public oblivion and bliss. They have naturally been accused of being frivolous and never going beneath the brilliant surface of things. The reproach is justified, of course. But they are not frivolous because they cannot be anything else. Many great artists left private documents showing they were deeply tormented by the tragedy of their life. Italian literature is filled with anguished cries. Dante bitterly railed: 'Ah, slave Italy, the abode of sorrow, ship without a pilot in a tempest, not the ruler of domains but a brothel!' Petrarch saw her covered with sores no words could cure but only deeds: 'Valour will take up arms again and let the fighting be short as the ancient courage is not dead in Italian hearts!' Leopardi saw ruins and mementoes of past glories about him but not 'the laurel crowns of heroes and the steel weapons' which were to make a country free. And Filicaja found reasons for weeping in Italy's 'fatal gift of beauty', which attracted foreigners' appetites. Even the Popes sometimes raged against the conquerors from across the Alps. '*Fuori i barbari!*' was the battle cry of Julius II.

The reason why so many great or near-great Italian artists turned themselves into superior decorators and entertainers is that, *faute de mieux*, in the absence of any possibility of solving the national problem, they thought it was their moral duty to assuage their countrymen's suffering and to make them forget their unhappy and indecorous fate.

Italians were also accused of not having a sufficient respect for truth. Of course few people have a real respect for truth. The Italians are not alone. And yet they know truth when they see it. They are no fools. Each of them tries to steer his private boat by the light of truth, because anything else would be disastrous. But collectively they seem sometimes to forget truth's unique importance. They often ignore it, embellish it, embroider around it, deny it, as the case may be. They lie to please, to round off a picture, to provoke an emotion, to prove a point. Above all, they consider lying about their unfortunate country a sacred duty, as justified morally as the humane inventions one tells a dying man, to delude him and his relatives. This is another reason why the single Italian is almost always wise while his country, directed on the basis of flattering distortions and exaggerations, has fatally made so many disastrous mistakes down the centuries.

*

That Italians have been living in the Baroque age for the last four centuries can be proved by a cursory examination of all their régimes of the recent past. The eighteenth-century monarchies swept away by Napoleon, the united kingdom established after the Risorgimento, the veiled dictatorships of liberal statesmen at the end of the last century and the beginning of this one, the Fascist unconcealed dictatorship, and the Socialist and Catholic combinations ruling today are all specimens of pure Baroque. The names and the official rhetoric change. The recipe is always the same.

This is the formula. It was good in the past and it will probably be good enough for many years to come. Take a vast, hard-working, pliable, ingenious population, worried about its daily bread, capable at times of accepting untold sacrifices, but restless and anxious for novelties. Keep the people ignorant by providing the minimum amount of schools. Keep them in want by regimenting with an iron hand or persecuting industry and trade. Keep them bewildered and insecure by the arbitrary manipulation of vaguely worded laws. See that there never are clearly defined rights and duties, but always favours from above or abuses of power. Keep the people happy with a steady rain of miserable alms, distracted with many holidays, more holidays than any other nation in Europe, feasts, the inauguration of splendidly decorated and sometimes useful public works. Spend most of the money on superfluous things, the armed forces and insensate wars in the past, and now on entertainments, public spectacles, games; spend as little as possible on improving the people's moral and physical conditions. Keep them always drunk with stirring appeals to their more primitive emotions.

Then take a small oligarchy of leaders, eternally squabbling among themselves, frightened for their position and, often enough, for their life, whose power depends precariously on the favour of a few or of one man, sometimes even a foreign chief, residing abroad. Put these leaders above the law. This tends to make the best of them wary, pitiless, overbearing, unscrupulous and avaricious. In the old days such men were courtiers, landowning aristocrats, high dignitaries and generals; later they were also bankers, shipowners, industrialists; yesterday they were Fascist chieftains. Today they are the heads of mass parties, exponents of organizations turning out millions of votes, controllers of industrial empires privately- or State-owned and trades union chiefs. The *grands seigneurs* of old had better taste, were braver, more polite, and carried themselves with greater dignity; the liberal patriots of the nineteenth century often loved their country, encouraged industry and trade, and tried at times to do something to better the people's living conditions; today's leaders are more intelligent, efficient and have studied more. But such differences are as unimportant as the fashions of the clothes they wore.

When one forgets superficial variations, one can see that the Italian leaders of today behave more or less as their predecessors have always behaved. They manage Italy as if it were *cosa nostra*; carry out vast, ambitious, impressive political designs, which are described as essential to the welfare of the country but are brutally and transparently conceived mainly to reinforce their own power. They use the people as if they were extras on a Graeco-Roman film set, to be moved by remote control, to whom nobody explains the plot. Anything else would be unthinkable. To persuade their countrymen to cultivate the arts of reading and writing, to allow them to gain and enjoy a moderate prosperity, to encourage as many as possible to become soberly responsible would endanger the hold of the élite, or, as the élite prefers to say, weaken the social structure. There is, however, this to be said in the leaders' defence. They are the product of their society. The *grands seigneurs* of old as well as the contemporary cabinet ministers or controllers of State monopolies share the qualities and defects of the people, nourish the same ideals. They are, in fact, what the Italians make them.

It was always obvious to clear-thinking Italians that their country was the unfortunate victim of a vicious circle: the national character fatally generated tyrannies, tyrannies strengthened and exasperated the defects of the national character and inevitably led the country to catastrophe. If Italy was to be saved one day from her disgraceful destiny, the vicious circle had to be smashed. Patriots agreed from the earliest times that only the conquest of independence, the establishment of a national unified state (or a close confederation of Italian states), and the acceptance by the people of their civic and military duties would in the end regenerate the country. All this, however, could not be gained by luck or imposed by external agents, with little Italian collaboration, otherwise its results would be ephemeral at best, the usual dazzling show, one more spectacle behind which the old reality would have persisted practically unchanged.

All this had to be done the hard way. It had to come about through a spontaneous process of Italian history, provoked by a slow rising tide of popular indignation, and was to be purchased by blood, in victorious wars or revolts. Italian political thinkers, of course, knew that successful revolutions and victorious wars were not desirable *per se*. They were merely the ultimate proofs of the people's whole-hearted solidarity, of their belief in their common destiny, of their acceptance of a common law and common duties. They were the sign that the individual Italian had abandoned the struggle for his own private welfare and had begun to think in collective terms. But how could the Italians be brought to fight and die for their country? Clearly, if they could be persuaded to do that, there was, after all, no need for them to do so, as they would already be what the best of them hoped they would become.

This, it must be pointed out with solemnity, was in the past and still is today the crux of the Italian problem, of *all* Italian problems, the heart of the matter, the only significance in many apparently meaningless and disorderly intricacies of Italian history. It is the only explanation of many otherwise puzzling aspects of the national behaviour, the question people debated passionately down the centuries and are still debating today in cafés and Parliament, the thorn in the heart of all good Italians of all ages. Why did Italy, a land notoriously teeming with vigorous, wide-awake and intelligent people, always behave so feebly? Why was she invaded, ravaged, sacked, humiliated in every century, and yet failed to do the simple things necessary to defend herself?

The hope of achieving national unity and of conquering independence seemed to thinking Italians a dear but unattainable dream. To begin with the people never seriously felt the need to become one nation. After a survey of his country's history, Guicciardini bitterly admitted: 'This was never an easy country to reduce under one rule.' Even in the days of Imperial Rome, in fact, she successfully resisted being blanketed by uniform laws. When Gaul, Spain, Germany and Britain were, administratively speaking, compact and orderly provinces, she managed somehow to remain a vast mosaic of free cities, partially autonomous regions, rebellious mountain tribes, almost independent peoples with their dialects, gods and customs. Later, during the Middle Ages, unification of sorts could have been brought about any number of times by the Emperors of Germany. They came, in the spring, when the snows melted, to conquer, pillage and try to weld the mutable populations into a manageable system of feudal fiefs. The Germans were occasionally repulsed in bloody battles, and, when this was not possible, flattered by treacherous negotiations, deceived by fragile and ambiguous treaties, betrayed or corrupted. The results of their many military successes were inevitably short-lived. Most conquered cities put up a good show of loyalty as long as the imperial forces were around, but reverted to their customary seditiousness as soon as they turned their backs.

There were many reasons for this. Not only had the Italians always been, as Guicciardini says, generally difficult 'to reduce under one rule', but they also never felt they were a 'new' people, one of those immature and semi-barbaric nations which needed harsh laws and iron discipline in order to maintain a semblance of civilized order when the Roman Empire disappeared. The Italians felt much too old and wise to become imitation northerners. They clung to the decayed remnants of Roman ways, which, like all decayed remnants, were sweet and comfortable enough for them. Neither could they abandon the memory of their past greatness, a memory which was strong even when, in the darkest ages, it was but a dim and fabulous legend. It was not only strong enough to prevent the victory of foreign ideas and institutions, but was also a good substitute for them. The Italians felt themselves sufficiently unified, morally and culturally, anyway, to want political and military unification. They were held together by their language, ruins, arts, literature, habits, ruses, the fame of their great men and the memory of their great saints.

Later still, when other European nations were unified by powerful monarchies, the Italians still struggled to maintain their political divisions. Native princes and dynasties often tried to found unified kingdoms or confederations. The roster is a long one. It starts with Ardoin, Marquis of Ivrea, who almost managed it, and died in 1015; includes Frederick II, King of Sicily and Emperor of Germany,

Italian born and educated, the 'wonder of the world'; the Visconti of Milan, the Medici of Florence, and many others. Joachim Murat, King of Naples, tried to conquer the country in 1814, taking advantage of the defeat of his brother-in-law Napoleon. Even an Englishman dabbled with the problem, Lord William Bentinck, His Britannic Majesty's Minister to the exiled court of Naples during the Napoleonic wars, who thought of setting up an independent Italy, after 1815, in opposition to the Austrians and the French. Nobody down the centuries, no prince, revolutionary chief, republic or princely family was ever allowed to become strong enough to congregate all Italians under one flag and one law, until Victor Emmanuel of Savoy, King of Sardinia, became King of Italy, in 1861, with the aid of the French army, Garibaldi's volunteers, and republican revolutionaries.

The Popes, of course, were at all times among the most powerful and influential Italian princes. The Church was at all times the most vigorous and lively of Italian institutions. All Italians whole-heartedly belonged to it and served it. A Pope could presumably have unified the country without many difficulties. Why did this never happen? The Church was the people's traditional ally against the Empire. It led coalitions against the northern invaders, time and again. But the people were never durably grateful for the help received. They were never the Church's partisans for long. They became Guelphs for no longer than the situation required and as long as it suited them, turned Ghibellines as soon as the Church's political supremacy became threatening, and went back to being Guelphs when the Germans came once again over the Alps. In fact, Italians fought to prevent either of the two great rival institutions gaining the upper hand. The people considered their country with equal pride both the Garden of the Empire and the Throne of God on Earth, but not one of these things exclusively for all times.

It must be admitted that these unconscious patterns of behaviour are still valid today. As Italy is now indirectly being governed by the Church, through the Christian Democrat Party, a growing number of Italians instinctively join the party which can be considered the contemporary equivalent of the Ghibellines, a powerful organization sustained by an alien power which is hostile to the Vatican and the temporal influence of priests in Italian and world affairs. Should the Communists eventually gain the upper hand some day, any student of Italian history knows what will happen. The people will, secretly or openly, as the case may be, go to swell the Church's organizations in ever-increasing numbers, daring persecution and death if necessary, in order to fight what they consider an alien and hateful tyranny.

Machiavelli had not quite understood this pendular mechanism of Italian history. He thought the national ills had all been caused solely by the Church. This is what he wrote in a famous passage:

'No province was ever united and prosperous unless it was under the sway of one republic or one monarch, as is the case of France and Spain. And the reason why Italy is not in this condition is none other than the Church, for the Church has never had the vigour to extend its sway over the whole country. . . . Nor, on the other hand, has it been so feeble as not to be able, when afraid of losing its temporal power, to call in a foreign potentate, as counterpoise in its defence against those powers which threatened to become supreme. The Church has kept us under sundry lords and princes. These have caused so much discord and debility that Italy has become the prey not only of powerful barbarians but also of every assailant.'

This over-simple thesis is important because it is still held by many good Italians, who cannot easily admit that the people could, at any time, if they had wanted to, have won their independence and liberty against both foreign powers and the Church. It is comforting to think that priestly intrigues were too strong for any spontaneous movement to arise and develop. And yet the thesis is not wholly wrong, not wrong all the time. The Church's power was always strong, not because the Popes were great statesmen, the Curia a far-seeing body, and the Italians frightened of religious sanctions, but because the Italians never really wanted to become the actors of their own history, the arbiters of their destiny, and used the Church (as they used the Empire at different times) to prevent unification or, when unification was achieved, to undermine and weaken it.

This is illustrated by what happened in the last century and a half.

It took three generations of patriots, thinkers, dreamers, soldiers, poets, musicians, statesmen, revolutionaries, and adventurers to achieve unity in 1861. And yet, in spite of the great number of people who contributed to it, it was not won by the Italians as a whole. No rising tide of popular indignation animated the movement. The people believing in the Risorgimento, or the rebirth of their country, were the liberal and progressive minorities of the aristocracy and the enlightened bourgeoisie. The great masses, the majority of the élite and the peasants, watched the events with scepticism and diffidence. As a result the national state, the new Kingdom of Italy, was a fragile and unsafe structure. The *liberali* managed to maintain themselves in power by means of subterfuges, the same subterfuges and police methods the foreign oppressors or the small and weak princes had employed before them. They were forced at all times to stir up strong patriotic emotions, to keep the people in a frenzy, as all feeble governments do, by spending a lot of money on the armed forces and waging disastrous wars. They exhausted most of their energies mainly trying to put up a show as Italy the great world power.

The Kingdom was undermined by the alliance of the popular classes with the Church, the incredulity of the majority of citizens, and the national character. It struggled for decades, trying to educate an élite, improve the state administration, encourage commerce and industry. Its achievements were many, some were unique and admirable. But it never really solved fundamental problems. Its highest moment came in November 1918, when the army triumphed over their broken-down and dispirited Austrian and Hungarian enemies. But the effort had been too much for such a brittle and recent country. The unified state practically collapsed. The Fascist dictatorship was a police superstructure which postponed the ruin of the new Italy and propped it up as wooden beams support a crumbling wall. The moment of truth came in 1945 with the defeat in the last war. With the allies' invasion, the Italians understood that what they had believed to be the final solution of their century-old problems, the regeneration of the country and the people, the formation of a modern nation, had been but a heart-rending Baroque structure, which had cost the lives of millions, had wasted a precious part of the available resources, and had deluded for a century the best Italians. At the end, Italy was left without illusions to contemplate herself as she had always been. Anarchy prevailed, the Italian anarchy of all times, sweet anarchy at times, invisibly and spontaneously regulated by secret rules and customs, always mitigated by scepticism, forbearance, indulgence for man's foibles. It is often pleasant, definitely more satisfactory, in the short run, than the rigid rule of law, but the cause, in the long run, of untold suffering, humiliations, injustice, and outrages.

Foreign visitors are fascinated. They are won over, as they have always been, by the 'charm of Italy'. Italian life is gay, effervescent, intoxicating. The *dolce vita* looks now more *dolce* than it ever was. Very few travellers see the ugliness underneath, the humiliation, the suffering. Not one in a hundred perceives the fundamental dreariness of everything under the glittering ormolu, the bitter fate of men who are condemned perennially to amuse themselves and the world, to hide their innermost feelings, to be *simpatici* at all costs in order to make a living. What do they know of the peculiar feeling of frustration and resigned discontent which paralyses the best Italians? One of Ignazio Silone's characters describes it: 'There is a sadness, a subtle sadness that's not to be mistaken for the more ordinary kind that is the result of remorse, disillusionment or suffering; there is an intimate sadness which comes to chosen souls simply from their consciousness of man's fate. . . . This sort of sadness has always prevailed among intelligent Italians, but most of them, to evade suicide or madness, have taken to every known means of escape: they feign exaggerated gaiety, awkwardness, a passion for women, for food, for their country, and, above all, for fine-sounding words; they become, as chance may have it, policemen, monks, terrorists, war heroes. I think that there has never been a race of men so fundamentally desolate and desperate as these gay Italians.'

It is not surprising that few foreigners see these things when only a tiny minority of the natives are aware of them. Foreigners are delighted also because they always find themselves, without knowing it, in a favoured position. The Italian social structure can be compared to the olive tree, that most Italian of all trees, which looks entirely different when seen from above from what it looks when seen from below. The leaves are glossy dark-green on top and powdery grey underneath. The faces of the Italians look flattering, smiling, and kindly from above but overbearing, insolent, pitiless from below. Foreigners are automatically promoted to be honorary members of the ruling class. They occupy a position of vantage. Theirs is the bird's-eye view of the olive tree.

The illusion Italy creates is a relief. Countries which believe in discipline, the meticulous administration of justice, the cultivation of unbending moral virtues, universal education, the conquest of military glory and the diligent accumulation, distribution and administration of wealth, whether they really achieve their ideals or merely pay respect to them, can be worthy of esteem but are seldom amusing. Even those countries which pursue the ideal of liberty can be stifling and oppressive, for liberty is after all assured only by the impartial enforcement of the law. The Italian way of life down the centuries attracted people who wanted to take a holiday from their national virtues. In the heart of every man, wherever he is born, whatever his education and tastes, there is one small corner which is Italian, that part which finds regimentation irksome, the dangers of war frightening, strict morality stifling, that part which loves frivolous and entertaining art, admires larger-than-life-size solitary heroes, and dreams of an impossible liberation from the strictures of a tidy existence.

The consolations which Italy afforded at all times have become infinitely more precious today than they ever were. The Western world is deeply uneasy. It is coming to doubt the utility and sanctity of some of its traditional virtues, those on which it based its moral tranquillity and its self-respect. The bourgeois' industry and thrift are considered more and more injurious to society; the soldier's undaunted heroism is no longer required; unbridled patriotism has led men and nations to tragic mistakes; morality has lost some of its shining certainty; laws have become fluid; nobody really knows any more whether one truth exists. The era of powerful nations, proud of their racial superiority, masters of their own destinies, is at an end. Everybody's life is governed by the decisions of distant and practically unknown men, as powerful and out of reach as Charles V seemed to the Italians in the sixteenth century, who can make us rich or poor, can make us live or can kill all of us in our beds while we sleep. The regimentation of an industrial mass society is becoming more and more stifling. Men are kept working like galley slaves of old by their desire to conquer more and more garish material possessions. They are fed ready-made ideas, they are supplied with art approved by the authorities, entertained by the same shows, dazzled by the same ceremonies, stirred by the same slogans, moved by the same collective emotions. Modern men get lost in a maze of larger and larger anonymous organizations. Loneliness and tedium envelop each of them whenever he can get out of the uproar long enough to think about himself.

The art of living, this disreputable art developed by the Italians to defeat regimentation, is now becoming an invaluable guide for survival for many people. *La dolce vita* is spreading to countries which despised it and feared it, or coming to the surface in countries which liked to think it did not exist. Tax-payers are trying to avoid their sacred duty everywhere. The little pleasures of life have acquired a new importance, food, wines, a day in the sun, a pretty girl, the defeat of a rival, good music. Naturally more and more people flock to Italy every year. Most of them do not exactly know why. They think it is a wonderful place for a holiday. They are attracted by the pleasant sensation of peace, the lightness in their hearts. In reality they are drawn to the place where the new perplexing problems of the contemporary world are familiar monsters, problems with which the natives learned to live long ago. Other Western men are newcomers in the New Baroque age. Many are still reluctant, incredulous and unprepared newcomers, who cling to the old approved ways of doing things and are perpetually surprised to discover that they no longer have the same power to attain results. The Italians have invented ancient ruses to defeat boredom and discipline, to forget disgrace and misfortune, to lull man's *angst* to sleep and comfort him in his solitude. They still remember the age of Saturn, and reconstruct it longingly in a perennial Saturnalia. They do not make the mistakes some eager foreigners make, who rush blindly into new paths and accept indiscriminately all corrupt and cynical solutions. The Italians know the relative utility of all the tricks, know which ones are dangerous and which are deceptive. They know where to stop. In a minor way, Italy has perhaps become once again a teacher of nations.

*

The Italian way of life cannot be considered a success except by temporary visitors. It solves no problems. It makes them worse. It would be a success of sorts if at least it made Italians happy. It does not. Its effects are costly, flimsy and short-range. The people enjoy its temporary advantages, to be sure, without which they could not endure life, but are constantly tormented by discontent. They rage against their fate today as they have always done. They have been on the verge of revolution for the last one hundred and sixty odd years, against kings, foreign dominations, the Church, disunity, landowners, capitalists, centralization in turn. All these, of course, at one time or another contributed something to the national ills. Politicians eternally tinker with laws and institutions. But the fundamental cause escapes everybody. It is the Italian way of life which makes all laws and institutions function defectively. It is the illusion of a solution, lotus-eating, the resigned acceptance of the very evils man has tried to defeat, the art of decorating, ennobling them, calling them by different names and living with them. The unsolved problems pile up and inevitably produce catastrophes at regular intervals. The Italians always see the next one approaching with a clear eye, but, like sleepers in a nightmare, cannot do anything to ward it off. They can only play their amusing games, try to secure their families against the coming storm, and delude themselves for a time. They console themselves with the thought that, when the smoke clears, Italy can rise again like a phoenix from its ashes. Has she not always done so? The tenacity and the eagerness with which the individual pursues his private interests and defends himself from society, his mistrust of noble ideals and motives, the splendid show, the all-pervading indulgence for man's foibles make Italian life pleasant and bearable in spite of poverty, tyranny and injustice. They also waste the efforts and the sacrifices of the best Italians and make poverty, tyranny and injustice very difficult to defeat.

INDEX

341

THE HOLY ROMAN EMPIRE

The Swiss Federation THE ALPS
Brenner Pass
County of Tyrol
B. of Bressanone
Adige

THE ALPS

DUCHY
OF
SAVOY
Duchy
of Aosta
L.Maggiore
L.Como
B. of
Trent

Friuli

County of
Gorizia & Grad
Trieste

DUCHY
Valtellina
Bergamo
REPUB. OF VENICE

L.Garda

Milan
Monza
Brescia
Verona
Padua
Venice

OF
Pavia
1525
M. OF MANTUA
Mantua
Adige
Istria

Mont
Cenis Pass
Turin
M. OF
Asti
MILAN
Parma
Fornovo
1495
DUCHY
OF
MODENA
Modena
D. OF FERRARA

FRANCE
Montgenevre
Pass
MONT
OF GEN
Cisa
Pass
Bologna
A REGGIO
Romagna
Ferrara
Ravenna

SALUZZO
CITY OF NIZZA
REPUB OF GEN
Genoa
Savona
Sarzana
Faenza

Lerici
Massa
LUCCA
Pistoia
Florence
Rimini
Pesaro
REPUB OF SAN MARINO

PRINC. OF MONACO
Pisa
Arno
REP OF FLORENCE
Urbino

Leghorn
Siena
Trasimeno
Loreto
DALMATIA

REP OF
SIENA
Assisi
Perugia

Grosseto
Maremma
Spoleto

Elba

Viterbo

Corsica

Pescara

Civitavecchia
Rome
Frascati
Velletri
Campagna
Abruzzi

OTTOMAN
EMPIRE

KINGDOM OF HUNGARY

ADRIATIC SEA

REP OF RAGUSA
Ragusa

TYRRHENIAN SEA

Sardinia

Formia
Gaeta
Benevento
Naples
Salerno
Amalfi
Paestum

Foggia
Barletta
1503
Bari

APULIA

KINGDOM OF NAPLES

Taranto

Cosenza

Calabria

IONIAN SEA

MEDITERRANEAN

Palermo
Partinico
Villalba
Pietrasanta
Agrigento
KINGDOM OF
SICILY
Catania
Syracuse
Comiso
Noto

Messina
Reggio
Taormina

SEA

Malta

Italy 1500

Miles
0   50   100

THE HOLY ROMAN EMPIRE

THE ALPS • Brenner Pass

SWITZERLAND

B. of Bressanone

THE ALPS L. Maggiore L. Como

B. of Trent

DUCHY OF SAVOY

Cty of Anghiera

DUCHY OF Milan

REPUBLIC OF VENICE

L. Garda

Trieste

KINGDOM OF HUNGARY

PRINC. OF PIEDMONT

Mont Cenis Pass

MILAN

Brescia

Verona

Mantua

Padua

Adige

Venice

Istria

Turin

DUCHY OF Parma

DUCHY OF MODENA

Modena

Bologna

Romagna

Ferrara

Ravenna

OTTOMAN EMPIRE

FRANCE

REPUBLIC OF GENOA

PARMA

Genoa

Po

PAPAL

Dalmatia

PRINC. OF MONACO

DUC. OF MASSA

Leghorn

Pisa

Massa

LUCCA

Arno

Florence

REP. OF SAN MARINO

ADRIATIC SEA

REP. OF RAGUSA

PRINC. OF PIOMBINO

GRAND DUCHY OF TUSCANY

Siena

Perugia

Assisi

Spoleto

STATES

Tiber

Elba

Corsica

Civitavecchia

Rome

Abruzzi

KINGDOM

Apulia

Campagna

Benevento

Bari

TYRRHENIAN SEA

Naples

OF NAPLES

KINGDOM OF SARDINIA

Calabria

IONIAN SEA

Messina

Reggio

MEDITERRANEAN

Palermo

Sicily

Catania

Syracuse

Italy 1714

Miles
0   50   100

SEA

Malta

KINGDOM OF BAVARIA
THE ALPS
HELVETIC REPUB.
Tyrol
Brenner Pass
THE ALPS
L.Maggiore
L.Como
L.Garda
Mont
Cenis,
Pass
Milan
Brescia
Verona
Padua
Venice
Trieste
Turin
Po
Mantua
Parma
Ferrara
Modena
Bologna
Ravenna
Genoa
Liguria
Lucca
Princ.of Lucca
Florence
REP. OF SAN MARINO
Pisa
Arno
Leghorn
Siena
Perugia
Assisi
Princ. of
Piombino
Spoleto
Elba
Corsica
Civitavecchia
Rome
Campagna
Princ.of
Pontecorvo
Pr. of
Benevento
Bari
Apulia
Naples

AUSTRIAN
EMPIRE
K. of Hungary

Illyrian Provinces

OTTOMAN
EMPIRE

KINGDOM OF ITALY

KINGDOM OF NAPLES

FRENCH EMPIRE

ADRIATIC SEA

KINGDOM
OF
SARDINIA

TYRRHENIAN SEA

Palermo
Messina
Reggio
Calabria
KINGDOM OF
SICILY
Catania
Syracuse

IONIAN SEA

MEDITERRANEAN SEA

Italy 1810

Miles
0   50   100

Malta

Italy Today

Miles
0   50   100